Advances in Classical and Applied Mathematics

Advances in Classical and Applied Mathematics

Guest Editors

Cristina Flaut
Dana Piciu
Murat Tosun

MDPI

Basel • Beijing • Wuhan • Barcelona • Belgrade • Novi Sad • Cluj • Manchester

Guest Editors
Cristina Flaut
Faculty of Mathematics and
Computer Science
Ovidius University
Constanța
Romania

Dana Piciu
Faculty of Science
University of Craiova
Craiova
Romania

Murat Tosun
Department of Mathematics
Sakarya University
Sakarya
Turkey

Editorial Office
MDPI AG
Grosspeteranlage 5
4052 Basel, Switzerland

This is a reprint of the Special Issue, published open access by the journal *Axioms* (ISSN 2075-1680), freely accessible at: www.mdpi.com/journal/axioms/special_issues/YYXW321YX2.

For citation purposes, cite each article independently as indicated on the article page online and using the guide below:

Lastname, A.A.; Lastname, B.B. Article Title. *Journal Name* **Year**, *Volume Number*, Page Range.

ISBN 978-3-7258-3580-5 (Hbk)
ISBN 978-3-7258-3579-9 (PDF)
https://doi.org/10.3390/books978-3-7258-3579-9

Contents

George Georgescu, Leonard Kwuida and Claudia Mureşan
Congruence Extensions in Congruence–Modular Varieties
Reprinted from: *Axioms* **2024**, *13*, 824, https://doi.org/10.3390/axioms13120824 . . . . **1**

Yanlin Li, Kemal Eren, Soley Ersoy and Ana Savić
Modified Sweeping Surfaces in Euclidean 3-Space
Reprinted from: *Axioms* **2024**, *13*, 800, https://doi.org/10.3390/axioms13110800 . . . . **29**

Hidayet Hüda Kösal, Emre Kişi, Mahmut Akyiğit and Beyza Çelik
Elliptic Quaternion Matrices: A MATLAB Toolbox and Applications for Image Processing
Reprinted from: *Axioms* **2024**, *13*, 771, https://doi.org/10.3390/axioms13110771 . . . . **44**

Violeta Leoreanu-Fotea and Sarka Hoskova-Mayerova
Join Spaces and Lattices
Reprinted from: *Axioms* **2024**, *13*, 705, https://doi.org/10.3390/axioms13100705 . . . . **70**

Hidayet Hüda Kösal, Emre Kişi, Mahmut Akyiğit and Beyza Çelik
Elliptic Quaternion Matrices: Theory and Algorithms
Reprinted from: *Axioms* **2024**, *13*, 656, https://doi.org/10.3390/axioms13100656 . . . . **81**

Soley Ersoy, Kemal Eren and Abdussamet Çalışkan
Characterizations of Spatial Quaternionic Partner-Ruled Surfaces
Reprinted from: *Axioms* **2024**, *13*, 612, https://doi.org/10.3390/axioms13090612 . . . . **98**

Said EL Fakkoussi, Ouadie Koubaiti, Ahmed Elkhalfi, Sorin Vlase and Marin Marin
Numerical Analysis of the Cylindrical Shell Pipe with Preformed Holes Subjected to a Compressive Load Using Non-Uniform Rational B-Splines and T-Splines for an Isogeometric Analysis Approach
Reprinted from: *Axioms* **2024**, *13*, 529, https://doi.org/10.3390/axioms13080529 . . . . **112**

Sakander Hayat, Asad Khan and Mohammed J. F. Alenazi
On Some Distance Spectral Characteristics of Trees
Reprinted from: *Axioms* **2024**, *13*, 494, https://doi.org/10.3390/axioms13080494 . . . . **134**

Dorin Andrica and Ovidiu Bagdasar
On Some Properties of the Equilateral Triangles with Vertices Located on the Support Sides of a Triangle
Reprinted from: *Axioms* **2024**, *13*, 478, https://doi.org/10.3390/axioms13070478 . . . . **158**

Cristina Flaut and Andreea Baias
Some Remarks Regarding Special Elements in Algebras Obtained by the Cayley–Dickson Process over Z_p
Reprinted from: *Axioms* **2024**, *13*, 351, https://doi.org/10.3390/axioms13060351 . . . . **173**

Sana Habib, Faiz Muhammad Khan and Violeta Leoreanu-Fotea
A Progressive Outlook on Possibility Multi-Fuzzy Soft Ordered Semigroups: Theory and Analysis
Reprinted from: *Axioms* **2024**, *13*, 340, https://doi.org/10.3390/axioms13060340 . . . . **183**

Thomas Moran and Susanne Pumpluen
A Generalization of the First Tits Construction
Reprinted from: *Axioms* **2024**, *13*, 299, https://doi.org/10.3390/axioms13050299 . . . . **201**

axioms

MDPI

Article

Congruence Extensions in Congruence–Modular Varieties

George Georgescu [1], Leonard Kwuida [2] and Claudia Mureşan [1,*]

[1] Faculty of Mathematics and Computer Science, University of Bucharest, 010014 Bucharest, Romania; georgescu.capreni@yahoo.com

[2] School of Business, Bern University of Applied Sciences, 3005 Bern, Switzerland; leonard.kwuida@bfh.ch

* Correspondence: cmuresan@fmi.unibuc.ro

Abstract: We investigate from an algebraic and topological point of view the minimal prime spectrum of a universal algebra, considering the prime congruences with respect to the term condition commutator. Then we use the topological structure of the minimal prime spectrum to study extensions of universal algebras that generalize certain types of ring extensions. Our results hold for semiprime members of semidegenerate congruence–modular varieties, as well as semiprime algebras whose term condition commutators are commutative and distributive with respect to arbitrary joins and satisfy certain conditions on compact congruences, even if those algebras do not generate congruence–modular varieties.

Keywords: (modular) commutator; (minimal) prime congruence; (Stone, Zariski, flat) topology; (ring) extension

MSC: 08A30; 08B10; 06B10; 13B99; 06F35; 03G25

1. Introduction

Inspired by group theory and initially developped in [1] for congruence–modular varieties, commutator theory has led to the solving of many deep universal algebra problems; it has subsequently been extended by adopting various definitions for the commutator, all of which collapse to the modular commutator in this congruence–modular case.

The congruence lattices of members of congruence–modular varieties, endowed with the modular commutator, form commutator lattices, in which we can introduce the prime elements with respect to the commutator operation. For the purpose of not restricting to this congruence–modular setting, we have introduced the notion of a prime congruence through the term condition commutator. Under certain conditions for this commutator operation which do not have to be satisfied throughout a whole variety, the thus defined set of the prime congruences of an algebra becomes a topological space when endowed with a generalization of the Zariski topology from commutative rings [2,3]. For members of semidegenerate congruence–modular varieties, this topological space has strong properties [4], some of which extend to more general cases.

The first goal of this paper is to study the topology this generalization induces on the antichain of the minimal prime congruences of an algebra whose term condition commutator satisfies certain conditions, all of which hold in any member of a semidegenerate congruence–modular variety.

The second goal of our present work is the study of certain types of extensions of algebras with "well–behaved" commutators, meaning term condition commutators that behave like the modular commutator, generalizing results on ring extensions from [5,6].

In Section 2 we recall some results on congruence lattices and the term condition commutator, as well as the particular case of the modular commutator, along with the prime and minimal prime spectra of congruences of an algebra with "well–behaved" commutators, where the prime congruences are defined with respect to the commutator operation, as well

check for updates

Citation: Georgescu, G.; Kwuida, L.; Mureşan, C. Congruence Extensions in Congruence–Modular Varieties. *Axioms* **2024**, *13*, 824. https://doi.org/10.3390/axioms13120824

Academic Editors: Cristina Flaut, Dana Piciu and Murat Tosun

Received: 2 September 2024
Revised: 20 October 2024
Accepted: 21 October 2024
Published: 25 November 2024

as the prime and minimal spectra of ideals of a bounded distributive lattice. The following sections are dedicated to our new results.

Section 3 contains arithmetical properties of commutator lattices of congruences and annihilators with respect to the commutator in such lattices, derived from the residuation operation and its associated negation introduced through these annihilators.

In Section 4 we obtain several algebraic properties of the minimal prime spectrum of congruences, including a characterization of minimal prime congruences through their behavior with respect to the negations of congruences, obtained in two different cases from a corresponding characterization of minimal prime ideals of bounded distributive lattices.

In Section 5 we study the Stone (also called spectral) and the flat (also called inverse) topology on the minimal prime spectrum of congruences of an algebra, establish homeomorphisms between these and the corresponding topologies on the minimal prime spectrum of ideals of the reticulation of that algebra (see [7] for the construction of the reticulation in the universal algebra setting) and obtain necessary and sufficient conditions for these two topologies to coincide.

In Section 6, starting from the study of ring extensions in [5,6], we define certain classes of extensions of universal algebras that generalize corresponding classes of ring extensions: m–extensions, rigid, quasirigid and weak rigid extensions, r–extensions and quasi/weak r–extensions, r^*–extensions and quasi/weak r^*–extensions, and, generalizing results from [5,6], we obtain relations between these types of extensions, characterizations for these kinds of extensions and topological properties of the minimal prime spectra of the universal algebras that form such extensions.

2. Preliminaries

We refer the reader to [4,8–10] for a further study of the following notions from universal algebra, to [11–14] for the lattice–theoretical ones, to [1,4,10,15] for the results on commutators and to [4,16–20] for the Stone topologies.

All algebras will be nonempty and they will be designated by their underlying sets. By *trivial algebra* we mean one–element algebra.

$\mathbb{N}$ denotes the set of the natural numbers, $\mathbb{N}^*= \mathbb{N}\setminus\{0\}$, and, for any $a,b\in\mathbb{N}$, we denote by $\overline{a,b}= \{n\in\mathbb{N}\mid a\leq n\leq b\}$ the interval in the lattice $(\mathbb{N},\leq)$ bounded by a and b, where $\leq$ is the natural order (this is to differentiate from the notation for commutators). Let M, N be sets and $S\subseteq M$. Then we denote by $\mathcal{P}(M)$ the set of the subsets of M, by $\Delta_M= \{(x,x)\mid x\in M\}$ and $\nabla_M= M^2$ the smallest and the largest equivalence on M, respectively, and by $i_{S,M}$: $S\rightarrow M$ the inclusion map. For any function $f: M\rightarrow N$, we denote by $\mathrm{Ker}(f)$ the kernel of f, by f the direct image of $f^2=f\times f$ and by f^* the inverse image of f^2.

For any poset P, $Max(P)$ and $Min(P)$ will denote the set of the maximal elements and that of the minimal elements of P, respectively. The order on congruences of an algebra or ideals or filters of a lattice will always be the set inclusion.

Let L be a lattice. Then $\mathrm{Cp}(L)$ and $\mathrm{Mi}(L)$ denote the set of the compact elements and that of the meet–irreducible elements of L, respectively. $\mathrm{Filt}(L)$, $\mathrm{Id}(L)$, $\mathrm{PId}(L)$ and $\mathrm{Spec}_{\mathrm{Id}}(L)$ denote the sets of the filters, ideals, principal ideals and prime ideals of L, respectively. We denote by $\mathrm{Min}_{\mathrm{Id}}(L)= Min(\mathrm{Spec}_{\mathrm{Id}}(L))$: the set of the minimal prime ideals of L. Let $U\subseteq L$ and $u\in L$. Then $[U)_L$ and $[u)_L$ denote the filters of L generated by U and by u, respectively, while $(U]_L$ and $(u]_L$ denote the ideals of L generated by U and by u, respectively. If L has a 0, then $\mathrm{Ann}_L(U)= \{a\in L\mid (\forall\, x\in U)\,(a\wedge x=0)\}$ is the annihilator of U and we denote by $\mathrm{Ann}_L(u)= \mathrm{Ann}_L(\{u\})$ the annihilator of u. The subscript L will be eliminated from these notations when the lattice L is clear from the context. Note that, if L has a 0 and it is distributive, then all annihilators in L are ideals of L. If L is a bounded lattice, then we denote by $\mathcal{B}(L)$ the set of the complemented elements of L, which, of course, is a Boolean sublattice of L if L is distributive.

Recall that a *frame* is a complete lattice with the meet distributive with respect to arbitrary joins.

(H) Throughout the rest of this paper: τ will be a universal algebras signature, $\mathcal{V}$ a variety of τ–algebras and A an arbitrary member of $\mathcal{V}$.

Everywhere in this paper, we will mark global assumptions as above, for better visibility.

Unless mentioned otherwise, by *morphism* we mean τ–morphism.

$\mathrm{Con}(A)$, $\mathrm{Max}(A)$, $\mathrm{PCon}(A)$ and $\mathcal{K}(A)$ denote the sets of the congruences, maximal (proper) congruences, principal congruences and finitely generated congruences of A, respectively; note that $\mathcal{K}(A) = \mathrm{Cp}(\mathrm{Con}(A))$. $\mathrm{Max}(A)$ is called the *maximal spectrum* of A. For any $X \subseteq A^2$ and any $a,b \in A$, $Cg_A(X)$ will be the congruence of A generated by X and we shall denote by $Cg_A(a,b) = Cg_A(\{(a,b)\})$.

For any $\theta \in \mathrm{Con}(A)$, $p_\theta\colon A \to A/\theta$ will be the canonical surjective morphism; given any $X \in A \cup A^2 \cup \mathcal{P}(A) \cup \mathcal{P}(A^2)$, we denote by $X/\theta = p_\theta(X)$. Note that $\mathrm{Ker}(p_\theta) = \theta$ for any $\theta \in \mathrm{Con}(A)$, and that $Cg_A(Cg_S(X)) = Cg_A(X)$ for any subalgebra S of A and any $X \subseteq S^2$.

(H) Throughout the rest of this paper, B will be a member of $\mathcal{V}$ and $f : A \to B$ a morphism.

Recall that, for any $\alpha \in \mathrm{Con}(A)$ and any $\beta \in \mathrm{Con}(B)$, we have $f^*(\beta) \in [\mathrm{Ker}(f)) \subseteq \mathrm{Con}(A)$, $f(f^*(\beta)) = \beta \cap f(A^2) \subseteq \beta$ and $\alpha \subseteq f^*(f(\alpha))$; if $\alpha \in [\mathrm{Ker}(f))$, then $f(\alpha) \in \mathrm{Con}(f(A))$ and $f^*(f(\alpha)) = \alpha$. Hence $\theta \mapsto f(\theta)$ is a lattice isomorphism from $[\mathrm{Ker}(f))$ to $\mathrm{Con}(f(A))$, having f^* as inverse, and thus it sets an order isomorphism from $\mathrm{Max}(A) \cap [\mathrm{Ker}(f))$ to $\mathrm{Max}(f(A))$. In particular, for any $\theta \in \mathrm{Con}(A)$, the map $\alpha \mapsto \alpha/\theta$ is an order isomorphism from $[\theta)$ to $\mathrm{Con}(A/\theta)$.

Lemma 1 ([21] (Lemma 1.11), [22] (Proposition 1.2))**.** *For any $X \subseteq A^2$ and any $\alpha, \theta \in \mathrm{Con}(A)$:*
- *$f(Cg_A(X) \vee \mathrm{Ker}(f)) = Cg_{f(A)}(f(X))$, so $Cg_B(f(Cg_A(X))) = Cg_B(f(X))$ and $(Cg_A(X) \vee \theta)/\theta = Cg_{A/\theta}(X/\theta)$;*
- *in particular, $f(\alpha \vee \mathrm{Ker}(f)) = Cg_{f(A)}(f(\alpha))$, so $(\alpha \vee \theta)/\theta = Cg_{A/\theta}(\alpha/\theta)$.*

For any nonempty family $(\alpha_i)_{i\in I} \subseteq [\mathrm{Ker}(f))$, we have, in $\mathrm{Con}(f(A))$: $f(\bigvee\limits_{i\in I} \alpha_i) = \bigvee\limits_{i\in I} f(\alpha_i)$.

Indeed, by Lemma 1,

$$f(\bigvee_{i\in I} \alpha_i) = f(Cg_A(\bigcup_{i\in I} \alpha_i)) = Cg_{f(A)}(f(\bigcup_{i\in I} \alpha_i)) = Cg_{f(A)}(\bigcup_{i\in I} f(\alpha_i)) = \bigvee_{i\in I} f(\alpha_i).$$

We denote by $f^\bullet\colon \mathrm{Con}(A) \to \mathrm{Con}(B)$ the map defined by $f^\bullet(\alpha) = Cg_B(f(\alpha))$ for all $\alpha \in \mathrm{Con}(A)$. By the above, if f is surjective, then $f^\bullet\mid_{[\mathrm{Ker}(f))}\colon [\mathrm{Ker}(f)) \to \mathrm{Con}(B)$ is the inverse of the lattice isomorphism $f^*\mid_{\mathrm{Con}(B)}\colon \mathrm{Con}(B) \to [\mathrm{Ker}(f))$.

We use the following definition from [23] for the *term condition commutator*: let $\alpha, \beta \in \mathrm{Con}(A)$. For any $\mu \in \mathrm{Con}(A)$, by $C(\alpha, \beta; \mu)$ we denote the fact that the following condition holds: for all $n,k \in \mathbb{N}$ and any term t over τ of arity $n+k$, if $(a_i, b_i) \in \alpha$ for all $i \in \overline{1,n}$ and $(c_j, d_j) \in \beta$ for all $j \in \overline{1,k}$, then $(t^A(a_1,\ldots,a_n,c_1,\ldots,c_k), t^A(a_1,\ldots,a_n,d_1,\ldots,d_k)) \in \mu$ if and only if $(t^A(b_1,\ldots,b_n,c_1,\ldots,c_k), t^A(b_1,\ldots,b_n,d_1,\ldots,d_k)) \in \mu$. We denote by $[\alpha,\beta]_A$ the *commutator of α and β* in A, defined by $[\alpha,\beta]_A := \bigcap\{\mu \in \mathrm{Con}(A) \mid C(\alpha,\beta;\mu)\}$. The operation $[\cdot,\cdot]_A\colon \mathrm{Con}(A) \times \mathrm{Con}(A) \to \mathrm{Con}(A)$ is called the *commutator of A*.

By [1], if $\mathcal{V}$ is congruence–modular, then, for each member M of $\mathcal{V}$, $[\cdot,\cdot]_M$ is the unique binary operation on $\mathrm{Con}(M)$ such that, for all $\alpha, \beta \in \mathrm{Con}(M)$, $[\alpha,\beta]_M = \min\{\mu \in \mathrm{Con}(M) \mid \mu \subseteq \alpha \cap \beta$ and, for any member N of $\mathcal{V}$ and any surjective morphism $h : M \to N$ in $\mathcal{V}$, $\mu \vee \mathrm{Ker}(h) = h^*([h(\alpha \vee \mathrm{Ker}(h)), h(\beta \vee \mathrm{Ker}(h))]_N)\}$. Therefore, if $\mathcal{V}$ is congruence–modular, $\alpha, \beta, \theta \in \mathrm{Con}(A)$ and f is surjective, then

$$[f(\alpha \vee \mathrm{Ker}(f)), f(\beta \vee \mathrm{Ker}(f))]_B = f([\alpha,\beta]_A \vee \mathrm{Ker}(f)).$$

In particular, $[(\alpha \vee \theta)/\theta, (\beta \vee \theta)/\theta]_{A/\theta} = ([\alpha,\beta]_A \vee \theta)/\theta$, thus, if $\theta \subseteq \alpha \cap \beta$, then $[\alpha/\theta, \beta/\theta]_{A/\theta} = ([\alpha,\beta]_A \vee \theta)/\theta$; if, moreover, $\theta \subseteq [\alpha,\beta]_A$, then $[\alpha/\theta, \beta/\theta]_{A/\theta} = [\alpha,\beta]_A/\theta$.

By [23] [Lemma 4.6, Lemma 4.7, Theorem 8.3], the commutator is smaller than the intersection and increasing in both arguments; if $\mathcal{V}$ is congruence–modular, then the commutator is also commutative and distributive in both arguments with respect to arbitrary joins.

Hence, if $\mathcal{V}$ is congruence–modular and the commutator of A coincides to the intersection of congruences, then $\mathrm{Con}(A)$ is a frame, in particular it is distributive. Therefore, if $\mathcal{V}$ is congruence–modular and the commutator coincides to the intersection in each member of $\mathcal{V}$, then $\mathcal{V}$ is congruence–distributive. By [24], the converse holds, as well: if $\mathcal{V}$ is congruence–distributive, then, in each member of $\mathcal{V}$, the commutator coincides to the intersection of congruences.

For any $\alpha, \beta \in \mathrm{Con}(A)$, we denote by $[\alpha,\beta]^1_A = [\alpha,\beta]_A$ and, for any $n \in \mathbb{N}^*$, by $[\alpha,\beta]^{n+1}_A = [[\alpha,\beta]^n_A, [\alpha,\beta]^n_A]_A$.

Recall that $\mathcal{V}$ is said to be *semidegenerate* if and only if no nontrivial algebra in $\mathcal{V}$ has one–element subalgebras. Recall from [10] that, if $\mathcal{V}$ is congruence–modular, then the following are equivalent:

- $\mathcal{V}$ is semidegenerate;
- for all members M of $\mathcal{V}$, $\nabla_M \in \mathcal{K}(M)$.

If $[\cdot,\cdot]_A$ is distributive with respect to the join, in particular if $\mathcal{V}$ is congruence–modular, then, if A has *principal commutators*, that is its set $\mathrm{PCon}(A)$ of principal congruences is closed with respect to the commutator, then its set $\mathcal{K}(A)$ of compact congruences is closed with respect to the commutator.

Recall that a *prime congruence* of A is a proper congruence ϕ of A such that, for any $\alpha, \beta \in \mathrm{Con}(A)$, if $[\alpha,\beta]_A \subseteq \phi$, then $\alpha \subseteq \phi$ or $\beta \subseteq \phi$ [1]. It actually suffices that we enforce this condition for principal congruences α, β of A:

Lemma 2 ([7,18])**.** *A proper congruence ϕ of A is prime if and only if for any $\alpha, \beta \in \mathrm{PCon}(A)$, if $[\alpha,\beta]_A \subseteq \phi$, then $\alpha \subseteq \phi$ or $\beta \subseteq \phi$.*

We denote by $\mathrm{Spec}(A)$ the *(prime) spectrum* of A, that is the set of the prime congruences of A. Recall that $\mathrm{Spec}(A)$ is not necessarily nonempty. However, by [4] [Theorem 5.3], if the commutator of A is distributive with respect to the join of congruences, $\nabla_A \in \mathcal{K}(A)$ and $[\nabla_A, \nabla_A]_A = \nabla_A$, in particular if $\mathcal{V}$ is congruence–modular and semidegenerate, then:

- $\mathrm{Max}(A) \subseteq \mathrm{Spec}(A)$;
- any proper congruence of A is included in a maximal, thus prime congruence of A;
- hence $\mathrm{Max}(A)$ and thus $\mathrm{Spec}(A)$ is nonempty whenever A is nontrivial.

For all $\theta \in \mathrm{Con}(A)$, we set $V_A(\theta) := \mathrm{Spec}(A) \cap [\theta)$ and $D_A(\theta) := \mathrm{Spec}(A) \setminus V_A(\theta) = \mathrm{Spec}(A) \setminus [\theta)$.

For all $X \subseteq A^2$ and $a, b \in A$, we set $V_A(X) := V_A(Cg_A(X))$, $D_A(X) := D_A(Cg_A(X))$, $V_A(a,b) := V_A(Cg_A(a,b))$ and $D_A(a,b) := D_A(Cg_A(a,b))$.

For any $\theta \in \mathrm{Con}(A)$, we set $\rho_A(\theta) := \bigcap V_A(\theta)$ and call this congruence the *radical* of θ. We denote by $\mathrm{RCon}(A) = \{\rho_A(\theta) \mid \theta \in \mathrm{Con}(A)\} = \{\theta \in \mathrm{Con}(A) \mid \rho_A(\theta) = \theta\}$. We call the elements of $\mathrm{RCon}(A)$ the *radical congruences* of A. Obviously, any prime congruence of A is radical.

By [4] [Lemma 1.6, Proposition 1.2], if the commutator of A is commutative and distributive with respect to arbitrary joins, in particular if $\mathcal{V}$ is congruence–modular, then:

(i) a congruence θ of A is radical if and only if it is *semiprime*, that is, for any $\alpha \in \mathrm{Con}(A)$, if $[\alpha,\alpha]_A \subseteq \theta$, then $\alpha \subseteq \theta$;
(ii) hence $\mathrm{Spec}(A) = \mathrm{Mi}(\mathrm{Con}(A)) \cap \mathrm{RCon}(A)$.

A is called a *semiprime algebra* if and only if $\rho_A(\Delta_A) = \Delta_A$. By statement (i) above, if the commutator of A equals the intersection, in particular if $\mathcal{V}$ is congruence–distributive, then $\mathrm{RCon}(A) = \mathrm{Con}(A)$, thus A is semiprime.

Let us denote by $\mathcal{S}_{\mathrm{Spec}}(A)=\{D_A(\theta)\mid\theta\in\mathrm{Con}(A)\}$. If the commutator of A is commutative and distributive with respect to arbitrary joins, in particular if $\mathcal{V}$ is congruence–modular, then, by [4,7,18], $\mathcal{S}_{\mathrm{Spec}}(A)$ is a topology on $\mathrm{Spec}(A)$, called the *Stone topology* or the *spectral topology*, which satisfies, for all $\alpha,\beta\in\mathrm{Con}(A)$ and any family $(\alpha_i)_{i\in I}\subseteq\mathrm{Con}(A)$:

- $D_A(\alpha)\subseteq D_A(\beta)$ if and only if $V_A(\alpha)\supseteq V_A(\beta)$ if and only if $\rho_A(\alpha)\subseteq\rho_A(\beta)$;
- thus $D_A(\alpha)=D_A(\beta)$ if and only if $V_A(\alpha)=V_A(\beta)$ if and only if $\rho_A(\alpha)=\rho_A(\beta)$;
- clearly, $\alpha\subseteq\beta$ implies $\rho_A(\alpha)\subseteq\rho_A(\beta)$;
- clearly, $\alpha\subseteq\rho_A(\alpha)$, thus $\rho_A(\alpha)=\Delta_A$ implies $\alpha=\Delta_A$;
- $D_A(\nabla_A)=\mathrm{Spec}(A)=V_A(\Delta_A)$ and $D_A(\Delta_A)=\emptyset=V_A(\nabla_A)$;
- if A is semiprime, then: $D_A(\alpha)=\emptyset$ if and only if $V_A(\alpha)=\mathrm{Spec}(A)$ if and only if $\rho_A(\alpha)=\Delta_A$ if and only if $\alpha=\Delta_A$;
- if $\nabla_A\in\mathcal{K}(A)$ and $[\nabla_A,\nabla_A]_A=\nabla_A$, in particular if $\mathcal{V}$ is congruence–modular and semidegenerate, then: $D_A(\alpha)=\mathrm{Spec}(A)$ if and only if $V_A(\alpha)=\emptyset$ if and only if $\rho_A(\alpha)=\nabla_A$ if and only if $\alpha=\nabla_A$;
- $D_A([\alpha,\beta]_A)=D_A(\alpha\cap\beta)=D_A(\alpha)\cap D_A(\beta)$ and $D_A(\alpha\vee\beta)=D_A(\alpha)\cup D_A(\beta)$; thus $V_A([\alpha,\beta]_A)=V_A(\alpha\cap\beta)=V_A(\alpha)\cup V_A(\beta)$, $V_A(\alpha\vee\beta)=V_A(\alpha)\cap V_A(\beta)$, $\rho_A([\alpha,\beta]_A)=\rho_A(\alpha\cap\beta)=\rho_A(\alpha)\cap\rho_A(\beta)$ and $\rho_A(\alpha\vee\beta)=\rho_A(\rho_A(\alpha)\vee\rho_A(\beta))$;
- $D_A(\bigvee_{i\in I}\alpha_i)=D_A(\bigcup_{i\in I}\alpha_i)=\bigcup_{i\in I}D_A(\alpha_i)$, thus $V_A(\bigvee_{i\in I}\alpha_i)=V_A(\bigcup_{i\in I}\alpha_i)=\bigcap_{i\in I}V_A(\alpha_i)$ and $\rho_A(\bigvee_{i\in I}\alpha_i)=\rho_A(\bigcup_{i\in I}\alpha_i)=\rho_A(\bigcup_{i\in I}\rho_A(\alpha_i))=\rho_A(\bigvee_{i\in I}\rho_A(\alpha_i))$;
- hence, for any $\theta\in\mathrm{Con}(A)$, $V_A(\theta)=\bigcap_{(a,b)\in\theta}V_A(a,b)$ and $D_A(\theta)=\bigcup_{(a,b)\in\theta}D_A(a,b)$, therefore the Stone topology $\mathcal{S}_{\mathrm{Spec}}(A)$ has $\{D_A(a,b)\mid a,b\in A\}$ as a basis.

If $[\cdot,\cdot]_A$ is commutative and distributive with respect to arbitrary joins and $\mathrm{Max}(A)\subseteq\mathrm{Spec}(A)$, in particular if $\mathcal{V}$ is congruence–modular and semidegenerate, then the Stone topology $\mathcal{S}_{\mathrm{Spec}}(A)$ on $\mathrm{Spec}(A)$ induces the *Stone* or *spectral topology* on $\mathrm{Max}(A)$: $\mathcal{S}_{\mathrm{Max}}(A)=\{D_A(\theta)\cap\mathrm{Max}(A)\mid\theta\in\mathrm{Con}(A)\}$, having $\{D_A(a,b)\cap\mathrm{Max}(A)\mid a,b\in A\}$ as a basis. Note that $\mathrm{Max}(A)\subseteq\mathrm{Spec}(A)$ if $[\cdot,\cdot]_A$ is commutative and distributive with respect to arbitrary joins, $\nabla_A\in\mathcal{K}(A)$ and $[\nabla_A,\nabla_A]_A=\nabla_A$.

In the same way, but replacing congruences with ideals, one defines the Stone topology on the set of prime ideals and that of maximal ideals of a bounded distributive lattice.

We call f an *admissible morphism* if and only if $f^*(\mathrm{Spec}(B))\subseteq\mathrm{Spec}(A)$ [18,19]. Recall from [4] that, if $\mathcal{V}$ is congruence–modular, then the map $\alpha\mapsto f(\alpha)$ is an order isomorphism from $\mathrm{Spec}(A)\cap[\mathrm{Ker}(f))$ to $\mathrm{Spec}(f(A))$, thus to $\mathrm{Spec}(B)$ if f is surjective, case in which this map coincides with $f^\bullet$ and f^* is its inverse, hence f is admissible.

Remark 1. *By the above, if $\mathcal{V}$ is congruence–modular and f is surjective, then:*

- *for all $\alpha\in\mathrm{Con}(A)$, $f(V_A(\alpha))=V_B(f(\alpha))$ and $f(D_A(\alpha))=D_B(f(\alpha))$; in particular:*
- *for all $a,b\in A$, $f(V_A(a,b))=V_B(f(a),f(b))$ and $f(D_A(a,b))=D_B(f(a),f(b))$;*

thus, since $f=f^\bullet=(f^*)^{-1}$, the map $f^*\mid_{\mathrm{Spec}(B)}:\mathrm{Spec}(B)\to\mathrm{Spec}(A)$ is continuous with respect to the Stone topologies.

A subset S of A^2 is called an *m–system* for A if and only if, for all $a,b,c,d\in A$, if $(a,b),(c,d)\in S$, then $[Cg_A(a,b),Cg_A(c,d)]_A\cap S\neq\emptyset$. For instance, any congruence of A is an m–system. Also:

Remark 2 ([7,18]). *If $\phi\in\mathrm{Spec}(A)$, then $\nabla_A\setminus\phi$ is an m–system in A.*

Lemma 3 ([4]). *Let S be an m–system in A and $\alpha\in\mathrm{Con}(A)$ such that $\alpha\cap S=\emptyset$. If the commutator of A is distributive with respect to the join, in particular if $\mathcal{V}$ is congruence–modular, then:*

- $\mathrm{Max}\{\theta\in\mathrm{Con}(A)\mid\alpha\subseteq\theta,\theta\cap S=\emptyset\}\subseteq\mathrm{Spec}(A)$, *in particular, for the case $\alpha=\Delta_A$,* $\mathrm{Max}\{\theta\in\mathrm{Con}(A)\mid\theta\cap S=\emptyset\}\subseteq\mathrm{Spec}(A)$;

- *if* $\nabla_A \in \mathcal{K}(A)$, *in particular if* $\mathcal{V}$ *is congruence–modular and semidegenerate, then the set* $\mathrm{Max}\{\theta \in \mathrm{Con}(A) \mid \alpha \subseteq \theta, \theta \cap S = \emptyset\}$ *is nonempty; thus* $\mathrm{Max}\{\theta \in \mathrm{Con}(A) \mid \theta \cap S = \emptyset\}$ *is nonempty.*

We denote by $\mathrm{Min}(A) = Min(\mathrm{Spec}(A), \subseteq)$. Recall that $\mathrm{Min}(A)$ is called the *minimal prime spectrum* of A and its elements are called *minimal prime congruences* of A.

Now assume that the commutator of A is commutative and distributive with respect to arbitrary joins, which holds if $\mathcal{V}$ is congruence–modular. Then, by [25] [Proposition 5.9], if we define a binary relation $\equiv_A$ on $\mathrm{Con}(A)$ by: for any $\alpha, \beta \in \mathrm{Con}(A)$, $\alpha \equiv_A \beta$ if and only if $\rho_A(\alpha) = \rho_A(\beta)$, then $\equiv_A$ is a lattice congruence of $\mathrm{Con}(A)$ that preserves arbitrary joins such that $\mathrm{Con}(A)/\equiv_A$ is a frame; see also [7].

Following the notations from [25], if $(L, [\cdot,\cdot])$ is a *commutator lattice*, that is a complete lattice L endowed with a binary operation $[\cdot,\cdot]$ which is commutative, smaller than the meet and distributive with respect to arbitrary joins [16,26], then we denote by Spec_L the set of the prime elements of L with respect to the commutator $[\cdot,\cdot]$, by $\mathrm{Min}_L = Min(\mathrm{Spec}_L)$ the set of the minimal prime elements of L and by $R(L)$ the set of the *radical elements* of L, that is the meets of subsets of Spec_L.

Let $(L, [\cdot,\cdot])$ be a commutator lattice, $u \in L$ and $U \subseteq L$. The annihilators with respect to the commutator are defined by $\mathrm{Ann}_{(L,[\cdot,\cdot])}(U) := \{a \in L \mid (\forall x \in U)([a, x] = 0)\}$ and $\mathrm{Ann}_{(L,[\cdot,\cdot])}(u) := \mathrm{Ann}_{(L,[\cdot,\cdot])}(\{u\})$. Recall from [25] that $\equiv_A$ also preserves the commutator and the quotient algebra of $(\mathrm{Con}(A), [\cdot,\cdot]_A)$ through $\equiv_A$ is the commutator lattice $(\mathrm{Con}(A)/\equiv_A, \wedge)$. Note that L is a frame if its commutator $[\cdot,\cdot]$ equals the meet, case in which the annihilators in $(L, [\cdot,\cdot])$ coincide with those with respect to the meet and Spec_L is exactly the set of the meet–prime elements of L, thus $\mathrm{Spec}_L = \mathrm{Mi}(L)$ since L is distributive.

3. On the Residuated Structure of the Lattice of Congruences

Condition 1. *Let M be an arbitrary member of the variety $\mathcal{V}$. We will say that M satisfies condition:*

(i) *iff the commutator of M is commutative and distributive with respect to arbitrary joins;*
(ii) *iff* $[\theta, \nabla_M]_M = \theta$ *for all* $\theta \in \mathrm{Con}(M)$;
(iii) *iff, for all* $\alpha, \beta, \theta \in \mathrm{Con}(M)$, $([\alpha, \beta]_M \vee \theta)/\theta = [(\alpha \vee \theta)/\theta, (\beta \vee \theta)/\theta]_{M/\theta}$;
(iv) *iff* $\nabla_M \in \mathcal{K}(M)$ *and* $\mathcal{K}(M)$ *is closed with respect to the commutator of M;*
(v) *iff all principal ideals of* $\mathrm{Con}(M)/\equiv_M$ *generated by minimal prime elements are minimal prime ideals, that is: for any* $p \in \mathrm{Min}_{\mathrm{Con}(M)/\equiv_M}$, *we have* $(p] \in \mathrm{Min}_{\mathrm{Id}}(\mathrm{Con}(M)/\equiv_M)$;
(vi) *iff* $\alpha^{\perp} \in \mathcal{K}(M)$ *for any* $\alpha \in \mathcal{K}(M)$.

Recall from Section 2 and [1,10] that:

- if $\mathcal{V}$ is congruence–modular, then A satisfies (i) and (iii) from Condition 1;
- if $\mathcal{V}$ is congruence–modular and semidegenerate, then $\nabla_A \in \mathcal{K}(A)$ and A satisfies Condition 1.(ii);
- if $\mathcal{V}$ is congruence–distributive, then A satisfies Condition 1.(ii).

Recall that $\mathcal{K}(A) = \mathrm{Cp}(\mathrm{Con}(A))$. If the lattice $\mathrm{Con}(A)$ is compact, i.e., $\mathrm{Con}(A) = \mathcal{K}(A)$, then A trivially satisfies (iv) and (vi) from Condition 1. Recall from [7] that, if A satisfies Condition 1.(iv), then the *reticulation* $\mathcal{L}(A)$ of A can be constructed as $\mathcal{L}(A) = \mathcal{K}(A)/\equiv_A$, which is a bounded sublattice of the frame $\mathrm{Con}(A)/\equiv_A$ and thus $\mathcal{L}(A)$ is a bounded distributive lattice.

Since an element of a lattice is prime if and only if the principal ideal it generates is prime, we have that, whenever a principal ideal of a lattice is a minimal prime ideal, it follows that its generator is a minimal prime element of that lattice. Hence Condition 1.(v) for a member M of $\mathcal{V}$ is equivalent to:

- for any $p \in \mathrm{Con}(M)/\equiv_M$, $p \in \mathrm{Min}_{\mathrm{Con}(M)/\equiv_M}$ if and only if $(p] \in \mathrm{Min}_{\mathrm{Id}}(\mathrm{Con}(M)/\equiv_M)$.

Note that A satisfies Condition 1.(v) if all prime ideals of $\mathrm{Con}(A)/\equiv_A$ are principal, in particular if all ideals of $\mathrm{Con}(A)/\equiv_A$ are principal, that is if $\mathrm{Con}(A)/\equiv_A$ is compact, in particular if $\mathrm{Con}(A)/\equiv_A = \mathcal{K}(A)/\equiv_A$, that is if $\mathrm{Con}(A)/\equiv_A = \mathcal{L}(A)$ in the case when $\mathcal{K}(A)$ is closed with respect to the commutator of A, in particular if $\mathrm{Con}(A)$ is compact, that is if $\mathrm{Con}(A) = \mathcal{K}(A)$.

(H) Throughout this section, we will assume that A satisfies Condition 1.(i), which holds in the particular case when $\mathcal{V}$ is congruence–modular.

See [7] for the next results. Until mentioned otherwise, let $\alpha, \beta, \gamma, \theta \in \mathrm{Con}(A)$ and $n \in \mathbb{N}^*$, arbitrary. An induction argument shows that:

- $[\alpha, \beta]_A^{n+1} = [[\alpha, \beta]_A, [\alpha, \beta]_A]_A^n$;
- $\rho_A([\alpha, \beta]_A^n) = \rho_A([\alpha, \beta]_A) = \rho_A(\alpha \cap \beta) = \rho_A(\alpha) \cap \rho_A(\beta)$.

If A is semiprime, then $\rho_A(\theta) = \Delta_A$ if and only if $\theta = \Delta_A$, hence, by the above: $[\alpha, \beta]_A^n = \Delta_A$ if and only if $[\alpha, \beta]_A = \Delta_A$ if and only if $\alpha \cap \beta = \Delta_A$, so $\mathrm{Ann}_{\mathrm{Con}(A)}(\alpha) = \mathrm{Ann}_{(\mathrm{Con}(A),[\cdot,\cdot]_A)}(\alpha)$ and thus, for any $S \subseteq \mathrm{Con}(A)$, $\mathrm{Ann}_{\mathrm{Con}(A)}(S) = \mathrm{Ann}_{(\mathrm{Con}(A),[\cdot,\cdot]_A)}(S)$.

If $\mathcal{V}$ is congruence–modular and f is surjective, then, for any $X, Y \in \mathcal{P}(A^2)$ and any $a, b, c, d \in A$:

- $[f(\alpha \vee \mathrm{Ker}(f)), f(\beta \vee \mathrm{Ker}(f))]_B^n = f([\alpha, \beta]_A^n \vee \mathrm{Ker}(f))$, thus $[(\alpha \vee \theta)/\theta, (\beta \vee \theta)/\theta]_{A/\theta}^n = ([\alpha, \beta]_A^n \vee \theta)/\theta$;
- hence $[Cg_{A/\theta}(X/\theta), Cg_{A/\theta}(Y/\theta)]_{A/\theta}^n = ([Cg_A(X), Cg_A(Y)]_A^n \vee \theta)/\theta$, in particular $[Cg_{A/\theta}(a/\theta, b/\theta), Cg_{A/\theta}(c/\theta, d/\theta)]_{A/\theta}^n = ([Cg_A(a,b), Cg_A(c,d)]_A^n \vee \theta)/\theta$;
- $\mathrm{Spec}(B) = \{\phi/\mathrm{Ker}(f) \mid \phi \in V_A(\mathrm{Ker}(f))\}$, thus $\mathrm{Spec}(A/\theta) = \{\phi/\theta \mid \phi \in V_A(\theta)\}$.

We denote by $\beta \to \gamma = \bigvee\{\delta \in \mathrm{Con}(A) \mid [\delta, \beta]_A \subseteq \gamma\}$ and $\beta^\perp = \beta \to \Delta_A$.

Since $\theta = \bigvee\limits_{(a,b)\in\theta} Cg_A(a,b) = \bigvee\{\zeta \in \mathrm{PCon}(A) \mid \zeta \subseteq \theta\} = \bigvee\{\zeta \in \mathcal{K}(A) \mid \zeta \subseteq \theta\}$, it follows that:

$$\beta \to \gamma = \bigvee\{\zeta \in \mathcal{K}(A) \mid [\zeta, \beta]_A \subseteq \gamma\} = \bigvee\{\zeta \in \mathrm{PCon}(A) \mid [\zeta, \beta]_A \subseteq \gamma\},$$

$$\text{in particular } \beta^\perp = \bigvee\{\zeta \in \mathcal{K}(A) \mid [\zeta, \beta]_A = \Delta_A\} = \bigvee\{\zeta \in \mathrm{PCon}(A) \mid [\zeta, \beta]_A = \Delta_A\}.$$

Let us note that, for all $a, b \in A$, we have $(a,b) \in \beta^\perp$ if and only if $Cg_A(a,b) \subseteq \beta^\perp$ if and only if $[Cg_A(a,b), \beta]_A = \Delta_A$, hence $\beta^\perp = \{(a,b) \in A^2 \mid [Cg_A(a,b), \beta]_A = \Delta_A\}$.

Note that these operations can be defined for any commutator lattice $(L, [\cdot,\cdot])$ by: $b \to c = \bigvee\{a \in L \mid [a,b] \leq c\}$ and $b^\perp = b \to 0 = \bigvee\{a \in L \mid [a,b] = 0\}$ for any $b, c \in L$ and, if L is algebraic, that is compactly generated, then we also have equalities similar to the above.

Since $[\Delta_A, \beta]_A = \Delta_A \subseteq \gamma$ and, for any non–empty family $(\alpha_i)_{i\in I}$, $[\alpha_i, \beta]_A \subseteq \gamma$ for all $i \in I$ implies $[\bigvee\limits_{i\in I} \alpha_i, \beta]_A = \bigvee\limits_{i\in I} [\alpha_i, \beta]_A \subseteq \gamma$, it follows that:

$$\beta \to \gamma = \max\{\delta \in \mathrm{Con}(A) \mid [\delta, \beta]_A \subseteq \gamma\},$$

$$\text{in particular } \beta^\perp = \max\{\delta \in \mathrm{Con}(A) \mid [\delta, \beta]_A = \Delta_A\},$$

hence $\beta^\perp = \max(\mathrm{Ann}_{(\mathrm{Con}(A),[\cdot,\cdot]_A)}(\beta))$ and thus $\mathrm{Ann}_{(\mathrm{Con}(A),[\cdot,\cdot]_A)}(\beta) = (\beta^\perp] \in \mathrm{PId}(\mathrm{Con}(A))$.

Note that $[\beta, \beta \to \gamma]_A \subseteq \gamma$, in particular $[\beta, \beta^\perp]_A = \Delta_A$; moreover, for all $\delta \in \mathrm{Con}(A)$:

$$[\delta, \beta]_A \subseteq \gamma \text{ if and only if } \delta \subseteq \beta \to \gamma, \text{ in particular: } [\delta, \beta]_A = \Delta_A \text{ if and only if } \delta \subseteq \beta^\perp.$$

Therefore, in the particular case when the commutator of A is associative, $(\mathrm{Con}(A), \cap, \vee, \to, \Delta_A, \nabla_A)$ is a (bounded commutative integral) residuated lattice, in which $\cdot^\perp$ is the negation.

Lemma 4. *If the algebra A is semiprime, then $\theta^\perp \in \mathrm{RCon}(A)$ for any $\theta \in \mathrm{Con}(A)$.*

Proof. Let $\alpha, \theta \in \mathrm{Con}(A)$ such that $[\alpha, \alpha]_A \subseteq \theta^\perp$. Then, by the above and the fact that A is semiprime, $[[\alpha, \alpha]_A, \theta]_A = \Delta_A$, which is equivalent to $\rho_A([[\alpha, \alpha]_A, \theta]_A) = \Delta_A$, that is $\rho_A(\alpha \cap \theta) = \Delta_A$, that is $\rho_A([\alpha, \theta]_A) = \Delta_A$, which means that $[\alpha, \theta]_A = \Delta_A$, which in turn is equivalent to $\alpha \subseteq \theta^\perp$. Hence $\theta^\perp$ is a semiprime and thus a radical congruence of A. □

For any $X \subseteq A^2$, we set

$$X^\perp := \{(a, b) \in A^2 \mid (\forall (x, y) \in X) ([Cg_A(a, b), Cg_A(x, y)]_A = \Delta_A)\}.$$

Thus:

$$\begin{aligned} X^\perp &= \{(a, b) \in A^2 \mid [Cg_A(a, b), \bigvee_{(x,y)\in X} Cg_A(x, y)]_A = \Delta_A\} \\ &= \{(a, b) \in A^2 \mid [Cg_A(a, b), Cg_A(X)]_A = \Delta_A\} \\ &= \bigvee\{Cg_A(a, b) \mid (a, b) \in A^2, [Cg_A(a, b), Cg_A(X)]_A = \Delta_A\} \\ &= \bigvee\{\alpha \in \mathrm{Con}(A) \mid [\alpha, Cg_A(X)]_A = \Delta_A\} \\ &= \max\{\alpha \in \mathrm{Con}(A) \mid [\alpha, Cg_A(X)]_A = \Delta_A\} = Cg_A(X)^\perp. \end{aligned}$$

So this more general notation is consistent with the notation above for the particular case when $X \in \mathrm{Con}(A)$.

Lemma 5. *For any $\alpha, \beta, \theta \in \mathrm{Con}(A)$:*

(i) $\beta \subseteq \alpha \to \beta$;

(ii) $(\alpha \vee \theta) \to (\beta \vee \theta) = \alpha \to (\beta \vee \theta)$.

Proof. (i) $[\beta, \alpha]_A \subseteq \beta \cap \alpha \subseteq \beta$, thus $\beta \subseteq \max\{\zeta \in \mathcal{K}(A) \mid [\zeta, \alpha]_A \subseteq \beta\} = \alpha \to \beta$.
(ii) For all $\gamma \in \mathrm{Con}(A)$, we have, since $[\gamma, \theta]_A \subseteq \theta \subseteq \beta \vee \theta$: $\gamma \subseteq (\alpha \vee \theta) \to (\beta \vee \theta)$ if and only if $[\gamma, \alpha \vee \theta]_A \subseteq \beta \vee \theta$ if and only if $[\gamma, \alpha]_A \vee [\gamma, \theta]_A \subseteq \beta \vee \theta$ if and only if $[\gamma, \alpha]_A \subseteq \beta \vee \theta$ if and only if $\gamma \subseteq \alpha \to (\beta \vee \theta)$. By taking $\gamma = (\alpha \vee \theta) \to (\beta \vee \theta)$ and then $\gamma = \alpha \to (\beta \vee \theta)$ in the previous equivalences, we get: $\alpha \to (\beta \vee \theta) = (\alpha \vee \theta) \to (\beta \vee \theta)$. □

Proposition 1. *If A satisfies Condition 1.(iii), in particular if $\mathcal{V}$ is congruence–modular, then, for any $\alpha, \beta, \theta \in \mathrm{Con}(A)$:*

(i) $(\alpha \vee \theta)/\theta \to (\beta \vee \theta)/\theta = ((\alpha \vee \theta) \to (\beta \vee \theta))/\theta = (\alpha \to (\beta \vee \theta))/\theta$;

(ii) $((\alpha \vee \theta)/\theta)^\perp = (\alpha \to \theta)/\theta$.

Proof. By Lemma 5.(i), $\alpha \to (\beta \vee \theta) \supseteq \beta \vee \theta \supseteq \theta$ and $(\alpha \vee \theta) \to (\beta \vee \theta) \supseteq \beta \vee \theta \supseteq \theta$.
(i) For any $\gamma \in [\theta)$, by the inclusions above, the definition of the binary operation $\to$ on $\mathrm{Con}(A)$ and the assumption that A satisfies Condition 1.(iii), we have:

$$\begin{aligned} \gamma/\theta \subseteq (\alpha \vee \theta)/\theta \to (\beta \vee \theta)/\theta &\iff [\gamma/\theta, (\alpha \vee \theta)/\theta]_{A/\theta} \subseteq (\beta \vee \theta)/\theta \\ &\iff ([\gamma, \alpha \vee \theta]_A \vee \theta)/\theta \subseteq (\beta \vee \theta)/\theta \\ &\iff [\gamma, \alpha \vee \theta]_A \vee \theta \subseteq \beta \vee \theta \\ &\iff [\gamma, \alpha \vee \theta]_A \subseteq \beta \vee \theta \\ &\iff \gamma \subseteq (\alpha \vee \theta) \to (\beta \vee \theta) \\ &\iff \gamma/\theta \subseteq ((\alpha \vee \theta) \to (\beta \vee \theta))/\theta. \end{aligned}$$

Since $(\alpha \vee \theta)/\theta \to (\beta \vee \theta)/\theta, ((\alpha \vee \theta) \to (\beta \vee \theta))/\theta \in \mathrm{Con}(A/\theta) = \{\zeta/\theta \mid \zeta \in [\theta)\}$, we may take $\gamma/\theta = (\alpha \vee \theta)/\theta \to (\beta \vee \theta)/\theta$ and then $\gamma/\theta = ((\alpha \vee \theta) \to (\beta \vee \theta))/\theta$ in the equivalences above and obtain the first equality in the enunciation through double inclusion. The second equality follows from Lemma 5.(ii).
(ii) Take $\beta = \Delta_A$ in (i). □

Lemma 6. *Let $\alpha, \beta \in \mathrm{Con}(A)$. Then:*

(i) $\Delta_A^{\perp} = \nabla_A$ *and, if A satisfies Condition 1.(ii), in particular if $\mathcal{V}$ is either congruence–distributive or both congruence–modular and semidegenerate, then* $\nabla_A^{\perp} = \Delta_A$;

(ii) $\alpha \subseteq \beta$ *implies* $\beta^{\perp} \subseteq \alpha^{\perp}$, *and:* $\beta^{\perp} \subseteq \alpha^{\perp}$ *if and only if* $\alpha^{\perp\perp} \subseteq \beta^{\perp\perp}$, *in particular* $\alpha^{\perp} = \beta^{\perp}$ *if and only if* $\alpha^{\perp\perp} = \beta^{\perp\perp}$;

(iii) $\alpha \subseteq \alpha^{\perp\perp}$ *and* $\alpha^{\perp\perp\perp} = \alpha^{\perp}$;

(iv) $(\alpha \vee \beta)^{\perp} = \alpha^{\perp} \cap \beta^{\perp} = (\alpha^{\perp} \cap \beta^{\perp})^{\perp\perp}$;

(v) *if A is semiprime, then* $[\alpha, \beta]_A^{\perp} = (\alpha \cap \beta)^{\perp}$ *and* $(\alpha \cap \beta)^{\perp\perp} = \alpha^{\perp\perp} \cap \beta^{\perp\perp}$;

(vi) *if A is semiprime, then:* $\alpha^{\perp} \subseteq \beta^{\perp}$ *if and only if* $[\alpha, \beta]_A^{\perp} = \beta^{\perp}$;

(vii) *if A is semiprime, then:* $\alpha \subseteq \alpha^{\perp}$ *if and only if* $\alpha = \Delta_A$.

Proof. (i) $\Delta_A^{\perp} = \max\{\theta \in \mathrm{Con}(A) \mid [\theta, \Delta_A] = \Delta_A\} = \max(\mathrm{Con}(A)) = \nabla_A$.

If $[\theta, \nabla_A]_A = \theta$ for all $\theta \in \mathrm{Con}(A)$, then:

$\nabla_A^{\perp} = \max\{\theta \in \mathrm{Con}(A) \mid [\theta, \nabla_A] = \Delta_A\} = \max\{\theta \in \mathrm{Con}(A) \mid \theta = \Delta_A\} = \Delta_A$.

(ii), (iii) If $\alpha \subseteq \beta$, then $\{\theta \in \mathrm{Con}(A) \mid [\alpha, \theta]_A = \Delta_A\} \supseteq \{\theta \in \mathrm{Con}(A) \mid [\beta, \theta]_A = \Delta_A\}$, hence $\beta^{\perp} \subseteq \alpha^{\perp}$, which thus, in turn, implies $\alpha^{\perp\perp} \subseteq \beta^{\perp\perp}$.

Since $[\alpha, \alpha^{\perp}]_A = \Delta_A$, it follows that $\alpha \subseteq \alpha^{\perp\perp}$, hence $\alpha^{\perp} \subseteq \alpha^{\perp\perp\perp}$ if we replace α by $\alpha^{\perp}$ in this inclusion, but also $\alpha^{\perp\perp\perp} \subseteq \alpha^{\perp}$ by the above, therefore $\alpha^{\perp} = \alpha^{\perp\perp\perp}$.

Hence $\alpha^{\perp\perp} \subseteq \beta^{\perp\perp}$ implies $\beta^{\perp} = \beta^{\perp\perp\perp} \subseteq \alpha^{\perp\perp\perp} = \alpha^{\perp}$.

(iv) For any $\theta \in \mathrm{Con}(A)$, we have: $[\theta, \alpha]_A = [\theta, \beta]_A = \Delta_A$ if and only if $[\theta, \alpha \vee \beta]_A = \Delta_A$, hence: $\theta \subseteq \alpha^{\perp} \cap \beta^{\perp}$ if and only if $\theta \subseteq (\alpha \vee \beta)^{\perp}$, thus: $\alpha^{\perp} \cap \beta^{\perp} = (\alpha \vee \beta)^{\perp}$. By (iii), $(\alpha \vee \beta)^{\perp} = (\alpha \vee \beta)^{\perp\perp\perp} = (\alpha^{\perp} \cap \beta^{\perp})^{\perp\perp}$.

(v) If A is semiprime, then, for any $\theta, \zeta \in \mathrm{Con}(A)$, we have: $\theta \subseteq \zeta^{\perp}$ if and only if $[\theta, \zeta]_A = \Delta_A$ if and only if $\theta \cap \zeta = \Delta_A$.

Hence, for $\theta \in \mathrm{Con}(A)$: $\theta \subseteq [\alpha, \beta]_A^{\perp}$ if and only if $[\theta, [\alpha, \beta]_A]_A = \Delta_A$ if and only if $\theta \cap \alpha \cap \beta = \Delta_A$ if and only if $[\theta, \alpha \cap \beta]_A = \Delta_A$ if and only if $\theta \subseteq (\alpha \cap \beta)^{\perp}$. Taking $\theta = [\alpha, \beta]_A^{\perp}$ and then $\theta = (\alpha \cap \beta)^{\perp}$ in the previous equivalences, we obtain $[\alpha, \beta]_A^{\perp} = (\alpha \cap \beta)^{\perp}$.

If we denote by $\gamma = \alpha^{\perp\perp} \cap \beta^{\perp\perp}$ and $\delta = (\alpha \cap \beta)^{\perp} = [\alpha, \beta]_A^{\perp}$, then:

$\gamma \subseteq \alpha^{\perp\perp}$ and $\gamma \subseteq \beta^{\perp\perp}$, thus $[\gamma, \alpha^{\perp}]_A = \Delta_A$ and $[\gamma, \beta^{\perp}]_A = \Delta_A$;

$[\delta, \alpha \cap \beta]_A = \Delta_A$, so $\delta \cap \alpha \cap \beta = \Delta_A$, thus $[\alpha \cap \delta, \beta]_A = \Delta_A$, hence $\alpha \cap \delta \subseteq \beta^{\perp}$;

therefore $[\gamma, \alpha \cap \delta]_A = \Delta_A$, so $\gamma \cap \alpha \cap \delta = \Delta_A$, thus $[\gamma \cap \delta, \alpha]_A = \Delta_A$, so $\gamma \cap \delta \subseteq \alpha^{\perp}$;

hence $[\gamma, \gamma \cap \delta]_A = \Delta_A$, so $\gamma \cap \delta = \gamma \cap \gamma \cap \delta = \Delta_A$, thus $[\gamma, \delta]_A = \Delta_A$, hence $\alpha^{\perp\perp} \cap \beta^{\perp\perp} = \gamma \subseteq \delta^{\perp} = [\alpha, \beta]_A^{\perp\perp} = (\alpha \cap \beta)^{\perp\perp}$ by the above.

But $(\alpha \cap \beta)^{\perp\perp} \subseteq \alpha^{\perp\perp} \cap \beta^{\perp\perp}$ by (ii). Therefore $(\alpha \cap \beta)^{\perp\perp} = \alpha^{\perp\perp} \cap \beta^{\perp\perp}$.

(vi) By (v), $[\alpha, \beta]_A^{\perp\perp} = (\alpha \cap \beta)^{\perp\perp} = \alpha^{\perp\perp} \cap \beta^{\perp\perp}$, thus, according to (ii) and (iii): $\alpha^{\perp} \subseteq \beta^{\perp}$ if and only if $\beta^{\perp\perp} \subseteq \alpha^{\perp\perp}$ if and only if $\alpha^{\perp\perp} \cap \beta^{\perp\perp} = \beta^{\perp\perp}$ if and only if $[\alpha, \beta]_A^{\perp\perp} = \beta^{\perp\perp}$ if and only if $[\alpha, \beta]_A^{\perp} = \beta^{\perp}$.

(vii) If A is semiprime, then: $\alpha \subseteq \alpha^{\perp}$ if and only if $[\alpha, \alpha]_A = \Delta_A$ if and only if $\alpha \cap \alpha = \Delta_A$ if and only if $\alpha = \Delta_A$. □

Lemma 7 ([4] (Proposition 4.(1)), [7] (Proposition 18, Corollary 2))**.** *For any $\theta \in \mathrm{Con}(A)$:*

- $$\begin{aligned}\rho_A(\theta) &= \max\{\alpha \in \mathrm{Con}(A) \mid (\exists\, n \in \mathbb{N}^*)\,([\alpha, \alpha]_A^n \subseteq \theta)\}\\ &= \bigvee\{\alpha \in \mathrm{Con}(A) \mid (\exists\, n \in \mathbb{N}^*)\,([\alpha, \alpha]_A^n \subseteq \theta)\}\\ &= \bigvee\{\alpha \in \mathcal{K}(A) \mid (\exists\, n \in \mathbb{N}^*)\,([\alpha, \alpha]_A^n \subseteq \theta)\}\\ &= \bigvee\{\alpha \in \mathrm{PCon}(A) \mid (\exists\, n \in \mathbb{N}^*)\,([\alpha, \alpha]_A^n \subseteq \theta)\}\\ &= \{(a,b) \in A^2 \mid (\exists\, n \in \mathbb{N}^*)\,([Cg_A(a,b), Cg_A(a,b)]_A^n \subseteq \theta)\};\end{aligned}$$
- *for any $\alpha \in \mathrm{Con}(A)$, $\alpha \subseteq \rho_A(\theta)$ if and only if there exists an $n \in \mathbb{N}^*$ such that $[\alpha, \alpha]_A^n \subseteq \theta$;*
- *A is semiprime if and only if, for any $\alpha \in \mathrm{PCon}(A)$ and any $n \in \mathbb{N}^*$, $[\alpha, \alpha]_A^n = \Delta_A$ implies $\alpha = \Delta_A$.*

Proposition 2. *If A satisfies Condition 1.(ii), in particular if $\mathcal{V}$ is either congruence–distributive or both congruence–modular and semidegenerate, then: $A/\theta^{\perp}$ is semiprime for all $\theta \in \mathrm{Con}(A)$ if and only if A is semiprime.*

Proof. By [27] (Proposition 5.22) and Lemma 4, if A is semiprime, then A/ζ is semiprime for all $\zeta \in \mathrm{RCon}(A)$, in particular $A/\theta^{\perp}$ is semiprime for all $\theta \in \mathrm{Con}(A)$.

Conversely, if $A/\theta^{\perp}$ is semiprime for all $\theta \in \mathrm{Con}(A)$, then $A/\nabla_A^{\perp}$ is semiprime; but $\nabla_A^{\perp} = \Delta_A$ by Lemma 6.(i), and $A/\nabla_A^{\perp} = A/\Delta_A$, which is isomorphic to A, thus A is semiprime. □

See also [7] for the following properties. By [25] [Proposition 6.7], if A satisfies Condition 1.(ii), in particular if $\mathcal{V}$ is either congruence–distributive or both congruence–modular and semidegenerate, then:

- for any $\varepsilon \in \mathcal{B}(\mathrm{Con}(A))$ and any $\alpha \in \mathrm{Con}(A)$, $[\varepsilon, \alpha]_A = \varepsilon \cap \alpha$;
- $\mathcal{B}(\mathrm{Con}(A))$ is a Boolean sublattice of $\mathrm{Con}(A)$ whose complementation is $\cdot^{\perp}$ and in which, by the above, the commutator equals the intersection.

By [25] (Proposition 6.11), if $\nabla_A \in \mathcal{K}(A)$ and A satisfies Condition 1.(ii), in particular if $\mathcal{V}$ is congruence–modular and semidegenerate, then $\mathcal{B}(\mathrm{Con}(A)) \subseteq \mathcal{K}(A)$.

Let us also note that, if the commutator of A equals the intersection, in particular if $\mathcal{V}$ is congruence–distributive, then $\mathrm{Con}(A)$ is a frame, hence $\mathcal{B}(\mathrm{Con}(A))$ is a complete Boolean sublattice of $\mathrm{Con}(A)$.

Following [8], we say that an algebra A is *hyperarchimedean* if and only if, for all $\theta \in \mathrm{PCon}(A)$, there exists an $n \in \mathbb{N}^*$ such that $[\theta, \theta]_A^n \in \mathcal{B}(\mathrm{Con}(A))$.

By the above, if the commutator of A equals the intersection, in particular if $\mathcal{V}$ is congruence–distributive, then A is hyperarchimedean if and only if $\mathrm{PCon}(A) \subseteq \mathcal{B}(\mathrm{Con}(A))$ if and only if $\mathrm{Con}(A) \subseteq \mathcal{B}(\mathrm{Con}(A))$ if and only if $\mathcal{B}(\mathrm{Con}(A)) = \mathrm{Con}(A)$; furthermore, if the commutator of A equals the intersection and $\nabla_A \in \mathcal{K}(A)$, in particular if $\mathcal{V}$ is congruence–distributive and semidegenerate, then A is hyperarchimedean if and only if $\mathcal{B}(\mathrm{Con}(A)) = \mathcal{K}(A) = \mathrm{Con}(A)$. Thus the hyperarchimedean members of a congruence–distributive variety are those with Boolean lattices of congruences and, if the variety is also semidegenerate, then all congruences of its hyperarchimedean members are compact.

Extending the terminology used for rings in [25], we call A a *strongly Baer*, respectively *Baer algebra* if and only if, for all $\theta \in \mathrm{Con}(A)$, respectively all $\theta \in \mathrm{PCon}(A)$, we have $\theta^{\perp} \in \mathcal{B}(\mathrm{Con}(A))$, that is if and only if the commutator lattice $(\mathrm{Con}(A), [\cdot, \cdot]_A)$ is strongly Stone, respectively Stone.

Lemma 8. *If A satisfies Condition 1.(ii), in particular if $\mathcal{V}$ is either congruence–distributive or both congruence–modular and semidegenerate, then: A is Baer if and only if, for all $\theta \in \mathcal{K}(A)$, we have $\theta^{\perp} \in \mathcal{B}(\mathrm{Con}(A))$.*

Proof. The converse implication is trivial.

If A is Baer and $\theta \in \mathcal{K}(A)$, so that $\theta = \bigvee_{i=1}^{n} \theta_i$ for some $n \in \mathbb{N}^*$ and $\theta_1, \ldots, \theta_n \in \mathrm{PCon}(A)$, then $\theta_1^{\perp}, \ldots, \theta_n^{\perp} \in \mathcal{B}(\mathrm{Con}(A))$, hence $\theta^{\perp} = (\theta_1 \vee \ldots \vee \theta_n)^{\perp} = \theta_1^{\perp} \cap \ldots \cap \theta_n^{\perp} \in \mathcal{B}(\mathrm{Con}(A))$ by Lemma 6.(iv). □

Proposition 3. *If A satisfies Condition 1.(ii), in particular if $\mathcal{V}$ is either congruence–distributive or both congruence–modular and semidegenerate, then:*

(i) *if A is hyperarchimedean, then A is strongly Baer;*
(ii) *if A is strongly Baer, then A is semiprime;*
(iii) *if A is Baer and has principal commutators, then A is semiprime.*

Proof. (i) By the above, if A is hyperarchimedean, then $\mathcal{B}(\mathrm{Con}(A)) = \mathrm{Con}(A)$, thus A is strongly Baer.

(ii) Assume that A is strongly Baer and let $\theta \in \mathrm{Con}(A)$ such that $[\theta,\theta]^n_A = \Delta_A$ for some $n \in \mathbb{N}^*$. If $n \geq 2$, then $[\theta,\theta]^n_A = [[\theta,\theta]^{n-1}_A, [\theta,\theta]^{n-1}_A]_A$, hence $[\theta,\theta]^{n-1}_A \subseteq ([\theta,\theta]^{n-1}_A)^\perp$ by the properties of the implication. But, since A is strongly Baer, $([\theta,\theta]^{n-1}_A)^\perp \in \mathcal{B}(\mathrm{Con}(A))$, thus its commutator with any congruence of A equals the intersection, hence $[\theta,\theta]^{n-1}_A = [\theta,\theta]^{n-1}_A \cap ([\theta,\theta]^{n-1}_A)^\perp = [[\theta,\theta]^{n-1}_A, ([\theta,\theta]^{n-1}_A)^\perp]_A = \Delta_A$. By turning the above into a recursive argument we get that $[\theta,\theta]_A = \Delta_A$ and then that $\theta = \Delta_A$. By Lemma 7, it follows that A is semiprime.
(iii) By an analogous argument to that of (ii), taking $\theta \in \mathrm{PCon}(A)$, so that $[\theta,\theta]^n_A \in \mathrm{PCon}(A)$ for any $n \in \mathbb{N}^*$ since A has principal commutators. □

4. The Minimal Prime Spectrum

(H) Throughout this section, we will assume that A satisfies Condition 1.(i), which holds if $\mathcal{V}$ is congruence–modular.

By an argument based on Zorn's Lemma, it follows that:

- any prime congruence of A includes a minimal prime congruence, hence $\rho_A(\Delta_A) = \bigcap \mathrm{Spec}(A) = \bigcap \mathrm{Min}(A)$;
- moreover, for any $\theta \in \mathrm{Con}(A)$ and any $\psi \in V_A(\theta) = [\theta) \cap \mathrm{Spec}(A)$, there exists a $\phi \in Min(V_A(\theta)) = Min([\theta) \cap \mathrm{Spec}(A))$ such that $\phi \subseteq \psi$, hence:

Remark 3. *For any $\theta \in \mathrm{Con}(A)$, we have:*

- $\rho_A(\theta) = \bigcap Min(V_A(\theta)) = \bigcap Min([\theta) \cap \mathrm{Spec}(A))$;
- $D_A(\theta) \cap \mathrm{Min}(A) = \emptyset$ *if and only if* $V_A(\theta) \cap \mathrm{Min}(A) = \mathrm{Min}(A)$ *if and only if* $[\theta) \cap \mathrm{Min}(A) = \mathrm{Min}(A)$ *if and only if* $\mathrm{Min}(A) \subseteq [\theta)$ *if and only if* $\theta \subseteq \bigcap \mathrm{Min}(A)$ *if and only if* $\theta \subseteq \rho_A(\Delta_A)$ *if and only if* $\rho_A(\theta) = \rho_A(\Delta_A)$;
- $D_A(\theta) \cap \mathrm{Min}(A) = \mathrm{Min}(A)$ *if and only if* $V_A(\theta) \cap \mathrm{Min}(A) = \emptyset$. $V_A(\theta) = \emptyset$ *if and only if* $\rho_A(\theta) = \nabla_A$*, which holds if* $\theta = \nabla_A$*; recall from [7] that, if* $\nabla_A \in \mathcal{K}(A)$ *and* $[\nabla_A, \nabla_A]_A = \nabla_A$*, then* $\nabla_A / \equiv_A = \{\nabla_A\}$*, so:* $\rho_A(\theta) = \nabla_A$ *if and only if* $\theta = \nabla_A$*. Clearly,* $V_A(\theta) = \emptyset$ *implies* $V_A(\theta) \cap \mathrm{Min}(A) = \emptyset$*; the converse implication holds if and only if* $\mathrm{Min}(A) = \mathrm{Spec}(A)$ *if and only if* $\mathrm{Spec}(A)$ *is an antichain.*

Indeed, $\mathrm{Spec}(A)$ *is an antichain if and only if* $\mathrm{Min}(A) = \mathrm{Spec}(A)$*, case in which* $V_A(\theta) = V_A(\theta) \cap \mathrm{Min}(A)$.

Now, if $V_A(\theta) \cap \mathrm{Min}(A) = \emptyset$ *implies* $V_A(\theta) = \emptyset$*, then let us assume by absurdum that* $\mathrm{Min}(A) \neq \mathrm{Spec}(A)$*, that is* $\mathrm{Spec}(A) \not\subseteq \mathrm{Min}(A)$*, so that there exists* $\phi \in \mathrm{Spec}(A) \setminus \mathrm{Min}(A)$*. But then* $V_A(\phi) \cap \mathrm{Min}(A) = \emptyset$*, while* $V_A(\phi) \neq \emptyset$ *since* $\phi \in V_A(\phi)$*; a contradiction.*

Proposition 4. *If* $\nabla_A \in \mathcal{K}(A)$*, in particular if* $\mathcal{V}$ *is congruence–modular and semidegenerate, then, for any* $\theta \in \mathrm{Con}(A)$ *and any* $\phi \in V_A(\theta)$*, the following are equivalent:*

(i) $\phi \in Min(V_A(\theta))$;
(ii) $\nabla_A \setminus \phi$ *is a maximal element of the set of* m*–systems of* A *which are disjoint from* θ.

Proof. By Remark 2, $\nabla_A \setminus \phi$ is an m–system, which is, of course, disjoint from θ since $(\nabla_A \setminus \phi) \cap \theta \subseteq (\nabla_A \setminus \phi) \cap \phi = \emptyset$.
(i)⇒(ii): By an application of Zorn's Lemma, it follows that there exists a maximal element M of the set of m–systems of A which include $\nabla_A \setminus \phi$ and are disjoint from θ, so that $\nabla_A \setminus \phi \subseteq M \subseteq \nabla_A \setminus \theta$ and, furthermore, M is a maximal element of the set of m–systems of A which are disjoint from θ.

By Lemma 3, there is $\psi \in Max\{\alpha \in \mathrm{Con}(A) \mid \theta \subseteq \alpha, M \cap \alpha = \emptyset\} \subseteq \mathrm{Spec}(A)$, so that $\psi \in V_A(\theta)$ and $(\nabla_A \setminus \phi) \cap \psi \subseteq M \cap \psi = \emptyset$, thus $\nabla_A \setminus \phi \subseteq M \subseteq \nabla_A \setminus \psi$, hence $\psi \subseteq \phi$.

Since $\phi \in Min(V_A(\theta))$, it follows that $\phi = \psi$, thus $\nabla_A \setminus \phi = M$, which is a maximal element of the set of m–systems of A disjoint from θ.
(ii)⇒(i): Let μ be a minimal element of $V_A(\theta)$ with $\mu \subseteq \phi$.

By Remark 2, $\nabla_A \setminus \mu$ is an m–system, disjoint from θ since $(\nabla_A \setminus \mu) \cap \theta \subseteq (\nabla_A \setminus \mu) \cap \mu = \emptyset$, and $\nabla_A \setminus \phi \subseteq \nabla_A \setminus \mu$. Since $\nabla_A \setminus \phi$ is a maximal element of the set of m–systems of A which are disjoint from θ, it follows that $\nabla_A \setminus \phi = \nabla_A \setminus \mu$, thus $\phi = \mu \in Min(V_A(\theta))$. □

Corollary 1. *If $\nabla_A \in \mathcal{K}(A)$, in particular if $\mathcal{V}$ is congruence–modular and semidegenerate, then, for any $\phi \in \mathrm{Spec}(A)$, the following are equivalent:*
- *$\phi \in \mathrm{Min}(A)$;*
- *$\nabla_A \setminus \phi$ is a maximal element of the set of m–systems of A which are disjoint from Δ_A.*

Proof. By Proposition 4 for $\theta = \Delta_A$. □

Lemma 9 ([28]). *If L is a bounded distributive lattice and $P \in \mathrm{Spec}_{\mathrm{Id}}(L)$, then the following are equivalent:*
- *$P \in \mathrm{Min}_{\mathrm{Id}}(L)$;*
- *for any $x \in P$, $\mathrm{Ann}_L(x) \nsubseteq P$.*

Recall from Section 2 that $\mathrm{Spec}(A) = \mathrm{Mi}(\mathrm{Con}(A)) \cap \mathrm{RCon}(A)$. By [25] (Proposition 4.4), if A is semiprime, then all annihilators in $(\mathrm{Con}(A), [\cdot,\cdot]_A)$ are lattice ideals of $\mathrm{Con}(A)$.

Remember that, in the commutator lattice $(\mathrm{Con}(A), [\cdot,\cdot]_A)$, $R(\mathrm{Con}(A)) = \mathrm{RCon}(A)$ and $\mathrm{Spec}_{\mathrm{Con}(A)} = \mathrm{Spec}(A)$, and that, since $\mathrm{Con}(A)/\equiv_A$ is a frame, the elements of $\mathrm{Spec}_{\mathrm{Con}(A)/\equiv_A}$ are exactly the meet–prime elements of $\mathrm{Con}(A)/\equiv_A$, thus, by the distributivity of $\mathrm{Con}(A)/\equiv_A$, $\mathrm{Spec}_{\mathrm{Con}(A)/\equiv_A} = \mathrm{Mi}(\mathrm{Con}(A)/\equiv_A)$.

Lemma 10. *If A is semiprime, then:*
- *(i)* *for any $U \subseteq \mathrm{Con}(A)$, $\mathrm{Ann}_{\mathrm{Con}(A)/\equiv_A}(U/\equiv_A) = \mathrm{Ann}_{(\mathrm{Con}(A),[\cdot,\cdot]_A)}(U)/\equiv_A$;*
- *(ii)* $\mathrm{Spec}_{\mathrm{Con}(A)/\equiv_A} = \{\phi/\equiv_A \mid \phi \in \mathrm{Spec}(A)\}$;
- *(iii)* *for all $\theta \in \mathrm{RCon}(A)$, $\theta/\equiv_A \cap \mathrm{RCon}(A) = \{\theta\}$ and $\theta = \max(\theta/\equiv_A)$;*
- *(iv)* *$\phi \mapsto \phi/\equiv_A$ is an order isomorphism from $\mathrm{Spec}(A)$ to $\mathrm{Spec}_{\mathrm{Con}(A)/\equiv_A}$;*
- *(v)* *$R(\mathrm{Con}(A)/\equiv_A) = \{\phi/\equiv_A \mid \phi \in \mathrm{RCon}(A)\}$; moreover, for any $\phi \in \mathrm{Con}(A)$, we have: $\phi \in \mathrm{RCon}(A)$ if and only if $\phi/\equiv_A \in R(\mathrm{Con}(A)/\equiv_A)$; thus $\phi \mapsto \phi/\equiv_A$ is an order isomorphism from $\mathrm{RCon}(A)$ to $R(\mathrm{Con}(A)/\equiv_A)$.*

Proof. (i) By [25] (Lemma 4.2).
(ii) By [25] (Proposition 6.2).
(iii) By [25] (Remark 5.11).
(iv) By (ii),(iii) and the fact that $\mathrm{Spec}(A) \subseteq \mathrm{RCon}(A)$ and $\mathrm{Spec}_{\mathrm{Con}(A)/\equiv_A} \subseteq R(\mathrm{Con}(A)/\equiv_A)$.
(v) The equality follows from (ii) and the definition of radical elements; by (iii), we also obtain the equivalence and the order isomorphism. □

Remark 4. *For any $\alpha, \beta \in \mathrm{Con}(A)$, we have $\alpha/\equiv_A \leq \beta/\equiv_A$ if and only if $\rho_A(\alpha) \subseteq \rho_A(\beta)$. Indeed, $\alpha/\equiv_A \leq \beta/\equiv_A$ if and only if $\alpha/\equiv_A \wedge \beta/\equiv_A = \alpha/\equiv_A$ if and only if $(\alpha \cap \beta)/\equiv_A = \alpha/\equiv_A$ if and only if $\rho_A(\alpha \cap \beta) = \rho_A(\alpha)$ if and only if $\rho_A(\alpha) \cap \rho_A(\beta) = \rho_A(\alpha)$ if and only if $\rho_A(\alpha) \subseteq \rho_A(\beta)$.*

Proposition 5. *Assume that A is semiprime and let $\phi \in \mathrm{Spec}(A)$. Let us consider the following statements:*
- *(i)* $\phi \in \mathrm{Min}(A)$;
- *(ii)* *for any $\alpha \in \mathcal{K}(A)$, $\alpha \subseteq \phi$ implies $\alpha^{\perp} \nsubseteq \phi$;*
- *(iii)* *for any $\alpha \in \mathcal{K}(A)$, $\alpha \subseteq \phi$ if and only if $\alpha^{\perp} \nsubseteq \phi$;*
- *(iv)* *for any $\alpha \in \mathrm{Con}(A)$, $\alpha \subseteq \phi$ implies $\alpha^{\perp} \nsubseteq \phi$;*
- *(v)* *for any $\alpha \in \mathrm{Con}(A)$, $\alpha \subseteq \phi$ if and only if $\alpha^{\perp} \nsubseteq \phi$.*

If A satisfies Condition 1.(iv), then statements (i), (ii) and (iii) are equivalent.

If A satisfies Condition 1.(v), then statements (i), (iv) and (v) are equivalent.

Proof. Case 1: Assume that A satisfies Condition 1.(iv).
(i)⇔(ii): Recall from [7] [Lemma 11.(i)] that we have the following order–preserving maps: $\theta \mapsto \theta^*$ from $\mathrm{Con}(A)$ to $\mathrm{Id}(\mathcal{L}(A))$, defined by: $\theta^* = ((\theta] \cap \mathcal{K}(A))/\equiv_A$ for all $\theta \in \mathrm{Con}(A)$; $I \mapsto I_*$ from $\mathrm{Id}(\mathcal{L}(A))$ to $\mathrm{Con}(A)$, defined by: $I_* = \bigvee\{\gamma \in \mathcal{K}(A) \mid \gamma/\equiv_A \in I\}$ for all $I \in \mathrm{Id}(\mathcal{L}(A))$.

By [7] [Proposition 11], these maps restrict to order isomorphisms between $\mathrm{Spec}(A)$ and $\mathrm{Spec}_{\mathrm{Id}}(\mathcal{L}(A))$, inverses of each other, thus they further restrict to mutually inverse order isomorphisms between $\mathrm{Min}(A)$ and $\mathrm{Min}_{\mathrm{Id}}(\mathcal{L}(A))$.

Let $\beta \in \mathcal{K}(A)$ and $\psi \in \mathrm{Spec}(A)$, arbitrary. By the above, $(\psi^*)_* = \psi$. Since $\beta \in \mathcal{K}(A)$,

$$(\beta/\equiv_A]_{\mathcal{L}(A)} = (\beta/\equiv_A]_{\mathrm{Con}(A)/\equiv_A} \cap \mathcal{L}(A) =$$

$$(\beta]_{\mathrm{Con}(A)}/\equiv_A \cap \mathcal{K}(A)/\equiv_A = ((\beta]_{\mathrm{Con}(A)} \cap \mathcal{K}(A))/\equiv_A = \beta^*,$$

hence $\mathrm{Ann}_{\mathcal{L}(A)}(\beta/\equiv_A) = \mathrm{Ann}_{\mathcal{L}(A)}((\beta/\equiv_A]_{\mathcal{L}(A)}) = \mathrm{Ann}_{\mathcal{L}(A)}(\beta^*)$. By [7] [Lemma 27], since A is semiprime, we have: $\mathrm{Ann}_{\mathcal{L}(A)}(\beta^*) \subseteq \psi^*$ if and only if $\beta^\perp \subseteq (\psi^*)_*$, that is $\beta^\perp \subseteq \psi$.

Hence: $\phi \in \mathrm{Min}(A)$ if and only if $\phi^* \in \mathrm{Min}_{\mathrm{Id}}(\mathcal{L}(A))$. By Lemma 9, the latter is equivalent to $(\forall x \in \phi^*)(\mathrm{Ann}_{\mathcal{L}(A)}(x) \nsubseteq \phi^*)$, i.e., $(\forall \alpha \in (\phi] \cap \mathcal{K}(A))(\mathrm{Ann}_{\mathcal{L}(A)}(\alpha/\equiv_A) \nsubseteq \phi^*)$, which means that $(\forall \alpha \in (\phi] \cap \mathcal{K}(A))\,(\mathrm{Ann}_{\mathcal{L}(A)}(\alpha^*) \nsubseteq \phi^*)$, which is equivalent to $(\forall \alpha \in (\phi] \cap \mathcal{K}(A))\,(\alpha^\perp \nsubseteq \phi)$, that is $(\forall \alpha \in \mathcal{K}(A))\,(\alpha \subseteq \phi \Rightarrow \alpha^\perp \nsubseteq \phi)$.
(iii)⇒(ii): Trivial.
(ii)⇒(iii): If $\alpha \in \mathcal{K}(A)$ is such that $\alpha^\perp \nsubseteq \phi$, then, since $[\alpha, \alpha^\perp]_A = \Delta_A \subseteq \phi \in \mathrm{Spec}(A)$, it follows that $\alpha \subseteq \phi$.
Case 2: Now assume that A satisfies Condition 1.(v).
(v)⇒(iv): Trivial.
(iv)⇒(v): Analogous to the proof of (ii)⇒(iii).
(i)⇔(iv): By Lemma 10.(iv), the condition that $\phi \in \mathrm{Spec}(A)$ is equivalent to $\phi/\equiv_A \in \mathrm{Spec}_{\mathrm{Con}(A)/\equiv_A}$, which is equivalent to $(\phi/\equiv_A] \in \mathrm{Spec}_{\mathrm{Id}}(\mathrm{Con}(A)/\equiv_A)$.

Again by Lemma 10.(iv), $\phi \in \mathrm{Min}(A)$ if and only if $\phi/\equiv_A \in \mathrm{Min}_{\mathrm{Con}(A)/\equiv_A}$, which is equivalent to $(\phi/\equiv_A] \in \mathrm{Min}_{\mathrm{Id}}(\mathrm{Con}(A)/\equiv_A)$. By Lemma 9 and Lemma 10.(i), the latter is equivalent to the fact that, for any $\alpha \in (\phi]$, $(\alpha^\perp/\equiv_A] = (\alpha^\perp]/\equiv_A = \mathrm{Ann}_{(\mathrm{Con}(A),[\cdot,\cdot]_A)}(\alpha)/\equiv_A$ $= \mathrm{Ann}_{\mathrm{Con}(A)/\equiv_A}(\alpha/\equiv_A) \nsubseteq (\phi/\equiv_A] = (\phi]/\equiv_A$, that is $\alpha^\perp/\equiv_A \notin (\phi/\equiv_A] = (\phi]/\equiv_A$. Since $\phi \in \mathrm{Spec}(A) \subseteq \mathrm{RCon}(A)$ and thus $\phi = \max(\phi/\equiv_A)$ by Lemma 10.(iii), this condition is equivalent to $\alpha^\perp \notin (\phi]$, that is $\alpha^\perp \nsubseteq \phi$. □

Example 1. *Note that the equivalence in Proposition 5 for the case when A satisfies Condition 1.(iv) does not hold for $\alpha \in \mathrm{Con}(A)$, arbitrary. Indeed, if we let A be the Boolean subalgebra of the power set $\mathcal{P}(\mathbb{N})$ of the set $\mathbb{N}$ of natural numbers formed of the finite and the cofinite subsets of $\mathbb{N}$: $A = \{S \mid S \subseteq \mathbb{N}, |S| < \aleph_0$ or $|\mathbb{N} \setminus S| < \aleph_0\}$, then, since A is a Boolean algebra, its lattice of congruences is isomorphic to its lattice of filters, and obviously this lattice isomorphism φ : $\mathrm{Filt}(A) \to \mathrm{Con}(A)$ takes the set $\mathrm{Spec}_{\mathrm{Filt}(A)}$ of the prime elements of the lattice $\mathrm{Filt}(A)$ of the filters of A, which equals the set $\mathrm{Spec}_{\mathrm{Filt}}(A) = \mathrm{Max}_{\mathrm{Filt}}(A)$ of the prime and thus maximal filters of A by a routine proof, to $\mathrm{Spec}_{\mathrm{Con(A)}} = \mathrm{Spec}(A) = \mathrm{Max}(A) = \mathrm{Min}(A)$ since A is a Boolean algebra, therefore $\mathrm{Min}_{\mathrm{Filt}}(A) := Min(\mathrm{Spec}_{\mathrm{Filt}}(A)) = \mathrm{Spec}_{\mathrm{Filt}}(A) = \mathrm{Max}_{\mathrm{Filt}}(A) = Max(\mathrm{Filt}(A) \setminus \{A\})$. Now let us consider the filter $P := \{S \mid S \subseteq \mathbb{N}, |\mathbb{N} \setminus S| < \aleph_0\}$. It is well known that $\mathrm{Spec}_{\mathrm{Filt}}(A) = Max(\mathrm{Filt}(A) \setminus \{A\}) = \{M \cap A \mid M \in Max(\mathrm{Filt}(\mathcal{P}(\mathbb{N})) \setminus \{\mathcal{P}(\mathbb{N})\})\} \cup \{P\} = \{[\{a\})_{\mathcal{P}(\mathbb{N})} \cap A \mid a \in \mathbb{N}\} \cup \{P\}$, in particular P is a prime and thus a minimal prime filter of A. P is clearly not a principal, thus not a compact filter of A. Since Boolean algebras are congruence–distributive, the commutator $[\cdot,\cdot]_A$ of A equals the intersection, thus the commutator lattice $(\mathrm{Con}(A), [\cdot,\cdot]_A = \cap)$ is isomorphic to the commutator lattice $(\mathrm{Filt}(A), \cap)$, also endowed with the commutator operation equalling the intersection, in which $P^\perp = \max\{F \in \mathrm{Filt}(A) \mid P \cap F =$*

$\{\mathbb{N}\}\} = \max\{\{\mathbb{N}\}\} = \{\mathbb{N}\}$, since any nontrivial filter F of A contains a proper subset S of $\mathbb{N}$, which must thus be such that an $a \in \mathbb{N}$ does not belong to S, hence S is included in the proper cofinite subset $\mathbb{N} \setminus \{a\}$ of $\mathbb{N}$, so $\mathbb{N} \setminus \{a\} \in P \cap F$, which means that no nontrivial filter F of A satisfies $P \cap F = \{\mathbb{N}\}$. So $P^{\perp} = \{\mathbb{N}\} \subset P$; of course, $P \subseteq P$. Therefore, $\varphi(P) \in \mathrm{Spec}(A) = \mathrm{Min}(A)$, and $\varphi(P) \in \mathrm{Con}(A) \setminus \mathrm{Cp}(\mathrm{Con}(A)) = \mathrm{Con}(A) \setminus \mathcal{K}(A)$; thus $\varphi(P)^{\perp} = \varphi(P^{\perp}) = \varphi(\{\mathbb{N}\}) = \Delta_A \subset \varphi(P)$ and $\varphi(P) \subseteq \varphi(P)$, hence $\varphi(P) \subseteq \varphi(P)$ does not imply $\varphi(P)^{\perp} \nsubseteq \varphi(P)$.

Corollary 2. *Assume that A satisfies Condition 1.(iii), let $\phi \in \mathrm{Spec}(A)$ and let us consider the following statements:*

(i) $\phi \in \mathrm{Min}(A)$;
(ii) *for any $\alpha \in \mathcal{K}(A)$, $\alpha \subseteq \phi$ implies $\alpha \to \rho_A(\Delta_A) \nsubseteq \phi$;*
(iii) *for any $\alpha \in \mathrm{Con}(A)$, $\alpha \subseteq \phi$ implies $\alpha \to \rho_A(\Delta_A) \nsubseteq \phi$.*

If A satisfies Condition 1.(iv), then (i) is equivalent to (ii).
If A satisfies Condition 1.(v), then (i) is equivalent to (iii).

Proof. **Case 1:** Assume that A satisfies Condition 1.(iv). Then we have the following equivalences: $\phi \in \mathrm{Min}(A)$ if and only if $\phi/\rho_A(\Delta_A) \in \mathrm{Min}(A/\rho_A(\Delta_A))$, which, by Proposition 5, since $A/\rho_A(\Delta_A)$ is semiprime, is equivalent to the fact that, for any $\alpha \in \mathcal{K}(A)$, $(\alpha \vee \rho_A(\Delta_A))/\rho_A(\Delta_A) \subseteq \phi/\rho_A(\Delta_A)$ implies $((\alpha \vee \rho_A(\Delta_A))/\rho_A(\Delta_A))^{\perp} \nsubseteq \phi/\rho_A(\Delta_A)$, that is $\alpha \vee \rho_A(\Delta_A) \subseteq \phi$ implies $(\alpha \to \rho_A(\Delta_A))/\rho_A(\Delta_A) \nsubseteq \phi/\rho_A(\Delta_A)$ according to Proposition 1.(ii), that is $\alpha \subseteq \phi$ implies $\alpha \to \rho_A(\Delta_A) \nsubseteq \phi$ since ϕ is prime and thus $\rho_A(\Delta_A) \subseteq \phi$.
Case 2: Assume that A satisfies Condition 1.(v). Then the proof goes the same as above, but for all $\alpha \in \mathrm{Con}(A)$. □

5. Two Topologies on the Minimal Prime Spectrum

(H) Throughout this section, we will assume that A satisfies Condition 1.(i), which holds in the particular case when $\mathcal{V}$ is congruence–modular.

Clearly, the Stone topology $\mathcal{S}_{\mathrm{Spec}}(A)$ of $\mathrm{Spec}(A)$ induces the topology $\mathcal{S}_{\mathrm{Min}}(A) = \{D_A(\theta) \cap \mathrm{Min}(A) \mid \theta \in \mathrm{Con}(A)\}$ on $\mathrm{Min}(A)$, which has $\{D_A(a,b) \cap \mathrm{Min}(A) \mid a,b \in A\}$ as a basis and $\{V_A(\theta) \cap \mathrm{Min}(A) \mid \theta \in \mathrm{Con}(A)\}$ as the family of closed sets. $\mathcal{S}_{\mathrm{Min}}(A)$ is called the *Stone* or *spectral topology* on $\mathrm{Min}(A)$.

(H) Throughout the rest of this section, we will also assume that A is semiprime.

Lemma 11. $\theta^{\perp} = \bigcap(V_A(\theta^{\perp}) \cap \mathrm{Min}(A))$ *for every $\theta \in \mathrm{Con}(A)$.*

Proof. Let $\theta \in \mathrm{Con}(A)$. Clearly, $\theta^{\perp} \subseteq \bigcap(V_A(\theta^{\perp}) \cap \mathrm{Min}(A))$.

Let us denote by $\alpha = \bigcap(V_A(\theta^{\perp}) \cap \mathrm{Min}(A))$, so that $\alpha \subseteq \mu$ for any $\mu \in V_A(\theta^{\perp}) \cap \mathrm{Min}(A)$. Assume by absurdum that $\alpha \nsubseteq \theta^{\perp}$, so that $[\alpha,\theta]_A \neq \Delta_A = \rho_A(\Delta_A) = \bigcap \mathrm{Min}(A)$ since A is semiprime, therefore $[\alpha,\theta]_A \nsubseteq \phi$ for some $\phi \in \mathrm{Min}(A)$, which implies that $\theta \nsubseteq \phi$ and $\alpha \nsubseteq \phi$, hence $\phi \notin V_A(\theta^{\perp})$, that is $\theta^{\perp} \nsubseteq \phi$. So $\theta \nsubseteq \phi$ and $\theta^{\perp} \nsubseteq \phi$, while $[\theta,\theta^{\perp}]_A = \Delta_A \subseteq \phi$, which contradicts the fact that $\phi \in \mathrm{Min}(A) \subseteq \mathrm{Spec}(A)$. Therefore $\bigcap(V_A(\theta^{\perp}) \cap \mathrm{Min}(A)) = \alpha \subseteq \theta^{\perp}$, hence the equality. □

Remark 5. *By Lemma 11, for any $\alpha, \beta \in \mathrm{Con}(A)$, we have: $\alpha^{\perp} = \beta^{\perp}$ if and only if $V_A(\alpha^{\perp}) \cap \mathrm{Min}(A) = V_A(\beta^{\perp}) \cap \mathrm{Min}(A)$ if and only if $D_A(\alpha^{\perp}) \cap \mathrm{Min}(A) = D_A(\beta^{\perp}) \cap \mathrm{Min}(A)$.*

Proposition 6. *For any $\alpha, \beta, \gamma \in \mathrm{Con}(A)$, we consider the following statements:*

(i) $V_A(\alpha) \cap \mathrm{Min}(A) = V_A(\alpha^{\perp\perp}) \cap \mathrm{Min}(A) = D_A(\alpha^{\perp}) \cap \mathrm{Min}(A)$ *and* $D_A(\alpha) \cap \mathrm{Min}(A) = D_A(\alpha^{\perp\perp}) \cap \mathrm{Min}(A) = V_A(\alpha^{\perp}) \cap \mathrm{Min}(A)$;
(ii) $\alpha^{\perp} \cap \beta^{\perp} = \gamma^{\perp}$ *if and only if* $V_A(\alpha) \cap V_A(\beta) \cap \mathrm{Min}(A) = V_A(\gamma) \cap \mathrm{Min}(A)$;

(iii) $\alpha^{\perp\perp} = \beta^{\perp}$ *if and only if* $\alpha^{\perp} = \beta^{\perp\perp}$ *if and only if* $V_A(\alpha) \cap \text{Min}(A) = V_A(\beta^{\perp}) \cap \text{Min}(A)$ *if and only if* $V_A(\alpha) \cap \text{Min}(A) = D_A(\beta) \cap \text{Min}(A)$ *if and only if* $D_A(\alpha^{\perp}) \cap \text{Min}(A) = D_A(\beta) \cap \text{Min}(A)$.

If A satisfies Condition 1.(iv), then the statements above hold for all $\alpha, \beta, \gamma \in \mathcal{K}(A)$.
If A satisfies Condition 1.(v), then the statements above hold for all $\alpha, \beta, \gamma \in \text{Con}(A)$.

Proof. Let $\phi \in \text{Min}(A)$.
Case 1: Assume that A satisfies Condition 1.(iv) and let $\alpha, \beta, \gamma \in \mathcal{K}(A)$.
(i) By Proposition 5, $\phi \in V_A(\alpha)$ if and only if $\phi \in D_A(\alpha^{\perp})$, hence also $\phi \notin V_A(\alpha)$ if and only if $\phi \notin D_A(\alpha^{\perp})$, that is $\phi \in D_A(\alpha)$ if and only if $\phi \in V_A(\alpha^{\perp})$. Therefore $V_A(\alpha) \cap \text{Min}(A) = D_A(\alpha^{\perp}) \cap \text{Min}(A)$ and $D_A(\alpha) \cap \text{Min}(A) = V_A(\alpha^{\perp}) \cap \text{Min}(A)$, hence also $V_A(\alpha^{\perp\perp}) \cap \text{Min}(A) = D_A(\alpha^{\perp\perp\perp}) \cap \text{Min}(A) = D_A(\alpha^{\perp}) \cap \text{Min}(A)$ and $D_A(\alpha^{\perp\perp}) \cap \text{Min}(A) = V_A(\alpha^{\perp\perp\perp}) \cap \text{Min}(A) = V_A(\alpha^{\perp}) \cap \text{Min}(A)$ by Lemma 6.(iii).
(ii) By (i), along with Proposition 6.(iv), and Remark 5, $\alpha^{\perp} \cap \beta^{\perp} = \gamma^{\perp}$ if and only if $(\alpha \vee \beta)^{\perp} = \gamma^{\perp}$ if and only if $V_A((\alpha \vee \beta)^{\perp}) \cap \text{Min}(A) = V_A(\gamma^{\perp}) \cap \text{Min}(A)$ if and only if $(D_A(\alpha) \cap \text{Min}(A)) \cup (D_A(\beta) \cap \text{Min}(A)) = (D_A(\alpha) \cup D_A(\beta)) \cap \text{Min}(A) = D_A(\alpha \vee \beta) \cap \text{Min}(A) = D_A(\gamma) \cap \text{Min}(A)$ if and only if $\text{Min}(A) \setminus ((D_A(\alpha) \cap \text{Min}(A)) \cup (D_A(\beta) \cap \text{Min}(A))) = \text{Min}(A) \setminus (D_A(\gamma) \cap \text{Min}(A))$ if and only if $V_A(\alpha) \cap V_A(\beta) \cap \text{Min}(A) = (V_A(\alpha) \cap \text{Min}(A)) \cap (V_A(\beta) \cap \text{Min}(A)) = V_A(\gamma) \cap \text{Min}(A)$.
(iii) By (i) and Remark 5, $\alpha^{\perp\perp} = \beta^{\perp}$ if and only if $V_A(\alpha^{\perp\perp}) \cap \text{Min}(A) = V_A(\beta^{\perp}) \cap \text{Min}(A)$ if and only if $D_A(\alpha^{\perp}) \cap \text{Min}(A) = V_A(\alpha) \cap \text{Min}(A) = V_A(\beta^{\perp}) \cap \text{Min}(A) = D_A(\beta) \cap \text{Min}(A)$. By Lemma 6.(iii), $\alpha^{\perp\perp} = \beta^{\perp}$ implies $\alpha^{\perp} = \alpha^{\perp\perp\perp} = \beta^{\perp\perp}$, which also proves the converse.
Case 2: The proof goes similarly in the case when A satisfies Condition 1.(v), but for all $\alpha, \beta, \gamma \in \text{Con}(A)$. □

Let us denote by $\mathcal{F}_{\text{Min}}(A)$ the topology on $\text{Min}(A)$ generated by $\{V_A(a,b) \cap \text{Min}(A) \mid a, b \in A\}$, called the *flat topology* or the *inverse topology* on $\text{Min}(A)$. Also, we denote by $\mathcal{M}in(A)$, respectively $\mathcal{M}in(A)^{-1}$ the minimal prime spectrum of A endowed with the Stone, respectively the flat topology: $\mathcal{M}in(A) = (\text{Min}(A), \mathcal{S}_{\text{Min}}(A))$ and $\mathcal{M}in(A)^{-1} = (\text{Min}(A), \mathcal{F}_{\text{Min}}(A))$.

Remark 6. $\mathcal{F}_{\text{Min}}(A)$ *has* $\{V_A(\alpha) \cap \text{Min}(A) \mid \alpha \in \mathcal{K}(A)\}$ *as a basis, since* $V_A(\Delta_A) \cap \text{Min}(A) = \text{Min}(A)$ *and, for* $\alpha, \beta \in \mathcal{K}(A)$, $\alpha \vee \beta \in \mathcal{K}(A)$ *and* $V_A(\alpha) \cap \text{Min}(A) \cap V_A(\beta) \cap \text{Min}(A) = V_A(\alpha \vee \beta) \cap \text{Min}(A)$.

Recall that, for any $\alpha \in \text{Con}(A)$, $\alpha^{\perp}$ generates the annihilator of α in the commutator lattice $(\text{Con}(A), [\cdot,\cdot]_A)$ as a principal ideal.

Proposition 7.

(i) *The flat topology on* $\text{Min}(A)$ *is coarser than the Stone topology:* $\mathcal{F}_{\text{Min}}(A) \subseteq \mathcal{S}_{\text{Min}}(A)$.
(ii) *If A satisfies Condition 1.(vi), in particular if* $\text{Con}(A)$ *is compact, then the two topologies coincide:* $\mathcal{F}_{\text{Min}}(A) = \mathcal{S}_{\text{Min}}(A)$, *that is* $\mathcal{M}in(A) = \mathcal{M}in(A)^{-1}$.

Proof. (i) By Proposition 6.(i), $V_A(\alpha) \cap \text{Min}(A) = D_A(\alpha^{\perp}) \cap \text{Min}(A) \in \mathcal{S}_{\text{Min}}(A)$, for any $\alpha \in \mathcal{K}(A)$.
(ii) Again by Proposition 6.(i), for any $\alpha \in \mathcal{K}(A)$, $D_A(\alpha) \cap \text{Min}(A) = V_A(\alpha^{\perp}) \cap \text{Min}(A)$, which belongs to $\mathcal{F}_{\text{Min}}(A)$ if $\alpha^{\perp} \in \mathcal{K}(A)$. □

Now let L be a bounded distributive lattice. Following [7], we denote, for any $I \in \text{Id}(L)$ and $a \in L$, by $V_{\text{Id},L}(I) = \text{Spec}_{\text{Id}}(L) \cap [I)_{\text{Id}(L)}$, $D_{\text{Id},L}(I) = \text{Spec}_{\text{Id}}(L) \setminus V_{\text{Id},L}(I)$, $V_{\text{Id},L}(a) = V_{\text{Id},L}((a]_L)$ and $D_{\text{Id},L}(a) = D_{\text{Id},L}((a]_L)$.

Let us denote by $\mathcal{S}_{\text{Spec,Id}}(L)$ the Stone topology on $\text{Spec}_{\text{Id}}(L)$ and by $\mathcal{S}_{\text{Min,Id}}(L)$ the Stone topology on $\text{Min}_{\text{Id}}(L)$: $\mathcal{S}_{\text{Spec,Id}}(L) = \{D_{\text{Id},L}(I) \mid I \in \text{Id}(L)\}$, with $\{D_{\text{Id},L}(a) \mid a \in L\}$ as a basis; $\mathcal{S}_{\text{Min,Id}}(L) = \{D_{\text{Id},L}(I) \cap \text{Min}_{\text{Id}}(L) \mid I \in \text{Id}(L)\}$, with $\{D_{\text{Id},L}(a) \cap \text{Min}_{\text{Id}}(L) \mid a \in L\}$ as a basis.

And let $\mathcal{F}_{\mathrm{Min,Id}}(L)$ be the flat topology on $\mathrm{Min}_{\mathrm{Id}}(L)$, which has $\{V_{\mathrm{Id},L}(a) \cap \mathrm{Min}_{\mathrm{Id}}(L) \mid a \in L\}$ as a basis. Let $\mathcal{M}in_{\mathrm{Id}}(L)$, respectively $\mathcal{M}in_{\mathrm{Id}}(L)^{-1}$ be the minimal prime spectrum of ideals of L endowed with the Stone, respectively the flat topology: $\mathcal{M}in_{\mathrm{Id}}(L) = (\mathrm{Min}_{\mathrm{Id}}(L), \mathcal{S}_{\mathrm{Min,Id}}(L))$ and $\mathcal{M}in_{\mathrm{Id}}(L)^{-1} = (\mathrm{Min}_{\mathrm{Id}}(L), \mathcal{F}_{\mathrm{Min,Id}}(L))$.

Lemma 12. *If A satisfies Condition 1.(iv), then:*

(i) $\mathcal{M}in(A)$ *is homeomorphic to* $\mathcal{M}in_{\mathrm{Id}}(\mathcal{L}(A))$*;*

(ii) $\mathcal{M}in(A)^{-1}$ *is homeomorphic to* $\mathcal{M}in_{\mathrm{Id}}(\mathcal{L}(A))^{-1}$*.*

Proof. Assume that A satisfies Condition 1.(iv), so that its reticulation can be constructed as: $\mathcal{L}(A) = \mathcal{K}(A)/\equiv_A$. As in [7], let us denote by $u : \mathrm{Spec}(A) \to \mathrm{Spec}_{\mathrm{Id}}(\mathcal{L}(A))$ and $v : \mathrm{Spec}_{\mathrm{Id}}(\mathcal{L}(A)) \to \mathrm{Spec}(A)$ the mutually inverse homeomorphisms with respect to the Stone topologies mentioned in the proof of Proposition 5: $u(\phi) = \phi^*$ for all $\phi \in \mathrm{Spec}(A)$ and $v(P) = P_*$ for all $P \in \mathrm{Spec}_{\mathrm{Id}}(\mathcal{L}(A))$.
(i) u and v obviously restrict to homeomorphisms between $\mathcal{M}in(A)$ and $\mathcal{M}in_{\mathrm{Id}}(\mathcal{L}(A))$.
(ii) Recall that the flat topology $\mathcal{F}_{\mathrm{Min}(A)}$ has $\{V_A(\alpha) \cap \mathrm{Min}(A) \mid \alpha \in \mathcal{K}(A)\}$ as a basis, while the flat topology on $\mathcal{F}_{\mathrm{Min,Id}}(\mathcal{L}(A))$ has $\{V_{\mathrm{Id},\mathcal{L}(A)}((a]_{\mathcal{L}(A)}) \cap \mathrm{Min}_{\mathrm{Id}}(\mathcal{L}(A)) \mid a \in \mathcal{L}(A)\} = \{V_{\mathrm{Id},\mathcal{L}(A)}((\alpha/\equiv_A]_{\mathcal{L}(A)}) \cap \mathrm{Min}_{\mathrm{Id}}(\mathcal{L}(A)) \mid \alpha \in \mathcal{K}(A)\}$ as a basis.

In the proof of [7] [Proposition 11] we have obtained that $u(V_A(\alpha)) = V_{\mathrm{Id},\mathcal{L}(A)}(\alpha^*)$ for all $\alpha \in \mathrm{Con}(A)$. Note that, if $\alpha \in \mathcal{K}(A)$, then $\alpha^* = (\alpha/\equiv_A]_{\mathcal{L}(A)}$, thus $u(V_A(\alpha)) = V_{\mathrm{Id},\mathcal{L}(A)}((\alpha/\equiv_A]_{\mathcal{L}(A)})$, hence u is open with respect to the flat topologies on the minimal prime spectra.

Consequently, for all $\alpha \in \mathcal{K}(A)$, $v(V_{\mathrm{Id},\mathcal{L}(A)}((\alpha/\equiv_A]_{\mathcal{L}(A)})) = v(u(V_A(\alpha))) = V_A(\alpha)$, hence v is open with respect to the flat topologies on the minimal prime spectra.

Therefore u and v are mutually inverse homeomorphisms between $\mathcal{M}in(A)^{-1}$ and $\mathcal{M}in_{\mathrm{Id}}(\mathcal{L}(A))^{-1}$. □

Proposition 8. *If A satisfies Condition 1.(iv), then $\mathcal{M}in(A)^{-1}$ is a compact* T_1 *topological space.*

Proof. Assume that A satisfies Condition 1.(iv), and let us consider the reticulation of A: $\mathcal{L}(A) = \mathcal{K}(A)/\equiv_A$.

By Hochster's theorem [20] [Proposition 3.13], there exists a commutative unitary ring R such that the reticulation $\mathcal{L}(R)$ of R is lattice isomorphic to $\mathcal{L}(A)$. Recall that the commutator lattice of the ideals of R endowed with the multiplication of ideals as commutator operation is isomorphic to the commutator lattice of its congruences, $(\mathrm{Con}(R), [\cdot,\cdot]_R)$.

By Lemma 12.(ii), the minimal prime spectrum of R endowed with the flat topology, $\mathcal{M}in(R)^{-1}$, is homeomorphic to $\mathcal{M}in_{\mathrm{Id}}(\mathcal{L}(R))^{-1}$ and thus to $\mathcal{M}in_{\mathrm{Id}}(\mathcal{L}(A))^{-1}$, which in turn is homeomorphic to $\mathcal{M}in(A)^{-1}$, thus $\mathcal{M}in(R)^{-1}$ is homeomorphic to $\mathcal{M}in(A)^{-1}$.

By [29] [Theorem 3.1], $\mathcal{M}in(R)^{-1}$ is compact and T_1. Therefore $\mathcal{M}in(A)^{-1}$ is compact and T_1. □

Following [7], whenever A satisfies Condition 1.(iv), we will denote the lattice bounds of $\mathcal{L}(A)$ by $\mathbf{0}$ and $\mathbf{1}$, so $\mathbf{0} = \Delta_A/\equiv_A$ and $\mathbf{1} = \nabla_A/\equiv_A$.

Theorem 1. *If A satisfies Condition 1.(iv), then the following are equivalent:*

(i) $\mathcal{M}in(A) = \mathcal{M}in(A)^{-1}$*;*

(ii) $\mathcal{M}in(A)$ *is compact;*

(iii) *for any $\alpha \in \mathcal{K}(A)$, there exists $\beta \in \mathcal{K}(A)$ such that $\beta \subseteq \alpha^{\perp}$ and $(\alpha \vee \beta)^{\perp} = \Delta_A$.*

Proof. Assume that A satisfies Condition 1.(iv). Then the reticulation $\mathcal{L}(A)$ of A is a bounded distributive lattice and thus a distributive lattice with zero, hence, according to [30] (Proposition 5.1), the following are equivalent:

(a) $\mathcal{M}in_{\mathrm{Id}}(\mathcal{L}(A)) = \mathcal{M}in_{\mathrm{Id}}(\mathcal{L}(A))^{-1}$;

(b) $\mathcal{M}in_{\mathrm{Id}}(\mathcal{L}(A))$ is compact;

(c) for any $x \in \mathcal{L}(A)$, there exists $y \in \mathcal{L}(A)$ such that $x \wedge y = \mathbf{0}$ and $\mathrm{Ann}_{\mathcal{L}(A)}(x \vee y) = \{\mathbf{0}\}$.

By Lemma 12, (i) is equivalent to (a). By Lemma 12.(i), (ii) is equivalent to (b).

To prove that (iii) is equivalent to (c), let $\alpha, \beta \in \mathcal{K}(A)$, arbitrary, so that $\alpha/\equiv_A$ and $\beta/\equiv_A$ are arbitrary elements of $\mathcal{L}(A)$.

A is semiprime, that is $\rho_A(\Delta_A) = \Delta_A$, which is equivalent to $\Delta_A/\equiv_A = \{\Delta_A\}$ according to [25] (Remark 5.10), hence, for any $\theta \in \mathrm{Con}(A)$, $\theta = \Delta_A$ if and only if $\theta \in \Delta_A/\equiv_A$ if and only if $\theta/\equiv_A = \Delta_A/\equiv_A$, that is $\theta/\equiv_A = \mathbf{0}$.

Recall that $\beta \subseteq \alpha^\perp$ is equivalent to $[\alpha, \beta]_A = \Delta_A$ and thus to $[\alpha, \beta]_A/\equiv_A = \mathbf{0}$ by the above, that is $\alpha/\equiv_A \wedge \beta/\equiv_A = \mathbf{0}$.

Furthermore, since A is semiprime, we have, for all $\theta \in \mathrm{Con}(A)$: by [25] (Lemma 5.18.$(ii)$), $\mathrm{Ann}_{(\mathrm{Con}(A),[\cdot,\cdot]_A)}(\theta) = \mathrm{Ann}_{\mathrm{Con}(A)}(\theta)$, and, by Lemma 10.(i), $\mathrm{Ann}_{\mathrm{Con}(A)}(\theta) = \{\Delta_A\}$ if and only if $\mathrm{Ann}_{\mathrm{Con}(A)/\equiv_A}(\theta/\equiv_A) = \{\mathbf{0}\}$.

$(\alpha \vee \beta)^\perp = \Delta_A$ means that $\mathrm{Ann}_{(\mathrm{Con}(A),[\cdot,\cdot]_A)}(\alpha \vee \beta) = \{\Delta_A\}$, that is $\mathrm{Ann}_{\mathrm{Con}(A)}(\alpha \vee \beta) = \{\Delta_A\}$, which is equivalent to $\mathrm{Ann}_{\mathrm{Con}(A)/\equiv_A}(\alpha/\equiv_A \vee \beta/\equiv_A) = \{\mathbf{0}\}$, which in turn is equivalent to $\mathrm{Ann}_{\mathcal{L}(A)}(\alpha/\equiv_A \vee \beta/\equiv_A) = \{\mathbf{0}\}$, because, if we denote by $\theta = \alpha \vee \beta$, so that $\theta \in \mathcal{K}(A)$ and $\theta/\equiv_A = \alpha/\equiv_A \vee \beta/\equiv_A \in \mathcal{L}(A)$, we have:

since $\mathcal{L}(A)$ is a bounded sublattice of $\mathrm{Con}(A)/\equiv_A$, $\mathrm{Ann}_{\mathrm{Con}(A)/\equiv_A}(\theta/\equiv_A) = \{\mathbf{0}\}$ implies $\mathrm{Ann}_{\mathcal{L}(A)}(\theta/\equiv_A) = \mathrm{Ann}_{\mathrm{Con}(A)/\equiv_A}(\theta/\equiv_A) \cap \mathcal{L}(A) = \{\mathbf{0}\}$;

for the converse, recall that:

$$\max \mathrm{Ann}_{\mathrm{Con}(A)}(\theta) = \max \mathrm{Ann}_{(\mathrm{Con}(A),[\cdot,\cdot]_A)}(\theta) = \bigvee\{\gamma \in \mathcal{K}(A) \mid [\theta, \gamma]_A = \Delta_A\} =$$

$$\bigvee\{\gamma \in \mathcal{K}(A) \mid [\theta, \gamma]_A/\equiv_A = \mathbf{0}\} = \bigvee\{\gamma \in \mathcal{K}(A) \mid \theta/\equiv_A \wedge \gamma/\equiv_A = \mathbf{0}\},$$

thus, if $\theta \in \mathcal{K}(A)$, so that $\theta/\equiv_A \in \mathcal{L}(A)$, then

$$\max \mathrm{Ann}_{\mathrm{Con}(A)}(\theta) = \bigvee\{\gamma \in \mathcal{K}(A) \mid \gamma/\equiv_A \in \mathrm{Ann}_{\mathcal{L}(A)}(\theta/\equiv_A)\};$$

hence, if $\mathrm{Ann}_{\mathcal{L}(A)}(\theta/\equiv_A) = \{\mathbf{0}\}$, then

$$\max \mathrm{Ann}_{\mathrm{Con}(A)}(\theta) = \bigvee\{\gamma \in \mathcal{K}(A) \mid \gamma/\equiv_A \in \{\mathbf{0}\}\} = \bigvee\{\gamma \in \mathcal{K}(A) \mid \gamma/\equiv_A = \mathbf{0}\} =$$

$$\bigvee\{\gamma \in \mathcal{K}(A) \mid \gamma = \Delta_A\} = \Delta_A,$$

thus $\mathrm{Ann}_{\mathrm{Con}(A)}(\theta) = \{\Delta_A\}$, which is equivalent to $\mathrm{Ann}_{\mathrm{Con}(A)/\equiv_A}(\theta/\equiv_A) = \{\mathbf{0}\}$. □

Proposition 9. *If $\nabla_A \in \mathcal{K}(A)$ and $\mathrm{Spec}(A)$ is unordered, then $\mathcal{M}in(A)$ is compact.*

Proof. Assume that $\nabla_A \in \mathcal{K}(A)$ and $\mathrm{Spec}(A)$ is unordered, that is $\mathrm{Spec}(A) = \mathrm{Min}(A)$, and let $\mathrm{Min}(A) = \bigcup_{i \in I}(D_A(\alpha_i) \cap \mathrm{Min}(A))$ for some nonempty family $\{\alpha_i \mid i \in I\}$ of congruences of A. Then $\mathrm{Min}(A) = (\bigcup_{i \in I} D_A(\alpha_i)) \cap \mathrm{Min}(A) = D_A(\bigvee_{i \in I} \alpha_i) \cap \mathrm{Min}(A)$, thus $V_A(\bigvee_{i \in I} \alpha_i) \cap \mathrm{Min}(A) = \emptyset$. By Remark 3, this implies that $\bigvee_{i \in I} \alpha_i = \nabla_A \in \mathcal{K}(A)$, so that $\nabla_A = \bigvee_{i \in F} \alpha_i$ for some finite subset F of I, hence $\mathrm{Min}(A) = D_A(\bigvee_{i \in F} \alpha_i) \cap \mathrm{Min}(A) = (\bigcup_{i \in F} D_A(\alpha_i)) \cap \mathrm{Min}(A) = \bigcup_{i \in F}(D_A(\alpha_i) \cap \mathrm{Min}(A))$, therefore $\mathcal{M}in(A)$ is compact. □

Remark 7. *Clearly, if $\mathrm{Con}(A)$ is finite, in particular if A is finite, then $\mathcal{M}in(A)$ is compact.*

Of course, if $\mathrm{Con}(A)$ is finite, then $\mathrm{Con}(A) = \mathrm{Cp}(\mathrm{Con}(A)) = \mathcal{K}(A)$, thus $\nabla_A \in \mathcal{K}(A)$.

However, even if A is finite, its prime spectrum of congruences is not necessarily unordered. For instance, the five–element non–modular lattice $\mathcal{N}_5$ has $\mathrm{Con}(\mathcal{N}_5)$ isomorphic to the ordinal sum $\mathcal{L}_2 \oplus \mathcal{L}_2^2$ of the two–element chain with the four–element Boolean algebra, so, if we let $\mathrm{Con}(\mathcal{N}_5) =$

$\{\Delta_{\mathcal{N}_5}, \alpha, \beta, \gamma, \nabla_{\mathcal{N}_5}\}$, where $\text{Max}(\mathcal{N}_5) = \{\alpha, \beta\}$ and $\gamma = \alpha \cap \beta$, then $\text{Spec}(\mathcal{N}_5) = \{\Delta_{\mathcal{N}_5}, \alpha, \beta\} = \{\Delta_{\mathcal{N}_5}\} \cup \text{Max}(\mathcal{N}_5)$, which is obviously not unordered.

Therefore the converse of the implication in Proposition 9 does not hold.

Theorem 2. *If A satisfies (iv) and (vi) from Condition 1, in particular if the lattice $\text{Con}(A)$ is compact, then $\mathcal{M}in(A)$ is a Hausdorff topological space consisting solely of clopen sets, thus the Stone topology $\mathcal{S}_{\text{Min}(A)}$ is a complete Boolean sublattice of $\mathcal{P}(\text{Min}(A))$. If, moreover, $\text{Spec}(A)$ is unordered, then $\mathcal{M}in(A)$ is also compact.*

Proof. By Proposition 6.(i), the Stone topology $\mathcal{S}_{\text{Min}}(A)$ on $\text{Min}(A)$ consists entirely of clopen sets.

Let μ, ν be distinct minimal prime congruences of A. Then there exist $a, b \in A$ such that $(a,b) \in \mu \setminus \nu$, so that $Cg_A(a,b) \subseteq \mu$ and $Cg_A(a,b) \nsubseteq \nu$, so that $Cg_A(a,b)^{\perp} \nsubseteq \mu$ by Proposition 5, so $\mu \in D_A(Cg_A(a,b)^{\perp}) \cap \text{Min}(A)$ and $\nu \in D_A(Cg_A(a,b)) \cap \text{Min}(A)$. $D_A(Cg_A(a,b)) \cap \text{Min}(A) \cap D_A(Cg_A(a,b)^{\perp}) \cap \text{Min}(A) = D_A(Cg_A(a,b)) \cap D_A(Cg_A(a,b)^{\perp}) \cap \text{Min}(A) = D_A([Cg_A(a,b), Cg_A(a,b)^{\perp}]_A) \cap \text{Min}(A) = D_A(\Delta_A) \cap \text{Min}(A) = \emptyset \cap \text{Min}(A) = \emptyset$, therefore the topological space $(\text{Min}(A), \{D_A(\theta) \cap \text{Min}(A) \mid \theta \in \text{Con}(A)\})$ is Hausdorff.

By Proposition 9, if $\text{Spec}(A)$ is an antichain, then $\mathcal{M}in(A)$ is also compact. □

6. *m*–Extensions

(H) Throughout this section, we will assume that A is a subalgebra of B and that the algebras A and B are semiprime and they both satisfy Condition 1.(i).

In particular, the following results hold for extensions of semiprime algebras in congruence–modular varieties.

To avoid any danger of confusion, we will denote by $\alpha^{\perp A} = \alpha \rightarrow \Delta_A$ and $X^{\perp A} = Cg_A(X)^{\perp A}$ for any $\alpha \in \text{Con}(A)$ and any $X \subseteq A^2$ and by $\beta^{\perp B} = \beta \rightarrow \Delta_B$ and $Y^{\perp B} = Cg_B(Y)^{\perp B}$ for any $\beta \in \text{Con}(B)$ and any $Y \subseteq B^2$. See this notation for arbitrary subsets in Section 3.

We call the extension $A \subseteq B$:

- *admissible* if and only if the map $i_{A,B} : A \rightarrow B$ is admissible, that is if and only if $i^*_{A,B}(\phi) = \phi \cap \nabla_A \in \text{Spec}(A)$ for all $\phi \in \text{Spec}(B)$;
- Min–*admissible* or an *m–extension* if and only if $i^*_{A,B}(\mu) = \mu \cap \nabla_A \in \text{Min}(A)$ for all $\mu \in \text{Min}(B)$.

Lemma 13. *Assume that the extension $A \subseteq B$ is admissible and let us consider the following statements:*

(i) $A \subseteq B$ is an m–extension;

(ii) for any $\alpha \in \mathcal{K}(A)$ and any $\mu \in \text{Min}(B)$, if $\alpha \subseteq \mu$, then $\alpha^{\perp A} \nsubseteq \mu$;

(iii) for any $\alpha \in \mathcal{K}(A)$ and any $\mu \in \text{Min}(B)$, $\alpha \subseteq \mu$ if and only if $\alpha^{\perp A} \nsubseteq \mu$;

(iv) for any $\alpha \in \text{Con}(A)$ and any $\mu \in \text{Min}(B)$, if $\alpha \subseteq \mu$, then $\alpha^{\perp A} \nsubseteq \mu$;

(v) for any $\alpha \in \text{Con}(A)$ and any $\mu \in \text{Min}(B)$, $\alpha \subseteq \mu$ if and only if $\alpha^{\perp A} \nsubseteq \mu$.

If A satisfies Condition 1.(iv), then (i), (ii) and (iii) are equivalent.

If A satisfies Condition 1.(v), then (i), (iv) and (v) are equivalent.

Proof. For any $\alpha \in \text{Con}(A)$ and $\mu \in \text{Con}(B)$, we obviously have: $\alpha \subseteq \mu$ if and only if $\alpha \subseteq \mu \cap \nabla_A$, and $\alpha^{\perp A} \nsubseteq \mu$ if and only if $\alpha^{\perp A} \nsubseteq \mu \cap \nabla_A$.

Now assume that A satisfies (iv) or (v) from Condition 1, and let: $M = \mathcal{K}(A)$ if A satisfies (iv), and $M = \text{Con}(A)$ if A satisfies (v).

Since the extension $A \subseteq B$ is admissible, $\mu \cap \nabla_A \in \text{Spec}(A)$ for any $\mu \in \text{Spec}(B)$. $A \subseteq B$ is an m–extension if and only if $\mu \cap \nabla_A \in \text{Min}(A)$ for any $\mu \in \text{Min}(B)$, hence, by Proposition 5: $A \subseteq B$ is an m–extension if and only if, for all $\mu \in \text{Min}(B)$ and all $\alpha \in M$, the following equivalence holds: $\alpha \subseteq \mu \cap \nabla_A$ if and only if $\alpha^{\perp A} \nsubseteq \mu \cap \nabla_A$; by the above, this is equivalent to: $\alpha \subseteq \mu$ if and only if $\alpha^{\perp A} \nsubseteq \mu$. □

If $A \subseteq B$ is an m–extension, then the function $\Gamma = i^*_{A,B} \mid_{\mathrm{Min}(B)}: \mathrm{Min}(B) \to \mathrm{Min}(A)$, $\Gamma(\mu) = \mu \cap \nabla_A$ for all $\mu \in \mathrm{Min}(B)$, is well defined.

Proposition 10. *If the extension $A \subseteq B$ is admissible, then, for every $\psi \in \mathrm{Spec}(A)$, there exists a $\mu \in \mathrm{Min}(B)$ such that $\mu \cap \nabla_A \subseteq \psi$.*

Proof. Since $\psi \in \mathrm{Spec}(A)$, $\nabla_A \setminus \psi$ is an m–system in A, thus also in B, according to [18] [Lemma 4.18]. Hence there exists a $\nu \in \mathrm{Max}\{\gamma \in \mathrm{Con}(B) \mid \gamma \cap (\nabla_A \setminus \psi) = \emptyset\}$, so that $\nu \in \mathrm{Spec}(B)$ by Lemma 3, and thus there exists a $\mu \in \mathrm{Min}(B)$ with $\mu \subseteq \nu$, so that $\mu \cap (\nabla_A \setminus \psi) \subseteq \nu \cap (\nabla_A \setminus \psi) = \emptyset$ and thus $(\mu \cap \nabla_A) \setminus \psi = \emptyset$, so $\mu \cap \nabla_A \subseteq \psi$. □

Corollary 3.
- *If the extension $A \subseteq B$ is admissible, then, for every $\psi \in \mathrm{Min}(A)$, there exists a $\mu \in \mathrm{Min}(B)$ such that $\mu \cap \nabla_A = \psi$.*
- *If $A \subseteq B$ is an admissible m–extension, then $\Gamma : \mathrm{Min}(B) \to \mathrm{Min}(A)$ is surjective.*

Lemma 14. *If $A \subseteq B$ is an admissible m–extension, then, for any $\theta, \zeta \in \mathrm{Con}(A)$: $[\theta, \zeta]_A = \Delta_A$ if and only if $[Cg_B(\theta), Cg_B(\zeta)]_B = \Delta_B$.*

Proof. Since A and B are semiprime, we have $\Delta_A = \rho_A(\Delta_A) = \bigcap \mathrm{Min}(A)$ and $\Delta_B = \rho_B(\Delta_B) = \bigcap \mathrm{Min}(B)$, therefore: $[Cg_B(\theta), Cg_B(\zeta)]_B = \Delta_B$ if and only if $[Cg_B(\theta), Cg_B(\zeta)]_B \subseteq \nu$ for all $\nu \in \mathrm{Min}(B)$ if and only if, for all $\nu \in \mathrm{Min}(B)$, $Cg_B(\theta) \subseteq \nu$ or $Cg_B(\zeta) \subseteq \nu$ if and only if, for all $\nu \in \mathrm{Min}(B)$, $\theta \subseteq \nu$ or $\zeta \subseteq \nu$ if and only if, for all $\nu \in \mathrm{Min}(B)$, $\theta \subseteq \nu \cap \nabla_A$ or $\zeta \subseteq \nu \cap \nabla_A$; by Corollary 3, the latter is equivalent to: for all $\mu \in \mathrm{Min}(A)$, $\theta \subseteq \mu$ or $\zeta \subseteq \mu$, which in turn is equivalent to the fact that $[\theta, \zeta]_A \subseteq \mu$ for all $\mu \in \mathrm{Min}(A)$, that is $[\theta, \zeta]_A = \Delta_A$. □

Recall from [1] that, if $A \subseteq B$ is an extension of algebras from a congruence–modular variety, then, for all $\alpha, \beta \in \mathrm{Con}(B)$, $[\alpha \cap \nabla_A, \beta \cap \nabla_A]_A \subseteq [\alpha, \beta]_B \cap \nabla_A$. So, in this case, the right-to-left implication in Lemma 14 holds without admissibility or Min–admissibility:

Remark 8. *If the extension $A \subseteq B$ satisfies $[\alpha \cap \nabla_A, \beta \cap \nabla_A]_A \subseteq [\alpha, \beta]_B \cap \nabla_A$ for all $\alpha, \beta \in \mathrm{Con}(B)$, in particular if the variety $\mathcal{V}$ is congruence–modular, then, for any $\theta, \zeta \in \mathrm{Con}(A)$: $[Cg_B(\theta), Cg_B(\zeta)]_B = \Delta_B$ implies $[\theta, \zeta]_A = \Delta_A$.*

Indeed, since $\theta \subseteq Cg_B(\theta) \cap \nabla_A$ for all $\theta \in \mathrm{Con}(A)$ and the commutator is increasing in both arguments, it follows that, for all $\theta, \zeta \in \mathrm{Con}(A)$:

$[\theta, \zeta]_A \subseteq [Cg_B(\theta) \cap \nabla_A, Cg_B(\zeta) \cap \nabla_A]_A \subseteq [Cg_B(\theta), Cg_B(\zeta)]_B \cap \nabla_A$.

Thus, if $[Cg_B(\theta), Cg_B(\zeta)]_B = \Delta_B$, then $[\theta, \zeta]_A \subseteq \Delta_B \cap \nabla_A = \Delta_A$, so $[\theta, \zeta]_A = \Delta_A$.

Proposition 11. *If $A \subseteq B$ is an admissible m–extension, then, for any $\theta \in \mathrm{Con}(A)$:*

(i) $\theta^{\perp A} = \theta^{\perp B} \cap \nabla_A$ *and* $Cg_B(\theta^{\perp A}) \subseteq \theta^{\perp B}$*;*

(ii) *if, furthermore, $\theta^{\perp B} \in \{Cg_B(\alpha) \mid \alpha \in \mathrm{Con}(A)\}$, then $\theta^{\perp B} = Cg_B(\theta^{\perp A})$.*

Proof. (i) By Lemma 14 we have, for any $u, v \in A$: $(u, v) \in \theta^{\perp A}$ if and only if $[Cg_A(u, v), \theta]_A = \Delta_A$ if and only if $[Cg_B(Cg_A(u, v)), Cg_B(\theta)]_B = [Cg_B(u, v), Cg_B(\theta)]_B = \Delta_B$ if and only if $(u, v) \in \theta^{\perp B}$ if and only if $(u, v) \in \theta^{\perp B} \cap \nabla_A$. Therefore $\theta^{\perp A} = \theta^{\perp B} \cap \nabla_A$, hence $Cg_B(\theta^{\perp A}) = Cg_B(\theta^{\perp B} \cap \nabla_A) \subseteq \theta^{\perp B}$.
(ii) If $\theta^{\perp B}$ is generated by a congruence of A, then, by Lemma 14 and the fact that the map $\alpha \mapsto Cg_B(\alpha)$ from $\mathrm{Con}(A)$ to $\mathrm{Con}(B)$ is order-preserving, we have: $\theta^{\perp B} = Cg_B(\theta)^{\perp B} = \max\{\beta \in \mathrm{Con}(B) \mid [\beta, Cg_B(\theta)]_B = \Delta_B\} = \max\{Cg_B(\alpha) \mid \alpha \in \mathrm{Con}(A), [Cg_B(\alpha), Cg_B(\theta)]_B = \Delta_B\} = \max\{Cg_B(\alpha) \mid \alpha \in \mathrm{Con}(A), [\alpha, \theta]_A = \Delta_A\} = Cg_B(\max\{\alpha \in \mathrm{Con}(A) \mid [\alpha, \theta]_A = \Delta_A\}) = Cg_B(\theta^{\perp A})$. □

Corollary 4. *If $A \subseteq B$ is an admissible m–extension, then, for any $\theta, \zeta \in \mathrm{Con}(A)$:*

(i) $\theta^{\perp B} = \zeta^{\perp B}$ *implies* $\theta^{\perp A} = \zeta^{\perp A}$*;*

(ii) *if, furthermore,* $\theta^{\perp B}, \zeta^{\perp B} \in \{Cg_B(\alpha) \mid \alpha \in \mathrm{Con}(A)\}$, *then:* $\theta^{\perp A} = \zeta^{\perp A}$ *if and only if* $\theta^{\perp B} = \zeta^{\perp B}$.

Corollary 5. *If* $A \subseteq B$ *is an admissible m–extension such that A satisfies (v) and B satisfies (iv) or (v) from Condition 1, then, for any* $\psi \in \mathrm{Spec}(B)$, *we have:* $\psi \in \mathrm{Min}(B)$ *if and only if* $\psi \cap \nabla_A \in \mathrm{Min}(A)$.

Proof. We have the direct implication by the definition of an m–extension.

Now assume that $\psi \cap \nabla_A \in \mathrm{Min}(A)$ and let $\beta \in \mathrm{Con}(B)$, arbitrary. Then, by Proposition 5 and Proposition 11.(i): $\beta \subseteq \psi$ implies $\beta \cap \nabla_A \subseteq \psi \cap \nabla_A$, which is equivalent to $(\beta \cap \nabla_A)^{\perp A} \nsubseteq \psi \cap \nabla_A$, hence $(\beta \cap \nabla_A)^{\perp A} \nsubseteq \psi$, thus $\beta^{\perp B} \supseteq Cg_B((\beta \cap \nabla_A)^{\perp A}) \supseteq (\beta \cap \nabla_A)^{\perp A} \nsubseteq \psi$, so $\beta^{\perp B} \nsubseteq \psi$. Therefore, again by Proposition 5, $\psi \in \mathrm{Min}(B)$. □

Remark 9. *Note from the proof of Corollary 5 that, if* $A \subseteq B$ *is an admissible m–extension such that A satisfies (v) and B satisfies (iv) from Condition 1, then B satisfies the equivalence of all statements (i), (ii), (iii), (iv) and (v) in Proposition 5.*

By extending the terminology for ring extensions from [5], we call $A \subseteq B$:

- a *rigid*, a *quasirigid*, respectively a *weak rigid extension* if and only if, for any $\beta \in \mathrm{PCon}(B)$, there exists an $\alpha \in \mathrm{PCon}(A)$, an $\alpha \in \mathcal{K}(A)$, respectively an $\alpha \in \mathrm{Con}(A)$ such that $\alpha^{\perp B} = \beta^{\perp B}$;
- an *r–extension*, a *quasi r–extension*, respectively a *weak r–extension* if and only if, for any $\mu \in \mathrm{Min}(B)$ and any $\beta \in \mathrm{PCon}(B)$ such that $\beta \nsubseteq \mu$, there exists an $\alpha \in \mathrm{PCon}(A)$, an $\alpha \in \mathcal{K}(A)$, respectively an $\alpha \in \mathrm{Con}(A)$ such that $\alpha \nsubseteq \mu$ and $\beta^{\perp B} \subseteq \alpha^{\perp B}$;
- an *r^*–extension*, a *quasi r^*–extension*, respectively a *weak r^*–extension* if and only if, for any $\mu \in \mathrm{Min}(B)$ and any $\beta \in \mathrm{PCon}(B)$ such that $\beta \subseteq \mu$, there exists an $\alpha \in \mathrm{PCon}(A)$, an $\alpha \in \mathcal{K}(A)$, respectively an $\alpha \in \mathrm{Con}(A)$ such that $\alpha \subseteq \mu$ and $\alpha^{\perp B} \subseteq \beta^{\perp B}$.

Remark 10. *If* $A \subseteq B$ *is admissible or an m–extension, then, since any* $\alpha \in \mathrm{Con}(A)$ *and* $\mu \in \mathrm{Con}(B)$ *satisfy the equivalence* $\alpha \subseteq \mu$ *if and only if* $\alpha \subseteq \mu \cap \nabla_A$, *thus also the equivalence* $\alpha \nsubseteq \mu$ *if and only if* $\alpha \nsubseteq \mu \cap \nabla_A$, *it follows that* $A \subseteq B$ *is:*

- *an r–extension, a quasi r–extension, respectively a weak r–extension if and only if, for any* $\beta \in \mathrm{PCon}(B)$, $\{\mu \cap \nabla_A \mid \mu \in D_B(\beta) \cap \mathrm{Min}(B)\} \subseteq \bigcup\{D_A(\alpha) \mid \alpha \in M, \beta^{\perp B} \subseteq \alpha^{\perp B}\} = D_A(\bigvee\{\alpha \in M \mid \beta^{\perp B} \subseteq \alpha^{\perp B}\})$, *where M is equal to* $\mathrm{PCon}(A)$, $\mathcal{K}(A)$, *respectively* $\mathrm{Con}(A)$;
- *an r^*–extension, a quasi r^*–extension, respectively a weak r^*–extension if and only if, for any* $\beta \in \mathrm{PCon}(B)$, $\{\mu \cap \nabla_A \mid \mu \in V_B(\beta) \cap \mathrm{Min}(B)\} \subseteq \bigcup\{V_A(\alpha) \mid \alpha \in M, \alpha^{\perp B} \subseteq \beta^{\perp B}\}$, *where M is equal to* $\mathrm{PCon}(A)$, $\mathcal{K}(A)$, *respectively* $\mathrm{Con}(A)$;

thus, if $A \subseteq B$ *is an m–extension, then* $A \subseteq B$ *is:*

- *an r–extension, a quasi r–extension, respectively a weak r–extension if and only if, for any* $\beta \in \mathrm{PCon}(B)$, $\Gamma(D_B(\beta) \cap \mathrm{Min}(B)) \subseteq \bigcup\{D_A(\alpha) \mid \alpha \in M, \beta^{\perp B} \subseteq \alpha^{\perp B}\} = D_A(\bigvee\{\alpha \in M \mid \beta^{\perp B} \subseteq \alpha^{\perp B}\})$, *where M is equal to* $\mathrm{PCon}(A)$, $\mathcal{K}(A)$, *respectively* $\mathrm{Con}(A)$;
- *an r^*–extension, a quasi r^*–extension, respectively a weak r^*–extension if and only if, for any* $\beta \in \mathrm{PCon}(B)$, $\Gamma(V_B(\beta) \cap \mathrm{Min}(B)) \subseteq \bigcup\{V_A(\alpha) \mid \alpha \in M, \alpha^{\perp B} \subseteq \beta^{\perp B}\}$, *where M is equal to* $\mathrm{PCon}(A)$, $\mathcal{K}(A)$, *respectively* $\mathrm{Con}(A)$.

Remark 11. *Note from Lemma 1 that, for any set I and any* $\{a_i, b_i \mid i \in I\} \subseteq A$, $Cg_B(Cg_A(\{(a_i, b_i) \mid i \in I\})) = Cg_B(\{(a_i, b_i) \mid i \in I\})$, *hence, for any* $\alpha \in \mathrm{PCon}(A)$ *and any* $\beta \in \mathcal{K}(A)$, *it follows that* $Cg_B(\alpha) \in \mathrm{PCon}(B)$ *and* $Cg_B(\beta) \in \mathcal{K}(B)$.

Proposition 12. *If* $A \subseteq B$ *is an m–extension, then:*

(i) *if B satisfies Condition 1.(v) and* $A \subseteq B$ *is a weak rigid extension, then it is both a weak r–extension and a weak r^*–extension;*

(ii) *if B satisfies (iv) or (v) from Condition 1 and $A \subseteq B$ is a quasirigid extension, then it is both a quasi r–extension and a quasi r*–extension;*
(iii) *if B satisfies (iv) or (v) from Condition 1 and $A \subseteq B$ is a rigid extension, then it is both an r–extension and an r*–extension.*

Proof. (ii) Assume that $A \subseteq B$ is a quasirigid extension and let $\mu \in \mathrm{Min}(B)$ and $\beta \in \mathrm{PCon}(B)$, so that $Cg_B(\alpha)^{\perp B} = \beta^{\perp B}$ for some $\alpha \in \mathcal{K}(A)$, hence, according to Proposition 5 and Remark 11:
$\beta \nsubseteq \mu$ implies $Cg_B(\alpha)^{\perp B} = \beta^{\perp B} \subseteq \mu$, thus $Cg_B(\alpha) \nsubseteq \mu$, hence $\alpha \nsubseteq \mu$;
$\beta \subseteq \mu$ implies $Cg_B(\alpha)^{\perp B} = \beta^{\perp B} \nsubseteq \mu$, thus $\alpha \subseteq Cg_B(\alpha) \subseteq \mu$.
(i) and (iii) Analogously. □

Proposition 13. *If $A \subseteq B$ is an m–extension, then:*
(i) *Γ is continuous with respect to the Stone topologies and the inverse topologies;*
(ii) *if A satisfies (iv) or (v) or B satisfies (iv) or (v) from Condition 1, then $\Gamma : \mathcal{M}in(B) \to \mathcal{M}in(A)^{-1}$ is continuous;*
(iii) *if A satisfies (vi), along with one of (iv) and (v) from Condition 1, or B satisfies (vi), along with one of (iv) and (v) from Condition 1, then $\Gamma : \mathcal{M}in(B)^{-1} \to \mathcal{M}in(A)$ is continuous.*

Proof. Let $\alpha \in \mathrm{Con}(A)$, so that $D_A(\alpha) \cap \mathrm{Min}(A)$ is an arbitrary open set in $\mathcal{M}in(A)$, $D_B(Cg_B(\alpha)) \cap \mathrm{Min}(B)$ is an open set in $\mathcal{M}in(B)$ and, if $\alpha \in \mathcal{K}(A)$, so that $Cg_B(\alpha) \in \mathcal{K}(B)$, then $V_A(\alpha) \cap \mathrm{Min}(A)$ is an arbitrary basic open set in $\mathcal{M}in(A)^{-1}$ and $V_B(Cg_B(\alpha)) \cap \mathrm{Min}(B)$ is a basic open set in $\mathcal{M}in(B)^{-1}$.

Since $A \subseteq B$ is an m–extension, we have, for all $\nu \in \mathrm{Min}(B)$: $\nu \cap \nabla_A \in \mathrm{Min}(A)$, thus:

$\nu \in \Gamma^{-1}(V_A(\alpha) \cap \mathrm{Min}(A))$ if and only if $\nu \cap \nabla_A \in V_A(\alpha) \cap \mathrm{Min}(A) = [\alpha) \cap \mathrm{Min}(A)$ if and only if $\nu \cap \nabla_A \in [\alpha)$ if and only if $\alpha \subseteq \nu \cap \nabla_A$ if and only if $\alpha \subseteq \nu$ if and only if $Cg_B(\alpha) \subseteq \nu$ if and only if $\nu \in V_B(Cg_B(\alpha)) \cap \mathrm{Min}(B)$; hence $\Gamma^{-1}(V_A(\alpha) \cap \mathrm{Min}(A)) = V_B(Cg_B(\alpha)) \cap \mathrm{Min}(B)$;

similarly, $\nu \in \Gamma^{-1}(D_A(\alpha) \cap \mathrm{Min}(A))$ if and only if $\alpha \nsubseteq \nu \cap \nabla_A$ if and only if $\alpha \nsubseteq \nu$ if and only if $Cg_B(\alpha) \nsubseteq \nu$ if and only if $\nu \in D_B(Cg_B(\alpha)) \cap \mathrm{Min}(B)$; hence $\Gamma^{-1}(D_A(\alpha) \cap \mathrm{Min}(A)) = D_B(Cg_B(\alpha)) \cap \mathrm{Min}(B)$.

(i) Hence $\Gamma : \mathcal{M}in(B) \to \mathcal{M}in(A)$ and $\Gamma : \mathcal{M}in(B)^{-1} \to \mathcal{M}in(A)^{-1}$ are continuous.

(ii) Assume that $\alpha \in \mathcal{K}(A)$.

If A satisfies (iv) or (v) from Condition 1, then, by Proposition 5: $\alpha \subseteq \nu \cap \nabla_A$ if and only if $\alpha^{\perp A} \nsubseteq \nu \cap \nabla_A$ if and only if $\alpha^{\perp A} \nsubseteq \nu$ if and only if $Cg_B(\alpha^{\perp A}) \nsubseteq \nu$ if and only if $\nu \in D_B(Cg_B(\alpha^{\perp A})) \cap \mathrm{Min}(B)$; hence $\Gamma^{-1}(V_A(\alpha) \cap \mathrm{Min}(A)) = D_B(Cg_B(\alpha^{\perp A})) \cap \mathrm{Min}(B)$.

If B satisfies (iv) or (v) from Condition 1, then, by Proposition 5: $Cg_B(\alpha) \subseteq \nu$ if and only if $Cg_B(\alpha)^{\perp B} \nsubseteq \nu$ if and only if $\nu \in D_B(Cg_B(\alpha)^{\perp B}) \cap \mathrm{Min}(B)$; hence $\Gamma^{-1}(V_A(\alpha) \cap \mathrm{Min}(A)) = D_B(Cg_B(\alpha)^{\perp B}) \cap \mathrm{Min}(B)$.

Thus, in either of these cases, $\Gamma : \mathcal{M}in(B) \to \mathcal{M}in(A)^{-1}$ is continuous.

(iii) Analogous to the proof of (ii) or simply by applying (i), (ii) and Proposition 7.(ii). □

Proposition 14. *If $A \subseteq B$ is an admissible quasi r–extension and B satisfies (iv) or (v) from Condition 1, then: $A \subseteq B$ is an m–extension and Γ is a bijection.*

Proof. Assume that $A \subseteq B$ is an admissible quasi r–extension and B satisfies (iv) or (v) from Condition 1.

Assume by absurdum that there exists a $\nu \in \mathrm{Min}(B)$ with $\nu \cap \nabla_A \notin \mathrm{Min}(A)$, so that $\nu \cap \nabla_A \in \mathrm{Spec}(A) \setminus \mathrm{Min}(A)$ since $\mathrm{Min}(B) \subseteq \mathrm{Spec}(B)$ and $A \subseteq B$ is admissible, hence there exists $\mu \in \mathrm{Min}(A)$ such that $\mu \subsetneq \nu \cap \nabla_A$.

Since $A \subseteq B$ is admissible, by Corollary 3 it follows that $\mu = \varepsilon \cap \nabla_A$ for some $\varepsilon \in \mathrm{Min}(B)$. Thus $\varepsilon \cap \nabla_A = \mu \subsetneq \nu \cap \nabla_A$, therefore ε and ν are distinct minimal prime congruences of B, hence they are incomparable, thus $\varepsilon \setminus \nu \neq \emptyset$, so that $(x, y) \in \varepsilon \setminus \nu$ for some $x, y \in B$.

Then $Cg_B(x,y) \nsubseteq \nu$, so that, since $A \subseteq B$ is a quasi r–extension, there exists an $\alpha \in \mathcal{K}(A)$ such that $\alpha \nsubseteq \nu$ and $Cg_B(x,y)^{\perp B} \subseteq \alpha^{\perp B} = Cg_B(\alpha)^{\perp B}$. Then $Cg_B(\alpha) \in \mathcal{K}(B)$ and $\alpha \nsubseteq \nu$, thus $Cg_B(\alpha) \nsubseteq \nu$, hence $Cg_B(\alpha)^{\perp B} \subseteq \nu$ by Proposition 5 and the fact that B satisfies (iv) or (v) from Condition 1.

Also, $Cg_B(x,y) \subseteq \varepsilon$, thus, again by Proposition 5 and the fact that B satisfies (iv) or (v) from Condition 1, $Cg_B(\alpha)^{\perp B} \supseteq Cg_B(x,y)^{\perp B} \nsubseteq \varepsilon$, hence $\alpha \subseteq Cg_B(\alpha) \subseteq \varepsilon$, thus $\alpha \subseteq \varepsilon \cap \nabla_A = \mu \subset \nu \cap \nabla_A \subseteq \nu$, hence $Cg_B(\alpha) \subseteq \nu$, so that $Cg_B(\alpha)^{\perp B} \nsubseteq \nu$, which contradicts the above.

Therefore $A \subseteq B$ is an m–extension, hence Γ is surjective by Corollary 3 and the admissibility of $A \subseteq B$.

Now let $\phi, \psi \in \mathrm{Min}(B)$ such that $\Gamma(\phi) = \Gamma(\psi)$, that is $\phi \cap \nabla_A = \psi \cap \nabla_A$, and assume by absurdum that $\phi \neq \psi$, so that $\phi \setminus \psi \neq \emptyset$, that is $(u,v) \in \phi \setminus \psi$ for some $u, v \in B$, which thus satisfy $Cg_B(u,v) \subseteq \phi$ and $Cg_B(u,v) \nsubseteq \psi$, hence $Cg_B(u,v)^{\perp B} \nsubseteq \phi$ and $Cg_B(u,v)^{\perp B} \subseteq \psi$ by Proposition 5.

As above, it follows that there exists a $\gamma \in \mathcal{K}(A)$ such that $\gamma \nsubseteq \psi$ and $Cg_B(u,v)^{\perp B} \subseteq \gamma^{\perp B}$, so that $\gamma \nsubseteq \psi \cap \nabla_A$ and $Cg_B(\gamma)^{\perp B} = \gamma^{\perp B} \nsubseteq \phi$, thus $\gamma \subseteq Cg_B(\gamma) \subseteq \phi$ by Proposition 5, so $\gamma \subseteq \phi \cap \nabla_A$. We have obtained $\gamma \subseteq \phi \cap \nabla_A = \psi \cap \nabla_A \nsupseteq \gamma$; a contradiction. Therefore Γ is injective. □

Proposition 15. *If $A \subseteq B$ is an admissible quasi r^*–extension and B satisfies (iv) or (v) from Condition 1, then: $A \subseteq B$ is an m–extension and Γ is a bijection.*

Proof. Similar to the proof of Proposition 14. □

Theorem 3. *If $A \subseteq B$ is an admissible extension such that B satisfies (iv) or (v) from Condition 1, then the following are equivalent:*

(i) $A \subseteq B$ is an r–extension;
(ii) $A \subseteq B$ is a quasi r–extension;
(iii) $\Gamma : \mathcal{M}in(B) \to \mathcal{M}in(A)$ is a homeomorphism.

Proof. (i)⇒(ii): Trivial.
(ii)⇒(iii): If $A \subseteq B$ is an admissible quasi r–extension such that B satisfies (iv) or (v) from Condition 1, then, by Propositions 14 and 13, it follows that $A \subseteq B$ is an m–extension and $\Gamma : \mathcal{M}in(B) \to \mathcal{M}in(A)$ is a continuous bijection.

Let $\beta \in \mathrm{PCon}(B)$, so that $\Gamma(D_B(\beta) \cap \mathrm{Min}(B)) = \{\psi \cap \nabla_A \mid \psi \in D_B(\beta) \cap \mathrm{Min}(B)\} = \{\psi \cap \nabla_A \mid \psi \in \mathrm{Min}(B), \beta \nsubseteq \psi\}$. By Remark 10 and the fact that $A \subseteq B$ is a quasi r–extension and an m–extension, $\Gamma(D_B(\beta) \cap \mathrm{Min}(B)) \subseteq D_A(\bigvee\{\alpha \in \mathcal{K}(A) \mid \beta^{\perp B} \subseteq \alpha^{\perp B}\}) \cap \mathrm{Min}(A)$.

Now let $\phi \in D_A(\bigvee\{\alpha \in \mathcal{K}(A) \mid \beta^{\perp B} \subseteq \alpha^{\perp B}\}) \cap \mathrm{Min}(A)$, that is $\phi \in (\{\bigcup\{D_A(\alpha) \mid \alpha \in \mathcal{K}(A), \beta^{\perp B} \subseteq \alpha^{\perp B}\}) \cap \mathrm{Min}(A) = \bigcup\{D_A(\alpha) \cap \mathrm{Min}(A) \mid \alpha \in \mathcal{K}(A), \beta^{\perp B} \subseteq \alpha^{\perp B}\}\}$, so $\phi \in D_A(\alpha) \cap \mathrm{Min}(A)$ for some $\alpha \in \mathcal{K}(A)$ such that $\beta^{\perp B} \subseteq \alpha^{\perp B} = Cg_B(\alpha)^{\perp B}$. By Corollary 3, there exists $\psi \in \mathrm{Min}(B)$ such that $\Gamma(\psi) = \psi \cap \nabla_A = \phi \nsupseteq \alpha$, thus $\psi \nsupseteq Cg_B(\alpha)$, hence $\psi \supseteq Cg_B(\alpha)^{\perp B} = \beta^{\perp B}$ and thus $\psi \nsupseteq \beta$ by Proposition 5 and the fact that B satisfies (iv) or (v) from Condition 1, so that $\psi \in D_B(\beta) \cap \mathrm{Min}(B)$, thus $\phi \in \Gamma(D_B(\beta) \cap \mathrm{Min}(B))$.

Hence we also have the converse inclusion: $D_A(\bigvee\{\alpha \in \mathcal{K}(A) \mid \beta^{\perp B} \subseteq \alpha^{\perp B}\}) \cap \mathrm{Min}(A) \subseteq \Gamma(D_B(\beta) \cap \mathrm{Min}(B))$, so $\Gamma(D_B(\beta) \cap \mathrm{Min}(B)) = D_A(\bigvee\{\alpha \in \mathcal{K}(A) \mid \beta^{\perp B} \subseteq \alpha^{\perp B}\}) \cap \mathrm{Min}(A)$. Therefore $\Gamma : \mathcal{M}in(B) \to \mathcal{M}in(A)$ is also open, thus it is a homeomorphism.
(iii)⇒(i): Assume that Γ is a homeomorphism with respect to the Stone topologies, so $A \subseteq B$ is an m–extension and Γ maps basic open sets of $\mathcal{M}in(B)$ to basic open sets of $\mathcal{M}in(A)$.

Let $\beta \in \mathrm{PCon}(B)$, so that $D_B(\beta) \cap \mathrm{Min}(B)$ is a basic open set of $\mathcal{M}in(B)$. By the above, there exists $\alpha \in \mathrm{PCon}(A)$ such that $\{\mu \cap \nabla_A \mid \mu \in D_B(\beta) \cap \mathrm{Min}(B)\} = \Gamma(D_B(\beta) \cap \mathrm{Min}(B)) = D_A(\alpha) \cap \mathrm{Min}(A)$. Hence, for all $\mu \in D_B(\beta) \cap \mathrm{Min}(B)$, that is $\mu \in \mathrm{Min}(B)$ such that $\beta \nsubseteq \mu$, we have $\mu \cap \nabla_A \in D_A(\alpha) \cap \mathrm{Min}(A)$, so $\alpha \nsubseteq \mu \cap \nabla_A$, that is $\alpha \nsubseteq \mu$. Since B satisfies (iv) or (v) from Condition 1, we have, by Proposition 5: $\beta^{\perp B} \subseteq \mu$ and $\alpha^{\perp B} = Cg_B(\alpha)^{\perp B} \subseteq \mu$.

For any $\gamma \in \mathcal{K}(B)$ such that $\gamma \subseteq \beta^{\perp B}$, all $\varepsilon \in \mathrm{Min}(B)$ satisfy the following:

- if $Cg_B(\alpha) \subseteq \varepsilon$, then $[\gamma, Cg_B(\alpha)]_B \subseteq \varepsilon$;
- if $Cg_B(\alpha) \nsubseteq \varepsilon$, then $\alpha \nsubseteq \varepsilon \cap \nabla_A$, that is $\Gamma(\varepsilon) = \varepsilon \cap \nabla_A \in D_A(\alpha) \cap \mathrm{Min}(A) = \Gamma(D_B(\beta) \cap \mathrm{Min}(B))$, hence $\varepsilon \in D_B(\beta) \cap \mathrm{Min}(B)$ since Γ is a bijection, thus $\beta \nsubseteq \varepsilon$, so $\beta^{\perp B} \subseteq \varepsilon$, again by Proposition 5, thus $\gamma \subseteq \varepsilon$ by the above, hence $[\gamma, Cg_B(\alpha)]_B \subseteq \varepsilon$;

hence $[\gamma, Cg_B(\alpha)]_B \subseteq \bigcap \mathrm{Min}(B) = \Delta_B$ since B is semiprime, thus $[\gamma, Cg_B(\alpha)]_B = \Delta_B$, that is $\gamma \subseteq Cg_B(\alpha)^{\perp B} = \alpha^{\perp B}$.

Therefore $\beta^{\perp B} = \bigvee\{\gamma \in \mathcal{K}(B) \mid \gamma \subseteq \beta^{\perp B}\} \subseteq \alpha^{\perp B}$. Hence $A \subseteq B$ is an r–extension. □

Proposition 16. *If $A \subseteq B$ is an admissible r–extension such that B satisfies (iv) or (v) from Condition 1, then the following are equivalent:*

(i) *$A \subseteq B$ is a rigid extension;*

(ii) *Γ maps basic open sets of $\mathcal{M}in(B)$ to basic open sets of $\mathcal{M}in(A)$.*

Proof. By Proposition 14, $A \subseteq B$ is an m–extension and Γ is bijective.

(i)$\Rightarrow$(ii): Let $\beta \in \mathrm{PCon}(B)$, so that there exists $\alpha \in \mathrm{PCon}(A)$ with $\beta^{\perp B} = \alpha^{\perp B} = Cg_B(\alpha)^{\perp B}$ since $A \subseteq B$ is rigid. By Proposition 5, for any $\nu \in \mathrm{Min}(B)$, the following equivalences hold: $\beta \nsubseteq \nu$ if and only if $\beta^{\perp B} \subseteq \nu$ if and only if $Cg_B(\alpha)^{\perp B} \subseteq \nu$ if and only if $Cg_B(\alpha) \nsubseteq \nu$ if and only if $\alpha \nsubseteq \nu$ if and only if $\alpha \nsubseteq \nu \cap \nabla_A$, therefore, since Γ is bijective, we have $\Gamma(D_B(\beta) \cap \mathrm{Min}(B)) = \{\nu \cap \nabla_A \mid \nu \in \mathrm{Min}(B), \beta \nsubseteq \nu\} = \{\mu \in \mathrm{Min}(A) \mid \alpha \nsubseteq \mu\} = D_A(\alpha) \cap \mathrm{Min}(A)$.

(ii)$\Rightarrow$(i): Let $\beta \in \mathrm{PCon}(B)$. By the hypothesis of this implication, $\Gamma(D_B(\beta) \cap \mathrm{Min}(B)) = D_A(\alpha) \cap \mathrm{Min}(A)$ for some $\alpha \in \mathrm{PCon}(A)$, thus $\{\nu \cap \nabla_A \mid \nu \in \mathrm{Min}(A), \beta \nsubseteq \nu\} = \{\mu \mid \mu \in \mathrm{Min}(A), \alpha \nsubseteq \mu\}$. By Proposition 5, it follows that any $\nu \in \mathrm{Min}(B)$ satisfies: $\beta^{\perp B} \subseteq \nu$ if and only if $\beta \nsubseteq \nu$ if and only if $\alpha \nsubseteq \nu \cap \nabla_A$ if and only if $\alpha \nsubseteq \nu$ if and only if $Cg_B(\alpha) \nsubseteq \nu$ if and only if $Cg_B(\alpha)^{\perp B} \subseteq \nu$.

As in the proof of the implication (iii)$\Rightarrow$(i) from Theorem 3, it follows that $\beta^{\perp B} = \bigcap V_B(\beta^{\perp B}) = \bigcap V_B(Cg_B(\alpha)^{\perp B}) = Cg_B(\alpha)^{\perp B} = \alpha^{\perp B}$. Hence the extension $A \subseteq B$ is rigid. □

Proposition 17. *If $A \subseteq B$ is an admissible r^*–extension such that B satisfies (iv) or (v) from Condition 1, then the following are equivalent:*

(i) *$A \subseteq B$ is a quasirigid extension;*

(ii) *Γ maps basic open sets of $\mathcal{M}in(B)^{-1}$ to basic open sets of $\mathcal{M}in(A)^{-1}$.*

Proof. By Proposition 15, $A \subseteq B$ is an m–extension and Γ is bijective.

(i)$\Rightarrow$(ii): Let $\beta \in \mathcal{K}(B)$, so that $\beta = \bigvee_{i=1}^{n} \beta_i$ for some $n \in \mathbb{N}^*$ and some $\beta_1, \ldots, \beta_n \in \mathrm{PCon}(B)$. By the hypothesis of this implication, for each $i \in \overline{1,n}$, there exists $\alpha_i \in \mathcal{K}(A)$ such that $\beta_i^{\perp B} = \alpha_i^{\perp B} = (Cg_B(\alpha_i))^{\perp B}$.

Analogously to the proof of (i)$\Rightarrow$(ii) from Proposition 16, it follows that $\Gamma(V_B(\beta_i) \cap \mathrm{Min}(B)) = V_A(\alpha_i) \cap \mathrm{Min}(A)$ for all $i \in \overline{1,n}$, hence $\Gamma(V_B(\beta) \cap \mathrm{Min}(B)) = \Gamma(\bigcap_{i=1}^{n} V_B(\beta_i) \cap \mathrm{Min}(B)) = \bigcap_{i=1}^{n} \Gamma(V_B(\beta_i) \cap \mathrm{Min}(B)) = \bigcap_{i=1}^{n} V_A(\alpha_i) \cap \mathrm{Min}(A) = V_A(\alpha) \cap \mathrm{Min}(A)$, where $\alpha = \bigvee_{i=1}^{n} \alpha_i \in \mathcal{K}(A)$.

(ii)$\Rightarrow$(i): Similar to the proof of (ii)$\Rightarrow$(i) in Proposition 16. □

Corollary 6. *If $A \subseteq B$ is an admissible r–extension and r^*–extension such that B satisfies (iv) or (v) from Condition 1, then the following are equivalent:*

- *$A \subseteq B$ is a quasirigid extension;*
- *$A \subseteq B$ is a rigid extension.*

Proof. By Proposition 15, $A \subseteq B$ is an m–extension and Γ is bijective.

Clearly, if the extension $A \subseteq B$ is rigid, then it is quasirigid.

Now assume that $A \subseteq B$ is quasirigid. Then, by Proposition 17, Γ maps basic open sets of $\mathcal{M}in(B)^{-1}$ to basic open sets of $\mathcal{M}in(A)^{-1}$. Since Γ is bijective, it follows that Γ maps basic open sets of $\mathcal{M}in(B)$ to basic open sets of $\mathcal{M}in(A)$, hence $A \subseteq B$ is rigid according to Proposition 16. □

Theorem 4. *If $A \subseteq B$ is an admissible extension such that B satisfies (iv) or (v) from Condition 1, then the following are equivalent:*

(i) $A \subseteq B$ *is a quasi r^*–extension;*
(ii) $\Gamma : \mathcal{M}in(B)^{-1} \to \mathcal{M}in(A)^{-1}$ *is a homeomorphism.*

Proof. By adapting the proof of Theorem 3. □

We say that A satisfies the *annihilator condition* (AC for short) if for all $\alpha, \beta \in \text{PCon}(A)$ there exists $\gamma \in \text{PCon}(A)$ such that $\gamma^{\perp A} = \alpha^{\perp A} \cap \beta^{\perp A}$.

Remark 12. *By Proposition 6.(ii), A satisfies AC if and only if the family $\{V_A(\alpha) \cap \text{Min}(A) \mid \alpha \in \text{PCon}(A)\}$ is closed under finite intersections. Thus, for any semiprime algebra A that satisfies AC, the family $\{V_A(\alpha) \cap \text{Min}(A) \mid \alpha \in \text{PCon}(A)\}$ is a basis for the inverse topology $\mathcal{F}_{\text{Min}(A)}$ of $\text{Min}(A)$.*

Proposition 18. *Let $A \subseteq B$ be an admissible extension such that B satisfies (iv) or (v) from Condition 1.*

(i) *If A satisfies AC, then: $A \subseteq B$ is a quasi r^*–extension if and only if $A \subseteq B$ is an r^*–extension.*
(ii) *If $A \subseteq B$ is an r–extension and both A and B satisfy AC, then: $A \subseteq B$ is a quasirigid extension if and only if $A \subseteq B$ is a rigid extension.*

Proof. (i) Assume that $A \subseteq B$ is a quasi r^*–extension. Then, by Theorem 4, $\Gamma : \mathcal{M}in(B)^{-1} \to \mathcal{M}in(A)^{-1}$ is a homeomorphism.

Let $\nu \in \text{Min}(B)$ and $\beta \in \text{PCon}(B)$ such that $\beta \subseteq \nu$, so that $\nu \in V_B(\beta) \cap \text{Min}(B)$, thus, by the above, $\nu \cap \nabla_A = \Gamma(\nu) \in \Gamma(V_B(\beta) \cap \text{Min}(B))$, which, according to Remark 12, equals $V_A(\alpha) \cap \text{Min}(A)$ for some $\alpha \in \text{PCon}(A)$. As in the proof of (ii)⇒(i) from Proposition 16, it follows that $\alpha^{\perp B} \subseteq \beta^{\perp B}$. Therefore $A \subseteq B$ is an r^*–extension.

The converse implication is trivial.

(ii) By Propositions 16 and 17 and the clear fact that, in this case, condition (ii) from Proposition 16 is equivalent to (ii) from Proposition 17. □

Let us denote, for any subset $X \subseteq A^2$, by $S(X) = \{\psi \in \text{Min}(B) \mid X \nsubseteq \psi \cap \nabla_A\}$, thus $S(X) = \{\psi \in \text{Min}(B) \mid \psi \cap \nabla_A \in D_A(Cg_A(X))\}$.

Proposition 19. *Let $A \subseteq B$ be an admissible extension such that B is hyperarchimedean and satisfies (iv) or (v) from Condition 1. If the extension $A \subseteq B$ has the property that, for any $\theta, \zeta \in \text{Con}(A)$, $\theta^{\perp A} = \zeta^{\perp A}$ implies $\theta^{\perp B} = \zeta^{\perp B}$, in particular if $A \subseteq B$ is an m–extension such that $\{\beta^{\perp B} \mid \beta \in \text{Con}(B)\} \subseteq \{Cg_B(\alpha) \mid \alpha \in \text{Con}(A)\}$, then the following are equivalent:*

(i) $\mathcal{M}in(A)$ *is a compact space;*
(ii) $A \subseteq B$ *is an m–extension;*
(iii) *for any $\alpha \in \text{PCon}(A)$ there exists $\beta \in \mathcal{K}(A)$ such that $S(\beta) = \text{Spec}(B) \setminus S(\alpha)$;*
(iv) *for any $\alpha \in \text{PCon}(A)$ there exists $\beta \in \mathcal{K}(A)$ such that $\beta \subseteq \alpha^{\perp A}$ and $(\alpha \vee \beta)^{\perp A} = \Delta_A$.*

Proof. First, note from Corollary 4.(ii) that, if $A \subseteq B$ is an admissible m–extension such that $\beta^{\perp B}$ is generated by a congruence of A for every $\beta \in \text{Con}(B)$, then this extension satisfies the implication: $\theta^{\perp A} = \zeta^{\perp A}$ implies $\theta^{\perp B} = \zeta^{\perp B}$.

Now assume that $A \subseteq B$ is an admissible extension such that, for any $\theta, \zeta \in \text{Con}(A)$, $\theta^{\perp A} = \zeta^{\perp A}$ implies $\theta^{\perp B} = \zeta^{\perp B}$, and that B is hyperarchimedean and satisfies (iv) or (v) from Condition 1.

(i)⇔(iv) By Theorem 1.

(iv)⇒(iii): Assume that $\alpha \in PCon(A)$. By the hypothesis (iv), there exists $\beta \in \mathcal{K}(A)$ such that $\beta \subseteq \alpha^{\perp A}$ and $(\alpha \vee \beta)^{\perp A} = \Delta_A$.

To show that $Spec(B) \setminus S(\alpha) = S(\beta)$, let $\psi \in Spec(B) \setminus S(\alpha)$, hence $\alpha \subseteq \psi \cap \nabla_A$. Since $A \subseteq B$ satisfies the implication in the enunciation, by Proposition 5 it follows that these implications hold: if $(\alpha \vee \beta)^{\perp B} = \Delta_B$, i.e., $(Cg_B(\alpha \vee \beta))^{\perp B} = \Delta_B$, then $(Cg_B(\alpha \vee \beta))^{\perp B} \subsetneq \psi$, thus $Cg_B(\alpha \vee \beta) \nsubseteq \psi$, so $\alpha \vee \beta \nsubseteq \psi$, thus $\beta \nsubseteq \psi \cap \nabla_A$, so $\psi \in S(\beta)$, which proves the inclusion $Spec(B) \setminus S(\alpha) \subseteq S(\beta)$.

Conversely, let $\psi \in S(\beta)$, so that $\beta \nsubseteq \psi \cap \nabla_A$. But $[\alpha, \beta]_A = \Delta_A \subseteq \psi \cap \nabla_A \in Spec(A)$, hence $\alpha \subseteq \psi \cap \nabla_A$, so $\psi \in Spec(B) \setminus S(\alpha)$. Therefore $S(\beta) \subseteq Spec(B) \setminus S(\alpha)$.

(iii)⇒(ii): We have to prove that $\psi \cap \nabla_A \in Min(A)$ for any $\psi \in Min(B)$. Assume by absurdum that there exists $\psi \in Min(B)$ such that $\psi \cap \nabla_A \notin Min(A)$. But $\psi \cap \nabla_A \in Spec(A)$ since $A \subseteq B$ is admissible, thus $\phi \subsetneq \psi \cap \nabla_A$ for some $\phi \in Min(A)$. By Corollary 3, there exists $\varepsilon \in Min(B)$ such that $\phi = \varepsilon \cap \nabla_A$. So $\varepsilon \cap \nabla_A \subsetneq \psi \cap \nabla_A$, hence there exists $(a, b) \in (\psi \cap \nabla_A) \setminus (\varepsilon \cap \nabla_A)$, so that, if we denote by $\alpha = Cg_A(a, b) \in PCon(A)$, then $\alpha \nsubseteq \varepsilon \cap \nabla_A$ and $\alpha \subseteq \psi \cap \nabla_A$, therefore $\varepsilon \in S(\alpha)$ and $\psi \notin S(\alpha)$. Since $S(\beta) = Spec(B) \setminus S(\alpha)$, it follows that $\varepsilon \notin S(\beta)$ and $\psi \in S(\beta)$, hence $\beta \subseteq \varepsilon \cap \nabla_A \subseteq \psi \cap \nabla_A$ and $\beta \nsubseteq \psi \cap \nabla_A$. We have obtained a contradiction, thus $A \subseteq B$ is an m–extension.

(ii)⇒(i): Assume that $A \subseteq B$ is an m–extension, so the map Γ is surjective and continuous with respect to the Stone topologies by Corollary 3 and Proposition 13.(i).

By [7] [Theorem 8], it follows that the reticulation $\mathcal{L}(B)$ of the hyperarchimedean algebra B is a Boolean algebra. Since $\mathcal{M}in(B)$ and $\mathcal{M}in_{Id}(\mathcal{L}(B))$ are homeomorphic, it follows that $\mathcal{M}in(B)$ is a Boolean space, hence $\mathcal{M}in(B)$ is a compact space, therefore $\mathcal{M}in(A)$ is also a compact space. □

Remark 13. *Let A be a reduced (that is semiprime) commutative ring and $Q(A)$ the complete ring of A (see [3]). In this case, $Q(A)$ is a regular ring [3], i.e., a hyperarchimedean ring. In accordance with [6] [Proposition 7.2.(2)], $A \subseteq Q(A)$ is a Baer extension of rings, so one can apply our Proposition 6.18. Then we obtain [31] [Theorem 4.3] as a particular case. It also results that, if A is a reduced ring, then: $\mathcal{M}in(A)$ is compact if and only if $A \subseteq Q(A)$ is an m–extension.*

Theorem 5. *If $A \subseteq B$ is an admissible m–extension such that $\{\beta^{\perp B} \mid \beta \in Con(B)\} \subseteq \{Cg_B(\alpha) \mid \alpha \in Con(A)\}$, both A and B satisfy (v) and (vi) from Condition 1 and Γ is injective, then $\Gamma : \mathcal{M}in(B) \to \mathcal{M}in(A)$ is a homeomorphism and $A \subseteq B$ is a weak rigid extension.*

Proof. We will be using Proposition 5, Proposition 11.(ii) and Lemma 6.(ii).

Let $\alpha \in Con(A)$ and $\mu \in Min(A)$, so that $\mu = \nu \cap \nabla_A$ for some $\nu \in Min(B)$ by Corollary 3. Then the fact that $\mu \in D_A(\alpha) \cap Min(A)$, that is $\alpha \nsubseteq \mu$, is equivalent to $\alpha^{\perp A} \subseteq \mu$, which implies $\alpha^{\perp B} = Cg_B(\alpha)^{\perp B} = Cg_B(\alpha^{\perp A}) \subseteq Cg_B(\mu) \subseteq \nu$, thus $Cg_B(\alpha) \nsubseteq \nu$, that is $\nu \in D_B(Cg_B(\alpha)) \cap Min(B)$. On the other hand, $\nu \in D_B(Cg_B(\alpha)) \cap Min(B)$ means that $Cg_B(\alpha) \nsubseteq \nu$, so that $\alpha^{\perp B} = Cg_B(\alpha)^{\perp B} \subseteq \nu$, hence $\alpha^{\perp A} = \alpha^{\perp B} \cap \nabla_A \subseteq \nu \cap \nabla_A = \mu$, thus $\alpha \nsubseteq \mu$, that is $\mu \in D_A(\alpha) \cap Min(A)$.

Hence, $\nu \in D_B(Cg_B(\alpha)) \cap Min(B)$ if and only if $\Gamma(\nu) = \mu \in D_A(\alpha) \cap Min(A)$ if and only if $\nu \in \Gamma^{-1}(D_A(\alpha) \cap Min(A))$, therefore $\Gamma^{-1}(D_A(\alpha) \cap Min(A)) = D_B(Cg_B(\alpha)) \cap Min(B)$. Thus Γ is continuous and, by Proposition 6.(i), for all $\theta \in Con(A)$, $\Gamma^{-1}(V_A(\alpha) \cap Min(A)) = \Gamma^{-1}(D_A(\alpha^{\perp A}) \cap Min(A)) = D_B(Cg_B(\alpha^{\perp A})) \cap Min(B) = V_B(Cg_B(\alpha^{\perp A})^{\perp B}) \cap Min(B) = V_B(\alpha^{\perp B \perp B}) \cap Min(B) = V_B(Cg_B(\alpha)^{\perp B \perp B}) \cap Min(B) = V_B(Cg_B(\alpha)) \cap Min(B)$.

Hence, if Γ is injective and thus bijective according to Corollary 3, then Γ is a homeomorphism, in particular Γ is open, thus, for every $\beta \in Con(B)$, there is $\alpha \in Con(A)$ such that $\Gamma(D_B(\beta) \cap Min(B)) = D_A(\alpha) \cap Min(A)$, hence, by the above, along with Proposition 6.(i) and Proposition 11.(ii),

$$\begin{aligned} V_B(\beta^{\perp B}) \cap Min(B) &= D_B(\beta) \cap Min(B) = \Gamma^{-1}(D_A(\alpha) \cap Min(A)) \\ &= \Gamma^{-1}(D_A(\alpha^{\perp A \perp A}) \cap Min(A)) = D_B(Cg_B(\alpha^{\perp A \perp A})) \cap Min(B) \\ &= D_B(Cg_B(\alpha^{\perp A})^{\perp B}) \cap Min(B) = V_B(Cg_B(\alpha^{\perp A})) \cap Min(B) \\ &= V_B(Cg_B(\alpha)^{\perp B}) \cap Min(B). \end{aligned}$$

By Lemma 11, $\beta^{\perp B} = \bigcap(V_B(\beta^{\perp B}) \cap \mathrm{Min}(B)) = \bigcap(V_B(Cg_B(\alpha)^{\perp B}) \cap \mathrm{Min}(B)) = Cg_B(\alpha)^{\perp B}$ $= \alpha^{\perp B}$, thus $A \subseteq B$ is weak rigid. □

Theorem 6. *If $A \subseteq B$ is an admissible weak r–extension such that $\{\beta^{\perp B} \mid \beta \in \mathrm{Con}(B)\} \subseteq \{Cg_B(\alpha) \mid \alpha \in \mathrm{Con}(A)\}$ and both A and B satisfy (v) and (vi) from Condition 1, then $A \subseteq B$ is an m–extension and an r–extension and $\Gamma : \mathcal{M}in(B) \to \mathcal{M}in(A)$ is a homeomorphism.*

Proof. Assume that $A \subseteq B$ is an admissible weak r–extension, so that Γ is surjective by Corollary 3. We will apply Proposition 5.

Assume by absurdum that there exists a $\mu \in \mathrm{Min}(B)$ such that $\mu \cap \nabla_A \notin \mathrm{Min}(A)$, so that $\phi \subsetneq \mu \cap \nabla_A$ for some $\phi \in \mathrm{Min}(A)$. By the above, $\phi = \varepsilon \cap \nabla_A$ for some $\varepsilon \in \mathrm{Min}(B)$, so that $\varepsilon \cap \nabla_A \subsetneq \mu \cap \nabla_A$, thus $\varepsilon \neq \mu$, hence $\varepsilon \setminus \mu \neq \emptyset$, that is $(x,y) \in \varepsilon \setminus \mu$ for some $x, y \in B$.

We have $Cg_B(x,y) \nsubseteq \mu$, hence there exists an $\alpha \in \mathrm{Con}(A)$ such that $\alpha \nsubseteq \mu$ and $Cg_B(x,y)^{\perp B} \subseteq \alpha^{\perp B} = Cg_B(\alpha)^{\perp B}$ since $A \subseteq B$ is a weak r–extension. But $\alpha \nsubseteq \mu$ implies $Cg_B(\alpha) \nsubseteq \mu$, hence $Cg_B(\alpha)^{\perp B} \subseteq \mu$. Since $Cg_B(x,y) \subseteq \varepsilon$, we have $Cg_B(\alpha)^{\perp B} \supseteq Cg_B(x,y)^{\perp B} \nsubseteq \varepsilon$, thus $\alpha \subseteq Cg_B(\alpha) \subseteq \varepsilon$, hence $\alpha \subseteq \varepsilon \cap \nabla_A = \phi \subset \mu \cap \nabla_A \subseteq \mu$, hence $Cg_B(\alpha) \subseteq \mu$, thus $Cg_B(\alpha)^{\perp B} \nsubseteq \mu$, contradicting the above.

Therefore $A \subseteq B$ is an m–extension.

Now let $\mu, \nu \in \mathrm{Min}(B)$ such that $\mu \cap \nabla_A = \nu \cap \nabla_A$. Assume by absurdum that $\mu \neq \nu$, so that $\mu \setminus \nu \neq \emptyset$, that is $(u,v) \in \mu \setminus \nu$ for some $u, v \in B$. Then $Cg_B(u,v) \nsubseteq \nu$, thus, since $A \subseteq B$ is a weak r–extension, there exists a $\xi \in \mathrm{Con}(A)$ such that $\xi \nsubseteq \nu$ and $Cg_B(u,v)^{\perp B} \subseteq \xi^{\perp B}$. Since $Cg_B(u,v) \subseteq \mu$, $Cg_B(u,v)^{\perp B} \nsubseteq \mu$, hence, by Proposition 11.(ii), $Cg_B(\xi^{\perp A}) = Cg_B(\xi)^{\perp B} = \xi^{\perp B} \nsubseteq \mu$, thus $\xi \subseteq \xi^{\perp A \perp A} \subseteq Cg_B(\xi^{\perp A \perp A}) = Cg_B(\xi^{\perp A})^{\perp B} \subseteq \mu$, hence $\xi \subseteq \mu \cap \nabla_A = \nu \cap \nabla_A \subseteq \nu$, contradicting the above. Therefore Γ is injective and thus a homeomorphism by Theorem 5.

Finally, let $\mu \in \mathrm{Min}(B)$ and $\beta \in \mathrm{PCon}(B)$ such that $\beta \nsubseteq \mu$, so that, since $A \subseteq B$ is a weak r–extension, there exists a $\gamma \in \mathrm{Con}(A)$ such that $\gamma \nsubseteq \mu$ and $\beta^{\perp B} \subseteq \gamma^{\perp B}$. Then $(w,z) \in \gamma \setminus \mu$ for some $w, z \in A$, so that $Cg_A(w,z) \nsubseteq \mu$ and $Cg_A(w,z) \subseteq \gamma$, so that $Cg_B(Cg_A(w,z)) \subseteq Cg_B(\gamma)$ and thus $\beta^{\perp B} \subseteq \gamma^{\perp B} = Cg_B(\gamma)^{\perp B} \subseteq Cg_B(Cg_A(w,z))^{\perp B} = Cg_A(w,z)^{\perp B}$. Therefore $A \subseteq B$ is an r–extension. □

Theorem 7. *If $A \subseteq B$ is an admissible weak r^*–extension such that $\{\beta^{\perp B} \mid \beta \in \mathrm{Con}(B)\} \subseteq \{Cg_B(\alpha) \mid \alpha \in \mathrm{Con}(A)\}$ and both A and B satisfy (v) and (vi) from Condition 1, then $A \subseteq B$ is an m–extension and an r^*–extension and Γ is a homeomorphism with respect to the Stone topologies.*

Proof. By adapting the proof of Theorem 6. □

Corollary 7. *If $\{\beta^{\perp B} \mid \beta \in \mathrm{Con}(B)\} \subseteq \{Cg_B(\alpha) \mid \alpha \in \mathrm{Con}(A)\}$, both A and B satisfy (v) and (vi) from Condition 1 and $A \subseteq B$ is admissible and either a weak r–extension or a weak r^*–extension, then $A \subseteq B$ is a weak rigid extension.*

Corollary 8. *If $A \subseteq B$ is admissible, $\{\beta^{\perp B} \mid \beta \in \mathrm{Con}(B)\} \subseteq \{Cg_B(\alpha) \mid \alpha \in \mathrm{Con}(A)\}$ and both A and B satisfy (v) and (vi) from Condition 1, then the following are equivalent:*

- *$A \subseteq B$ is a weak rigid extension;*
- *$A \subseteq B$ is a weak r–extension;*
- *$A \subseteq B$ is a weak r^*–extension;*
- *$A \subseteq B$ is an r–extension;*
- *$A \subseteq B$ is an r^*–extension.*

7. Conclusions

Commutator theory, developed for different kinds of varieties, with congruence-modular varieties as an important case [1], is a powerful tool for extending properties of concrete algebraic structures to universal algebras. Our paper illustrates this by generalizing some results from [5] on classes of ring extensions to universal algebras whose commutators satisfy certain conditions; this includes members of semidegenerate congruence–modular varieties, but also applies to more general cases. We start by studying some algebraic and topological properties of the minimal prime spectrum of an algebra whose commutator operation is commutative and distributive with respect to arbitrary joins, then use these results on the minimal prime spectrum to obtain characterizations for some classes of extensions of such algebras. Our results can be applied to many kinds of structures, for instance to generalize those results in [5] to non–commutative rings or semirings.

In future work we will study the preservation of these properties of extensions of universal algebras by the reticulation, look for classes of universal algebras to which other results from [5] can be generalized and study abstractions of our results, using commutator lattices and lattice morphisms preserving the commutator operations, in the manner from [25].

Author Contributions: This research was initiated by George Georgescu, who also obtained the first form of the main results. The contributions of the three authors have been roughly equally important for this paper. All authors have read and agreed to the published version of the manuscript.

Funding: This work was partly supported by the research grant number IZSEZO_186586/1, awarded to the project *Reticulations of Concept Algebras* by the Swiss National Science Foundation, within the programme Scientific Exchanges.

Data Availability Statement: The original contributions presented in the study are included in the article; further inquiries can be directed to the corresponding author.

Acknowledgments: We thank the anonymous reviewers for making useful suggestions that helped us improve our paper.

Conflicts of Interest: The authors declare no conflicts of interest.

References

1. Freese, R.; McKenzie, R. *Commutator Theory for Congruence–Modular Varieties*; London Mathematical Society Lecture Note Series 125; Cambridge University Press: Cambridge, UK, 1987.
2. Kaplansky, J. *Commutative Rings*, 1st ed.; University of Chicago Press: Chicago, IL, USA, 1974.
3. Lambek, J. *Lectures on Rings and Modules*, 2nd ed.; Chelsea Publishing Company: New York, NY, USA, 1976.
4. Agliano, P. Prime Spectra in Modular Varieties. *Algebra Universalis* **2008**, *30*, 142–149. [CrossRef]
5. Bhattacharjee, P.; Dress, K.M.; McGovern, W.W. Extensions of Commutative Rings. *Topol. Its Appl.* **2011**, *158*, 1802–1814. [CrossRef]
6. Picavet, G. Ultrafiltres sur un Espace Spectral—Anneaux de Baer—Anneaux à Spectre Minimal Compact. *Math. Scand.* **1980**, *46*, 23–53. [CrossRef]
7. Georgescu, G.; Mureşan, C. The Reticulation of a Universal Algebra. *Sci. Ann. Comput. Sci.* **2018**, *28*, 67–113.
8. Burris, S.; Sankappanavar, H.P. *A Course in Universal Algebra*; Graduate Texts in Mathematics, 78; Springer–Verlag: New York, NY, USA; Berlin, Germany, 1981.
9. Grätzer, G. *Universal Algebra*, 2nd ed.; Springer Science+Business Media, LLC: New York, NY, USA, 2008.
10. Kollár, J. Congruences and One–element Subalgebras. *Algebra Universalis* **1979**, *9*, 266–267. [CrossRef]
11. Balbes, R.; Dwinger, P. *Distributive Lattices*; University of Missouri Press: Columbia, MO, USA, 1974.
12. Blyth, T.S. *Lattices and Ordered Algebraic Structures*; Springer–Verlag: London, UK, 2005.
13. Crawley, P.; Dilworth, R.P. *Algebraic Theory of Lattices*; Prentice Hall: Englewood Cliffs, NJ, USA, 1973.
14. Grätzer, G. *General Lattice Theory*; Birkhäuser Akademie–Verlag: Basel, Switzerland; Boston, MA, USA; Berlin, Germany, 1978.
15. Ouwehand, P. Commutator Theory and Abelian Algebras. *arXiv* **2013**, arXiv:1309.0662.
16. Czelakowski, J. Additivity of the Commutator and Residuation. *Rep. Math. Log.* **2008**, *43*, 109–132.
17. Czelakowski, J. *The Equationally–Defined Commutator. A Study in Equational Logic and Algebra*; Birkhäuser Mathematics: Basel, Switzerland, 2015.
18. Georgescu, G.; Mureşan, C. Going Up and Lying Over in Congruence–modular Algebras. *Math. Slovaca* **2019**, *69*, 275–296. [CrossRef]
19. Mureşan, C. Taking Prime, Maximal and Two–class Congruences Through Morphisms. *arXiv* **2016**, arXiv:1607.06901.
20. Johnstone, P.T. *Stone Spaces*; Cambridge Studies in Advanced Mathematics 3; Cambridge University Press: Cambridge, UK, 1982.
21. Baker, K.A. Primitive Satisfaction and Equational Problems for Lattices and Other Algebras. *Trans. Amer. Math. Soc.* **1974**, *190*, 125–150. [CrossRef]
22. Ursini, A. On Subtractive Varieties, V: Congruence Modularity and the Commutator. *Algebra Universalis* **2000**, *43*, 51–78. [CrossRef]
23. McKenzie, R.; Snow, J. *Congruence Modular Varieties: Commutator Theory and Its Uses, in Structural Theory of Automata, Semigroups, and Universal Algebra*; Springer: Dordrecht, The Netherlands, 2005.

24. Jónsson, B. Congruence–distributive Varieties. *Math. Japonica* **1995**, *42*, 353–401.
25. Mureşan, C. Stone Commutator Lattices and Baer Rings. *Discuss. Math. Gen. Algebra Appl.* **2022**, *42*, 51–96. [CrossRef]
26. Galatos, N.; Jipsen, P.; Kowalski, T.; Ono, H. *Residuated Lattices: An Algebraic Glimpse at Substructural Logics*; Studies in Logic and The Foundations of Mathematics 151; Elsevier: Amsterdam, The Netherlands, 2007.
27. Georgescu, G.; Kwuida, L.; Mureşan, C. Functorial Properties of the Reticulation of a Universal Algebra. *J. Appl. Logics. Spec. Issue Mult. Valued Log. Appl.* **2021**, *8*, 1123–1168.
28. Simmons, H. Reticulated Rings. *J. Algebra* **1980**, *66*, 169–192. [CrossRef]
29. Knox, M.L.; Levy, R.; McGovern, W.W.; Shapiro, J. Generalizations of Complemented Rings with Applications to Rings of Functions. *J. Algebra Its Appl.* **2009**, *8*, 17–40. [CrossRef]
30. Speed, T.P. Spaces of Ideals of Distributive Lattices II. Minimal Prime Ideals. *J. Aust. Math. Soc.* **1974**, *18*, 54–72. [CrossRef]
31. Huckaba, J.A. *Commutative Rings with Zero Divizors*; Monographs and Textbooks in Pure and Applied Mathematics 117; M. Dekker: New York, NY, USA, 1988.

axioms

MDPI

Article

Modified Sweeping Surfaces in Euclidean 3-Space

Yanlin Li [1,*], Kemal Eren [2], Soley Ersoy [2] and Ana Savić [3]

1 School of Mathematics, Hangzhou Normal University, Hangzhou 311121, China
2 Department of Mathematics, Faculty of Sciences, Sakarya University, 54050 Sakarya, Turkey; kemal.eren1@ogr.sakarya.edu.tr (K.E.); sersoy@sakarya.edu.tr (S.E.)
3 School of Electrical and Computer Engineering, Academy of Technical and Art Applied Studies, 11000 Belgrade, Serbia; ana.savic@viser.edu.rs
* Correspondence: liyl@hznu.edu.cn

Abstract: In this study, we explore the sweeping surfaces in Euclidean 3-space, utilizing the modified orthogonal frames with non-zero curvature and torsion, which allows us to consider the spine curves even if their second differentiations vanish. If the curvature of the spine curve of a sweeping surface has discrete zero points, the Frenet frame might undergo a discontinuous change in orientation. Therefore, the conventional parametrization with the Frenet frame of such a surface cannot be given. Thus, we introduce two types of modified sweeping surfaces by considering two types of spine curves; the first one's curvature is not identically zero and the second one's torsion is not identically zero. Then, we determine the criteria for classifying the coordinate curves of these two types of modified sweeping surfaces as geodesic, asymptotic, or curvature lines. Additionally, we delve into determining criteria for the modified sweeping surfaces to be minimal, developable, or Weingarten. Through our analysis, we aim to clarify the characteristics defining these surfaces. We present graphical representations of sample modified sweeping surfaces to enhance understanding and provide concrete examples that showcase their properties.

Keywords: sweeping surface; modified orthogonal frame; Gaussian and mean curvature

MSC: 53A04; 53A05

check for updates

Citation: Li, Y.; Eren, K.; Ersoy, S.; Savić, A. Modified Sweeping Surfaces in Euclidean 3-Space. *Axioms* **2024**, *13*, 800. https://doi.org/10.3390/axioms13110800

Academic Editors: Cristina Flaut, Dana Piciu and Murat Tosun

Received: 3 October 2024
Revised: 14 November 2024
Accepted: 14 November 2024
Published: 18 November 2024

1. Introduction

Sweeping is a widely used technique in geometric modeling to define the geometry of three-dimensional objects. The geometric and computational properties of this technique have been examined via various approaches where planar curves sweep along the trajectories called the spine curves. For instance, in the process of generating sweeping surfaces, the superiority of using the rotation minimizing frame (RMF) with the Frenet frame was compared in [1,2]. The sweeping surfaces are generated by a plane curve known as a profile curve or generatrix that is continuously moving in the same direction with the normal vector field. Strings, canal surfaces, and tubular (pipe) surfaces are prominent varieties of sweeping surfaces that are the ultimate outcomes of this process. In [3], Xu et al. represented the characterizations of a particular kind of sweeping surface known as a canal surface. Ro and Yoon provided an analysis of another type of sweeping surface called tube that satisfied particular equations based on surface curvatures in [4]. Research findings also suggest that sweeping surfaces generated by the use of RMF can also be categorized as developable surfaces [5]. The investigation of sweeping surfaces along a curve based on the Darboux frame was documented in [6]. Furthermore, the properties of right conoids hypersurfaces in Minkowski 4-space were studied in [7,8]. The theory of singularity has been thoroughly studied in [9] and it is a vital tool in many various fields of inquiry, including differential geometry, the field of optics, robotics, and visual computing. The involutive sweeping surfaces were presented as a novel surface type by Köseoğlu and Bilici, who also explored their singularities [10]. Several scholars have examined the singularities and characteristic features of the surfaces [11–17].

On the other hand, it is observed that at the points where a space curve's second derivative is zero, the Frenet frame becomes insufficient. That is, the principal normal and binormal vector fields of such a curve are not continuous at these points. Sasai created the modified orthogonal frame (MOF) and inferred the formulae corresponding to the Frenet formulae in [18] to address this problem. Recently, Bükcü and Karacan described two MOFs with non-zero curvature and non-zero torsion in Minkowski 3-space [19]. A number of investigations [20–25] revisited some specific curves as well as surfaces such as ruled surfaces, Hasimoto surfaces, tubular surfaces, and the evolution of curves using MOF.

In numerous above-mentioned investigations, RMF was typically utilized to generate sweeping surfaces to correct the unwanted rotation of the Frenet frame. In fact, RMF is a frame developed to minimize the rotation of the normal and binormal vectors as they move along the curve. On the other hand, to preserve orthogonality without requiring minimal rotation, the normal and binormal vectors are modified according to curvature and torsion in the MOFs with non-zero curvature and non-zero torsion, respectively.

In this study, we modify the parametric representation of a classical sweeping surface defined along a spine curve with non-zero curvatures everywhere. In this modification, the spine curve may have discrete zero curvatures. This can lead to a discontinuity in the directions of the principal normal vector, and thus, the binormal vector, when approaching a zero-curvature point from either side. Thus, the Frenet frame may not be well-defined, particularly because the normal and binormal directions can become ambiguous. Even if a spine curve has discrete zero curvatures, an MOF is well-defined at any point where the curvature is non-zero, and another MOF is also well-defined at any point where the torsion is non-zero. Thus, two types of modified surfaces occur since there are two types of MOFs with non-vanishing curvature and non-vanishing torsion. The novelty of our study is generating sweeping surfaces by using two types of MOFs, which ensure the orthogonality and continuity of the frame vectors of the spine curves. We determine the criteria for the coordinate curves of these types of modified sweeping surfaces to be geodesic, asymptotic, or lines of curvature. Furthermore, we derive criteria for the modified sweeping surfaces to be developable, minimal, or Weingarten. Finally, we provide examples of these sweeping surfaces and illustrate their graphical representations.

2. Preliminaries

Let β be a moving space curve with arc-length parameter s in E^3. If the tangent, principal normal, and binormal unit vectors of the space curve β are noted by t, n, and b, respectively, then the moving Frenet frame of the unit speed curve β satisfies

$$\begin{aligned} t_s &= \kappa n, \\ n_s &= -\kappa t + \tau b, \\ b_s &= -\tau n, \end{aligned}$$

where the curvature and torsion of β are κ and τ, respectively. The subscript symbol represents differentiation with respect to the variable s. However, if the principal normal or binormal vectors of a space curve are not continuous at the points where the curvature function has discrete zero points, the Frenet frame cannot be defined. Then, the alternative frame of Sasai can be used instead of the Frenet frame [18].

If $\kappa(s_0) = 0$, then the Frenet frame can display a change at the points $s \in (s_0 - \varepsilon, s_0 + \varepsilon)$ for any $\varepsilon > 0$. However, a frame can be defined at the points $s \in (s_0 - \varepsilon, s_0 + \varepsilon)\backslash\{s_0\}$ where $\kappa(s) \neq 0$ called MOF with non-vanishing curvature, and another frame can be defined for $\tau(s) \neq 0$ called MOF with non-vanishing torsion as explained subsequently. Assume that the curvature κ of a general analytic curve β is not identically zero; then, the elements of MOF with the non-vanishing curvature of a curve are defined as

$$T = \frac{d\beta}{ds}, \; N = \frac{dT}{ds}, \; B = T \times N$$

where "×" represents the vector product. At non-zero curvature values of κ, the frames $\{T, N, B\}$ and $\{t, n, b\}$ are related to each other as

$$T(s) = t(s),\ N(s) = \kappa(s)n(s),\ B(s) = \kappa(s)b(s).$$

Then, the derivative formulae of MOF are written in matrix form as follows:

$$\begin{bmatrix} T \\ N \\ B \end{bmatrix}_s = \begin{bmatrix} 0 & 1 & 0 \\ -\kappa^2 & \frac{\kappa_s}{\kappa} & \tau \\ 0 & -\tau & \frac{\kappa_s}{\kappa} \end{bmatrix} \begin{bmatrix} T \\ N \\ B \end{bmatrix} \tag{1}$$

when $\kappa \neq 0$ and

$$\tau = \frac{\det(\beta_s, \beta_{ss}, \beta_{sss})}{\kappa^2}$$

is the torsion of the space curve β. Moreover, the MOF with non-zero curvature satisfies

$$\langle T, T \rangle = 1,\ \langle N, N \rangle = \kappa^2 = \langle B, B \rangle.$$

On the other hand, the relations between the elements of the other MOF and the Frenet frame at non-zero torsion values of τ are

$$T(s) = t(s),\ \ N(s) = \tau(s)n(s),\ \ B(s) = \tau(s)b(s).$$

In this case, we obtain the following MOF with non-zero torsion hold:

$$\begin{bmatrix} T \\ N \\ B \end{bmatrix}_s = \begin{bmatrix} 0 & \frac{\kappa}{\tau} & 0 \\ -\kappa\tau & \frac{\tau_s}{\tau} & \tau \\ 0 & -\tau & \frac{\tau_s}{\tau} \end{bmatrix} \begin{bmatrix} T \\ N \\ B \end{bmatrix} \tag{2}$$

where

$$\langle T, T \rangle = 1,\ \langle N, N \rangle = \tau^2 = \langle B, B \rangle.$$

In the cases of $\kappa = 1$ and $\tau = 1$, respectively, the derivative Formulas (1) and (2) are coincident with Frenet derivative formulae.

Let $\varphi_s = \frac{\partial \varphi}{\partial s}$ and $\varphi_v = \frac{\partial \varphi}{\partial v}$ be tangent vectors of a surface M parametrized by $\varphi(s, v)$; then, the equation of the normal vector field of the surface is

$$\Delta(s, v) = \frac{\varphi_s \times \varphi_v}{\|\varphi_s \times \varphi_v\|}. \tag{3}$$

The Gaussian and mean curvatures of M are

$$K = \frac{km - l^2}{EG - F^2} \text{ and } H = \frac{Em - 2El + Gk}{2(EG - F^2)}, \tag{4}$$

respectively, where the elements of $\{E, F, G\}$ and $\{k, l, m\}$ denote the coefficients of the first and second fundamental forms of the surface with parametrization $\varphi(s, v)$ as

$$E = \left\langle \frac{\partial \varphi}{\partial s}, \frac{\partial \varphi}{\partial s} \right\rangle,\ F = \left\langle \frac{\partial \varphi}{\partial s}, \frac{\partial \varphi}{\partial v} \right\rangle,\ G = \left\langle \frac{\partial \varphi}{\partial v}, \frac{\partial \varphi}{\partial v} \right\rangle \tag{5}$$

and

$$k = \left\langle \frac{\partial^2 \varphi}{\partial s^2}, \Delta \right\rangle,\ l = \left\langle \frac{\partial^2 \varphi}{\partial s \partial v}, \Delta \right\rangle,\ m = \left\langle \frac{\partial^2 \varphi}{\partial v^2}, \Delta \right\rangle, \tag{6}$$

respectively. It is common knowledge that a surface M can be described by the following characterizations given in [13]:

- M is a developable surface if and only if $K = 0$ everywhere.

- M is a minimal surface if and only if $H = 0$ everywhere.
- M is a Weingarten-type surface if and only if $K_s H_v - K_v H_s = 0$ everywhere.

3. Modified Sweeping Surfaces Using the MOFs

In this section, the parametric expression of sweeping surfaces along a spine curve β is modified in order to fix the cases in which β has discrete zero curvatures. The modified sweeping surfaces are generated with the spine curves even if $\kappa(s_0) = 0$ for some s_0. A modified sweeping surface of the MOF with non-vanishing curvature κ along at least twice continuously differentiable spine curve β is defined by the modified principal normal and modified binormal vectors $N(s) = \kappa(s)n(s)$ and $B(s) = \kappa(s)b(s)$ when $\kappa(s) \neq 0$ at $s \in (s_0 - \varepsilon, s_0 + \varepsilon)\backslash\{s_0\}$ for any $\varepsilon > 0$. Moreover, a modified sweeping surface of the MOF with non-vanishing torsion τ along at least three times continuously differentiable spine curve β is defined by the modified principal normal and modified binormal vectors $N(s) = \tau(s)n(s)$ and $B(s) = \tau(s)b(s)$ when $\tau(s) \neq 0$ at $s \in (s_0 - \varepsilon, s_0 + \varepsilon)\backslash\{s_0\}$ for any $\varepsilon > 0$. Now, let us outline a simple method for illustrating the modified sweeping surfaces. The parameter along the curve β is chosen as one of the variables, and the position vector φ is established by connecting a point on the curve β to another point on the modified sweeping surface.

The parametric equation of a modified sweeping surface M, formed by the spine curve β and the planar profile (cross-section) curve $\delta(v) = (0, r(v), p(v))^{\perp}$, where the symbol "$^{\perp}$" represents transpose, is

$$\varphi(s,v) = \beta(s) + \delta(v)\Gamma(s) = \beta(s) + r(v)N(s) + p(v)B(s), \tag{7}$$

where $\Gamma(s) = (T(s), N(s), B(s))$ denotes the orthogonal matrix with the elements of MOFs with non-vanishing curvature and non-vanishing torsion along the spine curve $\beta(s)$. Thus, two types of modified sweeping surfaces exist that are investigated in the following subsections.

3.1. Modified Sweeping Surfaces of the MOF with Non-Vanishing Curvature κ

In this subsection, the modified sweeping surface M from (7) is investigated according to the MOF with non-vanishing curvature κ. Referring to (1), the first-order partial differentiations of $\varphi(s,v)$ with respect to s and v are found as

$$\varphi_s = \left(1 - r\kappa^2\right)T + \left(\frac{r\kappa_s}{\kappa} - p\tau\right)N + \left(r\tau + \frac{p\kappa_s}{\kappa}\right)B$$

and

$$\varphi_v = r_v N + p_v B.$$

Thus, by a straightforward computation from the last two equations and Equation (3), the unit normal vector field Δ of the surface is found as

$$\Delta(s,v) = \frac{(\lambda_2 p_v - \lambda_3 r_v)T - \lambda_1 p_v N + \lambda_1 r_v B}{\sqrt{{\lambda_1}^2\kappa^2({p_v}^2 + {r_v}^2) + (\lambda_2 p_v - \lambda_3 r_v)^2}}, \tag{8}$$

where

$$\lambda_1(s,v) = 1 - r\kappa^2, \quad \lambda_2(s,v) = \frac{r\kappa_s}{\kappa} - p\tau, \quad \text{and} \quad \lambda_3(s,v) = \frac{p\kappa_s}{\kappa} + r\tau. \tag{9}$$

Theorem 1. *Let M be a modified sweeping surface formed by the MOF with non-vanishing curvature κ. Then, the Gaussian curvature of M is given with:*

$$K(s,v) = \frac{\lambda_1\kappa^2\eta_2(p_v(\lambda_2\mu_1 - \kappa^2\lambda_1\mu_2) - r_v(\lambda_1\mu_1 - \kappa^2\lambda_1\mu_3)) - \begin{pmatrix} \lambda_1\kappa^2(r_v\lambda_{3v} - p_v\lambda_{2v}) \\ +\lambda_{1v}(\lambda_2 p_v - \lambda_3 r_v) \end{pmatrix}^2}{\|\varphi_s \times \varphi_v\|^2\kappa^2\left(\kappa^2(\lambda_2 p_v - \lambda_3 r_v)^2 + \lambda_1^2\eta_1\right)}.$$

The mean curvature of M is obtained as

$$H(s,v) = \frac{\eta_1 \begin{pmatrix} \mu_1 \\ -\lambda_1 \kappa^2 \end{pmatrix} \begin{pmatrix} p_v \lambda_2 \\ -r_v \lambda_3 \end{pmatrix} - \lambda_1 \eta_2 \begin{pmatrix} \lambda_1^2 \\ +\kappa^2 \left(\lambda_2^2 + \lambda_3^2 \right) \end{pmatrix} - 2 \begin{pmatrix} \lambda_3 p_v \\ +\lambda_2 r_v \end{pmatrix} \begin{pmatrix} p_v \left(\lambda_2 \lambda_{1v} - \kappa^2 \lambda_1 \lambda_{2v} \right) \\ +r_v \left(\kappa^2 \lambda_1 \lambda_{3v} - \lambda_3 \lambda_{1v} \right) \end{pmatrix}}{2 \|\varphi_s \times \varphi_v\| \left(\kappa^2 (\lambda_2 p_v - \lambda_3 r_v)^2 + \lambda_1^2 \eta_1 \right)}.$$

Here, the following notations are employed for the sake of brevity:

$$\begin{aligned}
\|\varphi_s \times \varphi_v\| &= \sqrt{\lambda_1{}^2 \kappa^2 (p_v{}^2 + r_v{}^2) + (\lambda_2 p_v - \lambda_3 r_v)^2}, \\
\mu_1(s,v) &= \lambda_{1s} - \kappa^2 \lambda_2, \\
\mu_2(s,v) &= \lambda_1 + \lambda_{2s} - \lambda_3 \tau + \frac{\lambda_2 \kappa_s}{\kappa}, \\
\mu_3(s,v) &= \lambda_2 \tau + \lambda_{3s} + \frac{\lambda_3 \kappa_s}{\kappa}, \\
\eta_1(v) &= p_v{}^2 + r_v{}^2, \\
\eta_2(v) &= r_v p_{vv} - p_v r_{vv}.
\end{aligned}$$

Proof. Let M be a modified sweeping surface generated by the MOF with non-vanishing curvature κ. From the Equation (5), the coefficients of the first fundamental form of M are

$$\begin{cases} E(s,v) = \lambda_1{}^2 + \kappa^2 \left(\lambda_2{}^2 + \lambda_3{}^2 \right), \\ F(s,v) = \kappa^2 (\lambda_2 r_v + \lambda_3 p_v), \\ G(s,v) = \kappa^2 \left(p_v{}^2 + r_v{}^2 \right). \end{cases}$$

By considering Equation (1), the second-order partial differentiations of $\varphi(s,v)$ given in (7) with respect to s and v are obtained as follows:

$$\begin{aligned}
\varphi_{ss} &= \mu_1 T + \mu_2 N + \mu_3 B, \\
\varphi_{sv} &= \lambda_{1v} T + \lambda_{2v} N + \lambda_{3v} B, \\
\varphi_{vv} &= r_{vv} N + p_{vv} B.
\end{aligned} \tag{10}$$

Note that for the sake of simplicity, we use the following notations:

$$\begin{aligned}
\mu_1(s,v) &= \lambda_{1s} - \kappa^2 \lambda_2, \\
\mu_2(s,v) &= \lambda_1 + \lambda_{2s} - \lambda_3 \tau + \frac{\lambda_2 \kappa_s}{\kappa}, \\
\mu_3(s,v) &= \lambda_2 \tau + \lambda_{3s} + \frac{\lambda_3 \kappa_s}{\kappa}.
\end{aligned}$$

From the Equation (6), the coefficients k, l, and m for M are found as follows:

$$\begin{cases} k(s,v) = \dfrac{\left(\mu_1 (\lambda_2 p_v - \lambda_3 r_v) - \kappa^2 \lambda_1 (\mu_2 p_v - \mu_3 r_v) \right)}{\|\varphi_s \times \varphi_v\|}, \\ l(s,v) = \dfrac{\left(\lambda_{1v} (\lambda_2 p_v - \lambda_3 r_v) - \kappa^2 \lambda_1 (\lambda_{2v} p_v - \lambda_{3v} r_v) \right)}{\|\varphi_s \times \varphi_v\|}, \\ m(s,v) = \dfrac{\kappa^2 \lambda_1 \eta_2}{\|\varphi_s \times \varphi_v\|}. \end{cases}$$

If the magnitudes E, F, G, k, l, and m are substituted into Equation (4), the Gaussian and mean curvatures K and H of M are obtained as in the hypothesis. □

Corollary 1. *Let M be a modified sweeping surface generated by the MOF with non-vanishing curvature κ. Then, M is developable if and only if*

$$\lambda_1\kappa^2\eta_2\Big(\lambda_2\mu_1 p_v - \lambda_3\mu_1 r_v + \lambda_1\kappa^2(-\mu_2 p_v + \mu_3 r_v)\Big) = \Big(\lambda_1\kappa^2(-p_v\lambda_{2v} + r_v\lambda_{3v}) + \lambda_{1s}(\lambda_2 p_v - \lambda_3 r_v)\Big)^2.$$

M is minimal if and only if

$$\begin{aligned}&\eta_1\Big(\mu_1(\lambda_2 p_v - \lambda_3 r_v) + \lambda_1\kappa^2(\mu_3 r_v - \mu_2 p_v)\Big) + \lambda_1\eta_2\Big(\lambda_1^2 + \kappa^2\big(\lambda_2^2 + \lambda_3^2\big)\Big)\\ &-2(\lambda_3 p_v + \lambda_2 r_v)\Big(\lambda_1\kappa^2(r_v\lambda_{3v} - p_v\lambda_{2v}) + (\lambda_2 p_v - \lambda_3 r_v)\lambda_{1s}\Big) = 0.\end{aligned}$$

Theorem 2. *Let M be a modified sweeping surface generated by the MOF with non-vanishing curvature κ. Then, M is a Weingarten-type surface if and only if*

$$\begin{pmatrix}\kappa^2\varepsilon_1(\lambda_1\eta_{2v} + \eta_2\lambda_{1v})\\ +\big(\lambda_1\kappa^2\eta_2 - 2\varepsilon_1\big)\varepsilon_{1v}\end{pmatrix}\begin{pmatrix}\eta_1\delta_{1s} - 2\delta_{3s}\\ -\eta_2(\delta_2\lambda_{1s} + \lambda_1\delta_{2s})\end{pmatrix} = \begin{pmatrix}\delta_1\eta_{1v} - \delta_2(\lambda_1\eta_{2v} + \eta_2\lambda_{1v})\\ +\eta_1\delta_{1v} - \lambda_1\eta_2\delta_{2v} - 2\delta_{3v}\end{pmatrix}\begin{pmatrix}\kappa\varepsilon_1\eta_2(2\lambda_1\kappa_s + \kappa\lambda_{1s})\\ +\varepsilon_{1s}\big(\lambda_1\kappa^2\eta_2 - 2\varepsilon_1\big)\end{pmatrix}$$

where

$$\begin{aligned}
\varepsilon_1(s,v) &= \frac{p_v(\lambda_2\mu_1 - \kappa^2\lambda_1\mu_2) - r_v(\lambda_1\mu_1 - \kappa^2\lambda_1\mu_3)}{\|\varphi_s \times \varphi_v\|^2\kappa^2\Big(\kappa^2(\lambda_2 p_v - \lambda_3 r_v)^2 + \lambda_1^2\eta_1\Big)},\\
\varepsilon_2(s,v) &= \frac{p_v(\lambda_2\mu_1 - \kappa^2\lambda_1\mu_2) - r_v(\lambda_1\mu_1 - \kappa^2\lambda_1\mu_3)}{\|\varphi_s \times \varphi_v\|\kappa\sqrt{\Big(\kappa^2(\lambda_2 p_v - \lambda_3 r_v)^2 + \lambda_1^2\eta_1\Big)}},\\
\delta_1(s,v) &= \frac{(\mu_1 - \lambda_1\kappa^2)(p_v\lambda_2 - r_v\lambda_3)}{2\|\varphi_s \times \varphi_v\|\Big(\kappa^2(\lambda_2 p_v - \lambda_3 r_v)^2 + \lambda_1^2\eta_1\Big)},\\
\delta_2(s,v) &= \frac{\lambda_1^2 + \kappa^2(\lambda_2^2 + \lambda_3^2)}{2\|\varphi_s \times \varphi_v\|\Big(\kappa^2(\lambda_2 p_v - \lambda_3 r_v)^2 + \lambda_1^2\eta_1\Big)},\\
\delta_3(s,v) &= \frac{(\lambda_3 p_v + \lambda_2 r_v)\big(p_v(\lambda_2\lambda_{1v} - \kappa^2\lambda_1\lambda_{2v}) + r_v(\kappa^2\lambda_1\lambda_{3v} - \lambda_3\lambda_{1v})\big)}{2\|\varphi_s \times \varphi_v\|\Big(\kappa^2(\lambda_2 p_v - \lambda_3 r_v)^2 + \lambda_1^2\eta_1\Big)}.
\end{aligned}$$

Proof. Let M be a modified sweeping surface formed by the MOF with non-vanishing curvature κ. If the Gaussian and mean curvatures K and H of M are differentiated in terms of s and v, we have

$$\begin{cases}
K_s = \kappa\varepsilon_1\eta_2(2\lambda_1\kappa_s + \kappa\lambda_{1s}) + \Big(-2\varepsilon_1 + \lambda_1\kappa^2\eta_2\Big)\varepsilon_{1s},\\
K_v = \kappa^2\varepsilon_1(\lambda_1\eta_{2v} + \eta_2\lambda_{1v}) + \Big(-2\varepsilon_1 + \lambda_1\kappa^2\eta_2\Big)\varepsilon_{1v},\\
H_s = \eta_1\delta_{1s} - \eta_2(\delta_2\lambda_{1s} + \lambda_1\delta_{2s}) - 2\delta_{3s},\\
H_v = \delta_1\eta_{1v} - \delta_2(\lambda_1\eta_{2v} + \eta_2\lambda_{1v}) + \eta_1\delta_{1v} - \lambda_1\eta_2\delta_{2v} - 2\delta_{3v}.
\end{cases}$$

By considering these equalities, the condition specified in the hypothesis is satisfied if and only if $K_s H_v - K_v H_s = 0$, which requires M to be a Weingarten-type surface. □

Theorem 3. *If M is a modified sweeping surface generated by the MOF with non-vanishing curvature κ, then, the s−coordinate curves of M are geodesic if and only if*

$$\frac{p_v}{r_v} = \frac{\lambda_1(\mu_1 - \mu_2) + \lambda_3(\mu_3 - \mu_2)}{\lambda_1(\mu_3 - \mu_1) + \lambda_2(\mu_3 - \mu_2)}.$$

The s−coordinate curves of M are asymptotic if and only if

$$\frac{p_v}{r_v} = \frac{\mu_1\lambda_3 - \kappa^2\mu_3\lambda_1}{\mu_1\lambda_2 - \kappa^2\mu_2\lambda_1}.$$

Proof. To ensure that the coordinate curves meet the criteria for being geodesic curves, the acceleration vector of the coordinate curve must be perpendicular to the surface, and, thereby, parallel to the surface's normal vector.

From the equation of the normal vector field given in (8) and the first equality of (10), the following equation is obtained:

$$\begin{aligned}\Delta \times \varphi_{ss} &= \lambda_1(\mu_3 p_v + \mu_2 r_v)T + (\mu_3\lambda_2 p_v - (\mu_3\lambda_3 + \mu_1\lambda_1)r_v)N \\ &+(\mu_2\lambda_3 r_v - (\mu_2\lambda_2 + \mu_1\lambda_1)p_v)B.\end{aligned}$$

By the fact that the vectors T, N, and B are linearly independent, if $\Delta \times \varphi_{ss} = 0$, then the last equation requires

$$\begin{aligned}&\lambda_1(\mu_3 p_v + \mu_2 r_v) = 0,\\ &\mu_3\lambda_2 p_v - (\mu_3\lambda_3 + \mu_1\lambda_1)r_v = 0,\\ &\mu_2\lambda_3 r_v - (\mu_2\lambda_2 + \mu_1\lambda_1)p_v = 0.\end{aligned}$$

Thus, the criterion in the hypothesis is verified by the common solution of these equalities. It is a fact that the $s-$coordinate curves are geodesics under the criterion stated in the hypothesis.

Moreover, a curve on a surface is classified as asymptotic if the acceleration vector of the curve lies entirely in the tangent plane of the surface, which means that the inner product of the second derivative of the curve and the normal vector field of the surface must be zero. To check the condition for the $s-$coordinate curves of M to be asymptotic, we take the Equation (8) and the first equality in (10) for Δ and φ_{ss}, respectively. Then, we obtain

$$\langle \Delta, \varphi_{ss} \rangle = \left(\mu_1\lambda_2 - \kappa^2\mu_2\lambda_1\right)p_v + \left(\kappa^2\mu_3\lambda_1 - \mu_1\lambda_3\right)r_v.$$

Thus, $(\mu_1\lambda_2 - \kappa^2\mu_2\lambda_1)p_v = (\mu_1\lambda_3 - \kappa^2\mu_3\lambda_1)r_v$ if and only if $\langle \Delta, \varphi_{ss} \rangle = 0$, and we can state that the $s-$coordinate curves are asymptotic under the criterion stated in the hypothesis. □

Theorem 4. *Let M be a modified sweeping surface generated by the MOF with non-vanishing curvature κ. Then, the $v-$coordinate curves of M are geodesic if and only if*

$$\lambda_2 p_v - \lambda_3 r_v = 0, \quad p_{vv} + r_{vv} = 0, \quad \text{and} \quad \lambda_1(p_v p_{vv} + r_v r_{vv}) = 0.$$

Also, the $v-$coordinate curves of M are asymptotic if and only if

$$r\kappa^2 = 1 \quad \text{or} \quad r_v p_{vv} - p_v r_{vv} = 0.$$

Proof. From the equation of the normal vector field given by (8) and the third equality of (10), the following equation is obtained:

$$\Delta \times \varphi_{vv} = \lambda_1(p_v p_{vv} + r_v r_{vv})T + p_{vv}(\lambda_2 p_v - \lambda_3 r_v)N - r_{vv}(\lambda_2 p_v - \lambda_3 r_v)B.$$

Since the vectors T, N, and B are linearly independent, if $\Delta \times \varphi_{vv} = 0$, we have

$$\begin{aligned}&(p_v p_{vv} + r_v r_{vv})\lambda_1 = 0,\\ &(\lambda_2 p_v - \lambda_3 r_v)p_{vv} = 0,\\ &(\lambda_2 p_v - \lambda_3 r_v)r_{vv} = 0.\end{aligned}$$

Thus, the criterion in the hypothesis is verified by these last three equations. Consequently, we can say that the $v-$coordinate curves of M are geodesics under the criterion stated in the hypothesis.

Now, let us check whether the $v-$coordinate curves of M are asymptotic. Therefore, we take the Equation (8) and the third equality in (10) and we obtain

$$\langle \Delta, \varphi_{vv} \rangle = \kappa^2\lambda_1(r_v p_{vv} - p_v r_{vv}).$$

This gives us $\lambda_1 = 0$ or $r_v p_{vv} - p_v r_{vv} = 0$ if and only if $\langle \Delta, \varphi_{vv} \rangle = 0$. Since $\lambda_1 = 1 - r\kappa^2$ from (9), it is obvious that the $v-$coordinate curves of M are asymptotic under the criteria stated in the hypothesis. □

Theorem 5. *Let M be a modified sweeping surface generated by the MOF with non-vanishing curvature κ. If the s and $v-$coordinate curves of M are lines of curvature, then*

$$\frac{\lambda_2}{\lambda_3} = \frac{\kappa^2 \lambda_1 \lambda_{3v} - \lambda_{1v} \lambda_3}{\lambda_{1v} \lambda_2 - \kappa^2 \lambda_1 \lambda_{2v}}.$$

Proof. It is known that the curves that are always tangent to a principal direction are known as lines of curvature. Each coordinate curve follows one of the principal curvature directions on the surface if and only if $F = l = 0$, because $F = 0$ ensures the orthogonality of the coordinate curves and $l = 0$ ensures that each coordinate direction is independent in terms of curvature. Let us recall the equations

$$F(s, v) = \kappa^2 (\lambda_3 p_v + \lambda_2 r_v)$$

and

$$l(s, v) = \frac{\lambda_{1v}(\lambda_2 p_v - \lambda_3 r_v) - \kappa^2 \lambda_1 (\lambda_{2v} p_v - \lambda_{3v} r_v)}{\| \varphi_s \times \varphi_v \|}.$$

Then, the common solution of $F = 0$ and $l = 0$ gives us

$$\frac{\lambda_2}{\lambda_3} = \frac{\kappa^2 \lambda_1 \lambda_{3v} - \lambda_{1v} \lambda_3}{\lambda_{1v} \lambda_2 - \kappa^2 \lambda_1 \lambda_{2v}}.$$

This completes the proof. □

3.2. *Modified Sweeping Surfaces of the MOF with Non-Vanishing Torsion τ*

In this section, the surface given by the Equation (7) is investigated using the MOF with non-vanishing torsion. The first order partial differentiations of $\varphi(s, v)$ with respect to s and v, are found as follows:

$$\varphi_s = (1 - r\kappa\tau) T + \left(\frac{r\tau_s}{\tau} - \tau p \right) N + \left(\frac{p\tau_s}{\tau} + r\tau \right) B$$

and

$$\varphi_v = r_v N + p_v B.$$

Thus, by a straightforward computation from the last equations and the Equation (3), the normal vector field Δ of M is obtained as

$$\Delta(s, v) = \frac{(f_2 p_v - f_3 r_v) T - f_1 p_v N + f_1 r_v B}{\sqrt{\tau^2 {f_1}^2 ({p_v}^2 + {r_v}^2) + (f_2 p_v - f_3 r_v)^2}}, \tag{11}$$

where

$$f_1(s, v) = 1 - r\kappa\tau, \; f_2(s, v) = \frac{r\tau_s}{\tau} - \tau p, \text{ and } f_3(s, v) = \frac{p\tau_s}{\tau} + r\tau.$$

Theorem 6. *Let M be a modified sweeping surface constructed by the MOF with non-vanishing torsion. Then, the Gaussian curvature of M is given by*

$$K(s, v) = \frac{f_1 \eta_2 ((f_2 g_1 - f_1 g_2) p_v + (f_1 g_3 - f_3 g_1) r_v) - ((f_2 p_v - f_3 r_v) f_{1v} - f_1 (p_v f_{2v} - r_v f_{3v}))^2}{\| \varphi_s \times \varphi_v \|^2 \tau^2 \left({f_1}^2 \eta_1 + \tau^2 \left(\left({f_2}^2 + {f_3}^2 \right) \eta_1 - (f_3 p_v + f_2 r_v)^2 \right) \right)}.$$

Under the same condition, the mean curvatures of M is given by

$$H(s,v)=\frac{\tau^2(f_3r_v-f_2p_v)\begin{pmatrix}2f_{1v}(f_3p_v+f_2r_v)\\ -\eta_1g_1\end{pmatrix}+f_1\left(f_1{}^2\eta_2+\tau^2\begin{pmatrix}\left(f_2{}^2+f_3{}^2\right)\eta_2+\eta_1(+g_3r_v-g_2p_v)\\ +2(f_3p_v+f_2r_v)(p_vf_{2v}-r_vf_{3v})\end{pmatrix}\right)}{2\|\varphi_x\times\varphi_v\|\tau^2\left(f_1{}^2\eta_1+\tau^2\left(\eta_1\left(f_2{}^2+f_3{}^2\right)-(f_3p_v+f_2r_v)^2\right)\right)}$$

where

$$\begin{aligned}\|\varphi_s\times\varphi_v\|&=\sqrt{\tau^2f_1{}^2(p_v{}^2+r_v{}^2)+(f_2p_v-f_3r_v)^2},\\ g_1(s,v)&=f_{1s}-f_2\kappa\tau,\\ g_2(s,v)&=f_{2s}-f_3\tau+\frac{f_1\kappa}{\tau}+\frac{f_2\tau_s}{\tau},\\ g_3(s,v)&=f_2\tau+f_{3s}+\frac{f_3\tau_s}{\tau}.\end{aligned}$$

Proof. Assume that M is a modified sweeping surface generated by the MOF with non-vanishing torsion. From the Equation (5), the coefficients of the first fundamental form of this sweeping surface are found as follows:

$$\begin{cases}E(s,v)=f_1{}^2+\tau^2\left(f_2{}^2+f_3{}^2\right),\\ F(s,v)=\tau^2(f_2r_v+f_3p_v),\\ G(s,v)=\tau^2\left(p_v{}^2+r_v{}^2\right),\end{cases}$$

where $f_1(s,v), f_2(s,v)$, and $f_3(s,v)$ are as mentioned above. The second-order partial differentiations of $\varphi(s,v)$ with respect to s and v are as follows:

$$\begin{aligned}\varphi_{ss}&=g_1T+g_2N+g_3B,\\ \varphi_{sv}&=f_{1v}T+f_{2v}N+f_{3v}B,\\ \varphi_{vv}&=r_{vv}N+p_{vv}B,\end{aligned}\qquad(12)$$

where

$$\begin{aligned}g_1(s,v)&=f_{1s}-f_2\kappa\tau,\\ g_2(s,v)&=f_{2s}-f_3\tau+\frac{f_1\kappa}{\tau}+\frac{f_2\tau_s}{\tau},\\ g_3(s,v)&=f_2\tau+f_{3s}+\frac{f_3\tau_s}{\tau}.\end{aligned}$$

By Equations (6) and (12), the second fundamental form coefficients of M are found as follows:

$$\begin{cases}k(s,v)=\dfrac{g_1(f_2p_v-f_3r_v)+\tau^2f_1(g_3r_v-g_2p_v)}{\|\varphi_s\times\varphi_v\|},\\ l(s,v)=\dfrac{f_{1v}(f_2p_v-f_3r_v)+\tau^2f_1(f_{3v}r_v-f_{2v}p_v)}{\|\varphi_s\times\varphi_v\|},\\ m(s,v)=\dfrac{\tau^2f_1\eta_2}{\|\varphi_s\times\varphi_v\|}.\end{cases}$$

If the coefficients of the first and second fundamental forms of this type of modified sweeping surface are substituted into Equation (4), the Gaussian and mean curvatures K and H of M are obtained as in the hypothesis. □

Corollary 2. *If M is a modified sweeping surface generated by the MOF with non-vanishing torsion, then, M is developable if and only if*

$$f_1\eta_2((f_2g_1-f_1g_2)p_v+(f_1g_3-f_3g_1)r_v)=((f_2p_v-f_3r_v)f_{1v}-f_1(p_vf_{2v}-r_vf_{3v}))^2.$$

The modified sweeping surface generated by the MOF with non-vanishing torsion is the minimal surface if and only if

$$\tau^2(f_3r_v - f_2p_v)(2f_{1v}(f_3p_v + f_2r_v) - \eta_1 g_1) = f_1\left(f_1{}^2\eta_2 + \tau^2\begin{pmatrix}\eta_2\left(f_2{}^2 + f_3{}^2\right) + \eta_1(g_3r_v - g_2p_v) \\ +2(f_3p_v + f_2r_v)(p_vf_{2v} - r_vf_{3v})\end{pmatrix}\right).$$

Theorem 7. *Let M be a modified sweeping surface generated by the MOF with non-vanishing torsion. M is a Weingarten-type surface if and only if*

$$\begin{pmatrix}\xi_1(f_1\eta_{2v} + \eta_2 f_{1v}) \\ +(f_1\eta_2 - 2\xi_1)\xi_{1v}\end{pmatrix}\begin{pmatrix}\zeta_3 f_{1s} + f_1\zeta_{3s} \\ +\tau(\tau\zeta_2\zeta_{1s} + \zeta_1(2\zeta_2\tau_s + \tau\zeta_{2s}))\end{pmatrix} = \begin{pmatrix}\zeta_3 f_{1v} + f_1\zeta_{3v} \\ +\tau^2(\zeta_2\zeta_{1v} + \zeta_1\zeta_{2v})\end{pmatrix}\begin{pmatrix}\eta_2\xi_1 f_{1s} \\ +(f_1\eta_2 - 2\xi_1)\xi_{1s}\end{pmatrix}$$

where

$$\xi_1(s,v) = \frac{(f_2g_1 - f_1g_2)p_v + (f_1g_3 - f_3g_1)r_v}{\|\varphi_s \times \varphi_v\|^2\tau^2\left(f_1{}^2\eta_1 + \tau^2\left(\left(f_2^2 + f_3^2\right)\eta_1 - (f_3p_v + f_2r_v)^2\right)\right)},$$

$$\xi_2(s,v) = \frac{(f_2p_v - f_3r_v)f_{1v} - f_1(p_vf_{2v} - r_vf_{3v})}{\|\varphi_s \times \varphi_v\|\tau\sqrt{\left(f_1{}^2\eta_1 + \tau^2\left(\left(f_2^2 + f_3^2\right)\eta_1 - (f_3p_v + f_2r_v)^2\right)\right)}},$$

$$\zeta_1(s,v) = \frac{f_3r_v - f_2p_v}{2\|\varphi_s \times \varphi_v\|\tau^2\left(f_1{}^2\eta_1 + \tau^2\left(\eta_1\left(f_2^2 + f_3^2\right) - (f_3p_v + f_2r_v)^2\right)\right)},$$

$$\zeta_2(s,v) = \frac{2f_{1v}(f_3p_v + f_2r_v) - \eta_1 g_1}{2\|\varphi_s \times \varphi_v\|\tau^2\left(f_1{}^2\eta_1 + \tau^2\left(\eta_1\left(f_2^2 + f_3^2\right) - (f_3p_v + f_2r_v)^2\right)\right)},$$

$$\zeta_3(s,v) = \frac{f_1{}^2\eta_2 + \tau^2\left(\left(f_2^2 + f_3^2\right)\eta_2 + \eta_1(+g_3r_v - g_2p_v) + 2(f_3p_v + f_2r_v)(p_vf_{2v} - r_vf_{3v})\right)}{2\|\varphi_s \times \varphi_v\|\tau^2\left(f_1{}^2\eta_1 + \tau^2\left(\eta_1\left(f_2^2 + f_3^2\right) - (f_3p_v + f_2r_v)^2\right)\right)}.$$

Proof. Let M be a modified sweeping surface generated by the MOF with non-vanishing torsion. By differentiating the curvatures K and H of M in terms of s and v, we obtain

$$\begin{cases} K_s = \eta_2\xi_1 f_{1s} + (f_1\eta_2 - 2\xi_1)\xi_{1s}, \\ K_v = \xi_1(f_1\eta_{2v} + \eta_2 f_{1v}) + (f_1\eta_2 - 2\xi_1)\xi_{1v}, \\ H_s = \zeta_3 f_{1s} + \tau(\tau\zeta_2\zeta_{1s} + \zeta_1(2\zeta_2\tau_s + \tau\zeta_{2s})) + f_1\zeta_{3s}, \\ H_v = \zeta_3 f_{1v} + \tau^2(\zeta_2\zeta_{1v} + \zeta_1\zeta_{2v}) + f_1\zeta_{3v}. \end{cases}$$

From here, the condition specified in the hypothesis is met if and only if $K_sH_v - K_vH_s = 0$. So, one can say that M generated by the MOF with non-vanishing torsion is a Weingarten-type surface under this condition. □

Theorem 8. *Let M be a modified sweeping surface generated by the MOF with non-vanishing torsion. Then, the $s-$coordinate curves of M are geodesic if and only if*

$$\frac{p_v}{r_v} = \frac{f_3(g_3 - g_2) + f_1g_1}{f_2(g_3 - g_2) - f_1g_1}.$$

Also, the $s-$coordinate curves of M are asymptotic if and only if

$$\frac{p_v}{r_v} = \frac{g_1f_3 - \tau^2 g_3 f_1}{g_1f_2 - \tau^2 g_2 f_1}.$$

Proof. Let M be a modified sweeping surface generated by the MOF with non-vanishing torsion. From (11) and the first equality in (12), the following equation is obtained:

$$\Delta \times \varphi_{ss} = f_1(g_3p_v + g_2r_v)T + (g_3f_2p_v - (g_1f_1 + g_3f_3)r_v)N$$
$$+(g_2f_3r_v - (g_1f_1 + g_2f_2)p_v)B.$$

By the linear independence of the elements of MOF, $\Delta \times \varphi_{ss} = 0$ requires

$$
\begin{aligned}
&f_1(g_3p_v+g_2r_v)=0,\\
&g_3f_2p_v-(g_1f_1+g_3f_3)r_v=0,\\
&g_2f_3r_v-(g_1f_1+g_2f_2)p_v=0.
\end{aligned}
$$

Thus, the criterion in the hypothesis is obtained by these last three equations. One can say that the $s-$coordinate curves of the modified sweeping surface are geodesics under the criterion stated in the hypothesis.

From Equations (11) and (12), we have

$$\langle \Delta, \varphi_{ss}\rangle = \left(g_1f_2-\tau^2g_2f_1\right)p_v+\left(\tau^2g_3f_1-g_1f_3\right)r_v.$$

Thus, $(g_1f_2-\tau^2g_2f_1)p_v=(g_1f_3-\tau^2g_3f_1)r_v$ if and only if $\langle\Delta,\varphi_{ss}\rangle=0$. Consequently, it is proved that the $s-$coordinate curves of M are asymptotic under the criterion stated in the hypothesis. □

Theorem 9. *Let M be a modified sweeping surface generated by the MOF with non-vanishing torsion. Then, the $v-$coordinate curves of M are geodesic if and only if*

$$f_2p_v-f_3r_v=0,\ p_{vv}-r_{vv}=0 \quad \textit{and} \quad f_1(p_vp_{vv}+r_vr_{vv})=0.$$

Also, the $v-$coordinate curves of M are asymptotic if and only if

$$r\kappa\tau=1 \quad \textit{or} \quad r_vp_{vv}-p_vr_{vv}=0.$$

Proof. The vector product of the normal vector Δ given by (11) and φ_{vv} given in the third equation of (12) is found as follows:

$$\Delta\times\varphi_{vv}=f_1(p_vp_{vv}+r_vr_{vv})T+p_{vv}(f_2p_v-f_3r_v)N+r_{vv}(f_3r_v-f_2p_v)B.$$

The condition for $v-$curve to be geodesic is $\Delta\times\varphi_{vv}=0$, which requires

$$
\begin{aligned}
&f_1(p_vp_{vv}+r_vr_{vv})=0,\\
&p_{vv}(f_2p_v-f_3r_v)=0,\\
&r_{vv}(f_3r_v-f_2p_v)=0.
\end{aligned}
$$

Thus, for $\Delta\times\varphi_{vv}=0$, the criterion in the hypothesis must be verified. It is obvious that the $v-$coordinate curves of M are geodesics under the criterion stated in the hypothesis. From Equation (11) and the third equality in (12), we have

$$\langle\Delta,\varphi_{vv}\rangle=\tau^2f_1(r_vp_{vv}-p_vr_{vv}).$$

Then, $f_1=0$ or $r_vp_{vv}-p_vr_{vv}=0$ if and only if $\langle\Delta,\varphi_{vv}\rangle=0$. Since $f_1=1-r\kappa\tau$, it is seen that the $v-$coordinate curves of M are asymptotic under the criteria stated in the hypothesis. □

Theorem 10. *Let M be a modified sweeping surface generated by the MOF with non-vanishing torsion τ. Then, the s and $v-$coordinate curves of M are lines of curvature if and only if*

$$\frac{p_v}{r_v}=\frac{\tau^2f_1f_{3v}-f_{1v}f_3}{f_{1v}f_2-\tau^2f_1f_{2v}}.$$

Proof. Let M be a modified sweeping surface generated by the MOF with non-vanishing torsion. Then, $F=l=0$ provided that the coordinate curves of M are lines of curvature. Taking into consideration $\tau\neq0$ and the equations

$$F=\tau^2(f_3p_v+f_2r_v) \quad \text{and} \quad l=\frac{f_{1v}(f_2p_v-f_3r_v)+\tau^2f_1(f_{3v}r_v-f_{2v}p_v)}{\|\varphi_s\times\varphi_v\|},$$

the common solution of $F = 0$ and $l = 0$ gives us

$$\frac{p_v}{r_v} = \frac{\tau^2 f_1 f_{3v} - f_{1v} f_3}{f_{1v} f_2 - \tau^2 f_1 f_{2v}}.$$

The last is the condition for the s and $v-$coordinate curves of M generated by the MOF with non-vanishing torsion to be the lines of curvature. □

Example 1. *Let us consider a curve β defined by the parametric equation*

$$\beta(s) = (\sin s, \sin s \cos s, s).$$

The Frenet apparatuses of β are found as $\{t, n, b, \kappa, \tau\}$ where $s \in (2k\pi, (2k+1)\pi)$ and $\{t, -n, -b, -\kappa, \tau\}$ where $s \in ((2k+1)\pi, (2k+2)\pi)$ for $k \in \mathbb{Z}$, such that

$$t = \left(\frac{\sqrt{2}\cos s}{\sqrt{4+\cos 2s+\cos 4s}}, \frac{\sqrt{2}\cos 2s}{\sqrt{4+\cos 2s+\cos 4s}}, \frac{\sqrt{2}}{\sqrt{4+\cos 2s+\cos 4s}} \right),$$

$$n = \begin{pmatrix} \dfrac{(4\cos 2s+\cos 4s-1)}{\sqrt{(4+\cos 2s+\cos 4s)(27+24\cos 2s+\cos 4s)}}, \\ \dfrac{-2\cos s(6+\cos 2s)}{\sqrt{(4+\cos 2s+\cos 4s)(27+24\cos 2s+\cos 4s)}}, \\ \dfrac{2\cos s(1+4\cos 2s)}{\sqrt{(4+\cos 2s+\cos 4s)(27+24\cos 2s+\cos 4s)}} \end{pmatrix},$$

$$b = \left(\frac{4\sqrt{2}\cos s}{\sqrt{27+24\cos 2s+\cos 4s}}, \frac{-\sqrt{2}}{\sqrt{27+24\cos 2s+\cos 4s}}, \frac{-4-2\cos 2s}{\sqrt{27+24\cos 2s+\cos 4s}} \right),$$

and

$$\kappa = \frac{2\sin s\sqrt{27+24\cos 2s+\cos 4s}}{(4+\cos 2s+\cos 4s)^{3/2}}, \quad \tau = -\frac{8\sin s}{27+24\cos 2s+\cos 4s}.$$

Moreover, at $s = k\pi$ for each $k \in \mathbb{Z}$, the curvature and torsion of β are zero. In addition, the Frenet frame cannot be constituted at these points since normal and binormal vectors are discontinuous, and it is impossible to refer to the Frenet frame in a unique way. So, this problem is solved via the MOF. Here, we express the elements of the MOF with non-zero curvatures for all s as follows:

$$T = \left(\frac{\sqrt{2}\cos s}{\sqrt{4+\cos 2s+\cos 4s}}, \frac{\sqrt{2}\cos 2s}{\sqrt{4+\cos 2s+\cos 4s}}, \frac{\sqrt{2}}{\sqrt{4+\cos 2s+\cos 4s}} \right),$$

$$N = \left(\frac{2\sin s(4\cos 2s+\cos 4s-1)}{(4+\cos 2s+\cos 4s)^2}, \frac{-2\sin 2s(6+\cos 2s)}{(4+\cos 2s+\cos 4s)^2}, \frac{2(\sin 2s+2\sin 4s)}{(4+\cos 2s+\cos 4s)^2} \right),$$

$$B = \left(\frac{4\sqrt{2}\sin 2s}{(4+\cos 2s+\cos 4s)^{3/2}}, \frac{-2\sqrt{2}\sin s}{(4+\cos 2s+\cos 4s)^{3/2}}, \frac{-\sqrt{2}(3\sin s+\sin 3s)}{(4+\cos 2s+\cos 4s)^{3/2}} \right).$$

If we take the planar profile (cross-section) curve $\delta(v) = (0, \cos v, \sin v)$, the equation of the modified sweeping surface (see Figure 1) generated by the MOF with non-vanishing curvature κ is represented by

$$\varphi(s,v) = \begin{pmatrix} \sin s + \dfrac{2\sin s\cos v(4\cos 2s+\cos 4s-1)}{(4+\cos 2s+\cos 4s)^2} + \dfrac{4\sqrt{2}\sin 2s\sin v}{(4+\cos 2s+\cos 4s)^{3/2}}, \\ \sin s\cos s + -\dfrac{2\sin 2s\cos v(6+\cos 2s)}{(4+\cos 2s+\cos 4s)^2} - \dfrac{2\sqrt{2}\sin s\sin v}{(4+\cos 2s+\cos 4s)^{3/2}}, \\ s + \dfrac{2\cos v(\sin 2s+2\sin 4s)}{(4+\cos 2s+\cos 4s)^2} - \dfrac{\sqrt{2}(3\sin s+\sin 3s)\sin v}{(4+\cos 2s+\cos 4s)^{3/2}} \end{pmatrix}. \quad (13)$$

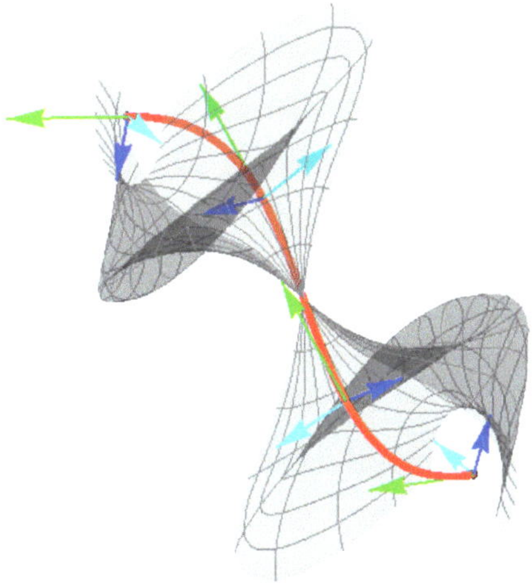

Figure 1. The sweeping surface modified by MOF in non-vanishing curvature case presented by (13), with the tangent (green), principal normal (blue), binormal (cyan) vectors of spine curve $\beta(s)$ (red) in front view with $s \in (-\pi/2, \pi/2)$ and $v \in (-2, 2)$.

Example 2. *Let us consider the Euler (Cornu) spiral parameterized by*

$$\beta(s) = \left(\frac{1}{\sqrt{2}} \int_0^s \cos \frac{\pi t^2}{2} dt, \frac{1}{\sqrt{2}} \int_0^s \sin \frac{\pi t^2}{2} dt, \frac{s}{\sqrt{2}} \right),$$

where the components $\int_0^s \cos \frac{\pi t^2}{2} dt$ *and* $\int_0^s \sin \frac{\pi t^2}{2} dt$ *of this curve are known as Fresnel integrals* [21]. *The Frenet apparatus of* β *are found as* $\{t, n, b, \kappa, \tau\}$ *for* $s \in \mathbb{R}^+$ *and* $\{t, -n, -b, -\kappa, \tau\}$ *for* $s \in \mathbb{R}^-$ *such that*

$$t = \left(\frac{1}{\sqrt{2}} \cos \frac{\pi s^2}{2}, \frac{1}{\sqrt{2}} \sin \frac{\pi s^2}{2}, \frac{1}{\sqrt{2}} \right), \; n = \left(-\sin \frac{\pi s^2}{2}, \cos \frac{\pi s^2}{2}, 0 \right),$$
$$b = \left(-\frac{1}{\sqrt{2}} \cos \frac{\pi s^2}{2}, -\frac{1}{\sqrt{2}} \sin \frac{\pi s^2}{2}, \frac{1}{\sqrt{2}} \right), \; \kappa = \frac{\pi s}{\sqrt{2}}, \; \tau = \frac{\pi s}{\sqrt{2}}.$$

Here, the Frenet frame does not occur at $s = 0$, *since the second derivative of* $\beta(s)$ *is zero. To fix this problem, we can refer to any MOF. The elements of MOF with non-zero torsion are obtained as*

$$T = \left(\frac{1}{\sqrt{2}} \cos \frac{\pi s^2}{2}, \frac{1}{\sqrt{2}} \sin \frac{\pi s^2}{2}, \frac{1}{\sqrt{2}} \right),$$
$$N = \left(-\frac{\pi s}{\sqrt{2}} \sin \frac{\pi s^2}{2}, \frac{\pi s}{\sqrt{2}} \cos \frac{\pi s^2}{2}, 0 \right),$$
$$B = \left(-\frac{\pi s}{2} \cos \frac{\pi s^2}{2}, -\frac{\pi s}{2} \sin \frac{\pi s^2}{2}, \frac{\pi s}{2} \right).$$

By taking spine curve β *and the planar profile curve* $\delta(v) = (0, \cos v, \sin v)$, *a modified sweeping surface (see Figure 2) generated by the MOF with non-vanishing torsion is given with the following equation:*

$$\varphi(s,v)=\begin{pmatrix}\frac{1}{\sqrt{2}}\int\limits_0^s\cos\frac{\pi t^2}{2}dt-\frac{\pi s\cos v}{\sqrt{2}}\sin\frac{\pi s^2}{2}-\frac{\pi s\sin v}{2}\cos\frac{\pi s^2}{2},\\ \frac{1}{\sqrt{2}}\int\limits_0^s\sin\frac{\pi t^2}{2}dt+\frac{\pi s\cos v}{\sqrt{2}}\cos\frac{\pi s^2}{2}-\frac{\pi s\sin v}{2}\sin\frac{\pi s^2}{2},\\ \frac{s}{\sqrt{2}}+\frac{\pi s\sin v}{2}\end{pmatrix}. \quad (14)$$

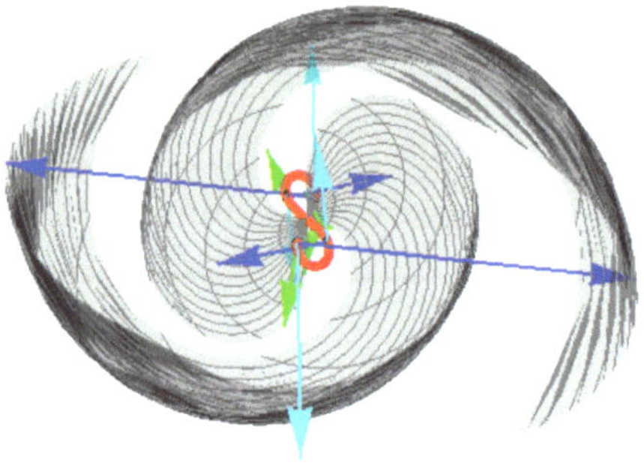

Figure 2. The sweeping surface modified by MOF in non-vanishing torsion case presented by (14), with the tangent (green), principal normal (blue), binormal (cyan) vectors of spine curve $\beta(s)$ (red) in front view with $s\in(-\pi/2,\pi/2)$ and $v\in(-1,1)$.

4. Conclusions

This study explores the application of modified orthogonal frames with non-vanishing curvature and non-vanishing torsion, enabling the generation of two types of modified sweeping surfaces, even when the second derivative of the spine curve is zero. The research involves the following processes:

- Deriving criteria for each type of modified sweeping surface with non-vanishing curvature and non-vanishing torsion to be minimal, developable, or Weingarten surfaces.
- Conducting a comprehensive analysis of the coordinate curves of these modified sweeping surfaces to determine criteria for geodesic, asymptotic, and curvature lines.
- Providing examples of the modified sweeping surfaces along with illustrated graphics.

Author Contributions: Conceptualization, K.E.; Formal analysis, Y.L., K.E., S.E., and A.S.; Investigation, Y.L., K.E., S.E., and A.S.; Methodology; Y.L., K.E., S.E., and A.S.; Supervision, S.E.; Writing—original draft, K.E.; Writing—review and editing, Y.L., K.E., S.E., and A.S. All authors have read and agreed to the published version of the manuscript.

Funding: This research received no external funding.

Data Availability Statement: The original contributions presented in the study are included in the article, further inquiries can be directed to the corresponding author.

Conflicts of Interest: The authors declare no conflicts of interest.

References

1. Flok, F. Two moving coordinate frames for sweeping along a 3D trajectory. *Comput. Aided Geom. Des.* **1986**, *3*, 217–229. [CrossRef]
2. Wang, W.; Joe, B. Robust computation of the rotation minimizing frame for sweep surface modeling. *Comput. Aided Geom. Des.* **1997**, *29*, 379–391. [CrossRef]
3. Xu, Z.; Feng, R.; Sun, J.G. Analytic and algebraic properties of canal surfaces. *J. Comput. Appl. Math.* **2006**, *195*, 220–228. [CrossRef]
4. Ro, J.S.; Yoon, D.W. Tubes of Weingarten types in Euclidean 3-space. *J. Chungcheong Math. Soc.* **2009**, *22*, 359–366. [CrossRef]
5. Abdel-Baky, R.A. Developable surfaces through sweeping surfaces. *Bull. Iran. Math. Soc.* **2019**, *45*, 951–963. [CrossRef]
6. Moraffeh, F.; Abdel-Baky, R.A.; Alluhaibi, N. Sweeping surfaces with Darboux frame in Euclidean 3-space. *Aust. J. Math. Anal. Appl.* **2021**, *18*, 1–10.

7. Li, Y.; Güler, E. Right Conoids Demonstrating a Time-like Axis within Minkowski Four-Dimensional Space. *Mathematics* **2024**, *12*, 2421. [CrossRef]
8. Li, Y.; Güler, E.; Toda, M. Family of right conoid hypersurfaces with light-like axis in Minkowski four-space. *AIMS Math.* **2024**, *9*, 18732–18745. [CrossRef]
9. Bruce, J.W.; Giblin, P.J. *Curves and Singularities;* Cambridge University Press: Cambridge, UK, 1992. [CrossRef]
10. Köseoğlu, G.; Bilici, M. Involutive sweeping surfaces with Frenet frame in Euclidean 3-space. *Heliyon* **2023**, *9*, e18822. [CrossRef]
11. Maekawa, T.; Patrikalakis, N.M.; Sakkalis, T.; Yu, G. Analysis and applications of pipe surfaces. *Comput. Aided Geom. Des.* **1998**, *15*, 437–458. [CrossRef]
12. Blaga, P.A. On tubular surfaces in computer graphics. *Stud. Univ. Babeş-Bolyai Inform.* **2005**, *50*, 81–90.
13. Kızıltuğ, S.; Kaya, S.; Tarakçı, Ö. Tube surfaces with type-2 Bishop frame of Weingarten types in E^3. *Int. J. Math. Anal.* **2013**, *7*, 9–18. [CrossRef]
14. Moraffeh, F.; Abdel-Baky, R.; Alluhall, N. Spacelike sweeping surfaces and singularities in Minkowski 3-space. *Math. Probl. Eng.* **2021**, *3*, 5130941. [CrossRef]
15. Li, Y.; Bouleryah, M.L.H.; Ali, A. On Convergence of Toeplitz Quantization of the Sphere. *Mathematics* **2024**, *12*, 3565. [CrossRef]
16. Li, Y.; Abdel-Aziz, H.; Serry, H.; El-Adawy, F.; Saad, M. Geometric visualization of evolved ruled surfaces via alternative frame in Lorentz-Minkowski 3-space. *AIMS Math.* **2024**, *9*, 25619–25635. [CrossRef]
17. Li, Y.; Turki, N.; Deshmukh, S.; Belova, O. Euclidean hypersurfaces isometric to spheres. *AIMS Math.* **2024**, *9*, 28306–28319. [CrossRef]
18. Sasai, T. The fundamental theorem of analytic space curves and apparent singularities of Fuchsian differential equations. *Tohoku Math. J.* **1984**, *36*, 17–24. [CrossRef]
19. Karacan, M.K.; Bükçü, B. On the modified orthogonal frame with curvature and torsion in 3-space. *Math. Sci. Appl. E-Notes* **2016**, *4*, 184–188.
20. Lone, M.S.; Hasan, E.S.; Karacan, M.K.; Bükçü, B. On some curves with modified orthogonal frame in Euclidean 3-space. *Iran J. Sci. Technol. Trans. A Sci.* **2019**, *43*, 1905–1916. [CrossRef]
21. Eren, K.; Kösal, H.H. Evolution of space curves and the special ruled surfaces with modified orthogonal frame. *AIMS Math.* **2020**, *5*, 2027–2039. [CrossRef]
22. Akyiğit, M.; Eren, K.; Kösal, H.H. Tubular surfaces with modified orthogonal frame. *Honam Math. J.* **2021**, *43*, 453–463. [CrossRef]
23. Eren, K. New representation of Hasimoto surfaces with the modified orthogonal frame. *Konuralp J. Math.* **2022**, *10*, 69–72.
24. Eren, K. A study of the evolution of space curves with modified orthogonal frame in Euclidean 3-space. *App. Math. E-Notes* **2022**, *22*, 281–286.
25. Eren, K.; Ersoy, S. On characterization of Smarandache curves constructed by modified orthogonal frame. *Math. Sci. Appl. E-Notes* **2024**, *12*, 101–112. [CrossRef]

Article

Elliptic Quaternion Matrices: A MATLAB Toolbox and Applications for Image Processing

Hidayet Hüda Kösal *[ ], Emre Kişi [ ], Mahmut Akyiğit [ ] and Beyza Çelik

Faculty of Sciences, Department of Mathematics, Sakarya University, Sakarya TR-54000, Türkiye; ekisi@sakarya.edu.tr (E.K.); makyigit@sakarya.edu.tr (M.A.); beyza.celik6@ogr.sakarya.edu.tr (B.Ç.)
* Correspondence: hhkosal@sakarya.edu.tr

Abstract: In this study, we developed a MATLAB 2024a toolbox that performs advanced algebraic calculations in the algebra of elliptic numbers and elliptic quaternions. Additionally, we introduce color image processing methods, such as principal component analysis, image compression, image restoration, and watermarking, based on singular-value decomposition theory for elliptic quaternion matrices; we added these to the newly developed toolbox. The experimental results demonstrate that elliptic quaternionic methods yield better image analysis and processing performance compared to other hypercomplex number-based methods.

Keywords: elliptic quaternion matrices; MATLAB toolbox; optimal p-value; singular value decomposition; least minimum error; image processing

MSC: 11R52; 15A60; 15A18

Citation: Kösal, H.H.; Kişi, E.; Akyiğit, M.; Çelik, B. Elliptic Quaternion Matrices: A MATLAB Toolbox and Applications for Image Processing. Axioms **2024**, *13*, 771. https://doi.org/10.3390/axioms13110771

Academic Editor: Fabio Caldarola

Received: 23 August 2024
Revised: 22 October 2024
Accepted: 27 October 2024
Published: 6 November 2024

Copyright: © 2024 by the authors. Licensee MDPI, Basel, Switzerland. This article is an open access article distributed under the terms and conditions of the Creative Commons Attribution (CC BY) license (https://creativecommons.org/licenses/by/4.0/).

1. Introduction

In 1843, Hamilton introduced the concept of real quaternions, expressed as

$$q_{(R)} = q_{(R),r} + q_{(R),i}i + q_{(R),j}j + q_{(R),k}k,$$

where $q_{(R),r}, q_{(R),i}, q_{(R),j}$, and $q_{(R),k}$ are real-valued components, and the imaginary units i, j, and k satisfy the relations

$$i^2 = j^2 = k^2 = -1, \ ij = -ji = k, \ jk = -kj = i, \ ki = -ik = j.$$

The absence of the commutative property in quaternion multiplication classifies real quaternions as a division ring or, more specifically, a skew field [1]. This mathematical structure finds its application across a broad spectrum of disciplines, including but not limited to quantum mechanics [2], computer graphics [3], signal and image processing [4], and the study of neural networks [5]. In 2005, Sangwine and Bihan introduced a MATLAB toolbox designed to facilitate the computational demands associated with real quaternions and their matrices. This toolbox, notable for its inclusion of image processing functionalities, has been subject to continuous refinement, with its most recent update occurring in February 2024 [6]. MATLAB introduced quaternion support in the R2018b release as part of the Aerospace Toolbox and, after that, incorporated it into several pivotal MATLAB toolboxes such as the Sensor Fusion and Tracking Toolbox, the Robotics System Toolbox, and the Navigation Toolbox. This expansion highlights the importance and applicability of real quaternions in various technological and scientific areas. However, the noncommutative nature of real quaternion multiplication not only introduces certain constraints in various applications but also causes difficulties in calculations. For instance, the inherent complexity in performing the singular-value decomposition of a real quaternion matrix is notably high, registering a computational complexity of $O(8n^3)$ for an $n \times n$ real quaternion matrix, considering that its complex representation is of size $2n \times 2n$. Additionally, the convolution theorem does not hold for real quaternion-valued signals; that is, the Fourier transform of the convolution products of two such signals does not equate to the dot products of their respective Fourier transforms. This deviation from the convolution theorem implies that the fast Fourier transform algorithm remains undeveloped for real quaternion-valued linear time-invariant systems, presenting challenges in their analysis [7].

As the need for more efficient and versatile algebraic structures grew, researchers sought alternatives to real quaternions that retained the benefits of hypercomplex numbers while mitigating some of the associated limitations. This search led to the development of generalized Segre quaternions, a class of four-dimensional commutative hypercomplex numbers. These quaternions have been gaining attention due to their ability to extend methodologies from the real and complex number domains to more versatile four-dimensional counterparts [8,9]. The definition of generalized Segre quaternions is as follows:

$$q_{(GS)} = q_{(GS),r} + q_{(GS),i}i + q_{(GS),j}j + q_{(GS),k}k,$$

where $q_{(GS),r}, q_{(GS),i}, q_{(GS),j}, q_{(GS),k} \in \mathbb{R}$ and $i, j, k \notin \mathbb{R}$. The multiplication rules for the units i, j, k are given by

$$i^2 = k^2 = p, \quad j^2 = 1, \quad ij = ji = k, \quad jk = kj = i, \quad ki = ik = pj,$$

where $p \in \mathbb{R}$. Based on the value of p, generalized Segre quaternions are classified into three categories: hyperbolic quaternions ($p > 0$), parabolic quaternions ($p = 0$), and elliptic quaternions ($p < 0$) [9]. Each of these systems has specific scientific and technological applications. For example, hyperbolic quaternions are used to solve problems in non-Euclidean geometry [10,11], while parabolic quaternions are applied in robotic control and spatial mechanics [10,12]. Due to the elliptic behavior of many physical systems, elliptic quaternions have significant practical applications in applied science. Additionally, elliptic quaternions offer a notable improvement over real quaternions, especially with their commutative multiplication and enhanced generalization capability [9,10,13,14]. These properties result in reduced computational complexity and improved performance across a range of computational tasks. Specifically, the process of singular-value decomposition within the context of elliptic quaternion matrices is characterized by an algorithmic complexity of $O(2n^3)$, as detailed in [15]. Furthermore, the applicability of the convolution theorem within this mathematical framework enables the formulation of a fast Fourier transform algorithm specifically designed for elliptic quaternion spaces. Consequently, recent developments in elliptic quaternion-valued methodologies have demonstrated their superiority over conventional real quaternion approaches in critical fields such as image processing, signal processing, and deep learning, as evidenced by [7,14–17].

In this paper, we present a MATLAB toolbox that we developed for performing advanced calculations in elliptic numbers and elliptic quaternions. The aim of this toolbox is to address and provide solutions to the computational challenges associated with these algebraic structures, thereby facilitating further scientific and technological research in this field. This development is fundamentally rooted in the theoretical framework and algorithms delineated in references [9,15,18]. Furthermore, by leveraging mathematical theory and algorithms elucidated in [15], we have enriched this toolbox with advanced color image processing methodologies, including but not limited to principal component analysis, image compression, image restoration, and watermarking techniques. We have observed that the proposed methods for image compression, image restoration, and watermarking exhibit better performance than existing techniques based on separable, real quaternions and reduced biquaternions (for comparison results, see Tables 4–8). Moreover, our performance analyses reveal that the p-value of elliptic quaternions directly affects the solution of the problem, with better results obtained by adjusting this p-value (for optimal p-value results, see Figures 11, 13 and 19.

Within the context of this paper, the following notations are employed. Let $\mathbb{R}$, $\mathbb{C}$, $\mathbb{C}_p$, and $\mathbb{H}_p$ denote the sets of real numbers, complex numbers, elliptic numbers, and elliptic quaternions, respectively. $\mathbb{R}^{m\times n}$, $\mathbb{C}^{m\times n}$, $\mathbb{C}_p^{m\times n}$, and $\mathbb{H}_p^{m\times n}$ denote the set of all $m\times n$ matrices on $\mathbb{R}$, $\mathbb{C}$, $\mathbb{C}_p$, and $\mathbb{H}_p$, respectively. Throughout the study, we use the following notations: $q_{(\square)}$ represents a complex number when $\square = c$, an elliptic number when $\square = e$, and an elliptic quaternion when $\square = E$. Similarly, $Q_{(\square)}$ denotes a complex matrix when $\square = c$, an elliptic matrix when $\square = e$, and an elliptic quaternion matrix when $\square = E$. This study was conducted using MATLAB 2024a (64-bit) on a system equipped with an Intel® Raptor Lake Core™ i7-13700H 14C/20T, NVIDIA® GeForce® RTX4060 and 32 GB of DDR5 RAM.

2. Mathematical Preliminaries

This section establishes the fundamental algebraic properties and the notations for elliptic numbers and elliptic quaternions.

2.1. Elliptic Numbers

An elliptic number $q_{(e)}$ is denoted by $q_{(e)} = q_{(e),r} + q_{(e),i}i$, where $i^2 = p < 0$ and $q_{(e),r}, q_{(e),i}, p \in \mathbb{R}$. The conjugate and norm of $q_{(e)} \in \mathbb{C}_p$ are defined as $\overline{q_{(e)}} = q_{(e),r} - q_{(e),i}i$ and $\left\|q_{(e)}\right\|_p = \sqrt{q_{(e),r}^2 - pq_{(e),i}^2}$, respectively [19]. The multiplication of the elliptic numbers $q_{1,(e)} = q_{1,(e),r} + q_{1,(e),i}i$ and $q_{2,(e)} = q_{2,(e),r} + q_{2,(e),i}i$ is defined as

$$q_{1,(e)}q_{2,(e)} = \left(q_{1,(e),r}q_{2,(e),r} + pq_{1,(e),i}q_{2,(e),i}\right) + i\left(q_{1,(e),r}q_{2,(e),i} + q_{2,(e),r}q_{1,(e),i}\right).$$

An elliptic matrix $Q_{(e)}$ is denoted as $Q_{(e)} = Q_{(e),r} + Q_{(e),i}i$, where $i^2 = p < 0$, $p \in \mathbb{R}$, and $Q_{(e),r}, Q_{(e),i} \in \mathbb{R}^{m\times n}$. The conjugate, transpose, conjugate transpose, and Frobenius norm of $Q_{(e)} \in \mathbb{C}_p^{m\times n}$ are defined by $\overline{Q_{(e)}} = Q_{(e),r} - Q_{(e),i}i$, $Q_{(e)}^T = Q_{(e),r}^T + Q_{(e),i}^T i$, $Q_{(e)}^* = Q_{(e),r}^T - Q_{(e),i}^T i$, and $\|Q_{(e)}\|_p = \sqrt{\|Q_{(e),r}\|^2 - p\|Q_{(e),i}\|^2}$, respectively [15,19]. The multiplication of two elliptic matrices $Q_{1,(e)} = Q_{1,(e),r} + Q_{1,(e),i}i$ and $Q_{2,(e)} = Q_{2,(e),r} + Q_{2,(e),i}i$ is defined as

$$Q_{1,(e)}Q_{2,(e)} = \left(Q_{1,(e),r}Q_{2,(e),r} + pQ_{1,(e),i}Q_{2,(e),i}\right) + i\left(Q_{1,(e),r}Q_{2,(e),i} + Q_{2,(e),r}Q_{1,(e),i}\right).$$

There exists an isomorphism between elliptic matrices and complex matrices, as depicted in the following:

$$\begin{aligned} \mathrm{H}_p : \mathbb{C}_p^{m\times n} &\to \mathbb{C}^{m\times n} \\ Q_{(e)} = Q_{(e),r} + Q_{(e),i}i &\to \mathrm{H}_p\left(Q_{(e)}\right) = Q_{(c)} = Q_{(e),r} + I\sqrt{-p}Q_{(e),i}, \end{aligned}$$

where I represents the complex unit ($I^2 = -1$) [15].

Lemma 1 ([15]). *Let the eigenvalues of a complex matrix $\mathrm{H}_p\left(Q_{(e)}\right)$ be denoted by $\lambda_{\mathrm{H}_p\left(Q_{(e)}\right)}$, and let the corresponding eigenvectors be represented by $x_{\mathrm{H}_p\left(Q_{(e)}\right)}$. Then, the eigenvalues of the elliptic matrix $Q_{(e)} \in \mathbb{C}_p^{n\times n}$ are given by*

$$\lambda_{(e)} = \mathrm{Re}(\lambda_{\mathrm{H}_p(Q_{(e)})}) + \frac{i}{\sqrt{-p}}\mathrm{Im}(\lambda_{\mathrm{H}_p(Q_{(e)})})$$

and the corresponding eigenvectors are given by

$$x_{(e)} = \mathrm{Re}(x_{\mathrm{H}_p(Q_{(e)})}) + \frac{i}{\sqrt{-p}}\mathrm{Im}(x_{\mathrm{H}_p(Q_{(e)})}).$$

Lemma 2 ([15])**.** *Let $Q_{(e)} \in \mathbb{C}_p^{m\times n}$. The pseudoinverse of $Q_{(e)}$ is given by*

$$\left(Q_{(e)}\right)^{\dagger} = \mathrm{Re}\left(\left(\mathrm{H_p}\left(Q_{(e)}\right)\right)^{\dagger}\right) + \frac{i}{\sqrt{-p}}\mathrm{Im}\left(\left(\mathrm{H_p}\left(Q_{(e)}\right)\right)^{\dagger}\right),$$

where $\left(\mathrm{H_p}\left(Q_{(e)}\right)\right)^{\dagger}$ is the pseudoinverse of the complex matrix $\mathrm{H_p}\left(Q_{(e)}\right)$.

Lemma 3 ([15])**.** *Let $Q_{(e)} \in \mathbb{C}_p^{m\times n}$. Suppose that the singular-value decomposition of the complex matrix $\mathrm{H}_p\left(Q_{(e)}\right)$ is given by $\mathrm{H_p}\left(Q_{(e)}\right) = U_{(c)}\Sigma V_{(c)}^{*}$. Then, the singular-value decomposition of the elliptic matrix $Q_{(e)}$ is $Q_{(e)} = U_{(e)}\Sigma V_{(e)}^{*}$, where*

$$U_{(e)} = \left(\mathrm{Re}\left(U_{(c)}\right) + \frac{i}{\sqrt{-p}}\mathrm{Im}\left(U_{(c)}\right)\right) \text{ and } V_{(e)} = \left(\mathrm{Re}\left(U_{(c)}\right) + \frac{i}{\sqrt{-p}}\mathrm{Im}\left(U_{(c)}\right)\right).$$

Lemma 4 ([15])**.** *Let $Q_{1,(e)} \in \mathbb{C}_p^{m\times n}$ and $Q_{2,(e)} \in \mathbb{C}_p^{m\times q}$. Suppose that $\mathrm{H_p}\left(Q_{1,(e)}\right) = U_{(c)}\Sigma V_{(c)}^{*}$. In this case, the least squares solution with the minimum norm $X_{(e)}$ of the elliptic matrix equation $Q_{1,(e)}X_{(e)} = Q_{2,(e)}$ is given by*

$$X_{(e)} = \left(\mathrm{Re}\left(V_{(e)}\right) + \frac{i}{\sqrt{-p}}\mathrm{Im}\left(V_{(e)}\right)\right)\Sigma^{\dagger}\left(\mathrm{Re}\left(U_{(e)}\right) + \frac{i}{\sqrt{-p}}\mathrm{Im}\left(U_{(e)}\right)\right)^{*}Q_{2,(e)}.$$

2.2. Elliptic Quaternions

An elliptic quaternion $q_{(E)}$ is denoted as $q_{(E)} = q_{(E),r} + q_{(E),i}i + q_{(E),j}j + q_{(E),k}k$, where $i^2 = k^2 = p < 0$, $j^2 = 1$, $ij = ji = k$, $jk = kj = i$, $ki = ik = pj$, and $q_{(E),r}, q_{(E),i}, q_{(E),j}, q_{(E),k}, p \in \mathbb{R}$. An elliptic quaternion $q_{(E)}$ is denoted in the following forms:

$$q_{(E)} = \left(q_{(E),r} + iq_{(E),i}\right) + \left(q_{(E),j} + iq_{(E),k}\right)j = q_{(e),1}e_1 + q_{(e),2}e_2,$$

where

$$q_{(e),1} = \left(q_{(E),r} + q_{(E),j}\right) + \left(q_{(E),i} + q_{(E),k}\right)i$$

and

$$q_{(e),2} = \left(q_{(E),r} - q_{(E),j}\right) + \left(q_{(E),i} - q_{(E),k}\right)i$$

are elliptic numbers and $e_1 = \frac{1+j}{2}$ and $e_2 = \frac{1-j}{2}$. Clearly, $e_1e_2 = 0$, $e_1 + e_2 = 1$, $e_1 - e_2 = j$ and $e_1^2 = e_1$, $e_2^2 = e_2$. As a result, e_1 and e_2 are disjoint idempotent units.

The multiplication of the two elliptic quaternions $q_{1,(E)} = q_{1,(e),1}e_1 + q_{1,(e),2}e_2$ and $q_{2,(E)} = q_{2,(e),1}e_1 + q_{2,(e),2}e_2$ is defined by

$$q_{1,(E)}q_{2,(E)} = \left(q_{1,(e),1}q_{2,(e),1}\right)e_1 + \left(q_{1,(e),2}q_{2,(e),2}\right)e_2.$$

The conjugate and norm of the elliptic quaternion $q_{(E)} = q_{(e),1}e_1 + q_{(e),2}e_2$ are defined by $\overline{q_{(E)}} = \overline{q_{(e),1}}e_1 + \overline{q_{(e),2}}e_2$ and $\left\|q_{(E)}\right\|_p = \frac{1}{\sqrt{2}}\sqrt{\left(\left\|q_{(e),1}\right\|_p^2 + \left\|q_{(e),2}\right\|_p^2\right)}$, respectively [10].

An elliptic quaternion matrix $Q_{(E)}$ is represented

$$\begin{aligned} Q_{(E)} &= Q_{(E),r} + Q_{(E),i}i + Q_{(E),j}j + Q_{(E),k}k = \left(Q_{(E),r} + Q_{(E),i}i\right) + \left(Q_{(E),j} + Q_{(E),k}i\right)j \\ &= Q_{(e),1}e_1 + Q_{(e),2}e_2, \end{aligned}$$

where

$$Q_{(e),1} = \left(Q_{(E),r} + Q_{(E),j}\right) + \left(Q_{(E),i} + Q_{(E),k}\right)i$$

and

$$Q_{(e),2} = \left(Q_{(E),r} - Q_{(E),j}\right) + \left(Q_{(E),i} - Q_{(E),k}\right)i$$

are elliptic matrices, and $Q_{(E),r}, Q_{(E),i}, Q_{(E),j}, Q_{(E),k} \in \mathbb{R}^{m \times n}$. The multiplication of the two elliptic quaternion matrices $Q_{1,(E)} = Q_{1,(e),1}e_1 + Q_{1,(e),2}e_2$ and $Q_{2,(E)} = Q_{2,(e),1}e_1 + Q_{2,(e),2}e_2$ is defined by

$$Q_{1,(E)}Q_{2,(E)} = \left(Q_{1,(e),1}Q_{2,(e),1}\right)e_1 + \left(Q_{1,(e),2}Q_{2,(e),2}\right)e_2.$$

The conjugate, transpose, conjugate transpose, and Frobenius norm of elliptic quaternion matrix $Q_{(E)} = Q_{(e),1}e_1 + Q_{(e),2}e_2 \in \mathbb{H}_p^{m \times n}$ are defined by $\overline{Q_{(E)}} = \overline{Q_{(e),1}}e_1 + \overline{Q_{(e),2}}e_2$, $Q^T_{(E)} = Q^T_{(e),1}e_1 + Q^T_{(e),2}e_2$, $Q^*_{(E)} = \overline{Q^T_{(e),1}}e_1 + \overline{Q^T_{(e),2}}e_2$ and $\left\|Q_{(E)}\right\|_p = \frac{1}{\sqrt{2}}\sqrt{\left\|Q_{(e),1}\right\|_p^2 + \left\|Q_{(e),2}\right\|_p^2}$, respectively [18,20].

Theorem 1 ([15]). *Let $Q_{(E)} = Q_{(e),1}e_1 + Q_{(e),2}e_2 \in \mathbb{H}_p^{n \times n}$. Suppose that $\lambda_{(e),1}$ and $\lambda_{(e),2}$ are eigenvalues of elliptic matrices $Q_{(e),1}$ and $Q_{(e),2}$ corresponding to the eigenvectors $x_{(e),1}$ and $x_{(e),2}$, respectively. Then, $\lambda_{(E)} = \lambda_{(e),1}e_1 + \lambda_{(e),2}e_2$ is an eigenvalue of $Q_{(E)}$ corresponding to the eigenvector $x_{(E)} = x_{(e),1}e_1 + x_{(e),2}e_2$.*

Theorem 2 ([15]). *Let $Q_{(E)} = Q_{(e),1}e_1 + Q_{(e),2}e_2 \in \mathbb{H}_p^{m \times n}$. Suppose that singular-value decompositions of $Q_{(e),1}$ and $Q_{(e),2}$ are $Q_{(e),1} = U_{(e),1}\Sigma_1 V^*_{(e),1}$ and $Q_{(e),2} = U_{(e),2}\Sigma_2 V^*_{(e),2}$, respectively. Then, the singular-value decomposition of the elliptic quaternion matrix $Q_{(E)}$ is given by $Q_{(E)} = U_{(E)}\Sigma_{(E)}V^*_{(E)}$, where $\Sigma_{(E)} = \Sigma_1 e_1 + \Sigma_2 e_2$ is hyperbolic matrix since Σ_1 and Σ_2 are real matrices ($\Sigma_{(E)}$ is real matrix if and only if $\Sigma_1 = \Sigma_2$). Moreover $U_{(E)} = U_{(e),1}e_1 + U_{(e),2}e_2$ and $V_{(E)} = V_{(e),1}e_1 + V_{(e),2}e_2$ are unitary matrices.*

Corollary 1 ([15]). *Let $Q_{(E)} = Q_{(e),1}e_1 + Q_{(e),2}e_2 \in \mathbb{H}_p^{m \times n}$ and $Q_{(E)} = U_{(E)}\Sigma_{(E)}V^*_{(E)}$. Then, the pseudoinverse of $Q_{(E)}$ is $Q^\dagger_{(E)} = V_{(E)}\Sigma^\dagger_{(E)}U^*_{(E)}$, where $\Sigma^\dagger_{(E)} = \Sigma_1^\dagger e_1 + \Sigma_2^\dagger e_2$ and $\Sigma_1, \Sigma_2 \in \mathbb{R}^{m \times n}$.*

Theorem 3 ([15]). *The least squares solution with the minimum norm of the elliptic quaternion matrix equation $Q_{1,(E)}X_{(E)} = Q_{2,(E)}$ is $X_{(E)} = Q^\dagger_{1,(E)}Q_{2,(E)} = V_{(E)}\Sigma^\dagger_{(E)}U^*_{(E)}Q_{2,(E)}$, where $Q_{1,(E)} \in \mathbb{H}_p^{m \times n}$ and $Q_{2,(E)} \in \mathbb{H}_p^{m \times q}$.*

3. MATLAB Toolbox for Elliptic Numbers and Elliptic Quaternions

Elliptic numbers and elliptic quaternions are number systems that confer significant advantages in solving certain mathematical and physical problems. In this section, we introduce a MATLAB toolbox (version 0.1) developed to facilitate computations involving these systems. As illustrated in Figure 1, elliptic quaternions generalize elliptic numbers, reduced biquaternions (commutative quaternions), complex numbers, and real numbers, thereby providing a more expansive computational framework. This generalization enhances the versatility and applicability of the developed toolbox.

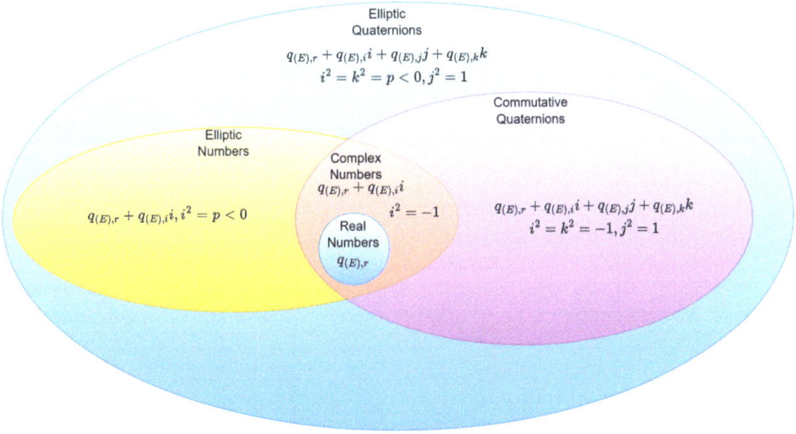

Figure 1. The set of elliptic quaternions and the number sets it contains.

Tables 1 and 2 show the signatures and their descriptions of the functions of the elliptic numbers and elliptic quaternions, respectively, in the toolbox.

Table 1. Key functions of the elliptic numbers.

Function Name	**Description**
ellipticcomplex2complexnumber($q_{(e)}$)	Returns the complex number (or matrix) to which the elliptic number (or matrix) is isomorphic.
complexnumber2ellipticcomplex(p-value, complex)	Returns the elliptic number (or matrix) to which the complex number (or matrix) is isomorphic.
elliptic_n_addition($q_{(e)}$,$p_{(e)}$)	Returns the sum of two elliptic numbers (or matrices).
elliptic_n_subtraction($q_{(e)}$,$p_{(e)}$)	Returns the difference of two elliptic numbers (or matrices).
elliptic_n_product($q_{(e)}$,$p_{(e)}$)	Returns the product of two elliptic numbers (or matrices).
elliptic_n_transpose($Q_{(e)}$)	Returns the transpose of the elliptic matrix $Q_{(e)}$.
elliptic_n_conjugate($Q_{(e)}$)	Returns the conjugate of the elliptic matrix $Q_{(e)}$.
elliptic_n_hermitianconjugate($Q_{(e)}$)	Returns the Hermitian conjugate of the elliptic matrix $Q_{(e)}$.
elliptic_n_eig($Q_{(e)}$)	$[D_{(e)}, V_{(e)}]$ = elliptic_n_eig($Q_{(e)}$) returns diagonal matrix $D_{(e)}$ of eigenvalues and matrix $V_{(e)}$ whose columns are the corresponding eigenvectors, so that $Q_{(e)}V_{(e)} = V_{(e)}D_{(e)}$.
elliptic_n_svd($Q_{(e)}$)	$[U_e, S_e, V_e]$ = elliptic_n_svd($Q_{(e)}$) performs a singular-value decomposition of elliptic matrix $Q_{(e)}$, such that $Q_{(e)} = U_{(e)}S_{(e)}V^*_{(e)}$.
elliptic_n_pinv($Q_{(e)}$)	Returns the pseudoinverse of the elliptic matrix $Q_{(e)}$.
elliptic_n_rank($Q_{(e)}$)	Returns the rank of the elliptic matrix $Q_{(e)}$.
elliptic_n_lss($Q_{(e)}$, $P_{(e)}$)	Returns the least squares solution of the elliptic matrix equation $Q_{(e)}X_{(e)} = P_{(e)}$ and the least squares error.

Table 2. Key functions of the elliptic quaternions.

Function Name	Description
e1e2form($q_{(E)}$)	Returns the elliptic quaternion (or elliptic quaternion matrix) given in ijk-form in e_1-e_2 form.
ijkform(e1_part,e2_part)	Returns the elliptic quaternion (or elliptic quaternion matrix) given in e_1-e_2 form in ijk form.
elliptic_q_conjugate_1($q_{(E)}$)	Returns the 1st conjugate of the elliptic quaternion (or elliptic quaternion matrix).
elliptic_q_conjugate_2($q_{(E)}$)	Returns the 2nd conjugate of the elliptic quaternion (or elliptic quaternion matrix).
elliptic_q_conjugate_3($q_{(E)}$)	Returns the 3rd conjugate of the elliptic quaternion (or elliptic quaternion matrix).
elliptic_q_addition($q_{(E)}$,$p_{(E)}$)	Returns the sum of two elliptic quaternions (or elliptic quaternion matrices).
elliptic_q_subtraction($q_{(E)}$,$p_{(E)}$)	Returns the difference of two elliptic quaternions (or elliptic quaternion matrices).
elliptic_q_product($q_{(E)}$,$p_{(E)}$)	Returns the product of two elliptic quaternions (or elliptic quaternion matrices).
elliptic_q_scalar(lamda,$q_{(E)}$)	Returns the lambda scalar multiple of the elliptic quaternion (or elliptic quaternion matrix).
elliptic_q_norm($q_{(E)}$)	Returns the norm of the elliptic quaternion (or elliptic quaternion matrix).
elliptic_q_transpose($Q_{(E)}$)	Returns the transpose of the elliptic quaternion matrix.
elliptic_q_hermitianconjugate($Q_{(E)}$)	Returns the conjugate transpose of the elliptic quaternion matrix.
elliptic_q_eig($Q_{(E)}$)	[$D_{(E)}$,$V_{(E)}$] = elliptic_q_eig($Q_{(E)}$) returns diagonal matrix $D_{(E)}$ of eigenvalues and matrix $V_{(E)}$ whose columns are the corresponding eigenvectors, so that $Q_{(E)}V_{(E)} = V_{(E)}D_{(E)}$.
elliptic_q_svd($Q_{(E)}$)	[$U_{(E)}$,$S_{(E)}$,$V_{(E)}$] = elliptic_q_svd($Q_{(E)}$) performs a singular-value decomposition of elliptic quaternion matrix $Q_{(E)}$, such that $Q_{(E)} = U_{(E)}S_{(E)}V^*_{(E)}$.
elliptic_q_pseudoinverse($Q_{(E)}$)	Returns the pseudoinverse of the elliptic quaternion matrix.
elliptic_q_lss($Q_{(E)}$,$P_{(E)}$)	Returns the least squares solution of the elliptic quaternion matrix equation $Q_{(E)}X_{(E)} = P_{(E)}$ and the least squares error.
elliptic_q_qrank($Q_{(E)}$)	Returns the rank of the elliptic matrix.

To enable the toolbox to process any elliptic number, the user must specify its real part, imaginary part, and the associated p-value. For example, to initialize the elliptic number $q_{(e)} = 1 + 2i$ and the elliptic matrix $Q_{(e)} \in \mathbb{C}^{3\times3}_{-5}$ (initialized with random numbers) for $p = -5$, the functions in the Listing 1 should be invoke.

Listing 1. MATLAB console output of the function elliptic_number().

```
>> q_e=elliptic_number(1,2,-5)
q_e =
  elliptic_number with properties:
    r_part: 1
    i_part: 2
    j_part: 0
    k_part: 0
         p: -5
>> Q_e=elliptic_number(rand(3),rand(3),-5);
>> Q_e.r_part
ans =
    0.8147    0.9134    0.2785
    0.9058    0.6324    0.5469
    0.1270    0.0975    0.9575
>> Q_e.i_part
ans =
    0.9649    0.9572    0.1419
    0.1576    0.4854    0.4218
    0.9706    0.8003    0.9157
```

Initializing the elliptic quaternions $q_{(E)} = 1 + 2i + 3j + 4k$ and $p_{(E)} = -1 + 3i + 2j + 5k$ for $p = -3$ and their multiplication is carried out as in the Listing 2:

Listing 2. MATLAB console output of the functions elliptic_quaternion() and elliptic_q_product().

```
>> q_E=elliptic_quaternion(1,2,3,4,-3)
q_E =
  elliptic_quaternion with properties:
    r_part: 1
    i_part: 2
    j_part: 3
    k_part: 4
         p: -3
>> p_E=elliptic_quaternion(-1,3,2,5,-3)
p_E =
  elliptic_quaternion with properties:
    r_part: -1
    i_part: 3
    j_part: 2
    k_part: 5
         p: -3
>> elliptic_q_product(q_E,p_E)
ans =
  elliptic_quaternion with properties:
    r_part: -73
    i_part: 24
    j_part: -67
    k_part: 14
         p: -3
```

The singular-value decomposition of the elliptic quaternion matrix $Q_{(E)} \in \mathbb{H}_{-3}^{3\times3}$, initialized with random numbers for $p = -3$, is conducted as in the Listing 3:

Listing 3. MATLAB console output of the functions elliptic_quaternion() and elliptic_q_svd().

```
>> Q_E=elliptic_quaternion(rand(3),rand(3),rand(3),rand(3),-3);
>> Q_E.r_part
ans =
    0.7094    0.6797    0.1190
    0.7547    0.6551    0.4984
    0.2760    0.1626    0.9597
>> Q_E.i_part
ans =
    0.3404    0.7513    0.6991
    0.5853    0.2551    0.8909
    0.2238    0.5060    0.9593
>> Q_E.j_part
ans =
    0.5472    0.2575    0.8143
    0.1386    0.8407    0.2435
    0.1493    0.2543    0.9293
>> Q_E.k_part
ans =
    0.3500    0.6160    0.8308
    0.1966    0.4733    0.5853
    0.2511    0.3517    0.5497
```

```
>> [U_E,S_E,V_E]=elliptic_q_svd(Q_E);
>> U_E.r_part
ans =
    0.0688    0.3288   -0.0097
   -0.4539    0.4338    0.2619
   -0.3010   -0.3188    0.0270
>> U_E.i_part
ans =
   -0.1527    0.0660    0.1851
   -0.2815    0.1238   -0.1460
   -0.1981   -0.2507    0.2152
>> U_E.j_part
ans =
   -0.4307   -0.2540   -0.5746
    0.1073    0.1145    0.0292
   -0.0673   -0.3711    0.3302
>> U_E.k_part
ans =
   -0.1469    0.1349    0.0244
    0.0346   -0.1510   -0.1751
   -0.0337    0.0732   -0.1741
>> S_E.r_part
ans =
    3.9299         0         0
         0    1.0719         0
         0         0    0.5868
>> S_E.j_part
ans =
    2.5800         0         0
         0    0.2531         0
         0         0    0.0769
>> V_E.r_part
ans =
   -0.4288    0.5420   -0.2491
   -0.0871    0.2363    0.6669
   -0.7349   -0.5820    0.1505
>> V_E.i_part
ans =
         0         0         0
   -0.0063    0.0205    0.0573
    0.1485    0.0211    0.0042
>> V_E.j_part
ans =
    0.0523   -0.2479   -0.6294
   -0.4315    0.4510   -0.2146
   -0.0037   -0.0433   -0.0434
>> V_E.k_part
ans =
         0         0         0
    0.0549    0.1030   -0.0367
   -0.0378   -0.0593   -0.0644
```

The minimum error and least squares solution of the matrix equation $Q_{(E)}X_{(E)} = P_{(E)}$, where $P_{(E)} \in \mathbb{H}_{-3}^{3\times 5}$ is initialized with random numbers for $p = -3$, are carried out as in the Listing 4:

Listing 4. MATLAB console output of the functions elliptic_quaternion() and elliptic_q_lss().

```
>> P_E=elliptic_quaternion(rand(3,5),rand(3,5),rand(3,5),rand(3,5),-
   3);
>> P_E.r_part
ans =
    0.1524    0.9961    0.1067    0.7749    0.0844
    0.8258    0.0782    0.9619    0.8173    0.3998
    0.5383    0.4427    0.0046    0.8687    0.2599
>> P_E.i_part
ans =
    0.8001    0.1818    0.1361    0.5499    0.6221
    0.4314    0.2638    0.8693    0.1450    0.3510
    0.9106    0.1455    0.5797    0.8530    0.5132
>> P_E.j_part
ans =
    0.4018    0.1233    0.4173    0.9448    0.3377
    0.0760    0.1839    0.0497    0.4909    0.9001
    0.2399    0.2400    0.9027    0.4893    0.3692
>> P_E.k_part
ans =
    0.1112    0.2417    0.1320    0.5752    0.3532
    0.7803    0.4039    0.9421    0.0598    0.8212
    0.3897    0.0965    0.9561    0.2348    0.0154
>> [Solution, e_error]=elliptic_q_lss(Q_E,P_E);
>> e_error=
  5.3613e-15
>> Solution.r_part
ans =
    0.2340    0.7035    0.8838   -0.1262   -0.2939
    0.8401    0.2717   -0.8857    0.9705    0.7762
    0.7036   -0.0697    0.3243    0.7171    0.4535
>> Solution.i_part
ans =
   -0.2895    0.0276   -0.8655   -0.0185   -0.0841
    0.3573   -0.2956    0.8372   -0.4357    0.3067
   -0.1816   -0.0402    0.3593   -0.0443   -0.1579
>> Solution.j_part
ans =
    0.1977    0.2637    0.5569   -0.3424    0.7052
   -0.8351   -0.7083   -0.0969   -0.1652   -0.4677
   -0.0960    0.2117    0.6330   -0.3586   -0.2543
>> Solution.k_part
ans =
   -0.2619    0.1894   -0.5397    0.1359   -0.1520
   -0.1278    0.2092   -0.1541   -0.0603    0.1394
    0.3473   -0.0198   -0.0614    0.1691   -0.0101
```

In the example above, the obtained minimum error value is 5.3613×10^{-15} for $p = -3$. However, changing the value of p can further reduce the minimum error. Figure 2 shows the minimum errors corresponding to p-values of the range $-5 \leq p \leq -0.1$ with a step size

0.2. The graph demonstrates that the minimum error 1.2057×10^{-15} obtained for $p = -0.8$ is smaller than the minimum error obtained for $p = -3$.

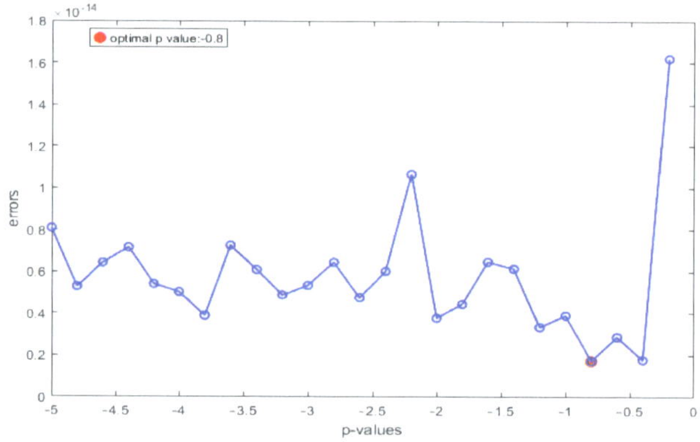

Figure 2. Minimum errors of least squares solution of the matrix equation $Q_{(E)}X_{(E)} = P_{(E)}$ according to p-values.

In conclusion, the value of p in the elliptic quaternion space emerges as a critical hyperparameter that directly affects the solution to a problem addressed in this space. This finding highlights the significant role of selecting the appropriate p-value in solving any problem and emphasizes that it is a key factor in reducing the error rate. Therefore, optimizing the p-value is important in enhancing solution quality and achieving lower error rates.

4. Color Image Processing Using Singular-Value Decomposition of Elliptic Quaternion Matrices

Elliptic quaternions are distinguished by their composition, comprising one real part alongside three imaginary counterparts. Within the realm of color imagery, particularly in the RGB color space framework, each pixel is constituted by three primary color components, namely red, green, and blue. By drawing an analogy from this, it can be postulated that each pixel within a color image can be analogously represented as a purely imaginary elliptic quaternion, wherein the real component is nullified. In such a representational schema, the red, green, and blue color components are analogically mapped to the i, j, and k components of the purely imaginary elliptic quaternions, respectively. By following this premise, it is possible to articulate that a color image, defined by a dimensional matrix of $m \times n$ pixels, can be succinctly expressed through an elliptic quaternion matrix:

$$f_{(E)} = R_{(E),i}i + G_{(E),j}j + B_{(E),k}k,$$

where the matrices $R_{(E),i}$, $G_{(E),j}$, and $B_{(E),k} \in \mathbb{R}^{m \times n}$ represent the red, green, and blue component matrices of a color image, respectively. This representation is visually illustrated in Figure 3 [18].

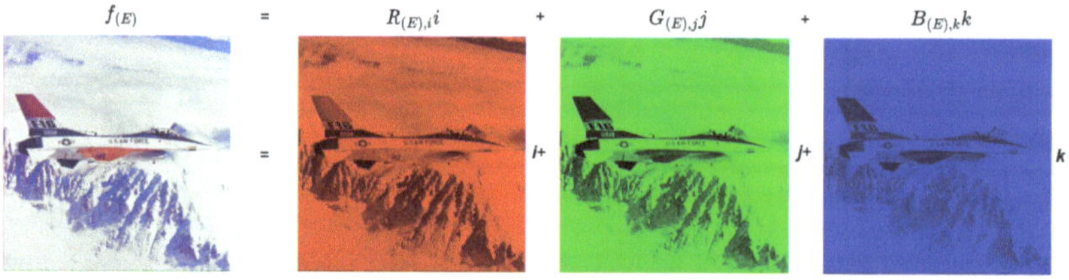

Figure 3. Elliptic quaternion matrix representation of the color image airplane.png.

The signatures and descriptions of the image processing functions in the Toolbox are presented in Table 3. The experimental results in this work demonstrate that elliptic quaternion methods outperform other hypercomplex number-based approaches in image analysis and processing (Tables 4–8). The test images used in the experiments of the developed techniques are given in Figure 4. On the other hand, the p-value in the algebra of elliptic quaternions directly affects the performance of the problem modeled in this space (see Figures 11, 13 and 19). As a result, choosing the most appropriate elliptic quaternion space for the problem under consideration (choosing the p-value that gives the most optimal solution to the problem) and the elliptical behavior of many physical systems make this number system more advantageous in image processing. Therefore, incorporating the elliptic quaternion number system into image processing may solve various problems related to time, memory, and performance.

Table 3. Key image processing functions in the toolbox.

Function Name	Description
`image2elliptic_q(I,p-value)`	Returns the elliptic quaternion matrix representation of the image. I (Type: uint8, array): The input image in RGB color space p-value (Type: negative double)
`elliptic_q2image(`$f_{(E)}$`)`	Returns the RGB space representation of an image represented by an elliptical quaternion matrix. $f_{(E)}$ (Type: Object): The elliptic quaternion matrix representation of the image.
`elliptic_q_eigenimage(`$f_{(E)}$`,h)`	Returns the desired eigenimages of the image in the elliptic quaternion matrix space. h (Type: integer): Specifies the index of the eigenimage to be computed.
`elliptic_q_singularvalues(`$f_{(E)}$`)`	It shows the change of singular values of the image in the elliptical quaternion matrix space.
`elliptic_q_image_reconstruction(`$f_{(E)}$`,k)`	It compresses the image according to the desired k value in the elliptical quaternion matrix space. k (Type: integer): The number of singular values to retain for the reconstruction.
`elliptic_q_optimal_p_for_psnr(`$f_{(E)}$`)`	Returns the optimal p (for psnr) value for image compression performed in elliptic quaternion matrix space.
`elliptic_q_optimal_p_for_mse(`$f_{(E)}$`)`	Returns the optimal p (for mse) value for image compression performed in elliptic quaternion matrix space.
`elliptic_q_embedding_watermarking(`$f_{(E)}$`,`$g_{(E)}$`,alpha)`	The embedding_elliptic_watermarking function embeds a watermark into an object using elliptic quaternion matrix algebra. $f_{(E)}$ (Type: Object): The primary object to be watermarked. $g_{(E)}$ (Type: Object): The watermark object to be embedded. alpha (Type: Double): The embedding strength parameter.
`elliptic_q_extraction_watermarking(`$f_{(E)}$`,`$g_{(E)}$`,U_w,V_w,alpha)`	The extraction_elliptic_watermarking function extracts a watermark from a watermarked object using the elliptic quaternion matrix algebra. $f_{(E)}$ (Type: Object): The watermarked object from which the watermark is to be extracted. $g_{(E)}$ (Type: Object): The original, unwatermarked object. U_w (Type: Object): The U component of the watermark's singular-value decomposition. V_w (Type: Object): The V component of the watermark's singular-value decomposition.
`elliptic_q_watermarking_optimal_p_for_psnr(`$f_{(E)}$`,`$g_{(E)}$`,alpha)`	Finds the optimal p (for psnr) for watermarking using the elliptic quaternion matrix algebra $f_{(E)}$ (Type: Object): The primary object to be watermarked. $g_{(E)}$ (Type: Object): The watermark object to be embedded.
`elliptic_q_watermarking_optimal_p_for_mse(`$f_{(E)}$`,`$g_{(E)}$`,alpha)`	Finds the optimal p (for mse) for watermarking using the elliptic quaternion matrix algebra. $f_{(E)}$ (Type: Object): The primary object to be watermarked. $g_{(E)}$ (Type: Object): The watermark object to be embedded.

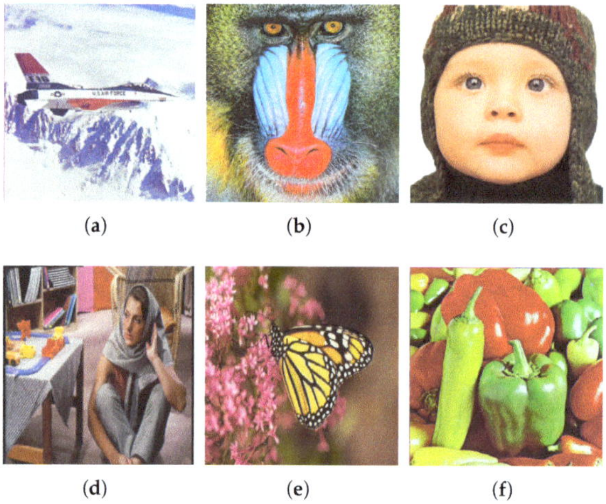

Figure 4. All experimental test images: (**a**) airplane.png (512×512), (**b**) baboon.png (512×512), (**c**) baby.png (512×512), (**d**) Barbara.png (576×720), (**e**) monarch.png (512×768), and (**f**) peppers.png (512×512).

For $p = -0.5$, the elliptic quaternion matrix representation of the test image airplane.png with a resolution of 512×512 pixels is obtained as in the Listing 5:

Listing 5. MATLAB console output of the function image2elliptic().

```
>> f_E=image2elliptic("test_images/airplane.png",-0.5)
f_E =
  elliptic_quaternion with properties:
    r_part: [512x512 double]
    i_part: [512x512 double]
    j_part: [512x512 double]
    k_part: [512x512 double]
         p: -0.5
```

On the other hand, a color image can also be represented using elliptic quaternionic singular-value decomposition (ESVD) as

$$f_{(E)} = U_{(E)}\Sigma_{(E)}V^*_{(E)},$$

where the matrices $U_{(E)}$ and $V_{(E)}$ are unitary matrices and $\Sigma_{(E)}$ is a hyperbolic matrix. Various image processing techniques can be applied to a color image after applying ESVD without decomposing it into three-channel images. In the subsequent section, principal component analysis, image compression, image restoration, and watermarking techniques were applied to a color image using ESVD.

4.1. Eigenimages of Color Images

The ESVD of any color image can be expressed as

$$f_{(E)} = U_{(E)}\Sigma_{(E)}V^*_{(E)} = \sum_{i=1}^{R} \sigma_{i(E)}\left(u_{i(E)} \otimes v^*_{i(E)}\right), \tag{1}$$

where $u_{i(E)} \in \mathbb{H}_p^{m\times 1}$ and $v_{i(E)} \in \mathbb{H}_p^{n\times 1}$ are elliptic quaternionic vectors, and R represents the rank of the elliptic quaternion matrix $f_{(E)}$. Each term $u_{i(E)} \otimes v^*_{i(E)}$ is called an elliptic quaternion-valued eigenimage of the image. Consequently, the color image $f_{(E)}$ can be thought of as a linear combination of R eigenimages. The first eigenimage, shown in Figure 5, of the test image baby.png is obtained with the function in Listing 6:

Listing 6. MATLAB console output of the functions image2elliptic() and elliptic_q_eigenimage().

```
>> f_E=image2elliptic("test_images/baby.png",-0.5)
>> elliptic_q_eigenimage(f_E,1)
```

Figure 5. The first eigenimage of the test image baby.png.

Moreover, normalized absolute versions of the third, tenth, and twenty-fifth eigenimages of the test image baby.png are also given in Figure 6.

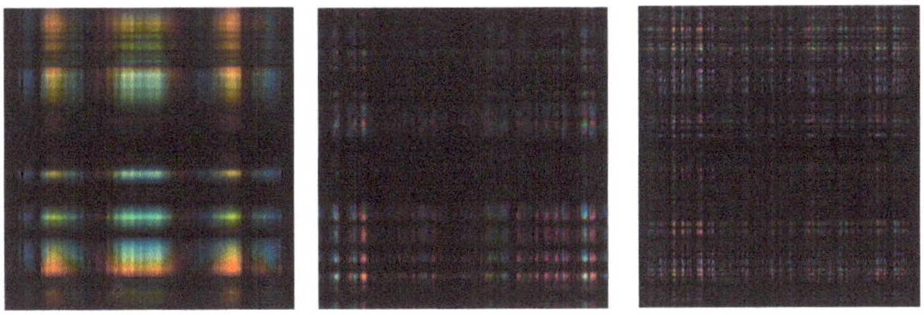

(**a**) (**b**) (**c**)

Figure 6. Third, tenth, and twenty-fifth eigenimages of the test image baby.png. (**a**) $u_{3(E)} \otimes v^*_{3(E)}$. (**b**) $u_{10(E)} \otimes v^*_{10(E)}$. (**c**) $u_{25(E)} \otimes v^*_{25(E)}$.

As seen in Figure 6, the initial eigenimages correspond to the low-frequency components of the original image, capturing the broad, smooth variations and overall structure. In contrast, the subsequent eigenimages represent the high-frequency components, which detail the finer, more intricate features and textures. This distinction between low- and high-frequency components allows for a more subtle analysis and manipulation of the image data.

4.2. Color Image Compression with ESVD

When color images are represented as illustrated in Equation (1), the variation in their singular values can be examined using the function provided in Listing 7. The graph depicted in Figure 7, generated by the function elliptic_q_singularvalues(), demonstrates the variation of the singular values for the test image airplane.png:

Listing 7. MATLAB console output of the functions image2elliptic() and elliptic_q_singularvalues().

```
>> f_E=image2elliptic("test_images/airplane.png",-0.5);
>> elliptic_q_singularvalues(f_E);
```

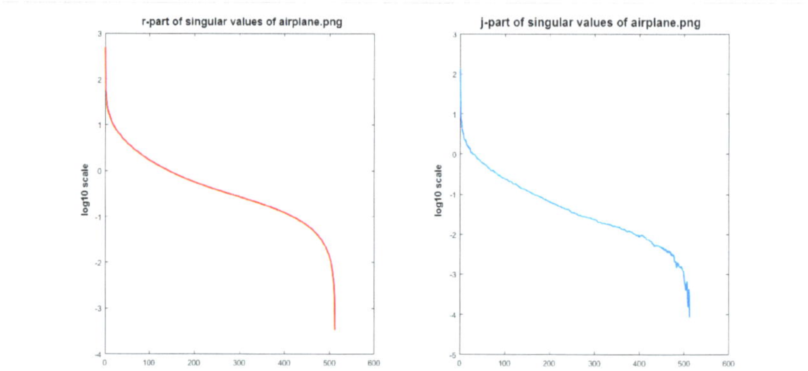

Figure 7. Graphs of singular values of the test images airplane.png.

The graphs of singular values of other test images for $p = -0.5$ are shown in Figure 8:

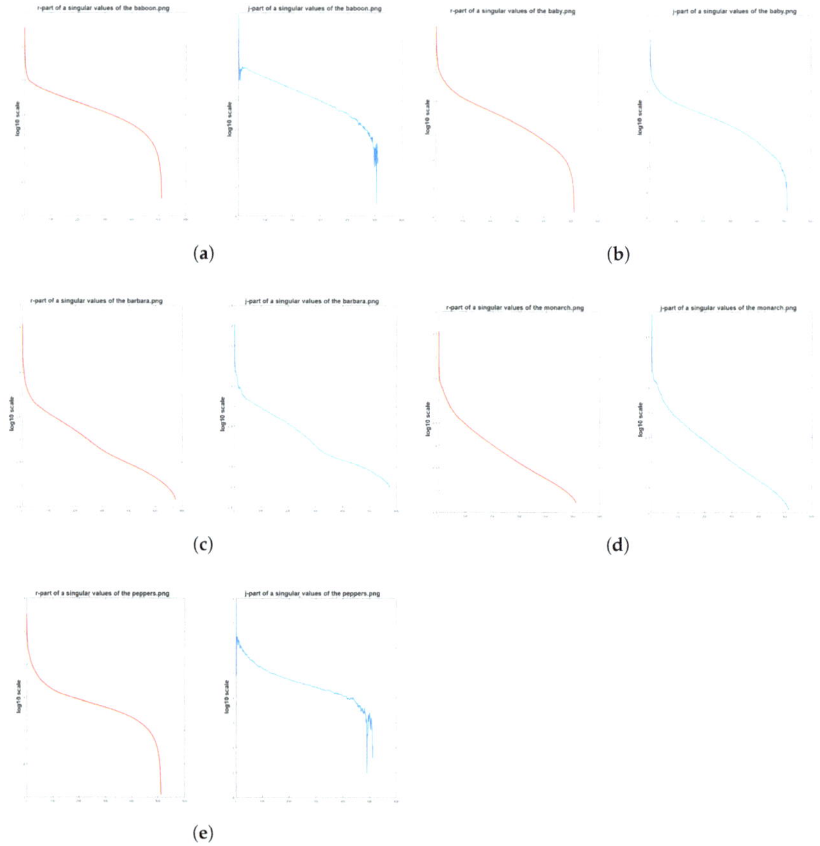

Figure 8. Graphs of singular values of test images: (**a**) baboon.png, (**b**) baby.png, (**c**) Barbara.png, (**d**) monarch.png, and (**e**) pepper.png.

As seen in Figures 7 and 8, the singular values of test images decrease very rapidly. Therefore, even for small values of K satisfying $K < R$, a good approximation of a color image can be achieved. To approximate the matrix $f_{(E)}$ in Equation (1) for $K < R$, the equation

$$f_{(E)} = \sum_{i=1}^{K} \sigma_{i(E)} \left(u_{i(E)} \otimes v_{i(E)}^{*} \right)$$

can be used. In this case, the storage space required to store a color image reduces from $3mn$ to $K(m+n+2)$. The steps for image compression with ESVD are provided in Figure 9:

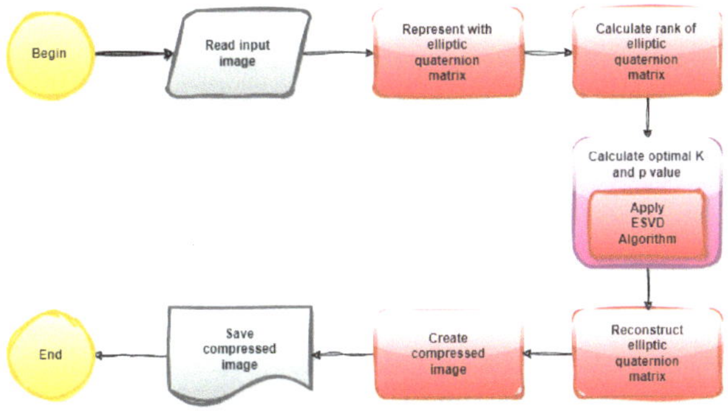

Figure 9. Flowchart of image compression using ESVD.

The function in Listing 8 reconstructs the test image airplane.png for $p = -0.5$ and $K = 50$. Figure 10 shows the original image airplane.png and the compressed version side-by-side.

Listing 8. MATLAB console output of the function elliptic_q_image_reconstruction().

```
>> [I_c,I_o,E_c,E_o]=elliptic_q_image_reconstruction(f_E,50);
```

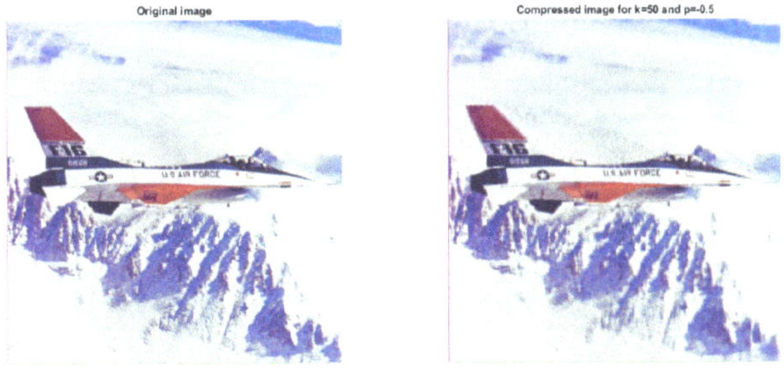

Figure 10. PSNR and MSE results of the reconstruction of the test image airplane.png for $p = -0.5$ and $K = 50$: PSNR = 30.4527; MSE = 9.0100×10^{-4}.

The functions in Listing 9 draw surfaces, which are represented in Figure 11, showing the PSNR (peak signal-to-noise ratio) and MSE (mean squared error) values corresponding to each K and p-value of the test image airplane.png for $K = 10:20:150$ and $p = -5:0.1:-0.1$. The red dots indicate optimal p-values.

Listing 9. MATLAB console output of the functions elliptic_q_optimal_p_for_psnr() and optimal_p_for_mse().

```
>> elliptic_q_optimal_p_for_psnr(f_E);
>> optimal_p_for_mse(f_E);
```

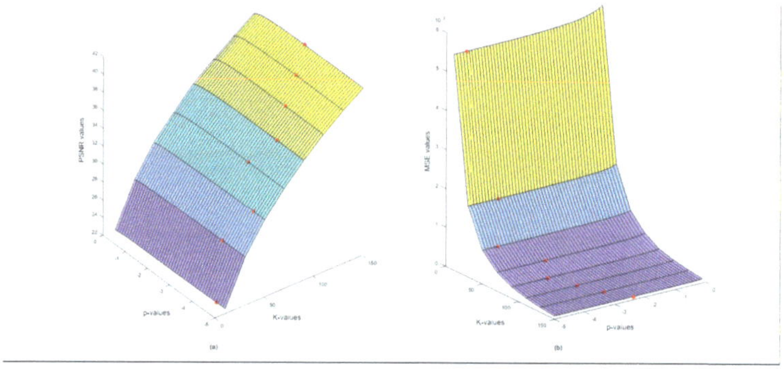

Figure 11. Optimal p-values for PSNR and MSE for the test image aiplane.png.

The run time comparison of the proposed ESVD compression method along with the Separable method (compression method obtained by applying singular-value decomposition separately to R, G, and B components) and hypercomplex-based compression methods, such as QSVD (performs singular-value decomposition on real quaternion matrices [21]) and RBSVD (performs singular-value decomposition on reduced biquaternion matrices [22]), on the test images are provided in Figure 12.

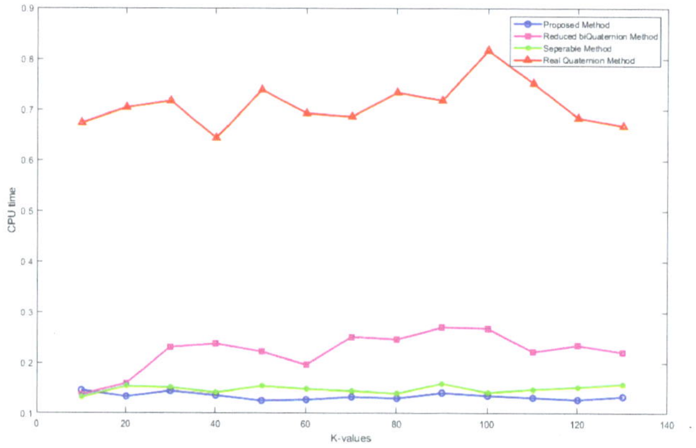

Figure 12. Run time comparison of the methods: Separable, QSVD, RBSVD, and ESVD (proposed method) on the test image airplane.png.

The PSNR and MSE values of all other test images according to the given K and p-values are given in Figure 13.

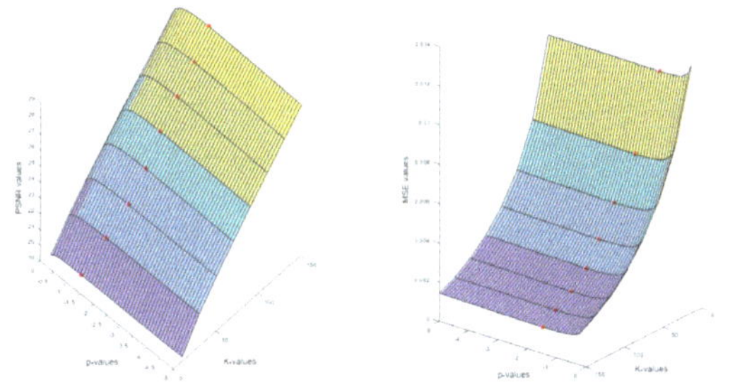

(**a**)

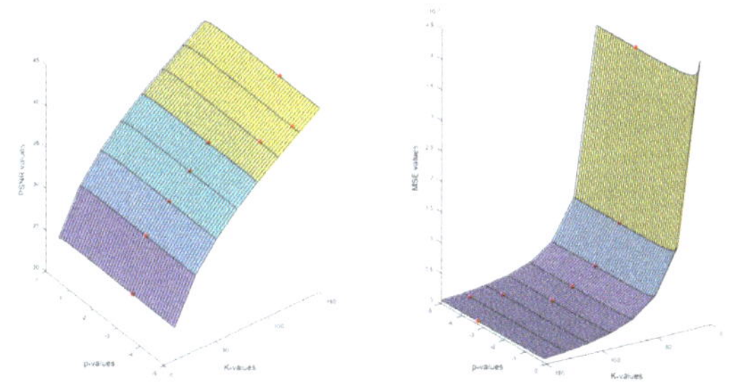

(**b**)

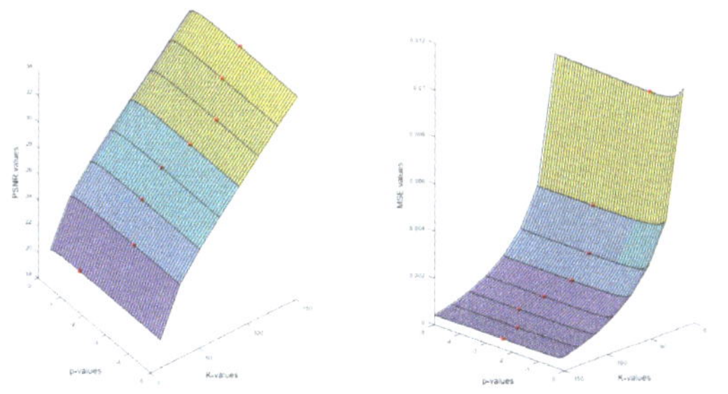

(**c**)

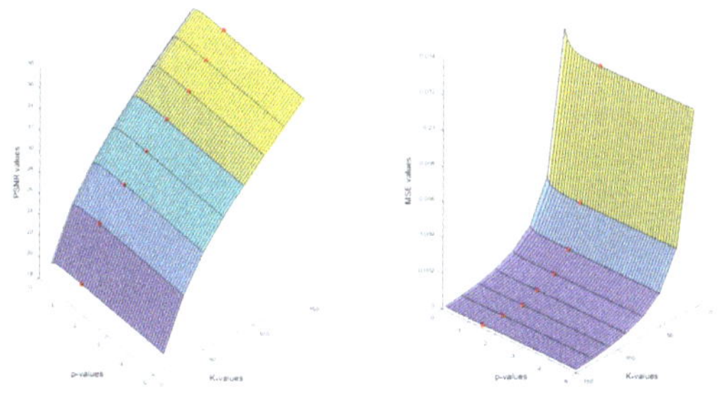

(**d**)

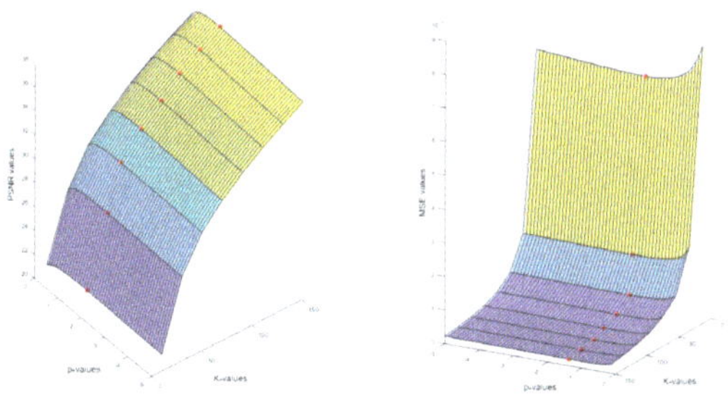

(**e**)

Figure 13. Optimal *p*-values for the PSNR and MSE values of the test images: (**a**) baboon.png, (**b**) baby.png, (**c**) Barbara.png, (**d**) monarch.png, and (**e**) pepper.png.

The PSNR and MSE values of the proposed ESVD compression method, along with the Separable method and hypercomplex-based compression methods, such as QSVD and RBSVD, on the test images are provided in Tables 4 and 5.

Table 4. Compression results (PSNR) of Separable, QSVD, RBSVD, and ESVD (proposed method) methods on the test images.

Methods	K	airplane.png	baboon.png	baby.png	Barbara.png	monarch.png	peppers.png
Seperable	10	22.47626	19.22365	23.97807	20.17889	19.47392	21.49341
QSVD	10	22.4593	19.2345	23.9613	20.1977	19.4925	21.4130
RBSVD	10	22.5009	19.3129	24.0043	20.2469	19.561	21.4875
ESVD (Proposed Method)	10	22.5705 ($p = -4.6$)	19.3139 ($p = -1.2$)	24.0406 ($p = -3.2$)	20.2534 ($p = -1.4$)	19.5665 ($p = -1.4$)	21.5484 ($p = -1.8$)
Seperable	50	30.53264	22.36072	32.18642	25.47954	27.17356	29.93859
QSVD	50	30.5012	22.3650	32.2036	25.5249	27.1818	29.9245
RBSVD	50	30.5456	22.504	32.2748	25.6348	27.2814	30.0184
ESVD (Proposed Method)	50	30.6426 ($p = -4.5$)	22.5321 ($p = -1.7$)	32.3295 ($p = -3$)	25.6730 ($p = -2.4$)	27.2899 ($p = -1.5$)	30.0510 ($p = -1.5$)
Seperable	90	35.29278	24.87109	36.67848	28.73954	31.59597	33.3296
QSVD	90	35.2712	24.8850	36.7164	28.7752	31.6127	33.3777
RBSVD	90	35.3386	25.0464	36.8034	28.9119	31.7219	33.4616
ESVD (Proposed Method)	90	35.4537 ($p = -3.8$)	25.0826 ($p = -1.7$)	36.8688 ($p = -2.9$)	28.9695 ($p = -2.8$)	31.7322 ($p = -1.6$)	33.4848 ($p = -1.5$)
Seperable	130	38.97289	27.25229	40.30344	31.8519	35.26918	35.70147
QSVD	130	38.9621	27.2877	40.3574	31.8910	35.3170	35.8012
RBSVD	130	39.0576	27.4817	40.4524	32.0467	35.4109	35.891
ESVD (Proposed Method)	130	39.1724 ($p = -2.9$)	27.5193 ($p = -1.6$)	40.5347 ($p = -4.7$)	32.1148 ($p = -2.5$)	35.4245 ($p = -1.6$)	35.9194 ($p = -1.4$)

Table 5. Compression results (MSE) of Separable, QSVD, RBSVD, and ESVD (proposed method) methods on the test images.

Methods	K	airplane.png	baboon.png	baby.png	Barbara.png	monarch.png	peppers.png
Seperable	10	0.00565	0.01196	0.004	0.0096	0.01129	0.00709
QSVD	10	0.0057	0.0119	0.0040	0.0096	0.0112	0.0072
RBSVD	10	0.0056	0.011714	0.004	0.00944	0.0111	0.0071
ESVD (Proposed Method)	10	0.00553 ($p = -4.6$)	0.011711 ($p = -1.2$)	0.00394 ($p = -3.2$)	0.00943 ($p = -1.4$)	0.01104 ($p = -1.4$)	0.00700 ($p = -1.8$)
Seperable	50	0.00088	0.00581	0.0006	0.00283	0.00192	0.00101
QSVD	50	0.00089	0.0058	0.000602	0.0028	0.0019	0.0010
RBSVD	50	0.00088	0.0056	0.00059	0.00273	0.0019	0.00099
ESVD (Proposed Method)	50	0.00086 ($p = -4.5$)	0.0055 ($p = -1.7$)	0.00058 ($p = -3$)	0.00270 ($p = -2.4$)	0.00186 ($p = -1.5$)	0.00098 ($p = -1.5$)
Seperable	90	0.0003	0.00326	0.00021	0.00134	0.00069	0.00046
QSVD	90	0.000297	0.0032	0.000212	0.0013	0.00068	0.000459
RBSVD	90	0.00029	0.00312	0.000208	0.0013	0.000672	0.00045
ESVD (Proposed Method)	90	0.00028 ($p = -3.8$)	0.00310 ($p = -1.7$)	0.000205 ($p = -2.9$)	0.00126 ($p = -2.8$)	0.000671 ($p = -1.6$)	0.00044 ($p = -1.5$)
Seperable	130	0.00013	0.00188	0.00009	0.00065	0.0003	0.0003
QSVD	130	0.000127	0.0019	0.000092	0.00064	0.000293	0.00026
RBSVD	130	0.000124	0.0018	0.00009	0.00062	0.000287	0.000257
ESVD (Proposed Method)	130	0.00012 ($p = -2.9$)	0.0017 ($p = -1.6$)	0.00008 ($p = -4.7$)	0.00061 ($p = -2.5$)	0.000286 ($p = -1.6$)	0.000256 ($p = -1.4$)

4.3. Color Image Restoration with ESVD

Image restoration is a significant concept in the field of image processing. It entails the estimation of a desired, enhanced image from its degraded version. By utilizing prior knowledge of the degradation phenomena, image restoration techniques aim to remove or reduce degradations introduced during image acquisition—such as noise, pixel value errors, out-of-focus blurring, or camera motion blurring. Generally, the degradation process of an image is nonlinear and spatially variant. However, in applied sciences, this process is often considered linear and spatially invariant, allowing it to be examined using the linear shift invariant (LSI) image restoration model [23].

For an LSI system, f is the original image, g is the observed image, H is the point spread function (PSF) of the imaging system, and n is the additional noise; the following matrix-vector formula expresses the process of image degradation: $g = Hf + n$. Image restoration methods attempt to construct an approximation to f from the observation $g = Hf$. The method of least squares estimator minimizes the sum of squared differences between the real observation g and the predicted observation Hf. The function to be minimized can be equivalently written as $\|g - Hf\|^2$ in matrix-vector notation [23].

Since the color image can be represented by the elliptic quaternion matrix, the image restoration problem is transformed into the elliptic least squares problem of the elliptic quaternion matrix equation $g_{(E)} = H_{(E)}f_{(E)}$. As a result, this subsection will present an image restoration model, referred to as ESVD-LSI, based on the singular-value decomposition theory of elliptic quaternion matrices.

In our simulation, Gaussian blur PSFs are employed. Gaussian blur is one of the most prevalent types of blurring that degrades images. It depends on two parameters: the kernel size (hsize) and the standard deviation sigma (σ) of the Gaussian function in MATLAB. The kernel size determines the dimensions of the pixel area considered during the application of the filter, while the sigma value dictates the amount of blurring; higher sigma values produce a more pronounced blurring effect. These parameters are utilized to simulate the effect of an out-of-focus image or to smooth fine details. The simulation steps are as follows:

Step 1: An experimental test image is acquired for the ESVD-LSI image restoration method.
Step 2: PSF is selected manually.
Step 3: The range of p and step size are selected.
Step 4: A degraded image is obtained.

In the backend coding, we denote the image matrix of the input image as f. In this case, the elliptic quaternion matrix representation matrix of f is $f_{(E)} = R_{(E),i}i + G_{(E),j}j + B_{(E),k}k$. The image matrix $R_{(E),i}$ was degraded with the 2-D Gaussian blur (hsize = 15, σ = 1) PSF H to obtain the degraded image matrix $R'_{(E),i}$. Let $H_{(E)} = R'_{(E),i}\left(R_{(E),i}\right)^{\dagger}$. In this case, with the help of $H_{(E)}$, we obtain the elliptic quaternion representation of the degraded image in the form of $g_{(E)} = H_{(E)}f_{(E)}$.

Step 5: According to Theorem 3, the least squares solution with the minimum norm of the elliptic quaternion matrix equation $H_{(E)}f_{(E)} = g_{(E)}$ is

$$f'_{(E)} = H^{\dagger}_{(E)}g_{(E)} = V_{(E)}\Sigma^{\dagger}_{(E)}U^{*}_{(E)}Q_{2,(E)},$$

where $H_{(E)} = U_{(E)}\Sigma_{(E)}V^{*}_{(E)}$.

Step 6: By using the step size and the range of p, the optimal p-value is obtained.
Step 7: Finally, the enhanced image is obtained by reverse sampling from the elliptic quaternion matrices, which will be obtained by choosing the optimal p-value that makes the least squares error the smallest for $\left\|g_{(E)} - H_{(E)}f_{(E)}\right\|^2$.

For the results of the simulation system, the test images are degraded according to the instructions in Step 4 for 2-D Gaussian blur (hsize = 15 and σ = 1). The degraded images are shown in Figure 14.

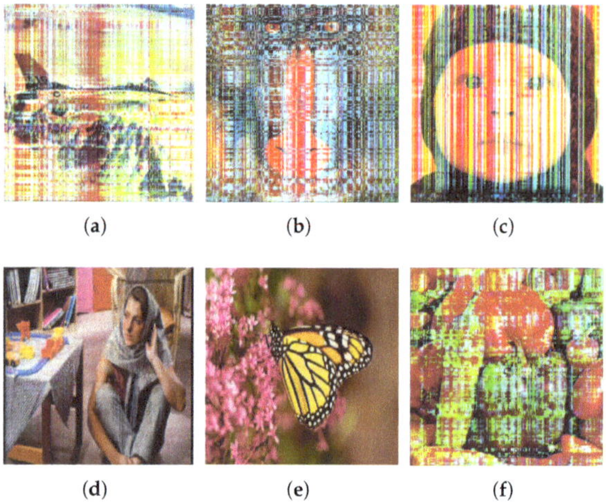

Figure 14. Degraded Images: (a) airplane.png, (b) baboon.png, (c) baby.png, (d) Barbara.png, (e) monarch.png, and (f) peppers.png.

After steps 5, 6, and 7, the restored test images according to optimal p-values are given in Figure 15.

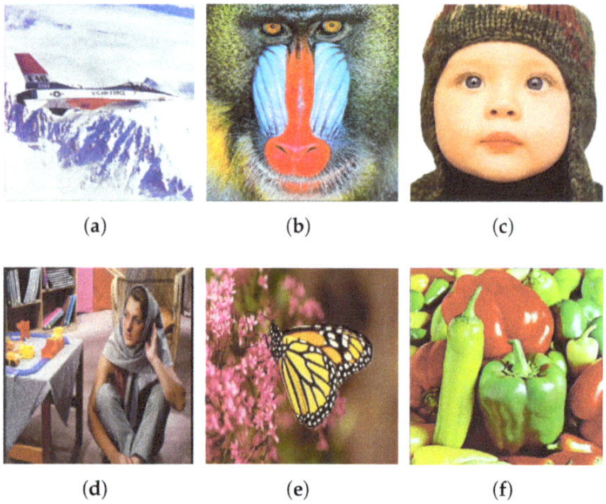

Figure 15. Restored images: (a) airplane.png, (b) baboon.png, (c) baby.png, (d) Barbara.png, (e) monarch.png, and (f) peppers.png.

The least squares errors of the QSVD-LSI and RBSVD-LSI restoration methods using the ESVD-LSI restoration method on the test images are provided in Table 6.

Table 6. Comparison of the least squares errors of QSVD-LSI, RBSVD-LSI, and ESVD-LSI (proposed method) on test images.

Methods	airplane.png	baboon.png	baby.png	Barbara.png	monarch.png	peppers.png
QSVD-LSI	4.1089×10^{-8}	5.6875×10^{-8}	8.9857×10^{-6}	5.5693×10^{-10}	1.7255×10^{-10}	1.1666×10^{-8}
RBSVD-LSI	4.1351×10^{-8}	4.4554×10^{-8}	8.6843×10^{-6}	6.6432×10^{-10}	1.4722×10^{-10}	8.7254×10^{-9}
ESVD-LSI (Proposed Method)	2.9479×10^{-8}	2.9227×10^{-8}	5.6462×10^{-6}	4.0293×10^{-16}	8.3596×10^{-11}	6.2201×10^{-9}

4.4. Color Image Watermarking with ESVD

Watermarking is a crucial technique in the field of digital image processing, used extensively for copyright protection, authentication, and data integrity verification. By embedding a watermark into a digital image, one can ensure the traceability and rightful ownership of the content. This technique finds applications in various domains, including media, healthcare, and secure communications. According to the algorithm in [24], we can give a similar algorithm for color image watermarking by using elliptic quaternion matrix algebra. The flowcharts in Figures 16 and 17 illustrate the elliptical quaternion matrix-based color image watermark embedding and extraction procedures, respectively.

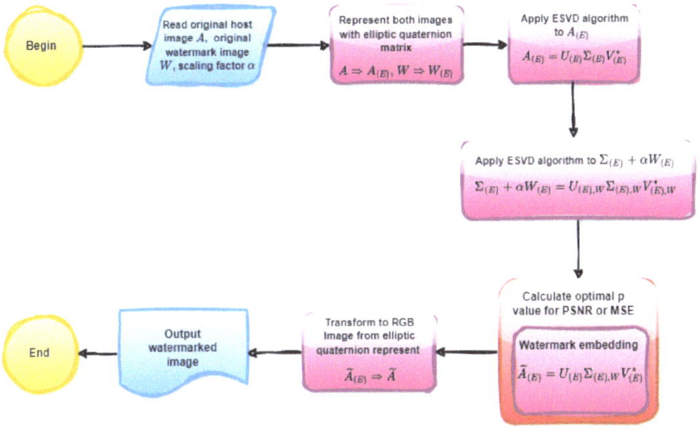

Figure 16. The flowchart of watermark embedding.

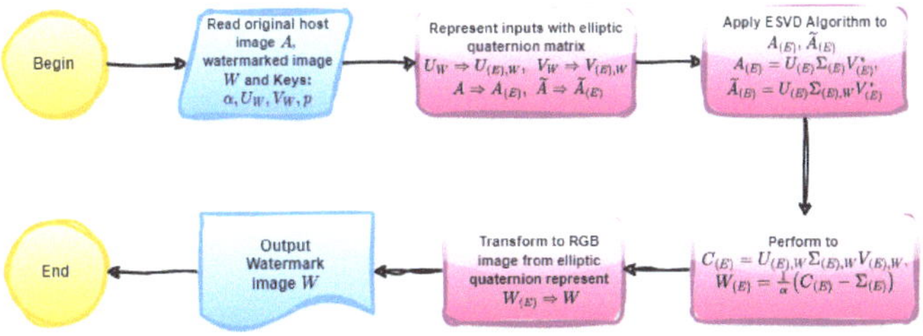

Figure 17. The flowchart of watermark extracting.

The watermark image sau.png in Figure 18b is embedded in the host image airplane.png via the function elliptic_q_embedding_watermarking() as represented in Listing 10.

Listing 10. MATLAB console output of the functions image2elliptic() and elliptic_q_embedding_watermarking().

```
>> f_E=image2elliptic("test_images/airplane.png",-0.5);
>> g_E=image2elliptic("test_images/sau.png",-0.5);
>> elliptic_q_embedding_watermarking(f_E,g_E,0.05);
```

With the parameters $p = -0.5$ and $\alpha = 0.05$. The watermarked image is as in Figure 18c. The PSNR and MSE values between the host and the watermarked images are 59.4340 and 1.1392×10^{-6}, respectively.

(**a**) (**b**) (**c**)

Figure 18. (**a**) Host image; (**b**) watermark image; (**c**) watermarked image.

Figure 19 shows the MSE and PSNR values between the host image and a watermarked image corresponding to p-values given in the range of $-1 \leq p \leq -0.001$ with a step size of 0.001 ($\alpha = 0.05$). According to the graphs, the least MSE is 7.03352×10^{-7}, and the maximum PSNR is 61.5283 for the optimal $p = -0.059$.

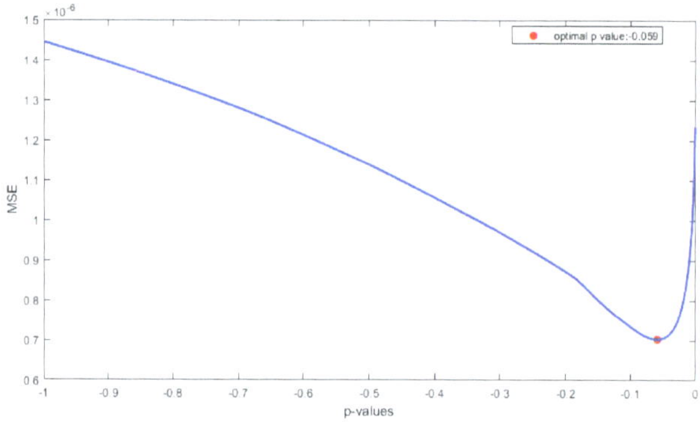

(**a**)

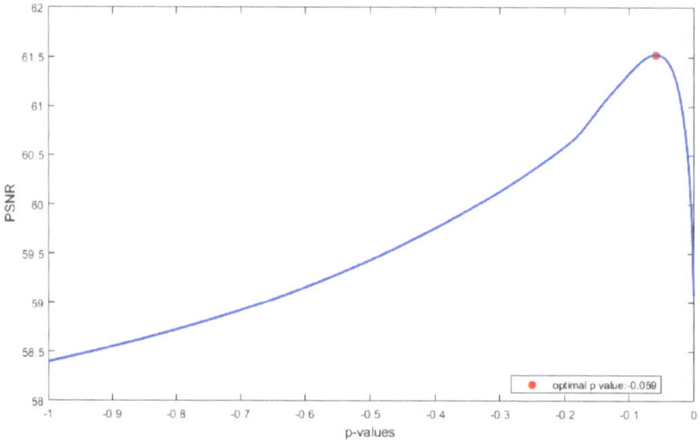

(**b**)

Figure 19. Change in the MSE (**a**) and PSNR (**b**) values between the host image and a watermarked image according to p-values.

A comparison of the watermarking methods based on Separable, QSVD, RBSVD, and ESVD in terms of PSNR and MSE on test images are given in Tables 7 and 8. The proposed method demonstrates better performance than the other approaches.

Table 7. PSNR comparison for the watermarking methods based on Separable, QSVD, RBSVD, and ESVD on the test images.

Methods	α	airplane.png	baboon.png	baby.png	Barbara.png	monarch.png	peppers.png
Seperable	0.05	56.9556	62.3572	56.5094	59.5572	58.6407	57.7683
QSVD	0.05	58.3759	65.2280	57.4869	60.8656	59.3973	59.7142
RBSVD	0.05	58.3989	64.8821	57.3881	60.6836	59.2756	59.7100
ESVD (Proposed Method)	0.05	61.5283 optimal $p = -0.059$	66.2703 optimal $p = -0.199$	58.9558 optimal $p = -0.075$	61.5525 optimal $p = -0.093$	60.9556 optimal $p = -0.099$	61.8606 optimal $p = -0.116$

Table 8. MSE comparison for the watermarking methods based on Separable, QSVD, RBSVD, and ESVD on the test images.

Methods	α	airplane.png	baboon.png	baby.png	Barbara.png	monarch.png	peppers.png
Separable	0.05	2.0158×10^{-6}	5.8114×10^{-7}	2.2339×10^{-6}	1.1073×10^{-6}	1.3675×10^{-6}	1.6717×10^{-6}
QSVD	0.05	1.4534×10^{-6}	3.0005×10^{-7}	1.7836×10^{-6}	8.1929×10^{-7}	1.1488×10^{-6}	1.0680×10^{-6}
RBSVD	0.05	1.4458×10^{-6}	3.2493×10^{-7}	1.8247×10^{-6}	8.5435×10^{-7}	1.1815×10^{-6}	1.0691×10^{-6}
ESVD (Proposed Method)	0.05	7.0335×10^{-7} optimal $p = -0.059$	2.3603×10^{-7} optimal $p = -0.199$	1.2718×10^{-6} optimal $p = -0.075$	6.9945×10^{-7} optimal $p = -0.093$	8.0249×10^{-7} optimal $p = -0.099$	6.5154×10^{-7} optimal $p = -0.116$

To evaluate the robustness of the proposed watermarking scheme, several attacks, including adding 2% Gaussian noise, cropping one-fourth of the upper-left area of the watermarked image, sharpening, and their sequential application, were performed. The robustness of the watermarking scheme was evaluated using the MSE between the extracted and original watermarks. Table 9 shows the results of the watermarked images for the test images after different attacks. From Table 9, it can be seen that the MSE error values are very small. This result demonstrates the robustness of the proposed scheme against attacks. The watermarks shown in Figure 20 were obtained from the test image airplane.png as a result of the attacks we considered.

Figure 20. The extracted watermarks from the test image airplane.png: (**a**) Noise, (**b**) Cropping, (**c**) Noise + Cropping, (**d**) Sharpening, (**e**) Noise + Sharpening, and (**f**) Noise + Cropping + Sharpening.

Table 9. Results of the MSE of the extracted watermark after different attacks.

Test Images	α	Noise 2% Gaussian	Cropping 25%	Noise + Cropping	Sharpening	Noise + Sharpening	Noise + Cropping + Sharpening
airplane.png	0.5	0.0142	0.0010	0.0086	0.0007	0.0396	0.0250
baby.png	0.5	0.0027	0.0017	0.0022	0.0018	0.0123	0.0071
baboon.png	0.5	0.0167	0.0005	0.0099	0.0006	0.0448	0.0281
Barbara.png	0.5	0.0104	0.0015	0.0072	0.0015	0.0313	0.0202
monarch.png	0.5	0.0131	0.0010	0.0077	0.0009	0.0354	0.0214
peppers.png	0.5	0.0088	0.0017	0.0066	0.0005	0.0256	0.0174

5. Conclusions

In color image processing, conventional sparse matrix models employed for representing color images often neglect the interdependencies among the three distinct color channels RGB. Consequently, in numerous image processing tasks, these channels are either processed separately, or the image is converted to grayscale. Such an approach can significantly limit the effectiveness of various image processing techniques, particularly those that rely on the complex interactions of color data. In this study, we applied various color image processing techniques—including principal component analysis, image compression, image restoration, and watermarking—directly to color images represented in the elliptic quaternion algebra without decomposing them into separate RGB channels. These methods were integrated into the MATLAB toolbox developed for this purpose. Extensive experiments were conducted on image compression, reconstruction, image restoration, and watermarking. A comparative performance analysis between the proposed method and other hypercomplex-based compression techniques demonstrated that our method outperformed existing approaches. The experiments also revealed that the choice of the p-value in the algebra of elliptic quaternions directly affects the performance of the solution of the problem under consideration. Selecting an optimal p-value for problem-solving, combined with the elliptic characteristics exhibited by many physical systems, renders this number system advantageous in image processing and other applied fields. Therefore, integrating the elliptic quaternions system into the image processing process can effectively address various challenges related to computational time, memory usage, and overall performance in fields such as machine learning, convolutional neural networks, etc.

On the other hand, the optimal p-values for the problems considered were selected via a brute-force approach by searching in a specific range with a certain step size. It was observed that, in certain cases, the optimal p-values clustered at specific points. Investigating the underlying reasons for this clustering, elucidating the relationship between the optimal p-values and the problems discussed, and developing analytical methods for determining the optimal p-values are proposed as subjects for future research in this article.

Author Contributions: Conceptualization, H.H.K.; Formal analysis, E.K. and M.A.; H.H.K., E.K., and B.Ç. wrote the main manuscript text. All authors reviewed the manuscript. All authors have read and agreed to the published version of the manuscript.

Funding: This paper was supported by the Scientific and Technological Research Institution of Türkiye (TUBITAK-1002-a-121F289).

Data Availability Statement: The original data presented in the study are openly available at https://github.com/hidayethuda/elliptic_quaternions_and_elliptic_numbers_toolbox, accessed on 22 August 2024.

Acknowledgments: This paper was supported by the Scientific and Technological Research Institution of Türkiye (TUBITAK-1002-a-121F289). We thank TÜBİTAK for their support. In addition, the authors would like to thank the anonymous referees for their helpful suggestions and comments, which significantly improved the presentation of the paper.

Conflicts of Interest: The authors declare no competing interests.

References

1. Hamilton, W.R. On a new species of imaginary quantities, connected with the theory of quaternions. *Proc. R. Ir. Acad.* **1840**, *2*, 424–434.
2. Adler, S. *Quaternionic Quantum Mechanics and Quantum Fields*; Oxford University Press: New York, NY, USA, 1995.
3. Mukundan, R. *Quaternions. Advanced Methods in Computer Graphics: With Examples in OpenGL*; Springer-Verlag London Limited: London, UK, 2012.
4. Ell, T. A.; Bihan, N.L.; Sangwine, S.J. *Quaternion Fourier Transforms for Signal and Image Processing*; Wiley: Hoboken, NJ, USA, 2014.
5. Parcollet, T.; Morchid, M.; Linares, G. A survey of quaternion neural networks. *Artif. Intell. Rev.* **2020**, *53*, 2957–2982. [CrossRef]
6. Sangwine, S.J.; Bihan N.L. Quaternion Toolbox for Matlab. Available online: http://qtfm.sourceforge.net/ (accessed on 22 August 2024).
7. Pei, S.C.; Chang, J.H.; Ding, J.J. Commutative Reduced Biquaternions and Their Fourier Transform for Signal and Image Processing Applications. *IEEE Trans. Signal Process* **2004**, *52*, 2012–2031. [CrossRef]
8. Navarro-Moreno, J.; Fernández-Alcalá, R.M.; Ruiz-Molina, J.C. Proper ARMA Modeling and Forecasting in the Generalized Segre's Quaternions Domain. *Mathematics* **2022** *10*, 1083. [CrossRef]
9. Catoni, F.; Cannata, R.; Zampetti, P. An introduction to commutative quaternions. *Adv. Appl. Clifford Algebr.* **2006**, *16*, 1–28. [CrossRef]
10. Catoni, F.; Boccaletti, D.; Cannata, R.; Catoni, V.; Nichelatti, E.; Zampetti, P. *The Mathematics of Minkowski Space–Time: With an Introduction to Commutative Hypercomplex Numbers*; Birkhäuser: Basel, Switzerland, 2008.
11. Yaglom, I.M. *A Simple Non-Euclidean Geometry and Its Physical Basis*; Springer: New York, NY, USA, 1979.
12. Condurache, D.; Burlacu, A. Dual tensors based solutions for rigid body motion parameterization. *Mech. Mach. Theory* **2014**, *74*, 390–412. [CrossRef]
13. Catoni, F.; Cannata, R.; Zampetti, P. An introduction to constant curvature spaces in the commutative (Segre) quaternion geometry. *Adv. Appl. Clifford Algebr.* **2006**, *16*, 85–101. [CrossRef]
14. Gai, S. Theory of reduced biquaternion sparse representation and its applications. *Expert Syst. Appl.* **2023**, *213*, 119245. [CrossRef]
15. Kosal, H.H.; Kisi, E.; Akyigit, M.; Celik, B. Elliptic Quaternion Matrices: Theory and Algorithms. *Axioms* **2024**, *13*, 656. [CrossRef]
16. Gai, S.; Huang, X. Reduced biquaternion convolutional neural network for color image processing. *IEEE Trans. Circuits Syst. Video Technol.* **2022**, *32*, 1061–1075. [CrossRef]
17. Kobayashi, M. Twin-multistate commutative quaternion Hopfield neural networks. *Neurocomputing* **2018**, *320*, 150–156. [CrossRef]
18. Atali, G.; Kosal, H.H.; Pekyaman, M. A new image restoration model associated with special elliptic quaternionic least-squares solutions based on LabVIEW. *J. Comput. Appl. Math.* **2023**, *425*, 115071. [CrossRef]
19. Harkin, A.A.; Harkin, J.B. Geometry of generalized complex numbers. *Math. Mag.* **2004**, *77*, 118–129. [CrossRef]
20. Tosun, M.; Kösal, H.H. An Algorithm for Solving the Sylvester s-Conjugate Elliptic Quaternion Matrix Equations. In *Algorithms as a Basis of Modern Applied Mathematics. Studies in Fuzziness and Soft Computing*; Hošková-Mayerová, Š., Flaut, C., Maturo, F., Eds.; Springer: Cham, Switzerland, 2021; Volume 404.
21. Chang, J.H.; Ding, J.J. Quaternion matrix singular value decomposition and its applications for color image processing. In Proceedings of the 2003 International Conference on Image Processing (Cat. No. 03CH37429), Barcelona, Spain, 14–17 September 2003; Volume 1, p. I-805.
22. Pei, S.C.; Chang, J.H.; Ding, J.J.; Chen, M.Y. Eigenvalues and singular value decompositions of reduced biquaternion matrices. *IEEE Trans. Circuits Syst. I Regul. Pap.* **2008**, *55*, 2673–2685.
23. Gunturk, B.K. Fundamental of image restoration. In *Image Restoration Fundamentals and Advances*; Gunturk, B.K., Li, X., Eds.; CRC Press: New York, NY, USA, 2013; pp. 25–61.
24. Abd El-Samie, F.E. An efficient singular value decomposition algorithm for digital audio watermarking. *Int. J. Speech Technol.* **2009**, *12*, 27–45. [CrossRef]

axioms

Review

Join Spaces and Lattices

Violeta Leoreanu-Fotea [1,*] and Sarka Hoskova-Mayerova [2]

1 Faculty of Mathematics, "Al.I. Cuza" University, Bd. Carol I, No. 11, 700506 Iaşi, Romania
2 Department of Mathematics and Physics, Faculty of Military Technology, University of Defence, 662 10 Brno, Czech Republic; sarka.mayerova@unob.cz
* Correspondence: violeta.fotea@uaic.ro

Abstract: Hypergroups represent a generalization of groups, introduced by Marty, that are rich in applications in several sectors of mathematics and in other fields. An important class of hypergroups called join spaces is presented in this paper, along with some connections to lattice theory, in particular, to modular and to distributive lattices. In particular, we study join spaces associated with chains through functions and we analyze when such join spaces are isomorphic. Moreover, a combinatorial problem is presented for a finite context, focusing on calculating the number of isomorphisms classes of join spaces.

Keywords: join space; hypergroup; chain; lattice

MSC: 20N20

check for updates

Citation: Leoreanu-Fotea, V.; Hoskova-Mayerova, S. Join Spaces and Lattices. *Axioms* **2024**, *13*, 705. https://doi.org/10.3390/axioms13100705

Academic Editors: Jorge Delgado Gracia and Salvador Hernández

Received: 16 August 2024
Revised: 1 October 2024
Accepted: 10 October 2024
Published: 12 October 2024

1. Introduction

The composition of two elements is an element in groups, while in an algebraic hypergroup, the composition of two elements is a nonempty subset. F. Marty observed that the elements of a factor group are subsets and this was the starting point for hypergroup theory, see [1].

He introduced the hypergroup concept in 1934 at the 8th Congress of the mathematicians from the Scandinavian countries. Over time, new results have also appeared interesting, but especially since the 1970s, this theory developed a lot in Europe, the United States, Asia, and Australia. Some sound names in this field such as Dresher, Ore, Koskas, and Krasner made contributions in the field of homomorphisms of hypergroups and in the theory of subhypergroups.

Hypergroups have applications in several sectors of mathematics and in other fields, see [2]. Complete parts were studied by Koskas, then by Corsini, Leoreanu, Davvaz, Vougiouklis, and Freni.

Fundamental equivalence relations are important in algebraic hyperstructures because they establish a natural connection between algebraic hyperstructures and classical algebraic structures. The relation β connects the class of hypergroups to the class of groups. More exactly, the quotient of a hypergroup has a group structure. Using relation β, Migliorato defines the notion of an n-complete hypergroup.

In [3], basic notions and results about algebraic hypergroups are presented, in particular about semihypergroups, hypergroups, subhypergroups, homomorphisms and isomorphisms, fundamental relations and the corresponding quotient structures, join spaces, canonical hypergroups, Rosenberg hypergroups, topological hypergroups, and also connections with hypergraphs and n-ary relations, while in [4] hyperstructures and their representations are studied.

Hyperlattices were introduced in 1994 by Mittas and Konstantinidou, see [5], and later on they were studied by many mathematicians, see, e.g., [6,7]. Connections between hypergroups and lattices or hyperlattices have been considered and analyzed by

Nakano [8] and Varlet [9], then by Comer [10] and later by Kehagias, Konstantinidou, and Serafimidis [11,12], Călugăreanu and Leoreanu [13], Tofan and Volf [14], and Njionou, Ngapeya and Leoreanu-Fotea [15].

2. Join Spaces and Connections with Lattices

In this section, we present the join space notion and we analyze some connections with lattice theory.

Let $H \neq \emptyset$. A function $\circ : H \times H \to \mathcal{P}^*(H)$ is called a *hyperoperation*, where $\mathcal{P}^*(H)$ denotes the set of nonempty subsets of H.

If S, T are subsets of H, then $S \circ T = \bigcup_{s \in S; t \in T} s \circ t$.

The structure $(H, \circ)$ is a *hypergroup* if for all u, v, w of H we have

$$(u \circ v) \circ w = u \circ (v \circ w) \text{ and } u \circ H = H \circ u = H.$$

For all elements $a, b \in H$, denote $a/b = \{u \in H \mid a \in u \circ b\}$.

Definition 1. *A hypergroup $(H, \circ)$ is called a join space if it is commutative and for all a, b, c, d of H, we have*

$$a/b \cap c/d \neq \emptyset \Rightarrow a \circ d \cap b \circ c \neq \emptyset. \tag{1}$$

In other words, $a \in u \circ b, c \in u \circ d \Rightarrow a \circ d \cap b \circ c \neq \emptyset$.

The condition (1) is often called the *join space condition.*

Join spaces were defined by W. Prenowitz. He and J. Jantosciak applied them in both Euclidean and non-Euclidean geometry, see [16]. Using join spaces, descriptive, projective, and spherical geometry were subsequently rebuilt.

Join spaces can be also studied in connections with binary relations, fuzzy sets, or rough sets, see [2,17].

We present here some examples of join spaces:

Example 1. *Let H be a non-empty set. If R is an equivalence relation on it, then denote the equivalence class of $a \in H$ by $[a]$ and define the next hyperoperation on H:*

$$\forall a, b \in H,\ a \circ b = [a] \cup [b].$$

Then, $(H, \circ)$ is a join space.

For all $a, b, c \in H$ we have $a \circ H = H,\ a \circ (b \circ c) = (a \circ b) \circ c = [a] \cup [b] \cup [c]$, whence $(H, \circ)$ is a commutative hypergroup. Moreover, if $a, b, c, d \in H$ and there is $u \in H$ such that $a \in u \circ b,\ c \in u \circ d$ then $a \in [u] \cup [b],\ c \in [u] \cup [d]$.

If $a \in [b]$, then $a \in a \circ d \cap b \circ d$. Similarly, if $c \in [d]$, then $c \in a \circ d \cap b \circ c$.

If $a \notin [b]$ and $c \notin [d]$, then $a \in [u]$ and $c \in [u]$, whence $[a] = [u] = [c]$, hence $u \in a \circ d \cap b \circ c$. Therefore, $(H, \circ)$ is a join space.

Example 2. *Let $(G, \cdot)$ be a commutative group. For all $x \in G$, consider a nonempty set $A(x)$, such that if $x, y \in G,\ x \neq y$, then $A(x) \cap A(y) = \emptyset$.*

Set $H_G = \cup_{x \in G} A(x)$ and $f : K_G \to G,\ f(a) = x \Leftrightarrow a \in A(x)$.

For all $a, b \in H_G$ we define $a \,\square\, b = A(f(a)f(b))$. Then, $(H_G, \square)$ is a join space.

Indeed, it can be checked that $\forall a \in H_G,\ a \,\square\, H_G = H_G$ and $\forall a, b, c \in H_G,\ (a \,\square\, b) \,\square\, c = a \,\square\, (b \,\square\, c) = A(f(a)f(b)f(c))$.

Now, if $a, b, c, d, u \in H_G$ are such that $a \in u \,\square\, b,\ c \in u \,\square\, d$ then $a \in A(f(u)f(b))$ and $c \in A(f(u)f(d))$, whence $f(a) = f(u)f(b)$ and $f(c) = f(u)f(d)$.

Hence, $f(a)f(d) = f(c)f(b)$, so $a \,\square\, d \cap b \,\square\, c \neq \emptyset$. Thus, $(H_G, \square)$ is a join space.

Example 3. *Consider* $(H, \circ)$ *a hypergroup and* $(G, \cdot)$ *a commutative group. Consider a family* $\{A_i\}_{i\in G}$ *of nonempty sets, such that* $A_1 = H$ *and for* $i, j \in G,\ i \neq j,\ A_i \cap A_j = \emptyset$. *We define the next hyperoperation on* $T = \cup_{i\in G} A_i$:

$$\forall a, b \in H,\ a \,\Box\, b = a \circ b;\ \forall a \in A_i,\ b \in A_j, (i,j) \neq (1,1), ij = k,\ a \,\Box\, b = A_k.$$

Then, $(T, \Box)$ *is a join space if and only if* $(H, \circ)$ *is a join space.*

Let $(H, \circ)$ be a join space.

We have $a \,\Box\, T = T$, since $(G, \cdot)$ is a group. The associativity law holds.

Moreover, if $a \in v \,\Box\, b,\ a \in A_i,\ b \in A_j$, then $v \in A_{ij^{-1}}$.

Similarly, if $c \in v \,\Box\, d,\ c \in A_k,\ d \in A_s$, then $v \in A_{ks^{-1}}$. Thus, $ij^{-1} = ks^{-1}$, whence $is = kj$.

If $(i, j, k, s) \neq (1, 1, 1, 1)$, then $a \,\Box\, d \cap c \,\Box\, b \neq \emptyset$.

If $(i, j, k, s) = (1, 1, 1, 1)$, then we use the fact $(H, \circ)$ is a join space.

Therefore, $(T, \Box)$ is a join space.

Conversely, suppose that $(T, \Box)$ is a join space. If $u \in H$ and $a \in u \circ b,\ c \in u \circ d$, then $a \in u \,\Box\, b,\ c \in u \,\Box\, d$, whence $a \,\Box\, d \cap c \,\Box\, b \neq \emptyset$, which means that $a \circ d \cap c \circ b \neq \emptyset$. Thus, $(H, \circ)$ is a join space.

The study of algebraic hypergroups and connections with lattices and ordered sets was initiated by J. Mittas and then by M. Konstantinidou and K. Serafimidis, Ch. Massouros, G. Massouros, and later by Ath. Kehagias. Connections between ordered sets, quasi-orders, and hypergroups were also studied by Chvalina.

In what follows, we present some connections with lattice theory, see [18]. Two important classes of lattices are characterized using hypergroups: distributive and modular lattices, see [9,10,19].

Connection 1. *In* [9], *J.Varlet provided the following characterization of distributive lattices:*

Consider the next hyperoperation on a lattice $\mathbf{L} = (L, \vee, \wedge)$:

$\forall a, b \in L$ *we set*

$$a \diamond b = [a \wedge b, a \vee b] = \{x \in L : a \wedge b \leq x \leq a \vee b\}.$$

Theorem 1. $\mathbf{L}$ *is a distributive lattice if and only if* $(L, \diamond)$ *is a join space.*

In [19], we considered and analyzed a family of hyperoperations $\{\diamond_{pq}\}_{p,q\in L}$ defined as follows.

Let $p, q \in L$ be arbitrary. For all $a, b \in L$ set

$$a \diamond_{pq} b = [a \wedge b \wedge p, a \vee b \vee q].$$

Theorem 2. *If the lattice* $\mathbf{L}$ *is distributive and* $p, q \in L$, *then* $(L, \diamond_{pq})$ *is a join space.*

We mention some important steps from the proof of this theorem:

First, check that

$$(a \diamond_{pq} b) \diamond_{pq} c = [a \wedge b \wedge c \wedge p, a \vee b \vee c \vee q].$$

In order to prove "$\supseteq$", we consider $t \in [a \wedge b \wedge c \wedge p, a \vee b \vee c \vee q]$ an arbitrary element and we set $s = (a \wedge b) \vee (a \wedge t) \vee (b \wedge t)$. Thus, $s \in a \diamond_{pq} b$ whence $t \in s \diamond_{pq} c$.

Now, we consider $a, b, c, d, u \in L$ that satisfy $a \in b \diamond_{pq} u$ and $c \in d \diamond_{pq} u$.

Set $z = (a \wedge d \wedge p) \vee (b \wedge c \wedge p)$. We obtain $z \in b \diamond_{pq} c$.

Hence, $z \in (a \diamond_{pq} d) \cap (b \diamond_{pq} c)$ and so $(L, \diamond_{pq})$ is a join space.

Connection 2. *The next example of a join space is useful to characterize modular lattices.*

Let $\mathbf{L} = (L, \vee, \wedge)$ *be a lattice. In* [8] *H. Nakano introduced the following hyperoperation on L:*

$$a \circ b = \{u \in H \mid a \vee b = a \vee u = b \vee u\}.$$

Later, S. Comer [10] showed that:

Theorem 3. $\mathbf{L}$ *is a modular lattice if and only if* $(L, \circ)$ *is a join space.*

Another interesting proof of the above theorem is given in [2]. Several properties of this join space were presented in [13].

In [19], a new family of hyperoperations determined by a lattice is analyzed. For all $p \in L$ set

$$a \circ_p b = \{u \in L \mid a \vee b \vee p = a \vee u \vee p = b \vee u \vee p\}.$$

Notice that $a \circ_p b \neq \emptyset$, since $a \vee b \in a \circ_p b$.

For $p \in L$ set $L_p = \{x \in L \mid x \geq p\}$ and denote by $\mathbf{L}_p$ the restriction of $\mathbf{L}$ to L_p.

Theorem 4. *Let* $p \in L$*. If* $\mathbf{L}_p$ *is modular, then* $(L, \circ_p)$ *is a join space.*

Similar results can be obtained by considering the hyperoperation:

$$a \square_p b = \{u \in L \mid a \wedge b \wedge p = a \wedge u \wedge p = b \wedge u \wedge p\}.$$

The hyperproduct is not empty since $a \wedge b \in a \square_p b$.

Connection 3. *Another connection between join spaces and lattices was highlighted by Tofan and Volf* [14]*, as follows:*

If $(L, \vee, \wedge)$ *is a lattice and* $f : H \to L$ *is a function, such that* $f(L)$ *is a distributive sublattice of* $(L, \vee, \wedge)$*, then define*

$$\forall a, b \in H,\ a \diamond_f b = \{c \in H \mid inf\,\{f(a), f(b)\} \leq f(c) \leq sup\{f(a), f(b)\}\}.$$

We obtain a commutative hypergroup $(H, \diamond_f)$*.*

Indeed, in the above conditions, the next equality is checked:

$$(a \diamond_f b) \diamond_f c = \{u \in H \mid \inf\,\{f(a), f(b), f(c)\} \leq f(u) \leq \sup\{f(a), f(b), f(b)\}\} =$$

$$= a \diamond_f (b \diamond_f c),\ \forall a, b, c \in H.$$

Moreover, we shall prove here the next result, as follows:

Theorem 5. *The next statements are equivalent:*

- $f(L)$ *is a distributive sublattice.*
- $\diamond_f$ *satisfies the join space condition.*

Proof. First, let us check that the join space condition is satisfied for a distributive sublattice $f(L)$. Let $u \in H$: $a \in u \diamond_f b$, $c \in u \diamond_f d$.

Then, we shall check that there is $v \in a \diamond_f d \cap b \diamond_f c$.

Since $\{\inf\{f(b), f(u)\} \leq f(a) \leq \sup\{f(b), f(u)\}$ and $\{\inf\{f(d), f(u)\} \leq f(c) \leq \sup\{f(d), f(u)\}$, according to the distributivity, it follows that

$$\inf\{f(a), f(d)\} \leq \inf\{\sup\{f(b), f(u)\}, f(d)\} \leq \sup\{\inf\{f(b), f(d)\}, f(c)\} \leq \sup\{f(b), f(c)\}.$$

From here we obtain $s = \sup\{\inf\{f(a), f(d)\}, \inf\{f(b), f(c)\}\} \leq \sup\{f(b), f(c)\}$.

Similarly, we have $s \leq \sup\{f(a), f(d)\}$.

Hence, $\sup\{\inf\{f(a), f(d)\}, \inf\{f(b), f(c)\}\} \leq \inf\{\sup\{f(a), f(d)\}, \sup\{f(b), f(c)\}$.

Therefore, $(a \diamond_f d) \cap (b \diamond_f c) \neq \emptyset$.

Now, let us note that the reciprocal statement also holds: if the join space condition is satisfied, then $f(L)$ is a distributive sublattice.

Indeed, if $f(L)$ is not distributive, then it will contain a sublattice

$$\{f(u), f(v), f(w), f(t), f(s)\} \text{ with } \sup\{f(u), f(w)\} = \sup\{f(v), f(w)\} = f(t),$$

$\inf\{f(u), f(w)\} = \inf\{f(v), f(w)\} = f(s)$ and $f(u) > f(v)$ of $f(u), f(v), f(w)$ are not comparable two by two.

In both situations, $w \in u/v \cap v/u$, since

$$\inf\{f(v), f(w)\} = f(s) \leq f(u) \leq \sup\{f(v), f(w)\} = f(t)$$

and

$$\inf\{f(u), f(w)\} = f(s) \leq f(v) \leq \sup\{f(u), f(w)\} = f(t).$$

Thus, $w \in u/v \cap v/u$, and $u \diamond_f u = \{u\} \neq \{v\} = v \diamond_f v$, a contradiction. Thus, the sublattice $f(L)$ is distributive. □

Canonical hypergroups are an important class of join spaces and were introduced by J. Mittas [20]. They are the additive structures of Krasner hyperrings and were used by R. Roth to obtain results in the finite group character theory, see [21]. McMullen and Price studied finite abelian hypergroups over splitting fields [22].

More recent studies of canonical hypergroups were conducted by C and G. Massouros (in connection with automata), P. Corsini (sd-hypergroups), and K. Serafimidis, M. Konstantinidou, and J. Mittas, while feebly canonical hypergroups were analyzed by P. Corsini and M. De Salvo.

Canonical hypergroups are exactly join spaces with a scalar identity e, which means that $\forall u,\ u \circ e = e \circ u = u$. Obviously, commutative groups are canonical hypergroups. Other examples of canonical hypergroups are given in [3].

More general structures were also considered, namely polygroups, also called quasi-canonical hypergroups, by Bonansinga, Corsini, and Ch. Massouros. Comer analyzed the applications of polygroups in the theory of graphs, relations, Boolean, and cylindrical algebras.

A particular type of polygroup, namely the hypergroup of bilateral classes, was investigated by Drbohlav, Harrison. and Comer. Polygroups satisfy the same conditions as canonical hypergroups, with the exception of commutativity.

In the next two sections, we associate join spaces with chains and we analyze when they are isomorphic. Moreover, a combinatorial problem is presented: we calculate how many isomorphism classes of join spaces are.

3. Join Spaces Associated with a Chain: The Finite Case

In what follows, we associate a join space structure with a chain, through a function. We then study under what conditions such join spaces, considered for different functions, are isomorphic, for the finite case.

Let H be finite and $f : H \to C$ where C is a chain. Consider the next hyperoperation on H:

$$\forall a, b \in H,\ a \diamond_f b = \{c \in H \mid f(a) \wedge f(b) \leq f(c) \leq f(a) \vee f(b)\}.$$

We have $f(a) \wedge f(b) = min\{f(a), f(b)\}$, $f(a) \vee f(b) = max\{f(a), f(b)\}$.

According to Theorem 5 or by a direct check, we then utilize the following theorem.

Theorem 6. *The structure $(H, \diamond_f)$ is a join space.*

Set $|H| = n$. We define the next equivalence relation on H:

$$h \sim_f k \Leftrightarrow f(h) = f(k).$$

Denote $s = |H/_\sim|$ and order $H/_\sim$ as follows: $\bar{h} \le \bar{k} \Leftrightarrow f(h) \le f(k)$, for $h, k \in H$.
We denote $H/_\sim = \{\bar{h_1}, \bar{h_2}, \dots, \bar{h_s}\}$ where $f(h_1) < f(h_2) < \dots < f(h_s)$.

For all $i \in \{1, \dots, s\}$ set $a_i = |f^{-1}(f(h_i))|$. We have $a_i \ge 1$, $\sum_{i=1}^{s} a_i = n$.
Denote $\lambda(f) = (a_1, a_2, \dots, a_s)$ the ordered partition of n into s parts and $\tau(a_1, a_2, \dots, a_s) = (b_1, b_2, \dots, b_s)$ where $\forall i, b_i = a_{s-i+1}$.

Theorem 7. *If $f, g : H \to C$ are two maps, then $(H, \diamond_f) \cong (H, \diamond_g) \Leftrightarrow \lambda(f) = \lambda(g)$ or $\lambda(g) = \tau(\lambda(f))$.*

Proof. "$\Leftarrow$"
Suppose $\lambda(f) = \lambda(g) = (a_1, a_2, \dots, a_s)$. Set $H = \cup_{j=1}^{s} A_j = \cup_{j=1}^{s} A'_j$, where for all $j \in \{1, 2, \dots, s\}$, $A_j = f^{-1}(f(h_j))$, $A'_j = g^{-1}(g(h_j))$.
Set $A_j = \{h_{1,j}, h_{2,j}, \dots, h_{a_j,j}\}$, $A'_j = \{h'_{1,j}, h'_{2,j}, \dots, h'_{a_j,j}\}$.
We order H as follows:
$\forall j \in \{1, 2, \dots, s\}$, $\forall k, k' \in \{1, 2, \dots, a_j\}$, $h_{k,j} < h_{k',j} \Leftrightarrow k < k'$,
$\forall j, j' \in \{1, 2, \dots, s\}, j \ne j'$, $\forall k \in \{1, 2, \dots, a_j\}, \forall k' \in \{1, 2, \dots, a'_j\}$, $h_{k,j} < h_{k',j'} \Leftrightarrow j < j'$.
For $i, j \in \{1, 2, \dots, s\}, k \in \{1, 2, \dots, a_i\}, l \in \{1, 2, \dots, a_j\}$ we have

$$h_{k,i} \diamond_f h_{l,j} = \cup_{t \in [i \wedge j, i \vee j]} A_t,$$

$$h_{k,i} \diamond_g h_{l,j} = \cup_{t \in [i \wedge j, i \vee j]} A'_t.$$

Consider the map: $\phi : (H, \diamond_f) \to (H, \diamond_g)$, $\phi(h_{k,i}) = h'_{k,i}$.
We have

$$\phi(h_{k,i} \diamond_f h_{l,j}) = h'_{k,i} \diamond_g h'_{l,j} = \phi(h_{k,i}) \diamond_g \phi(h_{l,j}),$$

which means that $(H, \diamond_f) \cong (H, \diamond_g)$.
Suppose now that $\lambda(g) = \tau(\lambda(f))$.
We have $H = \cup_{j=1}^{s} A_j = \cup_{j'=1}^{s} A'_{j'}$ where $j' = \tau(j) = s - j + 1$.
Moreover, $A_j = \{h_{1,j}, h_{2,j}, \dots, h_{a_j,j}\}$, $A'_{j'} = \{h'_{1,j'}, h'_{2,j'}, \dots, h'_{a'_{j'},j'}\}$ and $A_j = f^{-1}(f(h_j))$, $A'_{j'} = g^{-1}(g(h_{j'}))$ with $a'_{j'} = a_j$.
Consider the function: $\phi : (H, \diamond_f) \to (H, \diamond_g)$, $\phi(h_{k,j}) = h'_{k,j'}$. We obtain
$\phi(h_{k,i} \diamond_f h_{l,j}) = \phi(\cup_{i \wedge j \le t \le i \vee j} A_t) = \cup_{\tau(i \wedge j) \le \tau(t) \le \tau(i \vee j)} A'_{\tau(t)} = h'_{k,i'} \diamond_g h'_{l,j'} = \phi(h_{k,i}) \diamond_g \phi(h_{l,j})$.

Therefore, $(H, \diamond_f) \cong (H, \diamond_g)$.
"$\Rightarrow$"
Let $p : H \to \{1, 2, \dots, s\}$ be defined as follows: $p(h) = j$ such that $h \in A_j$. Similarly, $p' : H \to \{1, 2, \dots, s'\}$ is defined, where $s' = |H/_{\sim_g}|$.
Denote the isomorphism by $\phi : (H, \diamond_f) \to (H, \diamond_g)$.
Denote the set $\{t \mid u \wedge v \le t \le u \vee v\}$ by $I(u, v)$. For all $h, k \in H$ we have

$$\phi(h \diamond_f k) = \phi(\cup_{j \in I\left(p(h), p(k)\right)} A_j) = \cup_{j \in I\left(p(h), p(k)\right)} \phi(A_j).$$

On the other hand, $\phi(h) \diamond_g \phi(k) = \cup_{j \in I\left(p'(\phi(h)), p'(\phi(k))\right)} A'_j$.
For every $j \in \{1, 2, \dots, s\}$ and every $h \in A_j$ we have
$\phi(A_j) = \phi(h \diamond_f h) = \phi(h) \diamond_g \phi(h) = A'_{p'(\phi(h))}$.
Consider the function $\alpha : \{1, 2, \dots, s\} \to \{1, 2, \dots, s'\}, \alpha(p(h)) = p'(\phi(h))$. We obtain

$$\alpha : I(p(h), p(k)) \to I\Big(p'(\phi(h)), p'(\phi(k))\Big).$$

α is injective:

Indeed, if $\alpha(j_1) = \alpha(j_2)$ then $\phi(A_{j_1}) = \phi(A_{j_2})$. Hence, for every $n \in \{1, 2, \dots a_{j_1}\}$ there exists $t \in \{1, 2, \dots a_{j_2}\}$ such that $\phi(h_{n,j_1}) = \phi(h_{t,j_2})$ whence $j_1 = j_2$, which means that α is injective.

α is surjective:

Indeed, for each $t \in I(\alpha(i), \alpha(j))$, there is $u \in I(i,j)$ for which $\alpha(u) = t$ since $p'(\phi(A_i)) = \alpha(i)$.

Therefore, α is a bijective function from $I(i,j)$ to $I(\alpha(i), \alpha(j))$.

Particularly, $\alpha : I(1,s) \to I(\alpha(1), \alpha(s))$. We have

$$\phi(H) = H = \cup_{j \in \{1, \dots, s\}} \phi(A_j) = \cup_{j \in \{1, \dots, s\}} A'_{\alpha(j)} = \cup_{t \in I\left(\alpha(1), \alpha(s)\right)} A'_t.$$

So, $I\big(\alpha(1), \alpha(s)\big) = I(1, s')$, whence it follows that $\{\alpha(1), \alpha(s)\} = \{1, s'\}$. We have

$$s' = |H/\sim_g| = |\alpha(p(H))| = |p(H)| = s.$$

Hence, $\{\alpha(1), \alpha(s)\} = \{1, s\}$.

Moreover, for all $j \in \{1, \dots, s\}$, we have $a_j = |A_j| = |\phi(A_j)| = |A'_{\alpha(j)}| = a'_{\alpha(j)}$.

From $\{\alpha(1), \alpha(s)\} = \{1, s\}$ it follows that

$$\begin{aligned} I(2, s-1) &= I(\alpha(1), \alpha(s)) - \{\alpha(1), \alpha(s)\} \\ &= \alpha(I(1,s)) - \{\alpha(1), \alpha(s)\} \\ &= I(\alpha(2), \alpha(s-1)), \end{aligned}$$

so $\{\alpha(2), \alpha(s-1)\} = \{2, s-1\}$.

Hence,

$$\forall k,\ \alpha(k) = \{k, s-k+1\}. \tag{2}$$

Denote by B the set of bijections of $I(1,s)$ defined to itself.

We show that $\forall k,\ \alpha(k) = k$ or $\forall k,\ \alpha(k) = s-k+1$. Denote $s-k+1$ by $\tau(k)$.

For $s \leq 3$, we have $B = \{id_{I(1,s)}, \tau\}$.

If $s > 3$ and we suppose that $\alpha(1) = 1, \alpha(2) = \tau(2) = s-1$, then $\alpha(I(1,2)) = I(1, s-1)$, so $2 = |\alpha(I(1,2))| \neq |I(1,s-1)| \geq 3$, which is a contradiction.

Similarly, for $\alpha(1) = s, \alpha(2) = 2$, we obtain a contradiction.

Suppose now that there is $k \in I(1,s)$ such that

$$\alpha(I(1,k)) = id_{I(1,k)} \text{ and } \alpha(k+1) = \tau(k+1).$$

We obtain

$$\begin{aligned} k+1 &= |I(1,k+1)| \\ &= |\alpha(I(1,k+1))| \\ &= k+s-2k, \end{aligned}$$

whence $s = 2k+1$.

Therefore, $\alpha(k+1) = k+1$, which means that

$$\alpha(I(1,k+1)) = id_{I(1,k+1)}.$$

If $\alpha(I(1,k)) = \tau(I(1,k))$, $\alpha(k+1) = k+1$, then

$$k+1 = |\alpha(I(1,k+1))| = k+s-2k,$$

whence $s = 2k+1$. Thus, $\tau(k+1) = k+1$, that is $\alpha(I(1,s+1)) = \tau(I(1,k+1))$.

Hence, $\lambda(f) = \lambda(g)$ or $\lambda(g) = \tau(\lambda(f))$. □

Now we calculate how many isomorphism classes for join spaces can be constructed in this way.

Denote by $Q_f(n)$ the quotient set which contains classes of join spaces $(H, \diamond_f)$ associated with maps $f : H \to C$.

Theorem 8. *(i)* *If $n = 2k+1$ then $|Q_f(n)| = 2^{k-1}(2^k + 1)$.*
(ii) *If $n = 2k$ then $|Q_f(n)| = 2^{k-1}(2^{k-1} + 1)$.*

Proof. Denote by $(o.p.)(n)$ the set of ordered partitions of n.

According to [23], we have $|(o.p.)(n)| = 2^{n-1}$.

Let us number the symmetrical ordered partitions of n, that is partitions $(a_1, a_2, \ldots, a_s)$ for which $\tau(a_1, a_2, \ldots, a_s) = (a_1, a_2, \ldots, a_s)$.

Set $(s.o.p.)(n)$ the set of all symmetrical ordered partitions of n.

We have the two cases:

Case 1.

If $n = 2k+1$ and if $p \in (s.o.p.)(n)$, then $p = (2k+1)$ or $p = (i_1, \ldots, i_s, 2t+1, i_s, \ldots, i_1)$, where $t \in \{0, 1, \ldots, k-1\}$ and $s \in \{k-t, k-t-1, \ldots, 1\}$.

We have

$$2\sum_{j=1}^{s} i_j + 2t + 1 = 2k + 1 \text{ whence } \sum_{j=1}^{s} i_j = k - t.$$

According to [23], for all t we have $|(s.o.p.)(k-t)| = 2^{k-t-1}$. Hence,

$$|(s.o.p.)(n)| = \sum_{t=0}^{k-1} 2^{k-t-1} + 1 = 2^{(k-1)+1} = 2^k.$$

Case 2.

If $n = 2k$ and if $p \in (s.o.p.)(n)$, then $p = (2k)$ or $p = (i_1, \ldots, i_s, 2t, i_s, \ldots, i_1)$, where $t \in \{0, 1, \ldots, k-1\}$ and $s \in \{k-t, k-t-1, \ldots, 1\}$.

We obtain $\sum_{j=1}^{s} i_j = k - t$.

According to [23], for all t we have $|(s.o.p.)(k-t)| = 2^{k-t-1}$.

Hence,

$$|(s.o.p.)(n)| = \sum_{t=0}^{k-1} 2^{k-t-1} + 1 = 2^k.$$

Therefore, we can conclude:

- If $n = 2k+1$ then $|Q_f(n)| = 2^k + 1/2(2^{n-1} - 2^k) = 2^{k-1}(2^k + 1)$;
- If $n = 2k$ then $|Q_f(n)| = 2^k + 1/2(2^{n-1} - 2^k) = 2^{k-1}(2^{k-1} + 1)$.

□

4. Join Spaces Associated with a Chain: The General Case

In this section, we consider an arbitrary set H and we analyze when the join spaces associated with a chain are isomorphic.

Let us present first the context:

Let $f : H \to C$ and consider the equivalence relation on H:

$$h \sim_f k \Leftrightarrow f(h) = f(k).$$

We order $H/_{\sim_f}$ as follows: $[h]_f \le [k]_f \Leftrightarrow f(h) \le f(k)$, for $h, k \in H$.

Denote $H/_{\sim_f} = \{[h_i]_f \mid i \in I\}$ and $[h_i]_f$ by H_i, for all $i \in I$.

We order I as follows:

$$i \le j \Leftrightarrow \forall h \in H_i, \forall k \in H_j,\ f(h) \le f(k).$$

Since C is a chain, it follows that $(I, \le)$ is a chain, too.

Moreover, for all $i \in I$ denote $|H_i| = \alpha_i$.
If $g : H \to C$, then $H/_{\sim_g} = \{H'_{i'} \mid i' \in I'\}$. Similarly,

$$i' \leq j' \Leftrightarrow \forall h' \in H'_{i'}, \forall k' \in H'_{j'},\ g(h') \leq g(k')$$

and for all $i' \in I'$ denote $|H'_{i'}| = \alpha_{i'}$. We have that $(I', \leq)$ is a chain, too.

Theorem 9. *If $f, g : H \to C$ are two functions, then $(H, \diamond_f) \cong (H, \diamond_g)$ if and only if there exists a strictly monotonous bijection $\varphi : I \to I' :\ \forall i \in I, \alpha_i = \alpha'_{\varphi(i)}$.*

Proof. "$\Leftarrow$"
For all $i \in I,\ |H_i| = \alpha_i = \alpha'_{\varphi(i)} = |H'_{\varphi(i)}|$. Define
$\phi : (H, \diamond_f) \to (H, \diamond_g)$ as follows: $\forall i \in I, \forall h_i \in H_i, \phi(h_i) = h'_{\varphi(i)}$ where we choose $h'_{\varphi(i)} \in H'_{\varphi(i)}$. Now, $\forall i, j \in I$, $\forall h_i \in H_i, h_j \in H_j$ we have

$$\phi(h_i) \diamond_g \phi(h_j) = h'_{\varphi(i)} \diamond_g h'_{\varphi(j)} = \cup_{t \in [\varphi(i) \wedge \varphi(j), \varphi(i) \vee \varphi(j)]} H'_{t'},$$

$$\phi(h_i \diamond_f \phi h_j) = \cup_{k \in [i \wedge j, i \vee j} H'_{\varphi(k)]}.$$

If φ is strictly increasing, then $\varphi(i \wedge j) = \varphi(i) \wedge \varphi(j),\ \varphi(i \vee j) = \varphi(i) \vee \varphi(j)$.
Since φ is a bijective function, we have

$$\phi(h_i \diamond_f h_j) = \cup_{t' \in [\varphi(i) \wedge \varphi(j), \varphi(i) \vee \varphi(j)]} H'_{t'}.$$

Hence, $\phi(h_i \diamond_f h_j) = \phi(h_i) \diamond_g \phi(h_j)$.
If φ is strictly decreasing, then $\varphi(i \wedge j) = \varphi(i) \vee \varphi(j),\ \varphi(i \vee j) = \varphi(i) \wedge \varphi(j)$.
Since φ is a bijection, we have

$$\phi(h_i \diamond_f h_j) = \cup_{t' \in [\varphi(i) \wedge \varphi(j), \varphi(i) \vee \varphi(j)]} H'_{t'}.$$

Hence, $\phi(h_i \diamond_f h_j) = \phi(h_i) \diamond_g \phi(h_j)$.
Therefore, ϕ is an isomorphism.
"$\Rightarrow$"
Denote by ϕ the isomorphism from $(H, \diamond_f)$ to $(H, \diamond_g)$. Set $p : H \to I$ and $p' : H \to I'$, where for all $h_i \in H_i,\ h'_{i'} \in H'_{i'}$, we obtain $p(h_i) = i$ and $p'(h'_{i'}) = i'$.
For $h, k \in H_i$ we obtain $h \diamond_f h = h \diamond_f k = H_i$, whence

$$\phi(h) \diamond_g \phi(k) = \phi(h \diamond_f k) = \phi(h) \diamond_g \phi(k) = H'_{\varphi(i)}.$$

Hence, $p'(\phi(h)) = p'(\phi(k))$.
Define $\varphi : I \to I'$ by : $\varphi(i) = p'(\phi(x))$ where $p(x) = i$.
We check that φ is a bijective function.
Suppose that there are $i_1, i_2 \in I,\ i_1 \neq i_2$ such that $\varphi(i_1) = \varphi(i_2)$.
Thus, $\phi(H_{1_1}) = \phi(H_{i_2})$, which is a contradiction with $H_{i_1} \cap H_{i_2} = \emptyset$.
On the other hand, since $\phi(H) = H$ we obtain

$$H = \cup_{i' \in I'} H'_{i'} = \phi(\cup_{i \in I} H_i) = \cup_{i \in I} \phi(H_i) = \cup_{i \in I} H'_{\varphi(i)} = \cup_{i \in Im\varphi} H'_{\varphi(i)},$$

whence $I' = Im\varphi$. Hence, φ is bijective and $|I| = |I'|$.
Thus, $\forall i \in I,\ |H_{\varphi(i)}| = |\phi(H_i)| = |H_i|$.
Hence, $\forall i \in I, \alpha'_{\varphi(i)} = \alpha_i$. Let us prove now that φ is strictly monotonous.
If $i \leq j$ are elements of I, then we denote $[i, j] = \{t \in I | i \wedge j \leq t \leq i \vee j\}$ and for $i', j' \in I, i \leq j'$ then $[i', j'] = \{t' \in I' | i' \wedge j' \leq t' \leq i' \vee j'\}$.

If $i, j \in I, i \leq j$ and $h \in H_i, k \in H_j$, then $\phi(h \diamond_f k) = \phi(h) \diamond_g \phi(k)$ whence

$$\phi(\cup_{t\in[i,j]} H_t) = \cup_{t\in[i\wedge j, i\vee j]} H'_{\varphi(t)}.$$

We obtain that

$$\forall i \leq j,\ \varphi([i,j]) = [\varphi(i) \wedge \varphi(j), \varphi(i) \vee \varphi(j)]. \tag{3}$$

For $i \neq j$ we have $\varphi(i) < \varphi(j)$ or $\varphi(j) < \varphi(i)$.

If $\varphi(i) < \varphi(j)$, then φ is strictly increasing on I. Indeed, it follows from (3).

Similarly, if $\varphi(j) < \varphi(i)$, then φ is strictly decreasing on I.

Therefore, we obtain the thesis. □

Let us present some examples.

Example 4. *If $f, g : H \to [a,b]$, where $[a,b]$ is a real interval and $g(h) = a + b - f(h)$, then $[h]_f = [h]_g$, whence $I = I'$ and φ is the identity function. Hence, $(H, \diamond_f) \cong (H, \diamond_g)$.*

Example 5. *If $f, g : H \to \mathbb{R}$, where $\mathbb{R}$ is the real number set and $g(h) = -f(h)$, then $[h]_f = [h]_g$, and again $I = I'$, φ is the identity function and $(H, \diamond_f) \cong (H, \diamond_g)$.*

Example 6. *If $f, g : H \to C$ are such that $|H/\sim_f| = |H/\sim_g| = n$, $H/\sim_f = \{H_1, H_2, \ldots, H_n\}$, $H/\sim_g = \{H'_1, H'_2, \ldots, H'_n\}$ such that $|H_1| = |H'_n| = 1$, $|H_2| = |H'_{n-1}| = 2$, and so on.*

In general, $|H_i| = |H'_{n-i+1}| = i$ for all $i \in \{1, 2, \ldots, n\}$.

Then, $I = I' = \{1, 2, \ldots, n\}$ and $\varphi(i) = n - i + 1$ is a strictly decreasing function. Hence, $(H, \diamond_f) \cong (H, \diamond_g)$.

5. Conclusions

We study classes of isomorphism for join spaces associated with chains and a combinatorial problem is analyzed for the finite case, which is to determine the number of the classes of isomorphism.

As a future problem, we can study classes of isomorphism for join spaces associated with lattices. For two maps $f, g : H \to L$, where $(L, \vee, \wedge)$ is a lattice, we intend to determine when $(H, \diamond_f) \cong (H, \diamond_g)$, to consider the corresponding equivalence classes and examine the finite case.

Another study problem would be to determine hypergroups/join spaces associated with other classes of lattices, such as Boolean lattices and to obtain characterizations of these classes of lattices. In this way, some results of the lattice theory could be demonstrated with the help of the hypergroup theory. For example, in a modular lattice, the ideals are exactly the subhypergroups of the associated join space structure.

Author Contributions: Conceptualization, V.L.-F. and S.H.-M.; methodology, V.L.-F. and S.H.-M.; investigation, V.L.-F.; resources, V.L.-F.; writing—original draft preparation, V.L.-F.; writing—review and editing, V.L.-F. and S.H.-M.; project administration S.H.-M.; funding acquisition, S.H.-M. All authors have read and agreed to the published version of the manuscript.

Funding: The second author thanks to the Ministry of Defence of the Czech Republic for the support under the grant VAROPS.

Institutional Review Board Statement: Not applicable.

Informed Consent Statement: Not applicable.

Data Availability Statement: No new data were created or analyzed in this study. Data sharing is not applicable to this article.

Conflicts of Interest: The authors declare no conflicts of interest.

References

1. Marty, F. Sur une généralisation de la notion de groupe. In Proceedings of the Actes du IV Congrès des Mathématiciens Scandinaves, Stockholm, Sweden, 14–18 August 1934; pp. 45–49.
2. Corsini, P.; Leoreanu, V. *Applications of Hyperstructure Theory*; Advances in Mathematics; Kluwer Aademic Publishers: Dordrecht, The Netherlands; Boston, MA, USA, London, UK; 2003; Volume 5.
3. Davvaz, B.; Leoreanu-Fotea, V. *Hypergroup Theory*; Word Scientific: Singapore, 2022.
4. Vougiouklis, T. *Hyperstructures and Their Representations*; Hadronic Press, Inc.: Palm Harbor, FL, USA, 1994.
5. Konstantinidou, M.; Mittas, J. Contributions à la théorie des treillis avec des structures hypercompositionnelles y attachées. *Riv. Mat. Pura Appl.* **1999**, *14*, 83–119.
6. Ameri, R.; Amiri-Bideshki, M.; Saeid, A.B.; Hoskova-Mayerova, S. Prime filters of hyperlattices. *An. Stiint. Univ. "Ovidius" Constanta Ser. Mat.* **2016**, *24*, 15–26. [CrossRef]
7. Ameri, R.; Amiri-Bideshki, M.; Hoskova-Mayerova, S.; Saeid, A.B. Distributive and Dual Distributive Elements in Hyperlattices. *An. Stiint. Univ. "Ovidius" Constanta Ser. Mat.* **2017**, *25*, 25–36. [CrossRef]
8. Nakano, T. Rings and partly ordered systems. *Math. Z.* **1967**, *99*, 355–376. [CrossRef]
9. Varlet, J.C. Remarks on Distributive Lattices. *Bull. l'Acad. Pol. des Sci. Sér. Sci. Math. Astr. Phys.* **1975**, *XXIII*, 1143–1147.
10. Comer, S.D. *Multi-Valued Algebras and Their Graphical Representations*; Preliminary Draft; Mathematics and Computer Science Department, The Citadel: Charleston, SC, USA, 1986.
11. Konstantinidou, M.; Serafimidis, K. Hyperstructures dérivées d'un treillis particulier. *Rend. Mat. Appl.* **1993**, *7*, 257–265.
12. Kehagias, A.; Serafimidis, K. The L-Fuzzy Nakano Hypergroup. *Inf. Sci.* **2005**, *169*, 305–327. [CrossRef]
13. Călugăreanu, G.; Leoreanu, V. Hypergroups associated with lattices. *Ital. J. Pure Appl. Math.* **2001**, *9*, 165–173.
14. Tofan, I.; Volf, A.C. On some connections between hyperstructures and fuzzy sets. *Ital. J. Pure Appl. Math.* **2000**, *7*, 63–68.
15. Njionou, B.B.K.; Ngapeya, A.A.C.; Leoreanu-Fotea, V. A New Approach on Derivations of Hyperlattices. *J. Mult.-Valued Log. Soft Comput.* **2022**, *39*, 467–488.
16. Prenowitz, W.; Jantosciak, J. *Join Geometries*; Undergraduate Texts in Mathematics; Springer: New York, NY, USA; Berlin/Heidelberg, Germany, 1979.
17. Corsini, P.; Leoreanu, V. Join spaces associated with fuzzy sets. *J. Comb. Inf. Syst. Sci.* **1995**, *20*, 293–303.
18. Fotea, V.L.; Rosenberg, I.G. Hypergroupoids determined by lattices. *Eur. J. Comb.* **2010**, *31*, 925–931. [CrossRef]
19. Leoreanu-Fotea, V.; Rosenberg, I.G. Join spaces determined by lattices. *J. Mult. Valued Log. Soft Comput.* **2010**, *16*, 7–16.
20. Mittas, J. Hypergroupes canoniques. *Math. Balk.* **1972**, *2*, 165–179.
21. Roth, R. Character and conjugacy class hypergroups of a finite group. *Ann. Mat. Pura Appl.* **1975**, *105*, 295–311. [CrossRef]
22. McMullen, J.; Price, J. Duality for finite abelian hypergroups over splitting fields. *Bull. Austral. Math. Soc.* **1979**, *20*, 57–70. [CrossRef]
23. Hall, M., Jr. *Combinatorial Theory*; John Wiley and Sons Inc.: Hoboken, NJ, USA, 1967.

axioms

Article

Elliptic Quaternion Matrices: Theory and Algorithms

Hidayet Hüda Kösal *, Emre Kişi, Mahmut Akyiğit and Beyza Çelik

Faculty of Sciences, Department of Mathematics, Sakarya University, Sakarya TR-54050, Türkiye; ekisi@sakarya.edu.tr (E.K.); makyigit@sakarya.edu.tr (M.A.); beyza.celik6@ogr.sakarya.edu.tr (B.Ç.)
* Correspondence: hhkosal@sakarya.edu.tr

Abstract: In this study, we obtained results for the computation of eigen-pairs, singular value decomposition, pseudoinverse, and the least squares problem for elliptic quaternion matrices. Moreover, we established algorithms based on these results and provided illustrative numerical experiments to substantiate the accuracy of our conclusions. In the experiments, it was observed that the p-value in the algebra of elliptic quaternions directly affects the performance of the problem under consideration. Selecting the optimal p-value for problem-solving and the elliptic behavior of many physical systems make this number system advantageous in applied sciences.

Keywords: elliptic quaternion matrix; optimal p-value; eigen-pairs; singular value decomposition; pseudoinverse; least squares solution

MSC: 11R52; 15A60; 15A18

1. Introduction

Eigenvalues and eigenvectors, singular value decomposition, the pseudoinverse, and the least squares solution form the foundational pillars of matrix theory, with significant applications in diverse fields such as theoretical and computational mathematics, image and signal processing, principal component analysis, data compression, machine learning, deep learning, etc. For example, Israel and Greville comprehensively treated eigenvalues, eigenvectors, singular value decomposition, the pseudoinverse, and the least squares solution. The book explores the interconnections between these concepts, presenting both their underlying theories and practical applications across various fields [1]. Samar et al. presented a K-weighted pseudoinverse and gave results for condition numbers for the solution of the least squares problem with equality constraint [2]. Samar et al. explored the conditioning theory of the $\mathcal{ML}$-weighted least squares and $\mathcal{ML}$-weighted pseudoinverse problems [3]. Simsek focused on obtaining least-squares solutions for generalized Sylvester-type quaternion matrix equations using pseudoinverses and applied these solutions to color image restoration processes [4]. Dian et al. presented a novel hyperspectral image and multispectral image fusion method based on the subspace representation and convolutional neural network denoiser. They obtained the subspaces via singular value decomposition of a high-resolution hyperspectral image [5]. Hashemipour et al. proposed a new lossy data compression framework centered on optimal singular value decomposition for big data compression [6]. Wang and Zhu focused on the implementation of data reduction algorithms in machine learning by using eigenvalues-eigenvectors, singular value decomposition, and principal component analysis [7].

These mathematical concepts not only form the basis of numerous applications but also extend to n-dimensional hypercomplex number systems. There is a generalization involving 2-dimensional hypercomplex numbers [8]. The following is the definition of these numbers, known as generalized complex numbers:

$$q_{(g)} = q_{(g),r} + q_{(g),i}i,$$

check for updates

Citation: Kösal, H.H.; Kişi, E.; Akyiğit, M.; Çelik, B. Elliptic Quaternion Matrices: Theory and Algorithms. *Axioms* **2024**, *13*, 656. https://doi.org/10.3390/axioms13100656

Academic Editor: Vladimir Rakocevic

Received: 30 July 2024
Revised: 16 September 2024
Accepted: 20 September 2024
Published: 24 September 2024

where $q_{(g),r}, q_{(g),i} \in \mathbb{R}, i \notin \mathbb{R}$ and $i^2 = p$ $(p \in \mathbb{R})$. Generalized Segre quaternions are generalized complex numbers extended to 4 dimensions. Generalized Segre quaternions are defined as follows:

$$q_{(GS)} = q_{(GS),r} + q_{(GS),i}i + q_{(GS),j}j + q_{(GS),k}k,$$

where $q_{(GS),r}, q_{(GS),i}, q_{(GS),j}, q_{(GS),k} \in \mathbb{R}, i, j, k \notin \mathbb{R}$. The multiplication rules for units i, j and k are given below:

$$i^2 = k^2 = p, \; j^2 = 1, \; ij = ji = k, \; jk = kj = i, \; ki = ik = pj, \; p \in \mathbb{R}.$$

Based on the value of p, generalized complex numbers and Segre quaternions are classified into three categories: they are referred to as hyperbolic complex numbers and hyperbolic quaternions when $p > 0$, parabolic complex numbers and parabolic quaternions when $p = 0$, and elliptic complex numbers and elliptic quaternions when $p < 0$, [8,9]. Each number system has various scientific and technological applications. For example, some problemsin non-Euclidean geometries can be solved by hyperbolic complex numbers and hyperbolic quaternions [10]. In domains like robotic control and spatial mechanics, parabolic complex (dual) numbers and parabolic quaternions are employed [11]. On the other hand, as numerous physical systems demonstrate elliptical behavior, the practical applications of elliptic complex numbers and elliptic quaternions in applied science are noteworthy. One of the examples is that, Ozdemir defined elliptic quaternions (non-commutative) and generated an elliptical rotation matrix for the motion of a point on an ellipse through some angle about a vector using those quaternions [12]. Dundar et al. studied elliptical harmonic motion, which is the superposition of two simple harmonic motions in perpendicular directions with the same angular frequency and phase difference of $\frac{\pi}{2}$ using elliptic complex numbers [13]. Derin and Gungor proposed the generalization of gravity, including the Proca-type and gravitomagnetic monopole by means of elliptic biquaternions [14]. Catoni et al. introduced algebraic properties and the differential conditions of elliptic quaternionic systems [9]. Additionally, Catoni et al. studied the constant curvature spaces associated with the geometry generated by elliptic quaternions. They formulated geodesic equations within the context of Riemann geometry [15]. Gua et al. defined the elliptic quaternionic canonical transform and investigated Parseval's theorem with the help of this transform [16]. Yuan et al. obtained the Hermitian solutions of the elliptic quaternion matrix equation $(AXB, CXD) = (E, G)$ [17]. Tosun and Kosal characterized the existence of the solution to Sylvester s-conjugate elliptic quaternion matrix equations. They obtained the solution explicitly using a real representation of an elliptic quaternion matrix [18]. Gai and Huang developed a new convolutional neural network with elliptic quaternion values. They conducted extensive experiments on colour image classification and colour image denoising to evaluate the performance of the proposed convolutional neural network [19]. Guo et al. studied the problem of solutions to Maxwell's equations of elliptic quaternions using a real representation of elliptic quaternion matrices [20]. Atali et al. obtained the elliptic quaternionic least-squares solution with the minimum norm of the elliptic quaternion matrix equation $AX = B$. Furthermore, leveraging the insights derived from their theories, they developed a novel color image restoration model known as the elliptical quaternionic least squares restoration filter [21].

As observed, the elliptic quaternions and their matrices find numerous practical applications in various branches of applied sciences. Thus, further study of the theoretical properties and numerical computations of elliptic quaternions and their matrices is becoming increasingly necessary. In this regard, we derive outcomes concerning the computation of eigen-pairs, singular value decomposition, pseudoinverse, and least squares solutions with the minimum norm for elliptic quaternion matrices. Additionally, algorithms are formulated based on these results, accompanied by illustrative numerical experiments to validate our findings' precision empirically. Within the context of this paper, the following notations are employed. Let $\mathbb{R}$, $\mathbb{C}$, $\mathbb{C}_p$, and $\mathbb{H}_p$ denote the sets of real numbers, complex numbers, elliptic complex numbers, and elliptic quaternions, respectively. $\mathbb{R}^{m\times n}$, $\mathbb{C}^{m\times n}$, $\mathbb{C}_p^{m\times n}$, and $\mathbb{H}_p^{m\times n}$ denote the set of all $m \times n$ matrices on $\mathbb{R}$, $\mathbb{C}$, $\mathbb{C}_p$ and $\mathbb{H}_p$, respectively. Throughout the study, we will also denote elliptic complex numbers as *EC* numbers and elliptic quaternions as *EQs* for short. Also, we use the following notations: $q_{(\square)}$ represents a complex number when $\square = c$, an *EC* number when $\square = e$, and an *EQ* when $\square = E$. Similarly, $Q_{(\square)}$ denotes a complex matrix when $\square = c$, an *EC* matrix when $\square = e$, and an *EQ* matrix when $\square = E$.

2. Preliminaries

In this section, some basic algebraic properties and notations for *EC* numbers and *EQs* are given. This section provides the basis for further operations, which are discussedin the following sections.

An *EC* number $q_{(e)}$ is denoted by $q_{(e)} = q_{(e),r} + q_{(e),i}i$, where $i^2 = p < 0$ and $q_{(e),r}, q_{(e),i}, p \in \mathbb{R}$. The real and imaginary parts of $q_{(e)}$ are denoted by $\mathrm{Re}\left(q_{(e)}\right) = q_{(e),r}$ and $\mathrm{Im}\left(q_{(e)}\right) = q_{(e),i}$, respectively. The conjugate and norm of $q_{(e)} \in \mathbb{C}_p$ are defined as $\overline{q_{(e)}} = q_{(e),r} - q_{(e),i}i$ and $\left\|q_{(e)}\right\|_p = \sqrt{q_{(e),r}^2 - pq_{(e),i}^2}$, respectively [22]. The multiplication of two *EC* numbers $q_{1,(e)} = q_{1,(e),r} + q_{1,(e),i}i$ and $q_{2,(e)} = q_{2,(e),r} + q_{2,(e),i}i$ is defined as

$$q_{1,(e)}q_{2,(e)} = \left(q_{1,(e),r}q_{2,(e),r} + pq_{1,(e),i}q_{2,(e),i}\right) + i\left(q_{1,(e),r}q_{2,(e),i} + q_{2,(e),r}q_{1,(e),i}\right).$$

An *EC* matrix $Q_{(e)}$ is denoted as $Q_{(e)} = Q_{(e),r} + Q_{(e),i}i$, where $i^2 = p < 0$, $p \in \mathbb{R}$, and $Q_{(e),r}, Q_{(e),i} \in \mathbb{R}^{m\times n}$. The conjugate, transpose, conjugate transpose and Frobenius norm of $Q_{(e)} \in \mathbb{C}_p^{m\times n}$ are defined by $\overline{Q_{(e)}} = Q_{(e),r} - Q_{(e),i}i$, $Q_{(e)}^T = Q_{(e),r}^T + Q_{(e),i}^T i$, $Q_{(e)}^* = Q_{(e),r}^T - Q_{(e),i}^T i$, and $\|Q_{(e)}\|_p = \sqrt{\|Q_{(e),r}\|^2 - p\|Q_{(e),i}\|^2}$, respectively. The multiplication of two *EC* matrices $Q_{1,(e)} = Q_{1,(e),r} + Q_{1,(e),i}i$ and $Q_{2,(e)} = Q_{2,(e),r} + Q_{2,(e),i}i$ is defined as

$$Q_{1,(e)}Q_{2,(e)} = \left(Q_{1,(e),r}Q_{2,(e),r} + pQ_{1,(e),i}Q_{2,(e),i}\right) + i\left(Q_{1,(e),r}Q_{2,(e),i} + Q_{2,(e),r}Q_{1,(e),i}\right).$$

There exists an isomorphism between *EC* matrices and complex matrices, as depicted in the following:

$$\begin{aligned} &\mathrm{H}_p : \mathbb{C}_p^{m\times n} \to \mathbb{C}^{m\times n} \\ &Q_{(e)} = Q_{(e),r} + Q_{(e),i}i \to \mathrm{H}_p\left(Q_{(e)}\right) = Q_{(c)} = Q_{(e),r} + I\sqrt{-p}Q_{(e),i}, \end{aligned}$$

where I represents the complex unit ($I^2 = -1$). Some algebraic operations of this isomorphism are listed below, where $Q_{(e),1}$ and $Q_{(e),2}$ are *EC* matrices of appropriate sizes:

(a) $H_p\left(Q_{(e),1}Q_{(e),2}\right) = H_p\left(Q_{(e),1}\right)H_p\left(Q_{(e),2}\right)$,

(b) $\left(H_p\left(Q_{(e),1}\right)\right)^T = H_p\left(Q_{(e),1}^T\right)$,

(c) $\left(H_p\left(Q_{(e),1}\right)\right)^* = H_p\left(Q_{(e),1}^*\right)$,

(d) $\overline{\left(H_p\left(Q_{(e),1}\right)\right)} = H_p\left(\overline{Q_{(e),1}}\right)$.

Many algebraic properties of *EC* numbers (or matrices) can be derived from their corresponding complex counterparts using this isomorphism [8,23].

An *EQ* $q_{(E)}$ is denoted as $q_{(E)} = q_{(E),r} + q_{(E),i}i + q_{(E),j}j + q_{(E),k}k$, where $i^2 = k^2 = p < 0$, $j^2 = 1$, $ij = ji = k$, $jk = kj = i$, $ki = ik = pj$, and $q_{(E),r}, q_{(E),i}, q_{(E),j}, q_{(E),k}, p \in \mathbb{R}$ [9,22]. An *EQ* $q_{(E)}$ is denoted in the forms:

$$q_{(E)} = \left(q_{(E),r} + iq_{(E),i}\right) + \left(q_{(E),j} + iq_{(E),k}\right)j = q_{(e),1}e_1 + q_{(e),2}e_2,$$

where

$$q_{(e),1} = \left(q_{(E),r} + q_{(E),j}\right) + \left(q_{(E),i} + q_{(E),k}\right)i$$

and

$$q_{(e),2} = \left(q_{(E),r} - q_{(E),j}\right) + \left(q_{(E),i} - q_{(E),k}\right)i,$$

are *EC* numbers and $e_1 = \frac{1+j}{2}$, $e_2 = \frac{1-j}{2}$. Clearly, $e_1 e_2 = 0$, $e_1 + e_2 = 1$, $e_1^2 = e_1$ and $e_2^2 = e_2$. As a result, e_1 and e_2 are disjoint idempotent units. The multiplication of two *EQ*s $q_{1,(E)} = q_{1,(e),1}e_1 + q_{1,(e),2}e_2$ and $q_{2,(E)} = q_{2,(e),1}e_1 + q_{2,(e),2}e_2$ is defined by

$$q_{1,(E)}q_{2,(E)} = \left(q_{1,(e),1}q_{2,(e),1}\right)e_1 + \left(q_{1,(e),2}q_{2,(e),2}\right)e_2.$$

The conjugate and norm of the *EQ* $q_{(E)} = q_{(e),1}e_1 + q_{(e),2}e_2$ are defined by $\overline{q_{(E)}} = \overline{q_{(e),1}}e_1 + \overline{q_{(e),2}}e_2$ and $\left\|q_{(E)}\right\|_p = \frac{1}{\sqrt{2}}\sqrt{\left(\left\|q_{(e),1}\right\|_p^2 + \left\|q_{(e),2}\right\|_p^2\right)}$, respectively.

An *EQ* matrix $Q_{(E)}$ is represented as

$$\begin{aligned} Q_{(E)} = Q_{(E),r} + Q_{(E),i}i + Q_{(E),j}j + Q_{(E),k}k &= \left(Q_{(E),r} + Q_{(E),i}i\right) + j\left(Q_{(E),j} + Q_{(E),k}i\right) \\ &= Q_{(e),1}e_1 + Q_{(e),2}e_2, \end{aligned} \tag{1}$$

where

$$Q_{(e),1} = \left(Q_{(E),r} + Q_{(E),j}\right) + \left(Q_{(E),i} + Q_{(E),k}\right)i$$

and

$$Q_{(e),2} = \left(Q_{(E),r} - Q_{(E),j}\right) + \left(Q_{(E),i} - Q_{(E),k}\right)i$$

are *EC* matrices and $Q_{(E),r}, Q_{(E),i}, Q_{(E),j}, Q_{(E),k} \in \mathbb{R}^{m\times n}$ [18,21]. The multiplication of two *EQ* matrices $Q_{1,(E)} = Q_{1,(e),1}e_1 + Q_{1,(e),2}e_2$ and $Q_{2,(E)} = Q_{2,(e),1}e_1 + Q_{2,(e),2}e_2$ is defined by

$$Q_{1,(E)}Q_{2,(E)} = \left(Q_{1,(e),1}Q_{2,(e),1}\right)e_1 + \left(Q_{1,(e),2}Q_{2,(e),2}\right)e_2.$$

The conjugate, transpose, conjugate transpose, and Frobenius norm of *EQ* matrix $Q_{(E)} = Q_{(e),1}e_1 + Q_{(e),2}e_2 \in \mathbb{H}_p^{m\times n}$ are defined by $\overline{Q_{(E)}} = \overline{Q_{(e),1}}e_1 + \overline{Q_{(e),2}}e_2$, $Q_{(E)}^T = Q_{(e),1}^T e_1 + Q_{(e),2}^T e_2$, $Q_{(E)}^* = \overline{Q_{(e),1}^T}e_1 + \overline{Q_{(e),2}^T}e_2$ and $\left\|Q_{(E)}\right\|_p = \frac{1}{\sqrt{2}}\sqrt{\left(\left\|Q_{(e),1}\right\|_p^2 + \left\|Q_{(e),2}\right\|_p^2\right)}$.

3. Eigenvalues and Eigenvectors, Singular Value Decomposition, Pseudoinverse, and Least Squares Problem for *EQ* Matrices

In the ensuing discourse, we delineate a series of lemmas pivotal for the computation of eigen-pairs, singular value decomposition, pseudoinverse, and the resolution of the least squares problem specifically tailored for *EC* matrices. Subsequently, leveraging these foundational lemmas, we derive the pertinent theoretical framework associated with elliptic quaternion matrices.

3.1. EC Matrices

Lemma 1. *A polynomial function of degree N with EC number coefficients presented by*

$$f_p(x_{(e)}) = x_{(e)}^N + q_{(e),N-1}x_{(e)}^{N-1} + \ldots + q_{(e),1}x_{(e)} + q_{(e),0}$$

has exactly N zeros in the set of EC numbers.

Proof. Let

$$f_p(x_{(e)}) = x_{(e)}^N + q_{(e),N-1}x_{(e)}^{N-1} + \ldots + q_{(e),1}x_{(e)} + q_{(e),0}$$

be a polynomial of degree N with EC coefficients and values. Its complex representation is as follows:

$$\mathrm{H}_p\left(f_p(x_{(e)})\right) = \mathrm{H}_p\left(x_{(e)}\right)^N + \mathrm{H}_p\left(q_{(e),N-1}\right)\mathrm{H}_p\left(x_{(e)}\right)^{N-1} + \ldots + \mathrm{H}_p\left(q_{(e),1}\right)\mathrm{H}_p\left(x_{(e)}\right) + \mathrm{H}_p\left(q_{(e),0}\right).$$

Since this representation is a polynomial of degree N with complex coefficients and values, the fundamental theorem of algebra tells us that it has exactly N roots. Suppose that the complex number $x_{(c)} = x_{(c),r} + x_{(c),i}I$ is a root of the polynomial $\mathrm{H}_p\left(f_p(x_{(e)})\right)$. Then, we have:

$$\mathrm{H}_p\left(f_p(x_{(e)})\right) = \left(x_{(c)}\right)^N + \mathrm{H}_p\left(q_{(e),N-1}\right)\left(x_{(c)}\right)^{N-1} + \ldots + \mathrm{H}_p\left(q_{(e),1}\right)\left(x_{(c)}\right) + \mathrm{H}_p\left(q_{(e),0}\right) = 0.$$

Applying the inverse of the isomorphism H_p to both sides of the above equation, we get:

$$f_p(x_{(e)}) = \mathrm{H}_\mathrm{p}^{-1}\left(\mathrm{x}_{(\mathrm{c})}\right)^\mathrm{N} + \mathrm{q}_{(\mathrm{e}),\mathrm{N}-1}\mathrm{H}_\mathrm{p}^{-1}\left(\mathrm{x}_{(\mathrm{c})}\right)^{\mathrm{N}-1} + \ldots + \mathrm{q}_{(\mathrm{e}),1}\mathrm{H}_\mathrm{p}^{-1}\left(\mathrm{x}_{(\mathrm{c})}\right) + \mathrm{q}_{(\mathrm{e}),0}.$$

This simplifies to:

$$f_p(x_{(e)}) = \left(x_{(c),r} + \frac{i}{\sqrt{-p}}x_{(c),i}\right)^N + q_{(e),N-1}\left(x_{(c),r} + \frac{i}{\sqrt{-p}}x_{(c),i}\right)^{N-1} + \ldots + q_{(e),1}\left(x_{(c),r} + \frac{i}{\sqrt{-p}}x_{(c),i}\right) + q_{(e),0} = 0.$$

Therefore, if $x_{(c)} = x_{(c),r} + x_{(c),i}I$ is a root of the polynomial $\mathrm{H}_p\left(f_p(x_{(e)})\right)$, then the EC number $x_{(e)} = x_{(c),r} + \frac{i}{\sqrt{-p}}x_{(c),i}$ is a root of the polynomial $f_p(x_{(e)})$. As a result, $f_p(x_{(e)})$ has exactly N roots. □

Lemma 2. *An EC matrix $Q_{(e)} \in \mathbb{C}_p^{n\times n}$ has at most n elliptic eigenvalues.*

Proof. Since the characteristic polynomial $f_p(\lambda_{(e)}) = \det(Q_{(e)} - \lambda_{(e)}I_n)$ of the matrix $Q_{(e)} \in \mathbb{C}_p^{n\times n}$ is an n-th order polynomial with EC coefficients and values, by Lemma 1, the EC matrix $Q_{(e)}$ has at most n eigenvalues. □

Lemma 3. *Let the eigenvalues of an complex matrix $\mathrm{H}_p\left(Q_{(e)}\right)$ be denoted by $\lambda_{\mathrm{H}_p(Q_{(e)})}$, and let the corresponding eigenvectors be represented by $x_{\mathrm{H}_p(Q_{(e)})}$. Then, the eigenvalues of the EC matrix $Q_{(e)} \in \mathbb{C}_p^{n\times n}$ are given by*

$$\lambda_{(e)} = \mathrm{Re}(\lambda_{\mathrm{H}_p(Q_{(e)})}) + \frac{i}{\sqrt{-p}}\mathrm{Im}(\lambda_{\mathrm{H}_p(Q_{(e)})})$$

and the corresponding eigenvectors are given by

$$x_{(e)} = \mathrm{Re}(x_{\mathrm{H}_p(Q_{(e)})}) + \frac{i}{\sqrt{-p}}\mathrm{Im}(x_{\mathrm{H}_p(Q_{(e)})}).$$

The converse of this lemma is also true.

Proof. Let $Q_{(e)} \in \mathbb{C}_p^{n\times n}$ be an EC matrix, and the eigenvalues of an complex matrix $\mathrm{H}_p\left(Q_{(e)}\right)$ be denoted by $\lambda_{\mathrm{H}_p(Q_{(e)})}$, and let the corresponding eigenvectors be represented by $x_{\mathrm{H}_p(Q_{(e)})}$. Then, we have $\mathrm{H}_p\left(Q_{(e)}\right)x_{\mathrm{H}_p(Q_{(e)})} = \lambda_{\mathrm{H}_p(Q_{(e)})}x_{\mathrm{H}_p(Q_{(e)})}$. Applying the inverse of the isomorphism H_p to both sides of the last equation, we get:

$$Q_{(e)}\mathrm{H}_p^{-1}\left(x_{\mathrm{H}_p(Q_{(e)})}\right) = \mathrm{H}_p^{-1}\left(\lambda_{\mathrm{H}_p(Q_{(e)})}\right)\mathrm{H}_p^{-1}\left(x_{\mathrm{H}_p(Q_{(e)})}\right).$$

Thus, we get

$$\lambda_{(e)} = \mathrm{Re}\Big(\lambda_{\mathrm{H}_p(Q_{(e)})}\Big) + \frac{i}{\sqrt{-p}}\mathrm{Im}\Big(\lambda_{\mathrm{H}_p(Q_{(e)})}\Big),$$

and

$$x_{(e)} = \mathrm{Re}\Big(x_{\mathrm{H}_p(Q_{(e)})}\Big) + \frac{i}{\sqrt{-p}}\mathrm{Im}\Big(x_{\mathrm{H}_p(Q_{(e)})}\Big).$$

□

Lemma 4. *Let $Q_{(e)} \in \mathbb{C}_p^{n\times n}$. An EC matrix $Q_{(e)}$ is nonsingular if and only if the complex matrix $\mathrm{H}_p(Q_{(e)})$ is nonsingular. If $\mathrm{H}_p(Q_{(e)})$ is nonsingular, then*

$$Q_{(e)}^{-1} = \mathrm{Re}\Big(\big(\mathrm{H}_p\big(Q_{(e)}\big)\big)^{-1}\Big) + \frac{i}{\sqrt{-p}}\mathrm{Im}\Big(\big(\mathrm{H}_p\big(Q_{(e)}\big)\big)^{-1}\Big).$$

Proof. Let the *EC* matrix $\mathrm{Q}_{(e)} = \mathrm{Q}_{(e),r} + \mathrm{Q}_{(e),i}i$ be nonsingular. Then, there exists an inverse matrix $\mathrm{Q}_{(e)}^{-1} \in \mathbb{C}_p^{n\times n}$ such that $\mathrm{Q}_{(e)}\mathrm{Q}_{(e)}^{-1} = \mathrm{Q}_{(e)}^{-1}\mathrm{Q}_{(e)} = I_n$. If we apply the isomorphism $\mathrm{H_p}$ to both sides of the last equation, we obtain:

$$\mathrm{H}_p\big(\mathrm{Q}_{(e)}\big)\mathrm{H}_p\big(\mathrm{Q}_{(e)}^{-1}\big) = \mathrm{H}_p\big(\mathrm{Q}_{(e)}^{-1}\big)\mathrm{H}_p\big(\mathrm{Q}_{(e)}\big) = I_n.$$

Hence, we conclude that $\big(\mathrm{H}_p\big(\mathrm{Q}_{(e)}\big)\big)^{-1} = \mathrm{H}_p\big(\mathrm{Q}_{(e)}^{-1}\big)$. On the other hand, since

$$\mathrm{H}_p\big(\mathrm{Q}_{(e)}^{-1}\big) = \mathrm{Re}\Big(\big(\mathrm{H}_p\big(\mathrm{Q}_{(e)}\big)\big)^{-1}\Big) + I\,\mathrm{Im}\Big(\big(\mathrm{H}_p\big(\mathrm{Q}_{(e)}\big)\big)^{-1}\Big),$$

we can apply the inverse of the isomorphism H_p to this equation, yielding:

$$\mathrm{Q}_{(e)}^{-1} = \mathrm{Re}\Big(\big(\mathrm{H}_p\big(\mathrm{Q}_{(e)}\big)\big)^{-1}\Big) + \frac{i}{\sqrt{-p}}\mathrm{Im}\Big(\big(\mathrm{H}_p\big(\mathrm{Q}_{(e)}\big)\big)^{-1}\Big).$$

□

Lemma 5. *Let $Q_{(e)} \in \mathbb{C}_p^{m\times n}$ be an EC matrix. The pseudoinverse of $Q_{(e)}$, denoted by $\big(Q_{(e)}\big)^{\dagger}$, is given by*

$$\big(Q_{(e)}\big)^{\dagger} = \mathrm{Re}\Big(\big(\mathrm{H_p}\big(Q_{(e)}\big)\big)^{\dagger}\Big) + \frac{i}{\sqrt{-p}}\mathrm{Im}\Big(\big(\mathrm{H_p}\big(Q_{(e)}\big)\big)^{\dagger}\Big),$$

where $\big(\mathrm{H_p}\big(Q_{(e)}\big)\big)^{\dagger}$ is the pseudoinverse of the complex matrix $\mathrm{H_p}\big(Q_{(e)}\big)$.

Proof. Suppose that $Q_{(e)}^{\dagger}$ is the pseudoinverse of the matrix $Q_{(e)}$. In that case, the following equations hold:

$$Q_{(e)}Q_{(e)}^{\dagger}Q_{(e)} = Q_{(e)}, \quad Q_{(e)}^{\dagger}Q_{(e)}Q_{(e)}^{\dagger} = Q_{(e)}^{\dagger},$$
$$\big(Q_{(e)}Q_{(e)}^{\dagger}\big)^{*} = Q_{(e)}Q_{(e)}^{\dagger}, \quad \big(Q_{(e)}^{\dagger}Q_{(e)}\big)^{*} = Q_{(e)}^{\dagger}Q_{(e)}.$$

Applying the isomorphism H_p to the above equations, we get the following results:

$$\begin{aligned}
&\mathrm{H}_p\left(Q_{(e)}\right)\mathrm{H}_p\left(Q_{(e)}^{\dagger}\right)\mathrm{H}_p\left(Q_{(e)}\right) = \mathrm{H}_p\left(Q_{(e)}\right),\\
&\mathrm{H}_p\left(Q_{(e)}^{\dagger}\right)\mathrm{H}_p\left(Q_{(e)}\right)\mathrm{H}_p\left(Q_{(e)}^{\dagger}\right) = \mathrm{H}_p\left(Q_{(e)}^{\dagger}\right),\\
&\left(\mathrm{H}_p\left(Q_{(e)}\right)\mathrm{H}_p\left(Q_{(e)}^{\dagger}\right)\right)^* = \mathrm{H}_p\left(Q_{(e)}\right)\mathrm{H}_p\left(Q_{(e)}^{\dagger}\right),\\
&\left(\mathrm{H}_p\left(Q_{(e)}^{\dagger}\right)\mathrm{H}_p\left(Q_{(e)}\right)\right)^* = \mathrm{H}_p\left(Q_{(e)}^{\dagger}\right)\mathrm{H}_p\left(Q_{(e)}\right).
\end{aligned}$$

As a result, we obtain the following pseudoinverse transformation under the isomorphism H_p:

$$\left(\mathrm{H}_p\left(Q_{(e)}\right)\right)^{\dagger} = \mathrm{H}_p\left(Q_{(e)}^{\dagger}\right),$$

and

$$\left(Q_{(e)}\right)^{\dagger} = \mathrm{Re}\left(\left(\mathrm{H}_p\left(Q_{(e)}\right)\right)^{\dagger}\right) + \frac{i}{\sqrt{-p}}\mathrm{Im}\left(\left(\mathrm{H}_p\left(Q_{(e)}\right)\right)^{\dagger}\right).$$

□

Lemma 6. *Let $Q_{(e)} \in \mathbb{C}_p^{m\times n}$. Suppose that the singular value decomposition of the complex matrix $\mathrm{H}_p\left(Q_{(e)}\right)$ is given by $\mathrm{H}_\mathrm{p}\left(Q_{(e)}\right) = U_{(c)}\Sigma V_{(c)}^*$. Then, the singular value decomposition of the EC matrix $Q_{(e)}$ is*

$$Q_{(e)} = U_{(e)}\Sigma V_{(e)}^*,$$

where

$$U_{(e)} = \left(\mathrm{Re}\left(U_{(c)}\right) + \frac{i}{\sqrt{-p}}\mathrm{Im}\left(U_{(c)}\right)\right) \text{ and } V_{(e)} = \left(\mathrm{Re}\left(U_{(c)}\right) + \frac{i}{\sqrt{-p}}\mathrm{Im}\left(U_{(c)}\right)\right).$$

The converse of this statement is also true.

Proof. Suppose that the singular value decomposition of the complex representation $\mathrm{H}_\mathrm{p}\left(Q_{(e)}\right)$ is given by:

$$\mathrm{H}_\mathrm{p}\left(Q_{(e)}\right) = U_{(c)}\Sigma V_{(c)}^*.$$

Now, using the expansion of the real and imaginary parts of the unitary matrices, we have:

$$\mathrm{H}_\mathrm{p}\left(Q_{(e)}\right) = \left(\mathrm{Re}\left(U_{(c)}\right) + i\,\mathrm{Im}\left(U_{(c)}\right)\right)\Sigma\left(\mathrm{Re}\left(V_{(c)}^*\right) + i\,\mathrm{Im}\left(V_{(c)}^*\right)\right).$$

Applying the inverse of the isomorphism H_p to both sides of the last equation, we obtain:

$$Q_{(e)} = \left(\mathrm{Re}\left(U_{(c)}\right) + \frac{i}{\sqrt{-p}}\mathrm{Im}\left(U_{(c)}\right)\right)\Sigma\left(\mathrm{Re}\left(V_{(c)}^*\right) + \frac{i}{\sqrt{-p}}\mathrm{Im}\left(V_{(c)}^*\right)\right).$$

On the other hand, since $U_{(c)}$ and $V_{(c)}$ are unitary matrices, we have

$$\begin{aligned}
U_{(e)}U_{(e)}^* &= \left(\mathrm{Re}\left(U_{(c)}\right) + \frac{i}{\sqrt{-p}}\mathrm{Im}\left(U_{(c)}\right)\right)\left(\mathrm{Re}\left(U_{(c)}^T\right) - \frac{i}{\sqrt{-p}}\mathrm{Im}\left(U_{(c)}^T\right)\right)\\
&= I_n
\end{aligned}$$

and

$$V_{(e)}V^{*}_{(e)} = \left(\mathrm{Re}\left(V_{(c)}\right) + \frac{i}{\sqrt{-p}}\,\mathrm{Im}\left(V_{(c)}\right)\right)\left(\mathrm{Re}\left(V^{T}_{(c)}\right) - \frac{i}{\sqrt{-p}}\,\mathrm{Im}\left(V^{T}_{(c)}\right)\right)$$
$$= I_n.$$

□

Corollary 1. *Let* $Q_{(e)} \in \mathbb{C}_p^{m\times n}$. *Then* $rank\left(Q_{(e)}\right) = rank\left(\mathrm{H_p}\left(Q_{(e)}\right)\right)$.

Proof. Since matrices $Q_{(e)}$ and $\mathrm{H}_p\left(Q_{(e)}\right)$ have the same number of nonzero singular values, we have $rank\left(Q_{(e)}\right) = rank\left(\mathrm{H_p}\left(Q_{(e)}\right)\right)$. □

Lemma 7. *Let* $Q_{(e)} \in \mathbb{C}_p^{m\times n}$. *Suppose that* $\mathrm{H_p}\left(Q_{(e)}\right) = U_{(c)}\Sigma V^{*}_{(c)}$. *In this case, the pseudoinverse of EC matrix* $Q_{(e)}$ *is given by*

$$\left(Q_{(e)}\right)^{\dagger} = \left(\mathrm{Re}\left(V_{(c)}\right) + \frac{i}{\sqrt{-p}}\mathrm{Im}\left(V_{(c)}\right)\right)\Sigma^{\dagger}\left(\mathrm{Re}\left(U_{(c)}\right) + \frac{i}{\sqrt{-p}}\mathrm{Im}\left(U_{(c)}\right)\right)^{*}.$$

Proof. Let $\mathrm{H_p}\left(Q_{(e)}\right) = U_{(c)}\Sigma V^{*}_{(c)}$. Then the pseudoinverse of the complex matrix $\mathrm{H_p}\left(Q_{(e)}\right)$ is $\left(\mathrm{H_p}(Q_{(e)})\right)^{\dagger} = V_{(c)}\Sigma^{\dagger}U^{*}_{(c)}$. From Lemma 5, we have $\left(\mathrm{H_p}(Q_{(e)})\right)^{\dagger} = \mathrm{H_p}(Q^{\dagger}_{(e)})$. Substituting this into the previous equation, we have: $\mathrm{H_p}(Q^{\dagger}_{(e)}) = V_{(c)}\Sigma^{\dagger}U^{*}_{(c)}$. Applying the inverse of the isomorphism $\mathrm{H_p}$ to both sides, we conclude that

$$Q^{\dagger}_{(e)} = \left(\mathrm{Re}(V_{(c)}) + \frac{i}{\sqrt{-p}}\mathrm{Im}(V_{(c)})\right)\Sigma^{\dagger}\left(\mathrm{Re}(U_{(c)}) + \frac{i}{\sqrt{-p}}\mathrm{Im}(U_{(c)})\right)^{*}.$$

□

Lemma 8. *Let* $Q_{1,(e)} \in \mathbb{C}_p^{m\times n}$ *and* $Q_{2,(e)} \in \mathbb{C}_p^{m\times q}$. *Suppose that* $\mathrm{H_p}\left(Q_{1,(e)}\right) = U_{(c)}\Sigma V^{*}_{(c)}$. *In this case, the least squares solution with the minimum norm* $X_{(e)}$ *of the EC matrix equation* $Q_{1,(e)}X_{(e)} = Q_{2,(e)}$ *is given by*

$$X_{(e)} = \left(\mathrm{Re}\left(V_{(e)}\right) + \frac{i}{\sqrt{-p}}\mathrm{Im}\left(V_{(e)}\right)\right)\Sigma^{\dagger}\left(\mathrm{Re}\left(U_{(e)}\right) + \frac{i}{\sqrt{-p}}\mathrm{Im}\left(U_{(e)}\right)\right)^{*}Q_{2,(e)}.$$

Proof. Let $Q_{1,(e)} \in \mathbb{C}_p^{m\times n}$ and $Q_{2,(e)} \in \mathbb{C}_p^{m\times q}$, and suppose that $\mathrm{H_p}\left(Q_{1,(e)}\right) = U_{(c)}\Sigma V^{*}_{(c)}$. Given the *EC* matrix equation $Q_{1,(e)}X_{(e)} = Q_{2,(e)}$, the complex representation of this equation is $\mathrm{H_p}\left(Q_{1,(e)}\right)\mathrm{H_p}\left(X_{(e)}\right) = \mathrm{H_p}\left(Q_{2,(e)}\right)$. The least-norm least-squares solution to this complex matrix equation is given by $\mathrm{H_p}\left(X_{(e)}\right) = V_{(c)}\Sigma^{\dagger}U^{*}_{(c)}\mathrm{H_p}\left(Q_{2,(e)}\right)$. If we apply the inverse of the isomorphism $\mathrm{H_p}$ to above equation, we get

$$X_{(e)} = \left(\mathrm{Re}\left(V_{(e)}\right) + \frac{i}{\sqrt{-p}}\mathrm{Im}\left(V_{(e)}\right)\right)\Sigma^{\dagger}\left(\mathrm{Re}\left(U_{(e)}\right) + \frac{i}{\sqrt{-p}}\mathrm{Im}\left(U_{(e)}\right)\right)^{*}Q_{2,(e)}.$$

□

3.2. EQ Matrices

Let $Q_{(E)} = Q_{(e),1}e_1 + Q_{(e),2}e_2 \in \mathbb{H}_p^{m\times n}$. Since e_1 and e_2 are disjoint idempotent units, the mathematical properties associated with *EQ* matrices are closely related to *EC* matrices

$Q_{(e),1}$, $Q_{(e),2}$. In this subsection, results related to eigen-pairs, singular value decomposition, pseudoinverse, and least squares solution with the minimum norm for EQ matrices have been derived from this fact.

Theorem 1. *A polynomial function of degree N with EQ number coefficients presented by*

$$f_p\left(x_{(E)}\right) = x_{(E)}^N + q_{(N-1),(E)}x_{(E)}^{N-1} + \ldots + q_{1,(E)}x_{(E)} + q_{0,(E)}$$

has exactly N^2 zeros in the set of EQs.

Proof. The polynomial $f_p\left(x_{(E)}\right)$ can be written in the form

$$\begin{aligned}
f_p\left(x_{(E)}\right) &= \left(x_{(e),1}e_1 + x_{(e),2}e_2\right)^N + \left(q_{(N-1),(e),1}e_1 + q_{(N-1),(e),2}e_2\right)\left(x_{(e),1}e_1 + x_{(e),2}e_2\right)^{N-1} \\
&\quad + \cdots + \left(q_{1,(e),1}e_1 + q_{1,(e),2}e_2\right)\left(x_{(e),1}e_1 + x_{(e),2}e_2\right) + \left(q_{0,(e),1}e_1 + q_{0,(e),2}e_2\right) \\
&= \left(\left(x_{(e),1}\right)^N + \left(q_{(N-1),(e),1}\right)\left(x_{(e),1}\right)^{N-1} + \ldots + \left(q_{1,(e),1}\right)\left(x_{(e),1}\right) + q_{0,(e),1}\right)e_1 \\
&+ \left(\left(x_{(e),2}\right)^N + \left(q_{(N-1),(e),2}\right)\left(x_{(e),2}\right)^{N-1} + \ldots + \left(q_{1,(e),2}\right)\left(x_{(e),2}\right) + q_{0,(e),2}\right)e_2 \\
&= f_p\left(x_{(e),1}\right)e_1 + f_p\left(x_{(e),2}\right)e_2,
\end{aligned}$$

where $f_p\left(x_{(e),1}\right)$ and $f_p\left(x_{(e),2}\right)$ are polynomials of degree N with EC number coefficients and values. Then, these polynomials have exactly N zeros each from Lemma 1. Suppose that the roots of $f_p\left(x_{(e),1}\right)$ are $x_{\alpha,(e),1}$ and the roots of $f_p\left(x_{(e),2}\right)$ are $x_{\beta,(e),1}$, where $\alpha, \beta \in \{1, 2, 3, \ldots, N\}$. From the last equation, we deduce that the roots of the polynomial $f_p\left(x_{(E),1}\right)$ are $x_{(E)} = x_{\alpha,(e),1}e_1 + x_{\beta,(e),2}e_2$. Since the number of possible different $\left(x_{\alpha,(e),1}, x_{\beta,(e),2}\right)$ pairs is N^2, the polynomial $f_p\left(x_{(E),1}\right)$ has exactly N^2 zeros in the set of EQs. □

Theorem 2. *An EQ matrix $Q_{(E)} = Q_{(e),1}e_1 + Q_{(e),2}e_2 \in \mathbb{H}_p^{n\times n}$ is nonsingular if and only if the EC matrices $Q_{(e),1}, Q_{(e),2} \in \mathbb{C}_p^{n\times n}$ are nonsingular. If $Q_{(e),1}, Q_{(e),2} \in \mathbb{C}_p^{n\times n}$ are nonsingular, then*

$$Q_{(E)}^{-1} = Q_{(e),1}^{-1}e_1 + Q_{(e),2}^{-1}e_2.$$

Proof. Suppose that $Q_{(E)} = Q_{(e),1}e_1 + Q_{(e),2}e_2 \in \mathbb{H}_p^{n\times n}$ is nonsingular and $Q_{(E)}^{-1} = P_{(e),1}e_1 + P_{(e),2}e_2$ is inverse of $Q_{(E)}$. In this case,

$$Q_{(E)}Q_{(E)}^{-1} = \left(Q_{(e),1}P_{(e),1}e_1 + Q_{(e),2}P_{(e),2}e_2\right) = I_n e_1 + I_n e_2$$

holds. By this fact,

$$Q_{(e),1}P_{(e),1} = I_n \text{ and } Q_{(e),2}P_{(e),2} = I_n$$

are obtained. Then, we get

$$Q_{(e),1}^{-1} = P_{(e),1} \text{ and } Q_{(e),2}^{-1} = P_{(e),2}.$$

Conversely, let's assume that $Q_{(e),1}, Q_{(e),2} \in \mathbb{C}_p^{n\times n}$ are nonsingular EC matrices. In this case,

$$\left(Q_{(e),1}e_1 + Q_{(e),2}e_2\right)\left(Q_{(e),1}^{-1}e_1 + Q_{(e),2}^{-1}e_2\right) = I_n e_1 + I_n e_2$$

holds. Consequently, $Q_{(E)} = Q_{(e),1}e_1 + A_{(e),2}e_2 \in \mathbb{H}_p^{n\times n}$ is nonsingular and

$$Q_{(E)}^{-1} = Q_{(e),1}^{-1}e_1 + Q_{(e),2}^{-1}e_2$$

is valid. □

Theorem 3. *Let $Q_{(E)} = Q_{(e),1}e_1 + Q_{(e),2}e_2 \in \mathbb{H}_p^{n\times n}$. Suppose that $\lambda_{(e),1}$ and $\lambda_{(e),2}$ are eigenvalues of EC matrices $Q_{(e),1}$ and $Q_{(e),2}$ corresponding to the eigenvectors $x_{(e),1}$ and $x_{(e),2}$, respectively. Then $\lambda_{(E)} = \lambda_{(e),1}e_1 + \lambda_{(e),2}e_2$ is an eigenvalue of $Q_{(E)}$ corresponding to the eigenvector $x_{(E)} = x_{(e),1}e_1 + x_{(e),2}e_2$ and its converse is also true.*

Proof. Suppose $\left(\lambda_{(e),1}, x_{(e),1}\right)$ and $\left(\lambda_{(e),2}, x_{(e),2}\right)$ are the eigen-pairs of *EC* matrices $Q_{(e),1}$ and $Q_{(e),2}$, respectively. Then,

$$\begin{aligned} Q_{(E)}x_{(E)} = Q_{(E)}\left(x_{(e),1}e_1 + x_{(2),2}e_2\right) &= \left(Q_{(e),1}e_1 + Q_{(e),2}e_2\right)\left(x_{(e),1}e_1 + x_{(e),2}e_2\right) \\ &= Q_{(e),1}x_{(e),1}e_1 + Q_{(e),2}x_{(e),2}e_2 \\ &= \lambda_{(e),1}x_{(e),1}e_1 + \lambda_{(e),2}x_{(e),2}e_2 \\ &= \left(\lambda_{(e),1}e_1 + \lambda_{(e),2}e_2\right)\left(x_{(e),1}e_1 + x_{(e),2}e_2\right) = \lambda_{(E)}x_{(E)}. \end{aligned}$$

Thus, $\left(\lambda_{(E)}, x_{(E)}\right)$ is an eigen-pair of $Q_{(E)}$. Conversely, assume that $\left(\lambda_{(E)}, x_{(E)}\right)$ is an eigen-pair of $Q_{(E)}$. Then, we get $Q_{(E)}x_{(E)} = \lambda_{(E)}x_{(E)}$ and

$$Q_{(e),1}x_{(e),1}e_1 + Q_{(e),2}x_{(e),2}e_2 = \lambda_{(e),1}x_{(e),1}e_1 + \lambda_{(e),2}x_{(e),2}e_2$$

which implies

$$Q_{(e),1}x_{(e),1} = \lambda_{(e),1}x_{(e),1} \text{ and } Q_{(e),2}x_{(e),2} = \lambda_{(e),2}x_{(e),2}.$$

□

Corollary 2. *Let $Q_{(E)} = Q_{(e),1}e_1 + Q_{(e),2}e_2 \in \mathbb{H}_p^{n\times n}$. Then, the EQ matrix $Q_{(E)}$ has at most n^2 eigenvalues.*

Proof. Let $Q_{(E)} = Q_{(e),1}e_1 + Q_{(e),2}e_2 \in \mathbb{H}_p^{n\times n}$. Then, *EC* matrices $Q_{(e),1}$ and $Q_{(e),2}$ have at most n eigenvalues from Lemma 2. Suppose that eigenvalues of $Q_{(e),1}$ are $\lambda_{\alpha,(e),1}$ and eigenvalues of $Q_{(e),2}$ are $\lambda_{\beta,(e),1}$, where $\alpha, \beta \in \{1, 2, 3, \ldots, n\}$. From Theorem 3, we deduce that eigenvalues of *EQ* matrix $Q_{(E)} = Q_{(e),1}e_1 + Q_{(e),2}e_2 \in \mathbb{H}_p^{n\times n}$ are $\lambda_{(E)} = \lambda_{\alpha,(e),1}e_1 + \lambda_{\beta,(e),2}e_2$. Since the number of possible different $\left(\lambda_{\alpha,(e),1}, \lambda_{\beta,(e),2}\right)$ pairs is n^2, *EQ* matrix $Q_{(E)} = Q_{(e),1}e_1 + Q_{(e),2}e_2 \in \mathbb{H}_p^{n\times n}$ has at most n^2 eigenvalues. □

Theorem 4. *Let $Q_{(E)} = Q_{(e),1}e_1 + Q_{(e),2}e_2 \in \mathbb{H}_p^{m\times n}$. Suppose that singular value decompositions of $Q_{(e),1}$ and $Q_{(e),2}$ are $Q_{(e),1} = U_{(e),1}\Sigma_1 V_{(e),1}^*$ and $Q_{(e),2} = U_{(e),2}\Sigma_2 V_{(e),2}^*$, respectively. Then, the singular value decomposition of EQ matrix $Q_{(E)}$ is given by*

$$Q_{(E)} = U_{(E)}\Sigma_{(E)}V_{(E)}^*,$$

where $\Sigma_{(E)} = \Sigma_1 e_1 + \Sigma_2 e_2$, $U_{(E)} = U_{(e),1}e_1 + U_{(e),2}e_2$ and $V_{(E)} = V_{(e),1}e_1 + V_{(e),2}e_2$ such that $U_{(E)}$ and $V_{(E)}$ are unitary matrices.

Proof. Let the singular value decompositions of $Q_{(e),1}$ and $Q_{(e),2}$ be $Q_{(e),1} = U_{(e),1}\Sigma_1 V^*_{(e),1}$ and $Q_{(e),2} = U_{(e),2}\Sigma_2 V^*_{(e),2}$, respectively. Then, the singular value decomposition of $Q_{(E)}$ is as follows:

$$\begin{aligned} Q_{(E)} = Q_{(e),1}e_1 + Q_{(e),2}e_2 &= \left(U_{(e),1}\Sigma_1 V^*_{(e),1}\right)e_1 + \left(U_{(e),2}\Sigma_2 V^*_{(e),2}\right)e_2 \\ &= \left(U_{(e),1}e_1 + U_{(e),2}e_2\right)(\Sigma_1 e_1 + \Sigma_2 e_2)\left(V_{(e),1}e_1 + V_{(e),2}e_2\right)^* \\ &= U_{(E)}\Sigma_{(E)}V^*_{(E)}, \end{aligned}$$

where

$$\begin{aligned} U_{(E)}U^*_{(E)} &= \left(U_{(e),1}e_1 + U_{(e),2}e_2\right)\left(U_{(e),1}e_1 + U_{(e),2}e_2\right)^* \\ &= U_{(e),1}U^*_{(e),1}e_1 + U_{(e),2}U^*_{(e),2}e_2 \\ &= I_n e_1 + I_n e_2 = I_n, \end{aligned}$$

$$\begin{aligned} V_{(E)}V^*_{(E)} &= \left(V_{(e),1}e_1 + V_{(e),2}e_2\right)\left(V_{(e),1}e_1 + V_{(e),2}e_2\right)^* \\ &= V_{(e),1}V^*_{(e),1}e_1 + V_{(e),2}V^*_{(e),2}e_2 \\ &= I_n e_1 + I_n e_2 = I_n, \end{aligned}$$

and $\Sigma_{(E)}$ is hyperbolic matrix. ($\Sigma_{(E)}$ is real matrix if and only if $\Sigma_1 = \Sigma_2$.) □

Corollary 3. *Let* $Q_{(E)} = Q_{(e),1}e_1 + Q_{(e),2}e_2 \in \mathbb{H}_p^{m\times n}$. *Then*

$$rank\left(Q_{(E)}\right) = \max\left(rank\left(Q_{(e),1}\right), rank\left(Q_{(e),2}\right)\right).$$

Proof. Let $Q_{(E)} = U_{(E)}\Sigma_{(E)}V^*_{(E)}$, $Q_{(e),1} = U_{(e),1}\Sigma_1 V^*_{(e),1}$ and $Q_{(e),2} = U_{(e),2}\Sigma_2 V^*_{(e),2}$. In this case, the ranks of matrices $Q_{(E)}$, $Q_{(e),1}$, and $Q_{(e),2}$, are equal to the rank of matrix $\Sigma_{(E)}$, Σ_1, and Σ_2, respectively. Since $\Sigma_{(E)} = \Sigma_1 e_1 + \Sigma_2 e_2$, we get

$$rank\left(\Sigma_{(E)}\right) = \max(rank(\Sigma_1), rank(\Sigma_2)) = \max\left(rank\left(Q_{(e),1}\right), rank\left(Q_{(e),2}\right)\right).$$

Thus, we have

$$rank\left(Q_{(E)}\right) = \max\left(rank\left(Q_{(e),1}\right), rank\left(Q_{(e),2}\right)\right).$$

□

Corollary 4. *Let* $Q_{(E)} = Q_{(e),1}e_1 + Q_{(e),2}e_2 \in \mathbb{H}_p^{m\times n}$ *and* $Q_{(E)} = U_{(E)}\Sigma_{(E)}V^*_{(E)}$. *Then, the pseudoinverse of* $Q_{(E)}$ *is* $Q^\dagger_{(E)} = V_{(E)}\Sigma^\dagger_{(E)}U^*_{(E)}$, *where* $\Sigma^\dagger = \Sigma_1^\dagger e_1 + \Sigma_2^\dagger e_2$ *and* $\Sigma_1, \Sigma_2 \in \mathbb{R}^{m\times n}$.

Proof. Since the units e_1 and e_2 are adjoint idempotent, we get $Q^\dagger_{(E)} = Q^\dagger_{(e),1}e_1 + Q^\dagger_{(e),2}e_2$. Then, the pseudoinverse of $Q_{(E)}$ is as follows:

$$
\begin{aligned}
Q^{\dagger}_{(E)} = Q^{\dagger}_{(e),1}e_1 + Q^{\dagger}_{(e),2}e_2 &= \left(V_{(e),1}\Sigma_1^{\dagger}U^*_{(e),1}\right)e_1 + \left(V_{(e),2}\Sigma_2^{\dagger}U^*_{(e),2}\right)e_2 \\
&= \left(V_{(e),1}e_1 + V_{(e),2}e_2\right)\left(\Sigma_1^{\dagger}e_1 + \Sigma_2^{\dagger}e_2\right)\left(U_{(e),1}e_1 + U_{(e),2}e_2\right)^* \\
&= V_{(E)}\Sigma^{\dagger}_{(E)}U^*_{(E)}.
\end{aligned}
$$

□

Theorem 5. *The least squares solution with the minimum norm of the EQ matrix equation* $Q_{1,(E)}X_{(E)} = Q_{2,(E)}$ *is*

$$X_{(E)} = Q^{\dagger}_{1,(E)}Q_{2,(E)} = V_{(E)}\Sigma^{\dagger}_{(E)}U^*_{(E)}Q_{2,(E)},$$

where $Q_{1,(E)} \in \mathbb{H}_p^{m\times n}$ *and* $Q_{2,(E)} \in \mathbb{H}_p^{m\times q}$.

Proof. Let the least squares solution with the minimum norm of the EQ matrix equation $Q_{1,(E)}X_{(E)} = Q_{2,(E)}$ be $X_{(E)}$. Then we get $\left\|Q_{1,(E)}X_{(E)} - Q_{2,(E)}\right\|_p = \min$ and

$$
\begin{aligned}
\left\|Q_{1,(E)}X_{(E)} - Q_{2,(E)}\right\|_p^2 &= \left\|\left(Q_{1,(e),1}e_1 + Q_{1,(e),2}e_2\right)\left(X_{(e),1}e_1 + X_{(e),2}e_2\right) - \left(Q_{2,(e),1}e_1 + Q_{2,(e),2}e_2\right)\right\|_p^2 \\
&= \left\|\left(Q_{1,(e),1}X_{(e),1}e_1 + Q_{1,(e),2}X_{(e),2}e_2\right) - \left(Q_{2,(e),1}e_1 + Q_{2,(e),2}e_2\right)\right\|_p^2 \\
&= \left\|\left(Q_{1,(e),1}X_{(e),1} - Q_{2,(e),1}\right)e_1 + \left(Q_{1,(e),2}X_{(e),2} - Q_{2,(e),2}\right)e_2\right\|_p^2.
\end{aligned}
$$

From the definition of the Frobenius norm of EQ matrices, we have

$$\left\|Q_{1,(E)}X_{(E)} - Q_{2,(E)}\right\|_p^2 = \frac{1}{2}\left(\left\|Q_{(e),1}X_{(e),1} - Q_{2,(e),1}\right\|_p^2 + \left\|Q_{1,(e),2}X_{(e),2} - Q_{2,(e),2}\right\|_p^2\right).$$

Hence, $\left\|Q_{1,(E)}X_{(E)} - Q_{2,(E)}\right\|_p = \min$ if and only if

$$\left\|Q_{1,(e),1}X_{(e),1} - Q_{2,(e),1}\right\|_p = \min, \quad \text{and} \quad \left\|Q_{1,(e),2}X_{(e),2} - Q_{2,(e),2}\right\|_p = \min.$$

If $\left\|Q_{1,(e),1}X_{(e),1} - Q_{2,(e),1}\right\|_p = \min$, then $X_{(e),1} = Q^{\dagger}_{1,(e),1}Q_{2,(e),1}$ and similarly, $X_{(e),2} = Q^{\dagger}_{1,(e),2}Q_{2,(e),2}$, where $Q^{\dagger}_{1,(e),1} = V_{(e),1}\Sigma_1U^*_{(e),1}$ and $Q^{\dagger}_{1,(e),2} = V_{(e),2}\Sigma_2U^*_{(e),2}$. Therefore, the least squares solution of the equation $Q_{1,(E)}X_{(E)} = Q_{2,(E)}$ is

$$
\begin{aligned}
X_{(E)} &= \left(V_{(e),1}\Sigma_1U^*_{(e),1}Q_{2,(e),1}\right)e_1 + \left(V_{(e),2}\Sigma_2U^*_{(e),2}Q_{2,(e),2}\right)e_2 \\
&= \left(\left(V_{(e),1}\Sigma_1U^*_{(e),1}\right)e_1 + \left(V_{(e),2}\Sigma_2U^*_{(e),2}\right)e_2\right)\left(Q_{2,(e),1}e_1 + Q_{2,(e),2}e_2\right) \\
&= \left(V_{(e),1}e_1 + V_{(e),2}e_2\right)\left(\Sigma_1e_1 + \Sigma_2e_2\right)\left(U^*_{(e),1}e_1 + U^*_{(e),2}e_2\right)\left(Q_{2,(e),1}e_1 + Q_{2,(e),2}e_2\right) \\
&= V_{(E)}\Sigma^{\dagger}_{(E)}U^*_{(E)}Q_{2,(E)} = Q^{\dagger}_{1,(E)}Q_{2,(E)}
\end{aligned}
$$

which completes the proof. □

3.2.1. Algorithms

The following algorithms delineate the computational procedures for determining eigen-pairs, singular value decomposition, pseudoinverse computation, and the derivation of least squares solution with the minimum norm for *EQ* matrices.

Algorithm 1 This algorithm calculates the eigenvalues and eigenvectors of the *EQ* matrix $Q_{(E)} \in \mathbb{H}_p^{n\times n}$.

Start
Input $Q_{(E),r}, Q_{(E),i}, Q_{(E),j}, Q_{(E),k}$ and p
Form $Q_{(e),1}$ and $Q_{(e),2}$ according to Equation (1)
Compute $\lambda_{(e),1}$ and $\lambda_{(e),2}$ according to Lemma 3 and Theorem 3
Compute $x_{(e),1}$ and $x_{(e),2}$ according to Lemma 3 and Theorem 3
Form $\lambda_{(E)} = \lambda_{(e),1}e_1 + \lambda_{(e),2}e_2$ according to Theorem 3
Form $x_{(E)} = x_{(e),1}e_1 + x_{(e),2}e_2$ according to Theorem 3
Output $\lambda_{(E)}$ and $x_{(E)}$
End

Algorithm 2 This algorithm performs the singular value decomposition of the *EQ* matrix $Q_{(E)} \in \mathbb{H}_p^{m\times n}$.

Start
Input $Q_{(E),r}, Q_{(E),i}, Q_{(E),j}, Q_{(E),k}$ and p
Form $Q_{(e),1}$ and $Q_{(e),2}$ according to Equation (1)
Compute $Q_{(e),1} = U_{(e),1}\Sigma_1 V^*_{(e),1}$ and $Q_{(e),2} = U_{(e),2}\Sigma_2 V^*_{(e),2}$ according to Lemma 6
Form $U_{(E)} = \left(U_{(e),1}e_1 + U_{(e),2}e_2\right)$, $\Sigma_{(E)} = (\Sigma_1 e_1 + \Sigma_2 e_2)$, and $V_{(E)} = \left(V_{(e),1}e_1 + V_{(e),2}e_2\right)$ according to Theorem 4
Output $U_{(E)}$, $\Sigma_{(E)}$, $V_{(E)}$
End

Algorithm 3 This algorithm calculates the pseudoinverse of the *EQ* matrix $Q_{(E)} \in \mathbb{H}_p^{m\times n}$.

Start
Run the Algorithm 2 for *EQ* matrix $Q_{(E)}$
Form $Q_{(E)} = U_{(E)}\Sigma_{(E)}V^*_{(E)}$
Compute $Q^\dagger_{(E)} = V_{(E)}\Sigma^\dagger_{(E)}U^*_{(E)}$
Output $Q^\dagger_{(E)}$
End

Algorithm 4 This algorithm calculates the minimum norm least squares solution of the *EQ* matrix equation $Q_{1,(E)}X_{(E)} = Q_{2,(E)}$.

Start
Input $Q_{1,(E),r}, Q_{1,(E),i}, Q_{1,(E),j}, Q_{1,(E),k}, Q_{2,(E),r}, Q_{2,(E),i}, Q_{2,(E),j}, Q_{2,(E),k}$ and p
Run the Algorithm 3 for *EQ* matrix $Q_{1,(E)}$
Compute $X_{(E)} = Q^\dagger_{1,(E)}Q_{2,(E)} = V_{(E)}\Sigma^\dagger_{(E)}U^*_{(E)}Q_{2,(E)}$
Output $X_{(E)}$
End

The fact that *EQ*s are commutative with respect to multiplication, can be written as a linear combination of two adjoint idempotent units, can choose the most appropriate p-value for the solution of the problem under consideration, and many physical systems exhibit elliptical behavior make this number system advantageous in applied sciences.

Therefore, using the algorithms given above in applied sciences will solve many problems related to time, memory, and performance in the problem-solving processes.

3.2.2. Numerical Examples

In this subsection, some illustrative examples are given to prove the authenticity of our results and distinguish them from existing ones. Moreover, all computations are performed using the MATLAB® 2024a (64 bit) on an Intel(R) Xeon(R) CPU E5-1650 v4 @3.60 GHz (12 CPUs)/16 GB (DDR3) RAM computer.

Example 1. *Given the EQ matrices* $Q_{1,(E)}$ *and* $Q_{2,(E)}$ *as follows:*

$$Q_{1,(E)} = \begin{pmatrix} 9+i-7j+2k & 2-7i+j+5k & 8-4i+7j-4k \\ 5+8i-j+4k & 4+7i+j-k & 9-6i-3j+8k \\ 8+9i+3j-4k & 9-2i+8j+2k & 6-5i+9j-6k \end{pmatrix} \in \mathbb{H}^{3\times 3}_{-0.5},$$

and

$$Q_{2,(E)} = \begin{pmatrix} 7+2i+3j+k \\ 7-6i+j+4k \\ 3+3i-5j-8k \end{pmatrix} \in \mathbb{H}^{3\times 1}_{-0.5}.$$

Let's find the least squares solution with the minimum norm by using Algorithms 2–4 for $p=-0.5$. *By the Algorithm 2, we get the singular value decomposition of EQ matrix* $Q_{1,(E)}$ *as follows:*

$$\Sigma = \begin{pmatrix} 27.1507+5.1850j & 0 & 0 \\ 0 & 13.3956-3.6604j & 0 \\ 0 & 0 & 3.5511+0.0727j \end{pmatrix},$$

$$U = \begin{pmatrix} -0.5887-0.0895i+0.1905j-0.1797k & 0.5737+0.2198i+0.2880j-0.0213k & -0.1504-0.0811i+0.3531j+0.1408k \\ -0.2573-0.4628i+0.0895j-0.0090k & -0.2014-0.8270i+0.0050j+0.3648k & 0.1490+0.6752i+0.1013j+0.4671k \\ -0.4969-0.4443i-0.2639j+0.0273k & -0.1356+0.2676i-0.1680j-0.2529k & -0.1172+0.4220i-0.326j-0.7217k \end{pmatrix},$$

and

$$V = \begin{pmatrix} -0.6674+0.2309j & -0.1204-0.3768j & 0.5534+0.1965j \\ -0.3280-0.3659i-0.1703j+0.0553k & -0.4857+0.1440i-0.0426j+0.0036k & -0.3596-0.6220i-0.2807j+0.5391k \\ -0.2692-0.5713i-0.2100j-0.1815k & 0.4859-0.3190i+0.1157j+0.7682k & -0.1476-0.1702i+0.2676j+0.0299k \end{pmatrix}.$$

By Algorithms 3 and 4, the least squares solution and minimum norm are found as

$$\begin{aligned} X_{(E)} = & Q^{\dagger}_{1,(E)} Q_{2,(E)} = V_{(E)} \Sigma^{\dagger}_{(E)} U^{*}_{(E)} Q_{2,(E)} \\ = & \begin{pmatrix} 0.7612-1.5582i-0.1979j-0.5332k \\ -1.4757-0.2366i+0.1496j+1.2282k \\ 0.0461+0.2919i+0.4652j-0.0282k \end{pmatrix} \end{aligned}$$

and

$$\left\| Q_{1,(E)} X_{(E)} - Q_{2,(E)} \right\|_p = 1.1801 \times 10^{-14},$$

respectively.

Example 2. *Let's define the dimensions of the EQ matrices* $Q_{1,(E)}$ *and* $Q_{2,(E)}$ *given by:*

$$\begin{aligned} & m = 50:50:1000, \\ & Q_{1,(E)} = rand(m,m) + rand(m,m)i + rand(m,m)j + rand(m,m)k, \\ & Q_{2,(E)} = rand(m,1) + rand(m,1)i + rand(m,1)j + rand(m,1)k. \end{aligned}$$

Then, the errors (or minimum norms) corresponding p and m-values are shown in Figure 1. Here, Algorithm 4 was executed for each m-value, iterating over each p-value in the range $-1 \leq p \leq -0.1$ *with a step size of* 0.1*. The minimal errors were identified and highlighted on the surface plot with red dots. Also, we compare our new proposed Algorithm 4 and the Algorithm documented by Atali et al. in [21], focusing on CPU time and error metrics. The experimental results of this comparison are depicted in Figure 2 (CPU times) and Figure 3 (Errors). Figures 2 and 3 show that our proposed algorithm outperforms the algorithm presented by Atali et al. in [21] regarding computational efficiency and accuracy.*

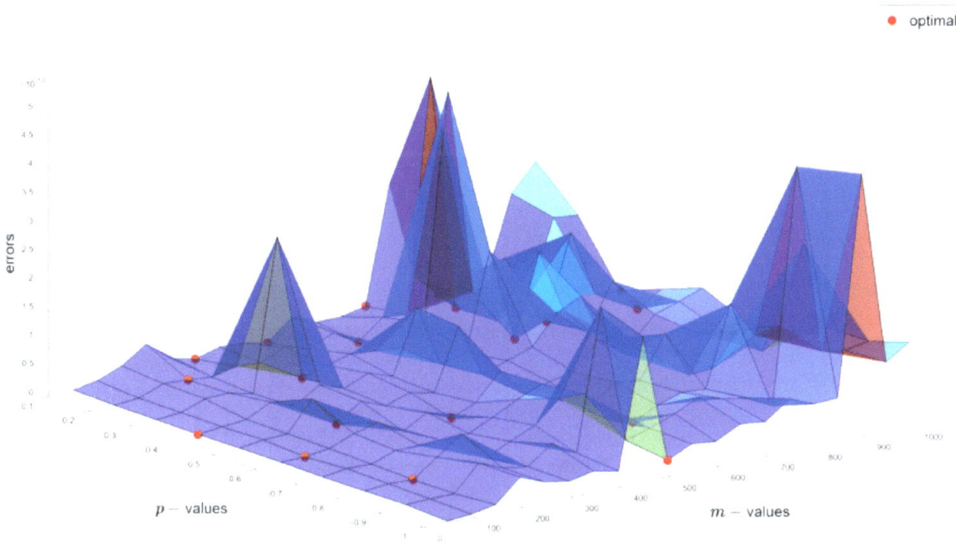

Figure 1. Errors corresponding p and m-values.

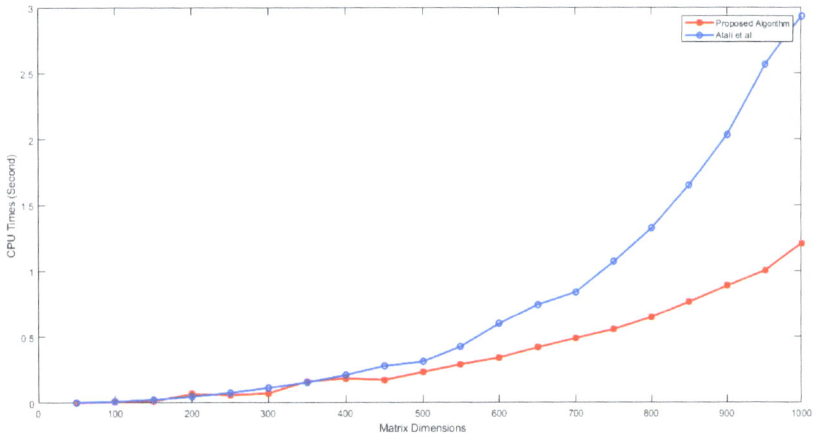

Figure 2. CPU times comparison proposed algorithm with the algorithm in [21].

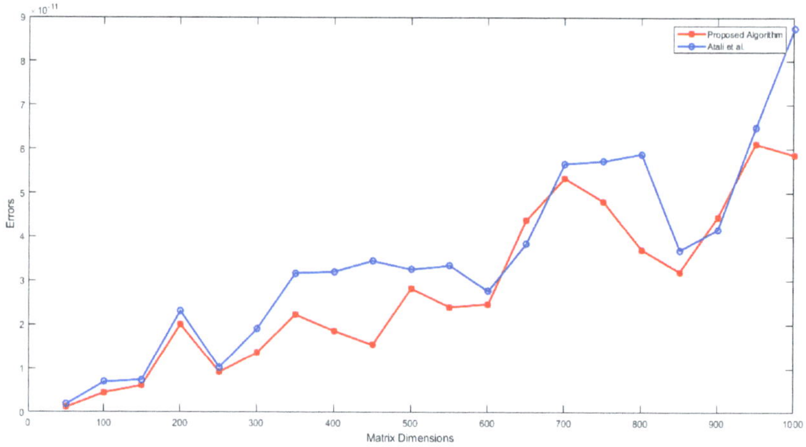

Figure 3. Errors comparison proposed algorithm with the algorithm in [21].

4. Conclusions

In this study, we derived outcomes for determining eigen-pairs, performing singular value decomposition, obtaining pseudoinverse, and finding the least squares solution with the minimum norm for *EQ* matrices. Additionally, we developed algorithms grounded on these outcomes and presented illustrative numerical instances to validate our results. This number system is more useful in applied sciences since it allows one to select the ideal p-value suited for the type of problem, considering the elliptical behavior of many physical systems. As a result, the use of *EQ*s in today's critical technology fields—information security, data analytics, simulation technologies, robotics, signal processing, image processing, artificial intelligence, and machine learning—may effectively solve many problems related to time, memory, and performance.

Author Contributions: Conceptualization, H.H.K.; Formal analysis, E.K. and M.A.; H.H.K., E.K. and B.Ç. wrote the main manuscript text. All authors reviewed the manuscript. All authors have read and agreed to the published version of the manuscript.

Funding: This research received no external funding .

Data Availability Statement: The data used to support the findings of this study are available from the corresponding author upon request.

Acknowledgments: This paper was supported by the Scientific and Technological Research Institution of TÜRKİYE (TUBITAK-1002-a-121F289). We thank TÜBİTAK for their support.

Conflicts of Interest: The authors declare no conflict of interest.

References

1. Ben-Israel, A.; Greville, T.N. *Generalized Inverses: Theory and Applications*; Springer Science Business Media: Berlin/Heidelberg, Germany, 2006.
2. Samar, M.; Li, H.; Wei, Y. Condition numbers for the *K*-weighted pseudoinverse and their statistical estimation. *Linear Multilinear Algebra* **2021**, *69*, 752–770. [CrossRef]
3. Samar, M.; Zhu, X.; Xu, H. Conditioning Theory for $\mathcal{ML}$-Weighted Pseudoinverse and $\mathcal{ML}$-Weighted Least Squares Problem. *Axioms* **2021**, *13*, 345. [CrossRef]
4. Simsek, S. Least-squares solutions of generalized Sylvester-type quaternion matrix equations. *Adv. Appl. Clifford Algebr.* **2023**, *33*, 28. [CrossRef]
5. Dian, R.; Li, S.; Kang, X. Regularizing hyperspectral and multispectral image fusion by CNN denoiser. *IEEE Trans. Neural Netw. Learn. Syst.* **2021**, *32*, 1124–1135. [CrossRef] [PubMed]
6. Hashemipour, N.; Aghaei, J.; Kavousi-Fard, A.; Niknam, T.; Salimi, L.; del Granado, P.C.; Shafie-Khah, M.; Wang, F.; Catalão, J.P.S. Optimal Singular value decomposition based big data compression approach in smart grids. *IEEE Trans. Ind. Appl.* **2021**, *32*, 1124–1135. [CrossRef]

7. Wang, Y.C.; Zhu, L. Research and implementation of SVD in machine learning. In Proceedings of the 2017 IEEE/ACIS 16th International Conference on Computer and Information Science, Wuhan, China, 24–26 May 2017; pp. 471–475.
8. Harkin, A.A.; Harkin, J.B. Geometry of generalized complex numbers. *Math. Mag.* **2004**, *77*, 118–129. [CrossRef]
9. Catoni, F.; Cannata, R.; Zampetti, P. An introduction to commutative quaternions. *Adv. Appl. Clifford Algebr.* **2006**, *16*, 1–28. [CrossRef]
10. Yaglom, I.M. *A Simple Non-Euclidean Geometry and Its Physical Basis*; Springer: New York, NY, USA, 1979.
11. Condurache, D.; Burlacu, A. Dual tensors based solutions for rigid body motion parameterization. *Mech. Mach. Theory* **2014**, *74*, 390–412. [CrossRef]
12. Ozdemir, M. An alternative approach to elliptical motion. *Adv. Appl. Clifford Algebr.* **2016**, *26*, 279–304. [CrossRef]
13. Dundar, F.S.; Ersoy, S.; Pereira, N.T.S. Bobillier formula for the elliptical harmonic motion. *An. St. Univ. Ovidius Constanta* **2018**, *26*, 103–110. [CrossRef]
14. Derin, Z.; Gungor, M.A. Elliptic biquaternionic equations of gravitoelectromagnetism. *Math. Methods Appl. Sci.* **2022**, *45*, 4231–4243. [CrossRef]
15. Catoni, F.; Cannata, R.; Zampetti, P. An introduction to constant curvature spaces in the commutative (Segre) quaternion geometry. *Adv. Appl. Clifford Algebr.* **2006**, *16*, 85–101. [CrossRef]
16. Guo, L.; Zhu, M.; Ge, X. Reduced biquaternion canonical transform, convolution and correlation. *Signal Process.* **2011**, *91*, 2147–2153. [CrossRef]
17. Yuan, S.F.; Tian, Y.; Li, M.Z. On Hermitian solutions of the reduced biquaternion matrix equation $(AXB, CXD) = (E, G)$. *Linear Multilinear Algebra* **2020**, *68*, 1355–1373. [CrossRef]
18. Tosun, M.; Kosal, H.H. An algorithm for solving the Sylvester s-conjugate elliptic quaternion matrix equations. In *Algorithms as a Basis of Modern Applied Mathematics*; Hošková-Mayerová, Š., Flaut, C., Maturo, F., Eds.; Springer International Publishing: Cham, Switzerland, 2021; pp. 279–292
19. Gai, S.; Huang, X. Reduced biquaternion convolutional neural network for color image processing. *IEEE Trans. Circuits Syst. Video Technol.* **2022**, *32*, 1061–1075. [CrossRef]
20. Guo, Z.; Zhang, D.; Vasiliev, V.I.; Jiang, T. Algebraic techniques for Maxwell's equations in commutative quaternionic electromagnetics. *Eur. Phys. J. Plus* **2022**, *137*, 577–1075.
21. Atali, G.; Kosal, H.H.; Pekyaman, M. A new image restoration model associated with special elliptic quaternionic least-squares solutions based on LabVIEW. *J. Comput. Appl. Math.* **2023**, *425*, 115071. [CrossRef]
22. Catoni, F.; Boccaletti, D.; Cannata, R.; Catoni, V.; Nichelatti, E.; Zampetti, P. *The Mathematics of Minkowski Space–Time: With an Introduction to Commutative Hypercomplex Numbers*; Birkhäuser: Basel, Switzerland, 2008.
23. Surekci, A.; Kosal, H.H.; Gungor, M.A. A Note on Gershgorin disks in the elliptic plane. *J. Math. Sci. Model.* **2021**, *4*, 104–109.

axioms

Article

Characterizations of Spatial Quaternionic Partner-Ruled Surfaces

Soley Ersoy [1,*], Kemal Eren [2] and Abdussamet Çalışkan [3]

[1] Department of Mathematics, Faculty of Sciences, Sakarya University, 54050 Sakarya, Turkey
[2] Sakarya University Technology Developing Zones Manager Company, 54050 Sakarya, Turkey; kemal.eren1@ogr.sakarya.edu.tr
[3] Fatsa Vocational School, Department of Accounting and Tax Applications, Ordu University, 52100 Ordu, Turkey; a.caliskan@odu.edu.tr
* Correspondence: sersoy@sakarya.edu.tr

Abstract: In this paper, we investigate the spatial quaternionic expressions of partner-ruled surfaces. Moreover, we formulate the striction curves and dralls of these surfaces by use of the quaternionic product. Furthermore, the pitches and angles of pitches are interpreted for the spatial quaternionic ruled surfaces that are closed. Additionally, we calculate the integral invariants of these surfaces using quaternionic formulas. Finally, the partner-ruled surfaces of a given spatial quaternionic ruled surface are demonstrated as an example, and their graphics are drawn.

Keywords: spatial quaternion; quaternionic curve; partner-ruled surface; striction curves; pitches and angle of pitches

MSC: 53A04; 53A05

check for updates

Citation: Ersoy, S.; Eren, K.; Çalışkan, A. Characterizations of Spatial Quaternionic Partner-Ruled Surfaces. *Axioms* **2024**, *13*, 612. https://doi.org/10.3390/axioms13090612

Academic Editors: Anna Maria Fino, Dana Piciu, Murat Tosun and Cristina Flaut

Received: 3 August 2024
Revised: 2 September 2024
Accepted: 4 September 2024
Published: 9 September 2024

1. Introduction

In 1843, William Rowan Hamilton, an Irish mathematician, first introduced the concept of quaternions [1]. Quaternions have since found numerous applications across a wide range of disciplines, including computer graphics, vision device development, animation representations, control theory, molecular dynamics, quantum theory, robot kinematics, and navigation devices. These applications have been extensively considered and documented in various sources, including references [2–5]. Quaternions have also been applied to the theory of curves and surfaces, leading to new interpretations and results. In 1987, Bharathi and Nagaraj demonstrated the use of quaternions to express the Serret–Frenet invariants of any curve [6]. Subsequently, as well as quaternionic curves, rectifying and osculating quaternionic curves were given the attention of various researchers [7–13]. Furthermore, modified Korteweg-de Vries equations were used to describe the motions of inextensible quaternionic curves, and these findings were presented in a research article that outlines the evolutions of inextensible quaternionic curves based on the Frenet formulae [14].

Additionally, in 2005, Chen and Li established new correlations between quaternionic transformations and minimal surfaces, resulting in novel findings [15]. Hoffman and Wang introduced a new technique that uses dual-quaternion multiplication to describe rigid transformations with dual quaternions, resulting in a family of rational surfaces in an affine 3-space. They specifically employed an approach to calculate all base points of the homogeneous tensor product parameterization of the resultant surfaces, together with three rational space curves [16].

These examples highlight the versatility and utility of quaternions in diverse areas of mathematics and beyond. Ruled surfaces are structures that can be generated by moving a straight line along a curve. There have been numerous studies conducted in various spaces and frames. The concept of partner-ruled surfaces based on the Flc frame on a polynomial curve was introduced in [17]. They investigated the requirements for two of these surfaces to be simultaneously developable and minimal. Şenyurt and Çalışkan investigated the ruled surface with the theory of quaternions and dual quaternions. They expressed integral invariants and obtained the ruled surfaces drawn by spatial quaternionic curves [18,19]. In [20], the quaternionic ruled surfaces were analyzed according to the alternative frame. During this process, some noteworthy studies on quaternions and surfaces have been presented in [21–24].

In Section 2, we present the geometric concepts regarding the basic structures of the paper mentioned in the introduction. In Section 3, we investigate the spatial quaternionic expressions of partner-ruled surfaces. Moreover, we determine the striction curves, dralls, pitches, and angles of pitches for these surfaces. Section 4 consists of a special example of the findings with graphical representations. The last section provides a summary of the article and highlights its main contributions and implications.

2. Preliminaries

In this section, we recall the concepts of quaternions [1] and spatial quaternionic curves [6]. We then explain some of the properties of spatial quaternionic ruled surfaces [18]. Understanding these preliminary concepts is crucial for comprehending the subsequent discussions on the subject.

A real quaternion can be described as the sum of a scalar $S_q = q_0$ and a vector $V_q = q_1e_1 + q_2e_2 + q_3e_3$ such that

$$q = q_0 + q_1e_1 + q_2e_2 + q_3e_3,$$

where the components q_0, q_1, q_2, q_3 are real numbers, and $1, e_1, e_2, e_3$ are quaternionic units that satisfy the multiplication rules given in Table 1.

Table 1. Multiplication table.

$\times$	1	e_1	e_2	e_3
1	1	e_1	e_2	e_3
e_1	e_1	-1	e_3	$-e_2$
e_2	e_2	$-e_3$	-1	e_1
e_3	e_3	e_2	$-e_1$	-1

Here, the left column displays the left factor, and the top row displays the right factor. The complex conjugate $\bar{q}$ is defined by

$$\bar{q} = S_q - V_q = q_0 - q_1e_1 - q_2e_2 - q_3e_3.$$

Let Q denote the set of quaternions. The quaternion inner product is presented by the following real-valued, symmetric, and bilinear form:

$$h : Q \times Q \to \mathbb{R}$$
$$(p,q) \to h(p,q) = \frac{1}{2}(p \times \bar{q} + q \times \bar{p}).$$

For $p = S_p + V_p$ and $q = S_q + V_q$, the quaternionic product is given by

$$p \times q = S_pS_q + S_pV_q + S_qV_p - \langle V_p, V_q \rangle + V_p \wedge V_q,$$

where $\langle , \rangle$ and $\wedge$ denote the inner product and cross-product in $\mathbb{R}^3$. Thus, the quaternionic product satisfies

$$p \times q = -\langle V_p, V_q \rangle + V_p \wedge V_q.$$

The square of the norm of a quaternion q is

$$\rho(q)^2 = h(q,q) = q \times \bar{q} = \bar{q} \times q = {q_0}^2 + {q_1}^2 + {q_2}^2 + {q_3}^2.$$

Provided that $\rho(q) = 1$, the quaternion q is called the unit quaternion. The inverse of the quaternion q is given by $q^{-1} = \frac{\overline{q}}{\rho(q)}$ where $\rho(q) \neq 0$.

The space of the spatial quaternions is classified by $\{q \in Q | q + \overline{q} = 0\}$ where Q denotes the set of quaternions [6].

Definition 1. *A spatial quaternionic curve α is defined by*

$$\begin{aligned} \alpha : I &\to Q \\ s &\to \alpha(s) = \sum_{i=1}^{3} \alpha_i(s) e_i \end{aligned}$$

where I is an interval in real line $\mathbb{R}$ and $s \in I$ is the arc-length parameter [6].

Theorem 1. *Let α be a spatial quaternionic curve with the arc-length parameter s. Then, the Serret–Frenet formulae of the spatial quaternionic curve α at any point $\alpha(s)$ are*

$$\begin{bmatrix} T \\ N \\ B \end{bmatrix}_s = \begin{bmatrix} 0 & \kappa & 0 \\ -\kappa & 0 & \tau \\ 0 & -\tau & 0 \end{bmatrix} \begin{bmatrix} T \\ N \\ B \end{bmatrix} \tag{1}$$

such that

$$T(s) = \alpha'(s),\ N(s) = \frac{\alpha''(s)}{\|\alpha''(s)\|},\ B(s) = T(s) \times N(s),$$

where the spatial quaternions $T, N,$ and B are the unit tangent, unit principal normal, and unit binormal of the spatial quaternionic curve α, respectively. Moreover, the scalar functions κ and τ are the curvature and torsion of α, respectively [6].

The spatial quaternion $w = N \times N' = \tau T + \kappa B$ is called the instantaneous Pfaffian quaternion along the motion of the Frenet frame $\{T, N, B\}$ of a spatial quaternionic curve α [18].

Definition 2. *A spatial quaternionic ruled surface is represented by*

$$\begin{aligned} \varphi : I \times \mathbb{R} &\to Q \\ (s, u) &\to \varphi(s, u) = \alpha(s) + uX(s) \end{aligned}$$

where α is a spatial quaternionic curve and X is a spatial quaternion [18].

Lemma 1. *The drall and the striction curve of a spatial quaternionic ruled surface φ are given by*

$$P = \frac{1}{2} \frac{(X \times X') \times \overline{\alpha'} + \alpha' \times \overline{(X \times X')}}{\rho(X')^2} \tag{2}$$

and

$$r(s) = \alpha(s) - \frac{1}{2} \frac{X' \times \overline{\alpha'} + \alpha' \times \overline{X'}}{\rho(X')^2} X, \tag{3}$$

respectively [18].

It is known that if a ruled surface satisfies $\varphi(s + 2\pi, u) = \varphi(s, u)$ for all $s \in I$, then the ruled surface is called closed.

Definition 3. *For a given closed spatial quaternionic ruled surface, the magnitude $l_X = \oint_{\alpha} h(d\alpha, X) ds$ is called the pitch of this surface [18].*

Definition 4. *The spatial quaternions D and V defined by*

$$D = \oint_{\alpha} w ds = \oint_{\alpha} (\tau T + \kappa B) ds \tag{4}$$

and

$$V = \oint_{\alpha} d\alpha \tag{5}$$

are called the Steiner rotation quaternion and Steiner translation quaternion of the closed motion of the Frenet frame of a closed spatial quaternionic curve α, respectively. Here, w is the instantaneous Pfaffian quaternion [18].

Theorem 2. *The angle of pitch and the pitch of a closed spatial quaternionic ruled surface λ_x and l_x are equal to*

$$\lambda_x = h(D, X) \tag{6}$$

and

$$l_x = h(V, X) \tag{7}$$

where D and V are the Steiner rotation and translation quaternions, respectively [18].

3. Characterizations of the Spatial Quaternionic Partner-Ruled Surfaces

In this section, we examine the spatial quaternionic expressions of partner-ruled surfaces. Then, we calculate the striction curves and dralls of these surfaces. Finally, our investigation focuses on closed quaternionic ruled surfaces. We analyze their pitches and pitch angles and interpret these properties. Additionally, we use quaternionic formulas to calculate the integral invariants of these surfaces.

3.1. TN-Spatial Quaternionic Partner-Ruled Surfaces

Definition 5. *Consider a differentiable spatial quaternionic curve $\alpha = \alpha(s)$ that moves with a unit speed for its parameter s, and let $\{T, N, B\}$ denote the Frenet frame of this curve. The two spatial quaternionic ruled surfaces defined by*

$$\begin{cases} \varphi_N^T(s,u) = T(s) + uN(s), \\ \varphi_T^N(s,u) = N(s) + uT(s), \end{cases}$$

are called TN-spatial quaternionic partner-ruled surfaces.

Theorem 3. *Let r_{TN} and r_{NT} be the striction curves of any TN-spatial quaternionic partner-ruled surfaces φ_N^T and φ_T^N. Then, the position vector of the striction curve on surface φ_N^T is equal to the tangent of the curve, and the position vector of the striction curve on surface φ_T^N is equal to the principal normal of the spatial quaternionic curve $\alpha = \alpha(s)$.*

Proof. Let $\alpha = \alpha(s)$ be a unit-speed spatial quaternionic curve with the Frenet frame $\{T, N, B\}$. If we consider Equation (3) and employ the quaternionic inner product, we find the equation of the striction curve of a spatial quaternionic ruled surface φ_N^T as follows:

$$r_{TN} = T - \frac{h(N', T')}{\rho(N')^2} N = T - \frac{1}{2} \frac{\left(N' \times \overline{T'} + T' \times \overline{N'}\right)}{\sqrt{h(N', N')}} N.$$

By taking the complex conjugate of a quaternion and applying Equation (1), we arrive at

$$r_{TN} = T + \frac{1}{2} \frac{(-\kappa T + \tau B) \times \kappa N + \kappa N \times (-\kappa T + \tau B)}{\sqrt{\kappa^2 + \tau^2}} N.$$

If we take the quaternionic product of the spatial quaternions, we obtain that the position vector of the striction curve corresponds to the tangent of the curve α.

Again, we calculate the position vector of the striction curve

$$r_{NT} = N - \frac{h(T', N')}{\rho(T')^2} T.$$

By a similar method, the striction curve of φ_T^N is found to be equal to the principal normal vector of the curve α, and this completes the proof. □

Theorem 4. *Let φ_N^T and φ_T^N be TN-spatial quaternionic partner-ruled surfaces; then, the dralls of the closed spatial quaternionic partner-ruled surfaces φ_N^T and φ_T^N are*

$$P_{TN} = 0, \;\; P_{NT} = \tau,$$

respectively.

Proof. Assuming $\alpha = \alpha(s)$ is a unit-speed spatial quaternionic curve with the Frenet frame $\{T, N, B\}$, the drall of the closed spatial quaternionic ruled surface φ_N^T can be obtained by considering Equation (2) and utilizing the quaternionic inner product. Specifically, the drall can be expressed as

$$P_{TN} = \frac{1}{2} \frac{(N \times N') \times \overline{T'} + T' \times \overline{(N \times N')}}{\rho(N')^2}.$$

We obtain the drall of the surface φ_N^T by utilizing the quaternionic product of the spatial quaternions and the Frenet invariants. The computation is carried out as follows:

$$P_{TN} = -\frac{1}{2} \frac{(\kappa B + \tau T) \times N + N \times (\kappa B + \tau T)}{\sqrt{\kappa^2 + \tau^2}} = 0.$$

In a similar way, the drall of the surface φ_T^N is determined by

$$\begin{aligned} P_{NT} &= \frac{1}{2} \frac{(T \times T') \times \overline{N'} + N' \times \overline{(T \times T')}}{\rho(T')^2} \\ &= \frac{\kappa}{2} \frac{(\kappa B \times (-\kappa T + \tau B) + (-\kappa T + \tau B) \times \kappa B)}{\kappa} \\ &= \tau. \end{aligned}$$

□

Corollary 1. *Let φ_N^T and φ_T^N be TN-spatial quaternionic partner-ruled surfaces; then, the TN-spatial quaternionic partner-ruled surfaces are developable surfaces if and only if the spatial quaternionic curve $\alpha = \alpha(s)$ is planar.*

Proof. The proof is obvious by the fact that the necessary and sufficient condition for a ruled surface to be developable is having a vanishing drall at each point of the surface, and the necessary and sufficient condition for a curve to be planar is having vanishing torsion at each point of the curve. □

Theorem 5. *Let φ_N^T and φ_T^N be TN-spatial quaternionic partner-ruled surfaces; then, the angles of the pitch of the closed spatial quaternionic partner-ruled surfaces are*

$$\lambda_{TN} = 0, \lambda_{NT} = \oint \tau ds,$$

respectively.

Proof. Assume $\alpha = \alpha(s)$ is a unit-speed spatial quaternionic curve with the Frenet frame $\{T, N, B\}$. By taking into consideration Equation (6), we can express the angle of the pitch of the closed spatial quaternionic ruled surface φ_N^T as

$$\lambda_{TN} = h(D, N) = \frac{1}{2}(D \times \overline{N} + N \times \overline{D}) = -\frac{1}{2}(D \times N + N \times D).$$

Using the quaternionic product of the spatial quaternions and Equation (4), we calculate the angle of the pitch as follows:

$$\lambda_{TN} = h(D, N) = h\left(\oint (\tau T + \kappa B)ds, N\right) = 0.$$

On the other hand, the angle of the pitch λ_{NT} of the ruled surface φ_T^N is maintained:

$$\begin{aligned} \lambda_{NT} &= h(D, T) = \frac{1}{2}(D \times \overline{T} + T \times \overline{D}) \\ &= h\left(\oint (\tau T + \kappa B)ds, T\right) \\ &= \oint \tau ds. \end{aligned}$$

□

Theorem 6. *Let φ_N^T and φ_T^N be TN-spatial quaternionic partner-ruled surfaces; then, the pitches of the closed spatial quaternionic partner-ruled surfaces φ_N^T and φ_T^N are*

$$l_{TN} = \oint \kappa ds,\ l_{NT} = -\oint \kappa ds,$$

respectively.

Proof. Assume that $\alpha = \alpha(s)$ is a unit-speed spatial quaternionic curve with the Frenet frame $\{T, N, B\}$. From Equation (5) we obtain $V = \oint dT = \oint \kappa N ds$, and from Equation (7), the pitch l_{TN} of the closed spatial quaternionic ruled surface φ_N^T is written by

$$l_{TN} = h(V, N) = h\left(\oint \kappa N ds, N\right).$$

By referring to the definition of the quaternion inner product, we find

$$l_{TN} = \frac{1}{2}\left(\oint \kappa N ds \times \overline{N} + N \times \overline{\oint \kappa N ds}\right).$$

Hence, using the quaternionic product and the conjugate of a quaternion, we obtain

$$l_{TN} = \oint \kappa ds.$$

By making similar calculations, the pitch l_{NT} of the closed spatial quaternionic ruled surface φ_T^N is found:

$$l_{NT} = h(V, T) = -\oint \kappa ds.$$

□

3.2. *TB*-Spatial Quaternionic Partner-Ruled Surfaces

Definition 6. *Consider a spatial quaternionic curve $\alpha = \alpha(s)$ that is differentiable and moves at a unit speed for its parameter s, and let $\{T, N, B\}$ be the Frenet frame of the curve. The two spatial quaternionic ruled surfaces defined by*

$$\begin{cases} \varphi_B^T(s,u) = T(s) + uB(s), \\ \varphi_T^B(s,u) = B(s) + uT(s), \end{cases}$$

are called TB-spatial quaternionic partner-ruled surfaces.

Theorem 7. *Let the surfaces φ_B^T and φ_T^B be spatial quaternionic partner-ruled surfaces; then, the striction curves r_{TB} and r_{BT} of the surfaces φ_B^T and φ_T^B are*

$$\begin{cases} r_{TB} = T(s) + \dfrac{\kappa}{\tau} B(s), \\ r_{BT} = B(s) + \dfrac{\tau}{\kappa} T(s), \end{cases}$$

where $\kappa \neq 0$ and $\tau \neq 0$, respectively.

Proof. Let $\alpha = \alpha(s)$ be a unit-speed spatial quaternionic curve with the Frenet frame $\{T, N, B\}$. By referring to Equation (3) and using the quaternionic inner product, the striction curve of the spatial quaternionic ruled surface φ_B^T can be written by

$$r_{TB} = T - \frac{h(B', T')}{\rho(B')^2} B = T - \frac{1}{2} \frac{\left(B' \times \overline{T'} + T' \times \overline{B'}\right)}{\sqrt{h(B', B')}} B.$$

Using the complex conjugate of a quaternion and Equation (1), we arrive at

$$r_{TB} = T + \frac{1}{2} \frac{(-\tau N) \times \kappa N + \kappa N \times (-\tau N)}{\tau} B.$$

Considering the quaternionic product of the spatial quaternions, the striction curve of φ_B^T is

$$r_{TB} = T(s) + \frac{\kappa}{\tau} B(s).$$

Similarly, from the equation $r_{BT} = B - \frac{h(T', B')}{\rho(T')^2} T$, one can easily find that the striction curve of φ_T^B is

$$r_{BT} = B(s) + \frac{\tau}{\kappa} T(s).$$

□

Theorem 8. *Let φ_B^T and φ_T^B be any TB-spatial quaternionic partner-ruled surfaces; then, the dralls of the closed spatial quaternionic partner-ruled surfaces φ_B^T and φ_T^B are*

$$P_{TB} = P_{BT} = 0,$$

respectively.

Proof. Let $\alpha = \alpha(s)$ be a unit-speed spatial quaternionic curve with the Frenet frame $\{T, N, B\}$. The drall of the closed spatial quaternionic ruled surface φ_B^T can be obtained by considering Equation (2) and utilizing the quaternionic inner product. Specifically, the drall is expressed as

$$P_{TB} = \frac{1}{2} \frac{(B \times B') \times \overline{T'} + T' \times \overline{(B \times B')}}{\rho(B')^2}.$$

We compute the drall of the surface φ_B^T by utilizing the quaternionic product of the spatial quaternions and the Frenet invariants. The computation is carried out as follows:

$$P_{TB} = \frac{1}{2}\frac{(\tau T \times \kappa N) + (\kappa N \times \tau T)}{\tau} = 0.$$

In a similar way, the drall of the surface φ_T^B is determined by

$$\begin{aligned} P_{BT} &= -\frac{1}{2}\frac{(T \times T') \times \overline{B'} + B' \times \overline{(T \times T')}}{\rho(T')^2} \\ &= -\frac{1}{2}\frac{(\kappa B \times \tau N) + (\tau N \times \kappa B)}{\kappa} \\ &= 0. \end{aligned}$$

□

Corollary 2. *Let φ_B^T and φ_T^B be any TB-spatial quaternionic partner-ruled surfaces; then, the TB-spatial quaternionic partner-ruled surfaces are developable surfaces.*

Proof. The proof is obvious by virtue that the necessary and sufficient condition for a ruled surface to be developable is having zero drall at each point of the surface. □

Theorem 9. *Let φ_B^T and φ_T^B be any TB-spatial quaternionic partner-ruled surfaces; the angles of the pitch of the closed spatial quaternionic partner-ruled surfaces are*

$$\lambda_{TB} = \oint \kappa ds,\ \lambda_{BT} = \oint \tau ds,$$

respectively.

Proof. Assume $\alpha = \alpha(s)$ is a unit-speed spatial quaternionic curve with the Frenet frame $\{T, N, B\}$. Taking into consideration Equation (6), the angle of pitch of the closed spatial quaternionic ruled surface φ_B^T is written by

$$\lambda_{TB} = h(D, B) = \frac{1}{2}(D \times \overline{B} + B \times \overline{D}) = -\frac{1}{2}(D \times B + B \times D).$$

By referring to Equation (4) and the definition of the quaternion inner product, we obtain

$$\lambda_{TB} = h(D, B\rangle = \left\langle \oint (\tau T + \kappa B)ds, B \right) = \oint \kappa ds.$$

In a similar manner, the angle of the pitch λ_{BT} of the closed spatial quaternionic ruled surface φ_T^B is calculated

$$\lambda_{BT} = h(D, T) = \left\langle \oint (\tau T + \kappa B)ds, T \right\rangle = \oint \tau ds.$$

□

Theorem 10. *Let φ_B^T and φ_T^B be TB-spatial quaternionic partner-ruled surfaces; then, the pitches of the closed spatial quaternionic partner-ruled surfaces φ_B^T and φ_T^B are*

$$l_{TB} = 0, l_{BT} = 0,$$

respectively.

Proof. Let $\alpha = \alpha(s)$ be a unit-speed spatial quaternionic curve with the Frenet frame $\{T, N, B\}$. From Equation (5), $V = \oint dT = \oint \kappa N ds$ is found, and from Equation (7), the pitch l_{TB} of the closed spatial quaternionic ruled surface φ_B^T is written by

$$l_{TB} = h(V, B) = h\left(\oint \kappa N ds, B\right).$$

From the definition of the quaternion inner product, it is found as

$$l_{TB} = \frac{1}{2}\left(\oint \kappa N ds \times \overline{B} + B \times \overline{\oint \kappa N ds}\right).$$

So, using the cross-product and the conjugate of a quaternion, we obtain

$$l_{TB} = 0.$$

By making similar calculations, the pitch l_{BT} of the closed spatial quaternionic ruled surface φ_T^B is determined as

$$l_{BT} = h(V, T) = 0,$$

where $V = \oint dB = -\oint \tau N ds$. □

Corollary 3. *Let φ_B^T and φ_T^B be any TB-spatial quaternionic partner-ruled surfaces. The TB-spatial quaternionic partner-ruled surfaces represent cones.*

Proof. The proof is obvious by virtue that the necessary and sufficient condition for a developable ruled surface to be a cone is having zero pitch at each point of the surface. □

3.3. NB-Spatial Quaternionic Partner-Ruled Surfaces

Definition 7. *Consider a spatial quaternionic curve $\alpha = \alpha(s)$ that is differentiable and moves at a unit speed for its parameter s, and let $\{T, N, B\}$ be Frenet frame of the curve. The two spatial quaternionic ruled surfaces defined by*

$$\begin{cases} \varphi_B^N(s,u) = N(s) + uB(s), \\ \varphi_N^B(s,u) = B(s) + uN(s), \end{cases}$$

are called NB-spatial quaternionic partner-ruled surfaces.

Theorem 11. *Let the surfaces φ_B^N and φ_N^B be spatial quaternionic partner-ruled surfaces; then, the striction curves r_{NB} and r_{BN} of the surfaces φ_B^N and φ_N^B are*

$$r_{NB} = N, r_{BN} = B,$$

respectively.

Proof. Let $\alpha = \alpha(s)$ be a unit-speed spatial quaternionic curve with the Frenet frame $\{T, N, B\}$. By considering Equation (3) and using the quaternionic inner product, the striction curve of the spatial quaternionic ruled surface φ_B^N can be written by

$$r_{NB} = N - \frac{h(B', N')}{\rho(B')^2} B = N - \frac{1}{2}\frac{\left(B' \times \overline{N'} + N' \times \overline{B'}\right)}{\sqrt{h(B', B')}} B.$$

If we consider Equations (1) and (3), we can prove using similar methods of Theorem 3. □

Theorem 12. *Let φ_B^N and φ_N^B be NB-spatial quaternionic partner-ruled surfaces; then, the dralls of the closed spatial quaternionic partner-ruled surfaces φ_B^N and φ_N^B are $P_{NB} = -\kappa$ and $P_{BN} = 0$, respectively.*

Proof. By considering Equation (2), the proof is completed in a similar way to the proof of Theorem 4. □

Corollary 4. *Let φ_B^N and φ_N^B be any NB-spatial quaternionic partner-ruled surfaces; then, the spatial quaternionic partner-ruled surfaces are developable surfaces if and only if the spatial quaternionic curve $\alpha = \alpha(s)$ is a straight line.*

Proof. The necessary and sufficient condition for a ruled surface to be developable is having zero drall at each point of the surface, and the necessary and sufficient condition for a curve to be a straight line is having zero curvature at each point of the curve. These prove the corollary. □

Theorem 13. *Let φ_B^N and φ_N^B be any NB-spatial quaternionic partner-ruled surfaces; then, the angles of the pitch of the closed spatial quaternionic partner-ruled surfaces are $\lambda_{NB} = \oint \kappa ds$ and $\lambda_{BN} = 0$, respectively.*

Proof. By considering Equations (4) and (6), the proof is completed similarly to the proof of Theorem 5. □

Theorem 14. *Let φ_B^N and φ_N^B be NB-spatial quaternionic partner-ruled surfaces; then, the pitches of the closed spatial quaternionic partner-ruled surfaces φ_B^N and φ_N^B are $l_{NB} = 0,\ l_{BN} = -\oint \tau ds$, respectively.*

Proof. By considering Equations (5) and (7), the proof is completed similarly to the proof of Theorem 6. □

Corollary 5. *Let φ_B^N and φ_N^B be NB-spatial quaternionic partner-ruled surfaces. Then, the following expressions are satisfied:*

i. *The surface φ_B^N is a cone if and only if the curve $\alpha = \alpha(s)$ is a straight line.*
ii. *The surface φ_N^B is a cone if and only if the curve $\alpha = \alpha(s)$ is a planar curve.*

Proof. The necessary and sufficient condition for a developable ruled surface to be a cone is having zero pitch at each point of the surface, and the necessary and sufficient condition a curve to be a straight line (planar) is having zero curvature (torsion) at each point of the curve. These prove the corollary. □

4. A Particular Example for Spatial Quaternionic Partner-Ruled Surfaces

Let us consider a spatial quaternionic curve given by the parametric equation

$$\alpha(s) = \frac{3}{4}\left(\cos s + \frac{\cos 3s}{9}, \sin s + \frac{\sin 3s}{9}, \frac{-2\cos s}{\sqrt{3}}\right).$$

The Frenet elements of the spatial quaternionic curves α are

$$\begin{aligned}
T(s) &= \left(\frac{-3\sin s - \sin 3s}{4}, \cos^3 s, \frac{\sqrt{3}\sin s}{2}\right), \\
N(s) &= \left(-\frac{\sqrt{3}\cos 2s}{2}, -\frac{\sqrt{3}\sin 2s}{2}, \frac{1}{2}\right), \\
B(s) &= \left(\frac{3\cos s - \cos 3s}{4}, \sin^3 s, \frac{\sqrt{3}\cos s}{2}\right), \\
\kappa &= \sqrt{3}\cos s,\ \tau = -\sqrt{3}\sin s.
\end{aligned}$$

and the TN-spatial quaternionic partner-ruled surfaces are found as

$$\begin{cases} \varphi_N^T = \left(\dfrac{-2\sqrt{3}u\cos 2s - 3\sin s - \sin 3s}{4}, \cos^3 s - \sqrt{3}u \sin s \cos s, \dfrac{u + \sqrt{3}\sin s}{2} \right), \\ \\ \varphi_T^N = \left(\dfrac{-2\sqrt{3}\cos 2s - u(3\sin s + \sin 3s)}{4}, u\cos^3 s - \dfrac{\sqrt{3}\sin 2s}{2}, \dfrac{1 + \sqrt{3}u\sin s}{2} \right). \end{cases}$$

Obviously, the striction curves of these TN-spatial quaternionic partner-ruled surfaces are

$$\begin{cases} r_{TN} = \left(\dfrac{-3\sin s - \sin 3s}{4}, \cos^3 s, \dfrac{\sqrt{3}\sin s}{2} \right) \\ r_{NT} = \left(-\dfrac{\sqrt{3}\cos 2s}{2}, -\dfrac{\sqrt{3}\sin 2s}{2}, \dfrac{1}{2} \right), \end{cases}$$

respectively; see Figure 1.

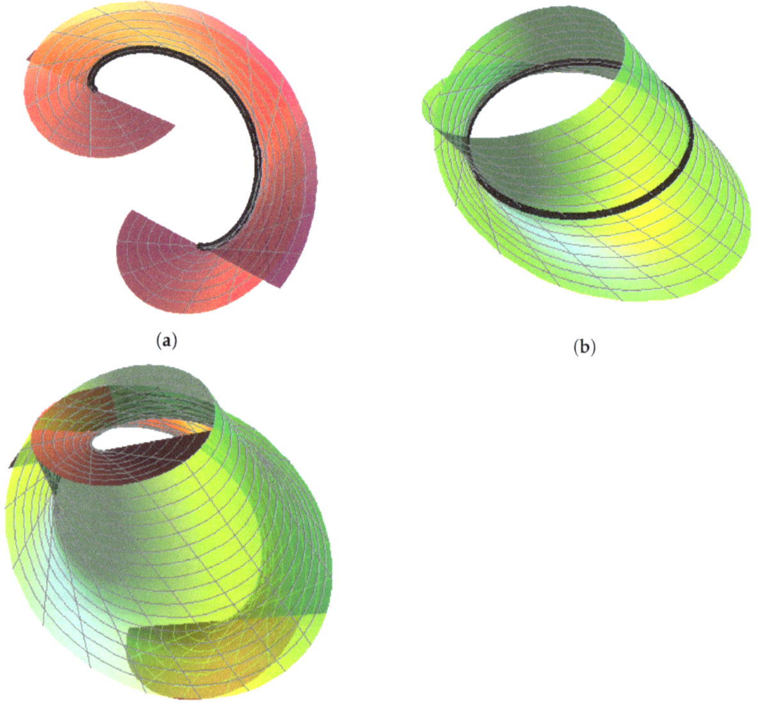

(a) (b) (c)

Figure 1. TN-spatial quaternionic partner-ruled surfaces for $s \in \left(-\frac{\pi}{2}, \frac{\pi}{2}\right)$ and $u \in (-1, 1)$. (**a**) φ_N^T and its striction curve (black). (**b**) φ_T^N and its striction curve (black). (**c**) The surfaces φ_N^T (red) and φ_N^T (green).

In a similar manner, the parametric forms of the TB-spatial quaternionic partner-ruled surfaces and their striction curves are found as

$$\begin{cases} \varphi_B^T = \left(\dfrac{u(3\cos s - \cos 3s) - 3\sin s - \sin 3s}{4}, \cos^3 s + u\sin^3 s, \dfrac{\sqrt{3}(u\cos s + \sin s)}{2} \right), \\ \\ \varphi_T^B = \left(\dfrac{3\cos s - \cos 3s - u(3\sin s + \sin 3s)}{4}, u\cos^3 s + \sin^3 s, \dfrac{\sqrt{3}(\cos s + u\sin s)}{2} \right), \end{cases}$$

$$\begin{cases} r_{TB} = \left(\dfrac{(-3 + \cos 4s)\csc s}{4}, \dfrac{\cos s + \cos 3s}{2}, -\dfrac{\sqrt{3}\cos 2s \csc s}{2} \right), \\ r_{BT} = \left(\dfrac{(3 - \cos 4s)\sec s}{4}, \dfrac{\sin s - \sin 3s}{2}, \dfrac{\sqrt{3}\cos 2s \sec s}{2} \right), \end{cases}$$

respectively; see Figure 2.

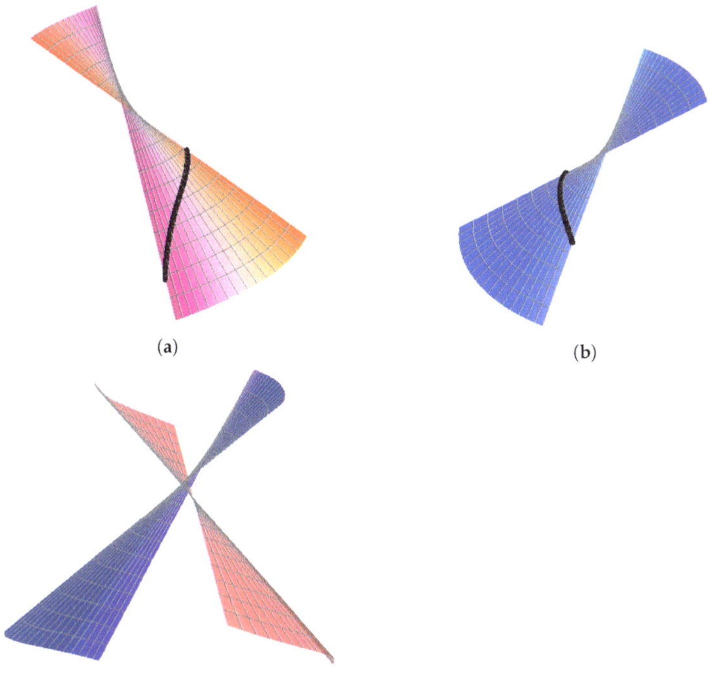

(**a**) (**b**) (**c**)

Figure 2. TB-spatial quaternionic partner-ruled surfaces for $s \in \left(\frac{\pi}{10}, \frac{\pi}{3}\right)$ and $u \in (-4, 4)$. (**a**) φ_B^T and its striction curve (black). (**b**) φ_T^B and its striction curve (black). (**c**) The surfaces φ_B^T (red) and φ_T^B (blue).

Similarly, the parametric forms for the NB-spatial quaternionic partner-ruled surfaces and their striction curves are found as

$$\begin{cases} \varphi_B^N = \left(\dfrac{u(3\cos s - \cos 3s) - 2\sqrt{3}\cos 2s}{4}, \dfrac{-\sqrt{3}\sin 2s}{2} + u\sin^3 s, \dfrac{1 + \sqrt{3}u\cos s}{2} \right), \\ \\ \varphi_N^B = \left(\dfrac{3\cos s - \cos 3s - 2\sqrt{3}u\cos 2s}{4}, \dfrac{-\sqrt{3}u\sin 2s}{2} + \sin^3 s, \dfrac{u + \sqrt{3}\cos s}{2} \right), \end{cases}$$

$$\begin{cases} r_{NB} = \left(-\frac{\sqrt{3}\cos 2s}{2}, -\frac{\sqrt{3}\sin 2s}{2}, \frac{1}{2} \right), \\ r_{BN} = \left(\frac{3\cos s - \cos 3s}{4}, \sin^3 s, \frac{\sqrt{3}\cos s}{2} \right), \end{cases}$$

respectively; see Figure 3.

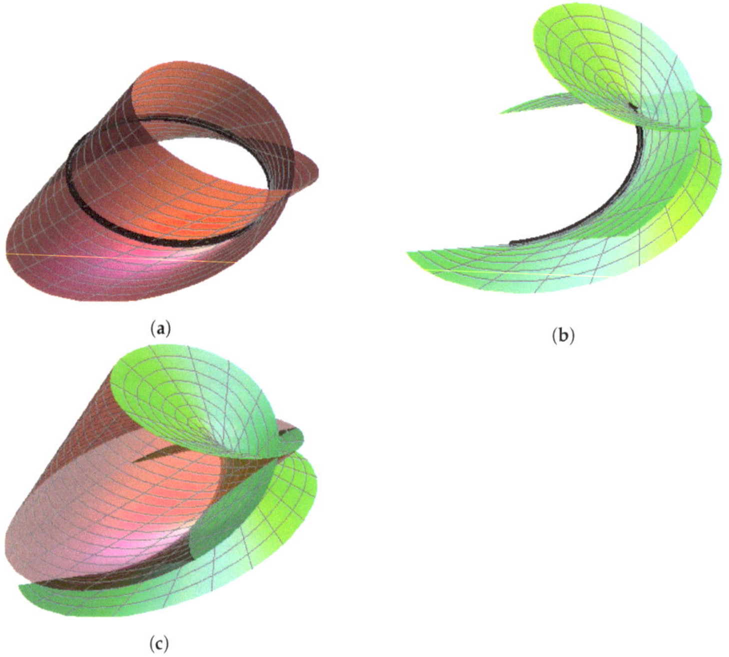

Figure 3. The NB-spatial quaternionic partner-ruled surfaces for $s \in \left(-\frac{\pi}{2}, \frac{\pi}{2}\right)$ and $u \in (-1, 1)$. (**a**) φ_B^N and its striction curve (black). (**b**) φ_N^B and its striction curve (black). (**c**) The surfaces φ_B^N (red) and φ_N^B (green).

5. Conclusions

In this paper, we derived the spatial quaternionic partner-ruled surfaces formed by spatial quaternions, which are Frenet elements of a spatial quaternionic base curve. Then, we determined the striction curves and dralls of these surfaces. Additionally, the conditions of these partner-ruled surfaces to be developable were investigated. Under consideration, the quaternionic partner-ruled surfaces were closed, and the pitches and angles of pitches of them were found. The integral invariants of these partner surfaces were calculated by using quaternionic products.

Author Contributions: Conceptualization, K.E.; formal analysis, S.E., K.E. and A.Ç.; investigation, S.E., K.E. and A.Ç.; methodology, S.E., K.E. and A.Ç.; supervision, S.E.; writing—original draft, K.E.; writing—review and editing, S.E., K.E. and A.Ç. All authors have read and agreed to the published version of the manuscript.

Funding: This work was funded by Sakarya University.

Data Availability Statement: The original contributions presented in the study are included in the article; further inquiries can be directed to the corresponding author.

Conflicts of Interest: Author Kemal Eren was employed by the Sakarya University Technology Developing Zones Manager Company. The remaining authors declare that the research was conducted in the absence of any commercial or financial relationships that could be construed as a potential conflict of interest.

References

1. Hamilton, W.R. *Elements of Quaternions*, 3rd ed.; Chelsea Publishing Co.: New York, NY, USA, 1969; Volume I–II.
2. Girard, P.R. The quaternion group and modern physics. *Eur. J. Phys.* **1984**, *5*, 25–32. [CrossRef]
3. Hanson, J.A.; Ma, H. Quaternion frame approach to streamline visualization. *IEEE Trans. Vis. Comput. Graph.* **1984**, *1*, 164–173. [CrossRef]
4. Kou, K.I.; Xia, Y.H. Linear quaternion differential equations: Basic theory and fundamental results. *Stud. Appl. Math.* **2018**, *141*, 3–45. [CrossRef]
5. Shoemake, K. Animating rotation with quaternionic curves. *ACM SIGGRAPH Comput. Graph.* **1985**, *9*, 245–253. [CrossRef]
6. Bharathi, K.; Nagaraj, M. Quaternion valued function of a real Serret-Frenet formulae. *Indian J. Pure Appl. Math.* **1985**, *16*, 741–756.
7. Soyfidan, T.; Parlatıcı, H.; Güngör, M.A. On the quaternionic curves according to parallel transport frame. *TWMS J. Pure Appl. Math.* **2013**, *4*, 194–203.
8. Erişir, T.; Güngör, M.A. Some characterizations of quaternionic rectifying curves in the semi-Euclidean space E_2^4. *Honam Math. J.* **2014**, *36*, 67–83. [CrossRef]
9. Güngör, M.A.; Erişir, T. On the quaternionic curves in the semi-Euclidean space E_2^4. *Casp. J. Math. Sci.* **2018**, *7*, 36–45. [CrossRef]
10. Giardino, S. A primer on the differential geometry of quaternionic curves. *Math. Methods Appl. Sci.* **2021**, *44*, 14428–14436. [CrossRef]
11. Giardino, S. Winding number and homotopy for quaternionic curves. *Int. J. Geom. Methods Mod. Phys.* **2022**, *19*, 2250087. [CrossRef]
12. Gök, İ.; Okuyucu, Z.; Kahraman, F.; Hacısalihoğlu, H.H. On the quaternionic B_2-slant helices in the Euclidean space E^4. *Adv. Appl. Clifford Algebr.* **2011**, *21*, 707–719. [CrossRef]
13. Kişi, İ.; Büyükkütük, S.; Öztürk, G. Quaternionic curves which lie on the special planes in 4-dimensional Euclidean space E^4. *J. Math.* **2024**, *2024*, 8. [CrossRef]
14. Eren, K. Motion of inextensible quaternionic curves and modified Korteweg-de Vries equation. *An. Ştiint. Univ. "Ovidius" Constanţa Ser. Mat.* **2022**, *30*, 91–101. [CrossRef]
15. Chen, J.; Li, J. Quaternionic maps and minimal surfaces. *Ann. Scuola Norm. Sup. Pisa Cl. Sci.* **2005**, *4*, 375–388. [CrossRef]
16. Hoffman, J.W.; Wang, H. Special syzygies of rational surfaces generated by dual quaternions. *J. Algebra Comput. Appl.* **2022**, *3*, 100004. [CrossRef]
17. Li, Y.; Eren, K.; Ayvacı, K.H.; Ersoy, S. Simultaneous characterizations of partner ruled surfaces using Flc frame. *AIMS Math.* **2022**, *7*, 20213–20229. [CrossRef]
18. Şenyurt, S.; Çalışkan, A. The quaternionic expression of ruled surfaces. *Filomat* **2018**, *32*, 5753–5766. [CrossRef]
19. Çalışkan, A.; Şenyurt, S. The dual spatial quaternionic expression of ruled surfaces. *Therm. Sci.* **2019**, *23*, 403–411. [CrossRef]
20. Çalışkan, A. The quaternionic ruled surfaces in terms of alternative frame. *Palest. J. Math.* **2022**, *11*, 406–412.
21. Gök, İ. Quaternionic approach of canal surfaces constructed by some new ideas. *Adv. Appl. Clifford Algebr.* **2017**, *27*, 1175–1190. [CrossRef]
22. Aslan, S.; Yaylı, Y. Canal surfaces with quaternions. *Adv. Appl. Clifford Algebr.* **2016**, *26*, 31–38. [CrossRef]
23. Çanakcı, Z.; Oğulcan, T.O.; Gök, İ.; Yaylı, Y. The construction of circular surfaces with quaternions. *Asian-Eur. J. Math.* **2019**, *12*, 1950091. [CrossRef]
24. Aslan, S.; Bekar, M.; Yaylı, Y. Ruled surfaces constructed by quaternions. *J. Geom. Phys.* **2021**, *161*, 104048. [CrossRef]

axioms

Article

Numerical Analysis of the Cylindrical Shell Pipe with Preformed Holes Subjected to a Compressive Load Using Non-Uniform Rational B-Splines and T-Splines for an Isogeometric Analysis Approach

Said EL Fakkoussi [1,*], Ouadie Koubaiti [2], Ahmed Elkhalfi [1], Sorin Vlase [3,4,*] and Marin Marin [5,6]

[1] Mechanical Engineering Laboratory, Faculty of Sciences and Techniques, Sidi Mohamed Ben Abdellah University of Fez, Fez 30000, Morocco; ahmed.elkhalfi@usmba.ac.ma
[2] Department of Mathematics, MSISI, Laboratory, Faculty of Sciences and Techniques of Errachidia, Moulay Ismail University of Meknes, B.P 509 Boutalamine, Errachidia 52000, Morocco; o.koubaiti@umi.ac.ma
[3] Department of Mechanical Engineering, Faculty of Mechanical Engineering, Transylvania University of Brasov, B-dul Eroilor 29, 500036 Brasov, Romania
[4] Technical Sciences Academy of Romania, 030167 Bucharest, Romania
[5] Department of Mathematics and Computer Science, Faculty of Mathematics and Informatics, Transylvania University of Brasov, B-dul Eroilor 29, 500036 Brasov, Romania; m.marin@unitbv.ro
[6] Academy of Romanian Scientist, Ilfov Street, No. 3, 050045 Bucharest, Romania
* Correspondence: said.elfakkoussi@usmba.ac.ma (S.E.F.); svlase@unitbv.ro (S.V.)

Abstract: In this paper, we implement the finite detail technique primarily based on T-Splines for approximating solutions to the linear elasticity equations in the connected and bounded Lipschitz domain. Both theoretical and numerical analyses of the Dirichlet and Neumann boundary problems are presented. The Reissner–Mindlin (RM) hypothesis is considered for the investigation of the mechanical performance of a 3D cylindrical shell pipe without and with preformed hole problems under concentrated and compression loading in the linear elastic behavior for trimmed and untrimmed surfaces in structural engineering problems. Bézier extraction from T-Splines is integrated for an isogeometric analysis (IGA) approach. The numerical results obtained, particularly for the displacement and von Mises stress, are compared with and validated against the literature results, particularly with those for Non-Uniform Rational B-Spline (NURBS) IGA and the finite element method (FEM) Abaqus methods. The obtained results show that the computation time of the IGA based on the T-Spline method is shorter than that of the IGA NURBS and FEM Abaqus/CAE (computer-aided engineering) methods. Furthermore, the highlighted results confirm that the IGA approach based on the T-Spline method shows more success than numerical reference methods. We observed that the NURBS IGA method is very limited for studying trimmed surfaces. The T-Spline method shows its power and capability in computing trimmed and untrimmed surfaces.

Keywords: isogeometric analysis; Reissner–Mindlin theory; NURBS; T-splines; Bézier extraction; linear elasticity; Abaqus/computer-aided engineering; MATLAB

MSC: 82C27; 65K15

Citation: EL Fakkoussi, S.; Koubaiti, O.; Elkhalfi, A.; Vlase, S.; Marin, M. Numerical Analysis of the Cylindrical Shell Pipe with Preformed Holes Subjected to a Compressive Load Using Non-Uniform Rational B-Splines and T-Splines for an Isogeometric Analysis Approach. *Axioms* **2024**, *13*, 529. https://doi.org/10.3390/axioms13080529

Academic Editors: Cristina Flaut, Dana Piciu and Murat Tosun

Received: 10 May 2024
Revised: 19 June 2024
Accepted: 20 June 2024
Published: 3 August 2024

1. Introduction

Isogeometric analysis (IGA) is a recently developed computational technique. This approach was supported by a study conducted by Hughes et al. [1] aiming to link computer-aided design (CAD) and finite element analysis (FEA). The IGA approach is primarily based on the isogeometric paradigm, approximating the unknown response of the partial differential equation using equal foundation features to symbolize the considered geometry. The IGA approach has been used to numerically approximate quite a few problems and has proved to be correct and environmentally friendly. A detailed discussion of the use of the IGA approach to solve linear and nonlinear equations for elastic or hydrodynamic problems can be found in [2,3].

In addition, the IGA approach optionally allows for the use of globally smooth basis functions. This gives benefits in the numerical approximation of higher-order PDEs inside the widespread Galerkin formulation. Due to the extensive use of NURBSs (Non-Uniform Rational B-Splines) [4] in CAD technology, we explicitly point out that IGA is primarily based on NURBSs, considering the mathematical properties of these basis functions.

One of the major capabilities of NURBSs that enables the numerical approximation of higher-order partial differential equations in the context of the Galerkin approach is the fact that the basic capability of NURBSs can be globally C^k non-stopping for $k \geq 0$ inside the computational domain. This property makes it possible to solve the problem with a weak form of direct discretization without resorting to mixed formulations, such as FEA [5,6]. In [7], the hull structure problem was solved using IGA, especially the Kirchhoff–Love model. In [8], a high-order formula, the stream function, was used to solve the plane elasticity problem in the IGA context, and an estimation of the error convergence rate with respect to the spot size was performed numerically.

T-Splines were developed by Sederberg et al. Introduced in [9] (2004), they have been extensively studied over the last decade by Y. Bazilevs et al. (2010) [1]. T-Splines are generalizations of NURBS surfaces, of which their mesh management permits for T-connections. T-Splines substantially lessen the range of needless manage factors in NURBS surfaces, permitting treasured operations that are inclusive of neighborhood refinement and merge a couple of B-Spline surfaces into a steady framework [10].

CAD-derived T-Splines triumph over the restrictions of tensor products inherent in NURBSs [11]. In fact, NURBSs shape a constrained subset of T-Splines. Additionally, T-Splines may be regionally refined [12] to generate fashions appropriate for studying topological complexity [13]. This makes T-Splines an excellent foundation for isogeometric evaluations. The extension of the isogeometric framework to superior T-Spline configurations was initiated in [14,15]. T-Spline discretization has been correctly implemented for fractures and injuries [16]. Efficient nearby refinement performs a key function in such applications. Early paintings extending the use of T-Splines have been primarily based on the isogeometric evaluation of arbitrary topological frameworks associated with hull structures and have been promising.

The widespread concept of Bézier extraction involves the creation of a linear map of the T-Spline foundation features and nearby Bernstein foundation features based on Bézier elements. Using Bézier extraction operators, preferred FEA applications may be reused in IGA by editing the most effective form feature subroutine [17].

IGA based on NUBRSs is limited to the evaluation of trimmed surfaces; it requires specific adjustments in terms of the interpolation domain, especially the B-Spline or NUBRS interpolation functions in order to consider the trimmed geometry [18]. Alternatively, MultiPatch specifically relies on Kirchhoff–Love shell theory for trimmed surfaces, as outlined by Reichle et al. [19]. The isogeometric analysis approach based on the use of T-Splines is designed to mitigate the limitations of NURBSs. T-Splines provide a high level of flexibility in 3D surface shaping, and they are often used in conjunction with subdivision surfaces. This combination allows for the creation of highly detailed models with smooth surfaces.

According to the literature review, several researchers are interested in investigating cylindrical shell structures (for example, aircraft fuselages, cooling towers, and reactor vessels) in the field of linear elasticity and elastoplastic behavior. These studies are based on experimental and numerical analyses employing the finite element method or the IGA approach, which are appropriate choices for modeling curved structures. One of the advantages of the IGA approach is that it allows us to approximate the exact geometry using NURBS functions. This provides better displacement and stress calculation results when compared to the finite element method. Du et al. [20] employed an IGA approach within MATLAB to investigate several benchmark examples in both 2D and 3D cases. In another work [21], the author developed the IGA method for thin-walled structures based on Bézier extraction in linear and nonlinear frameworks.

Pipes have been integrated into cylindrical shell structures. Used in various fields (naval, aeronautical, and mechanical structures), these structures are subjected to many mechanical [22,23], thermal [24], and earthquake [25] loads. These loadings reduce their performance. Due to the importance of these structures, several researchers and engineers have studied them in order to preserve their integrity and understand their mechanical behavior under various loads. Zhang et al. [26] studied the mechanical behavior of a pipeline buried under soil under traffic loads generated by the movement of vehicles above. The findings showed that the effects and impacts of vehicles are reduced when increasing the thickness and diameter of the pipelines. On the other hand, EL Fakkoussi et al. [27,28] investigated a cracked pipeline using the FEM and eXtended Finite Element Method (XFEM) to calculate the stress intensity factor (KI) in mode I. They also developed a method to calculate KI according to extended isogeometric analysis (XIGA), which is based on exact geometric modeling. Hussain et al. [29] predicted stress corrosion cracking in gas transportation pipelines using artificial intelligence, especially machine learning. These methods are based on several input data such as corrosion, cracking mechanisms, mechanical damage, and maintenance activities. These works contribute to investigating pipelines for potential issues and provide valuable input data for future studies utilizing machine learning and artificial intelligence methodologies.

The new IGA approach has become the most powerful numerical method in the field of computational modeling and simulation. Unlike the finite element method, the results of the IGA approach are not sensitive to mesh quality or local refinement. This gives us some confidence in terms of numerical stability and convergence. The mechanical performance analysis of 3D cylindrical shell pipes with and without preformed holes using the T-Spline approach for isogeometric analysis has been investigated little, as evidenced in the literature review.

This study investigated 3D cylindrical shell pipes with and without preformed holes under concentrated compression loading in relation to their linear elastic behavior, while also using the T-Spline approach for isogeometric analysis in the case of trimmed surfaces. Problems relating to cylinders that have preformed holes have never been studied using the T-Spline method, and this work will provide additional theoretical and numerical value to the literature, especially in terms of evaluating the mechanical performance of cylindrical shell pipes as well as evaluating and exploiting the robustness of the T-Spline method for the study of curved structures with untrimmed and trimmed surfaces. The results obtained were compared and validated with results found in the literature, especially those relating to the use of the NURBS IGA and Abaqus methods.

This paper is organized into three parts. The first section examines the mathematical equations, including the modified linear elasticity equation, the weak formulation, the Bézier extraction of T-Splines, and the parameters of the mechanical damage criterion. The following section explains the steps used to model a 3D cylindrical shell pipe subjected to a concentrated compressive load using the FEM based on Abaqus/computer-aided engineering (CAE), the IGA approach based on NURBS, and the T-Spline methods implemented in the MATLAB R2021a environment. The last section presents the results, focusing on the numerical results of displacement and stress in the cylindrical shell pipe subjected to a concentered compressive elastic load benchmark. The obtained results were compared and validated with the literature results, especially those relating to the use of NURBS IGA and FEM Abaqus/CAE methods. Additionally, we evaluated issues concerning a 3D cylindrical shell or pipe that has preformed holes.

2. Materials and Methods

In this paper, we present a comprehensive investigation of the Dirichlet boundary problem for linear elasticity systems in bounded Lipschitz domains with connected boundaries. This leads to the formulation of the following model:

$$\begin{cases} -\mu div(\nabla u) - (\mu+\lambda)\nabla(divu) = f \text{ } in \text{ } \Omega\,; \\ u = g \text{ } on \text{ } \Gamma_D; \\ \mu\frac{\partial u}{\partial n} + \lambda\nabla\cdot un = t \text{ } on \text{ } \Gamma_N. \end{cases} \quad (1)$$

Let $\Omega \rightarrow \mathbb{R}^n, n = 2, 3$ represent an elastic solid subjected to a surface or volume force f. Denote its boundary by $\Gamma = \partial\Omega = \Gamma_D \cup \Gamma_N$. Γ_D represents the Dirichlet boundary condition, Γ_N represents the Neumann boundary condition, μ represents a material property, and λ represents a material parameter.

The solid body is under the small deformation assumption. The displacement field u is, therefore, the solution of the following system [30]:

$$\text{Find } u\ : \Omega \ \rightarrow \ \mathbb{R}^n$$

where n is the normal vector directed toward the outside of the solid body, and t is the traction force applied to the surface of the solid body.

Weak formulation

We assume that we have $u = g$ and that it represents non-homogeneous Dirichlet boundary conditions for the displacement field. Then, we look for weak solutions to the Navier Lamé equation in the space

$$H = \left[H^1(\Omega)\right]^n \quad M = L^2(\Omega). \quad (2)$$

Then, we look to the solution in the space H_0 if $u = 0$:

$$H_0 := \left[H_0^1(\Omega)\right]^n, \text{ with}: \ n = 2 \text{ } or \text{ } 3. \quad (3)$$

For all $v \in H$,

$$-\mu\int_{\Omega} div(\nabla u)\cdot v dv - (\mu+\lambda)\int_{\Omega}\nabla(div(u))\cdot v \, dv = \int_{\Omega} f\cdot v \, dv. \quad (4)$$

We obtain that for all $\forall v \in H$,

$$\mu\int_{\Omega}\nabla(u):\nabla v \, dv + (\mu+\lambda)\int_{\Omega}\nabla\cdot u \, \nabla\cdot v \ dv - \mu\int_{\Gamma_N}(\nabla\cdot u)n\cdot v \, d\Gamma = \int_{\Omega} f\cdot v \, dv + \int_{\Gamma_N} t\cdot v \, d\Gamma. \quad (5)$$

Bilinear and linear forms:

Let us introduce the following bilinear forms:

$$a_1 : X_0 \times X_0 \rightarrow R, \ a(u,v) = \mu\int_{\Omega}\nabla u \ : \nabla v \, dv - \mu\int_{\Gamma_N}(\nabla\cdot u)n\cdot v \, d\Gamma; \quad (6)$$

$$a_2 : X_0 \times X_0 \rightarrow R, \ b(u,v) = (\mu+\lambda)\int_{\Omega}\nabla\cdot u \, \nabla\cdot v \ dv; \quad (7)$$

$$\Lambda : X_0 \times X_0 \rightarrow R, \ \Lambda(u,v) = a_1(u,v) + a_2(u,v). \quad (8)$$

Furthermore, we define the following linear form:

$$F : X_0 \rightarrow R, \ F(v) = \int_{\Omega} f\cdot v \, dv + \int_{\Gamma_N} t\cdot v \, d\Gamma. \quad (9)$$

Given f, find $u \in H$ such that $u = g$:

$$\forall v \in H, \ \Lambda(u,v) = F(v). \tag{10}$$

Applying non-homogeneous Dirichlet boundary conditions in the weak formulation of a problem using Lagrange multipliers is an elegant technique for systematically integrating these conditions. We construct an augmented formulation by adding a Lagrange term to impose $u = u_g$ on Γ_D; the Formulation (10) become:

$$\begin{cases} \Lambda + L^t \lambda = F \\ Lu = \mu \end{cases} \tag{11}$$

where L is the matrix associated with the Lagrange multipliers, and μ imposes Dirichlet conditions. The solution of this system allows us to find the displacements. u and the multipliers λ ensure that the boundary conditions are respected.

2.1. Bézier Extraction of T-Spline Basis

Like conventional finite detail analysis, the extracted Bezier factors of T-Splines are described as shown in Figure 1. A set of constant phrases in a polynomial foundation feature are referred to as a Bernstein foundation. Bezier factors may be processed in an identical manner as applied to widespread finite detail computer programs using identical information processing tables. In fact, it is convenient that only the form feature subprogram requires a change, as all of the different components relevant to the application of finite detail remain identical. A by-product of the extraction method is a detail extraction operator. This operator identifies detail-stage topology facts and worldwide smoothing facts and represents the canonical processing of T-joints. T-joints, referred to as "placing nodes" in finite detail analysis, are an essential characteristic of T-Splines.

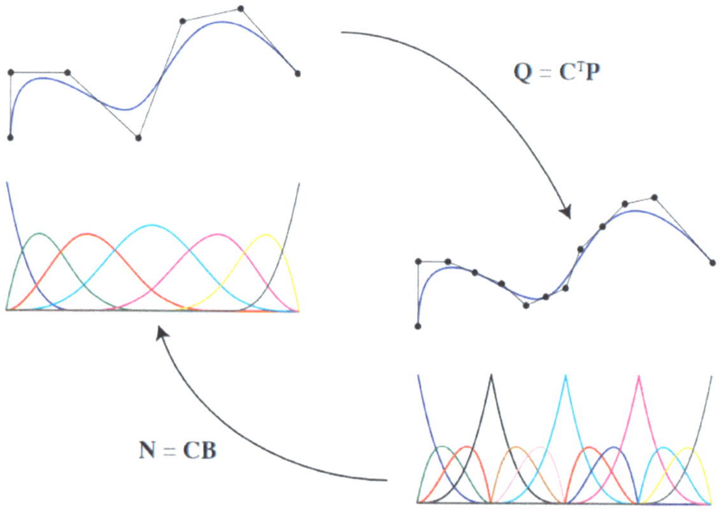

Figure 1. See [31] for a Bézier extraction diagram of the B-Spline curve. The basic capabilities and control points of the B-Spline are denoted as N and P, respectively. The Bernstein polynomial and the control points are denoted as B and Q, respectively.

The idea of Bezier extraction is to reduce the number of control points while respecting the geometry without modifying the domain we would like to study. Further, Bezier extraction applies a local refinement to some parts of the domain (in which there will be major displacements). This technique improves the resolution of the FEM and generates precise results since the number of degrees of freedom is reduced. Note that the geometry must not change when inserting nodes.

Bezier extraction is fundamentally based on knot insertion, which will be briefly outlined for the univariate case below. A new knot $\xi \in [\xi_i, \xi_{i+1}]$ can be inserted into the open node vector, resulting in the modified knot vector $\Psi = \{\xi_1, \xi_2, \ldots \cdot \xi_i, \xi, \xi_{i+1} \ldots \xi_{n+p+1}\}$, and n is the number of the basis function of order p, where $p < i < n + 1$.

This insertion produces a new set of basis functions. To preserve the geometry or approximation while altering the parametrization of the basis, new control point values, $\{Q_j\}$, $j = 1 \ldots m$, must be calculated from the original control points, $\{P_j\}, j = 1 \ldots m$, according to

$$Q_j = \begin{cases} P_1 \,,\; j = 1 \\ \delta_j P_j + (1 - \delta_j) P_{j-1}, \; 1 < \mathrm{j} < \mathrm{m} \\ P_n \,,\; j = n. \end{cases} \tag{12}$$

$$\delta_j = \begin{cases} 1 \,, 1 \leq j \leq i - p \\ \frac{\xi - \xi_j}{\xi_{j+p} - \xi_p} \qquad i - p + 1 < \mathrm{j} < \mathrm{i} \\ 0 \,,\; j \geq i \cdot \end{cases} \tag{13}$$

If we are able to convert the T-Spline basis functions of N to Bernstein polynomials B, this permits the replacement of the T-Spline surface with a series of Bézier patches utilizing the conventional parametric domain. According to the Cox–de Boor formula, this can be expressed as follows.

The new set of so-called Bézier control points Q is computed from B-Spline control points, resulting in the following: $Q = C^t P$. In remembering that the geometry must remain unchanged during the insertion of the nodes,

$$T(\xi) = Q^T B(\xi) = P^T N(\xi) = P^T C B(\xi) \tag{14}$$

where ξ is the coordinate in the standard domain of an individual Bézier patch, and $\mathrm{N}(\xi)$ is a T-Spline vector of the basis functions that are non-zero over the Bézier surface. However, $\mathrm{B}(\xi)$ is a vector of the tensor product of the basis functions of Bernstein polynomials associated with the Bézier surface. C is the extraction operator.

For each localized T-Spline over an element, it can be explained as a linear combination of these Bernstein polynomials. In fact, there exists a coefficient c_i, such that $T(\xi) = \sum_{i=0}^{N} c_i B_i(\xi)$, where the convention $N = (p+1)^d$ is typical in finite element analysis, p is the degree of the Bernstein polynomial, and d is the dimension of the domain; for example, for the surfaces, $d = 2$.

We propose that univariate Bernstein polynomials form the basis of the Bézier surface, which are defined over the biunit interval $[-1, 1]$, $B_{i,p}(\xi) = C_{i-1}^{p}(1 - \xi)^{p-i+1}(1 + \xi)^{i-1}$, with $1 \leq i \leq p + 1$, and C_{i-1}^{p}: binomial coefficient.

We can define the multivariate Bernstein basis functions of degree p as $B_{a(i,j),p}(\xi) = B_{i,p}(\xi_1) B_{j,p}(\xi_2)$, with $(\xi) = (\xi_1, \xi_2)$ representing a pair of variables, and $a(i,j)$ is a mapping from a pair of indices (i,j) to a single index. $a(i,j) = (p+1)(j-1) + i \cdot$.

The calculation of the element extraction operators is conducted function-by-function, each basis function adding a line to each extraction operator corresponding to the Bézier elements in its support.

In 3D cases, the T-Spline volume in the parametric domain can be defined as follows:

$$\mathrm{T}(\xi, \zeta, \eta) = \frac{\sum_{i=0}^{n} \mathrm{N_i}(\xi, \zeta, \eta) \omega_i \mathrm{P_i}}{\sum_{j=0}^{n} \mathrm{N_j}(\xi, \zeta, \eta) \omega_j}. \tag{15}$$

Weights ω_i are scalar weights associated with each control point $\mathrm{P_i}$ and T-Spline basis functions corresponding to control point $\mathrm{P_i}$:

$$N_i(\xi, \zeta, \eta) = N_{i,\xi}(\xi) N_{i,\zeta}(\zeta) N_{i,\eta}(\eta). \tag{16}$$

2.2. Incorporating Bézier Extraction of T-Splines into Finite Element Method

The Bezier extraction of T-Splines produces a fixed set of Bezier elements (defined using Bernstein terminology) and the corresponding element extraction operators C and IEN (index element node) arrays. This shape is equivalent to that derived for NURBSs in [31] and can be incorporated into the finite detail components in a similar way. We construct the functional subspace of finite dim $H_h \subset H$ from the T-Spline functions, forming the specified geometry. From problem (14), the approximate problem is written as follows: given f_h, find $u_h \in H_h$ such that $u_h = g_h$:

$$\forall\, v_h \in H_h,\ \Lambda(u_h, v_h) = F(v_h) \tag{17}$$

where $u_h = \sum_{i=1}^{n} \alpha_i T_i$, $v_h = \sum_{j=1}^{n} \beta_j T_j$, and $\Lambda(u_h, v_h)$ is a bilinear form that often arises from integrating the product of the derivatives of the trial function u_h and the test function v_h over the domain. $F(v_h)$ represents the right-hand side of the weak formulation.

With these combinations, problem (14) can be written in the form of a matrix problem:

$$Au = F. \tag{18}$$

We proceed as in the case of classical finite elements, with the global stiffness matrix A and the force vector F, which can be produced by performing an integration of the Bézier elements.

On each Bézier element, b, we have A^b, such as in the following: $\left(A^b\right)_{ij} = \Lambda\left(T_i^b, T_j^b\right)$, where the elementary stiffness matrix and the vector force $F_i^b = F\left(T_i^b\right)$ are assembled in the global matrix A and the vector F, respectively.

By taking into consideration the non-homogeneous Dirichlet boundary conditions and with the insertion of the Lagrange parameter, we obtain the following matrix problem that we wish to solve: $\begin{pmatrix} A & L^t \\ L & 0 \end{pmatrix} \binom{u}{\lambda} = \binom{F}{\mu}$.

We use the element extraction operators, and the T-Spline function is defined as follows:

$$T_i^b(\xi) = \mathrm{W^b C^b} \frac{\mathrm{B_i}(\xi)}{\Psi_{\mathrm{i}}(\xi)}, \tag{19}$$

where $\Psi_i(\xi) = \left(\omega^b\right)^T C^b B_i(\xi)$, and ω^b represents the weight vector corresponding to the T-Spline control points. W^b is the diagonal matrix form of vector ω^b.

We calculate the derivatives of the T-Splines with respect to the coordinates of the physical domain (x_1, x_2, x_3):

$$\frac{\partial T_i^b(\xi)}{\partial \mathrm{x_k}} = \sum_{\mathrm{j}=1}^{3} \frac{\partial T_i^b(\xi)}{\partial \xi_{\mathrm{j}}} \frac{\partial \xi_{\mathrm{j}}}{\partial \mathrm{x_k}},\ \text{for all } k = 1, 2, 3 \tag{20}$$

$$\frac{\partial T_i^b(\xi)}{\partial \xi_j} = W^b C^b \frac{\partial}{\partial \xi_j}\left(\frac{B_i(\xi)}{\left(\omega^b\right)^T C^b B_i(\xi)}\right) = \tag{21}$$

$$W^b C^b \left(\frac{1}{\Psi_i(\xi)} \frac{\partial B_i(\xi)}{\partial \xi_j} - \frac{\partial \Psi(\xi)}{\partial \xi_j} \frac{B_i(\xi)}{\left(\Psi_i(\xi)\right)^2}\right). \tag{22}$$

The approximation of the Bezier element is defined using a transformation to a reference element, which is the e $[0,1] \times [0,1] \times [0,1]\cdot$ The Jacobian determinant is defined as $|J| = \left|\frac{\partial x}{\partial \xi}\right|$.

To solve linear system (18), we must calculate the elements of the rigidity matrix corresponding to any Bezier element in order to assemble them in a global matrix.

$$(A^b)_{ij} = (A_1^b + A_2^b)_{ij},$$

such as:

$$\begin{aligned}(A_1^b)_{ij} = \\ \iiint_0^1 \mu\left(W^b C^b M_i J^{-1}\right)\left(W^b C^b M_j J^{-1}\right)^T |J| d\xi_1 d\xi_2 d\xi_3 - \\ \mu \iint_0^1 \left(\nabla \cdot W^b C^b \frac{B_i(\xi)}{\Psi_i(\xi)}\right) n \cdot W^b C^b \frac{B_j(\xi)}{\Psi_j(\xi)} |j| d\xi_1 d\xi_2\end{aligned} \tag{23}$$

n is the unit vector directed toward the outside of the domain, with the vector M_i written as follows:

$$\begin{aligned}(M_i)^T = \\ \frac{1}{\Psi_i(\xi)}\frac{\partial B_i(\xi)}{\partial \xi_1} - \frac{\partial \Psi(\xi)}{\partial \xi_1}\frac{B_i(\xi)}{(\Psi_i(\xi))^2} \quad \frac{1}{\Psi_i(\xi)}\frac{\partial B_i(\xi)}{\partial \xi_2} - \frac{\partial \Psi(\xi)}{\partial \xi_2}\frac{B_i(\xi)}{(\Psi_i(\xi))^2} \quad \frac{1}{\Psi_i(\xi)}\frac{\partial B_i(\xi)}{\partial \xi_3} - \frac{\partial \Psi(\xi)}{\partial \xi_3}\frac{B_i(\xi)}{(\Psi_i(\xi))^2}\end{aligned} \tag{24}$$

$$(A_2^b)_{ij} == (\mu + \lambda) \iiint_0^1 \nabla \cdot (W^b C^b \frac{B_i(\xi)}{\Psi_i(\xi)}) \nabla \cdot (W^b C^b \frac{B_j(\xi)}{\Psi_j(\xi)}) |J| d\xi_1 d\xi_2 d\xi_3 \tag{25}$$

$$F = \iiint_0^1 f \cdot (W^b C^b \frac{B_i(\xi)}{\Psi_i(\xi)}) |J| d\xi_1 d\xi_2 d\xi_3 + \iint_0^1 t \cdot (W^b C^b \frac{B_i(\xi)}{\Psi_i(\xi)}) |j| d\xi_1 d\xi_2. \tag{26}$$

The matrix j transforms the surface of the lateral domain to the reference surface $[0,1] \times [0,1]$.

To calculate all the elements of matrices, we use Gaussian quadrature.

2.3. Theoretically Stress Lateral Loading

The FEM analysis results are confirmed via comparison with the theoretically predicted tensile stress results and are presented according to the following equation [32,33]:

$$\sigma_{theo} = \frac{Px}{2S}, \tag{27}$$

with

$S = \frac{\pi\left(D_e^4 - D_i^4\right)}{32 D_e}$;

P: the concentered load (N);

X: the impact position;

S: the section modulus of a circular hollow section;

D_e: the outer diameter;

D_i: the inner diameters of the pipe.

2.4. Mechanical Failure Criteria

In the literature, several failure criteria can be found that are used to analyze the performance of structures. The von Mises stress criterion is more commonly used in the field of linear elasticity to determine whether failure will occur by comparing the failure limits of materials. Due to this criterion, it is possible to know whether the structure under study can function normally under load. The equation is expressed as follows:

$$\sigma_{Mises} = \frac{1}{\sqrt{2}}\sqrt{(\sigma_x - \sigma_y)^2 + (\sigma_x - \sigma_z)^2 + (\sigma_y - \sigma_z)^2}, \tag{28}$$

where σ_x, σ_y, and σ_z are the first, second, and third principal stresses.

3. Computational Modeling and Simulation

This section explains the steps used to model a 3D cylindrical shell pipe subjected to a concentrated and compressive load using the classic finite element method based on Abaqus/CAE and the IGA approach based on the NURBS and the T-Spline methods.

3.1. Cylindrical Shell 3D Pipe Geometry

The geometry of the 3D cylindrical shell pipe studied is shown in Figure 2.

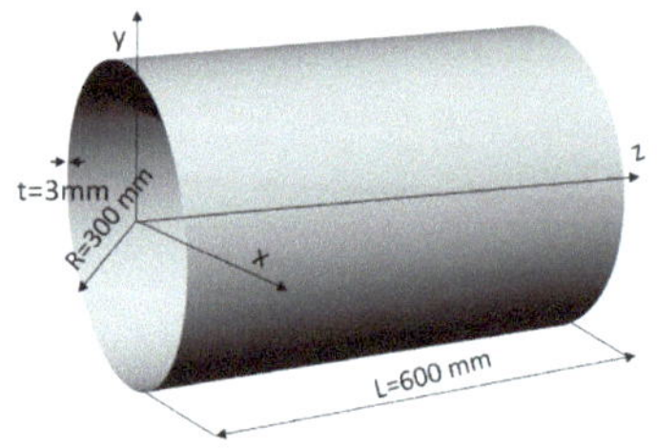

Figure 2. The geometry of the 3D cylindrical shell pipe.

3.2. Material

P264GH steel material [34] (Table 1) was used in this study. The stress–strain curve of the mechanical test is shown in Figure 3. The behavior of this material follows the Ramberg–Osgood law, which is described as follows:

$$\varepsilon = \frac{\sigma}{E} + \left(\frac{\sigma}{k}\right)^{1/n}, \tag{29}$$

where k = 494.54 MPa, and n = 0.068

Table 1. Mechanical properties of P264GH steel.

Young's modulus	E = 207 GPa
Poisson's ration	v = 0.3
Yield stress	Re = 340 MPa
Ultimate tensile strength	Rm = 440 MPa
Elongation to fracture	A = 35%

The stress–strain curve of the P264GH steel is illustrated in Figure 3:

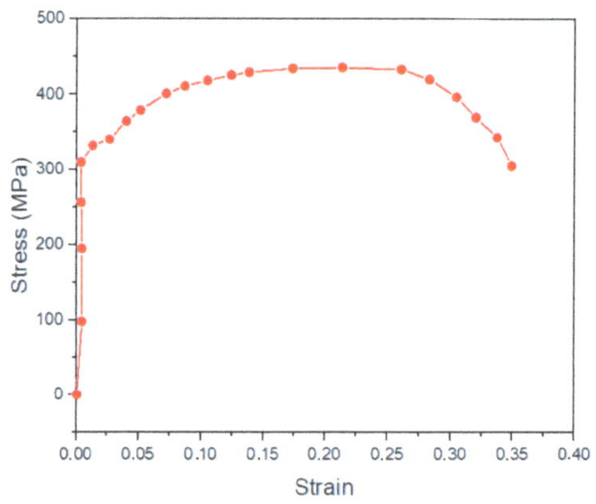

Figure 3. Stress–strain curve of P264GH steel.

3.3. Meshing, Loadings, and Boundary Conditions

To ensure a robust convergence of results in Abaqus/CAE and facilitate pertinent comparisons with the IGA approach based on the NURBS and T-Spline results, we performed a mesh convergence study for the proposed refinements. We established that a mesh size ranging from 0.15 mm to 0.09 mm for the calculation of stress is robust and consistent (Figure 4). Additionally, for an efficient computation time ratio, we used a mesh size of 0.15 mm for this investigation.

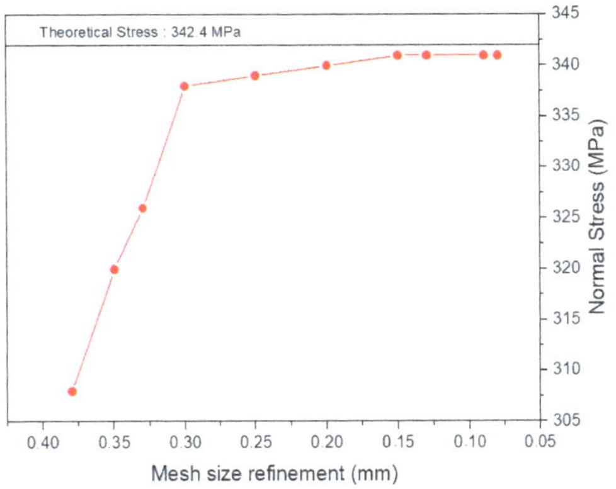

Figure 4. Mesh size convergence (finite element method (FEM) Abaqus/computer-aided engineering (CAE)).

In this study, we employed the IGA approach based on the T-Spline method to resolve industrial mechanical issues, particularly the failure of pipelines due to the side impact of excavation machines during installation, pipe–soil interactions, and preformed holes. The impact was modeled using an applied load (*F*) and a line compression load (Figure 5). It is important to note that this investigation was carried out in the linear elasticity domain.

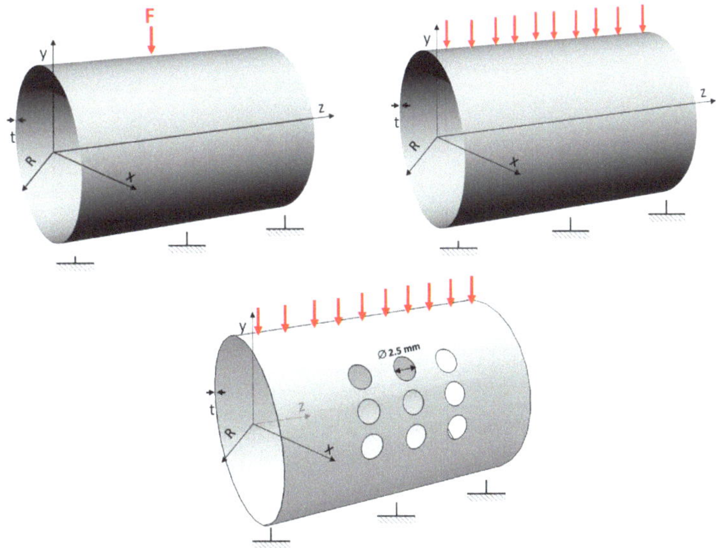

Figure 5. The geometry and loading conditions of the cylindrical shell pipe.

Considering geometric symmetry and to enable an efficient computation time ratio, we used half of a 3D cylindrical shell pipe (Figure 6) to model the impact for both numerical investigation methods, the finite element method (FEM) according to Abaqus/CAE and the IGA approach based on NURBSs and T-Splines.

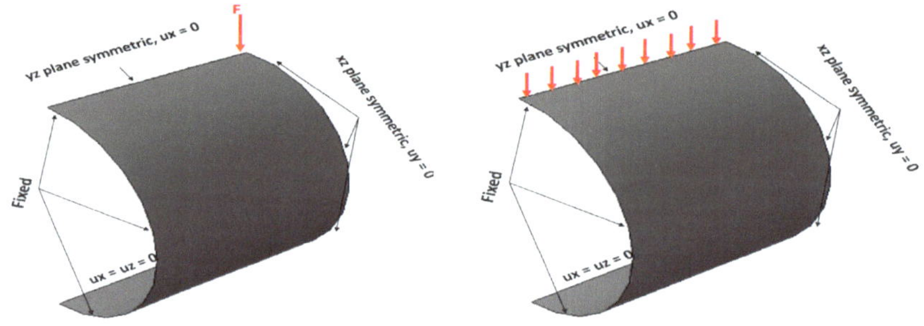

Figure 6. The boundary conditions for half of a cylindrical shell pipe.

After obtaining the efficient convergence of the numerical results in Abaqus/CAE, we locally refined the mesh where we applied the load, as shown in Figure 7. We used linear quadrilateral elements of type S4 to model the 3D cylindrical shell pipe case. This element is characterized by good computational time savings, is easier to mesh, and is less prone to negative Jacobian errors than 3D solid elements.

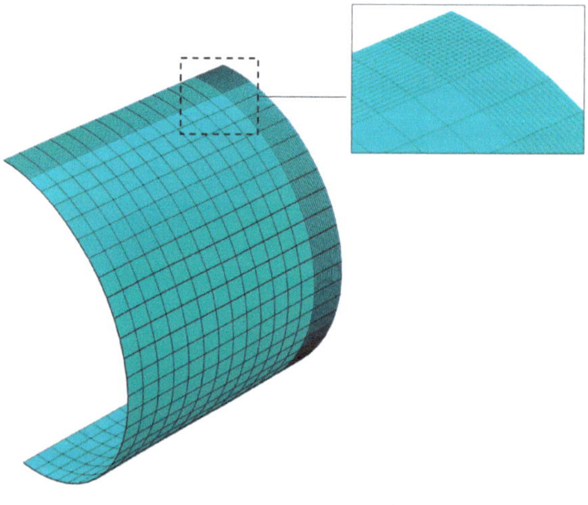

Figure 7. Mesh FEM (Abaqus/CAE); total number of nodes: 1197; total number of elements: 1176.

In the IGA approach, we used an exact mesh generated using NURBS functions (Figure 9a), and we took advantage of Bézier extraction for the T-Spline surfaces (Figure 8). Contrary to NURBS functions, T-Splines enable local adjustments by introducing additional control points only in areas where higher resolution is required (Figure 9d). This feature enhances the efficiency of capturing details during analysis.

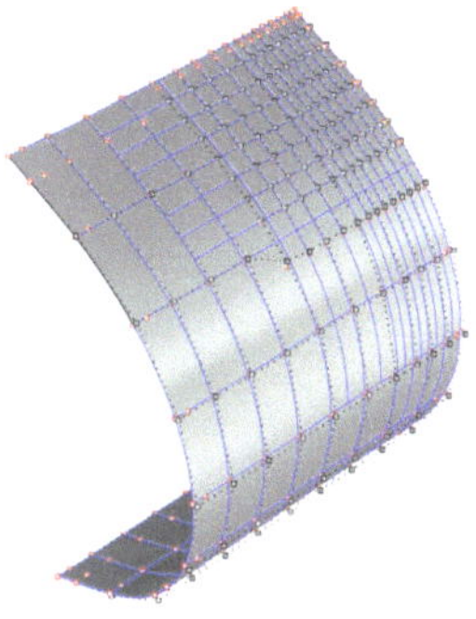

Figure 8. T-Spline surface with 112 control points and 88 T mesh elements.

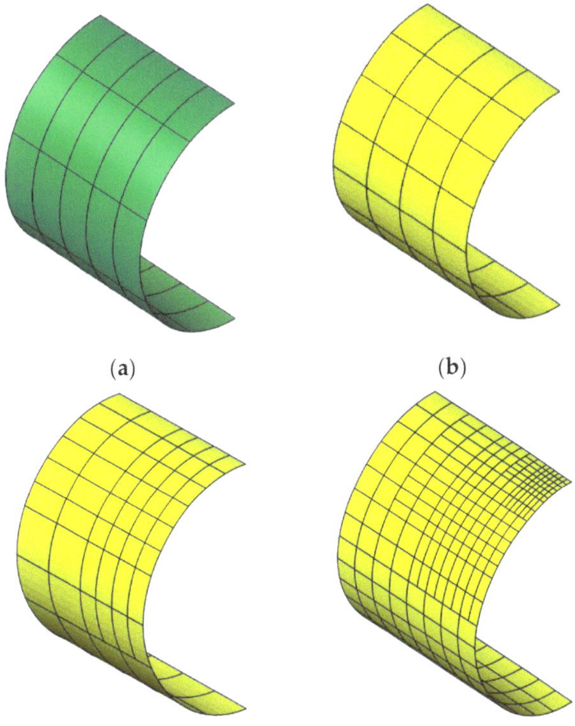

(a) (b) (c) (d)

Figure 9. The demi-cylinder with 15 Non-Uniform Rational B-Spline (NURBS) mesh elements and 32, 50, and 215 T mesh elements.

4. Numerical Results and Discussion

In this section, three numerical evaluations are introduced to highlight the primary advantages of employing the T-Spline approach for isogeometric analysis relating to 3D cylindrical shell pipe mechanical computation issues. Firstly, a 3D cylindrical shell pipe subjected to concentered elastic load and compressive load benchmarks was analyzed to verify the capability of the adaptive T-Spline approach for isogeometric analysis and to study the robustness of the 3D mechanical cylindrical shell pipe. The obtained results were compared and validated with results found in the literature, particularly those concerning the use of NURBS IGA and FEM Abaqus/CAE methods. In the final analysis, we will evaluate a 3D cylindrical shell involving the preformed hole issue. The goal is to provide further analysis evaluating the performance and robustness of T-Splines for the computational modeling of trimmed surfaces.

4.1. Cylindrical Shell 3D Pipe under Concentrated Load

We will study a cylindrical shell pipe without internal pressure subjected to compressive load in order to model impact machine excavation.

We performed a comparative study of the computation time between the different methods used in this investigation. The results show that the computation time (Table 2) of IGA based on the T-Spline method is shorter than that of IGA based on NURBS and FEM Abaqus/CAE. This confirms the results of Du et al. [20] and Guo et al. [35]. The better computation time of the T-Spline method is due to the use of fewer control points (Figure 10) compared to the NURBS method. Furthermore, T-Splines combine the advantages of NURBSs and polygonal modeling techniques, leading to better convergence of the results.

Table 2. Time calculation comparison for FEM, IGA NURBS, and IGA T-Splines carried out using Intel® Core ™ i5-8250U CPU 1.60 GHz (4 CPUs).

Method	FEM (Abaqus/CAE)	IGA NURBS	IGA T-Splines
Time Calculation (s)	3.30	0.99	0.42

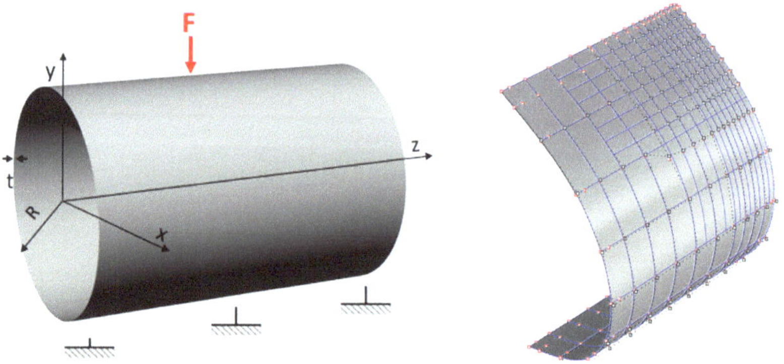

Figure 10. Boundary conditions and T-Spline surface with 326 control points and 215 T mesh elements.

Figure 11 illustrates a comparison of the displacement magnitude of a 3D cylindrical shell pipe subjected to a force of 1.6 kN computed using the FEM (Abaqus/CAE) ($u_{max} = 1.45 \times 10^{-3}$ mm), IGA NURBS ($u_{max} = 1.49 \times 10^{-3}$ mm), and IGA T-Spline ($u_{max} = 1.58 \times 10^{-3}$ mm) methods. The results show that the IGA T-Spline method yields better results than the IGA NURBS method, which is also a robust method. These results lead to the same conclusion reached by Du et al. [21]. The disparity between the T-Spline and NURBS methods is that the IGA approach based on T-Splines provides a high level of flexibility in 3D surface shaping, and T-Splines allow for the local refinement of the mesh (Figure 12). T-Splines are often used in conjunction with subdivision surfaces. This combination allows for the creation of highly detailed models with smooth surfaces.

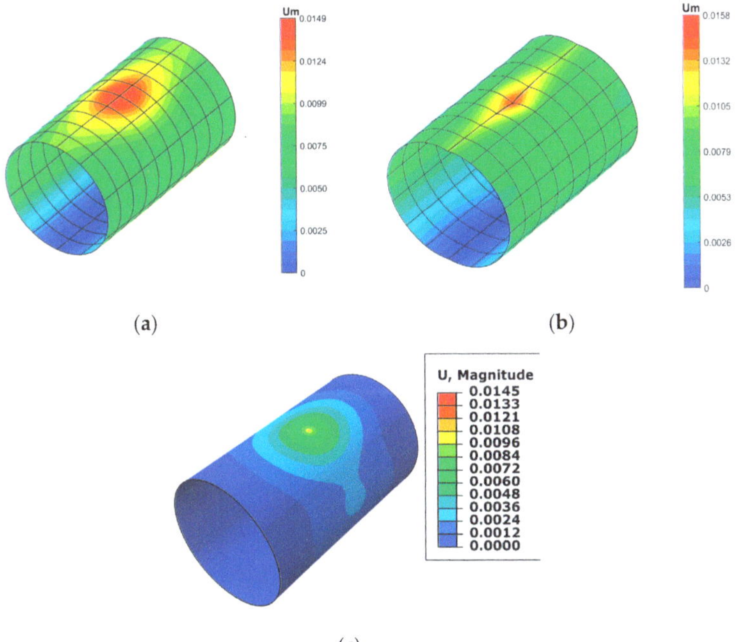

Figure 11. Displacement magnitude of 3D cylinder pipe: (**a**) result of NURBS; (**b**) result of T-Splines; (**c**) result of Abaqus/CAE finite element analysis (FEA).

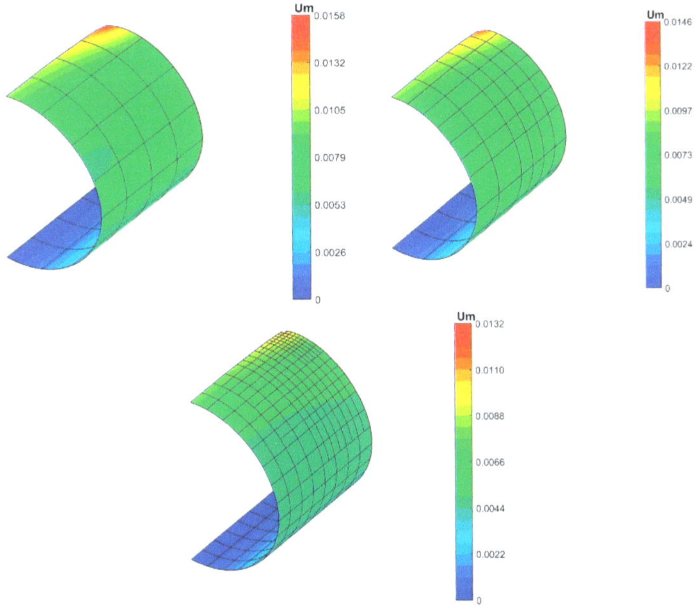

Figure 12. The displacement magnitude results for a 3D cylindrical pipe for various mesh refinements of 32, 50, and 215 T-Spline elements using the Bézier extraction method.

To complete the previously highlighted results and apply them to the study of the mechanical behavior and strength of a 3D pipe, we analyzed the load variation applied to the 3D cylindrical shell pipe as a function of displacement using the different FEM Abaqus/CAE, IGA NURBS, and T-Spline methods, as illustrated in Figure 13. Load magnitudes varying from 0 N to 1600 N were used to maintain linear elasticity and predict the impact of the excavator during work not subjected to internal pressure. The results show linearity between the load and displacement curves. Furthermore, it is important to point out that, after 1200 N, there is some variation in the results between the three methods. The divergence of the numerical results is explained by the influence of the proximity of the plastic zone.

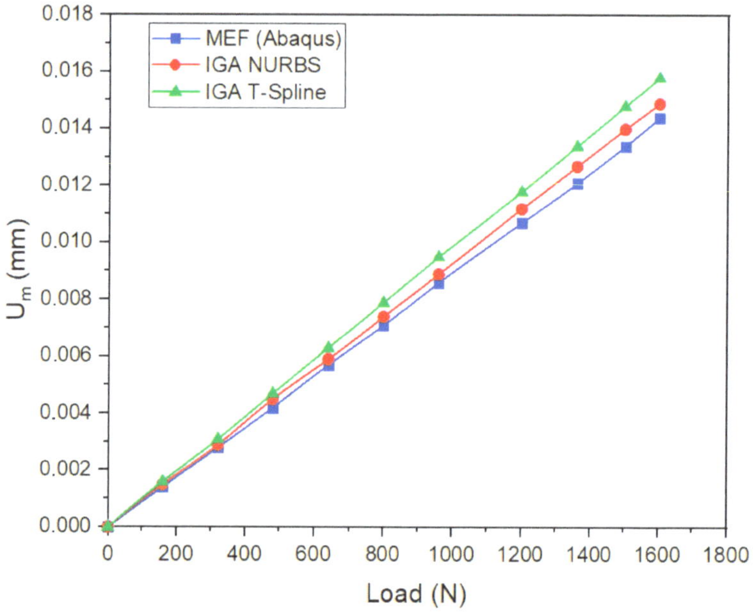

Figure 13. Load–displacement curves of the 3D cylindrical shell pipe.

Figure 14 illustrates the von Mises stress distribution around an applied radial load of 1.6 kN. Evaluations were performed for two numerical references methods, FEM Abaqus/CAE, IGA NURB and IGA T-Splines. The results confirm that the IGA approach based on the T-Spline method is successful compared to the numerical references methods. We conclude that, thanks to the T-Spline method, we obtain higher values of $\sigma_{vm} = 348$ MPa around the impact region than those found using FEM Abaqus/CAE ($\sigma_{vm} = 341$ MPa) and IGA NURBS ($\sigma_{vm} = 342$ MPa). The value found using the T-Splines method is in close proximity to the yield strength of the material. This allows us to provide pertinent information on fracture prediction and the robust convergence of the results that were undetected when using the FEM Abaqus/CAE and IGA NURBS methods. The robustness of the T-Spline method relates to its capability to introduce local control points, allowing for more detailed information to be obtained in certain regions without compromising the overall simplicity of the model. The local refinement feature of T-Splines is particularly useful for efficiently capturing geometric details in specific areas of a model.

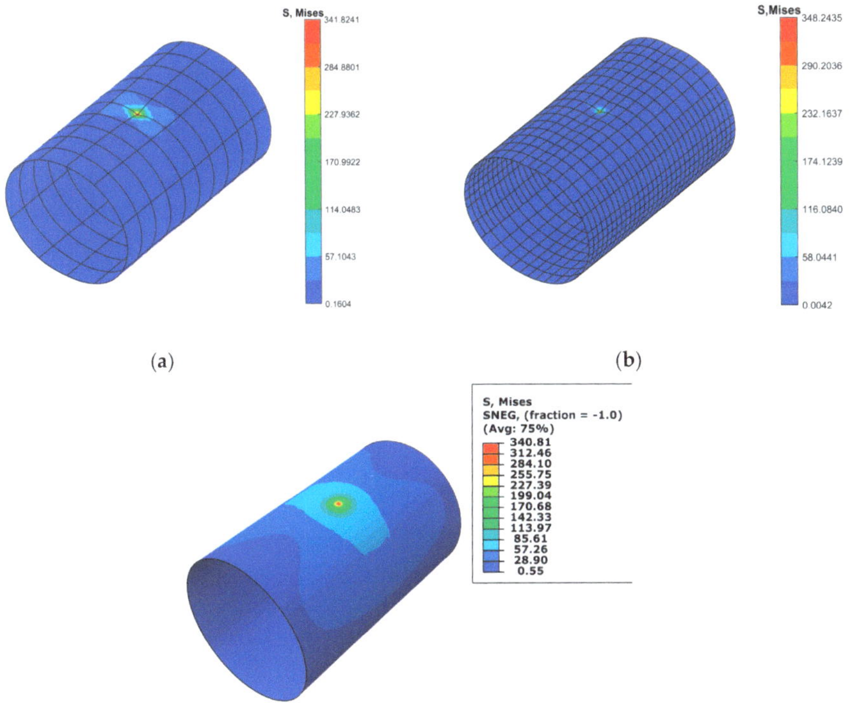

(**a**) (**b**)

(**c**)

Figure 14. von Mises stress of 3D cylindrical pipe: (**a**) result of NURBS; (**b**) result of T-Splines; (**c**) result of Abaqus/CAE FEA.

On the other hand, we evaluated the structural integrity of the 3D cylindrical shell pipe by applying various load values (from 0 N to 1600 N). We extracted different maximum values (denoted as 348 MPa) of the von Mises stress around the force impact region for various methods, especially using FEM Abaqus/CAE, IGA NURBSs, and IGA T-Splines (Figure 15). The results indicate that the stress curves converge closely with minor disparity. The value of 348 MPa obtained through the use of IGA T-Splines is higher than that of FEM Abaqus/CAE and IGA NURBSs.

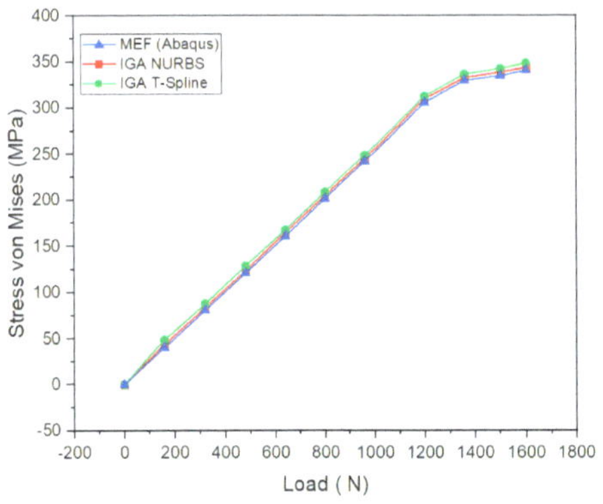

Figure 15. Load–von Mises stress curves of the 3D cylindrical shell pipe.

In addition, it was observed that the curve diverges from linearity when it exceeds the value of 340 MPa above 1200 N, suggesting a transition to the plastic region. This nonlinearity in the curve indicates a change in material behavior and signifies that the structural response is moving beyond the linear elastic domain.

4.2. Cylindrical 3D Shell Pipe under Compressive Loading

We studied a cylindrical shell pipe subjected to compressive load, modeling the pipe–soil interaction. The predicted load of this interaction between the pipe and the soil is 1.9 kN (Figure 16).

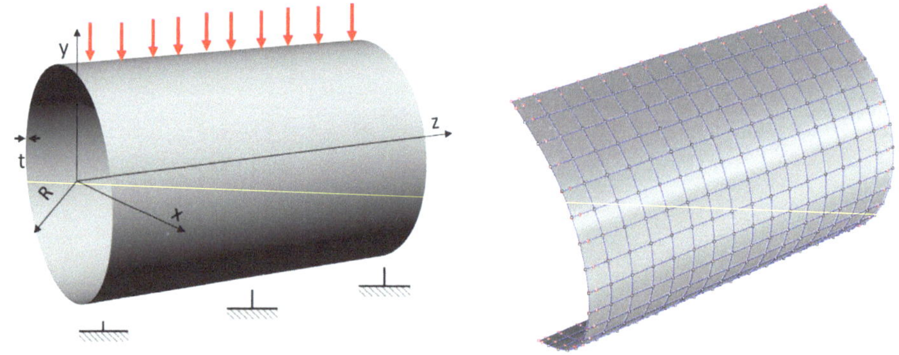

Figure 16. Boundary conditions and T-Spline surface with 361 control points and 256 T mesh elements.

T-Splines enable the addition of some local refinement control points in the area where good convergence is required (Figure 17), which is not available in IGA based on NURBS functions.

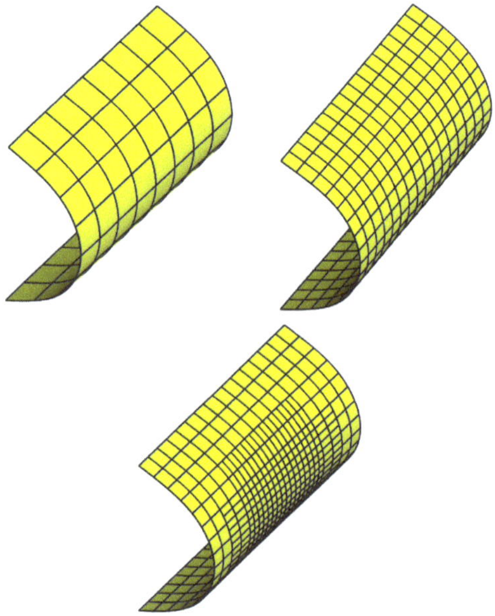

Figure 17. Mesh extraction Bézier of semi-cylinder with 64, 256, and 376 T mesh elements.

We compared the results found using T-Splines for different proposals for the local refinement of control points in a 3D cylinder (Figure 18). The obtained results show a dependence on the number of refinement control points. With 122 control points, the maximum displacement on the cylinder is 0.0728 mm, and when we refine up to 361 control points, the maximum displacement on the cylinder is reduced to 0.0693 mm.

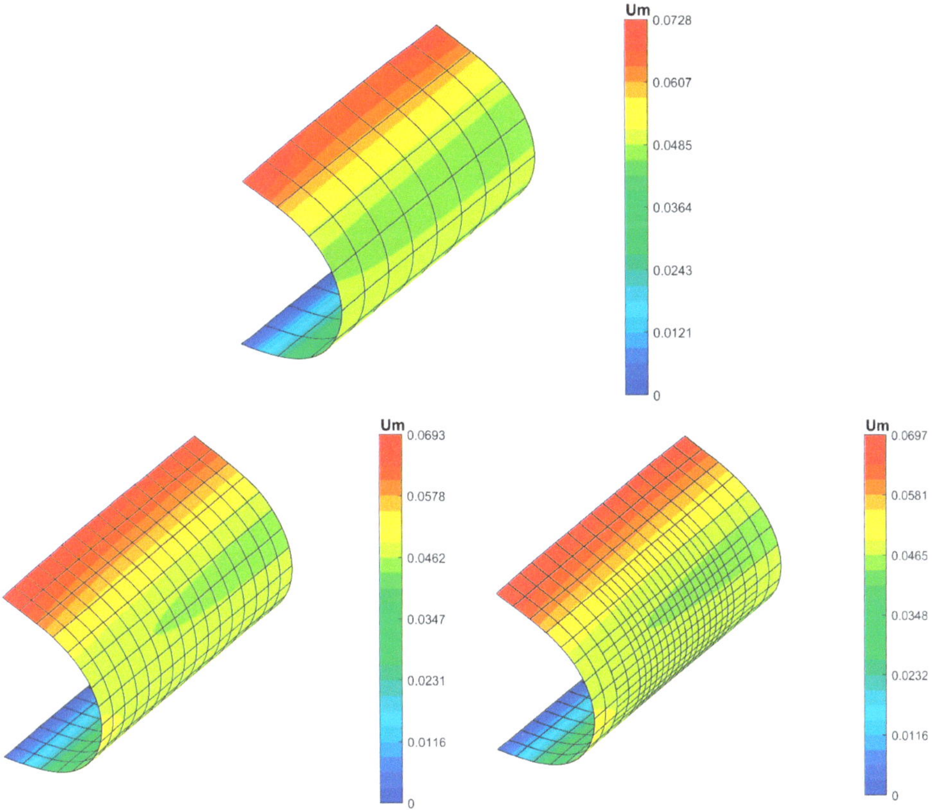

Figure 18. The displacement magnitude results of a 3D cylindrical pipe for various mesh refinements using the T-Spline method.

Further, we performed a comparative study using a T-Spline for comparison and validation with results found in the literature, especially those relating to the use of the NURBS IGA and FEM Abaqus/CAE methods (Figure 19). The amount of displacement calculated using the T-Spline method is 0.0728 mm, which is slightly higher than that found when using IGA NURBSs and FEM Abaqus at 0.0531 mm and 0.0626 mm, respectively. Note that in T-Splines with 361 control points, the maximum displacement per cylinder is reduced to 0.0693 mm. We conclude from all these results that we are confident in using the T-Spline method as an alternative method to investigate the mechanical performance of cylindrical shell structures.

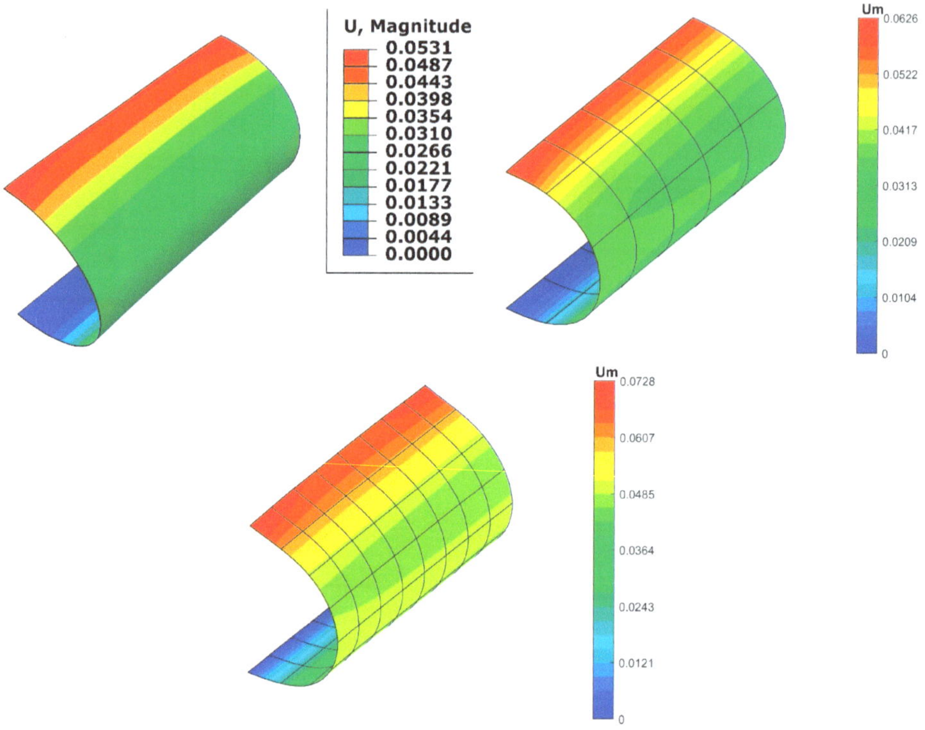

Figure 19. The displacement magnitude results of a 3D cylinder pipe for FEM Abaqus/CAE, IGA NURBSs, and T-Splines.

4.3. Three-Dimensional Cylindrical Shell Pipe with Preformed Holes and Pipe Junction under Compressive Loading

In this section, we evaluated a 3D cylindrical shell pipe with a preformed hole under a compressive load (Figure 20) in relation to structural engineering problems. The objective is to evaluate the efficiency and robustness of the T-Spline method in the field of trimmed surfaces. In this study, we compared the results found when using the T-Spline method with the Abaqus/CAE finite element method because IGA based on NUBRSs is too limited for the evaluation of the trimmed surfaces; it requires a specific adjustment of the interpolation domain, especially the B-Spline or NUBRS interpolation functions, when considering a trimmed geometry. A 3D cylindrical shell pipe (r = 300 mm; L = 600 mm; thickness = 3 mm) with nine holes with a 2.5 mm diameter was evaluated with the objective of assessing the mechanical robustness and structural integrity of pipes with preformed holes in cases of severe mechanical and chemical damage. This recent investigation completes the research conducted in [36–38].

In Figure 21, we compare the numerical results of the displacement between the T-Spline and FEM Abaqus methods, and in noting that the NURBS IGA method is very limited in terms of studying trimmed surfaces, it was not considered for comparison in this study. The maximum displacement value was found to be 7.7×10^{-2} mm higher than the FEM Abaqus displacement value 5.53×10^{-2} mm, and we concluded that, in the case of preformed holes, the displacement value increased by 7.7×10^{-3} mm; this suggests the performance degradation of a cylindrical shell pipe with preformed holes, leading to integrity issues.

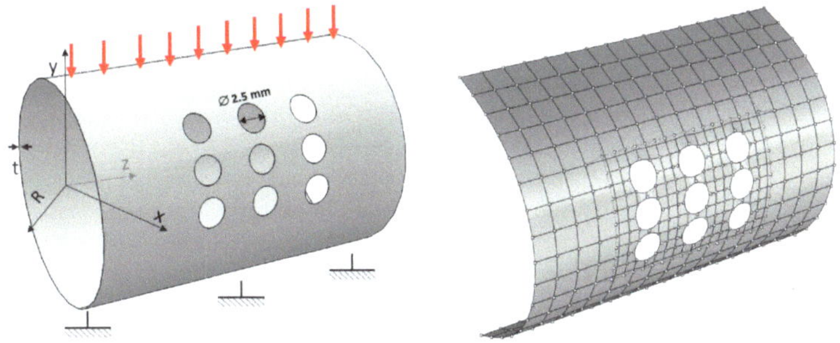

Figure 20. Boundary condition and T-Spline surface with 485 control points and 340 T mesh elements.

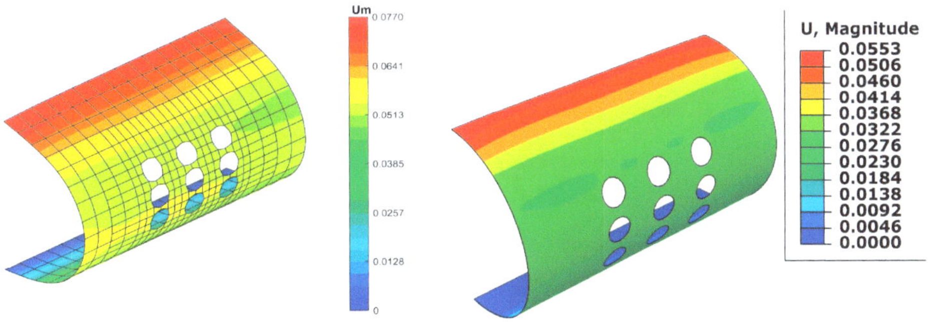

Figure 21. The displacement magnitude results of a 3D cylindrical pipe with holes calculated using the T-Spline method.

In addition, the T-Spline method once again shows its power and capability in terms of computing trimmed and untrimmed surfaces.

5. Conclusions

An investigation of the mechanical performance of a 3D cylindrical shell pipe with and without preformed holes under concentrated and compressive loading in terms of the linear elastic behavior in the cases of trimmed and untrimmed surfaces using the IGA method based on the T-Spline technique was successfully conducted. The numerical results obtained, especially relating to displacement and von Mises stress, were compared and validated with results found in the literature, particularly concerning the NURBS IGA and FEM Abaqus methods. The results show that the computation time of IGA based on T-Splines is shorter than the IGA NURBS and FEM Abaqus/CAE methods. Moreover, the results confirm that the IGA approach based on the T-Spline method shows successful achievements compared to numerical references found in the literature review.

The numerical results of von Mises stress found, through the use of the T-Spline method, are in close proximity to the yield strength of the material. This allows us to provide pertinent information on fracture prediction and the robust convergence of the results that were undetected when using the FEM Abaqus/CAE and the IGA NURBS methods. The robustness of the T-Spline method is based on its ability to introduce local control points in the area where robust convergence is required, which is too limited in IGA based on NURBS functions. In addition, through the use of T-Splines, we will end up with a linear system with a slightly lower degree of freedom with a stiffness matrix that is less full compared to the one obtained when using the NURBS method. This makes it easy to invert this matrix with a fairly small inversion error.

On the other hand, a 3D cylindrical shell pipe with a preformed hole under compressive load was studied as a structural engineering problem with the objective of evaluating the efficiency and robustness of the T-Spline method in the field of trimmed surfaces. We noticed that the NURBS IGA method is very limited when evaluating trimmed surfaces. The maximum displacement value was found to be higher than the FEM Abaqus displacement value; thus, we conclude that, in the case of preformed holes, the displacement value increased, which suggests the performance degradation of a cylindrical shell pipe with preformed holes, leading to integrity issues.

Future research work will involve the integration of a complementary investigation on the impact of machine excavation on pipes under internal pressure. This study will consider scenarios both with and without the presence of cracks using the IGA approach based on T-Splines. The aim is to evaluate the mechanical behavior and performance of cylindrical shell pipelines, addressing problems in both linear elastic and dynamic studies.

Author Contributions: Conceptualization, S.E.F., O.K. and A.E.; methodology, S.E.F., O.K. and A.E.; software, S.E.F., O.K. and A.E.; validation, S.E.F., O.K., A.E., S.V. and M.M.; formal analysis S.E.F., O.K., A.E., S.V. and M.M.; investigation, S.E.F., O.K. and A.E.; resources, A.E.; data curation, S.E.F., O.K. and A.E.; writing—original draft preparation, S.E.F., O.K., A.E., S.V. and M.M.; writing—review and editing, A.E. and S.V.; visualization, S.E.F., O.K., A.E., S.V. and M.M.; supervision, S.E.F., O.K., A.E., S.V. and M.M.; project administration, A.E.; funding acquisition, A.E., S.V. and M.M. All authors have read and agreed to the published version of the manuscript.

Funding: This research received no external funding.

Data Availability Statement: Data are contained within this article.

Conflicts of Interest: The authors declare no conflicts of interest.

References

1. Bazilevs, Y.; Calo, V.; Cottrell, J.; Evans, J.; Hughes, T.; Lipton, S.; Scott, M.; Sederberg, T. Isogeometric analysis using T-splines. *Comput. Methods Appl. Mech. Eng.* **2010**, *199*, 229–263. [CrossRef]
2. Cottrell, J.A.; Hughes, T.J.R.; Bazilevs, Y. *Isogeometric Analysis: Toward Integration of CAD and FEA*, 1st ed.; Wiley: Hoboken, NJ, USA, 2009.
3. Scutaru, M.L.; Guendaoui, S.; Koubaiti, O.; El Ouadefli, L.; El Akkad, A.; Elkhalfi, A.; Vlase, S. Flow of Newtonian Incompressible Fluids in Square Media: Isogeometric vs. Standard Finite Element Method. *Mathematics* **2023**, *11*, 3702. [CrossRef]
4. Oesterle, B.; Geiger, F.; Forster, D.; Fröhlich, M.; Bischoff, M. A study on the approximation power of NURBS and the significance of exact geometry in isogeometric pre-buckling analyses of shells. *Comput. Methods Appl. Mech. Eng.* **2022**, *397*, 115144. [CrossRef]
5. Koubaiti, O.; Elkhalfi, A.; El-Mekkaoui, J. WEB-Spline Finite Elements for the Approximation of Navier-Lamé System with *CA*, *B* Boundary Condition. *Abstr. Appl. Anal.* **2020**, *2020*, 1–14. [CrossRef]
6. Koubaiti, O.; El Fakkoussi, S.; El-Mekkaoui, J.; Moustachir, H.; Elkhalfi, A.; Pruncu, C.I. The treatment of constraints due to standard boundary conditions in the context of the mixed Web-spline finite element method. *Eng. Comput.* **2021**, *38*, 2937–2968. [CrossRef]
7. Farahat, A.; Verhelst, H.M.; Kiendl, J.; Kapl, M. Isogeometric analysis for multi-patch structured Kirchhoff–Love shells. *Comput. Methods Appl. Mech. Eng.* **2023**, *411*, 116060. [CrossRef]
8. Hattori, G.; Trevelyan, J.; Gourgiotis, P. An isogeometric boundary element formulation for stress concentration problems in couple stress elasticity. *Comput. Methods Appl. Mech. Eng.* **2023**, *407*, 115932. [CrossRef]
9. Sederberg, T.W.; Cardon, D.L.; Finnigan, G.T.; North, N.S.; Zheng, J.; Lyche, T. T-spline Simplification and Local Refinement. *ACM Trans. Graph.* **2004**, *23*, 239–247. [CrossRef]
10. Evans, E.; Scott, M.; Li, X.; Thomas, D. Hierarchical T-splines: Analysis-suitability, Bézier extraction, and application as an adaptive basis for isogeometric analysis. *Comput. Methods Appl. Mech. Eng.* **2015**, *284*, 1–20. [CrossRef]
11. Wei, X.; Zhang, Y.; Liu, L.; Hughes, T.J. Truncated T-splines: Fundamentals and methods. *Comput. Methods Appl. Mech. Eng.* **2017**, *316*, 349–372. [CrossRef]
12. Maier, R.; Morgenstern, P.; Takacs, T. Adaptive refinement for unstructured T-splines with linear complexity. *Comput. Aided Geom. Des.* **2022**, *96*, 102117. [CrossRef]
13. Toshniwal, D. Quadratic splines on quad-tri meshes: Construction and an application to simulations on watertight reconstructions of trimmed surfaces. *Comput. Methods Appl. Mech. Eng.* **2022**, *388*, 114174. [CrossRef]
14. Liu, Z.; Cheng, J.; Yang, M.; Yuan, P.; Qiu, C.; Gao, W.; Tan, J. Isogeometric analysis of large thin shell structures based on weak coupling of substructures with unstructured T-splines patches. *Adv. Eng. Softw.* **2019**, *135*, 102692. [CrossRef]

15. Dörfel, M.R.; Jüttler, B.; Simeon, B. Adaptive isogeometric analysis by local h-refinement with T-splines. *Comput. Methods Appl. Mech. Eng.* **2010**, *199*, 264–275. [CrossRef]
16. Fathi, F.; de Borst, R. Geometrically nonlinear extended isogeometric analysis for cohesive fracture with applications to delamination in composites. *Finite Elem. Anal. Des.* **2021**, *191*, 103527. [CrossRef]
17. Zhuang, C.; Xiong, Z.; Ding, H. Bézier extraction based isogeometric topology optimization with a locally-adaptive smoothed density model. *J. Comput. Phys.* **2022**, *467*, 111469. [CrossRef]
18. Coradello, L.; D'angella, D.; Carraturo, M.; Kiendl, J.; Kollmannsberger, S.; Rank, E.; Reali, A. Hierarchically refined isogeometric analysis of trimmed shells. *Comput. Mech.* **2020**, *66*, 431–447. [CrossRef]
19. Reichle, M.; Arf, J.; Simeon, B.; Klinkel, S. Smooth multi-patch scaled boundary isogeometric analysis for Kirchhoff–Love shells. *Meccanica* **2023**, *58*, 1693–1716. [CrossRef]
20. Du, X.; Zhao, G.; Wang, W.; Guo, M.; Zhang, R.; Yang, J. NLIGA: A MATLAB framework for nonlinear isogeometric analysis. *Comput. Aided Geom. Des.* **2020**, *80*, 101869. [CrossRef]
21. Du, X.; Zhao, G.; Zhang, R.; Wang, W.; Yang, J. Numerical implementation for isogeometric analysis of thin-walled structures based on a Bézier extraction framework: NligaStruct. *Thin-Walled Struct.* **2022**, *180*, 109844. [CrossRef]
22. Shan, X.; Yu, W.; Gong, J.; Wen, K.; Wang, H.; Ren, S.; Wei, S.; Wang, B.; Gao, G.; Zhang, G. A methodology to determine the target reliability of natural gas pipeline systems based on risk acceptance criteria of pipelines. *J. Pipeline Sci. Eng.* **2023**, *4*, 100150. [CrossRef]
23. El Fakkoussi, S.; Vlase, S.; Marin, M.; Koubaiti, O.; Elkhalfi, A.; Moustabchir, H. Predicting Stress Intensity Factor for Aluminum 6062 T6 Material in L-Shaped Lower Control Arm (LCA) Design Using Extended Finite Element Analysis. *Materials* **2023**, *17*, 206. [CrossRef] [PubMed]
24. Li, Y.; Chen, C.; Yao, L.; Fan, M.; Zhang, Y. Reliability analysis of gas pipelines under global bending and thermal loadings considering a high chloride ion environment. *Eng. Fail. Anal.* **2024**, *156*, 107802. [CrossRef]
25. Choudhury, D.; Chaudhuri, C.H. A critical review on performance of buried pipeline subjected to pipe bursting and earthquake induced permanent ground deformation. *Soil Dyn. Earthq. Eng.* **2023**, *173*, 108152. [CrossRef]
26. Zhang, J.; Gu, X.; Zhou, Y.; Wang, Y.; Zhang, H.; Zhang, Y. Mechanical Properties of Buried Gas Pipeline under Traffic Loads. *Processes* **2023**, *11*, 3087. [CrossRef]
27. El Fakkoussi, S.; Moustabchir, H.; Elkhalfi, A.; Pruncu, C.I. Computation of the stress intensity factor KI for external longitudinal semi-elliptic cracks in the pipelines by FEM and XFEM methods. *Int. J. Interact. Des. Manuf. IJIDeM* **2019**, *13*, 545–555. [CrossRef]
28. El Fakkoussi, S.; Moustabchir, H.; Elkhalfi, A.; Pruncu, C.I. Application of the Extended Isogeometric Analysis (X-IGA) to Evaluate a Pipeline Structure Containing an External Crack. *J. Eng.* **2018**, *2018*, 4125765. [CrossRef]
29. Hussain, M.; Zhang, T.; Chaudhry, M.; Jamil, I.; Kausar, S.; Hussain, I. Review of Prediction of Stress Corrosion Cracking in Gas Pipelines Using Machine Learning. *Machines* **2024**, *12*, 42. [CrossRef]
30. Koubaiti, O.; Elkhalfi, A.; El-Mekkaoui, J.; Mastorakis, N. Solving the Problem of Constraints Due to Dirichlet Boundary Conditions in the Context of the Mini Element Method. *Int. J. Mech.* **2020**, *14*, 12–22. [CrossRef]
31. Scott, M.A.; Borden, M.J.; Verhoosel, C.V.; Sederberg, T.W.; Hughes, T.J.R. Isogeometric finite element data structures based on Bézier extraction of T-splines. *Int. J. Numer. Methods Eng.* **2011**, *88*, 126–156. [CrossRef]
32. Xue, M.; Li, D.; Hwang, K. Theoretical stress analysis of intersecting cylindrical shells subjected to external loads transmitted through branch pipes. *Int. J. Solids Struct.* **2005**, *42*, 3299–3319. [CrossRef]
33. Tafsirojjaman, T.; Manalo, A.; Tien, C.M.T.; Wham, B.P.; Salah, A.; Kiriella, S.; Karunasena, W.; Dixon, P. Analysis of failure modes in pipe-in-pipe repair systems for water and gas pipelines. *Eng. Fail. Anal.* **2022**, *140*, 106510. [CrossRef]
34. Moustabchir, H.; Pruncu, C.I.; Azari, Z.; Hariri, S.; Dmytrakh, I. Fracture mechanics defect assessment diagram on pipe from steel P264GH with a notch. *Int. J. Mech. Mater. Des.* **2016**, *12*, 273–284. [CrossRef]
35. Guo, M.; Wang, W.; Zhao, G.; Du, X.; Zhang, R.; Yang, J. T-Splines for Isogeometric Analysis of the Large Deformation of Elastoplastic Kirchhoff–Love Shells. *Appl. Sci.* **2023**, *13*, 1709. [CrossRef]
36. Li, W.; Wang, P.; Feng, G.-P.; Lu, Y.-G.; Yue, J.-Z.; Li, H.-M. The deformation and failure mechanism of cylindrical shell and square plate with pre-formed holes under blast loading. *Def. Technol.* **2021**, *17*, 1143–1159. [CrossRef]
37. Marin, M.; Öchsner, A.; Bhatti, M.M. Some results in Moore-Gibson-Thompson thermoelasticity of dipolar bodies. *Zamm* **2020**, *100*, e202000090. [CrossRef]
38. Marin, M.; Hobiny, A.; Abbas, I. The Effects of Fractional Time Derivatives in Porothermoelastic Materials Using Finite Element Method. *Mathematics* **2021**, *9*, 1606. [CrossRef]

axioms

MDPI

Article

On Some Distance Spectral Characteristics of Trees

Sakander Hayat [1,†], Asad Khan [2,*,†] and Mohammed J. F. Alenazi [3]

[1] Mathematical Sciences, Faculty of Science, Univeriti Brunei Darussalam, Jln Tungku Link, Gadong, Bandar Seri Begawan BE1410, Brunei; sakander1566@gmail.com
[2] Metaverse Research Institute, School of Computer Science and Cyber Engineering, Guangzhou University, Guangzhou 510006, China
[3] Department of Computer Engineering, College of Computer and Information Sciences (CCIS), King Saud University, Riyadh 11451, Saudi Arabia; mjalenazi@ksu.edu.sa
* Correspondence: asad@gzhu.edu.cn
† These authors contributed equally to this work.

Abstract: Graham and Pollack in 1971 presented applications of eigenvalues of the distance matrix in addressing problems in data communication systems. Spectral graph theory employs tools from linear algebra to retrieve the properties of a graph from the spectrum of graph-theoretic matrices. The study of graphs with "few eigenvalues" is a contemporary problem in spectral graph theory. This paper studies graphs with few distinct distance eigenvalues. After mentioning the classification of graphs with one and two distinct distance eigenvalues, we mainly focus on graphs with three distinct distance eigenvalues. Characterizing graphs with three distinct distance eigenvalues is "highly" non-trivial. In this paper, we classify all trees whose distance matrix has precisely three distinct eigenvalues. Our proof is different from earlier existing proof of the result as our proof is extendable to other similar families such as unicyclic and bicyclic graphs. The main tools which we employ include interlacing and equitable partitions. We also list all the connected graphs on $\nu \leq 6$ vertices and compute their distance spectra. Importantly, all these graphs on $\nu \leq 6$ vertices are determined from their distance spectra. We deliver a distance cospectral pair of order 7, thus making it a distance cospectral pair of the smallest order. This paper is concluded with some future directions.

Keywords: graph; distance matrix; distance eigenvalues; interlacing; few eigenvalues

MSC: 05C12; 05C50

check for updates

Citation: Hayat, S.; Khan, A.; Alenazi, M.J.F. On Some Distance Spectral Characteristics of Trees. *Axioms* **2024**, *13*, 494. https://doi.org/10.3390/axioms13080494

Academic Editors: Cristina Flaut, Dana Piciu and Murat Tosun

Received: 2 May 2024
Revised: 13 July 2024
Accepted: 17 July 2024
Published: 23 July 2024

1. Introduction

All graphs in this article are undirected, finite, connected, and simple.

Spectral graph theory [1] employs tools from linear algebra to retrieve the properties of a graph from the spectrum of graph-theoretic matrices such as the adjacency, the distance, and the Laplacians, among others. In 1970, Doob [2] suggested the study of graphs with a few eigenvalues and proposed, at most, five. A connected regular graph with, at most, three distinct eigenvalues is known to be strongly regular; see, for example [3] for a survey on strongly regular graphs. Connected non-regular graphs with three distinct eigenvalues have been studied by, for example, De Caen, Van Dam and Spence [4], Bridges and Mena [5], Muzychuk and Klin [6], and Van Dam [7].Connected regular graphs with four distinct eigenvalues were studied by Van Dam [8], Van Dam and Spence [9] and Huang and Huang [10], among others. Cioabă et al. [11] (resp. Cioabă et al. [12]) studied connected graphs with, at most, two eigenvalues not equal to 1 and -1 (resp. 0 and -2). Haemers and Omidi [13] studied generalized adjacency matrices and characterized the graphs admitting two generalized adjacency eigenvalues. In this paper, we study graphs with three distinct generalized adjacency eigenvalues. For applications of graphical and, in general, mathematical models in machine learning and energy research, we refer to [14–17].

In case of connected graphs, the distance matrix [18] generalizes the adjacency matrix naturally as it delivers more information about pairs of vertices. Graham and Pollack [19], in 1971, put forward a relationship between the problem of addressing in systems of data communications and the number of negative eigenvalues of the distance matrix. In 1978, Graham and Lovász [20] precisely determined the characteristic polynomial of the distance matrix of a graph by providing explicit formulas for its coefficients. Merris [21] used the interlacing theorem to study properties of the distance eigenvalues of trees and their line graphs. The survey by Aouchiche and Hansen [22] covers the known results on the distance matrix and its spectrum till 2014.

The cospectrality of graphs with respect to the distance matrix has received researchers' attention recently. Lin et al. [23] showed that complete bipartite graphs are determined by their distance spectra and conjectured the same for complete multipartite graphs. Jin and Zhang [24] provided a proof for this conjecture. Heysse [25] proposed a method of constructing distance cospectral graphs. Aouchiche and Hansen [26] generated the distance, Laplacian distance, and signless Laplacian distance spectra of all the graphs up to 10 vertices and identified the ones which are distance cospectral. Zhang [27] investigated graphs with, at most, three distance eigenvalues, of which two are different from -1 and -2. Moreover, he identified all distance cospectral graphs among this class and showed the remaining can uniquely be determined from their distance spectra. Pokorný et al. [28] showed that non-trivial non-isomorphic trees are never distance integral. They also identify distance integral graphs among the class of complete split graphs.

Research on the study of graphs with few different eigenvalues corresponding to the distance matrix has been initiated recently. Lin et al. [23] classified graphs having three different distance eigenvalues and non-integral distance spectral radius. Aalipour et al. [29] constructed examples of non-regular graphs having a small number of different eigenvalues, showing that not all graphs with few distinct eigenvalues for the distance matrix are regular. Zhang et al. [30] proved some extremal results on the distance spectrum of graphs. They also delivered the first proof for the classification of trees with three distinct distance eigenvalues. In addition, Aalipour et al. [29] precisely determined the spectrum of the distance matrix of all the distance-regular graphs whose positive inertia is exactly one. For each $2 \leq k \leq 11$, Atik and Panigrahi [31] constructed infinite families of graphs with diameter of at least k and precisely k distinct distance eigenvalues. Lu et al. [32] classified graphs with exactly two distance eigenvalues different from -1 and -3.

In continuation of the study of graphs whose distance matrix has few distinct eigenvalues, in this note, we characterize trees having precisely three different distance eigenvalues. This paper studies the contemporary problem of "few eigenvalues" for the distance matrix of trees. The classification of general graphs with three distinct distance eigenvalues is highly non-trivial. In light of this, we solve this problem for the case of trees. Our proof is extendable to other families of graphs such as unicyclic and bicyclic graphs. The main result of this study is as follows:

Theorem 1. *Let T be a tree on $v \geq 2$ vertices. Then, T has three distinct distance eigenvalues if and only if T is a star graph.*

The organization of the note goes like this: In Section 2, we define all the necessary terminologies and present preliminary results needed in the subsequent section. Section 3 then provides a proof to Theorem 1.

2. Preliminaries

For standard notations and terminologies, the reader is referred to the standard graph theory textbook by West [33].

Let $\Gamma = (V_\Gamma, E_\Gamma)$ be a ν-vertex graph with V_Γ as its vertex set and $E_\Gamma \subseteq \binom{V_\Gamma}{2}$ as its edge set. The adjacency matrix $A = A_\Gamma$ of a graph Γ is defined as

$$(A)_{xy} = \begin{cases} 1, & xy \in E; \\ 0, & \text{Otherwise.} \end{cases}$$

Similarly, the distance matrix $\mathcal{D} = \mathcal{D}(\Gamma)$ of an ν-vertex graph Γ is defined as vertices of Γ and defined as

$$(\mathcal{D})_{xy} = \begin{cases} k, & d(x,y) = k; \\ 0, & x = y. \end{cases}$$

Let $\theta_0 \geq \ldots \geq \theta_t$ (resp. $\mu_0 \geq \ldots \geq \mu_t$) be the eigenvalues of A (resp. $\mathcal{D}$) called A-eigenvalues (resp. $\mathcal{D}$-eigenvalues) of Γ. Note that both of the adjacency and distance matrices are nonnegative irreducible real symmetric matrices.

Next, we present some tools from linear algebra which we use later on. The following is the so-called Perron–Frobenius Theorem.

Theorem 2. ([1], Theorem 2.2.1) *Let M be a nonnegative irreducible matrix of order $\nu \times \nu$. Let $\rho(M)$ be the largest eigenvalue of M such that $M\mathbf{x} = \rho\mathbf{x}$. Then,*

(i) Both geometric and algebraic multiplicity of $\rho(M)$ is one. Moreover, $\mathbf{x}$ is a strictly positive real vector.
(ii) For each eigenvalue θ of M, we have $\rho \geq |\theta|$. If M is primitive, then $\rho = |\theta|$ implies $\rho = \theta$.
(iii) Assume M_1 is a nonnegative $\nu \times \nu$ real matrix such that $M - M_1$ is nonnegative. Then, $\rho(M) \geq \rho(M_1)$ with $\rho(M) = \rho(M_1)$ if and only if $M = M_1$.

The following is the so-called Cauchy Interlacing Theorem of real symmetric matrices.

Theorem 3. ([34], Theorem 9.3.3) *Let M be an $m \times m$ principle submatrix of an $\nu \times \nu$ real symmetric matrix N. Assume that $\theta_i(N)$ $(1 \leq i \leq \nu)$ (resp. $\mu_i(M)$ $(1 \leq i \leq m)$ be a non-increasing sequence of the eigenvalues of N (resp. M). Then,*

$$\theta_{\nu-m+i}(N) \leq \mu_i(M) \leq \theta_i(N) \ \text{ for } i = 1, 2, \ldots, m.$$

Let $\chi_A(x)$ be the characteristic polynomial of a matrix A. The proof of the following result is a merely a modification of [34], Theorem 9.1.1.

Theorem 4. ([34], Theorem 9.1.1) *Assume π is an equitable partition for a Hermitian matrix M. Let Q be the quotient matrix of M corresponding to π. Then, we have $\chi_Q(x) \mid \chi_M(x)$.*

In 1971, Graham and Pollack [19] calculated the determinant of $\mathcal{D}(T)$ of a ν-vertex tree T as follows:

Theorem 5. ([19]) *If $\mathcal{D} = \mathcal{D}(T)$ is the distance matrix of a ν-vertex tree T, where $\nu \geq 2$. Then,*

$$\det(\mathcal{D}) = (-1)^{\nu-1}(\nu-1)2^{\nu-2}.$$

Let A be a real symmetric matrix. Then, the eigenvalues of A are all real. Assume $\nu_+(A)$ (resp. $\nu_-(A)$) is the number of positive (resp. negative) eigenvalues of A. If $\nu_0(A)$ is the dimension of the null space of A i.e., the number of zero eigenvalues of A, then, $(\nu_+(A), \nu_0(A), \nu_-(A))$ is said to be the inertia of the matrix A.

Theorem 5 immediately implies that the inertia of $\mathcal{D}(T)$ of a ν-vertex tree T is independent of the structural of T, i.e., only depends on ν.

Corollary 1. ([19]) *Let $\mathcal{D} = \mathcal{D}(T)$ be the distance matrix of a ν-vertex tree T, where $\nu \geq 2$. Then, the inertia of $\mathcal{D}$ is $(1, 0, \nu - 1)$.*

3. Main Results

For a graph Γ, let $\delta_\Gamma(\mathcal{D})$ be the number of distinct distance eigenvalues of Γ. Note that the distance matrix $\mathcal{D}$ is an irreducible nonnegative integer symmetric (and thus Hermitian) matrix. Thus, if $\mathcal{D}$ has one distinct eigenvalue μ, then, its minimal polynomial $m(x) = x - \mu$. This implies that $\mathcal{D} = \mu I$, and since the main diagonal of $\mathcal{D}$ is zero, we obtain that $\mu = 0$ and $\mathcal{D} = \mathbf{0}$. This shows that Γ is an isolated vertex, as Γ is connected. Thus, we have the following lemma.

Lemma 1. *Let Γ be a connected graph. Then, $\delta_\Gamma(\mathcal{D}) = 1$ if and only if $\Gamma = K_1$.*

Stevanović and Indulal [35] calculated the distance spectra of the combination of two regular graphs and, as its application, computed the distance spectra of the complete bipartite graphs. Here, we provide a different proof of this result using equitable partitions of the distance matrix.

Lemma 2. *Let $K_{s,t}$ be the complete bipartite graph. Then, the distance spectrum of $K_{s,t}$ is as follows:*

$$\{[s+t-2+\sqrt{s^2-st+t^2}]^1, [-2]^{s+t-2}, [s+t-2-\sqrt{s^2-st+t^2}]^1\}.$$

Proof. Consider the equitable partition $\pi = \{V_1, V_2\}$, where V_1 and V_2 are the partite sets of $K_{s,t}$. The quotient matrix Q of π is

$$Q = \begin{pmatrix} 2(s-1) & t \\ s & 2(t-1) \end{pmatrix}.$$

The eigenvalues of Q are $s+t-2 \pm \sqrt{s^2-st+t^2}$. By Theorem 4, these are also the distance eigenvalues of $K_{s,t}$ each with multiplicity 1. By Lemma 3.4 in [23], $K_{s,t}$ has three distinct eigenvalues. By using the trace of the distance matrix of $K_{s,t}$, we obtain that -2 with multiplicity $s+t-2$ is the other distinct distance eigenvalue of $K_{s,t}$. □

Indulal [36] characterized graphs with two distinct distance eigenvalues. We provide a short proof of this characterization.

Lemma 3. ([36]) *A graph Γ has $\delta_\Gamma(\mathcal{D}) = 2$ if and only if $\Gamma = K_\nu$, $\nu \geq 2$.*

Proof. If $\Gamma = K_\nu$, then $\mathcal{D}(\Gamma) = A(\Gamma)$ where $A(\Gamma)$ is the adjacency matrix of Γ. Thus, Γ has two distinct distance eigenvalues i.e., $\nu - 1$ and -1.

For the converse, assume that Γ has two distinct distance eigenvalues, say, $\mu_0 > \mu_1$. Let m_i be the multiplicity of μ_i. By Theorem 2, $m_1 = 1$, and thus, $m_2 = \nu - 1$. We show that Γ does not contain $K_{1,2}$ as an induced subgraph. On the contrary, we assume that it is true. Let P be the principle submatrix of $\mathcal{D}(\Gamma)$ induced by $K_{1,2}$. Then, by Theorem 3, we obtain that P has only two distinct distance eigenvalues. However, by Lemma 2, $\mathcal{D}(K_{1,2})$ has precisely three distinct distance eigenvalues. This implies that $K_{1,2}$ is not an induced subgraph of Γ. And thus, $D(\Gamma) = 1$ and $\Gamma = K_\nu$, $\nu \geq 2$. □

The problem of characterizing graphs with three distinct distance eigenvalues is, in fact, very hard. This problem was solved for trees by Zhang and Lin [30] in 2023. Here, we deliver an alternative proof which is extendable to other families of graphs such as unicyclic and bicyclic graphs.

Proof of Theorem 1. The 'only if part' of the statement follows from Lemma 2 by considering either $s = 1$ or $t = 1$.

For the 'if part' of the statement, we assume T to be a tree with three distinct distance eigenvalues. Let D (resp. $\mathcal{D}$) be the diameter (resp. distance matrix) of T. Since T is non-complete, we obtain that T is non-regular. Let $\mu_0 > \mu_1 > \mu_2$ be the distinct eigenvalues of T with respective multiplicities m_0, m_1, m_2. By the Perron–Frobenius Theorem 2, we have $m_0 = 1$. Moreover, by Corollary 1, we have $\mu_0 > 0$ and $\mu_1 < 0$. Let $\mathbf{x} > 0$ be the Perron–Frobenius eigenvector of $\mathcal{D}$, then

$$(J - I)\mathbf{x} \leq \mathcal{D}\mathbf{x} \leq D(J - I)\mathbf{x},$$

and $\mathcal{D}\mathbf{x} = D(J - I)\mathbf{x}$ if and only if $D = 1$. This implies that $\mu_0 \leq D(\nu - 1)$. We discuss the following two possible cases:

Case 1 . μ_0 is not an integer.

Since μ_0 is simple and non-integral, one of μ_i $(1 \leq i \leq 2)$ is also simple. Let $\{\mu, \mu'\} = \{\mu_1, \mu_2\}$, and assume μ is the simple eigenvalue. This implies that $\mu' \in \mathbb{Z}$ and has multiplicity $\nu - 2$. Since $(\mathcal{D}) = 0$, we obtain that $\mu_0 + \mu_1 = -\mu'(\nu - 2)$. Note that $\text{rank}(\mathcal{D} - \mu' I) = 2$. Moreover, $K_{1,2}$ is an induced subgraph of T as it is non-regular and non-complete. This implies that

$$\text{rank}\big(D(K_{1,2}) - \mu' I\big) \leq 2,$$

where $\mathcal{D}(K_{1,2})$ is a principle submatrix of $\mathcal{D}(T)$. Therefore, by interlacing, $\mu' \in \{1 \pm \sqrt{3}, -2\}$ since $Spec_{\mathcal{D}}(K_{1,2}) = \{1 \pm \sqrt{3}, -2\}$. However, since $\mu' \in \mathbb{Z}$, we obtain that $\mu' = -2$. By Theorem 2.6 from [23], T is a complete multipartite graph. Since T is a non-regular graph having three distinct distance eigenvalues, by Lemma 3.4 from [23], $T = K_{s,t}$, $s, t \geq 2$ is complete bipartite. By Lemma 2 and Corollary 1, we obtain that $\mu_1 = s + t - 2 - \sqrt{s^2 - st + t^2} < 0$ and $\mu_2 = s + t - 2 + \sqrt{s^2 - st + t^2} > 0$. By solving these inequalities, we obtain that either $s = 1$ or $t = 1$. This implies that T is the star graph.

Case 2. μ_0 is an integer.

In this case, we may assume that $m_i \geq 2$ for $i = 1, 2$. Based on m_i, we consider the following subcases.

Subcase 2.1. Assume that $m_1 \neq m_2$.

In this case, the corresponding distance eigenvalues μ_1 and μ_2 are integral such that $\mu_1 \geq 0$ and $\mu_2 \leq -2$. If $\mu_2 = -2$, then, by Theorem 2.6 from [23], T is a complete multipartite graph. Since T is a non-regular graph having three distinct distance eigenvalues, by Lemma 3.4 from [23], $T = K_{s,t}, s, t \geq 2$ is complete bipartite. By Lemma 2 and Corollary 1, we obtain that $\mu_1 = s + t - 2 - \sqrt{s^2 - st + t^2} < 0$ and $\mu_2 = s + t - 2 + \sqrt{s^2 - st + t^2} > 0$. By solving these inequalities, we obtain that either $s = 1$ or $t = 1$. This implies that T is a star graph.

Thus, we have $\mu_1 \geq 0$ and $\mu_2 \leq -3$. By Corollary 1, this is not possible, as the graph is a tree.

Subcase 2.2. Assume that $m_1 = m_2 \geq 2$.

Then, $m_1 = m_2 = m = \frac{1}{2}(\nu - 1)$, and hence, $\nu = 2m + 1$ is odd. Note that $(\mathcal{D}) = 0$ implies that $\sum_{i=1}^{\nu} \mu_i = 0$. This gives us

$$\mu_0 + \frac{1}{2}(\nu - 1)(\mu_1 + \mu_2) = 0. \tag{1}$$

As $\mu_1 + \mu_2 \in \mathbb{Z}^-$, we obtain $\mu_0 = c\frac{1}{2}(\nu - 1)$, where c is a positive integer by Equation (1). Since T is non-complete, there exist vertices x, y, and z in T such that $x \sim y \sim z$. Note that the set $S = \{x, y, z\}$ induces a path of length two in T. This implies that, by interlacing, we obtain $-1 < \mu_1 < 0$, as $Spec_{\mathcal{D}}(K_{1,2}) = \{1 \pm \sqrt{3}, -2\}$. Moreover, since ν is odd and $m_1 = m_2 = m = \frac{1}{2}(\nu - 1)$, by Theorem 5, we obtain

$$2^{2m} = -(\mu_1\mu_2)^m(\mu_1 + \mu_2). \tag{2}$$

By Equation (2), we obtain that $\mu_1\mu_2 \in \{1, 2, 4\}$ as $\mu_1 + \mu_2 \in \mathbb{Z}^-$. Next, we discuss all these possibilities one by one:

Subsubcase 2.2.1. $\mu_1\mu_2 = 4$.

By Equation (2), we obtain that $\mu_1 + \mu_2 = -1$, which is not possible as $\mu_1 > -1$ and $\mu_2 \leq -2$.

Subsubcase 2.2.2. $\mu_1\mu_2 = 1$.

In this case, by Equation (2), we obtain $\mu_1 + \mu_2 = -2^{2m}$. As a consequence of Theorem 5, one could show that T has $\lceil \frac{D}{2} \rceil$ distinct distance eigenvalues. Using this fact with $\mu_0 \leq D(\nu - 1)$, we find that $\mu_0 \leq D(\nu - 1) \leq 12m$. By using $\mu_0 \leq 12m$ and Theorem 2, we obtain

$$12m \geq |\mu_2| > 2^{2m} - 1$$

This implies that $m \leq 3$ and, thus, $\nu \leq 7$. Tables 1 and 2 present all the trees on $\nu \leq 7$ vertices and their distance spectra. It is easy to check that this case is not possible.

Subsubcase 2.2.3. $\mu_1\mu_2 = 2$.

In this case, we obtain that $\mu_1 + \mu_2 = -2^m$. By using a similar argument as in Subcase 2.1, we find that, in this case, we have $m \leq 6$. Note that μ_1 and μ_2 are the roots of

$$x^2 - (\mu_1 + \mu_2)x + \mu_1\mu_2 = 0. \tag{3}$$

From (3), we obtain $\mu_1, \mu_2 = \frac{-2^m \pm \sqrt{2^{2m} - 8}}{2}$. For $m \leq 6$, the number $2^{2m} - 8$ is not a perfect square. Thus, μ_i $(i = 1, 2)$ is not integral which is a contradiction to the fact that all μ_i's are integral. This shows that μ_0 is not integral which completes the proof. □

Table 1. Trees on $\nu \leq 7$ vertices and their distance spectra.

ν	Tree	Distance Spectrum
2		$\{[1]^1, [-1]^1\}$
3		$\{[2.7320]^1, [-0.7320]^1, [-2]^1\}$
4		$\{[4.6457]^1, [-0.6457]^1, [-2]^2, \}$
4		$\{[5.1623]^1, [-0.5858]^1, [-1.1623]^1, [-3.41421]^1, \}$
5		$\{[6.60555]^1, [-0.60555]^1, [-2]^3\}$
5		$\{[7.45929]^1, [-0.51198]^1, [-1.0846]^1, [-2]^1, [-3.8627]^1\}$
5		$\{[8.2882]^1, [-0.5578]^1, [-0.7639]^1, [-1.7304]^1, [-5.2361]^1\}$
6		$\{[8.5826]^1, [-0.5826]^1, [-2]^4\}$
6		$\{[9.6702]^1, [-0.4727]^1[-1.0566]^1, [-2]^2, [-4.1409]^1\}$
6		$\{[11.0588]^1, [-0.5114]^1, [-0.67301]^1, [-1.7026]^1[-2]^1, [-6.1717]^1\}$

Table 1. *Cont.*

ν	Tree	Distance Spectrum
6		$\{[10]^1, [-0.4384]^1, [-1]^1, [-2]^2, [-4.5615]^1\}$
6		$\{[10.7424]^1, [-0.4754]^1, [-0.7639]^1, [-1.3363]^1, [-5.2360]^1\}$
6		$\{[12.1093]^1, [-0.5358]^1, [-0.6798]^1, [-1]^1, [-2.4295]^1, [-7.4641]^1\}$
7		$\{[10.5678]^1, [-0.5678]^1, [-2]^5\}$
7		$\{[11.8281]^1, [-0.4488]^1, [-1.0423]^1, [-2]^3, [-4.3368]^1\}$
7		$\{[13.6353]^1, [-0.4703]^1, [-0.6481]^1, [-1.6923]^1, [-2]^2, [-6.8245]^1\}$
7		$\{[12.3945]^1, [-0.3973]^1, [-0.9692]^1, [-2]^3, [-5.02789]^1\}$

Table 2. Trees on $\nu \leq 7$ vertices and their distance spectra.

ν	Tree	Distance Spectrum
7		$\{[14.1759]^1, [-0.5073]^1, [-0.5359]^1, [-1.6687]^1, [-2]^2, [-7.464]^1\}$
7		$\{[13.0698]^1, [-0.4307]^1, [-0.7639]^1, [-1.2626]^1, [-2]^1, [-3.3764]^1, [-5.2360]^1\}$
7		$\{[15.4048]^1, [-0.4943]^1, [-0.62420]^1, [-0.9174]^1, [-2]^1, [-2.4757]^1, [-8.8932]^1\}$
7		$\{[14.863]^1, [-0.4749]^1, [-0.6461]^1, [-0.9171]^1, [-1.7796]^1, [-3.3529]^1, [-7.6929]^1\}$
7		$\{[13.6346]^1, [-0.43245]^1, [-0.6651]^1, [-1.3089]^1, [-2]^1, [-3.0055]^1, [-6.223]^1\}$
7		$\{[14.2969]^1, [-0.4559]^1, [-0.76393]^2, [-1.8410]^1, [-5.2361]^2\}$
7		$\{[16.6253]^1, [-0.52720]^1, [-0.6159]^1, [-0.8405]^1, [-1.2862]^1, [-3.2576]^1, [-10.0978]^1\}$

4. Distance Spectra of Small Graphs

In this section, we deliver all the connected graphs (excluding trees) on $\nu \leq 6$ vertices and their distance spectra. For trees, we refer to Tables 1 and 2. Tables 3–16 comprise these data. Note that these data are generated by using nauty-geng generators on Sage [37] software. The first column depicts their unique graph6 string. Researchers may use these data for their research on spectral graph theory of the distance matrix.

There are some interesting observations which we make based on the data in Tables 3–16. Before we elaborate these observations, we note some necessary definitions. Two non-isomorphic connected graphs Γ and Ω are said to be distance cospectral (or distance cospectral mates), if both Γ and Ω have the same multiset of distance eigenvalues. A graph Γ is said to be determined from its distance spectrum, if it has no distance cospectral mates.

From Tables 1–16, we notice that all the connected graphs on $\nu \leq 6$ vertices are determined from their distance spectra. We also deliver a distance cospectral pair on $\nu = 7$ vertices, making a distance cospectral pair of the smallest possible order. Figure 1 depicts that distance cospectral pair on $\nu = 7$ vertices.

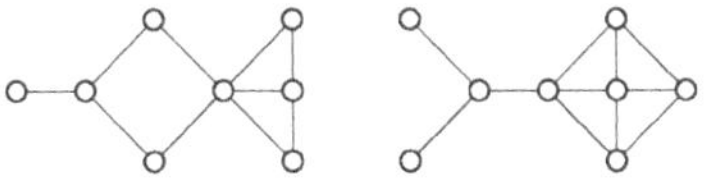

Figure 1. A distance cospectral pair of smallest order.

Table 3. Distance spectra of small graphs.

Graph6 String	ν	Graph	Distance Spectrum
`Bw`	3	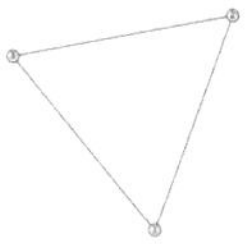	$\{[2]^1, [-1]^2\}$
`CV`	4	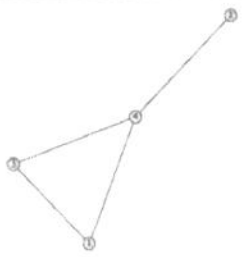	$\{[4.0996]^1, [-0.7165]^1, [-1]^1, [-2.3832]^1\}$
`C]`	4	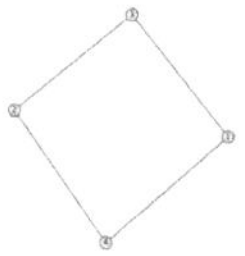	$\{[4.0]^1, [0.0]^1, [-2.0]^2, \}$
`C^`	4	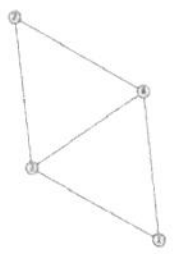	$\{[3.5616]^1, [-0.5616]^1, [-1.0]^1, [-2.0]^1, \}$
`C~`	4	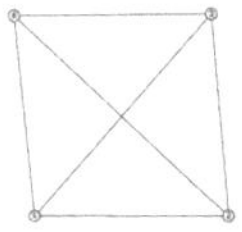	$\{[3.0]^1, [-1.0]^3\}$

Table 4. Distance spectra of small graphs.

Graph6 String	v	Graph	Distance Spectrum
DC{	5	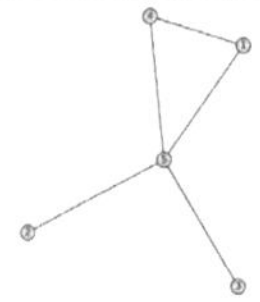	$\{[6.1764]^1, [-0.6378]^1, [-1.0]^1, [-2.0]^1, [-2.5387]^1\}$
DEw	5	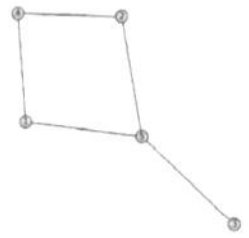	$\{[6.5381]^1, [0.0]^1, [-1.0534]^1, [-2.0]^1, [-3.4847]^1\}$
DEk	5	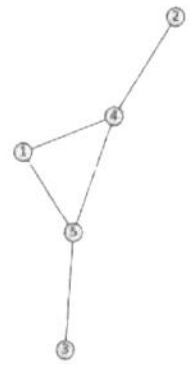	$\{[6.6375]^1, [-0.5858]^1, [-0.8365]^1, [-1.801]^1, [-3.4142]^1\}$
DE{	5	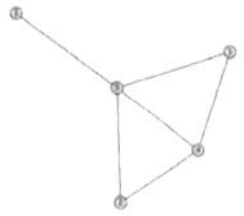	$\{[5.7596]^1, [-0.558]^1, [-0.7667]^1, [-2.0]^1, [-2.4348]^1\}$
DFw	5	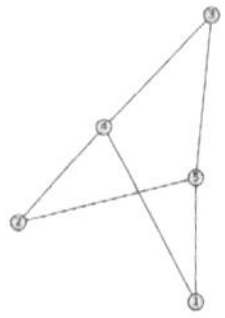	$\{[5.6458]^1, [0.3542]^1, [-2.0]^3\}$
DF{	5	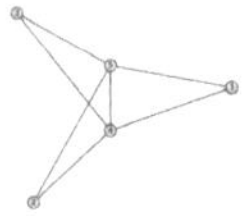	$\{[5.3723]^1, [-0.3723]^1, [-1.0]^1, [-2.0]^2\}$
DQw	5		$\{[7.0086]^1, [-0.5686]^1, [-1.0]^1, [-1.1774]^1, [-4.2626]^1\}$
DQ{	5	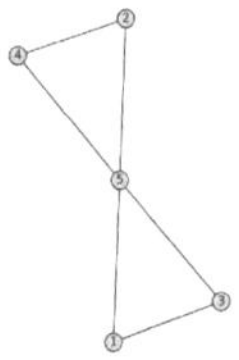	$\{[5.7016]^1, [-0.7016]^1, [-1.0]^2, [3.0]^1\}$

Table 5. Distance spectra of small graphs.

Graph6 String	v	Graph	Distance Spectrum
`DUW`	5		$\{[6.0]^1, [-0.382]^2, [-0.618]^2\}$
`DUw`	5	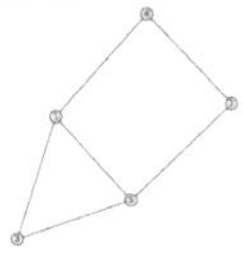	$\{[5.6351]^1, [0.0]^1, [-0.9125]^1, [-2.0]^1, [-2.7226]^1\}$
`DU{`	5		$\{[5.2926]^1, [-0.382]^1, [-0.7217]^1, [-1.5709]^1, [-2.618]^1\}$
`DTW`	5		$\{[6.2161]^1, [-0.4521]^1, [-1.0]^1, [-1.1971]^1, [-3.5669]^1\}$
`DT{`	5	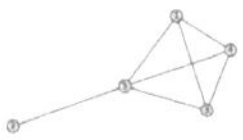	$\{[5.3441]^1, [-0.7105]^1, [-1.0]^2, [-2.6336]^1\}$
`DV{`	5	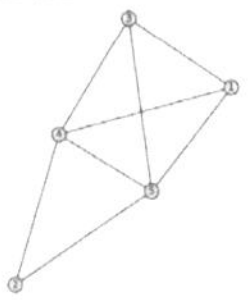	$\{[4.9018]^1, [-0.5122]^1, [-1.0]^2, [-2.3896]^1\}$
`D}w`	5	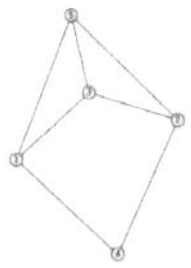	$\{[[5.2239]^1, [0.1606]^1, [-1.0]^1, [-2.0]^1, [-2.3844]^1\}$
`D}{`	5	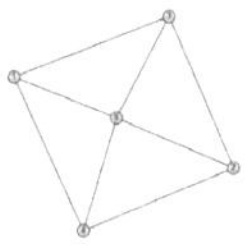	$\{[4.8284]^1, [0.0]^1, [-0.8284]^1, [-2.0]^2\}$
`D^{`	5	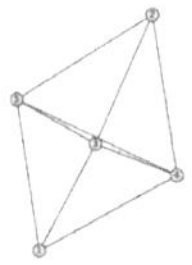	$\{[4.4495]^1, [-0.4495]^1, [-1.0]^2, [-2.0]^1\}$

Table 6. Distance spectra of small graphs.

Graph6 String	v	Graph	Distance Spectrum
D~{	5	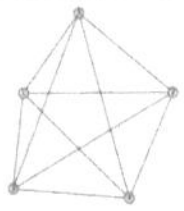	$\{[4.0]^1, [-1.0]^4\}$
E?bw	6	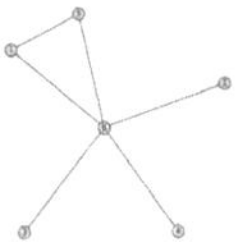	$\{[8.2297]^1, [-0.6009]^1, [-1.0]^1, [-2.0]^2, [-2.6288]^1\}$
E?ro	6	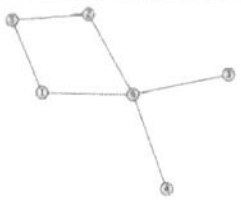	$\{[8.899]^1, [0.0]^1, [-0.899]^1, [-2.0]^2, [-4.0]^1\}$
E?qw	6	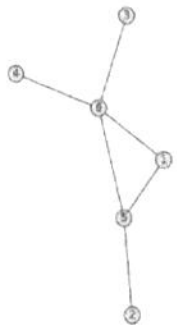	$\{[8.9909]^1, [-0.512]^1, [-0.8175]^1, [-1.7801]^1, [-2.0]^1, [-3.8813]^1\}$
E?rw	6	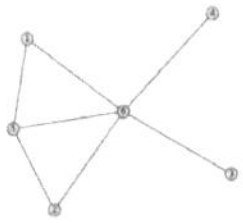	$\{[7.8888]^1, [-0.5542]^1, [-0.6926]^1, [-2.0]^2, [-2.642]^1\}$
E?zO	6	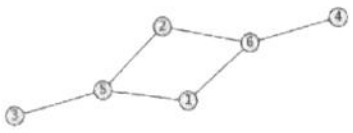	$\{[9.6569]^1, [0.0]^1, [-0.7639]^1, [-1.6569]^1, [-2.0]^1, [-5.2361]^1\}$
E?zo	6	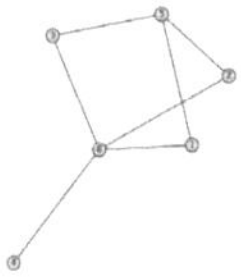	$\{[8.1468]^1, [0.4057]^1, [-1.0308]^1, [-2.0]^2, [-3.5217]^1\}$
E?zW	6	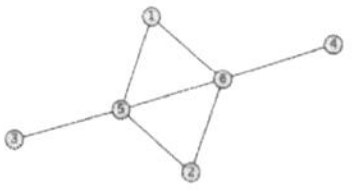	$\{[8.2882]^1, [-0.5578]^1, [-0.5858]^1, [-1.7304]^1, [-2.0]^1, [-3.4142]^1\}$
E?zw	6	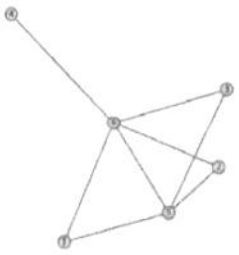	$\{[7.5673]^1, [-0.358]^1, [-0.7507]^1, [-2.0]^2, [-2.4586]^1\}$
E?~o	6	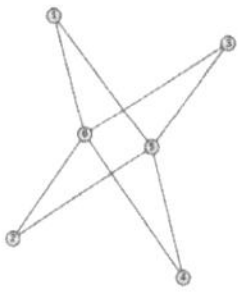	$\{[7.4641]^1, [0.5359]^1, [-2.0]^4\}$

Table 7. Distance spectra of small graphs.

Graph6 String	ν	Graph	Distance Spectrum
`E?~w`	6	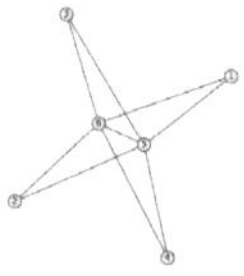	$\{[7.2749]^1, [-0.2749]^1, [-1.0]^1, [-2.0]^3\}$
`ECRo`	6	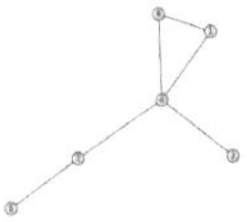	$\{[9.3154]^1, [-0.5023]^1, [-1.0]^1, [-1.0865]^1, [-2.3224]^1, [-4.4042]^1\}$
`ECRw`	6	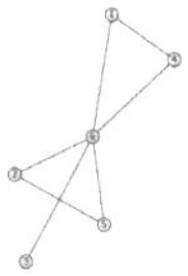	$\{[7.8526]^1, [-0.6303]^1, [-1.0]^2, [-2.2223]^1, [-3.0]^1\}$
`ECr_`	6		$\{[9.2606]^1, [0.0]^1, [-1.0]^1, [-1.0898]^1, [-3.1708]^1, [-4.0]^1\}$
`ECpo`	6	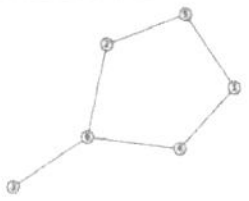	$\{[8.8219]^1, [-0.3559]^1, [-0.382]^1, [-1.2995]^1, [-2.618]^1, [-4.1664]^1\}$
`ECqg`	6	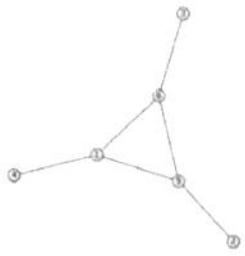	$\{[9.3852]^1, [-0.5858]^2, [-1.3852]^1, [-3.4142]^2\}$
`ECro`	6	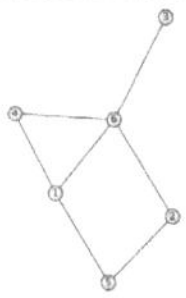	$\{[8.1822]^1, [0.0]^1, [-0.8303]^1, [-1.3401]^1, [-2.5075]^1, [-3.5042]^1\}$
`ECrg`	6	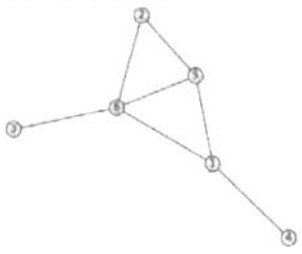	$\{[8.6632]^1, [-0.4351]^1, [-0.7665]^1, [-1.1966]^1, [-2.3862]^1, [-3.8789]^1\}$
`ECrw`	6	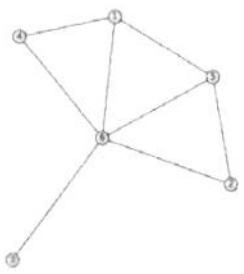	$\{[7.5222]^1, [-0.382]^1, [-0.6395]^1, [-1.4565]^1, [-2.4261]^1, [-2.618]^1\}$
`ECZ_`	6	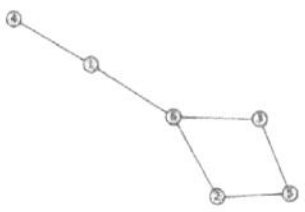	$\{[9.9713]^1, [0.0]^1, [-0.6685]^1, [-1.7199]^1, [-2.0]^1, [-5.5829]^1\}$

Table 8. Distance spectra of small graphs.

Graph6 String	ν	Graph	Distance Spectrum
ECZO	6	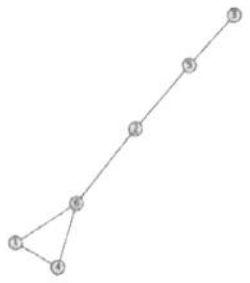	$\{[10.668]^1, [-0.5501]^1, [-0.7462]^1, [-1.0]^1, [-1.8096]^1, [-6.562]^1\}$
ECZG	6	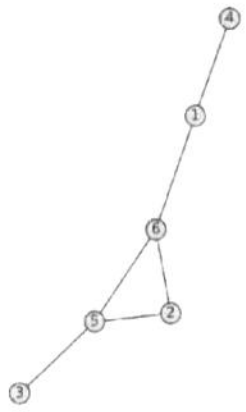	$\{[10.0548]^1, [-0.552]^1, [-0.6878]^1, [-1.1178]^1, [-2.2283]^1, [-5.4689]^1\}$
ECYW	6	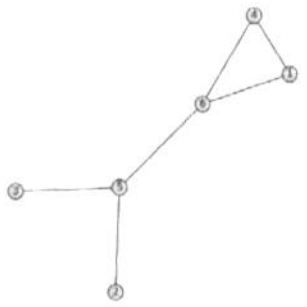	$\{[9.6088]^1, [-0.4931]^1, [-1.0]^1, [-1.0924]^1, [-2.0]^1, [-5.0233]^1\}$
ECZo	6	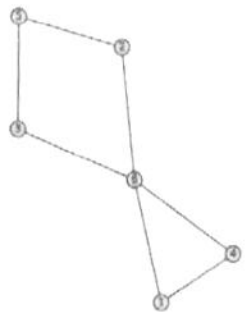	$\{[8.497]^1, [0.0]^1, [-1.0]^1, [-1.0613]^1, [-2.0]^1, [-4.4357]^1\}$
ECZg	6	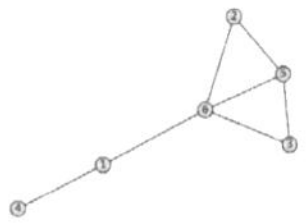	$\{[8.9694]^1, [-0.4807]^1, [-0.6851]^1, [-1.1687]^1, [-2.0]^1, [-4.6349]^1\}$
ECZW	6	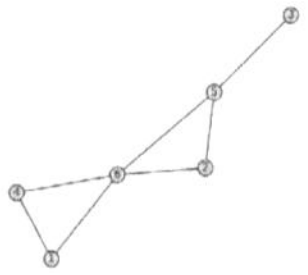	$\{[8.5936]^1, [-0.5686]^1, [-0.8339]^1, [-1.0]^1, [-1.8778]^1, [-4.3134]^1\}$
ECZw	6	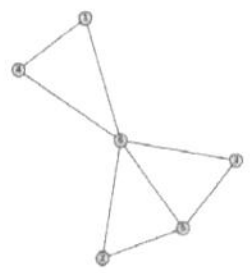	$\{[7.4864]^1, [-0.5574]^1, [-0.7551]^1, [-1.0]^1, [-2.0]^1, [-3.1739]^1\}$
ECfo	6	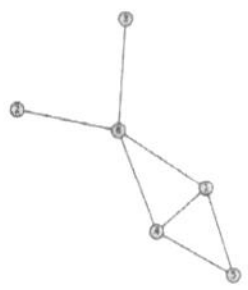	$\{[8.6378]^1, [-0.4043]^1, [-1.0]^1, [-1.1116]^1, [-2.0]^1, [-4.1219]^1\}$

Table 9. Distance spectra of small graphs.

Graph6 String	ν	Graph	Distance Spectrum
ECfw	6	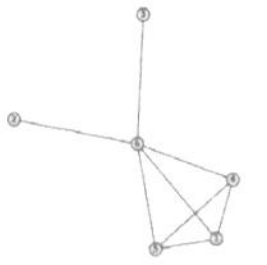	$\{[7.5546]^1, [-0.6347]^1, [-1.0]^2, [-2.0]^1, [-2.9199]^1\}$
ECxo	6	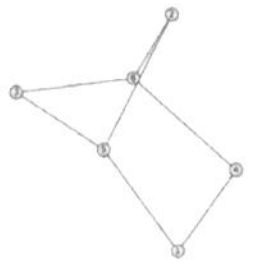	$\{[7.6952]^1, [0.0932]^1, [-0.382]^1, [-2.0]^1, [-2.618]^1, [-2.7884]^1\}$
ECzo	6	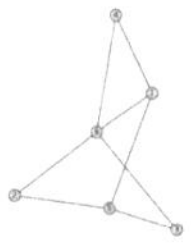	$\{[7.4058]^1, [0.3642]^1, [-0.9064]^1, [-2.0]^2, [-2.8636]^1\}$
ECzg	6	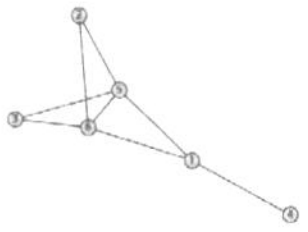	$\{[8.3569]^1, [-0.2733]^1, [-1.0]^1, [-1.0985]^1, [-2.0]^1, [-3.985]^1\}$
ECzW	6	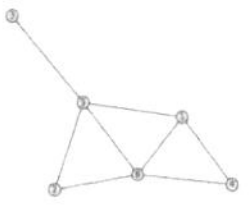	$\{[7.9151]^1, [-0.3566]^1, [-0.6712]^1, [-1.1846]^1, [-2.1064]^1, [-3.5963]^1\}$
ECxw	6	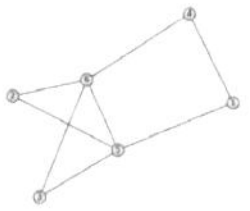	$\{[7.4417]^1, [0.0]^1, [-0.5595]^1, [-2.0]^2, [-2.8823]^1\}$
ECzw	6	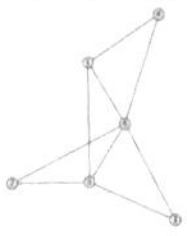	$\{[7.1742]^1, [-0.1943]^1, [-0.6764]^1, [-1.5289]^1, [-2.0]^1, [-2.7745]^1\}$
ECvo	6	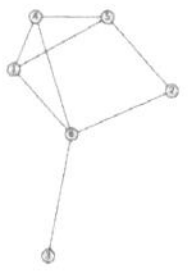	$\{[7.837]^1, [0.1708]^1, [-1.0]^1, [-1.0545]^1, [-2.377]^1, [-3.5763]^1\}$
ECuw	6	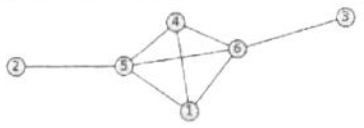	$\{[7.9777]^1, [-0.5858]^1, [-0.8093]^1, [-1.0]^1, [-2.1683]^1, [-3.4142]^1\}$
ECvw	6	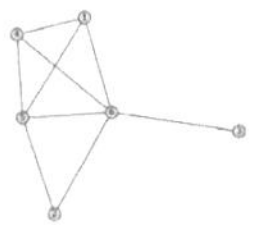	$\{[7.2057]^1, [-0.5121]^1, [-0.763]^1, [-1.0]^1, [-2.2667]^1, [-2.6639]^1\}$

Table 10. Distance spectra of small graphs.

Graph6 String	v	Graph	Distance Spectrum
EC~o	6	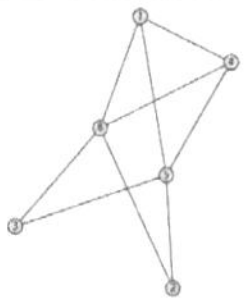	$\{[7.0959]^1, [0.4439]^1, [-1.0]^1, [-2.0]^2, [-2.5398]^1\}$
EC~w	6	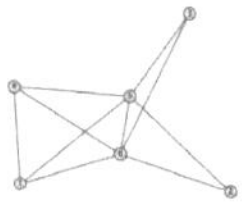	$\{[6.8858]^1, [-0.3426]^1, [-1.0]^2, [-2.0]^1, [-2.5432]^1\}$
EEr_	6		$\{[8.5704]^1, [0.3566]^1, [-1.0]^1, [-2.0]^2, [-3.927]^1\}$
EEro	6	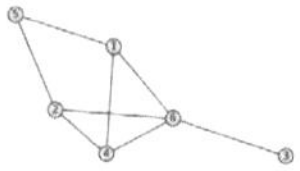	$\{[7.8759]^1, [0.1611]^1, [-0.7551]^1, [-1.7972]^1, [-2.0]^1, [-3.4847]^1\}$
EErw	6	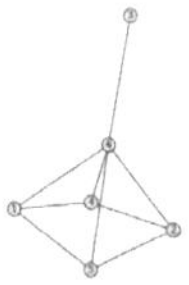	$\{[7.1648]^1, [0.0]^1, [-0.6718]^1, [-2.0]^2, [-2.4929]^1\}$
EEh_	6	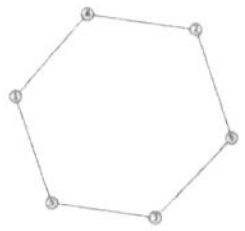	$\{[9.0]^1, [0.0]^2, [-1.0]^1, [-4.0]^2\}$
EEj_	6	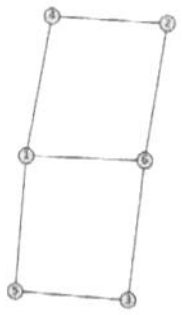	$\{[8.4244]^1, [0.0]^2, [-1.4244]^1, [-3.0]^1, [-4.0]^1\}$
EEio	6	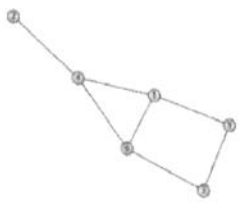	$\{[8.5543]^1, [0.0]^1, [-0.6439]^1, [-1.7422]^1, [-2.0]^1, [-4.1682]^1\}$
EEho	6	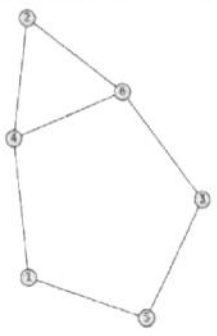	$\{[8.0741]^1, [-0.3258]^1, [-0.382]^1, [-0.8858]^1, [-2.618]^1, [-3.8625]^1\}$

Table 11. Distance spectra of small graphs.

Graph6 String	v	Graph	Distance Spectrum
EEiW	6		$\{[9.4244]^1, [-0.4244]^1, [-0.7639]^1, [-1.0]^1, [-2.0]^1, [-5.2361]^1\}$
EEhW	6		$\{[8.5237]^1, [0.0]^1, [-0.8401]^1, [-1.1598]^1, [-2.2582]^1, [-4.2656]^1\}$
EEjo	6	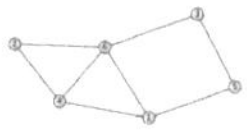	$\{[7.8043]^1, [0.0]^1, [-0.6535]^1, [-1.0921]^1, [-2.2817]^1, [-3.7771]^1\}$
EEjW	6	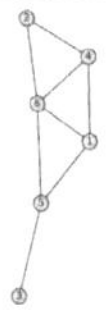	$\{[8.2723]^1, [-0.3698]^1, [-0.601]^1, [-1.1477]^1, [-1.8894]^1, [-4.2644]^1\}$
EEhw	6	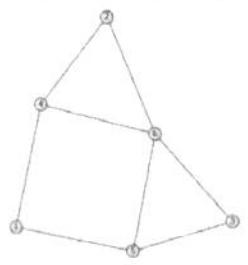	$\{[7.4002]^1, [0.0]^1, [-0.8467]^1, [-1.0]^1, [-2.5535]^1, [-3.0]^1\}$
EEjw	6	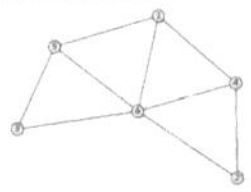	$\{[7.1287]^1, [-0.279]^1, [-0.7025]^1, [-1.0]^1, [-2.1472]^1, [-3.0]^1\}$
EEz_	6	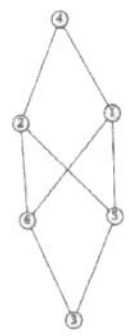	$\{[7.772]^1, [0.5616]^1, [-0.772]^1, [-2.0]^2, [-3.5616]^1\}$
EEzO	6	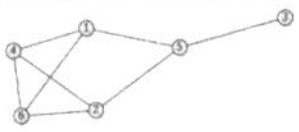	$\{[8.2037]^1, [0.1607]^1, [-1.0]^1, [-1.0566]^1, [-2.0]^1, [-4.3078]^1\}$
EEzo	6	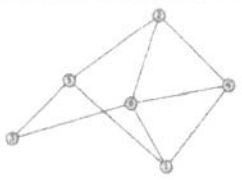	$\{[7.0425]^1, [0.4744]^1, [-0.76]^1, [-2.0]^2, [-2.7569]^1\}$
EEzg	6		$\{[7.5169]^1, [0.2038]^1, [-1.0]^1, [-1.0737]^1, [-2.0]^1, [-3.6471]^1\}$

Table 12. Distance spectra of small graphs.

Graph6 String	v	Graph	Distance Spectrum
EEzw	6	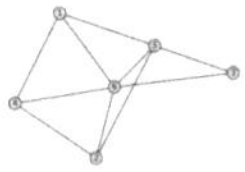	$\{[6.7884]^1, [0.1022]^1, [-0.7201]^1, [-1.4974]^1, [-2.0]^1, [-2.6732]^1\}$
EEvo	6	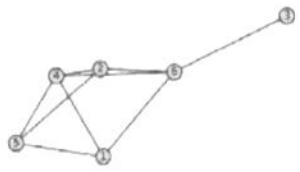	$\{[7.5455]^1, [0.0]^1, [-0.7465]^1, [-1.176]^1, [-2.0]^1, [-3.6229]^1\}$
EEuw	6	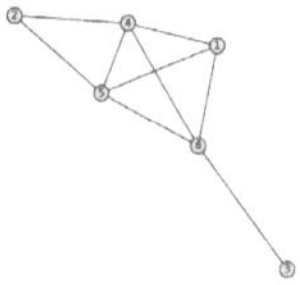	$\{[7.6235]^1, [-0.4235]^1, [-0.8097]^1, [-1.0]^1, [-1.8233]^1, [-3.567]^1\}$
EEvw	6	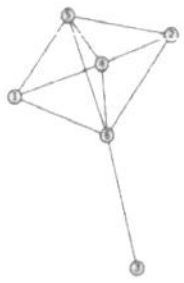	$\{[6.8601]^1, [-0.4485]^1, [-0.7263]^1, [-1.0]^1, [-2.0]^1, [-2.6853]^1\}$
EEno	6	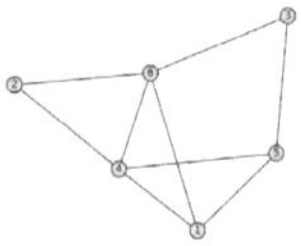	$\{[7.0835]^1, [0.1639]^1, [-0.5993]^1, [-1.5688]^1, [-2.3433]^1, [-2.7361]^1\}$
EElw	6	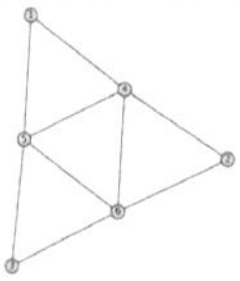	$\{[7.1231]^1, [-0.382]^1, [-0.382]^1, [-1.1231]^1, [-2.618]^1, [-2.618]^1\}$
EEnw	6	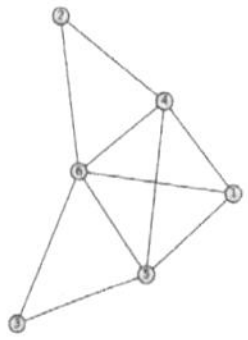	$\{[6.8289]^1, [-0.382]^1, [-0.5882]^1, [-1.0]^1, [-2.2407]^1, [-2.618]^1\}$
EEnw	6	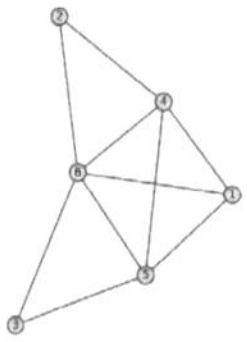	$\{[6.8289]^1, [-0.382]^1, [-0.5882]^1, [-1.0]^1, [-2.2407]^1, [-2.618]^1\}$
EE~w	6	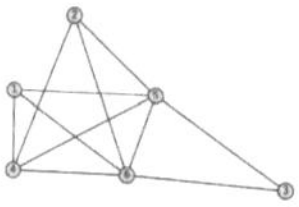	$\{[6.5109]^1, [-0.3512]^1, [-0.7158]^1, [-1.0]^1, [-2.0]^1, [-2.4439]^1\}$

Table 13. Distance spectra of small graphs.

Graph6 String	ν	Graph	Distance Spectrum
EFz_	6	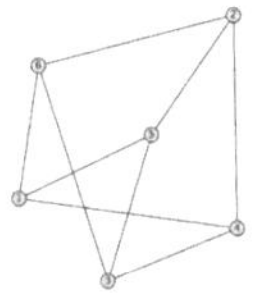	$\{[7.0]^1, [1.0]^1, [-2.0]^4\}$
EFzo	6	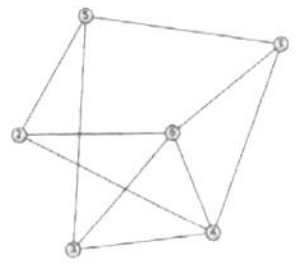	$\{[6.6961]^1, [0.6888]^1, [-1.0]^1, [-2.0]^2, [-2.3849]^1\}$
EFzW	6	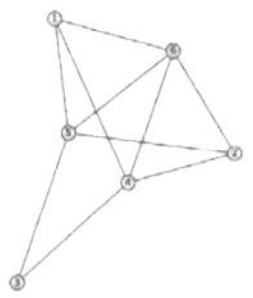	$\{[6.744]^1, [0.3631]^1, [-0.6703]^1, [-2.0]^2, [-2.4368]^1\}$
EFzw	6	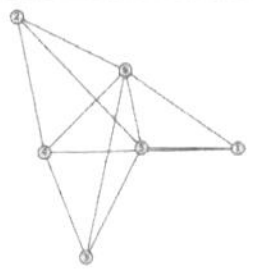	$\{[6.4188]^1, [0.3868]^1, [-0.8056]^1, [-2.0]^3\}$
EF~w	6	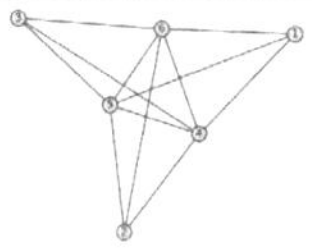	$\{[6.1623]^1, [-0.1623]^1, [-1.0]^2, [-2.0]^2\}$
EQj_	6		$\{[9.6964]^1, [-0.4484]^1, [-0.7224]^1, [-1.0]^1, [-1.7703]^1, [-5.7553]^1\}$
EQjO	6	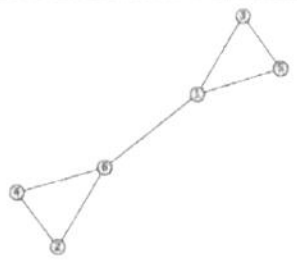	$\{[9.1962]^1, [-0.5505]^1, [-1.0]^2, [-1.1962]^1, [-5.4495]^1\}$
EQjo	6	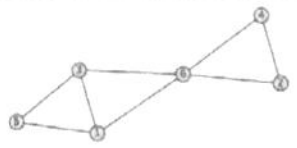	$\{[8.217]^1, [-0.4384]^1, [-1.0]^2, [-1.217]^1, [-4.5616]^1\}$
EQjg	6	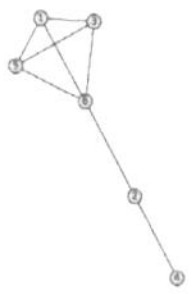	$\{[8.6279]^1, [-0.5617]^1, [-1.0]^2, [-1.1831]^1, [-4.883]^1\}$

Table 14. Distance spectra of small graphs.

Graph6 String	v	Graph	Distance Spectrum
`EQjw`	6	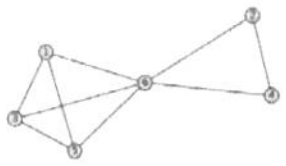	$\{[7.1246]^1, [-0.6959]^1, [-1.0]^3, [-3.4287]^1\}$
`EQZo`	6	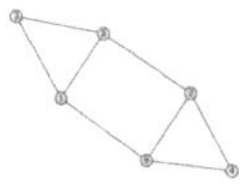	$\{[7.772]^1, [0.0]^1, [-0.772]^1, [-1.0]^1, [-2.0]^1, [-4.0]^1\}$
`EQzo`	6	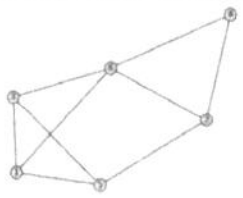	$\{[7.0418]^1, [0.1621]^1, [-0.912]^1, [-1.0]^1, [-2.1204]^1, [-3.1715]^1\}$
`EQzg`	6	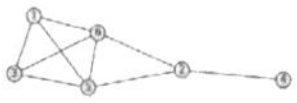	$\{[7.9676]^1, [-0.4017]^1, [-1.0]^1, [-1.223]^1, [-4.3429]^1\}$
`EQzW`	6	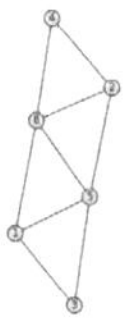	$\{[7.5165]^1, [-0.3389]^1, [-0.4679]^1, [-1.1776]^1, [-1.6527]^1, [-3.8794]^1\}$
`EQyw`	6	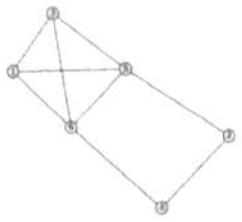	$\{[7.0747]^1, [0.0]^1, [-0.8868]^1, [-1.0]^1, [-2.0]^1, [-3.1879]^1\}$
`EQzw`	6	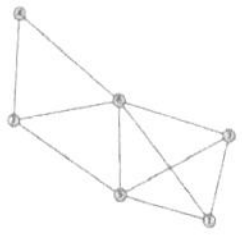	$\{[6.783]^1, [-0.3274]^1, [-0.711]^1, [-1.0]^1, [-1.6232]^1, [-3.1214]^1\}$
`EQ~o`	6	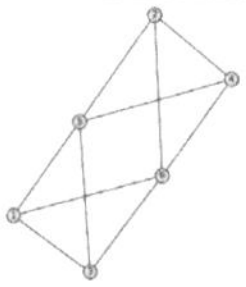	$\{[6.7016]^1, [0.2984]^1, [-1.0]^2, [-2.0]^1, [-3.0]^1\}$
`EQ~w`	6	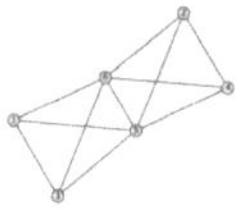	$\{[6.4641]^1, [-0.4641]^1, [-1.0]^3, [-3.0]^1\}$
`EUZ_`	6	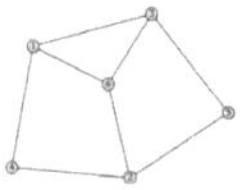	$\{[7.3594]^1, [0.1919]^1, [-0.382]^1, [-1.8043]^1, [-2.618]^1, [-2.7471]^1\}$
`EUZO`	6	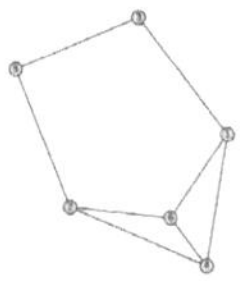	$\{[7.3554]^1, [-0.2166]^1, [-0.382]^1, [-1.0]^1, [-2.618]^1, [-3.1388]^1\}$

Table 15. Distance spectra of small graphs.

Graph6 String	v	Graph	Distance Spectrum
EUZo	6	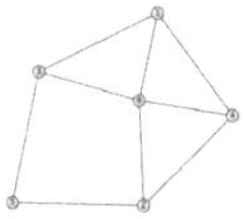	$\{[7.0372]^1, [0.0]^1, [-0.382]^1, [-1.2036]^1, [-2.618]^1, [-2.8336]^1\}$
EUZw	6	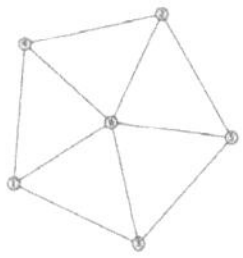	$\{[6.7417]^1, [-0.382]^1, [-0.382]^1, [-0.7417]^1, [-2.618]^1, [-2.618]^1\}$
EUxo	6	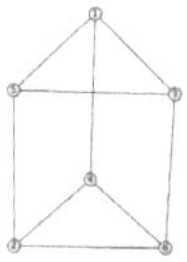	$\{[7.0]^1, [0.0]^2, [-2.0]^2, [-3.0]^1\}$
EUzo	6	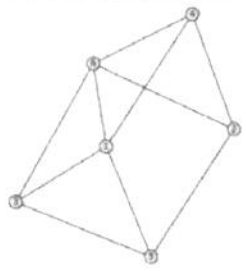	$\{[6.6953]^1, [0.247]^1, [-0.4698]^1, [-1.445]^1, [-2.2255]^1, [-2.8019]^1\}$
EUzW	6	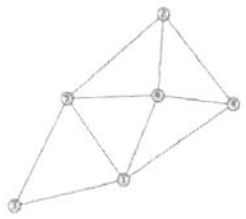	$\{[6.7363]^1, [0.0]^1, [-0.4464]^1, [-1.3637]^1, [-2.0]^1, [-2.9263]^1\}$
EUzw	6	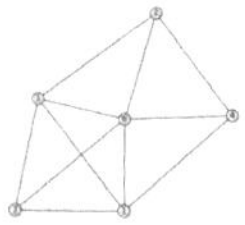	$\{[6.4114]^1, [0.0]^1, [-0.687]^1, [-1.0]^1, [-2.0]^1, [-2.7244]^1\}$
EU~w	6	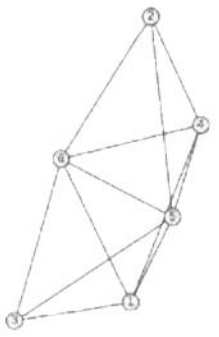	$\{[6.1012]^1, [-0.382]^1, [-0.5175]^1, [-1.0]^1, [-1.5837]^1, [-2.618]^1\}$
ETzo	6	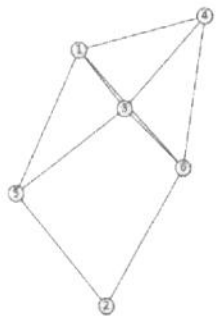	$\{[6.7321]^1, [0.187]^1, [-0.8992]^1, [-1.0]^1, [-2.1674]^1, [-2.8525]^1\}$
ETzg	6	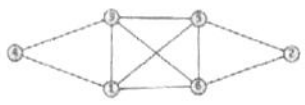	$\{[7.2426]^1, [-0.2679]^1, [-1.0]^2, [-1.2426]^1, [-3.7321]^1\}$

Table 16. Distance spectra of small graphs.

Graph6 String	v	Graph	Distance Spectrum
ETzw	6	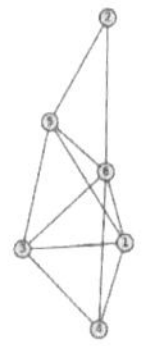	$\{[6.4523]^1, [-0.2263]^1, [-0.7212]^1, [-1.0]^1, [-1.6828]^1, [-2.8221]^1\}$
ETno	6	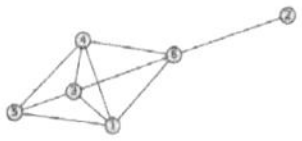	$\{[7.2675]^1, [-0.3691]^1, [-1.0]^2, [-1.2143]^1, [-3.6841]^1\}$
ETnw	6	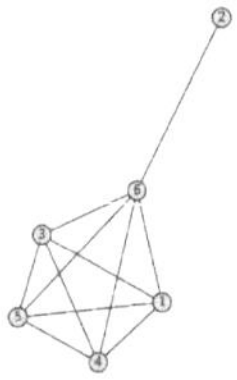	$\{[6.5242]^1, [-0.7074]^1, [-1.0]^3, [-2.8168]^1\}$
ET~w	6	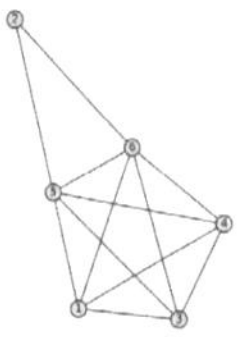	$\{[6.1425]^1, [-0.4913]^1, [-1.0]^3, [-2.6512]^1\}$
EV~w	6	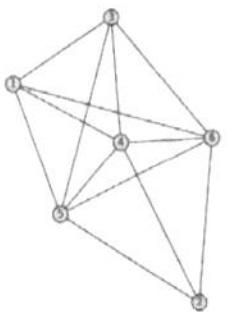	$\{[5.7566]^1, [-0.3629]^1, [-1.0]^3, [-2.3937]^1\}$
E]zo	6	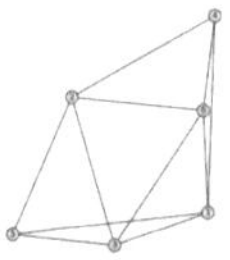	$\{[6.3647]^1, [0.2007]^1, [-0.382]^1, [-1.5654]^1, [-2.0]^1, [-2.618]^1\}$
E]zg	6	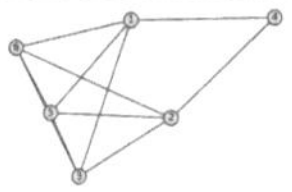	$\{[6.4017]^1, [0.2368]^1, [-1.0]^2, [-2.0]^1, [-2.6385]^1\}$
E]yw	6	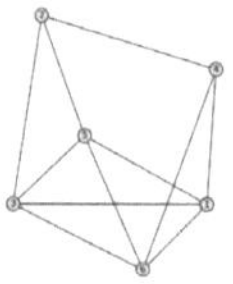	$\{[6.3589]^1, [0.4142]^1, [-1.0]^2, [-2.3589]^1, [-2.4142]^1\}$
E]zw	6	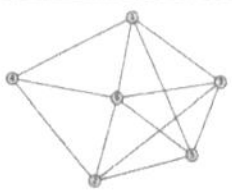	$\{[6.0479]^1, [0.1676]^1, [-0.8252]^1, [-1.0]^1, [-2.0]^1, [-2.3904]^1\}$

Table 16. *Cont.*

Graph6 String	ν	Graph	Distance Spectrum
`E]~o`	6	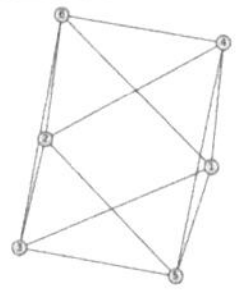	$\{[6.0]^1, [0.0]^2, [-2.0]^3\}$
`E]~w`	6	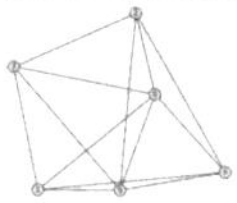	$\{[5.7016]^1, [0.0]^1, [-0.7016]^1, [-1.0]^1, [-2.0]^2\}$
`E^~w`	6	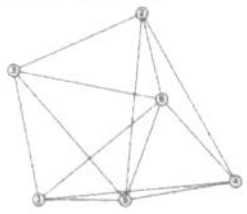	$\{[5.3723]^1, [-0.3723]^1, [-1.0]^3, [-2.0]^1\}$
`E^~w`	6	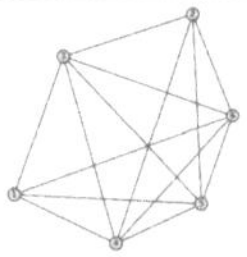	$\{[5.3723]^1, [-0.3723]^1, [-1.0]^3, [-2.0]^1\}$
`E~~w`	6	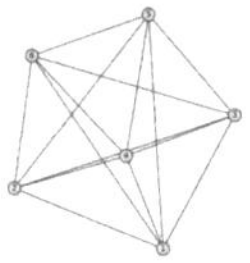	$\{[5.0]^1, [-1.0]^5\}$

5. Conclusions

The "few eigenvalues" problem is one of the contemporary problems in spectral graph theory. This paper investigates certain mathematical characteristics of the distance matrix of trees. In particular, this paper studies the "few eigenvalues" problem regarding the distance matrix. The main result of this paper classifies all the trees having precisely three distinct eigenvalues of their distance matrix. Our proof is different from the one delivered by Zhang and Lin [30]. Our proof employs interlacing and equitable partitions and can be extended to other families such as unicyclic and bicyclic graphs. We also list all the connected graphs on $\nu \leq 6$ vertices and compute their distance spectra. Some important observations on distance cospectrality are made based on these numerical data.

Based on these remarks, we propose the following open problems for future studies:

Problem 1. *Characterize all unicyclic graphs having precisely three distinct distance eigenvalues.*

Problem 2. *Solve Problem 1 for the case of bicyclic graphs.*

Problem 3. *Construct an infinite family of non-regular non-bipartite graphs with exactly three distance eigenvalues.*

Author Contributions: Conceptualization, S.H. and A.K.; methodology, S.H.; software, A.K.; validation, S.H., A.K. and M.J.F.A.; formal analysis, M.J.F.A.; investigation, S.H.; resources, A.K.; data curation, A.K.; writing—original draft preparation, S.H.; writing—review and editing, S.H., M.J.F.A.; visualization, A.K.; supervision, M.J.F.A.; project administration, M.J.F.A.; funding acquisition, A.K. All authors have read and agreed to the published version of the manuscript.

Funding: A. Khan was sponsored by the Key Laboratory of Philosophy and Social Sciences in Guangdong Province of Maritime Silk Road of Guangzhou University, grant No. GD22TWCXGC15, the National Natural Science Foundation of China grant No. 622260-101, and also by the Ministry of Science and Technology of China, grant No. WGXZ2023054L. S. Hayat is supported by UBD Faculty Research Grant with Grant Number UBD/RSCH/1.4/FICBF(b)/2022/053 the National Natural Science Foundation of China (Grant No. 622260-101). M.J.F. Alenazi extends his appreciation to Researcher Supporting Project number (RSPD2024R582), King Saud University, Riyadh, Saudi Arabia.

Data Availability Statement: There are no data associated with this manuscript.

Acknowledgments: We thank the reviewers whose deep insights significantly improved the paper.

Conflicts of Interest: The authors declare no conflicts of interest.

References

1. Brouwer, A.E.; Haemers, W.H. *Spectra of Graphs*; Springer: Berlin/Heidelberg, Germany, 2012.
2. Doob, M. Graphs with a small number of distinct eigenvalues. *Ann. N. Y. Acad. Sci.* **1970**, *175*, 104–110. [CrossRef]
3. Brouwer, A.E.; van Lint, J.H. Strongly regular graphs and partial geometries, In *Enumeration and Design: Papers from the Conference on Combinatorics Held at the University of Waterloo, Waterloo, ON, Canada, 14 June–2 July 1982*; Jackson, D.M., Vanstone, S.A., Eds.; Academic Press: Toronto, ON, Canada, 1984; pp. 85–122.
4. de Caen, D.; van Dam, E.R.; Spence, E. A nonregular analogue of conference graphs. *J. Combin. Theory Ser. A* **1999**, *88*, 194–204. [CrossRef]
5. Bridges, W.G.; Mena, R.A. Multiplicative cones—A family of three eigenvalue graphs. *Aequationes Math.* **1981**, *22*, 208–214. [CrossRef]
6. Muzychuk, M.; Klin, M. On graphs with three eigenvalues. *Discret. Math.* **1998**, *189*, 191–207. [CrossRef]
7. van Dam, E.R. Nonregular graphs with three eigenvalues. *J. Combin. Theory Ser. B* **1998**, *73*, 101–118. [CrossRef]
8. van Dam, E.R. Regular graphs with four eigenvalues. *Linear Algebra Its Appl.* **1995**, *226–228*, 139–162. [CrossRef]
9. van Dam, E.R.; Spence, E. Small regular graphs with four eigenvalues. *Discret. Math.* **1998**, *189*, 233–257. [CrossRef]
10. Huang, X.; Huang, Q. On regular graphs with four distinct eigenvalues. *Linear Algebra Its Appl.* **2017**, *512*, 219–233. [CrossRef]
11. Cioabă, S.M.; Haemers, W.H.; Vermette, J.R.; Wong, W. The graphs with all but two eigenvalues equal to ± 1. *J. Algebr. Comb.* **2015**, *41*, 887–897. [CrossRef]
12. Cioabă, S.M.; Haemers, W.H.; Vermette, J.R. The graphs with all but two eigenvalues equal to -2 or 0. *Des. Codes Cryptogr.* **2017**, *84*, 153–163. [CrossRef]
13. Haemers, W.H.; Omidi, G.R. Universal adjacency matrix with two eigenvalues. *Linear Algebra Its Appl.* **2011**, *435*, 2520–2529. [CrossRef]
14. Chang, L.; Wu, Z.; Ghadimi, N. A new biomass-based hybrid energy system integrated with a flue gas condensation process and energy storage option: An effort to mitigate environmental hazards. *Process Saf. Environ. Prot.* **2023**, *177*, 959–975. [CrossRef]
15. Ghiasi, M.; Niknam, T.; Wang, Z.; Mehrandezh, M.; Dehghani, M.; Ghadimi, N. A comprehensive review of cyber-attacks and defense mechanisms for improving security in smart grid energy systems: Past, present and future. *Electr. Power Syst. Res.* **2023**, *215*, 108975. [CrossRef]
16. Liu, H.; Ghadimi, N. Hybrid convolutional neural network and flexible dwarf Mongoose optimization algorithm for strong kidney stone diagnosis. *Biomed. Signal Process. Control* **2024**, *91*, 106024. [CrossRef]
17. Zhang, J.; Khayatnezhad, M., Ghadimi, N. Optimal model evaluation of the proton exchange membrane fuel cells based on deep learning and modified African vulture optimization algorithm. *Energy Sources A* **2022**, *44*, 287–305. [CrossRef]
18. Hakimi, S.L.; Yau, S.S. Distance matrix of a graph and its realizability. *Quart. Appl. Math.* **1964**, *22*, 305–317. [CrossRef]
19. Graham, R.L.; Pollack, H.O. On the addressing problem for loop switching. *Bell Syst. Tech. J.* **1971**, *50*, 2495–2519. [CrossRef]
20. Graham, R.L.; Lovász, L. Distance matrix polynomials of trees. *Adv. Math.* **1978**, *29*, 60–88. [CrossRef]
21. Merris, R.; The distance spectrum of a tree. *J. Graph Theory* **1990**, *14*, 365–369. [CrossRef]
22. Aouchiche, M.; Hansen, P. Distance spectra of graphs: A survey. *Linear Algebra Its Appl.* **2014**, *458*, 301–386. [CrossRef]
23. Lin, H.; Hong, Y.; Wang, J.; Shu, J. On the distance spectrum of graphs. *Linear Algebra Its Appl.* **2013**, *439*, 1662–1669. [CrossRef]
24. Jin, Y.-L.; Zhang, X.-D. Complete multipartite graphs are determined by their distance spectra. *Linear Algebra Its Appl.* **2014**, *448*, 285–291. [CrossRef]
25. Heysse, K. A construction of distance cospectral graphs. *Linear Algebra Its Appl.* **2017**, *535*, 195–212. [CrossRef]
26. Aouchiche, M.; Hansen, P. Cospectrality of graphs with respect to distance matrices. *Appl. Math. Comput.* **2018**, *325*, 309–321. [CrossRef]
27. Zhang, X. Graphs with few distinct D-eigenvalues determined by their D-spectra. *Linear Algebra Its Appl.* **2021**, *628*, 42–55. [CrossRef]
28. Pokorný, M.; Híc, P.; Stevanović, D.; Miloševic, M. On distance integral graphs. *Discret. Math.* **2015**, *338*, 1784–1792. [CrossRef]
29. Aalipour, G.; Abiad, A.; Berikkyzy, Z.; Cummings, J.; De Silva, J.; Gao, W.; Heysse, K.; Hogben, L.; Kenter, F.H.J.; Lin, J.C.-H.; Tait, M. On the distance spectra of graphs. *Linear Algebra Its Appl.* **2016**, *497*, 66–87. [CrossRef]

30. Zhang, Y.; Lin, H. Graphs with three distinct distance eigenvalues. *Appl. Math. Comput.* **2023**, *445*, 127848. [CrossRef]
31. Atik, F.; Panigrahi, P.; Graphs with few distinct distance eigenvalues irrespective of the diameters. *Electron. J. Linear Algebra* **2016**, *29*, 124–205. [CrossRef]
32. Lu, L.; Huang, Q.; Huang, X. The graphs with exactly two distance eigenvalues different from -1 and -3. *J. Algebr. Comb.* **2017**, *45*, 629–647. [CrossRef]
33. West, D.B. *Introduction to Graph Theory*; Prentice Hall: Upper Saddle River, NJ, USA, 2001; Volume 2.
34. Godsil, C.D.; Royle, G. *Algebraic Graph Theory*; Springer: Berlin/Heidelberg, Germany, 2001.
35. Stevanović, D.; Indulal, G. The distance spectrum and energy of the compositions of regular graphs. *Appl. Math. Lett.* **2009**, *22*, 1136–1140. [CrossRef]
36. Indulal, G. Sharp bounds on the distance spectral radius and the distance energy of graphs. *Linear Algebra Its Appl.* **2009**, *430*, 106–113. [CrossRef]
37. Stein, W.A. Sage Mathematics Software (Version 9.2), The Sage Development Team, 2024. Available online: http://www.sagemath.org (accessed on 5 July 2024).

axioms

MDPI

Article

On Some Properties of the Equilateral Triangles with Vertices Located on the Support Sides of a Triangle

Dorin Andrica [1] and Ovidiu Bagdasar [2,3,*]

[1] Faculty of Mathematics and Computer Science, Babeş-Bolyai University, 400084 Cluj-Napoca, Romania; dandrica@math.ubbcluj.ro
[2] School of Computing, University of Derby, Derby DE22 1GB, UK
[3] Department of Mathematics, Faculty of Exact Sciences, "1 Decembrie 1918" University of Alba Iulia, 510009 Alba Iulia, Romania
* Correspondence: o.bagdasar@derby.ac.uk

Abstract: The possible positions of an equilateral triangle whose vertices are located on the support sides of a generic triangle are studied. Using complex coordinates, we show that there are infinitely many such configurations, then we prove that the centroids of these equilateral triangles are collinear, defining two lines perpendicular to the Euler's line of the original triangle. Finally, we obtain the complex coordinates of the intersection points and study some particular cases.

Keywords: inscribed equilateral triangle; Euler line; complex coordinates

MSC: 51K99; 51M16; 51P99

check for updates

Citation: Andrica, D.; Bagdasar, O. On Some Properties of the Equilateral Triangles with Vertices Located on the Support Sides of a Triangle. *Axioms* **2024**, *13*, 478. https://doi.org/10.3390/axioms13070478

Academic Editors: Cristina Flaut, Dana Piciu and Murat Tosun

Received: 12 May 2024
Revised: 10 July 2024
Accepted: 12 July 2024
Published: 17 July 2024

1. Introduction

Let ΔABC be a triangle in the Euclidean plane, and denote the complex coordinates of the vertices A, B, and C by a, b, and c, respectively. We examine some geometric properties of the equilateral triangles ΔMNP whose vertices are located on the support sides of ΔABC, that is, $M \in BC$, $N \in AC$, and $P \in AB$.

The problem studied in this paper is related to a known general topological property. The polygon $\mathcal{P}$ is said to be inscribed in the Jordan curve γ (not necessarily contained in the interior of γ) if all the vertices of $\mathcal{P}$ are located on γ [1]. While Jordan curves can be complicated, they satisfy certain regular properties in this respect. For example, Meyerson [2] showed that an equilateral triangle can be inscribed in every Jordan curve, as illustrated in Figure 1. Later on, Nielsen proved the following result ([3], [Theorem 1.1]): *Let $J \subset \mathbb{R}^2$ be a Jordan curve and let Δ be any triangle. Then infinitely many triangles similar to Δ can be inscribed in γ.* Similar results exist for Jordan curves in $\mathbb{R}^n$ [4]. Interestingly, Toeplitz's statement from 1911 that *every Jordan curve admits an inscribed square* is still a conjecture in the general case. Just recently, it was proved for convex or piecewise smooth curves, while extensions exist for rectangles, curves, and Klein bottles (see, e.g., [5,6]).

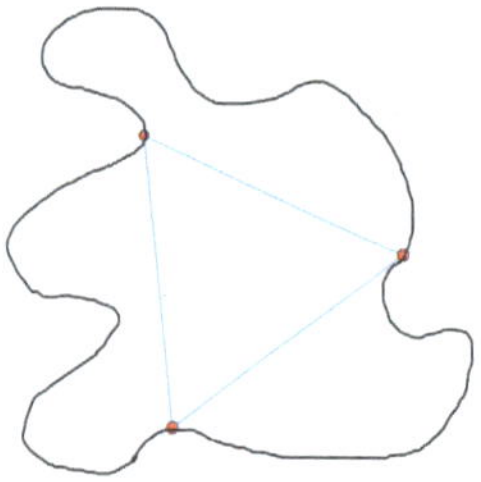

Figure 1. Inscribed equilateral triangle in a Jordan curve.

The triangle is the simplest example of a non-smooth and piecewise linear Jordan curve; while the equilateral triangle appears to be a simple configuration, it can generate very interesting properties and applications [7]. In the sense of the above definition for polygons, an equilateral triangle MNP inscribed in a given triangle ABC can have two vertices on the same side, a situation that does not present much interest from the geometric point of view. This is why in the present paper we consider the case $M \in BC$, $N \in CA$, and $P \in AB$, as seen in Figures 2 and 3 for an acute triangle ABC and in Figure 4 for an obtuse triangle, respectively. Similar to Nielsen's result, there are infinitely many such triangles, generating interesting properties in the triangle geometry [8–11]. Recently, in [12], we studied the equilateral triangles inscribed in the interior of arbitrary triangles, describing them by a single parameter and examining some extremal properties (e.g., the angles for which the minimum inscribed equilateral triangles are obtained). A summary of the results obtained in [12] is presented in Section 2.

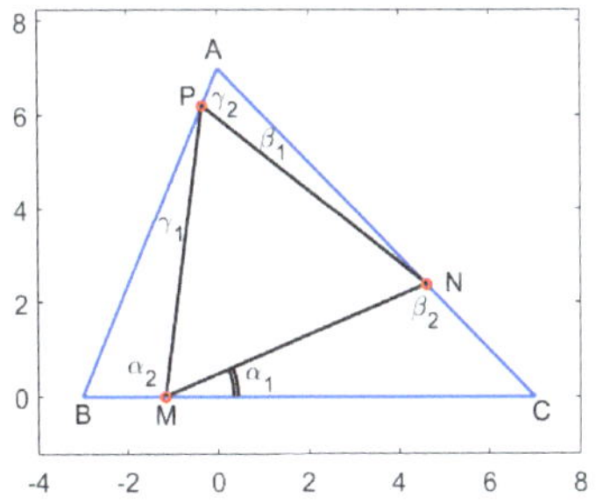

Figure 2. Equilateral triangle MNP inscribed in the triangle ABC. In our example, the initial triangle has the coordinates $A(0,7)$, $B(-3,0)$, $C(7,0)$, for which the angles in degrees measure $\widehat{A} = 68.1986°$, $\widehat{B} = 66.8014°$, and $\widehat{C} = 45°$, while $\widehat{M} = \widehat{N} = \widehat{P} = 60°$.

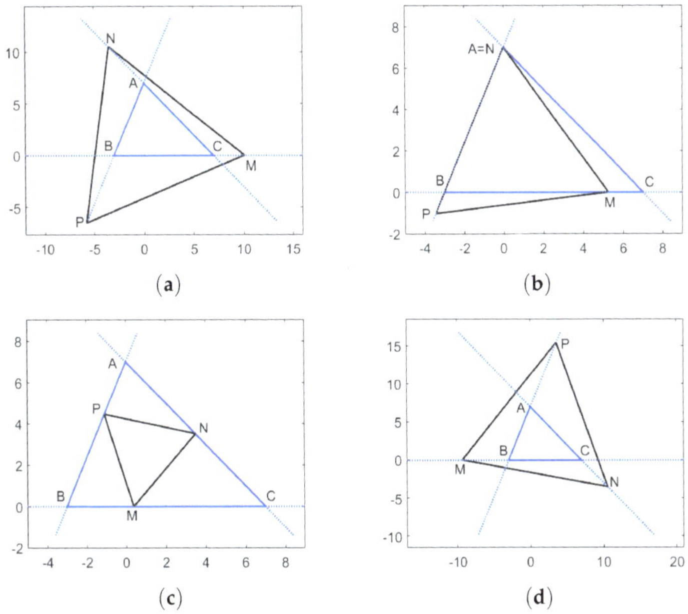

Figure 3. Figures corresponding to equilateral triangles ΔMNP with vertices on the lines BC, CA, and AB. (**a**) $\lambda = -0.5$; (**b**) $\lambda = 0$; (**c**) $\lambda = 0.5$; (**d**) $\lambda = 1.5$.

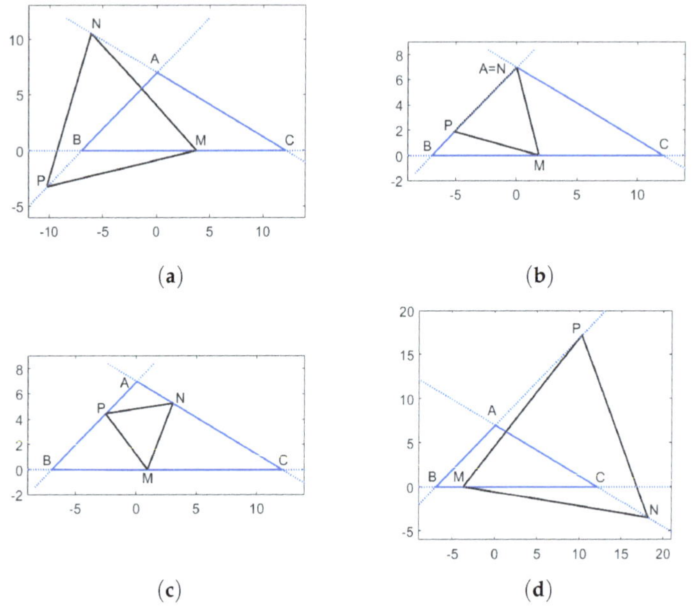

Figure 4. Figures corresponding to equilateral triangles ΔMNP with vertices on the lines BC, CA, and AB of an obtuse triangle ΔABC for (**a**) $\lambda = -0.5$; (**b**) $\lambda = 0$; (**c**) $\lambda = 0.5$; (**d**) $\lambda = 1.5$.

In this paper, we explore the equilateral triangles whose vertices are located on the support lines of the sides of an arbitrary triangle. While this configuration does not represent a Jordan curve, this presents interesting geometric properties. We prove that the centers of these triangles are situated on two parallel lines, which are perpendicular to the Euler's line of the original triangle.

The structure of this paper is as follows. In Section 2, we review some results obtained in [12], devoted to exact formulas for the lengths of the sides of inscribed equilateral triangles as a function of a unique parameter and to extremal properties of the side length. In Section 3, we obtain the complex coordinates of the centroids of the equilateral triangles having vertices on the support lines of a given triangle. The main result concerning the locus of these centroids is presented in Section 4. Furthermore, in Section 5 we prove that the locus of centroids consists of two parallel lines perpendicular to the Euler's line of the original triangle. Alternative derivations and particular cases are provided in Section 6, while conclusions are formulated in Section 7.

The adoption of complex coordinates instead of Cartesian coordinates considerably simplifies the computations.

2. Inscribed Equilateral Triangles

The particular case when the inscribed equilateral triangle MNP is nested, i.e., $M \in (BC)$, $N \in (CA)$, and $P \in (AB)$, was studied in [12] by a trigonometric approach. Related investigations by other means can be consulted in [8,10,11,13].

Let ΔABC be a triangle in the Euclidean plane, and denote by A, B, and C the measures of the angles from vertices A, B, and C, respectively. Without loss of generality, one may assume that $A \geq B \geq C$; therefore, $C \leq 60^\circ \leq A$. In the notation of Figure 2, one obtains the system

$$\begin{cases} \alpha_1 + \alpha_2 = \frac{2\pi}{3} \\ \beta_1 + \beta_2 = \frac{2\pi}{3} \\ \gamma_1 + \gamma_2 = \frac{2\pi}{3} \\ \beta_1 + \gamma_2 = \pi - A \\ \gamma_1 + \alpha_2 = \pi - B \\ \alpha_1 + \beta_2 = \pi - C. \end{cases} \tag{1}$$

The system can be written in matrix form as

$$\begin{pmatrix} 1 & 1 & 0 & 0 & 0 & 0 \\ 0 & 0 & 1 & 1 & 0 & 0 \\ 0 & 0 & 0 & 0 & 1 & 1 \\ 0 & 0 & 0 & 1 & 1 & 0 \\ 1 & 0 & 0 & 0 & 0 & 1 \\ 0 & 1 & 1 & 0 & 0 & 0 \end{pmatrix} \begin{pmatrix} \alpha_1 \\ \alpha_2 \\ \beta_1 \\ \beta_2 \\ \gamma_1 \\ \gamma_2 \end{pmatrix} = \begin{pmatrix} \frac{2\pi}{3} \\ \frac{2\pi}{3} \\ \frac{2\pi}{3} \\ \pi - A \\ \pi - B \\ \pi - C \end{pmatrix}. \tag{2}$$

By simple calculation, one can show that the system (2) is compatible and it has infinitely many solutions. Moreover, since the rank of the matrix is 5, the solutions are fully determined by a single variable chosen as the parameter. From the first three equations, one can substitute α_2, β_2, and γ_2 into the last three and obtain the reduced system

$$\begin{cases} \gamma_1 - \beta_1 = \frac{\pi}{3} - A \\ \alpha_1 - \gamma_1 = \frac{\pi}{3} - B \\ \beta_1 - \alpha_1 = \frac{\pi}{3} - C, \end{cases} \tag{3}$$

which can be written in matrix form as

$$\begin{pmatrix} 0 & -1 & 1 \\ 1 & 0 & -1 \\ -1 & 1 & 0 \end{pmatrix} \begin{pmatrix} \alpha_1 \\ \beta_1 \\ \gamma_1 \end{pmatrix} = \begin{pmatrix} \frac{\pi}{3} - A \\ \frac{\pi}{3} - B \\ \frac{\pi}{3} - C \end{pmatrix}. \tag{4}$$

Fixing the parameter $\alpha_1 = \alpha \in [0, 120^\circ] = m(\angle NMC)$, the system (3) has the solution

$$\beta_1 = \alpha + C - 60^\circ, \quad \gamma_1 = \alpha + 60^\circ - B.$$

From the conditions $0 \le \beta_1, \gamma_1 \le 120^\circ$ one obtains $\alpha + 60^\circ - B \le 120^\circ$. The geometric constraints illustrated in Figure 2

$$60^\circ - C \le \alpha \le \min\{60^\circ + B, 120^\circ\}, \tag{5}$$

show that there are infinitely many possible configurations.

In our recent paper [12], we obtained the following explicit formula for the side length of the inscribed equilateral triangle as a function of the parameter α:

$$\begin{aligned} l(\alpha) &= \frac{2R \cdot \sin A \cdot \sin B \cdot \sin C}{\sin C \cdot \sin(\alpha + 60^\circ - B) + \sin B \cdot \sin(\alpha + C)} \\ &= \frac{2R \cdot \sin A \cdot \sin B \cdot \sin C}{\sin A \cdot \sin\alpha + \sin C \cdot \sin(60^\circ + B - \alpha)} \\ &= \frac{2R \cdot \sin A \cdot \sin B \cdot \sin C}{\sin B \cdot \sin(\alpha + C - 60^\circ) + \sin A \cdot \sin(\alpha + 60^\circ)}, \end{aligned}$$

where R is the circumradius of triangle ABC. Denote $K[ABC]$ as the area of triangle ABC, and from the relation $K[ABC] = \frac{AB \cdot BC \cdot CA}{4R^2}$ and the Law of Sines, one obtains

$$l(\alpha) = \frac{2K[ABC]}{AB \cdot \sin(\alpha + 60^\circ - B) + AC \cdot \sin(\alpha + C)} \tag{6}$$
$$= \frac{2K[ABC]}{BC \cdot \sin\alpha + AB \cdot \sin(60^\circ + B - \alpha)}$$
$$= \frac{2K[ABC]}{AC \cdot \sin(\alpha + C - 60^\circ) + BC \cdot \sin(\alpha + 60^\circ)}.$$

Furthermore, we showed in [12] that the minimal triangle MNP is obtained for

$$\alpha^* = \arctan \frac{\frac{\sqrt{3}}{2}\sin B \cdot \sin C + \frac{1}{2}\cos B \sin C + \sin B \cos C}{\frac{\sqrt{3}}{2}\cos B \sin C + \frac{1}{2}\sin B \sin C}.$$

Numerous illustrative examples are also provided in [12].

3. Coordinates of the Centroids of the Triangle MNP

The complex coordinates of the vertices of ΔMNP are denoted by m, n, and p. As seen in Figure 3 for an acute triangle and in Figure 4 for an obtuse triangle, such triangles can be constructed starting from the points N on AC and P on the side AB, with the condition that the third point M on BC is obtained by a rotation of angle $\pi/3$, which in complex numbers can be performed by multiplying with (see, for example, [14]):

$$\omega = \cos\frac{\pi}{3} + i\sin\frac{\pi}{3} = \frac{1}{2} + \frac{\sqrt{3}}{2}i.$$

Clearly, if $N \in AC$ and $P \in AB$, there exist the scalars λ and μ such that

$$n = a + \lambda(c - a), \quad p = a + \mu(b - a), \quad \lambda, \mu \in \mathbb{R}.$$

In this notation, note that, as seen in Figure 3, we have

1. If $\lambda < 0$, then $A \in (NC)$;
2. If $\lambda = 0$, then $A = N$;
3. If $0 < \lambda < 1$, then $N \in (AC)$ (the case presented in Section 2);
4. If $\lambda = 1$, then $N = C$;
5. If $\lambda > 1$, then $C \in (AN)$.

Then, the point M of the equilateral triangle MNP is obtained by rotating segment (PN) around point N through an angle of $\pi/3$, clockwise or anticlockwise.

3.1. First Orientation of Triangle MNP: Anticlockwise Rotation

For anticlockwise rotation, we obtain the complex coordinate

$$\begin{aligned} m &= n + (p - n)\omega \\ &= [(1-\mu)a + \mu b]\omega + [(1-\lambda)a + \lambda c]\overline{\omega} \\ &= a + \mu\omega(b - a) + \lambda\overline{\omega}(c - a) = c + s(b - c), \end{aligned}$$

where we use the relation $\omega + \overline{\omega} = 1$. Since $M \in (BC)$, one must have $s \in \mathbb{R}$, hence $s = \overline{s}$. From here it follows that

$$\begin{aligned} s &= \frac{a - c + \mu\omega(b - a) + \lambda\overline{\omega}(c - a)}{b - c} \\ &= \frac{\overline{a} - \overline{c} + \mu\overline{\omega}\left(\overline{b} - \overline{a}\right) + \lambda\omega(\overline{c} - \overline{a})}{\overline{b} - \overline{c}} = \overline{s}. \end{aligned}$$

This condition can be written as

$$\left[(a-c)+\mu\omega(b-a)+\lambda\overline{\omega}(c-a)\right]\left(\overline{b}-\overline{c}\right)=\left[(\overline{a}-\overline{c})+\mu\overline{\omega}\left(\overline{b}-\overline{a}\right)+\lambda\omega(\overline{c}-\overline{a})\right](b-c),$$

which reduces to

$$\mu=\frac{y}{x}\lambda+\frac{z}{x}=k\lambda+l, \tag{7}$$

where x, y, and z are given by

$$\begin{aligned} x &= \omega(b-a)\left(\overline{b}-\overline{c}\right)-\overline{\omega}\left(\overline{b}-\overline{a}\right)(b-c)\in i\cdot\mathbb{R}, \\ y &= \omega(b-c)(\overline{c}-\overline{a})-\overline{\omega}\left(\overline{b}-\overline{c}\right)(c-a)\in i\cdot\mathbb{R}, \\ z &= (b-c)(\overline{a}-\overline{c})-\left(\overline{b}-\overline{c}\right)(a-c)\in i\cdot\mathbb{R}. \end{aligned} \tag{8}$$

Clearly, this shows that the coordinates m, n, p depend linearly on $\lambda\in\mathbb{R}$, as

$$\begin{aligned} n(\lambda) &= a+\lambda(c-a), \\ p(\lambda) &= a+(k\lambda+l)(b-a), \\ m(\lambda) &= a+(k\lambda+l)\omega(b-a)+\lambda\overline{\omega}(c-a), \quad \lambda\in\mathbb{R}, \end{aligned}$$

where the values k and l are real numbers obtained from (7) and (8), as

$$\begin{aligned} k &= \frac{\omega(b-c)(\overline{c}-\overline{a})-\overline{\omega}\left(\overline{b}-\overline{c}\right)(c-a)}{\omega(b-a)\left(\overline{b}-\overline{c}\right)-\overline{\omega}\left(\overline{b}-\overline{a}\right)(b-c)}, \\ l &= \frac{(b-c)(\overline{a}-\overline{c})-\left(\overline{b}-\overline{c}\right)(a-c)}{\omega(b-a)\left(\overline{b}-\overline{c}\right)-\overline{\omega}\left(\overline{b}-\overline{a}\right)(b-c)}, \end{aligned} \tag{9}$$

which are ratios of purely imaginary numbers.

3.2. Second Orientation of Triangle MNP: Clockwise Rotation

An alternative configuration is obtained when the rotation of P around N is taken with an angle of 60° clockwise. Similar to Section 3.1, we obtain

$$\begin{aligned} m_2 &= n+(p_2-n)\overline{\omega} \\ &= [(1-\mu)a+\mu b]\overline{\omega}+[(1-\lambda)a+\lambda c]\omega \\ &= a+\mu\overline{\omega}(b-a)+\lambda\omega(c-a)=c+s(b-c), \end{aligned}$$

where we use the fact that $\omega+\overline{\omega}=1$. Imposing the condition $s=\overline{s}$, for $\lambda\in\mathbb{R}$, the coordinates of the vertices of ΔMNP can be written explicitly

$$\begin{aligned} n(\lambda) &= a+\lambda(c-a), \\ p_2(\lambda) &= a+(k_2\lambda+l_2)(b-a), \\ m_2(\lambda) &= a+(k_2\lambda+l_2)\overline{\omega}(b-a)+\lambda\omega(c-a). \end{aligned} \tag{10}$$

The coefficients are related through the formula

$$\mu_2=\frac{y_2}{x_2}\lambda+\frac{z_2}{x_2}=k_2\lambda+l_2, \tag{11}$$

where x_2, y_2, and z_2 are obtained from

$$x_2 = \overline{\omega}(b-a)\left(\overline{b}-\overline{c}\right) - \omega\left(\overline{b}-\overline{a}\right)(b-c) \in i \cdot \mathbb{R}, \tag{12}$$
$$y_2 = \overline{\omega}(b-c)(\overline{c}-\overline{a}) - \omega\left(\overline{b}-\overline{c}\right)(c-a) \in i \cdot \mathbb{R},$$
$$z_2 = (b-c)(\overline{a}-\overline{c}) - \left(\overline{b}-\overline{c}\right)(a-c) = z.$$

Using (11) and (12), the values k_2 and l_2 are the real numbers given by

$$k_2 = \frac{\overline{\omega}(b-c)(\overline{c}-\overline{a}) - \omega\left(\overline{b}-\overline{c}\right)(c-a)}{\overline{\omega}(b-a)\left(\overline{b}-\overline{c}\right) - \omega\left(\overline{b}-\overline{a}\right)(b-c)}, \tag{13}$$
$$l_2 = \frac{(b-c)(\overline{a}-\overline{c}) - \left(\overline{b}-\overline{c}\right)(a-c)}{\overline{\omega}(b-a)\left(\overline{b}-\overline{c}\right) - \omega\left(\overline{b}-\overline{a}\right)(b-c)}.$$

These formulas allow a convenient calculation for the coordinates of the centroids. For a given point $N \in AC$, the possible equilateral triangles are shown in Figure 5.

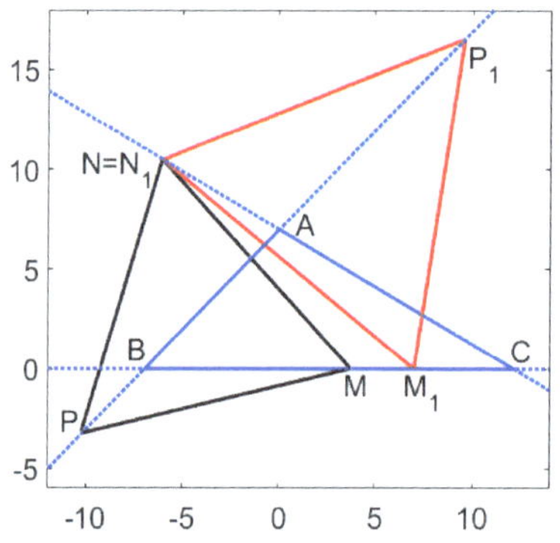

Figure 5. Inscribed equilateral triangles with distinct orientations.

4. The Collinearity of the Centroids of Triangle MNP

In this section, we show that for each orientation of the triangles MNP (clockwise and anticlockwise), the corresponding centroids are collinear.

4.1. The First Line of Centroids

As a function of λ, the coordinate of the centroid of triangle ΔMNP is given by

$$\begin{aligned} g_1(\lambda) &= \frac{m+n+p}{3} \\ &= \frac{[a+\mu\omega(b-a)+\lambda\overline{\omega}(c-a)]+[a+\lambda(c-a)]+[a+\mu(b-a)]}{3} \\ &= a+\frac{\mu(1+\omega)(b-a)+\lambda(1+\overline{\omega})(c-a)}{3} \\ &= [k(1+\omega)(b-a)+(1+\overline{\omega})(c-a)]\cdot\frac{\lambda}{3}+\frac{l(1+\omega)(b-a)}{3}+a, \end{aligned} \tag{14}$$

where we use (7) for k and l. By this formula, it follows that the centroids of the equilateral triangles ΔMNP situated on the support lines BC, CA, and AB, are collinear, as depicted in Figures 6 and 7, for a specified range of values λ.

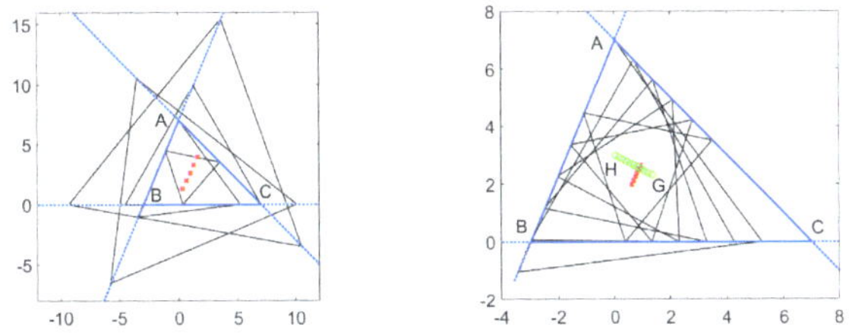

(a) (b)

Figure 6. Equilateral triangles ΔMNP with the vertices on the lines BC, CA, and AB, with centroids represented by red "x" symbols. (**a**) $\lambda = -0.5, 0, 0.5, 1, 1.5$; (**b**) $\lambda = 0, 0.1, 0.2, 0.3, 0.4, 0.5$. Also plotted are the centroid G and orthocenter H of ΔABC.

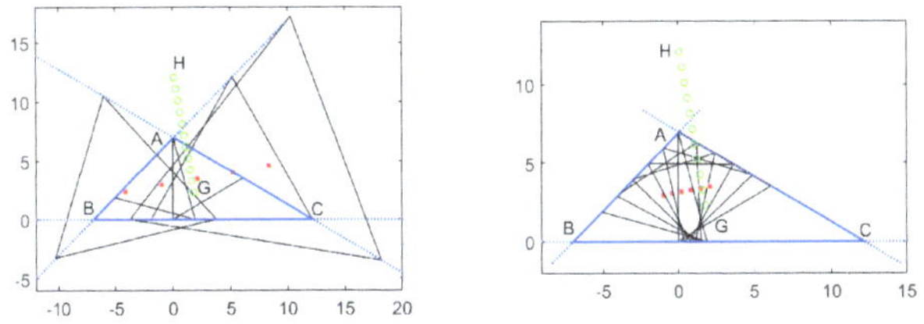

(a) (b)

Figure 7. Equilateral triangles ΔMNP with the vertices on the lines BC, CA, and AB, with centroids represented by red "x" symbols. (**a**) $\lambda = -0.5, 0, 0.5, 1, 1.5$; (**b**) $\lambda = 0, 0.1, 0.2, 0.3, 0.4, 0.5$. Also plotted are the centroid G and orthocenter H of ΔABC.

4.2. The Second Line of Centroids

For the second line, using (10), we have the formula

$$\begin{aligned} g_2(\lambda) &= \frac{m_2 + n + p_2}{3} \\ &= \frac{[a + \mu_2\overline{\omega}(b-a) + \lambda\omega(c-a)] + [a + \lambda(c-a)] + [a + \mu_2(b-a)]}{3} \\ &= a + \frac{\mu_2(1+\overline{\omega})(b-a) + \lambda(1+\omega)(c-a)}{3} \\ &= [k_2(1+\overline{\omega})(b-a) + (1+\omega)(c-a)] \cdot \frac{\lambda}{3} + \frac{l_2(1+\overline{\omega})(b-a)}{3} + a, \end{aligned} \tag{15}$$

where we use (11) and the coefficients k_2 and l_2 given by (13).

5. Perpendicularity and Intersection with Euler's Line

The following auxiliary result is useful in proving the main results of this section.

Lemma 1. *Let u_1, u_2, v_1, and v_2 be complex numbers and consider the lines (α_1) and (α_2) given in parametric form by $z = u_1 t + v_1$, $t \in \mathbb{R}$ and $\zeta = u_2 s + v_2$, $s \in \mathbb{R}$, respectively. The following properties hold:*

(1) If $\overline{u_1}u_2 + u_1\overline{u_2} = 0$, then (α_1) and (α_2) are perpendicular.
(2) If $\overline{u_1}u_2 - u_1\overline{u_2} \neq 0$, then (α_1) and (α_2) intersect at the point

$$Z = \frac{u_1(u_2\overline{v_2} - \overline{u_2}v_2) - u_2(u_1\overline{v_1} - \overline{u_1}v_1)}{\overline{u_1}u_2 - u_1\overline{u_2}}. \tag{16}$$

Proof. (1) Let us consider the points $z' = u_1 t_1 + v_1$ and $z'' = u_1 t_2 + v_1$ on (α_1) and the points $\zeta' = u_2 s_1 + v_2$ and $\zeta'' = u_2 s_2 + v_2$ on (α_2). The lines are perpendicular if and only if

$$\frac{\zeta'' - \zeta'}{z'' - z'} = \frac{(u_2 s_2 + v_2) - (u_2 s_1 + v_2)}{(u_1 t_2 + v_1) - (u_1 t_1 + v_1)} = \frac{u_2(s_2 - s_1)}{u_1(t_2 - t_1)} \in i \cdot \mathbb{R},$$

which reduces to $\frac{u_2}{u_1} \in i \cdot \mathbb{R}$. Therefore,

$$0 = \frac{u_2}{u_1} + \overline{\left(\frac{u_2}{u_1}\right)} = \frac{u_2}{u_1} + \frac{\overline{u_2}}{\overline{u_1}} = \frac{\overline{u_1} u_2 + u_1 \overline{u_2}}{|u_1|^2} = 0,$$

from where the conclusion follows.

(2) If the point of coordinate Z is located on both lines, it means that there exist real numbers t and s such that $Z = u_1 t + v_1 = u_2 s + v_2$. By conjugation, one obtains $\overline{u_1} t + \overline{v_1} = \overline{u_2} s + \overline{v_2}$, from where we can solve for t and s the system

$$\begin{cases} u_2 s - u_1 t = v_1 - v_2 \\ \overline{u_2} s - \overline{u_1} t = \overline{v_1} - \overline{v_2}. \end{cases} \tag{17}$$

The system (17) has the solution

$$s = \frac{\overline{u_1}(v_1 - v_2) - u_1(\overline{v_1} - \overline{v_2})}{(\overline{u_1} u_2 - u_1 \overline{u_2})}, \quad t = \frac{\overline{u_2}(v_1 - v_2) - u_2(\overline{v_1} - \overline{v_2})}{(\overline{u_1} u_2 - u_1 \overline{u_2})},$$

and by substitution, one obtains

$$Z = u_1 t + v_1 = u_1 \cdot \frac{\overline{u_2}(v_1 - v_2) - u_2(\overline{v_1} - \overline{v_2})}{(\overline{u_1} u_2 - u_1 \overline{u_2})} + v_1,$$

which after simplifications recovers formula (16). □

A special case is when (α_2) passes through the origin.

Recall that in every triangle ABC, the circumcenter O, the centroid G, and the orthocenter H are collinear on the Euler line of the triangle. Without loss of generality, we can choose the circumcenter O of ΔABC as the origin of the complex plane. Under this assumption, we obtain the coordinates $o = 0$, $g = \frac{a+b+c}{3}$, and $h = a + b + c$; hence, Euler's line is defined by the formula $u(a + b + c)$, $u \in \mathbb{R}$. Furthermore, the circumradius of the triangle ABC can be set to 1, in which case we have $|a| = |b| = |c| = 1$, or

$$\overline{a} = \frac{1}{a}, \quad \overline{b} = \frac{1}{b}, \quad \overline{c} = \frac{1}{c}.$$

5.1. The First Line of Centroids

For the first centroid line, by substituting, we obtain

$$\begin{aligned}
x &= \omega(b - a)\left(\frac{1}{b} - \frac{1}{c}\right) - \overline{\omega}\left(\frac{1}{b} - \frac{1}{a}\right)(b - c) \\
&= \frac{1}{abc}(b - a)(c - b)(\omega a - \overline{\omega} c) \\
y &= \omega(b - c)\left(\frac{1}{c} - \frac{1}{a}\right) - \overline{\omega}\left(\frac{1}{b} - \frac{1}{c}\right)(c - a) \\
&= \frac{1}{abc}(b - c)(a - c)(\omega b - \overline{\omega} a) = \frac{1}{abc}(c - b)(c - a)(\omega b - \overline{\omega} a) \\
z &= (b - c)\left(\frac{1}{a} - \frac{1}{c}\right) - \left(\frac{1}{b} - \frac{1}{c}\right)(a - c) \\
&= \frac{1}{abc}(b - a)(b - c)(c - a) = \frac{1}{abc}(b - a)(c - b)(a - c).
\end{aligned}$$

Substituting in (7), we obtain

$$k = \frac{y}{x} = \frac{c-a}{b-a} \cdot \frac{\omega b - \overline{\omega} a}{\omega a - \overline{\omega} c}, \tag{18}$$

$$l = \frac{z}{x} = \frac{a-c}{\omega a - \overline{\omega} c}. \tag{19}$$

Therefore, the first line of centroids depicted in Figure 8 has the equation

$$\begin{aligned} g_1(\lambda) &= \frac{c-a}{\omega a - \overline{\omega} c} \cdot (a+b+c) \cdot \sqrt{3} i \cdot \frac{\lambda}{3} + \frac{a-c}{\omega a - \overline{\omega} c} \cdot \frac{(1+\omega)(b-a)}{3} + a \\ &= -(a+b+c) \cdot \lambda \sqrt{3} i \cdot \frac{l}{3} + \frac{l(1+\omega)(b-a)}{3} + a = u_1 \lambda + v_1, \end{aligned} \tag{20}$$

while Euler's line is given by

$$E(s) = (a+b+c)s = u_2 s + v_2. \tag{21}$$

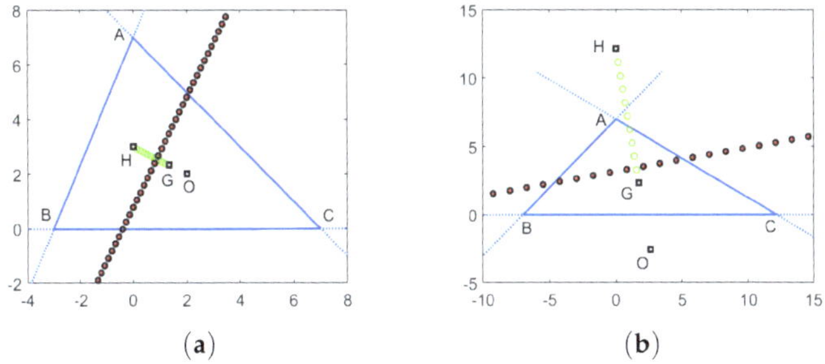

Figure 8. First line of centroids $g_1(\lambda)$ given by (14), represented by red "x" symbols. (**a**) Acute triangle; (**b**) obtuse triangle. Also plotted are the centroid G, orthocenter H, and centre O of ΔABC.

By Formulas (20) and (21) for the line of centroids and Euler's line, we obtain

$$\begin{aligned} u_1 &= -(a+b+c) \cdot \sqrt{3} i \cdot \frac{l}{3}, \\ v_1 &= \frac{l(1+\omega)(b-a)}{3} + a, \\ u_2 &= a+b+c, \\ v_2 &= 0, \end{aligned}$$

where $l \in \mathbb{R}$ is given by (19). First, notice that

$$u_1 = -\frac{\sqrt{3} l}{3} i \cdot u_2, \quad \overline{u_1} = \frac{\sqrt{3} l}{3} i \cdot \overline{u_2}. \tag{22}$$

By Lemma 1, we obtain the following result.

Theorem 1. (1) *The first line of centroids $g_1(\lambda)$ is perpendicular to Euler's line.*

(2) *The intersection point between the line $g_1(\lambda)$, $\lambda \in \mathbb{R}$ and Euler's line is*

$$Z = \Re\left(\frac{v_1}{u_2}\right) \cdot u_2,$$

where $\Re(z)$ denotes the real part of the complex number z.

Proof. (1) Substituting (22) in Lemma 1 (1), one obtains

$$\overline{u_1}u_2 + u_1\overline{u_2} = \frac{\sqrt{3}l}{3}i \cdot \overline{u_2} \cdot u_2 + \left(-\frac{\sqrt{3}l}{3}i \cdot u_2\overline{u_2}\right) = 0.$$

(2) Since $v_2 = 0$, the formula (16) reduces to

$$Z = -\frac{u_2(u_1\overline{v_1} - \overline{u_1}v_1)}{(\overline{u_1}u_2 - u_1\overline{u_2})}. \tag{23}$$

Therefore, we obtain

$$\overline{u_1}u_2 - u_1\overline{u_2} = \frac{2\sqrt{3}l}{3}i \cdot u_2 \cdot \overline{u_2} = \frac{2\sqrt{3}l}{3}i \cdot |u_2|^2. \tag{24}$$

After simplifications, one obtains

$$Z = u_2 \cdot \frac{\frac{\overline{v_1}}{\overline{u_2}} + \frac{v_1}{u_2}}{2} = \Re\left[\frac{v_1}{u_2}\right] \cdot u_2. \tag{25}$$

This ends the proof. □

5.2. The Second Line of Centroids

For the second centroid line, similar calculations show that

$$\begin{aligned}
x_2 &= \frac{1}{abc}(b-a)(c-b)(\overline{\omega}a - \omega c), \\
y_2 &= \frac{1}{abc}(c-b)(c-a)(\overline{\omega}b - \omega a), \\
z_2 = z &= \frac{1}{abc}(b-a)(c-b)(a-c),
\end{aligned}$$

from where, through (11), we have

$$k_2 = \frac{y_2}{x_2} = \frac{c-a}{b-a} \cdot \frac{\overline{\omega}b - \omega a}{\overline{\omega}a - \omega c}, \tag{26}$$

$$l_2 = \frac{z_2}{x_2} = \frac{a-c}{\overline{\omega}a - \omega c}. \tag{27}$$

The second line of centroids has the equation

$$\begin{aligned}
g_2(\lambda) &= \frac{c-a}{\overline{\omega}a - \omega c} \cdot (a+b+c) \cdot \sqrt{3}i \cdot \frac{\lambda}{3} + \frac{a-c}{\overline{\omega}a - \omega c} \cdot \frac{(1+\overline{\omega})(b-a)}{3} + a \\
&= -(a+b+c) \cdot \lambda\sqrt{3}i \cdot \frac{l_2}{3} + \frac{l_2(1+\overline{\omega})(b-a)}{3} + a = u_3\lambda + v_3,
\end{aligned} \tag{28}$$

where the coefficients are

$$u_3 = -(a+b+c) \cdot \sqrt{3}i \cdot \frac{l_2}{3}, \quad v_3 = \frac{l_2(1+\overline{\omega})(b-a)}{3} + a,$$

where $l_2 \in \mathbb{R}$ is given by (27). Again, one may notice that

$$u_3 = -\frac{\sqrt{3}l_2}{3}i \cdot u_2, \quad \overline{u_3} = \frac{\sqrt{3}l_2}{3}i \cdot \overline{u_2}, \tag{29}$$

so by Lemma 1, the perpendicularity follows from the relation

$$\overline{u_3}u_2 + u_3\overline{u_2} = \frac{\sqrt{3}l_2}{3}i \cdot \overline{u_2} \cdot u_2 + \left(-\frac{\sqrt{3}l_2}{3}i \cdot u_2\overline{u_2}\right) = 0.$$

The two parallel lines of centroids $g_1(\lambda)$ and $g_2(\lambda)$ are shown in Figure 9.

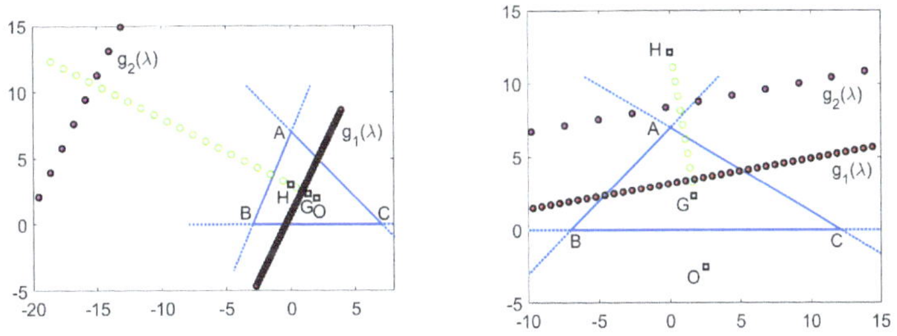

Figure 9. First and second lines of centroids $g_1(\lambda)$ and $g_2(\lambda)$ given by (14) and (28), respectively, represented by red "x" symbols. (**a**) Acute triangle; (**b**) obtuse triangle. Also plotted are the centroid G, orthocenter H, and centre O of ΔABC.

The coordinates of this intersection point are given by

$$Z_2 = u_2 \cdot \frac{\frac{\overline{v_3}}{\overline{u_2}} + \frac{v_3}{u_2}}{2} = \Re\left(\frac{v_3}{u_2}\right) \cdot u_2. \tag{30}$$

We have an analogous result to Theorem 1, for the second line of centroids.

Theorem 2. (1) *The second line of centroids $g_2(\lambda)$ is perpendicular to Euler's line.*
(2) *The intersection point between the line $g_2(\lambda)$, $\lambda \in \mathbb{R}$ and Euler's line is*

$$Z_2 = \Re\left(\frac{v_3}{u_2}\right) \cdot u_2.$$

6. Alternative Approaches and Particular Examples

This section presents alternative proofs of the results.

6.1. Perpendicularity to Euler's Line

For a direct proof of the result in Theorem 1 (1), without using Lemma 1, it suffices to show that for $\lambda_1 \neq \lambda_2$ we obtain

$$\frac{g_1(\lambda_1) - g_1(\lambda_2)}{a+b+c} \in i \cdot \mathbb{R}.$$

Indeed, by formula (14), one obtains

$$g_1(\lambda_1) - g_1(\lambda_2) = [k(1+\omega)(b-a) + (1+\overline{\omega})(c-a)] \cdot \frac{\lambda_1 - \lambda_2}{3}.$$

Furthermore, one can write

$$k(1+\omega)(b-a)+(1+\overline{\omega})(c-a)=(c-a)\cdot\left[\frac{\omega b-\overline{\omega}a}{\omega a-\overline{\omega}c}(1+\omega)+(1+\overline{\omega})\right]$$
$$=\frac{c-a}{\omega a-\overline{\omega}c}\cdot[(\omega b-\overline{\omega}a)(1+\omega)+(\omega a-\overline{\omega}c)(1+\overline{\omega})]$$
$$=\frac{c-a}{\omega a-\overline{\omega}c}\cdot\left[(\omega-\overline{\omega})a+\left(\omega+\omega^2\right)b+\left(-\overline{\omega}-\overline{\omega}^2\right)c\right]$$
$$=\frac{c-a}{\omega a-\overline{\omega}c}\cdot(a+b+c)\cdot\sqrt{3}i,$$

where for $\omega=\frac{1}{2}+\frac{\sqrt{3}}{2}i$, we use the identities

$$\omega-\overline{\omega}=\omega+\omega^2=-\overline{\omega}-\overline{\omega}^2=\sqrt{3}i.$$

Clearly, this shows that

$$\frac{g_1(\lambda_1)-g_1(\lambda_2)}{a+b+c}=\frac{\lambda_1-\lambda_2}{3}\cdot\frac{c-a}{\omega a-\overline{\omega}c}\cdot\sqrt{3}i,$$

which is purely imaginary since

$$\frac{\overline{c}-\overline{a}}{\overline{\omega}\overline{a}-\omega\overline{c}}=\frac{\frac{1}{c}-\frac{1}{a}}{\frac{\overline{\omega}}{a}-\frac{\omega}{c}}=\frac{c-a}{\omega a-\overline{\omega}c}.$$

This ends the proof. A proof based on trilinear coordinates was provided in [8]. Similarly, one can prove the result for the second line of centroids.

6.2. Intersection Points

From the condition $s\in\mathbb{R}$ (i.e., $s=\overline{s}$), we obtain

$$s=\frac{g_1(\lambda)}{a+b+c}=\frac{\overline{g_1(\lambda)}}{\overline{a}+\overline{b}+\overline{c}}=\overline{s}.$$

This condition reduces to

$$\frac{l(1+\omega)(b-a)+3a}{a+b+c}-\frac{l(1+\overline{\omega})\left(\overline{b}-\overline{a}\right)+3\overline{a}}{\overline{a}+\overline{b}+\overline{c}}=2l\sqrt{3}i\cdot\lambda,$$

which gives (using that $l\in\mathbb{R}$)

$$[l(1+\omega)(b-a)+3a]\left(\overline{a}+\overline{b}+\overline{c}\right)-\left[l(1+\overline{\omega})\left(\overline{b}-\overline{a}\right)+3\overline{a}\right](a+b+c)$$
$$=2l\mid a+b+c\mid^2\sqrt{3}i\cdot\lambda,$$

or

$$2\cdot\lambda\sqrt{3}i=\frac{(1+\omega)(b-a)}{a+b+c}-\frac{(1+\overline{\omega})\left(\overline{b}-\overline{a}\right)}{\overline{a}+\overline{b}+\overline{c}}+\frac{1}{l}\left[\frac{3a}{a+b+c}-\frac{3\overline{a}}{\overline{a}+\overline{b}+\overline{c}}\right].$$

By substituting $\lambda\sqrt{3}i$ in (20) and dividing by $a+b+c$, one obtains

$$s=\Re\left[\frac{l(1+\omega)(b-a)+3a}{3(a+b+c)}\right],$$

from where we deduce the following result.

Theorem 3. *The intersection point between the first line of centroids $g_1(\lambda)$, $\lambda \in \mathbb{R}$ and Euler's line of $\triangle ABC$ has the complex coordinates*

$$Z = \Re\left[\frac{l(1+\omega)(b-a)+3a}{3(a+b+c)}\right] \cdot (a+b+c)$$

$$= \Re\left[\frac{\frac{a-c}{\omega a - \overline{\omega} c}(1+\omega)(b-a)+3a}{3(a+b+c)}\right] \cdot (a+b+c).$$

Similarly, one can prove the coordinate of the intersection between the second line of centroids $g_2(\lambda)$, $\lambda \in \mathbb{R}$ and Euler's line of $\triangle ABC$ as

$$Z_2 = \Re\left[\frac{l_2(1+\overline{\omega})(b-a)+3a}{3(a+b+c)}\right] \cdot (a+b+c)$$

$$= \Re\left[\frac{\frac{a-c}{\overline{\omega} a - \omega c}(1+\overline{\omega})(b-a)+3a}{3(a+b+c)}\right] \cdot (a+b+c).$$

6.3. Particular Examples and Formulas

In this section, we derive some particular formulas for the lines of centroids and their intersection with Euler's line obtained for $a = 0$. From (14), we obtain

$$g_1(\lambda) = \frac{m+n+p}{3} = [k(1+\omega)b + (1+\overline{\omega})c] \cdot \frac{\lambda}{3} + \frac{l(1+\omega)b}{3}, \tag{31}$$

where by (9) and using $\omega - \overline{\omega} = \sqrt{3}i$, the values k and l are given by

$$k = \frac{\omega(b-c)\overline{c} - \overline{\omega}(\overline{b}-\overline{c})c}{\omega b(\overline{b}-\overline{c}) - \overline{\omega}\overline{b}(b-c)} = \frac{-|c|^2\sqrt{3}i + (\omega b\overline{c} - \overline{\omega}\overline{b}c)}{|b|^2\sqrt{3}i - (\omega b\overline{c} - \overline{\omega}\overline{b}c)}, \tag{32}$$

$$l = \frac{c(\overline{b}-\overline{c}) - \overline{c}(b-c)}{\omega b(\overline{b}-\overline{c}) - \overline{\omega}\overline{b}(b-c)} = \frac{c\overline{b} - b\overline{c}}{|b|^2\sqrt{3}i - (\omega b\overline{c} - \overline{\omega}\overline{b}c)}.$$

For the second line of centroids, we obtain

$$g_2(\lambda) = \frac{m_2+n+p_2}{3} = [k_2(1+\overline{\omega})b + (1+\omega)c] \cdot \frac{\lambda}{3} + \frac{l_2(1+\overline{\omega})b}{3}, \tag{33}$$

where by (13), the coefficients k_2 and l_2 are given by

$$k_2 = \frac{\overline{\omega}(b-c)\overline{c} - \omega(\overline{b}-\overline{c})c}{\overline{\omega} b(\overline{b}-\overline{c}) - \omega\overline{b}(b-c)} = \frac{|c|^2\sqrt{3}i - (\omega c\overline{b} - \overline{\omega}\overline{c}b)}{-|b|^2\sqrt{3}i + (\omega c\overline{b} - \overline{\omega}\overline{c}b)}, \tag{34}$$

$$l_2 = \frac{(\overline{b}-\overline{c})c - (b-c)\overline{c}}{\overline{\omega} b(\overline{b}-\overline{c}) - \omega\overline{b}(b-c)} = \frac{c\overline{b} - b\overline{c}}{-|b|^2\sqrt{3}i + (\omega c\overline{b} - \overline{\omega}\overline{c}b)}.$$

We notice that these parametrizations are different from those in Section 5.

7. Conclusions

In this paper, we studied the equilateral triangles whose vertices are located on the support lines of a given arbitrary triangle. Using complex coordinates and a parametrization, we proved that the centers of these triangles are located on two lines, which are perpendicular to the Euler's line of the given triangle, and we also computed the coordinates of these intersections.

It is interesting to investigate geometric properties related to triangles similar to a prototype whose vertices are located on the support lines of a given triangle.

Author Contributions: Conceptualization, D.A. and O.B.; methodology, D.A. and O.B.; software, O.B.; validation, D.A. and O.B.; formal analysis, D.A. and O.B.; investigation, D.A. and O.B.; resources, D.A. and O.B.; data curation, O.B.; writing—original draft preparation, D.A. and O.B.; writing—review and editing, D.A. and O.B.; project administration, D.A. and O.B. All authors have read and agreed to the published version of the manuscript.

Funding: This research received no external funding.

Data Availability Statement: The work did not report any data, apart from the Matlab plots.

Acknowledgments: The authors are grateful to the anonymous referees, whose comments and suggestions helped to improve this work.

Conflicts of Interest: The authors declare no conflicts of interest.

References

1. Apró, J. Triangles and Quadrilaterals Inscribed in Jordan Curves, Ph.D. Thesis, Eötvös Loránd University, Budapest, Hungary, 2023.
2. Meyerson, M.D. Equilateral triangles and continuous curves. *Fund. Math.* **1980**, *110*, 1–9. [CrossRef]
3. Nielsen, M.J. Triangles inscribed in simple closed curves. *Geom. Dedicata* **1992**, *43*, 291–297. [CrossRef]
4. Gupta, A.; Rubinstein-Salzedo, S. Inscribed triangles of Jordan curves in $\mathbb{R}^n$. *arXiv*, **2021**, arXiv:2102.03953v1.
5. Schwartz, R.E. Rectangles, curves, and Klein bottles. *Bull. Amer. Math. Soc.* **2022**, *59*, 1–17. [CrossRef]
6. Stromquist, W. Inscribed squares and square-like quadrilaterals in closed curves. *Mathematika* **1989**, *36*, 187–197. [CrossRef]
7. McCartin, B.J. *Mysteries of the Equilateral Triangle*; Hikari Ltd.: Rousse, Bulgaria, 2010.
8. Capitán, F.J.G. Locus of centroids of similar inscribed triangles. *Forum Geom.* **2016**, *16*, 257–267.
9. Kiss, N.S. Equal area triangles inscribed in a triangle. *Int. J. Geom.* **2016**, *5*, 19–30.
10. Russell, R.A. Inscribed Equilateral Triangles. *J. Classic Geom.* **2015**, *4*, 1–6.
11. Yaglom, I.M. *Geometric Transformations II*; Random House: London, UK, 1968; Translated from Russian.
12. Andrica, D.; Bagdasar, O.; Marinescu, D.-Ş. Inscribed equilateral triangles in general triangles. *Int. J. Geom.* **2024**, *13*, 113–124.
13. Čerin, Z. Configurations of inscribed equilateral triangles. *J Geom.* **2007**, *87*, 14–30. [CrossRef]
14. Andreescu, T.; Andrica, D. *Complex Numbers from A to ... Z*, 2nd ed.; Birkhäuser: Boston, MA, USA, 2014.

Article

Some Remarks Regarding Special Elements in Algebras Obtained by the Cayley–Dickson Process over Z_p

Cristina Flaut [1,*,†] and Andreea Baias [2,†]

Citation: Flaut, C.; Baias, A. Some Remarks Regarding Special Elements in Algebras Obtained by the Cayley–Dickson Process over Z_p. *Axioms* **2024**, *13*, 351. https://doi.org/10.3390/axioms13060351

Academic Editor: Florin Felix Nichita

Received: 27 March 2024
Revised: 19 May 2024
Accepted: 21 May 2024
Published: 24 May 2024

Copyright: © 2024 by the authors. Licensee MDPI, Basel, Switzerland. This article is an open access article distributed under the terms and conditions of the Creative Commons Attribution (CC BY) license (https://creativecommons.org/licenses/by/4.0/).

[1] Faculty of Mathematics and Computer Science, Ovidius University, Bd. Mamaia 124, 900527 Constanța, Romania
[2] Doctoral School of Mathematics, Ovidius University of Constanța, 900470 Constanța, Romania
* Correspondence: cflaut@univ-ovidius.ro or cristina_flaut@yahoo.com
† These authors contributed equally to this work.

Abstract: In this paper, we provide some properties of *k*-potent elements in algebras obtained by the Cayley–Dickson process over $\mathbb{Z}_p$. Moreover, we find a structure of nonunitary ring over Fibonacci quaternions over $\mathbb{Z}_3$ and we present a method to encrypt plain texts, by using invertible elements in some of these algebras.

Keywords: k-potent elements; algebras obtained by the Cayley–Dickson process; quaternion Fibonacci elements

MSC: 17A35; 11B39

1. Preliminaries

In [1], the authors provided some properties regarding quaternions over the field $\mathbb{Z}_p$. Since quaternions are special cases of algebras obtained by the Cayley–Dickson process, in this paper, we extend the study of *k*-potent elements over quaternions to an arbitrary algebra obtained by the Cayley–Dickson process. These algebras, in general, are poor in properties, are not commutative, starting with dimension 4 (the quaternions), are not associative, starting with dimension 8 (the octonions) and lost alternativity, starting with dimension 16 (the sedionions). The good news is that all algebras obtained by the Cayley–Dickson process are power-associative and this is the property that will be used when we study the *k*-potent elements in these algebras. For other details regarding the power-associative algebras and their properties and applications, the reader is referred to [2–4].

The paper is organized as follows: in the Introduction, we present basic properties of algebras obtained by the Cayley–Dickson process, in Section 3, we characterize the *k*-potent elements in these algebras, in Section 4, we give a structure of non-unitary and noncommutative ring over the Fibonacci quaternions over $\mathbb{Z}_3$, and in the last section, we provide an encryption method by using invertible elements in some of these algebras.

2. Introduction

In the following, we consider A, a finite-dimensional unitary algebra over a field K with $char K \neq 2$.

An algebra A is called *alternative* if $x^2 y = x(xy)$ and $xy^2 = (xy)y$, for all $x, y \in A$, *flexible* if $x(yx) = (xy)x = xyx$, for all $x, y \in A$ and *power-associative* if the subalgebra $<x>$ of A generated by any element $x \in A$ is associative. Each alternative algebra is a flexible algebra and a power-associative algebra [3].

We consider the algebra $A \neq K$ such that for each element $x \in A$, the following relation is true

$$x^2 + t_x x + n_x = 0,$$

for all $x \in A$ and $t_x, n_x \in K$. This algebra is called a *quadratic algebra*. For other details regarding quadratic algebras, the reader is referred to [3].

It is well known that a finite-dimensional algebra A is *a division* algebra if and only if A does not contain zero divisors [3].

A *composition algebra* A over the field K is an algebra, not necessarily associative, with a nondegenerate quadratic form n which satisfies the relation

$$n(xy) = n(x)n(y), \forall x, y \in A.$$

Unital composition algebras are called *Hurwitz algebras*. We denote with $\mathbb{R}$, $\mathbb{C}$, $\mathbb{H}$ and $\mathbb{O}$ the real field, the complex field, the real quaternion algebra and the real octonion algebra.

Hurwitz's Theorem [5]. $\mathbb{R}$, $\mathbb{C}$, $\mathbb{H}$ *and* $\mathbb{O}$ *are the only real alternative division algebras.*

Theorem 1 (Theorem 2.14, [6]). *A is a composition algebra if and only if A is an alternative quadratic algebra.*

An element x in a ring R is called *nilpotent* if we can find a positive integer n such that $x^n = 0$. The number n, the smallest with this property, is called the *nilpotency index*. A power-associative algebra A is called a *nil algebra* if and only if each element of this algebra is nilpotent. An element x in a ring R is called *k-potent*, for $k > 1$, a positive integer, if k is the smallest number such that $x^k = x$. The number k is called the *k-potency index*. For $k = 2$, we have idempotent elements, and for $k = 3$, we have tripotent elements, etc.

Let A be an algebra over the field K and a *scalar involution* over A,

$$^{-} : A \to A, a \to \bar{a},$$

that means a linear map with the following properties

$$\overline{ab} = \bar{b}\bar{a},\ \bar{\bar{a}} = a,$$

and

$$a + \bar{a}, a\bar{a} \in K \cdot 1, \text{ for all } a, b \in A.$$

For the element $a \in A$, the element $\bar{a}$ is called the *conjugate* of the element a. The linear form

$$\mathbf{t} : A \to K,\ \mathbf{t}(a) = a + \bar{a}$$

and the quadratic form

$$\mathbf{n} : A \to K,\ \mathbf{n}(a) = a\bar{a}$$

are called the *trace* and the *norm* of the element a, respectively. From here, the results show that an algebra A with a scalar involution is a quadratic algebra. Indeed, if in the relation $\mathbf{n}(a) = a\bar{a}$, we replace $\bar{a} = \mathbf{t}(a) - a$, we obtain

$$a^2 - \mathbf{t}(a)a + \mathbf{n}(a) = 0. \tag{1}$$

Let $\delta \in K$ be a fixed non-zero element. We define the following algebra multiplication on the vector space $A \oplus A$

$$(a_1, a_2)(b_1, b_2) = \left(a_1 b_1 + \delta \bar{b}_2 a_2, a_2 \overline{b_1} + b_2 a_1\right). \tag{2}$$

The obtained algebra structure over $A \oplus A$, denoted by (A, δ), is called the *algebra obtained from A by the Cayley–Dickson process.* We have that $\dim(A, \delta) = 2 \dim A$.

Let $x \in (A, \delta)$, $x = (a_1, a_2)$. The map

$$^{-} : (A, \delta) \to (A, \delta),\ x \to \bar{x} = (\bar{a}_1, -a_2),$$

is a scalar involution of the algebra (A,δ), extending the involution $^-$ of the algebra A. We consider the maps

$$\mathbf{t}(x)=\mathbf{t}(a_1)$$

and

$$\mathbf{n}(x)=\mathbf{n}(a_1)-\delta\mathbf{n}(a_2)$$

called the *trace* and the *norm* of the element $x\in(A,\delta)$,, respectively.

If we consider $A=K$ and we apply this process t times, $t\geq 1$, we obtain an algebra over K,

$$A_t=\left(\frac{\delta_1,\ldots,\delta_t}{K}\right). \tag{3}$$

Using induction in this algebra, the set $\{1,f_1,\ldots,f_{n-1}\},n=2^t$ generates a basis with the properties:

$$f_i^2=\delta_i 1,\ {}_i\in K,\delta_i\neq 0,\ i=1,\ldots,t \tag{4}$$

and

$$f_if_j=-f_jf_i=\alpha_{ij}f_k,\ \alpha_{ij}\in K,\ \alpha_{ij}\neq 0,i\neq j,i,j=\ 1,\ldots n-1, \tag{5}$$

α_{ij} and f_k being uniquely determined by f_i and f_j.

From [7], Lemma 4, the results show that in any algebra A_t with the basis $\{1,f_1,\ldots,f_{n-1}\}$ satisfying relations (4) and (5), we have:

$$f_i(f_ix)=\delta_ix=(xf_i)f_i, \tag{6}$$

for all $i\in\{1,2,\ldots,n-1\}$ and for every $x\in A$.

The field K is the center of the algebra A_t,for $t\geq 2$ [7]. Algebras A_t of dimension 2^t obtained by the Cayley–Dickson process, described above, are flexible and power-associative, for all $t\geq 1$, and, in general, are not division algebras, for all $t\geq 1$.

For $t=2$, we obtain the generalized quaternion algebras over the field K. If we take $K=\mathbb{R}$ and $\delta_1=\delta_2=-1$, we obtain the real quaternion algebra over $\mathbb{R}$. This algebra is an associative and a noncommutative algebra and will be denoted with $\mathbb{H}$.

Let $\mathbb{H}$ be the real quaternion algebra with basis $\{1,i,j,k\}$, where

$$i^2=j^2=k^2=-1,ij=-ji,ik=-ki,jk=-kj. \tag{7}$$

Therefore, each element from $\mathbb{H}$ has the following form

$$q=a+bi+cj+dk,a,b,c,d\in\mathbb{R}.$$

We remark that $\mathbb{H}$ is a vector space of dimension 4 over $\mathbb{R}$ with the addition and scalar multiplication. Moreover, $\mathbb{H}$ has a ring structure with multiplication given by (7) and the usual distributivity law.

If we consider K a finite field with $charK\neq 2$, due to the Wedderburn's Theorem, a quaternion algebra over K is always a non division algebra or a split algebra.

For other details regarding Cayley–Dickson process and the properties of obtained algebras, the reader is referred to [3] and to the book [4], p. 28–50.

3. Characterization of k-Potent Elements in Algebras Obtained by the Cayley–Dickson Process

In the paper [8], the author gave several characterizations of k-potent elements in associative rings from an algebraic point of view. In [9], the authors presented some properties of (m,k)-type elements over the ring of integers modulo n and in [10], the author emphasize the applications of k-potent matrices to digital image encryption.

In the following, we will study the properties of k-potent elements in a special case of nonassociative structures, which means we characterize the k-potent elements in algebras obtained by the Cayley–Dickson process over the field of integers modulo p, p a prime number greater than 2, $K = \mathbb{Z}_p$.

Remark 1. *Since algebras obtained by the Cayley–Dickson process are power-associative, we can define the power of an element. In this paper, we consider A_t such an algebra, given by the relation (3), with $\delta_i = -1$, for all i, $i \in \{1, \dots, t\}$. We consider $x \in A_t$, a k-potent element, which means k is the smallest positive integer with this property. Since A_t is a quadratic algebra, from relation (1), we have that $x^2 - \mathbf{t}(x)x + \mathbf{n}(x) = 0$, with $\mathbf{t}(x) \in K$, the trace, and $\mathbf{n}(x) \in K$. the norm of the element x. To make calculations easier, we will denote $\mathbf{t}(x) = t_x$ and $\mathbf{n}(x) = n_x$.*

Remark 2. *(i) In general, algebras obtained by the Cayley–Dickson process are not composition algebras, but the following relation*

$$\mathbf{n}(x^m) = (\mathbf{n}(x))^m$$

is true, for m a positive integer. Indeed, we have $\mathbf{n}(x^m) = x^m\overline{x^m}$ and $(\mathbf{n}(x))^m = (x\overline{x})^m = x\overline{x} \cdot \dots \cdot x\overline{x}$, m-times with $\overline{x} = t_x - x$, $t_x \in K$. Since x and $\overline{x}$ are in the algebra generated by x, they associate and commute, due to the power-associativity property. If $x \in A_t$ is an invertible element, which means $n_x \neq 0$, then the same remark is also true for $x^{-1} = \frac{\overline{x}}{n_x}$, the inverse of the element x. The element x^{-1} is in the algebra generated by x, therefore associate and commute with x.

(ii) We know that $x^2 - t_x x + n_x = 0$. If $x \in A_t$ is a nonzero k-potent element, then, from the above, we have $n_x = 0$ or $n_x \neq 0$ and $n_x^{k-1} = 1$.

(iii) Let $x \in A_t$ be a nonzero k-potent element such that $n_x \neq 0$. Then, the element x is an invertible element in A_t such that $x^{k-1} = 1$. Indeed, if $x^k = x$, multiplying with x^{-1} we have $x^{k-1} = 1$.

(iv) For a nilpotent element $x \in A_t$ there is a positive integer $k \geq 2$ such that $x^k = 0$, k the smallest with this property. From here, we have that $n_x = 0$; therefore, $x^2 = t_x x$. It results that $x^k = t_x x^{k-1}$, then $t_x x^{k-1} = 0$ with $x^{k-1} \neq 0$. We find that $t_x = 0$ and $x^2 = 0$. Therefore, we can say that in an algebra A_t, if exist, we have only nilpotent elements of index two.

In the following, we will characterize the k-potent elements in the case when $n_x = 0$.

Proposition 1. *The element $x \in A_t$, $x \neq 0$, with $n_x = 0$ and $t_x \neq 0$ is a k-potent element in A_t if and only if t_x is a k-potent element in $\mathbb{Z}_p^*$, $2 \leq k \leq p$ (t_x has $k-1$ as multiplicative order in $\mathbb{Z}_p^*$).*

Proof of Proposition 1. We must prove that if k is the smallest positive integer such that $x^k = x$, then $t_x^k = t_x$; therefore, $t_x^{k-1} = 1$, with k the smallest positive integer with this property. We have $x^k = x^{k-2}x^2 = x^{k-2}t_x x = t_x x^{k-1} = t_x x^{k-3}x^2 = t_x^2 x^{k-2} = \dots = t_x^{k-1}x$. If $t_x^{k-1} = 1$, we have $x^k = x$ and if $x^k = x$, we have $x = t_x^{k-1}x$; therefore, $t_x^{k-1} = 1$.

Now, we must prove that $k \leq p$. We know that in $\mathbb{Z}_p$ the multiplicative order of a nonzero element is a divisor of $p-1$. If the order is $p-1$, the element is called a primitive element. If $t_x \neq 0$ in $\mathbb{Z}_p$ and $t_x^{k-1} = 1$, the results show that $(k-1) \mid (p-1)$, then $k-1 \leq p-1$ and $k \leq p$. □

Remark 3. *For elements x with $n_x = 0$ and $t_x \neq 0$, from the above theorem, we remark that in an algebra A_t over $\mathbb{Z}_p$ we have $k \leq p$, where k is the potency index. That means the k-potency index in these conditions does not exceed the prime number p. Since $a^{p-1} \equiv 1 \bmod p$, for all nonzero $a \in \mathbb{Z}_p$, always the results show that $x^p = x$. It is not necessary for p to be the smallest with this property.*

Remark 4. *If we take $p = 5$ and we have $x \in A_t$ such that $x^{38} = x$, since we known that $x^5 = x$, we obtain $x^{38} = x^{35}x^3 = \left(x^5\right)^7 x^3 = x^7 x^3 = x^{10} = x^5 x^5 = x^2$. Therefore, $x^2 = x$ and the k-potency index is 2.*

In the following, we will characterize the k-potent elements when $n_x \neq 0$ and $n_x^{k-1} = 1$. We suppose that $k \geq 3$. Indeed, if $k = 2$, we have $x^2 = x$, then $x = 1$.

The following result it is well known from the literature. We reproduce here the proof.

Proposition 2. *Each element of a finite field K can be expressed as a sum of two squares from K.*

Proof of Proposition 2. If $charK = 2$, we have that the map $f : K \to K, f(x) = x^2$ is an injective map; therefore, is bijective and each element from K is a square. Indeed, if $f(x) = f(y)$, we have that $x^2 = y^2$ and $x = y$ or $x = -y = y$,since $-1 = 1$ in $charK = 2$.

Assuming that $charK = p \neq 2$. We suppose that K has $q = p^n$ elements, then K^* has $q-1$ elements. Since $(K^*, \cdot)$ is a cyclic group with $q-1$ elements, $K^* = \{1, v, v^2, \ldots, v^{q-2}\}$, half of them, namely the even powers are squares. The zero element is also a square, then we have $\frac{q-1}{2} + 1 = \frac{q+1}{2}$ square elements from K which are squares. We know that from a finite group $(G, *)$ if S and T are two subsets of G and $|S| + |T| > |G|$, we have that each $x \in G$ can be expresses as $x = s * t$, $s \in S, t \in T$. For $g \in G$, we consider the set $gS^{-1} = \{g * s^{-1}, s \in S\}$, which has the same cardinal as the set T. Since $|S| + |T| > |G|$, the results show that $|T| + |gS^{-1}| > |G|$; therefore, $T \cap gS^{-1} \neq \emptyset$. Then, there are the elements $s \in S$ and $t \in T$ such that $t = g * s^{-1}$ and $g = s * t$. Now, if we consider S and T two sets equal with the multiplicative. In the group $(K, +)$, we have that $|S| + |T| = q + 1 > |K|$; therefore, each $x \in K$ can be written as $x = s^2 + t^2$, with $s \in S, t \in T$. □

Remark 5. *(i) We can find an element $w \in A_t$, different from elements of the base, such that $w^2 = -1$. Indeed, such an element has $n_w = 1$ and $t_x = 0$. With the above notations and from the above Proposition 7, since $1 = a^2 + b^2$, we can take $w_{ij} = af_i + bf_j$, $a, b \in \mathbb{Z}_p$ and f_i, f_j elements from the basis in A_t, given by (4). Therefore, $w_{ij}^2 = -1$.*

(ii) The group $\left(\mathbb{Z}_p^*, \cdot\right)$ is cyclic and has $p-1$ elements. Elements of order $p-1$ are primitive elements. The rest of the elements have orders divisors of $p-1$.

Now, we consider the equation in A_t

$$x^n = 1, n \text{ a positive integer.} \tag{8}$$

In the following, we will find some conditions such that this equation has solutions different from 1.

Remark 6. *(i) With the above notations, we consider $w \in A_t$, a nilpotent element (it has the norm and the trace zero). Therefore, the element $z = 1 + w$ has the property that $z^n = 1 + nw$; therefore, if $n = pr, r$ a positive integer, Equation (8) has solutions of the form $z = 1 + w$, for all nilpotent elements $w \in A_t$. It is clear that z has the norm equal with 1 and $z^p = 1$; therefore, $z^{p+1} = z$, is a p-potent element.*

(ii) If we consider $\eta \in \mathbb{Z}_p^*$ with the multiplicative order θ and $z = \eta + w$, w nilpotent, we have that $(\eta + w)^p = \eta^p + pw = \eta^p$ and $(\eta + w)^{p\theta} = 1$. Therefore, if $n = pr, r$ a positive integer, Equation (8) has solutions of the form $z = 1 + w$, for all nilpotent elements $w \in A_t$. If r is a multiplicative order of an element from $\mathbb{Z}_p^*$ and $n = pr, r$ a positive integer, then Equation (8) has solutions of the form $z = \eta + w$, for all $\eta \in A_t$, η of order r, w a nilpotent element in A_t.

(iii) With the above notations, we consider the element $w \in A_t$ such that $w^2 = -1$ and $z = 1 + w$. We have that $z^2 = (1+w)^2 = 2w, z^3 = (1+w)^3 = 2w - 2$ and $z^4 = \left(z^2\right)^2 = -4$ modulo p. Let $\eta = -4 \in \mathbb{Z}_p^*$ with the multiplicative order θ, θ is always an even number. We have that $z^{4\theta} = 1$.

(iv) Let $z = a + w \in A_t$, where $a \in \mathbb{Z}_p$ and $w \in A_t$, with $t_w = 0$ and $n_w \neq 0$. We have that $w^2 = \alpha \in \mathbb{Z}_p^2$; therefore, $z^r = C_r + D_r w$. If $z^s = 1$, then there is a positive integer $m \leq s$ such that $C_m = 0$ or $D_m = 0$. Indeed, if $m = s$, we have $D_s = 0$ and $C_s = 1$.

Proposition 3. *By using the above notations, we consider the element $z = a + w$, where $a \in \mathbb{Z}_p$ and $w \in A_t$ with the trace zero. Assuming that there is a nonnegative integer m such that C_m or D_m is zero, then there is a positive integer k such that $z^k = 1$ and z is $(k+1)$-potent element.*

Proof of Proposition 3. Since w has the trace zero, let $w^2 = \beta$, with τ the multiplicative order of β. We have that $z^m = C_m + D_m w, C_m, D_m \in \mathbb{Z}_p$. Supposing that C_m is zero, then we have $z^m = D_m w$, with θ the multiplicative order of D_m. Therefore $z^{mM} = 1$, where $M = lcm\ \{2\tau, \theta\}$. If D_m is zero, then we have $z^m = C_m$ with v the multiplicative order of C_m. It results that $z^{vm} = 1$. □

Now, we can say that we proved the following theorem.

Theorem 2. *With the above notations, an element $z \in A_t$ is a k-potent element, if z is of one of the forms:*

Case 1. $n_z \neq 0$.

(i) $z = 1 + w$, with $w \in A_t$, w is a nilpotent element. In this case, z is $(p+1)$-potent;

(ii) $z = 1 + w$, with $w \in A_t$ such that $w^2 = -1$. Since $z^4 = -4$ modulo p and θ is the multiplicative order of -4 in $\mathbb{Z}_p^*$, we have that z is $(4\theta + 1)$-potent.

(iii) $z = a + w$, where $a \in \mathbb{Z}_p$, $w \in A_t$ with $t_w = 0$, $w^2 = \beta \in \mathbb{Z}_p^*$, with τ the multiplicative order of β, and $z^r = C_r + D_r w$. Assuming that there is a nonnegative integer m such that C_m or D_m is zero, then there is a positive integer k such that $z^k = 1$ and z is $(k+1)$-potent element. If $C_m = 0$, then $k = mM$, where $M = lcm\ \{2\tau, \theta\}$ and θ is the multiplicative order of D_m. If $D_m = 0$, then we have $k = vm$, with v the multiplicative order of C_m.

Case 2. $n_z = 0$. The element $z \in A_t$ is k-potent if and only if t_z is k-potent element in $\mathbb{Z}_p^*$, which means $k-1$ is a divisor of $p-1$.

Example 1. *In the following, we will give some examples of values of the potency index k.*

(i) Case $p = 5$ and $t = 2$; therefore, we work on quaternions. We consider $z = 2 + i + j + k$ with the norm $n_x = 2 \neq 0$. We have $w = i + j + k$ and $z = 2 + w$. We have $z^2 = 1 + 4w, z^3 = 4w$; therefore, $m = 3$ and $D_m = 4$, with $\theta = 4$. Since $w^2 = 2$, the results show that $\tau = 4$ and $M = 4$. We have that $z^{24} = 1$, then $z^{25} = z$ and z is 25-potent element, $k = 25$.

(ii) Case $p = 7$, $t = 2$ and $z = 2 + i + j + k$. The norm is zero and the trace is 4. Since 4 has multiplicative order equal with 3, from Proposition 4, we have $z^4 = z$. Indeed, $z^2 = 1 + 4w, z^3 = 4 + 2w, z^4 = 2 + w = z$ and $k = 4$.

(iii) Case $p = 5$ and $t = 2$. The element $z = 1 + 3i + 4j$ has $n_z = 1, w = 3i + 4j$, with $n_w = t_w = 0$; therefore, w is a nilpotent element. We have $z^5 = 1$, $z^6 = z$ and $k = 6$.

(iv) Case $p = 3$ and $t = 2$. The element $z = 1 + i + j + k$ has $n_z = 1$ and $w = i + j + k$. We have $z^2 = (1+w)^2 = 1 + 2w$, $z^3 = (1+w)(1+2w) = 1 + 2w + w = 1$; therefore, $z^4 = z$ and $k = 4$.

(v) Case $p = 5, t = 2$. We consider the element $z = 2 + 3i + j + 3k = 2 + 3w$, $w = i + 2j + k, n_z = 3, n_w = 1, t_w = 0$, then $w^2 = -1$. We have that $\tau = 2$ and $z^2 = 2w$. Therefore $m = 2, C_2 = 0, D_2 = 2$, then $\theta = 4$ and, therefore we work on quaternions. It results $z^{mM} = z^8 = 1$, therefore $z^9 = z$ and $k = 9$.

(vi) Case $p = 5, t = 2$. We consider the element $z = 2 + i + j + k = 2 + w$ with $n_z = 2$, $n_w = 3, t_w = 0, w^2 = 2$ and $\tau = 4$, the order of $\beta = 2$. We have $z^2 = 3 + 4w, z^3 = 4 + w$, $z^4 = 1 + 4w, z^5 = 4w$; therefore, $m = 5, C_5 = 0, D_5 = 4, \theta = 2, M = lcm\{2\tau, \theta\} = 8$. It results that $z^{mM} = z^{40} = 1$, then $z^{41} = z$ and $k = 42$.

(vii) Case $p = 11, t = 2$. We consider the element $z = 2i + 7j + 3k$ with $n_z = 7, z^2 = 4$; therefore, $m = 2, D_2 = 0, C_2 = 4, v = 5$, the multiplicative order of $C_2 = 4$. We have $z^{mv} = z^{10} = 1$ and $k = 11$.

(viii) Case $p = 13, t = 3$; therefore, we work on octonions. We consider the element $z = 3 + 2f_1 + f_2 + f_3 + f_4 + f_5 + f_6 + f_7 = 3 + w$, $w = 2f_1 + f_2 + f_3 + f_4 + f_5 + f_6 + f_7$, with $n_z = 6$, $n_w = 10, t_w = 0$. We have $w^2 = 3$ and $\tau = 3$, the order of $\beta = 3$. It results, $z^2 = 12 + 2w, z^3 = 3 + 5w, z^4 = 9w$, then $m = 4, C_4 = 0.D_4 = 9, \theta = 3, M = lcm\{2\tau, \theta\} = 6$. We obtain $z^{mM} = z^{24} = 1$, then $z^{25} = z$ and $k = 25$.

(ix) Case $p = 17, t = 4$; therefore, we work on sedenions. The Sedenion algebra is a noncommutative, nonassociative and nonalternative algebra of dimension 16. We consider the element

$z = 1 + w, w = \sum_{i=1}^{15} f_i$, *with* $w^2 = 2$ *and* $\tau = 8$. *It results* $z^2 = 3 + 2w, z^3 = 4w$. *Then* $m = 3, C_3 = 0, D_3 = 4, \theta = 4$. *We have* $M = \text{lcm}\{2\tau, \theta\} = \text{lcm}\{16, 4\} = 16$ *and* $z^{mM} = z^{48} = 1$. *It results* $z^{49} = z$ *and* $k = 49$.

Remark 7. *The* (m,k)*-type elements in* A_t*, with* m*,* n *positive integers, are the elements* $x \in A_t$ *such that* $x^m = x^k$*,* $m \geq k$*, smallest with this property. If* $n_x \neq 0$*, then* $x^{m-k} = 1$ *and* x *is an* $(m-k+1)$*-potent element. If* $n_x = 0$ *and* $t_x \neq 0$*, we have that* $t_x^{m-k} = 1$*, then* x *is an* $(m-k+1)$*-potent element. Therefore, an* (m,k)*-type element in* A_t *is an* $(m-k+1)$*-potent element in* A_t*.*

4. A nonunitary Ring Structure of Quaternion Fibonacci Elements over $\mathbb{Z}_p$

The Fibonacci numbers was introduced by *Leonardo of Pisa (1170–1240)* in his book *Liber abbaci*, a book published in 1202 AD (see [11], p. 1–3). The nth term of these numbers is given by the formula:

$$f_n = f_{n-1} + f_{n-2}, n \geq 2,$$

where $f_0 = 0, f_1 = 1$.

Fibonacci numbers have many applications. One of them was when Horadam connected Fibonacci numbers with real quaternions. In [12], Fibonacci quaternions over $\mathbb{H}$ were defined and studied, which are defined as follows

$$F_n = f_n 1 + f_{n+1} i + f_{n+2} j + f_{n+3} k, \tag{9}$$

called the nth Fibonacci quaternions.

In the same paper, the norm formula for the nth Fibonacci quaternions was found:

$$\boldsymbol{n}(F_n) = F_n \overline{F}_n = 3 f_{2n+3},$$

where $\overline{F}_n = f_n \cdot 1 - f_{n+1} i - f_{n+2} j - f_{n+3} k$ is the conjugate of the F_n in the algebra $\mathbb{H}$.

Fibonacci sequence is also studied when it is reduced modulo m. This sequence is periodic and this period is called *Pisano's period*, $\pi(m)$. In the following, we consider $m = p$, a prime number and $(f_n)_{n \geq 0}$, the Fibonacci numbers over $\mathbb{Z}_p$. It is clear that, in general, the sum of two arbitrary Fibonacci numbers is not a Fibonacci numbers, but if these numbers are consecutive Fibonacci numbers, the sentence is true. In the following, we will find conditions when the product of two Fibonacci numbers is also a Fibonacci number. In the following, we work on $A_t, t = 2$, over the field $\mathbb{Z}_p$. We denote this algebra with $\mathbb{H}_p$.

Let $F_1 = a + bi + (a+b)j + (a+2b)k$ and $F_2 = c + di + (c+d)j + (c+2d)k$, two Fibonacci quaternions in $\mathbb{H}_p$. We will find conditions such that $F_1 F_2$ and $F_2 F_1$ are also Fibonacci quaternion elements, which means elements of the same form:

$$A + Bi + (A+B)j + (A+2B)k. \tag{10}$$

We compute $F_1 F_2$ and $F_2 F_1$ and we obtain that

$$F_1 F_2 = (-ac - 3ad - 3bc - 6bd) + 2adi + 2a(c+d)j + (2ac + ad + 3bc)k \tag{11}$$

and

$$F_2 F_1 = (-ac - 3ad - 3bc - 6bd) + 2bci + 2c(a+b)j + (2ac + 3ad + bc)k. \tag{12}$$

By using relation (10), we obtain the following systems, with c, d as unknowns. From relation (11), we obtain:

$$\begin{cases} (-3a - 3b)c + (-3a - 6b)d = 0 \\ (-6b - 3a)c + (-6b)d = 0 \end{cases} \tag{13}$$

From relation (12), we obtain the system:

$$\begin{cases} (-3a+3b)c+(-3a)d=0 \\ (-3a)c+(-6a-6b)d=0 \end{cases} \tag{14}$$

We remark that for $p=3$, the systems (13) and (14) have solutions; therefore, for $p=3$, there is a chance to obtain an algebraic structure on the set $\mathcal{F}_{\pi(p)}$, the set of Fibonacci quaternions over $\mathbb{Z}_p$.

For $p=3$, the Pisano's period is 8, then we have the following Fibonacci numbers: $0,1,1,2,0,2,2,1$. We obtain the following Fibonacci quaternion elements: $F_0=i+j+2$,, $F_1=1+i+2j, F_2=1+2i+2k, F_3=2+2j+2k, F_4=2i+2j+k, F_5=2+2i+j$, $F_6=2+i+k, F_7=1+j+k$; therefore, $\mathcal{F}_{\pi(p)}=\{F_i, i\in\{0,1,2,3,4,5,6,7\}\}$. All these elements are zero norm elements. F_0 and F_4 are nilpotents, F_3, F_5 and F_6 are idempotent elements, F_1, F_2, F_7 are three potent elements. By using $C++$ software (https://www.programiz.com/cpp-programming/online-compiler/, accessed on 20 May 2024), we computed the sum and the product of these eight elements. Therefore, we have $F_0F_i=0$, for $i\in\{0,1,\ldots,7\}, F_4F_i=0$, for $i\in\{0,1,\ldots,7\}, F_5F_i=F_i$, for $i\in\{0,1,\ldots,7\}, F_6F_i=F_i$, for $i\in\{0,1,\ldots,7\}$ and

$$\begin{aligned}
F_1F_0 &= F_4, F_1^2=F_5, F_1F_2=F_6, F_1F_3=F_7,\\
F_1F_4 &= F_0, F_1F_5=F_1, F_1F_6=F_2, F_1F_7=F_3,\\
F_2F_0 &= F_4, F_2F_1=F_5, F_2^2=F_6, F_2F_3=F_7,\\
F_2F_4 &= F_0, F_2F_5=F_1, F_2F_6=F_2, F_2F_7=F_3,\\
F_3F_0 &= F_0, F_3F_1=F_1, F_3F_2=F_2, F_3^2=F_3,\\
F_3F_4 &= F_4, F_3F_5=F_5, F_3F_6=F_6, F_3F_7=F_7,\\
F_7F_0 &= F_4, F_7F_1=F_5, F_7F_2=F_6, F_7F_3=F_7,\\
F_7F_4 &= F_0, F_7F_5=F_1, F_7F_6=F_2, F_7^2=F_3.
\end{aligned}$$

Regarding the sum of two Fibonacci quaternions over $\mathbb{Z}_3$, we obtain:

$$\begin{aligned}
2F_0 = F_4, F_0+F_1 &= F_2, F_0+F_2=F_7, F_0+F_3=F_6, F_0+F_4=0,\\
F_0+F_5 &= F_3, F_0+F_6=F_5, F_0+F_7=F_1, 2F_1=F_5, F_1+F_2=F_3,\\
F_1+F_3 &= F_0, F_1+F_4=F_7, F_1+F_5=0, F_1+F_6=F_4, F_1+F_7=F_6,\\
2F_2 &= F_6, F_2+F_3=F_4, F_2+F_4=F_1, F_2+F_5=F_0, F_2+F_6=0,\\
F_2+F_7 &= F_5, 2F_3=F_7, F_3+F_4=F_5, F_3+F_5=F_2, F_3+F_6=F_1,\\
F_3+F_7 &= 0, 2F_4=F_0, F_4+F_5=F_6, F_4+F_6=F_0, F_4+F_7=F_2,\\
2F_5 &= F_1, F_5+F_6=F_7, F_5+F_7=F_4, 2F_6=F_2, F_6+F_7=F_0,\\
2F_7 &= F_3.
\end{aligned}$$

From here, we have the following result.

Proposition 4. *$\left(\mathcal{F}_{\pi(3)}\cup\{0\},+\right)$ is an abelian group of order 9, isomorphic to $\mathbb{Z}_3\times\mathbb{Z}_3$ and $\left(\mathcal{F}_{\pi(3)}\cup\{0\},+,\cdot\right)$ is a nonunitary and noncommutative ring.*

5. An Application in Cryptography

As an application of quaternions and octonions, in the following, we present a method to encrypt and decrypt texts by using these elements. For this purpose, we consider an algebra A_t over $\mathbb{Z}_p$, of dimension $2^t, t\in\{2,3\}$. We suppose that we have a text m to be encrypted and the alphabet has p elements, p being a prime number. Each letter of the alphabet will correspond a label from 0 to $p-1$, which means we work on $\mathbb{Z}_p$. The encryption algorithm is the following.

1. We will split m in blocks and we will choose the length of the blocks of the form 2^t. For a fixed t, we will find an invertible element $q, q \in A_t$, which means $n_q \neq 0$. This element will be the encryption key.
2. Supposing that $m = m_1 m_2 \ldots m_r$ is the plain text, with m_i blocks of length 2^t, formed by the labels of the letters, to each $m_i = m_{i0} m_{i1} \ldots m_{i2^t-1}$ we will associate an element

$$v_i \in A_t, v_i = \sum_{j=0}^{2^t-1} m_{ij} f_j.$$

3. We compute $qv_i = w_i$, for all $i \in \{1, 2, \ldots, r\}$. We obtain $w = w_1 w_2 \ldots w_r$, the encrypted text.

To decrypt the text, we use the decryption key, then we compute $d = q^{-1}$ and $v_i = dw_i$, for all $i \in \{1, 2, \ldots, r\}$.

Example 2. *We consider the word MATHEMATICS and the key SINE. We work on an alphabet with 29 letters, including blank space, denoted with "*", "." and ",". The labels of the letters are shown in the below table*

A	B	C	D	E	F	G	H	I	J
0	1	2	3	4	5	6	7	8	9
K	L	M	N	O	P	Q	R	S	T
10	11	12	13	14	15	16	17	18	19
U	V	W	X	Y	Z	*	.	,	
20	21	22	23	24	25	26	27	28	

We consider $t = 2$; therefore, we work on quaternions. We will add an "A" at the end of word "MATHEMATICS", to have multiple of 4 length text, therefore, we will encode the text "MATHEMATICSA". We have the following blocks MATH, EMAT, ICSA, with the corresponding quaternions $v_1 = 12 + 19j + 7k$, for MATH, $v_2 = 4 + 12i + 19k$, for EMAT and $v_3 = 8 + 2i + 18j$ for ICSA. The key is $q = 18 + 8i + 13j + 4k$, it is an invertible element, with the nonzero norm, $n_q = 22$. We have $w_1 = qv_1 = 28 + 24i + 7j + 7k$, corresponding to the message, "YHH", $w_2 = qv_2 = 16 + 2i + 6j + 28k$, corresponding to the message "QCG," and $w_3 = qv_3 = 10 + 28i + j + 5k$, corresponding to the message "K,BF". Therefore, the encrypted message is, "YHHQCG,K,BF". The decryption key is $d = q^{-1} = 14 + 26i + 6j + 13k$. For decryption, we will compute $dw_1 = 12 + 19j + 7k = v_1$, $dw_2 = 4 + 12i + 19k = v_2$, $dw_3 = 8 + 2i + 18j = v_3$, and we find the initial text "MATHEMATICSA".

6. Conclusions

In this paper, we studied properties of some special elements in algebras obtained by the Cayley–Dickson process and we find an algebraic structure (nonunitary and noncommutative ring) for Fibonacci quaternions over $\mathbb{Z}_3$. Moreover, an encryption method using these elements is also provided. As a further research, we intend to study other special elements in the idea of finding other good properties.

Author Contributions: Conceptualization, C.F. and A.B.; Methodology, C.F.; Validation, C.F.; Formal analysis, C.F.; Investigation, C.F. and A.B.; Writing original draft, C.F. and A.B.; Supervision, C.F. All authors have read and agreed to the published version of the manuscript.

Funding: This research received no external funding.

Data Availability Statement: Data are contained within the article.

Conflicts of Interest: The authors declare no conflicts of interest.

References

1. Miguel, C.J.; Serodio, R. On the Structure of Quaternion Rings over $\mathbb{Z}p$. *Int. J. Algebra* **2011**, *5*, 1313–1325.
2. Murakami, L.S.I.; Nascimento, P.S.M.; Shestakov, I.; da Silva, J.P. Commutative power-associative representations of symmetric matrices. *J. Algebra* **2024**, *644*, 411–427. [CrossRef]
3. Schafer, R.D. *An Introduction to Nonassociative Algebras*; Academic Press: New York, NY, USA, 1966.
4. Zhevlakov, K.A.; Slin'ko, A.M.; Shestakov, I.P.; Shirshov, A.I. *Rings That Are Nearly Associative*; Academic Press: New York, NY, USA, 1982.
5. Baez, J.C. The Octonions. *Bull. Am. Math. Soc.* **2001**, *39*, 145–205. Available online: http://www.ams.org/journals/bull/2002-39-02/S0273-0979-01-00934-X/S0273-0979-01-00934-X.pdf (accessed on 10 January 2024).
6. McCrimmon, K. Pre-Book on Alternative Algebras. 1980. Available online: http://mysite.science.uottawa.ca/neher/Papers/\alternative/2.2.Composition20algebras.pdf (accessed on 10 January 2024).
7. Schafer, R.D. On the algebras formed by the Cayley–Dickson process. *Am. J. Math.* **1954**, *76*, 435–446. [CrossRef]
8. Mosić, D. Characterizations of k-potent elements in rings. *Ann. Di Mat.* **2015**, *194*, 1157–1168. [CrossRef]
9. Ratanaburee, P.; Petapirak, M.; Chuysurichay, S. On (m, k)-type elements in the ring of integers modulo n. *Songklanakarin J. Sci. Technol.* **2022**, *44*, 1179–1184.
10. Wu, Y. k-Potent Matrices—Construction and Applications in Digital Image Encryption. In Proceedings of the 2010 American Conference on Applied Mathematics, Cambridge, MA, USA, 27–29 January 2010; pp. 455–460.
11. Koshy, T. *Fibonacci and Lucas Numbers with Applications*; A Wiley-Interscience Publication; John Wiley & Sons: Hoboken, NJ, USA, 2001.
12. Horadam, A.F. Complex Fibonacci Numbers and Fibonacci Quaternions. *Am. Math. Mon.* **1963**, *70*, 289–291. [CrossRef]

axioms

MDPI

Article

A Progressive Outlook on Possibility Multi-Fuzzy Soft Ordered Semigroups: Theory and Analysis

Sana Habib [1], Faiz Muhammad Khan [2] and Violeta Leoreanu-Fotea [3,*]

1 School of Mathematics and Statistics, Shaanxi Normal University, Xi'an 710119, China; sanahabib@snnu.edu.cn
2 Department of Mathematics and Statistics, University of Swat, Charbagh 19120, Pakistan; drfaiz@uswat.edu.pk
3 Faculty of Mathematics, Al. I. Cuza University of Iasi, Bd Carol I, No. 11, 700506 Iasi, Romania
* Correspondence: violeta.fotea@uaic.ro

Abstract: The concept of possibility fuzzy soft sets is a step in a new direction towards a soft set approach that can be used to solve decision-making issues. In this piece of research, an innovative and comprehensive conceptual framework for possibility multi-fuzzy soft ordered semigroups by making use of the notions that are associated with possibility multi-fuzzy soft sets as well as ordered semigroups is introduced. Possibility multi-fuzzy soft ordered semigroups mark a newly developed theoretical avenue, and the central aim of this paper is to investigate it. The focus lies on investigating this newly developed theoretical direction, with practical examples drawn from decision-making and diagnosis practices to enhance understanding and appeal to researchers' interests. We strictly build the notions of possibility multi-fuzzy soft left (right) ideals, as well as l-idealistic and r-idealistic possibility multi-fuzzy soft ordered semigroups. Furthermore, various algebraic operations, such as union, intersection, as well as AND and OR operations are derived, while also providing a comprehensive discussion of their properties. To clarify these innovative ideas, the theoretical constructs are further reinforced with a set of demonstrative examples in order to guarantee deep and improved comprehension of the proposed framework.

Keywords: fuzzy soft sets; multi-fuzzy soft set; ordered semigroups; possibility multi-fuzzy soft ordered semigroups; possibility multi-fuzzy soft left (resp. right) ideals

MSC: 03E72; 06F05; 90C70

Citation: Habib, S.; Khan, F.M.; Leoreanu-Fotea, V. A Progressive Outlook on Possibility Multi-Fuzzy Soft Ordered Semigroups: Theory and Analysis. *Axioms* **2024**, *13*, 340. https://doi.org/10.3390/axioms13060340

Academic Editors: Cristina Flaut, Dana Piciu, Murat Tosun, Hsien-Chung Wu and Javier Montero

Received: 8 March 2024
Revised: 2 May 2024
Accepted: 14 May 2024
Published: 21 May 2024

1. Introduction

The concept of possibility multi-fuzzy soft ordered semigroups is emerging as a promising avenue for addressing uncertainty in decision-making processes. The quest to address the challenges posed by uncertainty in problem solving, traditional mathematical methodologies have often proven insufficient as these methods do not always work in ambiguous and unpredictable situations. Realizing this fact has led scientists to create new approaches for dealing with uncertainty. In this context, we introduce the novel concept of possibility multi-fuzzy soft ordered semigroups. These structures combine elements of possibility theory, fuzzy sets and soft computing. By incorporating graded membership and possibility measures, they provide a robust framework for handling uncertainty in ordered semigroups.

One of the pioneers was Lotfi Zadeh, who in 1965 introduced fuzzy set theory, which opened up many fields to new ways of thinking about them. Fuzzy logic reflects the way that things are uncertain by allowing for degrees of membership rather than just yes/no inclusion or exclusion [1]. Moldstov [2,3] built on Zadeh's ideas when he put forward the concept of soft sets in 1999; these include tools for parameterization designed to cope with decision-making queries under conditions of limited information or lots of alternatives. Soft set theory has been shown by subsequent applications to be useful practically speaking; it can handle imprecise data and deal with incompleteness (P.K. Maji et al.) [4–6]. Alkalzaleh et al. [7,8] extended the framework by introducing ideas like soft multisets and interval-valued fuzzy soft sets. At the same time, fuzzy mathematics developed further and led to fuzzy soft set theory as a better way of dealing with uncertainty.

Currently, the fuzzy soft set approach has been bolstered by relating different new techniques such as interval-valued fuzzy soft sets, possibility intuitionistic fuzzy soft sets, intuitionistic fuzzy soft expert sets, soft expert sets, possibility fuzzy soft expert sets, neutrosophic sets, complex neutrosophic soft expert sets, neutrosophic vague soft expert sets, multi-fuzzy soft sets and many more [9–29].

Multi-fuzzy sets are an extension of ordinary fuzzy set theory that provided a new approach for certain problems that were previously unable to be resolved, such as color pixels [30]. Later, Yang et al. [31] combined the multi-fuzzy set theory with a soft set approach and provided its more precise applications in decision-making problems.

The concept of possibility fuzzy soft sets was broached by Alkalzaleh [32]. He also described some of the applications of this notion in decision making. Possibility fuzzy soft set theory states that for every element of set of parameters, there exists a degree of membership as well as a degree of possible membership value for all the elements of the universe U. Thus, the existence of two membership values will help the experts to choose well in decision-making problems. Recently, a new generalization to this study known as possibility multi-fuzzy soft sets is determined [33].

Rosenfeld in 1971 [12] was the first to study algebraic structures in terms of Zadeh's approach. He named these structures as fuzzy groups. One of the most adapted algebraic structures, i.e., the ordered semigroup, has a close connection with theoretical computer science including different code-correcting languages, sequential machines and arithmetical study, etc. The initial concept of ordered semigroups was introduced by Kehayopulu [34]. Jun et al. [35] instigated a new generalization of ordered semigroups by relating them with soft set theory. Kehayopulu [36] further generalized the concept of the ordered semigroup by relating its ideals with Green's relation. Later, the concept of fuzzy soft ordered semigroups, fuzzy soft left (resp. right) ideals and many more were introduced, and readers refer to [37–39]. Recently Habib et al. give the concept of possibility fuzzy soft ordered semigroups and described their applications [40,41].

The main purpose of this paper is to introduce a new theory by compiling possibility multi-fuzzy soft sets and ordered semigroups. For every element of a set of parameters in a possibility multi-fuzzy soft set, there exists multiple degrees of membership as well as multiple degrees of possible membership for all the elements of the universal set. This quantitative analysis will lead to obtaining an appropriate value that would further help experts in decision making. This paper is structured into multiple sections, beginning with a preliminary segment that establishes fundamental definitions and concepts necessary for grasping the new theory. Subsequent sections delve into the core principles and practical applications of the proposed theory. These discussions include an exploration of possibility multi-fuzzy soft ordered semigroups, emphasizing their significant roles in medical diagnosis and decision-making contexts. Moreover, the paper examines the process of homogenization of possibility multi-fuzzy soft sets and possibility multi-fuzzy soft l-ideals (resp. r-ideals) of ordered semigroups, and the notion of l-idealistic (resp. r-idealistic) possibility multi-fuzzy soft ordered semigroups is proposed, and some of the related properties using these notions are determined. Each section contributes to a comprehensive understanding of the proposed theory, elucidating its implications and potential applications. Finally, this paper concludes with a recapitulation of key insights and concluding remarks, providing a cohesive summary of the theory's significance and suggesting future research directions.

2. Preliminaries

This section relates some important notions and definitions, in light of which some important results are generated. An ordered semigroup is defined as a combination of a partially ordered set $(S, \leq)$ and a semigroup $(S, .)$ with $x \leq y$ $(\forall x, y \in S)$, implying $ax \leq ay,\ xa \leq ya,\ \forall a \in S$ [23]. Throughout the paper, an ordered semigroup $(S, ., \leq)$ is denoted by S. A non-empty subset X of an ordered semigroup S is called a left (resp. right) ideal of S [20] and is denoted by $X \lhd_l S$ (resp. $X \lhd_r S$) if it satisfies the following:

a. $SX \subseteq X$ (resp. $XS \subseteq X$);
b. $(\forall x \in X,\ y \in S)\ (y \leq x \Rightarrow y \in X)$.

Let S and T be two ordered semigroups. Then, a mapping $H : S \to T$ is called homomorphism if it satisfies the following:

a. $H(ab) = H(a)H(b)\ \forall a, b \in S$;
b. If $a \leq b \Rightarrow H(a) \leq H(b)\ \forall a, b \in S$.

A set of all the elements in S which are mapped to the identity element of T under a homomorphism H is known as the kernel of H, represented as $ker(H)$. More precisely, $ker(H) = \{s \in S | H(s) = e_T\}$, where e_T is the identity element of T.

Let U be a universal set, Q be the set of parameters and let $A \subseteq Q$. Then, a pair (f, A) is called a soft set of U if f is a mapping from A to P(U), i.e., $f : A \to P(U)$, where $P(U)$ is the power set of U [5].

Let A be a non-empty subset of a universal set U. Then, the characteristic function for A is defined as

$$\chi_A(x) = \left\{ {}^{1}_{0}\ if\ {}^{x \epsilon A}_{x \notin A} \right.$$

Definition 1 ([6]). *A pair of set (U, Q) is known as a soft universe, where U is a universal set and Q is a set of parameters. If $A \subseteq Q$, $f : A \to F(U)$, where $F(U)$ is the power set of all fuzzy subset of U, then (f, A) is called a fuzzy soft set.*

Definition 2 ([30]). *For any universal set U, a multi-fuzzy set $(\overline{\psi}, A)$ with index n is defined by a mapping $\overline{\psi} : A \to M^n FS(U)$, where n is a positive integer and $\overline{\psi}$ is of ordered sequences, $\overline{\psi} = \{u/v_1(u), v_2(u), \ldots, v_n(u)\} \forall u \epsilon U$, where $v_i(u)$ is the multi-membership values of the multi-fuzzy soft set.*

Definition 3 ([11]). *If $U = \{u_1, u_2, \ldots, u_n\}$ is the universal set and $Q = \{e_1, e_2, \ldots, e_n\}$ is the set of parameters, then a mapping $\overline{f}_{\overline{v}} : Q \to F(U) \times I(U)$ ($\overline{v}$ is the fuzzy subset of Q) is defined by $\overline{f}_{\overline{v}}(e_i) = (\overline{f}(e_i)(u),\ \overline{v}(e_i)(u)) \forall i = 1, 2, \ldots, m$ and is known as a possibility fuzzy soft set denoted by $(\overline{f}_{\overline{v}}, Q)$. A possibility fuzzy soft set is used to introduce a degree of membership value coupled with the possibility of a degree of membership of element denoted by $\overline{f}(e_i)$ and $\overline{v}(e_i)$, respectively.*

Note that if (f, Q) is a soft set over an ordered semigroup S and f(e) is a subsemigroup of S such that $\forall$e $\in$ Q f(e) $\neq \emptyset$, then (f, Q) is called a soft ordered semigroup over S [38].

Definition 4 ([35]). *If $(\overline{f}, Q|_1)$ and $(\overline{g}, Q|_2)$ are two soft sets over U, then their union is represented as $(\overline{f}, Q|_1) \cup (\overline{g}, Q|_2) = (\overline{h}, Q)$, which satisfies the following conditions:*

a. $Q = Q|_1 \cup Q|_2$;
b. $\overline{h}(e) = \begin{cases} \overline{f}(e) & e \in Q|_1 - Q|_2 \\ \overline{g}(e) & if\ e \in Q|_2 - Q|_1\ \forall e \in Q. \\ \overline{f}(e) \cup \overline{g}(e) & e \in Q|_1 \cap Q|_2 \end{cases}$

Definition 5 ([35]). *If $(\overline{f}, Q|_1)$ and $(\overline{g}, Q|_2)$ are two soft sets over U, then their intersection is represented as $(\overline{f}, Q|_1) \cap (\overline{g}, Q|_2) = (\overline{h}, Q)$, which satisfies the following conditions:*

a. $Q = Q|_1 \cap Q|_2$;
b. $\overline{h}(e) = \overline{f}(e)$ *or* $\overline{h}(e) = \overline{g}(e)\ \forall e \in Q$.

Definition 6 ([11]). *If (U, Q) is a pair of sets known as a soft universe, where $U = \{u_1, u_2, \ldots, u_n\}$ is the universal set and $Q = \{e_1, e_2, \ldots, e_m\}$ is the set of parameters, then define a mapping $\overline{\psi}_{\overline{f}} : Q \to M^n FS(U) \times M^n FS(U)$, where $\overline{\psi} : Q \to M^n FS(U)$ and $\overline{f} : Q \to M^n FS(U)$ ($\overline{f}$ and $\overline{\psi}$ are the fuzzy subsets of Q, and $M^n FS(U)$ represents the set of all multi-fuzzy sets with dimension n). $\overline{\psi}_{\overline{f}}(e_i) = (\overline{\psi}(e_i)(u), \overline{f}(e_i)(u)) \forall u \epsilon U$ is known as a possibility multi-fuzzy soft set denoted by $(\overline{\psi}_{\overline{f}}, Q)$ with dimension n. Note that $\overline{\psi}_{\overline{f}}(e_i)$ represents the degree of multi-membership value and $\overline{f}(e_i)$ represents the possibility of a degree of multi-membership for all the elements of U.*

In generalized form, a possibility multi-fuzzy soft set is represented as

$$\overline{\psi}_{\overline{f}}(e_i) = \left\{ \left({}^{u}/_{v_{\overline{\psi}(e_i)}(u), v_{\overline{f}(e_i)}(u)} \right) : u \epsilon U \right\}$$

where

$$v_{\overline{\psi}(e_i)}(u) = (v^1_{\overline{\psi}(e_i)}(u), v^2_{\overline{\psi}(e_i)}(u), \ldots, v^n_{\overline{\psi}(e_i)}(u))$$

and

$$v_{\overline{f}(e_i)}(u) = (v^1_{\overline{f}(e_i)}(u), v^2_{\overline{f}(e_i)}(u), \ldots, v^n_{\overline{f}(e_i)}(u)) \; i = 1, 2, \ldots, m$$

The possibility multi-fuzzy soft set is called a possibility fuzzy soft set with index n = 1.

Definition 7 ([11]). *If $\overline{\psi}_{\overline{f}}$ and $\overline{\xi}_{\overline{g}}$ are two possibility multi-fuzzy soft sets over U, then their union is denoted by $\overline{\psi}_{\overline{f}} \cup \overline{\xi}_{\overline{g}} = \overline{\eta}_{\overline{h}}$, where $\overline{\eta}_{\overline{h}} : Q \to M^n FS(U) \times M^n FS(U)$ is defined as $\overline{\eta}_{\overline{h}}(e) = \overline{\eta}(e)(u), \overline{h}(e)(u)$. The union must satisfy the following conditions:*

a. $\overline{\psi}(e) \cup \overline{\xi}(e) = \overline{\eta}(e)$;
b. $\overline{h}(e) = \overline{f}(e) \cup \overline{g}(e) \forall e \in Q$.

Definition 8 ([11]). *If $\overline{\psi}_{\overline{f}}$ and $\overline{\xi}_{\overline{g}}$ are two possibility multi-fuzzy soft sets over U, then their intersection is denoted as $\overline{\psi}_{\overline{f}} \cap \overline{\xi}_{\overline{g}} = \overline{\eta}_{\overline{h}}$, where $\overline{\eta}_{\overline{h}} : Q \to M^n FS(U) \times M^n FS(U)$ is defined as $\overline{\eta}_{\overline{h}}(e) = \overline{\eta}(e)(u), \overline{h}(e)(u)$. The intersection must satisfy the following:*

a. $\overline{\psi}(e) \cap \overline{\xi}(e) = \overline{\eta}(e)$;
b. $\overline{h}(e) = \overline{f}(e) \cap \overline{g}(e) \forall e \in Q$.

Definition 9 ([11]). *For two possibility multi-fuzzy soft sets $(\overline{\psi}_{\overline{f}}, A)$ and $(\overline{\xi}_{\overline{g}}, B)$ over U with index j, the similarity measure is defined as*

$$\overline{s}(\overline{\psi}_{\overline{f}}, \overline{\xi}_{\overline{g}}) = \frac{\sum_{j=1}^{n} (\varphi_j(\overline{\psi}, \overline{\xi})) \cdot (\phi_j(\overline{f}, \overline{g}))}{j}$$

where

$$\varphi_j(\overline{\psi}, \overline{\xi}) = \frac{\sum_{i=1}^{n} max_{x \epsilon U} \left\{ min\left(v^j_{\overline{\psi}(e_i)}(x), v^j_{\overline{\xi}(e_i)}(x) \right) \right\}}{\sum_{i=1}^{n} max_{x \epsilon U} \left\{ max\left(v^j_{\overline{\psi}(e_i)}(x), v^j_{\overline{\xi}(e_i)}(x) \right) \right\}},$$

$$\phi_j(\overline{f}, \overline{g}) = \frac{\sum_{i=1}^{n} max_{x \epsilon U} \left\{ min(v^j_{\overline{f}(e_i)}(x), v^j_{\overline{g}(e_i)}(x)) \right\}}{\sum_{i=1}^{n} max_{x \epsilon U} \left\{ max(v^j_{\overline{f}(e_i)}(x), v^j_{\overline{g}(e_i)}(x)) \right\}}.$$

For all $v^j_{\overline{\psi}(e_i)}(x) \neq 0, v^j_{\overline{\xi}(e_i)}(x) \neq 0, v^j_{\overline{f}(e_i)}(x) \neq 0$ and $v^j_{\overline{g}(e_i)}(x) \neq 0$,.

The possibility multi-fuzzy soft set is the most appropriate method used to solve decision-making problems more efficiently.

3. Possibility Multi-Fuzzy Soft Ordered Semigroups

This section provides an overview of possibility multi-fuzzy soft ordered semigroups. Additionally, it introduces new generalized concepts such as homomorphism in possibility multi-fuzzy soft ordered semigroups and possibility multi-fuzzy soft l-ideals (or r-ideals) of ordered semigroups. These concepts will be elucidated further through algebraic results employing fundamental operations like union, intersection, AND and OR operations.

Definition 10. *Let $(S,\cdot,\leq)$ be an ordered semigroup and R be a set of parameters of S, then a mapping $\overline{\psi}_{\overline{f}}: R \to M^nFS(S) \times M^nFS(S)$ is defined, where $\overline{\psi}: R \to M^nFS(S)$ and $\overline{f}: R \to M^nFS(S)$. Then, $(\overline{\psi}_{\overline{f}}, R)$ is called a possibility multi-fuzzy soft ordered semigroup of S if it satisfies $\forall e \epsilon R$ $(\overline{\psi}(e) \neq \varnothing, \overline{f}\ (e) \neq \varnothing)$ or $\overline{\psi}_{\overline{f}}(e_i) \neq \varnothing$ (if $\overline{\psi}_{\overline{f}}(e)$ are fuzzy subsemigroups of S). Possibility multi-fuzzy soft ordered semigroup is represented as PMFSS unless otherwise stated.*

Definition 11 . *Let $\overline{\psi}$ and $\overline{f}$ be two multi-fuzzy subsets of S and $(\overline{\psi}_{\overline{f}}, R)$ be a possibility multi-fuzzy soft ordered semigroup over S. Then, $\forall t \in [0,1]$; we define possibility multi-fuzzy soft level set of $\overline{\psi}_{\overline{f}}$ as $U(\overline{\psi}_{\overline{f}}; t) = \left\{ s\epsilon S \middle| \overline{\psi}(s) \geq t, \overline{f}(s) \geq t \right\}$.*

Example 1. *Let $S = \{a_1, a_2, a_3, a_4\}$ be an ordered semigroup under the following multiplication table and ordered relation:*

$$\leq := \{(a_1,a_1),(a_2,a_2),(a_3,a_3),(a_4,a_4),(a_1,a_2)$$

Multiplication Table

	a_1	a_2	a_3	a_4
a_1	a_1	a_1	a_1	a_1
a_2	a_1	a_1	a_1	a_1
a_3	a_1	a_1	a_2	a_1
a_4	a_1	a_1	a_2	a_2

For a set of parameters $R = \{e_1, e_2, e_3\}$, a possibility multi-fuzzy soft set $(\overline{\psi}_{\overline{f}}, R)$ is defined by mapping

$$\overline{\psi}: R \to M^nFS(S)\ , \overline{f}: R \to M^nFS(S)$$

Here, we obtain

$$\overline{\psi}(e) = \begin{bmatrix} (0.8,0.7,0.5) & (0.7,0.6,0.3) & (0.6,0.4,0.2) & (0.6,0.5,0.1) \\ (0.7,0.7,0.9) & (0.6,0.6,0.8) & (0.3,0.5,0.7) & (0.4,0.5,0.2) \\ (0.9,0.8,0.8) & (0.6,0.7,0.7) & (0.4,0.6,0.2) & (0.4,0.3,0.1) \end{bmatrix},$$

$$\overline{f}(e) = \begin{bmatrix} (0.7,0.6,0.5) & (0.6,0.5,0.4) & (0.4,0.3,0.3) & (0.5,0.3,0.2) \\ (0.8,0.7,0.8) & (0.7,0.3,0.6) & (0.5,0.1,0.3) & (0.6,0.2,0.5) \\ (0.8,0.8,0.7) & (0.6,0.7,0.5) & (0.4,0.6,0.2) & (0.2,0.3,0.1) \end{bmatrix}.$$

Thus,

$$\overline{\psi}_{\overline{f}}(e) = \begin{bmatrix} (0.8,0.7,0.5),\ (0.7,0.6,0.5) & (0.7,0.6,0.3),(0.6,0.5,0.4) & (0.6,0.4,0.2),(0.4,0.3,0.3) & (0.6,0.5,0.1),(0.5,0.3,0.2) \\ (0.7,0.7,0.9),(0.8,0.7,0.8) & (0.6,0.6,0.8),(0.7,0.3,0.6) & (0.3,0.5,0.7),(0.5,0.1,0.3) & (0.4,0.5,0.2),(0.6,0.2,0.5) \\ (0.9,0.8,0.8),(0.8,0.8,0.7) & (0.6,0.7,0.7),(0.6,0.7,0.5) & (0.4,0.6,0.2),(0.4,0.6,0.2) & (0.4,0.3,0.1),(0.2,0.3,0.1) \end{bmatrix}$$

Here, $\overline{\psi}_{\overline{f}}(e) \neq \varnothing$ and $\overline{\psi}_{\overline{f}}(e)(a), \forall a \in S$ are fuzzy subsemigroups of S. Hence, by Definition 10, $(\overline{\psi}_{\overline{f}}, R)$ is a PMFSS over S.

Theorem 1. *Let $(\overline{\psi}_{\overline{f}}, A)$ be a possibility multi-fuzzy soft ordered semigroup of S. Then, for any subset B of A, $(\overline{\xi}_{\overline{g}}, B)$ is also a possibility multi-fuzzy soft ordered semigroup of S.*

Proof. The proof follows directly from Definition 10. □

Example 2. *If S is an ordered semigroup and* $(\overline{\psi}_{\overline{f}}, A)$ *is a possibility multi-fuzzy soft ordered semigroup over S as defined in Example 1, then*

$$\overline{\psi}_{\overline{f}}(e) = \begin{bmatrix} (0.8,0.7,0.5),\ (0.7,0.6,0.5) & (0.7,0.6,0.3),(0.6,0.5,0.4) & (0.6,0.4,0.2),(0.4,0.3,0.3) & (0.6,0.5,0.1),(0.5,0.3,0.2) \\ (0.7,0.7,0.9),(0.8,0.7,0.8) & (0.6,0.6,0.8),(0.7,0.3,0.6) & (0.3,0.5,0.7),(0.5,0.1,0.3) & (0.4,0.5,0.2),(0.6,0.2,0.5) \\ (0.9,0.8,0.8),(0.8,0.8,0.7) & (0.6,0.7,0.7),(0.6,0.7,0.5) & (0.4,0.6,0.2),(0.4,0.6,0.2) & (0.4,0.3,0.1),(0.2,0.3,0.1) \end{bmatrix}$$

Let $B \subseteq A$; then, we define another mapping $\overline{\xi}_{\overline{g}} : B \to M^nFS(S) \times M^nFS(S)$ defined as $\overline{\xi}_{\overline{g}}(e) = \overline{\xi}(e)(s), \overline{g}(e)(s)$ for all $s \in S$.

$$\overline{\xi}(e) = \begin{bmatrix} (0.7,0.6,0.3) & (0.6,0.4,0.2) & (0.5,0.3,0.1) & (0.5,0.3,0.1) \\ (0.6,0.6,0.7) & (0.5,0.5,0.6) & (0.2,0.4,0.5) & (0.4,0.4,0.1) \\ (0.8,0.7,0.6) & (0.5,0.6,0.5) & (0.3,0.5,0.1) & (0.3,0.2,0.1) \end{bmatrix}$$

$$\overline{g}(e) = \begin{bmatrix} (0.6,0.5,0.4) & (0.5,0.5,0.3) & (0.4,0.3,0.2) & (0.4,0.2,0.1) \\ (0.5,0.4,0.6) & (0.4,0.3,0.5) & (0.3,0.1,0.2) & (0.5,0.1,0.3) \\ (0.7,0.6,0.5) & (0.5,0.5,0.4) & (0.2,0.3,0.1) & (0.2,0.2,0.1) \end{bmatrix}.$$

Combining above two matrices we obtain

$$\overline{\xi}_{\overline{g}}(e) = \begin{bmatrix} (0.7,0.6,0.3)(0.6,0.5,0.4) & (0.6,0.4,0.2)(0.5,0.5,0.3) & (0.5,0.3,0.1)(0.4,0.3,0.2) & (0.5,0.3,0.1)(0.4,0.2,0.1) \\ (0.6,0.6,0.7)(0.5,0.4,0.6) & (0.5,0.5,0.6)(0.4,0.3,0.5) & (0.2,0.4,0.5)(0.3,0.1,0.2) & (0.4,0.4,0.1)(0.5,0.1,0.3) \\ (0.8,0.7,0.6)(0.7,0.6,0.5) & (0.5,0.6,0.5)(0.5,0.5,0.4) & (0.3,0.5,0.1)(0.2,0.3,0.1) & (0.3,0.2,0.1)(0.2,0.2,0.1) \end{bmatrix}$$

Here, $\overline{\xi}_{\overline{g}}(e) \neq \emptyset$ and $\overline{\xi}_{\overline{g}}(e)(a), \forall a \in S$ are fuzzy subsemigroups of S. Hence, by Definition 10, $(\overline{\xi}_{\overline{g}}, B)$ is a PMFSS over S.

Theorem 2. *Let* $(\overline{\psi}_{\overline{f}}, A)$ *and* $(\overline{\xi}_{\overline{g}}, B)$ *be two PMFSSs over S. If* $A \cap B = \phi$*, then* $(\overline{\psi}_{\overline{f}}, A) \cup (\overline{\xi}_{\overline{g}}, B)$ *is also possibility multi-fuzzy soft ordered semigroup over S.*

Proof. Union of any two possibility multi-fuzzy soft sets is denoted by $(\overline{\psi}_{\overline{f}}, A) \cup (\overline{\xi}_{\overline{g}}, B)$. Let $(\overline{\psi}_{\overline{f}}, A) \cup (\overline{\xi}_{\overline{g}}, B) = (\overline{\sigma}_{\overline{h}}, C)$ where $C = A \cup B$; then, $\forall e \in C$.

$$(\overline{\sigma}_{\overline{h}}, C) = \begin{cases} (\overline{\psi}_{\overline{f}}, A) & e \in A - B, \\ (\overline{\xi}_{\overline{g}}, B) & \text{if} e \in B - A, \\ (\overline{\psi}_{\overline{f}}, A) \cup (\overline{\xi}_{\overline{g}}, B) & e \in A \cap B. \end{cases}$$

As $A \cap B = \emptyset \Rightarrow$ either $e \in A - B$ or $e \in B - A$; in other words, either $\overline{\sigma}_{\overline{h}}(e) = \overline{\psi}_{\overline{f}}(e)$ or $\overline{\sigma}_{\overline{h}}(e) = \overline{\xi}_{\overline{g}}(e)$. Then, a mapping $\overline{\sigma}_{\overline{h}} : C \to M^nFS(S) \times M^nFS(S)$ is defined as $\overline{\sigma}_{\overline{h}}(e) = \overline{\sigma}(e)(s), \overline{h}(e)(s) \forall s \in S$. Hence, $\overline{\sigma}_{\overline{h}}(e) \neq \emptyset$ also implies $\overline{\sigma}(e)(s)$, and $\overline{h}(e)(s)$ is a fuzzy subsemigroup over S. Then, using Definition 10, $(\overline{\sigma}_{\overline{h}}, C)$ is a PMFSS over S. Thus, the union of two PMFSSs over S is also a PMFSS over S. □

Example 3. *Let* $(\overline{\psi}_{\overline{f}}, A)$ *and* $(\overline{\xi}_{\overline{g}}, B)$ *be two possibility multi-fuzzy soft sets over S. Where S is defined under the same ordered relation as defined in Example 1,*

$$\overline{\psi}_{\overline{f}}(e) = \begin{bmatrix} (0.8,0.7,0.5),\ (0.7,0.6,0.5) & (0.7,0.6,0.3),(0.6,0.5,0.4) & (0.6,0.4,0.2),(0.4,0.3,0.3) & (0.6,0.5,0.1),(0.5,0.3,0.2) \\ (0.7,0.7,0.9),(0.8,0.7,0.8) & (0.6,0.6,0.8),(0.7,0.3,0.6) & (0.3,0.5,0.7),(0.5,0.1,0.3) & (0.4,0.5,0.2),(0.6,0.2,0.5) \\ (0.9,0.8,0.8),(0.8,0.8,0.7) & (0.6,0.7,0.7),(0.6,0.7,0.5) & (0.4,0.6,0.2),(0.4,0.6,0.2) & (0.4,0.3,0.1),(0.2,0.3,0.1) \end{bmatrix}$$

$$\overline{\xi}_{\overline{g}}(e) = \begin{bmatrix} (0.7,0.6,0.3)(0.6,0.5,0.4) & (0.6,0.4,0.2)(0.5,0.5,0.3) & (0.5,0.3,0.1)(0.4,0.3,0.2) & (0.5,0.3,0.1)(0.4,0.2,0.1) \\ (0.6,0.6,0.7)(0.5,0.4,0.6) & (0.5,0.5,0.6)(0.4,0.3,0.5) & (0.2,0.4,0.5)(0.3,0.1,0.2) & (0.4,0.4,0.1)(0.5,0.1,0.3) \\ (0.8,0.7,0.6)(0.7,0.6,0.5) & (0.5,0.6,0.5)(0.5,0.5,0.4) & (0.3,0.5,0.1)(0.2,0.3,0.1) & (0.3,0.2,0.1)(0.2,0.2,0.1) \end{bmatrix}.$$

Then, $(\psi_{\overline{f}}, A) \cup (\overline{\xi}_{\overline{g}}, B) = (\overline{\sigma}_{\overline{h}}, C)$; using Theorem 2, we obtain

$$\overline{\sigma}_{\overline{h}}(e) = \begin{bmatrix} (0.8,0.7,0.5),\ (0.7,0.6,0.5) & (0.7,0.6,0.3),(0.6,0.5,0.4) & (0.6,0.4,0.2),(0.4,0.3,0.3) & (0.6,0.5,0.1),(0.5,0.3,0.2) \\ (0.7,0.7,0.9),(0.8,0.7,0.8) & (0.6,0.6,0.8),(0.7,0.3,0.6) & (0.3,0.5,0.7),(0.5,0.1,0.3) & (0.4,0.5,0.2),(0.6,0.2,0.5) \\ (0.9,0.8,0.8),(0.8,0.8,0.7) & (0.6,0.7,0.7),(0.6,0.7,0.5) & (0.4,0.6,0.2),(0.4,0.6,0.2) & (0.4,0.3,0.1),(0.2,0.3,0.1) \end{bmatrix}.$$

Here, it is easily notified that $\overline{\sigma}_{\overline{h}}(e) \neq \emptyset$ also implies $\overline{\sigma}(e)(s)$ and $\overline{h}(e)(s)$ are fuzzy subsemigroups over S. Then, by Definition 10, $(\overline{\sigma}_{\overline{h}}, C)$ is a PMFSS over S. Thus, the union of two PMFSSs over S is also a PMFSS over S.

Theorem 3. *Let $(\overline{\psi}_{\overline{f}}, A)$ and $(\overline{\zeta}_{\overline{g}}, B)$ be two PMFSS over S. If $A \cap B \neq \emptyset$, then their intersection $((\overline{\psi}_{\overline{f}}, A) \cap (\overline{\zeta}_{\overline{g}}, B))$ is also possibility multi-fuzzy soft ordered semigroup over S.*

Proof. Intersection of any two possibility multi-fuzzy soft set is denoted as $(\overline{\psi}_{\overline{f}}, A) \cap (\overline{\zeta}_{\overline{g}}, B)$. Let $(\overline{\psi}_{\overline{f}}, A) \cap (\overline{\zeta}_{\overline{g}}, B) = (\overline{\sigma}_{\overline{h}}, C)$ where $C = A \cap B$ then $\forall e \in C$ implies $e \in A$ and $e \in B$ or in other words $\overline{\psi}_{\overline{f}}(e) \cap \overline{\zeta}_{\overline{g}}(e) = \overline{\sigma}_{\overline{h}}(e)$ implies $(\overline{\sigma}(e), \overline{h}(e)) = (\overline{\psi}(e), \overline{f}(e))$ and $(\overline{\sigma}(e), \overline{h}(e)) = (\overline{\xi}(e), \overline{g}(e))$. Thus, there exists a mapping $\overline{\sigma}_{\overline{h}} : C \to M^nFS(S) \times M^nFS(S)$ defined as $\overline{\sigma}_{\overline{h}}(e) = \overline{\sigma}(e)(s), \overline{h}(e)(s)\ \forall s \in S$. Where, $\overline{\sigma}_{\overline{h}}(e) \neq \emptyset$ also implies $\overline{\sigma}(e)(s)$ and $\overline{h}(e)(s)$ are fuzzy subsemigroups over S then by Definition 10 $(\overline{\sigma}_{\overline{h}}, C)$ is a PMFSS over S. Thus intersection of two PMFSS over S is also a PMFSS over S. □

Example 4. *Let $(\overline{\psi}_{\overline{f}}, A)$ and $(\overline{\zeta}_{\overline{g}}, B)$ be two possibility multi-fuzzy soft sets over S. Where S is defined under the same ordered relation as defined in Example 1,*

$$\psi_{\overline{f}}(e) = \begin{bmatrix} (0.8,0.7,0.5),\ (0.7,0.6,0.5) & (0.7,0.6,0.3),(0.6,0.5,0.4) & (0.6,0.4,0.2),(0.4,0.3,0.3) & (0.6,0.5,0.1),(0.5,0.3,0.2) \\ (0.7,0.7,0.9),(0.8,0.7,0.8) & (0.6,0.6,0.8),(0.7,0.3,0.6) & (0.3,0.5,0.7),(0.5,0.1,0.3) & (0.4,0.5,0.2),(0.6,0.2,0.5) \\ (0.9,0.8,0.8),(0.8,0.8,0.7) & (0.6,0.7,0.7),(0.6,0.7,0.5) & (0.4,0.6,0.2),(0.4,0.6,0.2) & (0.4,0.3,0.1),(0.2,0.3,0.1) \end{bmatrix},$$

$$\overline{\zeta}_{\overline{g}}(e) = \begin{bmatrix} (0.7,0.6,0.3)(0.6,0.5,0.4) & (0.6,0.4,0.2)(0.5,0.5,0.3) & (0.5,0.3,0.1)(0.4,0.3,0.2) & (0.5,0.3,0.1)(0.4,0.2,0.1) \\ (0.6,0.6,0.7)(0.5,0.4,0.6) & (0.5,0.5,0.6)(0.4,0.3,0.5) & (0.2,0.4,0.5)(0.3,0.1,0.2) & (0.4,0.4,0.1)(0.5,0.1,0.3) \\ (0.8,0.7,0.6)(0.7,0.6,0.5) & (0.5,0.6,0.5)(0.5,0.5,0.4) & (0.3,0.5,0.1)(0.2,0.3,0.1) & (0.3,0.2,0.1)(0.2,0.2,0.1) \end{bmatrix}$$

Then, their intersection is denoted as $(\psi_{\overline{f}}, A) \cap (\overline{\zeta}_{\overline{g}}, B) = (\overline{\sigma}_{\overline{h}}, C)$.
So here,

$$\overline{\sigma}_{\overline{h}}(e) = \begin{bmatrix} (0.7,0.6,0.3)(0.6,0.5,0.4) & (0.6,0.4,0.2)(0.5,0.5,0.3) & (0.5,0.3,0.1)(0.4,0.3,0.2) & (0.5,0.3,0.1)(0.4,0.2,0.1) \\ (0.6,0.6,0.7)(0.5,0.4,0.6) & (0.5,0.5,0.6)(0.4,0.3,0.5) & (0.2,0.4,0.5)(0.3,0.1,0.2) & (0.4,0.4,0.1)(0.5,0.1,0.3) \\ (0.8,0.7,0.6)(0.7,0.6,0.5) & (0.5,0.6,0.5)(0.5,0.5,0.4) & (0.3,0.5,0.1)(0.2,0.3,0.1) & (0.3,0.2,0.1)(0.2,0.2,0.1) \end{bmatrix}$$

As $\overline{\sigma}_{\overline{h}}(e) \neq \emptyset$ also implies $\overline{\sigma}(e)$ and $\overline{h}(e)$ are fuzzy subsemigroups over S, then by Definition 10, $(\overline{\sigma}_{\overline{h}}, C)$ is a PMFSS over S.

Next, we discuss the logical operators, i.e., AND and OR, for possibility multi-fuzzy soft sets and characterized possibility multi-fuzzy soft ordered semigroups by the properties of these newly defined notions.

Theorem 4. *If $(\overline{\psi}_{\overline{f}}, A)$ and $(\overline{\zeta}_{\overline{g}}, B)$ are two possibility multi-fuzzy soft ordered semigroups over S, then $(\overline{\psi}_{\overline{f}}, A) \wedge (\overline{\zeta}_{\overline{g}}, B)$ is also a PMFSS over S.*

Proof. As AND operation in possibility multi-fuzzy soft sets is defined as $(\overline{\psi}_{\overline{f}}, A) \wedge (\overline{\zeta}_{\overline{g}}, B) = (\overline{\sigma}_{\overline{h}}, C)$, where $C = A \times B$ and $\overline{\sigma}(a,b) = \overline{\psi}(a) \cap \overline{\zeta}(b)$, similarly $\overline{h}(a,b) = \overline{f}(a) \cap \overline{g}(b)\ \forall (a,b) \in A \times B$. Since $(\overline{\psi}_{\overline{f}}, A)$ and $(\overline{\zeta}_{\overline{g}}, B)$ are PMFSSs over S, we can say that $\overline{\psi}_{\overline{f}}(a)$ and $\overline{\zeta}_{\overline{g}}(b)$ are multi-fuzzy subsemigroups of S, and the intersection of $(\overline{\psi}_{\overline{f}}(a)) \cap (\overline{\zeta}_{\overline{g}}(b)) \forall (a,b) \in A \times B$ is also a fuzzy subsemigroup of S. Hence, $\overline{\sigma}_{\overline{h}}(a,b) = (\overline{\sigma}(a,b)(s), \overline{h}(a,b)(s)) \forall s \in S$ is also a fuzzy subsemigroup of S $\forall (a,b) \in A \times B$. Thus, $(\overline{\psi}_{\overline{f}}, A) \wedge (\overline{\zeta}_{\overline{g}}, B) = (\overline{\sigma}_{\overline{h}}, C)$ is also a PMFSS over S. □

Example 5. *Let $(\overline{\psi}_{\overline{f}}, A)$ and $(\overline{\zeta}_{\overline{g}}, B)$ be two PMFSSs over S as defined in Example 2. Then, we can define its AND operation as $(\overline{\psi}_{\overline{f}}, A) \wedge (\overline{\zeta}_{\overline{g}}, B) = (\overline{\sigma}_{\overline{h}}, C)$, where $\overline{\sigma}_{\overline{h}}$ for all pair of parameters can be concluded, and we obtain*

$$\overline{\sigma}_{\overline{h}}(e_1,e_1) = \left\{\left(\frac{s_1}{(0.7,0.6,0.3)},(0.6,0.5,0.4)\right),\left(\frac{s_2}{(0.6,0.4,0.2)},(0.5,0.5,0.3)\right),\left(\frac{s_3}{(0.5,0.3,0.1)},(0.4,0.3,0.2)\right),\left(\frac{s_4}{(0.5,0.3,0.1)},(0.4,0.2,0.1)\right)\right\},$$

$$\overline{\sigma}_{\overline{h}}(e_1,e_2) = \left\{\left(\frac{s_1}{(0.6,0.6,0.5)},(0.5,0.4,0.5)\right),\left(\frac{s_2}{(0.5,0.5,0.3)},(0.4,0.3,0.4)\right),\left(\frac{s_3}{(0.2,0.4,0.2)},(0.3,0.1,0.2)\right),\left(\frac{s_4}{(0.4,0.4,0.1)},(0.5,0.1,0.2)\right)\right\}$$

$$\overline{\sigma}_{\overline{h}}(e_1,e_3) = \left\{\left(\frac{s_1}{(0.8,0.8,0.5)},(0.7,0.6,0.5)\right),\left(\frac{s_2}{(0.5,0.6,0.3)},(0.5,0.5,0.4)\right),\left(\frac{s_3}{(0.3,0.4,0.1)},(0.2,0.3,0.1)\right),\left(\frac{s_4}{(0.3,0.2,0.1)},(0.2,0.2,0.1)\right)\right\}.$$

Similarly, we can calculate the values for every pair of parameters.
In matrix form,

$$\overline{\sigma}_{\overline{h}} = \begin{bmatrix}
(0.7,0.6,0.3),(0.6,0.5,0.4) & (0.6,0.4,0.2),(0.5,0.5,0.3) & (0.5,0.3,0.1),(0.4,0.3,0.2) & (0.5,0.3,0.1),(0.4,0.2,0.1) \\
(0.6,0.6,0.5),(0.5,0.4,0.5) & (0.5,0.5,0.3),(0.4,0.3,0.4) & (0.2,0.4,0.2),(0.3,0.1,0.2) & (0.4,0.4,0.1),(0.5,0.1,0.2) \\
(0.8,0.7,0.5),(0.7,0.6,0.5) & (0.5,0.6,0.3),(0.5,0.5,0.4) & (0.3,0.4,0.1),(0.2,0.3,0.1) & (0.3,0.2,0.1),(0.2,0.2,0.1) \\
(0.7,0.6,0.3),(0.6,0.5,0.4) & (0.6,0.4,0.2),(0.5,0.3,0.3) & (0.3,0.3,0.1),(0.4,0.1,0.2) & (0.4,0.3,0.1),(0.4,0.2,0.1) \\
(0.6,0.6,0.7),(0.5,0.4,0.6) & (0.5,0.5,0.6),(0.4,0.3,0.5) & (0.2,0.4,0.5),(0.3,0.1,0.2) & (0.4,0.4,0.1),(0.5,0.1,0.3) \\
(0.7,0.7,0.6),(0.7,0.6,0.5) & (0.5,0.6,0.5),(0.5,0.3,0.4) & (0.3,0.5,0.1),(0.2,0.1,0.1) & (0.3,0.2,0.1),(0.2,0.2,0.1) \\
(0.7,0.6,0.3),(0.6,0.5,0.4) & (0.6,0.4,0.2),(0.5,0.5,0.3) & (0.4,0.3,0.1),(0.4,0.3,0.2) & (0.4,0.3,0.1),(0.2,0.2,0.1) \\
(0.6,0.6,0.7),(0.5,0.4,0.6) & (0.5,0.5,0.6),(0.4,0.3,0.5) & (0.2,0.4,0.2),(0.3,0.1,0.2) & (0.4,0.3,0.1),(0.2,0.1,0.1) \\
(0.8,0.7,0.6),(0.7,0.6,0.5) & (0.5,0.6,0.5),(0.5,0.5,0.4) & (0.3,0.5,0.1),(0.2,0.3,0.1) & (0.3,0.2,0.1),(0.2,0.2,0.1)
\end{bmatrix}$$

As $\overline{\sigma}_{\overline{h}}(e_i,e_j) \neq \phi$, $\overline{\sigma}_{\overline{h}}(e_i,e_j)$ is a fuzzy subsemigroup of S. Thus, $(\overline{\psi}_{\overline{f}}, A) \wedge (\overline{\zeta}_{\overline{g}}, B) = (\overline{\sigma}_{\overline{h}}, C)$ is a PMFSS over S.

Definition 12. *Let $(\overline{\psi}_{\overline{f}}, A)$ be a PMFSS over S. Then, $(\overline{\psi}_{\overline{f}}, A)$ is said to be trivial if $\overline{\psi}_{\overline{f}}(e) = \{T\}$ for all $e \in A$, where T stands for a trivial ordered semigroup.*

Lemma 1. Let us define homomorphism as a mapping $H : S \to T$ from an ordered semigroup S to a trivial ordered semigroup T. If $(\overline{\psi}_{\overline{f}}, R)$ is a PMFSS over S, then $(H(\overline{\psi}_{\overline{f}}), R)$ also defines a PMFSS over T.

Proof. As the definition of homomorphism states that $\forall e \in R$, $H(\overline{\psi}_{\overline{f}})(e) = H(\overline{\psi}_{\overline{f}}(e)) = H(\overline{\psi}(e), \overline{f}(e))$ is a subsemigroup of T. If $(\overline{\psi}_{\overline{f}}, R)$ defines a PMFSS over S, then by definition its homomorphic image is a fuzzy subsemigroup of T. Hence, $H(\overline{\psi}_{\overline{f}}(e))$ is a fuzzy subsemigroup of T. Thus, it implies that $(H(\overline{\psi}_{\overline{f}}), R)$ is a possibility multi-fuzzy soft ordered semigroup over T. □

Theorem 5. *Let $(\overline{\psi}_{\overline{f}}, R)$ be a PMFSS over S and $H : S \to T$ be a homomorphic image from an ordered semigroup S to a trivial ordered semigroup T. Then, if $\overline{\psi}_{\overline{f}}(e) \subseteq ker(H), \forall e \in R$, then $(H(\overline{\psi}_{\overline{f}}), R)$ is a trivial PMFSS over T.*

Proof. As $\overline{\psi}_{\overline{f}}(e) \subseteq ker(H), \forall e \in R$, also by definition of homomorphism, $H(\overline{\psi}_{\overline{f}})(e) = H(\overline{\psi}_{\overline{f}}(e)) = H(\overline{\psi}(e), \overline{f}(e)), \forall e \in R$. As defined earlier for a trivial PMFSS $(\overline{\psi}_{\overline{f}}, R)$ over S,

$\overline{\psi}_{\overline{f}}(e) = \{T\}$. Thus, by using the Lemma 1, it is concluded that $H(\overline{\psi}_{\overline{f}})(e) = H(\overline{\psi}_{\overline{f}}(e)) = \{T\}, \forall e \in R$. Hence, $(H(\overline{\psi}_{\overline{f}}), R)$ is a trivial PMFSS over T. □

Theorem 6. *Let $(\overline{\psi}_{\overline{f}}, A)$ and $(\overline{\zeta}_{\overline{g}}, B)$ be two PMFSSs over S. Then, for all $B \subseteq A$, $(\overline{\zeta}_{\overline{g}}, B)$ is a multi-fuzzy subsemigroup of $(\overline{\psi}_{\overline{f}}, A)$ or $(\overline{\zeta}_{\overline{g}}, B) \leq (\overline{\psi}_{\overline{f}}, A)$ if and only if $\overline{\zeta}_{\overline{g}}(e)$ is a fuzzy subsemigroup of $\overline{\psi}_{\overline{f}}(e)$*
$\forall e \in R$.

Proof. The theorem can be directly proved by using Theorem 1. □

Example 6. *Let us consider two PMFSSs $(\overline{\psi}_{\overline{f}}, A)$ and $(\overline{\zeta}_{\overline{g}}, B)$ over S (defined as in Example 1) defined as*

$$\overline{\psi}_{\overline{f}}(e) = \begin{bmatrix} (0.8,0.7,0.5),(0.7,0.6,0.5) & (0.7,0.6,0.3),(0.6,0.5,0.4) & (0.6,0.4,0.2),(0.4,0.3,0.3) & (0.6,0.5,0.1),(0.5,0.3,0.2) \\ (0.7,0.7,0.9),(0.8,0.7,0.8) & (0.6,0.6,0.8),(0.7,0.3,0.6) & (0.3,0.5,0.7),(0.5,0.1,0.3) & (0.4,0.5,0.2),(0.6,0.2,0.5) \\ (0.9,0.8,0.8),(0.8,0.8,0.7) & (0.6,0.7,0.7),(0.6,0.7,0.5) & (0.4,0.6,0.2),(0.4,0.6,0.2) & (0.4,0.3,0.1),(0.2,0.3,0.1) \end{bmatrix}$$
$$\overline{\zeta}_{\overline{g}}(e) = \begin{bmatrix} (0.7,0.6,0.3),(0.6,0.5,0.4) & (0.6,0.4,0.2),(0.5,0.5,0.3) & (0.5,0.3,0.1),(0.4,0.3,0.2) & (0.5,0.3,0.1),(0.4,0.2,0.1) \\ (0.6,0.6,0.7),(0.5,0.4,0.6) & (0.5,0.5,0.6),(0.4,0.3,0.5) & (0.2,0.4,0.5),(0.3,0.1,0.2) & (0.4,0.4,0.1),(0.5,0.1,0.3) \\ (0.8,0.7,0.6),(0.7,0.6,0.5) & (0.5,0.6,0.5),(0.5,0.5,0.4) & (0.3,0.5,0.1),(0.2,0.3,0.1) & (0.3,0.2,0.1),(0.2,0.2,0.1) \end{bmatrix}$$

It can easily be analyzed that for each parameter, $\overline{\psi}_{\overline{f}}(e)$ is multi-fuzzy subsemigroup of $\overline{\zeta}_{\overline{g}}(e)$ over S. Conversely, for any two $\overline{\psi}_{\overline{f}}(e)$ and $\overline{\zeta}_{\overline{g}}(e)$ that are multi-fuzzy subsets of an ordered semigroup S, $\overline{\zeta}_{\overline{g}}(e)$ is a fuzzy subsemigroup of $\overline{\psi}_{\overline{f}}(e)$, then $\overline{\zeta}(e) \leq \overline{\psi}(e)$, $\overline{g}(e) \leq \overline{f}(e)\ \forall e \in B$. Also, $(\overline{\psi}_{\overline{f}}, A)$ and $(\overline{\xi}_{\overline{g}}, B)$ satisfy the definition of PMFSS. Thus, for $B \subseteq A$, $(\overline{\xi}_{\overline{g}}, B)$ is a fuzzy subsemigroup of $(\overline{\psi}_{\overline{f}}, A)$.

Theorem 7. *Suppose $(\overline{\psi}_{\overline{f}}, A)$ is a PMFSS over S and let $(\overline{\zeta}_{\overline{g}}|_1, B_1)$ and $(\overline{\zeta}_{\overline{g}}|_2, B_2)$ be the two possibility multi-fuzzy soft ordered subsemigroups of $(\overline{\psi}_{\overline{f}}, A)$, then*

(1) $(\overline{\zeta}_{\overline{g}}|_1, B_1) \cap (\overline{\zeta}_{\overline{g}}|_2, B_2) \leq (\overline{\psi}_{\overline{f}}, A)$;

(2) If $B_1 \cap B_2 = \phi$, then $\left(\overline{\zeta}_{\overline{g}}|_1, B_1\right) \cup \left(\overline{\zeta}_{\overline{g}}|_2, B_2\right) \leq \left(\overline{\psi}_{\overline{f}}, A\right)$.

Proof. (1) The intersection of any two possibility multi-fuzzy soft sets is defined as $(\overline{\zeta}_{\overline{g}}|_1, B_1) \cap (\overline{\zeta}_{\overline{g}}|_2, B_2) = (\overline{\zeta}_{\overline{g}}, B)$, where $B_1 \cap B_2 = B, \forall e \in B$ implies $e \in B_1$ and $e \in B_2$, or in other words, either $\overline{\zeta}_{\overline{g}}(e) = \overline{\zeta}_{\overline{g}}|_1(e)$ or $\overline{\zeta}_{\overline{g}}(e) = \overline{\zeta}_{\overline{g}}|_2(e)$. Since $(\overline{\zeta}_{\overline{g}}|_1, B_1) \leq (\overline{\psi}_{\overline{f}}, A)$ and $(\overline{\zeta}_{\overline{g}}|_2, B_2) \leq (\overline{\psi}_{\overline{f}}, A)$, $\overline{g}_{\overline{\mu}}(e)$ is a fuzzy subsemigroup of $\overline{f}_{\overline{v}}(e)$.
Thus, $(\overline{\zeta}_{\overline{g}}|_1, B_1) \cap (\overline{\zeta}_{\overline{g}}|_2, B_2) \leq (\overline{f}_{\overline{v}}, A)$..

(2) The union of any two possibility multi-fuzzy soft sets can be defined as $(\overline{\zeta}_{\overline{g}}|_1, B_1) \cup (\overline{\zeta}_{\overline{g}}|_2, B_2) = (\overline{\zeta}_{\overline{g}}, B)$, where $B_1 \cup B_2 = B$. As $\forall e \in B$, we obtain

$$\overline{\zeta}_{\overline{g}}(e) = \begin{cases} \overline{\zeta}_{\overline{g}}|_1(e) \text{if} e \in B_1 - B_2, \\ \overline{\zeta}_{\overline{g}}|_2(e) \text{if} e \in B_2 - B_1, \\ \overline{\zeta}_{\overline{g}}|_1(e) \cup \overline{\zeta}_{\overline{g}}|_2(e) \text{if} e \in B_1 \cap B_2. \end{cases}$$

Here, if $B_1 \cap B_2 = \phi$, either $e \in B_1 - B_2$ or $e \in B_2 - B_1$; thus, either $\overline{\zeta}_{\overline{g}}(e) = \overline{\zeta}_{\overline{g}}|_1(e)$ or $\overline{\zeta}_{\overline{g}}(e) = \overline{\zeta}_{\overline{g}}|_2(e)$, as $(\overline{\zeta}_{\overline{g}}|_1, B_1) \leq (\overline{\psi}_{\overline{f}}, A)$ and $(\overline{\zeta}_{\overline{g}}|_2, B_2) \leq (\overline{\psi}_{\overline{f}}, A)$, so $\overline{\zeta}_{\overline{g}}(e)$ is a fuzzy subsemigroup of $\overline{\psi}_{\overline{f}}(e)$. Hence, $(\overline{\zeta}_{\overline{g}}|_1, B_1) \cup (\overline{\zeta}_{\overline{g}}|_2, B_2) \leq (\overline{\psi}_{\overline{f}}, A)$. □

Theorem 8. *Let $H: S \rightarrow T$ define a homomorphic mapping of ordered semigroups. And let $(\overline{\psi}_{\overline{f}}, A)$ and $(\overline{\zeta}_{\overline{g}}, B)$ be two PMFSSs over S. Then, if $(\overline{\psi}_{\overline{f}}, A) \leq (\overline{\zeta}_{\overline{g}}, B)$, this implies $H(\overline{\psi}_{\overline{f}}, A) \leq H(\overline{\zeta}_{\overline{g}}, B)$.*

Proof. Let $(\overline{\psi}_{\overline{f}}, A) \leq (\overline{\zeta}_{\overline{g}}, B) \forall A \subseteq B$, then by Theorem 6 it is clear that $\overline{\psi}_{\overline{f}}(e)$ is a fuzzy subsemigroup of $\overline{\zeta}_{\overline{g}}(e)$. Also, according to the definition of homomorphism, $H(\overline{\psi}_{\overline{f}}(e))$ is a fuzzy subsemigroup of $H(\overline{\zeta}_{\overline{g}}(e))$. Therefore, it is concluded that $H(\overline{\psi}_{\overline{f}}, A) \leq H(\overline{\zeta}_{\overline{g}}, B)$. □

Definition 13. *Let $(\overline{\psi}_{\overline{f}}, A)$ be a PMFSS over S. Then, a possibility multi-fuzzy soft set $(\overline{\zeta}_{\overline{g}}, X)$ over S is called a possibility multi-fuzzy soft l-ideal (resp. r-ideal) of $(\overline{\psi}_{\overline{f}}, A)$ and is denoted $((\overline{\zeta}_{\overline{g}}, X) \lhd_l (\overline{\psi}_{\overline{f}}, A))$ (resp. $((\overline{\zeta}_{\overline{g}}, X) \lhd_r (\overline{\psi}_{\overline{f}}, A))$) if it follows*

(1) $X \subseteq A$;
(2) $\forall e \in X, \overline{\zeta}_{\overline{g}}(e)$ *is a fuzzy soft left ideal (resp. right ideal) of* $\overline{\psi}_{\overline{f}}(e) \Rightarrow ((\overline{\zeta}_{\overline{g}}, X) \lhd_l (\overline{\psi}_{\overline{f}}, A))$ *(resp.*$((\overline{\zeta}_{\overline{g}}, X) \lhd_r (\overline{\psi}_{\overline{f}}, A))$*).*

If $(\overline{\zeta}_{\overline{g}}, B)$ is both an l-ideal and r-ideal of $(\overline{\psi}_{\overline{f}}, A)$, then we can call $(\overline{\zeta}_{\overline{g}}, B)$ a possibility multi-fuzzy soft ideal of $(\overline{\psi}_{\overline{f}}, A)$, and it is denoted as $(\overline{\zeta}_{\overline{g}}, X) \lhd (\overline{\psi}_{\overline{f}}, A)$.

Example 7. *Suppose $S = \{s_1, s_2, s_3, s_4\}$ is an ordered semigroup under the following multiplication relation and order relation:*

$$\leq := \{(s_1,s_1), (s_2,s_2), (s_3,s_3), (s_4,s_4), (s_1,s_2)\}.$$

Multiplication table

$\cdot$	s_1	s_2	s_3	s_4
s_1	s_1	s_1	s_1	s_1
s_2	s_1	s_1	s_1	s_1
s_3	s_1	s_1	s_1	s_2
s_4	s_1	s_1	s_2	s_3

Let $(\overline{\psi}_{\overline{f}}, A)$ be a possibility multi-fuzzy soft set of S, where $A = \{e_1, e_2, e_3\}$ and $\overline{\psi}_{\overline{f}} : A \to M^nFSS(S) \times M^nFSS(S)$. Let us assume a set of parameters X, where $X \subseteq A$; then, a mapping $\overline{\zeta}_{\overline{g}} : X \to M^nFSS(S) \times M^nFSS(S)$ can be defined, where $\overline{\zeta}_{\overline{g}}(e) = (\overline{\zeta}(e)(s_i), \overline{g}(e)(s_i)) \forall s_i \in S$.

$$\overline{\zeta}_{\overline{g}}(e) = \begin{bmatrix} (0.7,0.6),(0.6,0.5) & (0.6,0.4),(0.5,0.5) & (0.5,0.3),(0.4,0.3) & (0.5,0.3),(0.4,0.2) \\ (0.6,0.6),(0.5,0.4) & (0.5,0.5),(0.4,0.3) & (0.2,0.4),(0.3,0.1) & (0.1,0.4),(0.2,0.1) \\ (0.8,0.7),(0.7,0.6) & (0.5,0.6),(0.5,0.5) & (0.3,0.5),(0.2,0.3) & (0.3,0.2),(0.2,0.2) \end{bmatrix}.$$

As $\overline{\zeta}_{\overline{g}}(e)(a_i \cdot a_j) \geq \overline{\zeta}_{\overline{g}}(e)(a_i) \ \forall a_i, a_j \in S$, $\overline{\zeta}_{\overline{g}}(e)$ is a fuzzy soft right ideal of $\overline{\psi}_{\overline{f}}(e)$. Similarly, $\overline{\zeta}_{\overline{g}}(e)(a_i \cdot a_j) \geq \overline{\zeta}_{\overline{g}}(e)(a_j)$ implies $\overline{\zeta}_{\overline{g}}(e)$ is a fuzzy soft left ideal of $\overline{\psi}_{\overline{f}}(e)$. Thus, $(\overline{\zeta}_{\overline{g}}, X) \lhd_r (\overline{\psi}_{\overline{f}}, A)$ and $(\overline{\zeta}_{\overline{g}}, X) \lhd_l (\overline{\psi}_{\overline{f}}, A)$. Thus, $(\overline{\zeta}_{\overline{g}}, X) \lhd (\overline{\psi}_{\overline{f}}, A)$.

Theorem 9. *Let $(\overline{\psi}_{\overline{f}}, A)$ be a PMFSS over S. Then, for any two possibility multi-fuzzy soft sets $(\overline{\zeta}_{\overline{g}}|_1, X_1)$ and $(\overline{\zeta}_{\overline{g}}|_2, X_2)$ of S, where $X_1 \cap X_2 \neq \phi$, we can prove following:*

(1) If $(\overline{\zeta}_{\overline{g}}|_1, X_1) \lhd_l (\overline{\psi}_{\overline{f}}, A)$ and $(\overline{\zeta}_{\overline{g}}|_2, X_2) \lhd_l (\overline{\psi}_{\overline{f}}, A)$, then $(\overline{\zeta}_{\overline{g}}|_1, X_1) \cap (\overline{\zeta}_{\overline{g}}|_2, X_2) \lhd_l (\overline{\psi}_{\overline{f}}, A)$.
(2) If $(\overline{\zeta}_{\overline{g}}|_1, X_1) \lhd_r (\overline{\psi}_{\overline{f}}, A)$ and $(\overline{\zeta}_{\overline{g}}|_2, X_2) \lhd_r (\overline{\psi}_{\overline{f}}, A)$, then $(\overline{\zeta}_{\overline{g}}|_1, X_1) \cap (\overline{\zeta}_{\overline{g}}|_2, X_2) \lhd_r (\overline{\psi}_{\overline{f}}, A)$.

Proof. (1) The intersection of any two possibility multi-fuzzy soft sets can be defined as $(\overline{\zeta}_{\overline{g}}|_1, X_1) \cap (\overline{\zeta}_{\overline{g}}|_2, X_2) = (\overline{\zeta}_{\overline{g}}, X)$, where $X_1 \cap X_2 = X$. Then, $\forall e \in X$ implies $e \in X_1$ and $e \in X_2$, so either $\overline{\zeta}_{\overline{g}}(e) = \overline{\zeta}_{\overline{g}}|_1(e)$ or $\overline{\zeta}_{\overline{g}}(e) = \overline{\zeta}_{\overline{g}}|_2(e)$, also $X \subseteq A$; hence, $(\overline{\zeta}_{\overline{g}}, X)$ is a

PMFSS over S. $(\overline{\zeta}_{\overline{g}}|_1, X_1) \lhd_l (\overline{\psi}_{\overline{f}}, A)$ implies $(\overline{\zeta}_{\overline{g}}, X) \lhd_l (\overline{\psi}_{\overline{f}}, A)$ as $(\overline{\zeta}_{\overline{g}}|_1, X_1) \cap (\overline{\zeta}_{\overline{g}}|_2, X_2) = (\overline{\zeta}_{\overline{g}}, X) \lhd_l (\overline{\psi}_{\overline{f}}, A)$.
(2) Similarly, we can prove the second relation. □

Theorem 10. *Let $(\overline{\psi}_{\overline{f}}, A)$ be a PMFSS over S. Then, for any two possibility multi-fuzzy soft sets $(\overline{\zeta}_{\overline{g}}, B)$ and $(\overline{\sigma}_{\overline{h}}, C)$ over S, where $B \cap C = \phi$, we can prove the following:*

(1) If $\left(\overline{\zeta}_{\overline{g}}, B\right) \lhd_l \left(\overline{\psi}_{\overline{f}}, A\right)$ and $(\overline{\sigma}_{\overline{h}}, C) \lhd_l \left(\overline{\psi}_{\overline{f}}, A\right)$, then $\left(\overline{\zeta}_{\overline{g}}, B\right) \cup (\overline{\sigma}_{\overline{h}}, C) \lhd_l \left(\overline{\psi}_{\overline{f}}, A\right)$.
(2) If $\left(\overline{\zeta}_{\overline{g}}, B\right) \lhd_r \left(\overline{\psi}_{\overline{f}}, A\right)$ and $(\overline{\sigma}_{\overline{h}}, C) \lhd_r \left(\overline{\psi}_{\overline{f}}, A\right)$, then $\left(\overline{\zeta}_{\overline{g}}, B\right) \cup (\overline{\sigma}_{\overline{h}}, C) \lhd_r \left(\overline{\psi}_{\overline{f}}, A\right)$.

Proof. (1) The union of any two possibility multi-fuzzy soft sets is defined as $\left(\overline{\zeta}_{\overline{g}}, B\right) \cup (\overline{\sigma}_{\overline{h}}, C) = (\overline{\omega}_{\overline{k}}, K)$, where $B \cup C = K, \forall e \in K$.

$$\overline{\omega}_{\overline{k}}(e) = \begin{cases} \overline{\zeta}_{\overline{g}}(e) \text{if} e \in B - C, \\ \overline{\sigma}_{\overline{h}}(e) \text{if} e \in C - B, \\ \overline{\zeta}_{\overline{g}}(e) \cup \overline{\sigma}_{\overline{h}}(e) \text{if} e \in B \cap C. \end{cases}$$

Here, $B \cap C = \phi$, so either $e \in B - C$ or $e \in C - B$. If $e \in B - C$, then $\overline{\omega}_{\overline{k}}€ = \overline{\zeta}_{\overline{g}}€$, where $\overline{\zeta}_{\overline{g}}€$ is a left ideal of $\overline{\psi}_{\overline{f}}€$. So, $\overline{\omega}_{\overline{k}}€$ is also a left ideal of $\overline{\psi}_{\overline{f}}€$. Thus, $(\overline{\omega}_{\overline{k}}, K) \lhd_l (\overline{\psi}_{\overline{f}}, A)$. If $e \in C - B$, then $\overline{\omega}_{\overline{k}}(e) = \overline{\sigma}_{\overline{h}}€$, where $\overline{\sigma}_{\overline{h}}€$ is a left ideal of $\overline{\psi}_{\overline{f}}€$. So, $\overline{\omega}_{\overline{k}}(e)$ is also a left ideal of $\overline{\psi}_{\overline{f}}€$. Thus, $(\overline{\omega}_{\overline{k}}, K) \lhd_l (\overline{\psi}_{\overline{f}}, A)$.
Hence, we have $(\overline{\zeta}_{\overline{g}}, B) \cup (\overline{\sigma}_{\overline{h}}, C) \lhd_l (\overline{\psi}_{\overline{f}}, A)$.

(2) Similarly, we can prove $(\overline{\zeta}_{\overline{g}}, B) \cup (\overline{\sigma}_{\overline{h}}, C) \lhd_r (\overline{\psi}_{\overline{f}}, A)$. □

4. Application of PMFSS in Decision Making and Medical Diagnosis

In this section, we showcase the application of PMFSSs in decision-making problems by examining the following examples.

Example 8. *Let three players give a test for their selection in a cricket team. The parameters required for the players are e_1, which is all-rounder, consisting of batsman, bowler and fielder; e_2, which is age, consisting of old, medium and young; and e_3, which is fitness, consisting of excellent, good and poor. Here, $U = \{P_1, P_2, P_3\}$ and $R = \{e_1, e_2, e_3\}$. We have defined the following multiplication and ordered relation on the basis of their average performance in the last ten matches.*

Multiplication table

·	P_1	P_2	P_3
P_1	P_1	P_2	P_1
P_2	P_2	P_2	P_3
P_3	P_3	P_3	P_3

$$\leq := \{(P_1,P_1), (P_2,P_2), (P_3,P_3), (P_1,P_3), (P_2,P_3)\}.$$

Keeping in view the order relation as shown in Figure 1, it is easily noticed that the third player is better than first two. We consider two observations $\overline{\psi}_{\overline{f}}$ and $\overline{\zeta}_{\overline{g}}$ as two committee members to decide the best player.

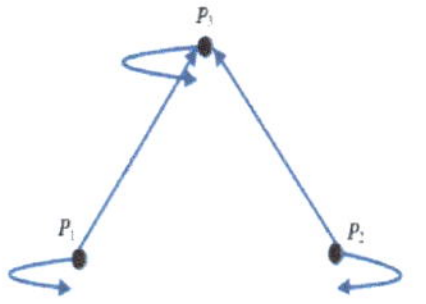

Figure 1. Hesse diagram for ordered relation of Z.

Here, possibility multi-fuzzy soft set technique is applied for both the observations. We obtain

$$\overline{\psi}_{\overline{f}}(e_1) = \left\{ \left(\frac{P_1}{(0.2,0.5,0.5)}, (0.6,0.9,0.1)\right), \left(\frac{P_2}{(0.9,0.8,0.3)}, (0.8,0.7,0.4)\right), \left(\frac{P_3}{(0.1,0.3,0.2)}, (0.5,0.2,0.3)\right) \right\},$$
$$\overline{\psi}_{\overline{f}}(e_2) = \left\{ \left(\frac{P_1}{(0.3,0.4,0.6)}, (0.2,0.3,0.7)\right), \left(\frac{P_2}{(0.3,0.4,0.7)}, (0.2,0.6,0.7)\right), \left(\frac{P_3}{(0.8,0.2,0.1)}, (0.7,0.3,0.2)\right) \right\}$$

and

$$\overline{\psi}_{\overline{f}}(e_3) = \left\{ \left(\frac{P_1}{(0.6,0.3,0.2)}, (0.7,0.4,0.3)\right), \left(\frac{P_2}{(0.9,0.7,0.2)}, (0.8,0.6,0.3)\right), \left(\frac{P_3}{(0.6,0.4,0.1)}, (0.7,0.5,0.1)\right) \right\},$$

In matrix form,

$$\overline{\psi}_{\overline{f}} = \begin{bmatrix} (0.2,0.5,0.5),(0.6,0.9,0.1) & (0.9,0.8,0.3),(0.8,0.7,0.4) & (0.1,0.3,0.2),(0.5,0.2,0.3) \\ (0.3,0.4,0.6),(0.2,0.3,0.7) & (0.3,0.4,0.7),(0.2,0.6,0.7) & (0.8,0.2,0.1),(0.7,0.3,0.2) \\ (0.6,0.3,0.2),(0.7,0.4,0.3) & (0.9,0.7,0.2),(0.8,0.6,0.3) & (0.6,0.4,0.1),(0.7,0.5,0.1) \end{bmatrix}.$$

Similarly, $\overline{\xi}_{\overline{g}}$ can be written as

$$\overline{\xi}_{\overline{g}} = \begin{bmatrix} (0.3,0.5,0.6),(0.7,0.8,0.2) & (0.9,0.9,0.2),(0.9,0.8,0.4) & (0.2,0.3,0.3),(0.6,0.3,0.2) \\ (0.2,0.4,0.6),(0.1,0.5,0.4) & (0.4,0.5,0.6),(0.2,0.5,0.7) & (0.7,0.3,0.2),(0.6,0.4,0.1) \\ (0.5,0.3,0.1),(0.6,0.4,0.1) & (0.9,0.8,0.1),(0.7,0.5,0.2) & (0.5,0.6,0.1),(0.7,0.4,0.3) \end{bmatrix}.$$

In order to calculate a mutual decision by both the members of committee, AND operation of possibility multi-fuzzy soft sets is applied. Defined as $\overline{\sigma}_{\overline{h}} = \overline{\psi}_{\overline{f}} \wedge \overline{\xi}_{\overline{g}}$,

$$\overline{\sigma}_{\overline{h}}(e_1,e_1) = \left\{ \left(\frac{P_1}{(0.2,0.5,0.5)}, (0.6,0.8,0.1)\right), \left(\frac{P_2}{(0.9,0.8,0.2)}, (0.8,0.7,0.4)\right), \left(\frac{P_3}{(0.1,0.3,0.2)}, (0.5,0.2,0.2)\right) \right\},$$
$$\overline{\sigma}_{\overline{h}}(e_1,e_2) = \left\{ \left(\frac{P_1}{(0.2,0.4,0.5)}, (0.1,0.5,0.1)\right), \left(\frac{P_2}{(0.4,0.5,0.3)}, (0.2,0.5,0.4)\right), \left(\frac{P_3}{(0.1,0.3,0.2)}, (0.5,0.2,0.1)\right) \right\},$$
$$\overline{\sigma}_{\overline{h}}(e_1,e_3) = \left\{ \left(\frac{P_1}{(0.2,0.3,0.1)}, (0.6,0.4,0.1)\right), \left(\frac{P_2}{(0.9,0.8,0.1)}, (0.7,0.5,0.2)\right), \left(\frac{P_3}{(0.1,0.3,0.1)}, (0.5,0.2,0.3)\right) \right\}.$$

And the values for all the other pairs of parameters can be evaluated in a similar manner. The values for all the pairs of parameters in matrix form are written as

$$\overline{\sigma}_{\overline{h}} = \begin{bmatrix} (0.2,0.5,0.5),(0.6,0.8,0.1) & (0.9,0.8,0.2),(0.8,0.7,0.4) & (0.1,0.3,0.2),(0.5,0.2,0.2) \\ (0.2,0.4,0.5),(0.1,0.5,0.1) & (0.4,0.5,0.3),(0.2,0.5,0.4) & (0.1,0.3,0.2),(0.5,0.2,0.1) \\ (0.2,0.3,0.1),(0.6,0.4,0.1) & (0.9,0.8,0.1),(0.7,0.5,0.2) & (0.1,0.3,0.1),(0.5,0.2,0.3) \\ (0.3,0.4,0.6),(0.2,0.3,0.2) & (0.3,0.4,0.2),(0.2,0.6,0.4) & (0.2,0.2,0.1),(0.6,0.3,0.2) \\ (0.2,0.4,0.6),(0.1,0.3,0.4) & (0.3,0.4,0.6),(0.2,0.5,0.7) & (0.7,0.2,0.1),(0.6,0.3,0.1) \\ (0.3,0.3,0.1),(0.2,0.3,0.1) & (0.3,0.4,0.1),(0.2,0.5,0.2) & (0.5,0.2,0.1),(0.7,0.3,0.2) \\ (0.3,0.3,0.2),(0.7,0.4,0.2) & (0.9,0.7,0.2),(0.8,0.6,0.3) & (0.2,0.3,0.1),(0.6,0.3,0.1) \\ (0.2,0.3,0.2),(0.1,0.4,0.3) & (0.4,0.5,0.2),(0.2,0.5,0.3) & (0.6,0.3,0.1),(0.6,0.4,0.1) \\ (0.5,0.3,0.1),(0.6,0.4,0.1) & (0.9,0.7,0.1),(0.7,0.5,0.2) & (0.5,0.4,0.1),(0.7,0.4,0.1) \end{bmatrix}$$

As we need to find the best player suitable for the team, we would compute the grades and possibility grades by the following formulas:

$$r_{ij}(u_k) = \sum_{u \in U} ((C_k^1 - v^1_{\overline{\sigma}(e_i,e_j)}(u)) + ((C_k^2 - v^2_{\overline{\sigma}(e_i,e_j)}(u)) + ((C_k^3 - v^3_{\overline{\sigma}(e_i,e_j)}(u))$$
$$\lambda_{ij}(u_k) = \sum_{u \in U} ((C_k^1 - v^1_{\overline{\sigma}(e_i,e_j)}(u)) + ((C_k^2 - v^2_{\overline{\sigma}(e_i,e_j)}(u)) + ((C_k^3 - v^3_{\overline{\sigma}(e_i,e_j)}(u))$$

By using these formulas, the grades and possibility grades for all possible values can be calculated.

$$r_{11}(P_1) = \sum_{P_1 \in U} ((C_1^1 - v^1_{\overline{\sigma}(e_1,e_1)}(P_1)) + ((C_1^2 - v^2_{\overline{\sigma}(e_1,e_1)}(P_1)) + ((C_1^3 - v^3_{\overline{\sigma}(e_1,e_1)}(P_1))$$
$$= (0.2 - 0.9) + (0.2 - 0.1) + (0.5 - 0.8) + (0.5 - 0.3) + (0.5 - 0.8) + (0.5 - 0.2)$$
$$= -0.7 + 0.1 - 0.3 + 0.2 + 0.3 + 0.3$$
$$= -0.1$$
$$\lambda_{11}(P_1) = \sum_{P_1 \in U} ((C_1^1 - v^1_{\overline{h}(e_1,e_1)}(P_1)) + ((C_1^2 - v^2_{\overline{h}(e_1,e_1)}(P_1)) + ((C_1^3 - v^3_{\overline{h}(e_1,e_1)}(P_1))$$
$$= (0.6 - 0.8) + (0.6 - 0.5) + (0.8 - 0.7) + (0.8 - 0.2) + (0.1 - 0.4) + (0.1 - 0.2)$$
$$= 0.2$$

Similarly, we can calculate the values for all the other possible points, which are given in Table 1. Now, we mark the highest numerical grade in each row and possibility grade related to that and then find the total score for each player by taking the sum of the product of these numerical grades with their respective possibility grades. Here, P_2 is the player with the highest score; thus, they will select P_2 for the team.

Table 1. Numerical and possibility grade table.

$\overline{\sigma}_{\overline{h}}$	P_1	P_2	P_3
(e_1, e_1)	−0.1, 0.2	0.2, 1.4	−0.1, −0.1
(e_1, e_2)	0.4, −0.5	0.7, 0.7	−1.1, −0.2
(e_1, e_3)	0.2,0.3	0.5, 0	−0.7, −0.4
(e_2, e_1)	1.2, −0.9	0.0, 0.6	−1.2, 0.5
(e_2, e_2)	0.1, −0.6	0.4, 1.0	−0.5, −0.2
(e_2, e_3)	0, −0.5	0, −0.5	0, 1
(e_3, e_1)	0.3,0.6	0.6, 0.3	−1.6, −0.9
(e_3, e_2)	−0.3, −0.2	0, −0.2	0.3, 0.4
(e_3, e_3)	1.5, 0.5	−0.9, −0.4	−0.6, −0.3

Example 9. *Suppose that we have a patient who is suffering with certain problem in his health, and he thinks that he might be suffering with hyperthyroidism or hypothyroidism. Let us consider all the symptoms he has as set of parameters as represented in Table 2, and the universal set for this case is yes or no. Here,* $R = \{e_1 + e_2 + e_3 + e_4 + e_5\}$ *and* $U = \{y, n\}$.

Table 2. Model table for a hyperthyroid patient.

h	y	$\overline{f}_y$	n	$\overline{f}_n$
e_1	(0,0,1)	(1,1,1)	(1,1,0)	(1,1,1)
e_2	(1,0,0)	(1,1,1)	(0,1,1)	(1,1,1)
e_3	(1,1,1)	(1,1,1)	(0,0,0)	(1,1,1)
e_4	(1,1,1)	(1,1,1)	(0,0,0)	(1,1,1)
e_5	(1,1,1)	(1,1,1)	(0,0,0)	(1,1,1)

For this case, we first have to construct a PMFSS model for a hyperthyroid and a hypothyroid patient by consulting a physician; then, we would construct a PMFSS model for the patient under observation.

Table 2 represents a possibility multi-fuzzy soft set model table for a hyperthyroid patient, and Table 3 represents a possibility multi-fuzzy soft set model table for a hypothyroid patient. Now, after constructing a model table for the patient under observation, we find the similarity measure between Tables 2 and 3 by using the Definition 9, and we obtain

$$\varphi_1(\overline{\psi}, \overline{\xi}) = \frac{\sum_{i=1}^{5} max_{u\epsilon U}\left\{min(v^1_{\overline{\psi}(e_i)}(u), v^1_{\overline{\xi}(e_i)}(u))\right\}}{\sum_{i=1}^{n} max_{u\epsilon U}\left\{max(v^1_{\overline{\psi}(e_i)}(u), v^1_{\overline{\xi}(e_i)}(u))\right\}}$$
$$= 4.3/5 = 0.86$$

$$\theta_1(\overline{f}, \overline{h}) = \frac{\sum_{i=1}^{5} max_{u\epsilon U}\left\{min(v^1_{\overline{f}(e_i)}(u), v^1_{\overline{h}(e_i)}(u))\right\}}{\sum_{i=1}^{5} max_{u\epsilon U}\left\{max(v^1_{\overline{f}(e_i)}(u), v^1_{\overline{h}(e_i)}(u))\right\}}$$
$$= 3.7/5 = 0.7$$

Table 3. Model table for a hypothyroid patient.

$\overline{\omega}_{\overline{g}}$	y	$\overline{g}_y$	n	$\overline{g}_n$
e_1	(1,0,0)	(1,1,1)	(0,0,1)	(1,1,1)
e_2	(0,0,1)	(1,1,1)	(1,0,0)	(1,1,1)
e_3	(1,1,1)	(1,1,1)	(0,0,0)	(1,1,1)
e_4	(1,1,1)	(1,1,1)	(0,0,0)	(1,1,1)
e_5	(1,1,1)	(1,1,1)	(0,0,0)	(1,1,1)

Similarly, $\varphi_2(\overline{\psi}, \overline{\xi}) = 0.62$, $\theta_2(\overline{f}, \overline{h}) = 0.66$, $\varphi_3(\overline{\psi}, \overline{\xi}) = 0.7$ and $\theta_3(\overline{f}, \overline{h}) = 0.72$. Thus, we can obtain $S(\overline{\psi}_{\overline{f}}, \overline{\xi}_{\overline{h}}) = (0.6364, 0.4092, 0.504)$. Hence, $s(\overline{\psi}_{\overline{f}}, \overline{\xi}_{\overline{h}}) = 0.514 > 0.5$. The result shows that the two possibility multi-fuzzy soft set models are significantly similar; thus, the patient is suffering with hyperthyroidism.

For the second case, we consider Figure 2 of the possibility multi-fuzzy soft set model for a hypothyroid patient with Table 4 of the possibility multi-fuzzy soft set model of the patient under observation. We find the similarity measure for the two models following the same method, and we conclude that $S(\overline{\omega}_{\overline{g}}, \overline{\xi}_{\overline{h}}) = (0.37, 0.4092, 0.288)$. Hence, $s(\overline{\omega}_{\overline{g}}, \overline{\xi}_{\overline{h}}) = 0.3557 < 0.5$. The result shows that the two possibility multi-fuzzy soft set models are not significantly similar; thus, the patient is not suffering from hypothyroidism.

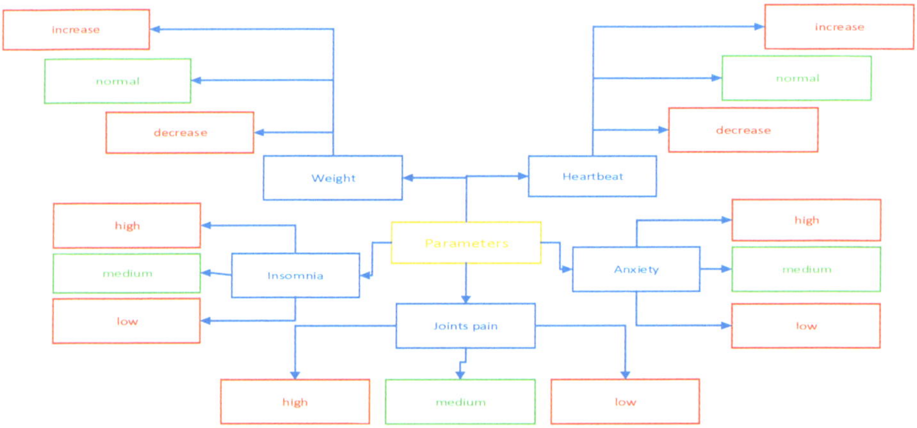

Figure 2. Set of parameters.

Table 4. Model table for the patient under observation.

$\overline{\xi}_{\overline{h}}$	y	$\overline{h}_y$	n	$\overline{h}_n$
e_1	(0.0,0.2,0.9)	(0.1,0.2,1.0)	(1.0,0.5,0.2)	(0.9,0.1,0.1)
e_2	(0.9,0.1,0.1)	(0.8,0.2,0.1)	(0.1,0.6,0.9)	(0.2,0.7,0.6)
e_3	(0.7,0.6,0.4)	(0.6,0.7,0.5)	(0.1,03,0.2)	(0,2,0.5,0.3)
e_4	(0.9,0.7,0.8)	(0,8,0.8,0,9)	(0.2,0.4,0.1)	(0.1,0.8,0.2)
e_5	(0.8,0.7,0.5)	(0.6,0.7,0.6)	(0.1,0.8,0.5)	(0.1,0.9,0.1)

5. Idealistic Possibility Multi-fuzzy Soft Ordered Semigroups

This section includes a new notion of idealistic possibility multi-fuzzy soft ordered semigroups. Further, some basic results are obtained using different operations including union, intersection, AND and OR operation with an idealistic PMFSS technique.

Definition 14. *Let $(\overline{\psi}_{\overline{f}}, A)$ be a possibility multi-fuzzy soft set over S. Then, $(\overline{\psi}_{\overline{f}}, A)$ is called an l-idealistic (resp. r-idealistic) possibility multi-fuzzy soft ordered semigroup over S if $\overline{\psi}_{\overline{f}}(e)$ is the left (resp. right) ideal of S, $\forall e \in A$.*

The example below will give a better understanding of this new concept.

Example 10. *Let S be an ordered semigroup with the multiplication and ordered relation as follows:*

$$\leq := \{(s_1,s_1),(s_2,s_2),(s_3,s_3),(s_4,s_4),(s_1,s_2)\}.$$

Multiplication table

$\cdot$	s_1	s_2	s_3	s_4
s_1	s_1	s_1	s_1	s_1
s_2	s_1	s_1	s_1	s_1
s_3	s_1	s_1	s_1	s_2
s_4	s_1	s_1	s_2	s_3

$(\overline{\psi}_{\overline{f}}, A)$ is a possibility multi-fuzzy soft set over S, where

$$\overline{\psi}_{\overline{f}}(e) = \begin{bmatrix} (0.8,0.7),(0.7,0.6) & (0.7,0.6),(0.6,0.5) & (0.6,0.5),(0.4,0.3) & (0.6,0.4),(0.3,0.1) \\ (0.7,0.7),(0.8,0.7) & (0.6,0.5),(0.7,0.4) & (0.3,0.5),(0.5,0.1) & (0.1,0.4),(0.2,0.1) \\ (0.9,0.7),(0.8,0.6) & (0.7,0.6),(0.6,0.5) & (0.4,0.5),(0.3,0.4) & (0.4,0.3),(0.2,0.2) \end{bmatrix}.$$

As here, $\overline{\psi}_{\overline{f}}(e)(s_i.s_j) \geq \overline{\psi}_{\overline{f}}(e)(s_i) \forall e \in A$, so $\overline{\psi}_{\overline{f}}(e)$ is the fuzzy right ideal of S by definition. Hence, $\overline{\psi}_{\overline{f}}(e)$ is an r-idealistic possibility multi-fuzzy soft ordered semigroup over S. Similarly, we can check it for an l-idealistic possibility multi-fuzzy soft ordered semigroup over S.

Theorem 11. *Let $(\overline{\psi}_{\overline{f}}, A)$ and $(\overline{\zeta}_{\overline{g}}, B)$ be l-idealistic (resp. r-idealistic) possibility multi-fuzzy soft ordered semigroups over S. If $A \cap B \neq \phi$, then their intersection $((\overline{\psi}_{\overline{f}}, A) \cap (\overline{\zeta}_{\overline{g}}, B))$ is also an l-idealistic (resp. r-idealistic) possibility multi-fuzzy soft ordered semigroup over S.*

Proof. As the intersection of any two possibility multi-fuzzy soft sets is defined as $(\overline{\psi}_{\overline{f}}, A) \cap (\overline{\zeta}_{\overline{g}}, B) = (\overline{\sigma}_{\overline{h}}, C)$, where $C = A \cap B$, then $\forall e \in C$ either $(\overline{\sigma}(e), \overline{h}(e)) = (\overline{\psi}(e), \overline{f}(e))$ or $(\overline{\sigma}(e), \overline{h}(e)) = (\overline{\zeta}(e), \overline{g}(e))$. $(\overline{\sigma}_{\overline{h}}, C)$ is a PMFSS over S as defined in Theorem 3. Since $(\overline{\psi}_{\overline{f}}, A)$ and $(\overline{\zeta}_{\overline{g}}, B)$ are both l-idealistic (resp. r-idealistic) PMFSSs over S, it follows that either $\overline{\sigma}_{\overline{h}}(e) = \overline{\psi}_{\overline{f}}(e)$ or $\overline{\sigma}_{\overline{h}}(e) = \overline{\zeta}_{\overline{g}}(e)$; hence, $\overline{\sigma}_{\overline{h}}(e)$ is also an l-idealistic (resp. r-idealistic)

PMFSS over S. So, we can say that the intersection of two l-idealistic (resp. r-idealistic) PMFSSs over S is also an l-idealistic (resp. r-idealistic) PMFSS over S. □

Theorem 12. *Let $(\overline{\psi}_{\overline{f}}, A)$ and $(\overline{\zeta}_{\overline{g}}, B)$ be l-idealistic (resp. r-idealistic) possibility multi-fuzzy soft ordered semigroups over S. If $A \cap B = \phi$, then their union $(\overline{\psi}_{\overline{f}}, A) \cup (\overline{\zeta}_{\overline{g}}, B)$ is also an l-idealistic (resp. r-idealistic) PMFSS over S.*

Proof. As the union of any two possibility multi-fuzzy soft sets is defined as $(\overline{\psi}_{\overline{f}}, A) \cup (\overline{\zeta}_{\overline{g}}, B) = (\overline{\sigma}_{\overline{h}}, C)$, where $C = A \cup B$, then $\forall e \in C$.

$$(\overline{\sigma}_{\overline{h}}, C) = \begin{cases} (\overline{\psi}_{\overline{f}}, A) \; if \; e \in A - B \\ (\overline{\zeta}_{\overline{g}}, B) \; if \; e \in B - A, \\ (\overline{\psi}_{\overline{f}}, A) \cup (\overline{\zeta}_{\overline{g}}, B) \; if \; e \in A \cap B \end{cases}$$

As $A \cap B = \phi \Rightarrow$ either $e \in A - B$ or $e \in B - A$. If $e \in A - B$, then $\overline{\sigma}_{\overline{h}}(e) = \overline{\psi}_{\overline{f}}(e)$, where $\overline{\psi}_{\overline{f}}(e)$ is an l-idealistic (resp. r-idealistic) PMFSS over S, so $\overline{\sigma}_{\overline{h}}(e)$ is also an l-idealistic (resp. r-idealistic) PMFSS over S. Similarly, if $e \in B - A$, then $\overline{\sigma}_{\overline{h}}(e) = \overline{\zeta}_{\overline{g}}(e)$, where $\overline{\zeta}_{\overline{g}}(e)$ is an l-idealistic (resp. r-idealistic) PMFSS over S, so $\overline{\sigma}_{\overline{h}}(e)$ is also an l-idealistic (resp. r-idealistic) PMFSS over S. Hence, $(\overline{\psi}_{\overline{f}}, A) \cup (\overline{\zeta}_{\overline{g}}, B) = (\overline{\sigma}_{\overline{h}}, C)$ is an l-idealistic (resp. r-idealistic) PMFSS over S. □

Theorem 13. *Let $(\overline{\psi}_{\overline{f}}, A)$ and $(\overline{\zeta}_{\overline{g}}, B)$ be l-idealistic (resp. r-idealistic) possibility multi-fuzzy soft ordered semigroups over S. Then, $(\overline{\psi}_{\overline{f}}, A) \wedge (\overline{\zeta}_{\overline{g}}, B)$ is an l-idealistic (resp. r-idealistic) possibility multi-fuzzy soft ordered semigroup over S.*

Proof. As the AND operation is defined as $(\overline{\psi}_{\overline{f}}, A) \wedge (\overline{\zeta}_{\overline{g}}, B) = (\overline{\sigma}_{\overline{h}}, C)$, where $C = A \times B$, then by definition, $\overline{\sigma}_{\overline{h}}(a,b) = \overline{\psi}_{\overline{f}}(a) \cap \overline{\zeta}_{\overline{g}}(b) \; \forall (a,b) \in A \times B$. Since $(\overline{\psi}_{\overline{f}}, A)$ and $(\overline{\zeta}_{\overline{g}}, B)$ are l-idealistic (resp. r-idealistic) PMFSSs over S, we can say that $(\overline{\psi}_{\overline{f}}, A)$ and $(\overline{\zeta}_{\overline{g}}, B)$ are possibility multi-fuzzy soft l-ideals (resp. r-ideals) over S; therefore, the intersection of $(\overline{\psi}_{\overline{f}}(a)) \cap (\overline{\zeta}_{\overline{g}}(b)) \forall (a,b) \in A \times B$ is a possibility multi-fuzzy soft l-ideal (resp. r-ideal) over S. Thus, the intersection of $(\overline{\psi}_{\overline{f}}(a)) \cap (\overline{\zeta}_{\overline{g}}(b)) \forall (a,b) \in A \times B$ is also an l-idealistic (resp. r-idealistic) PMFSS over S. Therefore, $(\overline{\psi}_{\overline{f}}, A) \wedge (\overline{\zeta}_{\overline{g}}, B) = (\overline{\sigma}_{\overline{h}}, C)$ is an l-idealistic (resp. r-idealistic) PMFSS over S. □

6. Conclusions

This paper presents a comprehensive exploration of the amalgamation of possibility multi-fuzzy soft sets with ordered semigroups. By synthesizing concepts from fuzzy mathematics, soft set theory and algebraic structures, this theory provides a powerful tool for addressing uncertainty in problem solving from different fields of applied sciences including medical diagnosis and decision making. This research will further lead to possibility multi-fuzzy soft interior ideals, possibility multi-fuzzy soft bi-ideals, possibility multi-fuzzy soft generalized bi-ideals, possibility multi-fuzzy soft quasi-ideals and several other algebraic structures, which will provide a platform for other researchers to further enhance this new theory, providing valuable insights and applications for future endeavors.

Author Contributions: Conceptualization, S.H. and F.M.K.; methodology, S.H. and V.L.-F.; validation, S.H., F.M.K. and V.L.-F.; formal analysis, S.H.; investigation, S.H.; resources, S.H.; data curation, S.H. and F.M.K.; writing—original draft preparation, S.H.; writing—review and editing, S.H.; visualization, S.H.; supervision, S.H.; project administration, S.H. and F.M.K. All authors have read and agreed to the published version of the manuscript.

Funding: This research received no external funding.

Data Availability Statement: Data are contained within the article.

Conflicts of Interest: The authors declare no conflict of interest.

References

1. Zadeh, L.A. Fuzzy sets. *Inf. Sci. Control* **1965**, *8*, 338–353. [CrossRef]
2. Molodtsov, D. Soft set theory first results. *Comput. Math. Appl.* **1999**, *37*, 19–31. [CrossRef]
3. Molodtsov, D. *The Theory of Soft Sets*; URSS Publishers: Moscow, Russia, 2004. (In Russian)
4. Maji, P.K.; Roy, A.R.; Biswas, R. Fuzzy soft sets. *J. Fuzzy Math.* **2001**, *9*, 589–602.
5. Maji, P.K.; Biswas, R.; Roy, A.R. Soft set theory. *Comput. Math. Appl.* **2003**, *45*, 555–562. [CrossRef]
6. Maji, P.K.; Roy, A.R.; Biswas, R. An application of soft sets in a decision making problems. *Comput. Math. Appl.* **2002**, *44*, 1077–1083. [CrossRef]
7. Alkhazaleh, S.; Salleh, A.R. Soft expert sets. *Adv. Decis. Sci.* **2011**, *2011*, 757868-1. [CrossRef]
8. Alkhazaleh, S.; Salleh, A.R.; Hassan, N. Soft multisets theory. *Appl. Math. Sci.* **2011**, *72*, 3561–3573.
9. Broumi, S.; Smarandache, F. Intuitionistic fuzzy soft expert sets and its application in decision making. *J. New Theory* **2015**, *1*, 89–105.
10. Al-Quran, A.; Hassan, N. Neutrosophic vague soft expert set theory. *J. Intell. Fuzzy Syst.* **2016**, *30*, 3691–3702. [CrossRef]
11. Khalil, A.M.; Hassan, N. A note on possibility multi-fuzzy soft set and its application in decision. *J. Intell. Fuzzy Syst.* **2017**, *32*, 2309–2314. [CrossRef]
12. Rosenfeld, A. Fuzzy groups. *J. Math. Anal. Appl.* **1971**, *35*, 512–517. [CrossRef]
13. Smarandache, F. Neutrosophic set—A generalization of the intuitionistic fuzzy sets. *Int. J. Pure Appl. Math.* **2005**, *24*, 287–297.
14. Selvachandran, G.; Singh, P.K. Interval-valued complex fuzzy soft set and its application. *Int. J. Uncertain. Quantifi.* **2018**, *8*, 101–117. [CrossRef]
15. Garg, H.; Khan, F.M.; Ahmed, W. Fermatean Fuzzy similarity measures-based group decision-making algorithm and its application to dengue disease. *Iran. J. Sci. Technol.* **2024**, 1–7. [CrossRef]
16. Wang, H.; Smarandache, F.; Zhang, Y.Q.; Sunderraman, R. Single valued neutrosophic sets. *Multispace Multistruct.* **2010**, *4*, 410–413.
17. Alhazaymeh, K.; Hassan, N. Vague soft expert set and its application in decision making. *Malays. J. Math. Sci.* **2017**, *11*, 23–39.
18. Alhazaymeh, K.; Hassan, N. Interval-valued vague soft sets and its application. *Adv. Fuzzy Syst.* **2012**, *2012*, 208489. [CrossRef]
19. Arshad, M.; Saeed, M.; Rahman, A.; Khalifa, H. Modeling uncertainties associated with multi-attribute decision-making based evaluation of cooling system using interval-valued complex intuitionistic fuzzy hypersoft settings. *AIMS Math.* **2024**, *9*, 11396–11422. [CrossRef]
20. Wang, D.; Yuan, Y.; Liu, Z. Novel Distance Measures of q-Rung Orthopair Fuzzy Sets and Their Applications. *Symmetry* **2024**, *16*, 574. [CrossRef]
21. Bashir, M.; Salleh, A.R.; Alkhazaleh, S. Possibility intuitionistic fuzzy soft set. *Adv. Decis. Sci.* **2012**, *2012*, 404325. [CrossRef]
22. Riaz, M.; Tanveer, S.; Pamucar, D.; Qin, D.S. Topological Data Analysis with Spherical Fuzzy Soft AHP-TOPSIS for Environmental Mitigation System. *MDPI Math.* **2022**, *10*, 1826. [CrossRef]
23. Khan, M.S.A.; Abdullah, S.; Lui, P. Grey method for multi-attribute decision making with incomplete weight information under Pythagorean fuzzy setting. *J. Intell. Syst.* **2018**, *221*, 245–252. [CrossRef]
24. Khan, M.S.A.; Ali, A.; Abdullah, S.; Amin, F.; Hussain, F. New extension of TOPSIS method based on Pythagorean hesitant fuzzy sets with incomplete weight information. *J. Intell. Fuzzy Syst.* **2018**, *35*, 5435–5448.
25. Farman, S.; Khan, F.M.; Bibi, N. T-Spherical fuzzy soft rough aggregation operators and their applications in multi-criteria group decision-making. *Granul. Comput.* **2023**, *9*, 6. [CrossRef]
26. Liang, R.X.; Wang, J.Q.; Zhang, H.Y. A multi-criteria decision-making method based on single-valued trapezoidal neutrosophic preference relations with complete weight information. *Neural Comput. Appl.* **2018**, *30*, 3383–3398. [CrossRef]
27. Yang, X.B.; Lin, T.Y.; Yang, J.Y.; Li, Y.; Yu, D. Combination of interval-valued fuzzy set and soft set. *Comput. Math. Appl.* **2009**, *58*, 521–527. [CrossRef]
28. Li, Y.Y.; Zhang, H.Y.; Wang, J.Q. Linguistic neutrosophic sets and their application in multicriteria decision-making problems. *Int. J. Uncertain. Quanti.* **2017**, *7*, 135–154. [CrossRef]
29. Broumi, S.; Smarandache, F. Single valued neutrosophic soft expert sets and their application in decision making. *J. New Theory* **2015**, *3*, 67–88.
30. Sebastian, S.; Ramakrishnan, T.V. Multi-fuzzy set: An extension of fuzzy sets. *J. Fuzzy Inf. Eng.* **2011**, *3*, 35–43. [CrossRef]
31. Yang, Y.; Tan, X.; Meng, C.C. The multi-fuzzy soft set and its application in decision making. *J. Appl. Math. Model.* **2013**, *37*, 4915–4923. [CrossRef]
32. Alkhazaleh, S.; Salleh, A.R.; Hassan, N. Possibility fuzzy soft set. *Adv. Decis. Sci.* **2011**, 3. [CrossRef]
33. Zhang, H.D.; Shu, L. Possibility multi-fuzzy soft set and its application in decision making. *J. Intell. Fuzzy Syst.* **2014**, *27*, 2115–2125. [CrossRef]
34. Kehayopulu, N. Ideals and Green's relations in ordered semigroups. *Int. J. Math.* **2006**, *61286*, 1–8. [CrossRef]
35. Jun, Y.B.; Lee, K.J.; Khan, A. Soft ordered semigroups. *J. Math. Log. Q.* **2009**, *56*, 42–50. [CrossRef]

36. Kehayopulu, N. On weakly prime ideals of ordered semigroups. *Jpn. J. Math.* **1990**, *35*, 1051–1056. [CrossRef]
37. Yin, Y.; Zhan, J. The characterization of ordered semigroups in terms of fuzzy soft ideals. *Bull. Malays. Math. Soc. Ser.* **2012**, *2*, 4.
38. Yang, C.F. Fuzzy soft semigroups and fuzzy soft ideals. *Comput. Math. Appl.* **2011**, *61*, 255–261. [CrossRef]
39. Khan, F.M.; Leoreanu-Fotea, V.; Ullah, S.; Ullah, A. A Benchmark Generalization of Fuzzy Soft Ideals in Ordered Semigroups, Analele Stiintifice ale Universitatii Ovidius Constanta. *Ser. Mat.* **2021**, *29*, 155–171.
40. Habib, S.; Khan, F.M.; Yufeng, N. A new concept of possibility fuzzy soft ordered semigroup via its application. *J. Intell. Fuzzy Syst.* **2019**, *36*, 3685–3696. [CrossRef]
41. Habib, S.; Garg, H.; Yufeng, N.; Khan, F.M. An Innovative Approach towards Possibility Fuzzy Soft Ordered Semigroups for Ideals and Its Application. *MDPI Math.* **2019**, *7*, 1183. [CrossRef]

axioms

MDPI

Article

A Generalization of the First Tits Construction

Thomas Moran [1] **and Susanne Pumpluen** [2,*]

1 Department of Mathematics and Statistics, University of Ottawa, 585 King Edward Avenue, Ottawa, ON K1N 7N5, Canada; tmora083@uottawa.ca
2 School of Mathematical Sciences, University of Nottingham, University Park, Nottingham NG7 2RD, UK
* Correspondence: susanne.pumpluen@nottingham.ac.uk

Abstract: Let F be a field of characteristic, not 2 or 3. The first Tits construction is a well-known tripling process to construct separable cubic Jordan algebras, especially Albert algebras. We generalize the first Tits construction by choosing the scalar employed in the tripling process outside of the base field. This yields a new family of non-associative unital algebras which carry a cubic map, and maps that can be viewed as generalized adjoint and generalized trace maps. These maps display properties often similar to the ones in the classical setup. In particular, the cubic norm map permits some kind of weak Jordan composition law.

Keywords: non-associative algebras; first Tits construction; Jordan algebras; generalized cubic algebras

MSC: 17A35

check for updates

Citation: Moran, T.; Pumpluen, S. A Generalization of the First Tits Construction. *Axioms* **2024**, *13*, 299. https://doi.org/10.3390/axioms13050299

Academic Editors: Dana Piciu, Murat Tosun and Cristina Flaut

Received: 26 March 2024
Revised: 22 April 2024
Accepted: 24 April 2024
Published: 29 April 2024

1. Introduction

Let F be a field of characteristic, not 2 or 3. Separable cubic Jordan algebras over F play an important role in Jordan theory (where separable means that their trace defines a non-degenerate bilinear form). It is well known that every separable cubic Jordan algebra can be obtained by either a first or a second Tits construction [1] (IX, Section 39). In particular, exceptional simple Jordan algebras, also called Albert algebras, are separable cubic Jordan algebras. The role of Albert algebras in the structure theory of Jordan algebras is similar to the role of octonion algebras in the structure theory of alternative algebras. Moreover, their automorphism group is an exceptional algebraic group of type F_4, and their cubic norms have isometry groups of type E_6. For some recent developments, see [2–6].

In this paper, we canonically generalize the first Tits construction $J(A,\mu)$. The first Tits construction starts with a separable associative cubic algebra A and uses a scalar $\mu \in F^\times$ in its definition. Our construction also starts with A and employs the same algebra multiplication as that used for the classical first Tits construction, but now allows also $\mu \in A^\times$.

We obtain a new class of non-associative unital algebras which we again denote by $J(A,\mu)$. They carry a cubic map $N : J(A,\mu) \to A$ that generalizes the classical norm, a map $T : J(A,\mu) \to F$ that generalizes the classical trace, and a map $\sharp : J(A,\mu) \to J(A,\mu)$ that generalizes the classical adjoint of a Jordan algebra. Starting with a cubic étale algebra E, the algebras obtained this way can be viewed as generalizations of special nine-dimensional Jordan algebras. Starting with a central simple algebra A of degree three, the algebras obtained this way can be viewed as generalizations of Albert algebras.

Cubic Jordan algebras carry a cubic norm that satisfies some Jordan composition law involving the U-operator. Curiously, the cubic map $N : J(A,\mu) \to A$ of our generalized construction still allows some sort of generalized weak Jordan composition law, and some of the known identities of cubic Jordan algebras involving a generalized trace map and adjoint can be at least partially recovered.

We point out that there already exists a canonical non-associative generalization of associative central simple cyclic algebras of degree three, involving skew polynomials: the non-associative cyclic algebras $(K/F, \sigma, \mu)$, where K/F is a cubic separable field extension or a C_3-Galois algebra, and $\mu \in K \setminus F$, were first studied over finite fields [7], and then later over arbitrary base fields and rings [8–11] and applied in space-time block coding [12,13]. Their "norm maps" reflect some of the properties of the non-associative cyclic algebra $(K/F, \sigma, \mu)$ and are isometric to the "norm maps" $N : J(K, \mu) \to K$ of the generalized Tits construction $J(K, \mu)$. We show that these algebras are not related, however.

Some obvious questions like if and when the algebras obtained through a generalized first Tits construction are division algebras seem to be very difficult to answer. We will not address these here and only discuss some straightforward implications.

The contents of the paper are as follows: After introducing the terminology in Section 2 and reviewing the classical first Tits construction, we generalize the classical construction in Section 3 and obtain unital non-associative algebras $J(A, \mu)$, where $\mu \in A^\times$. The algebras $J(A, \mu)$ carry maps that satisfy some of the same identities we know from the classical setup. If $A \neq F$, then $\mathrm{Nuc}_l(J(A, \mu)) = \mathrm{Nuc}_r(J(A, \mu)) = F$ for all $\mu \in A^\times$. If A is a central simple associative division algebra of degree three, then $\mathrm{Nuc}_m(J(A, \mu)) = F$ (Theorems 3 and 4). Some necessary conditions on when $J(A, \mu)$ is a division algebra are listed in Theorem 6: If $J(A, \mu)$ is a division algebra, then $\mu \notin N_A(A^\times)$ and A must be a division algebra. If N is anisotropic, then A is a division algebra and $\mu \notin N_A(A^\times)$. If there exist elements $0 \neq x = (x_0, x_1, x_2) \in J(A, \mu)$ such that $x^\sharp = 0$, we show that either A must have zero divisors, or A is a division algebra and $\mu \in N_A(A^\times)$. Moreover, if A is a division algebra over F and 1, μ, and μ^2 are linearly independent over F, then N must be anisotropic.

We investigate in which special cases several classical identities carry over in Section 4.

In Section 5, we compare the algebras obtained from a generalized first Tits construction starting with a cyclic field extension with the algebras $(K/F, \sigma, \mu)^+$, where $(K/F, \sigma, \mu)$ is a non-associative cyclic algebra over F of degree three. If $\mu \in F^\times$, then it is well known that these algebras are isomorphic. For $\mu \in K \setminus F$, they are not isomorphic, but their norms are isometric.

This construction was briefly investigated for the first time in Andrew Steele's PhD thesis [11]. We improved and corrected most of their results, and added many new ones.

2. Preliminaries

2.1. Non-Associative Algebras

Throughout the paper, F is a field of characteristic, not 2 or 3. An *algebra* over F is an F-vector space A together with an F-bilinear map $A \times A \to A$, $(x, y) \mapsto x \cdot y$, denoted simply by juxtaposition of xy, the *multiplication* of A. An algebra A is *unital* if there exists an element in A, denoted by 1, such that $1x = x1 = x$ for all $x \in A$.

A non-associative algebra $A \neq 0$ is called a *division algebra* if for any $a \in A$, $a \neq 0$, the left multiplication with a, $L_a(x) = ax$, and the right multiplication with a, $R_a(x) = xa$, are bijective. We will only consider unital finite-dimensional algebras, which implies that A is a division algebra if and only if A has no zero divisors. Define $[x, y, z] = (xy)z - x(yz)$. The subalgebras $\mathrm{Nuc}_l(A) = \{x \in A \,|\, [x, A, A] = 0\}$, $\mathrm{Nuc}_m(A) = \{x \in A \,|\, [A, x, A] = 0\}$, and $\mathrm{Nuc}_r(A) = \{x \in A \,|\, [A, A, x] = 0\}$ of A are called the *left*, *middle*, and *right nuclei* of A, $\mathrm{Nuc}(A) = \{x \in A \,|\, [x, A, A] = [A, x, A] = [A, A, x] = 0\}$ is called the *nucleus* of A. The *center* of A is defined as $C(A) = \{x \in A \,|\, xy = yx \text{ for all } y \in A\} \cap \mathrm{Nuc}(A)$ [14]. All algebras we consider will be unital.

A non-associative unital algebra J is called a *cubic Jordan algebra* over F, if J is a Jordan algebra, i.e., $xy = yx$ and $(x^2y)x = x^2(yx)$ for all $x, y \in J$, and if its generic minimal polynomial has degree three. Given an associative algebra A over F, its multiplication written simply by juxtaposition, we can define a Jordan algebra over F denoted by A^+ on the F-vector space underlying the algebra A via $x \cdot y = \frac{1}{2}(xy + yx)$. A Jordan algebra J is called *special*, if it is a subalgebra of A^+ for some associative algebra A over F; otherwise, J is *exceptional*. An exceptional Jordan algebra is called an *Albert algebra*.

The following easy observation is included for the sake of the reader:

Lemma 1. *Let A be an associative algebra over F such that A^+ is a division algebra. Then, A is a divison algebra.*

Proof. Suppose that $xy = 0$ for some $x, y \in A$. Then, $(yx) \cdot (yx) = y(xy)x = 0$, and since A^+ is a division algebra, we obtain $yx = 0$. This implies that $x \cdot y = \frac{1}{2}(xy + yx) = 0$. Using again that A^+ is a division algebra, we deduce that $x = 0$ or $y = 0$. □

A *non-associative cyclic algebra* $(K/F, \sigma, c)$ of degree m over F is an m-dimensional K-vector space $(K/F, \sigma, c) = K \oplus Kz \oplus Kz^2 \oplus \cdots \oplus Kz^{m-1}$, with multiplication given by the relations $z^m = c$, $zl = \sigma(l)z$ for all $l \in K$. The algebra $(K/F, \sigma, c)$ is a unital F-central algebra and associative if and only if $c \in F^\times$. The algebra $(K/F, \sigma, c)$ is a division algebra for all $c \in F^\times$, such that $c^s \notin N_{K/F}(K^\times)$ for all s which are prime divisors of m, $1 \leq s \leq m - 1$. If $c \in K \setminus F$, then $(K/F, \sigma, c)$ is a division algebra for all $c \in K \setminus F$ such that $1, c, \ldots, c^{m-1}$ are linearly independent over F [10]. If m is prime, then $(K/F, \sigma, c)$ is a division algebra for all $c \in K \setminus F$.

2.2. Cubic Maps

Let V and W be two finite-dimensional vector spaces over F. A trilinear map $M : V \times V \times V \to W$ is called *symmetric* if $M(x, y, z)$ is invariant under all permutations of its variables. A map $M : V \to W$ is called a *cubic map* over F, if $M(ax) = a^3 M(x)$ for all $a \in F$, $x \in V$, and if the associated map $M : V \times V \times V \to W$ defined by

$$M(x,y,z) = \frac{1}{6}(M(x+y+z) - M(x+y) - M(x+z) - M(y+z) + M(x) + M(y) + M(z))$$

is a (symmetric) F-trilinear map. We canonically identify symmetric trilinear maps $M : V \times V \times V \to W$ with the corresponding cubic maps $M : V \to W$.

A cubic map $M : V \to F$ is called a *cubic form* and a trilinear map $M : V \times V \times V \to F$ a *trilinear form* over F. A cubic map is called *non-degenerate* if $v = 0$ is the only vector such that $M(v, v_2, , v_3) = 0$ for all $v_i \in V$. A cubic map M is called *anisotropic* if $M(x) = 0$ implies that $x = 0$; otherwise, it is *isotropic*. For a non-associative algebra A over F together with a non-degenerate cubic form $M : A \to F$, M is called *multiplicative*, if $M(vw) = M(v)M(w)$ for all $v, w \in A$.

2.3. Associative Cubic Algebras

(cf. for Instance [1,15] (Chapter C.4)) Let A be a unital separable associative algebra over F with cubic norm $N_A : A \to F$. Let $x, y \in A$ and let Z be an indeterminate. The linearization $N_A(x + Zy) = N_A(x) + ZN_A(x; y) + Z^2 N_A(y; x) + Z^3 N_A(y)$ of N_A, i.e., the coefficient of Z in the above expansion, is quadratic in x and linear in y, and is denoted by $N_A(x; y)$. Indeed, we have

$$N_A(x + Zx) = N_A((1 + Z)x) = (1 + Z)^3 N_A(x) = (1 + 3Z + 3Z^2 + Z^3) N_A(x),$$

so $N_A(1; 1) = 3N_A(1) = 3$. Linearize $N_A(x; y)$ to obtain a symmetric trilinear map $N_A : A \times A \times A \to F$, $N_A(x, y, z) = N_A(x + z; y) - N_A(x; y) - N_A(z; y)$. We define

$$\begin{aligned} T_A(x) &= N_A(1; x), \\ T_A(x, y) &= T_A(x) T_A(y) - N_A(1, x, y), \\ S_A(x) &= N_A(x; 1), \\ x^\sharp &= x^2 - T_A(x)x + S_A(x)1, \end{aligned}$$

for all $x, y \in A$. We call $x^\sharp$ the *adjoint* of x, and define the *sharp map* $\sharp : A \times A \to A$, $x \sharp y = (x+y)^\sharp - x^\sharp - y^\sharp$ as the linearization of the adjoint. We observe that $T_A(1) = S_A(1) = 3$. Since the trilinear map $N_A(x, y, z)$ is symmetric,

$$T_A(x, y) = T_A(y, x) \tag{1}$$

for all $x, y \in A$.

The algebra A is called an (associative) *cubic algebra* (respectively, called an algebra *of degree three* in [15] (p. 490)), if the following three axioms are satisfied for all $x, y \in A$:

$$x^3 - T_A(x)x^2 + S_A(x)x - N_A(x)1 = 0 \text{ (degree 3 identity)}, \tag{2}$$
$$T_A(x^\sharp, y) = N_A(x; y) \text{ (trace-sharp formula)}, \tag{3}$$
$$T_A(x, y) = T_A(xy) \text{ (trace-product formula)}. \tag{4}$$

For the rest of Section 2.3, we assume that A is a separable cubic algebra over F with cubic norm $N_A : A \to F$. Note that (2) is equivalent to the condition that

$$xx^\sharp = x^\sharp x = N_A(x)1, \tag{5}$$

and combining (1) with (4) gives

$$T_A(xy) = T_A(yx). \tag{6}$$

An element $x \in A$ is invertible if and only if $N_A(x) \neq 0$. The inverse of $x \in A$ is $x^{-1} = N_A(x)^{-1}x^\sharp$. It can be shown that

$$(xy)^\sharp = y^\sharp x^\sharp \tag{7}$$

for all $x, y \in A$. Notice that

$$T_A(x^\sharp) = T_A(x^\sharp, 1) = N_A(x; 1) = S_A(x), \tag{8}$$

using (3) and (4). We also have $S_A(x) = T_A(x^\sharp) = T_A(x^2) - T_A(x)^2 + 3S_A(x)$, so

$$2S_A(x) = T_A(x)^2 - T_A(x^2). \tag{9}$$

A straightforward calculation shows that

$$x \sharp y = 2(x \cdot y) - T_A(x)y - T_A(y)x + (T_A(x)T_A(y) - T_A(x \cdot y))1 \tag{10}$$

for all $x, y \in A$. In particular,

$$x \cdot y = \frac{1}{2}(xy + yx) = \frac{1}{2}(x \sharp y + T_A(x)y + T_A(y)x - (T_A(x)T_A(y) - T_A(x, y))1)$$

for all $x, y \in A$ and by employing (5) and the adjoint identity in A, we see that the norm N_A satisfies the relation

$$N_A(x^\sharp) = N_A(x)^2. \tag{11}$$

A^+ satisfies the *adjoint identity*

$$(x^\sharp)^\sharp = N_A(x)x \tag{12}$$

for all $x \in A$. By (11), we have $N_A(x^\sharp)1 = x^\sharp(x^\sharp)^\sharp = x^\sharp N_A(x)x = N_A(x)^2 1$. For $x, y \in A$, we define the operators $U_x : A \to A$, $U_x(y) = T_A(x, y)x - x^\sharp \sharp y$ and $U_{x,y} : A \to A$, $U_{x,y}(z) = U_{x+y}(z) - U_x(z) - U_y(z)$. Then, we have $x \cdot y = \frac{1}{2}U_{x,y}(1)$ for all $x, y \in A$ and

$$xyx = T_A(x, y)x - x^\sharp \sharp y, \tag{13}$$

Hence, $U_x(y) = xyx$ for all $x, y \in A^\times$.

Define
$$x \times y = \frac{1}{2}(x \sharp y),$$
and
$$\bar{x} = \frac{1}{2}(T_A(x)1 - x)$$
for $x, y \in A$. (Note that some literature does not include the factor $\frac{1}{2}$ in the definition of $\times$, e.g., [16]). By (10), we then have
$$x \times y = x \cdot y - \frac{1}{2}T_A(x)y - \frac{1}{2}T_A(y)x + \frac{1}{2}(T_A(x)T_A(y) - T_A(x \cdot y))1$$
for all $x, y \in A$; hence,
$$x \times x = x^2 - T_A(x)x + \frac{1}{2}(T_A(x)^2 - T_A(x^2)) = x^\sharp, \tag{14}$$
using (9).

2.4. The First Tits Construction

Let A be a separable cubic associative algebra over F with norm N_A, trace T_A and adjoint map $\sharp$. Let $\mu \in F^\times$ and define the F-vector space $J = J(A, \mu) = A_0 \oplus A_1 \oplus A_2$, where $A_i = A$ for $i = 0, 1, 2$. Then, $J(A, \mu)$ together with the multiplication
$$\begin{aligned}&(x_0, x_1, x_2)(y_0, y_1, y_2)\\&= (x_0 \cdot y_0 + \overline{x_1 y_2} + \overline{y_1 x_2}, \overline{x_0} y_1 + \overline{y_0} x_1 + \mu^{-1}(x_2 \times y_2), x_2 \overline{y_0} + y_2 \overline{x_0} + \mu(x_1 \times y_1))\end{aligned}$$
becomes a separable cubic Jordan algebra over F. $J(A, \mu)$ is called a *first Tits construction*. A^+ is a subalgebra of $J(A, \mu)$ by canonically identifying it with A_0. If A is a cubic etale algebra, then $J(A, \mu) \cong D^+$ for with D an associative cyclic algebra D of degree three. If A is a central simple algebra of degree three then $J(A, \mu)$ is an Albert algebra.

We define the *cubic norm form* $N : J(A, \mu) \to F$, the *trace* $T : J(A, \mu) \to F$, and the quadratic map $\sharp : J(A, \mu) \to J(A, \mu)$ (the *adjoint*) by
$$\begin{aligned}N((x_0, x_1, x_2)) &= N_A(x_0) + \mu N_A(x_1) + \mu^{-1} N_A(x_2) - T_A(x_0 x_1 x_2)\\ T((x_0, x_1, x_2)) &= T_A(x_0),\\ (x_0, x_1, x_2)^\sharp &= (x_0^\sharp - x_1 x_2, \mu^{-1} x_2^\sharp - x_0 x_1, \mu x_1^\sharp - x_2 x_0).\end{aligned}$$

The *intermediate quadratic form* $S : J(A, \mu) \to F$, $S(x_0) = N(x; 1)$, linearizes to a map $S : J(A, \mu) \times J(A, \mu) \to F$. The *sharp map* $\sharp : J(A, \mu) \times J(A, \mu) \to J(A, \mu)$ is the linearization $x \sharp y = (x + y)^\sharp - x^\sharp - y^\sharp$ of the adjoint. For every $x = (x_0, x_1, x_2) \in J(A, \mu)$, we have $x \sharp 1 = T(x)1 - x$ and
$$x \sharp y = (x_0 \sharp y_0 - x_1 y_2 - y_1 x_2, \mu^{-1}(x_2 \sharp y_2) - x_0 y_1 - y_0 x_1, \mu(x_1 \sharp y_1) - x_2 y_0 - y_2 x_0)$$
for all $x = (x_0, x_1, x_2), y = (y_0, y_1, y_2) \in J(A, \mu)$. We define the *trace symmetric bilinear form* $T : J(A, \mu) \times J(A, \mu) \to F$, $T(x, y) = T_A(x_0 y_0) + T_A(x_1 y_2) + T_A(x_2 y_1)$. Then, for all $x, y \in J(A, \mu)$, we have
$$T(x, y) = T(xy). \tag{15}$$

Remark 1. *$(N, \sharp, 1)$ is a cubic form with adjoint and base point $(1, 0, 0)$ on $J(A, \mu)$ which makes $J(A, \mu)$ into a cubic Jordan algebra $J(N, \sharp, 1)$.*

3. The Generalized First Tits Construction $J(A,\mu)$

Let A be a separable associative cubic algebra over F with norm N_A, trace T_A and adjoint map $\sharp$.

We now generalize the first Tits construction by choosing the scalar $\mu \in A^\times$. Then, the F-vector space $J(A,\mu) = A_0 \oplus A_1 \oplus A_2$, where again $A_i = A$ for $i = 0,1,2$, becomes a unital non-associative algebra over F together with the multiplication given by

$$\begin{aligned}&(x_0,x_1,x_2)(y_0,y_1,y_2)\\&=(x_0\cdot y_0+\overline{x_1y_2}+\overline{y_1x_2},\overline{x_0}y_1+\overline{y_0}x_1+\mu^{-1}(x_2\times y_2),x_2\overline{y_0}+y_2\overline{x_0}+\mu(x_1\times y_1)).\end{aligned}$$

The algebra $J(A,\mu)$ is called a *generalized first Tits construction*. The special Jordan algebra A^+ is a subalgebra of $J(A,\mu)$ by canonically identifying it with A_0. If $\mu \in F^\times$, then $J(A,\mu)$ is the first Tits construction from Section 2.4.

We define a *(generalized) cubic norm map* $N : J(A,\mu) \to A$, a *(generalized) trace* $T : J(A,\mu) \to F$, and a quadratic map $\sharp : J(A,\mu) \to J(A,\mu)$ via

$$N((x_0,x_1,x_2)) = N_A(x_0) + \mu N_A(x_1) + \mu^{-1}N_A(x_2) - T_A(x_0x_1x_2) \tag{16}$$

$$T((x_0,x_1,x_2)) = T_A(x_0), \tag{17}$$

$$(x_0,x_1,x_2)^\sharp = (x_0^\sharp - x_1x_2, \mu^{-1}x_2^\sharp - x_0x_1, \mu x_1^\sharp - x_2x_0). \tag{18}$$

Put $\sharp : J(A,\mu) \times J(A,\mu) \to J(A,\mu)$, $x\sharp y = (x+y)^\sharp - x^\sharp - y^\sharp$; then, it can be verified by a direct computation that

$$x\sharp y = (x_0\sharp y_0 - x_1y_2 - y_1x_2, \mu^{-1}(x_2\sharp y_2) - x_0y_1 - y_0x_1, \mu(x_1\sharp y_1) - x_2y_0 - y_2x_0)$$

for all $x = (x_0,x_1,x_2), y = (y_0,y_1,y_2) \in J(A,\mu)$. We also define a symmetric F-bilinear form $T : J(A,\mu) \times J(A,\mu) \to F$ via $T(x,y) = T_A(x_0y_0) + T_A(x_1y_2) + T_A(x_2y_1)$.

The quadratic form $S_A : A \to F$, $S_A(x_0) = N_A(x;1)$, linearizes to $S_A : A \times A \to F$, and we have $S_A(x_0) = T_A(x_0^\sharp)$ for all $x_0 \in A$. We extend S_A to $J(A,\mu)$ by defining the quadratic map $S : J(A,a) \to A$, $S(x) = N(x;1)$. As in the classical case, we obtain:

Theorem 1.

(i) [11] *(Proposition 5.2.2) For all $x \in J(A,\mu)$, we have $S(x) = T(x^\sharp)$ and the linearization $S : J(A,\mu) \times J(A,\mu) \to A$ satisfies*

$$S(x,y) = T(x)T(y) - T(x,y)$$

for all $y \in J(A,\mu)$.

(ii) [11] *(Lemma 5.2.3) For all $x,y \in J(A,\mu)$, we have $T(x,Y) = T(xy)$.*

(iii) [11] *(Lemma 5.2.3) For all $x \in J(A,\mu)$, we have $x\sharp 1 = T(x)1 - x$.*

Proof.

(i) Let $x = (x_0,x_1,x_2), y = (y_0,y_1,y_2) \in J(A,a)$, then

$$\begin{aligned}N(x;y) =& N_A(x_0;y_0) + \mu N_A(x_1;y_1) + \mu^{-1}N_A(x_2;y_2)\\&- T_A(x_0x_1y_2) - T_A(x_0y_1x_2) - T_A(y_0x_1x_2),\end{aligned}$$

and since $S(x) = N(x;1)$ we obtain $S(x) = N_A(x_0;1) - T_A(x_1x_2) = S_A(x_0) - T_A(x_1x_2)$. On the other hand,

$$T(x^\sharp) = T_A(x_0^\sharp - x_1x_2) = T_A(x_0^\sharp) - T_A(x_1x_2) = S_A(x_0) - T_A(x_1x_2) = S(x).$$

We have $S_A(x_0,y_0) = T_A(x_0)T_A(y_0) - T_A(x_0,y_0)$ for all $x_0,y_0 \in A$. Linearizing S gives $S(x,y) = S_A(x_0,y_0) - T_A(x_1y_2) - T_A(y_1x_2) = T_A(x_0)T_A(y_0) - T_A(x_0,y_0) -$

$T_A(x_1y_2) - T_A(y_1x_2) = T(x)T(y) - T(x,y)$ using the definitions of $T_A(x_i)$ and $T_A(x_i, y_i)$ and the fact that $T_A(x_0, y_0) = T_A(x_0y_0)$.

(ii) Let $x = (x_0, x_1, x_2), y = (y_0, y_1, y_2) \in J(A, \mu)$. Since T_A is linear, we obtain

$$\begin{aligned} T(xy) &= T_A(x_0 \cdot y_0) + T_A(\overline{x_1y_2}) + T_A(\overline{y_1x_2}) \\ &= \frac{1}{2}(T_A(x_0y_0) + T_A(y_0x_0)) + \frac{1}{2}(T_A(x_1y_2)T_A(1) - T_A(x_1y_2)) \\ &+ \frac{1}{2}(T_A(y_1x_2)T_A(1) - T_A(y_1x_2)). \end{aligned}$$

By (6) we obtain $T_A(x_0y_0) = T_A(y_0x_0)$ and $T_A(y_1x_2) = T_A(x_2y_1)$. Since we have $T_A(1) = 3$ we obtain $T(xy) = T_A(x_0y_0) + T_A(x_1y_2) + T_A(x_2y_1) = T(x,y)$.

(iii) Let $x = (x_0, x_1, x_2) \in J(A, \mu)$. By (10), we have $x_0\sharp 1 = T_A(x_0)1 - x_0$. Thus, $x\sharp 1 = (x_0\sharp 1, -x_1, -x_2) = T(x)1 - x$.

□

Theorem 2. *Let $\mu \in A^\times$, and let $x, y \in J(A, \mu)$. Then,*

(i) $x^\sharp = x^2 - T(x)x + S(x)1$,

(ii) $S(x) = T(x^\sharp)$,

(iii) $T(x \times y) = \frac{1}{2}(T(x)T(y) - T(xy))$.

Note that these are relations that also hold for a cubic form with adjoint and base point $(N, \sharp, 1)$ [15,17].

Proof. Let $x = (x_0, x_1, x_2), y = (y_0, y_1, y_2) \in J(A, \mu)$.

(i) We have that $x^2 - T(x)x + S(x)1 = (x_0, x_1, x_2)^2 - T_A(x_0)(x_0, x_1, x_2) + (S_A(x_0)1 - T_A(x_1x_2)1, 0, 0) = (x_0^2 - T_A(x_0)x_0 + S_A(x_0)1 + 2\overline{x_1x_2} - T_A(x_1x_2)1, \mu^{-1}x_2^\sharp + 2\overline{x_0}x_1 - T_A(x_0)x_1, \mu x_1^\sharp + 2x_2\overline{x_0} - T_A(x_0)x_2) = (x_0^\sharp - x_1x_2, \mu^{-1}x_2^\sharp - x_0x_1, \mu x_1^\sharp - x_2\overline{x_0}) = x^\sharp$.

(ii) As for the classical construction,

$$T(x^\sharp) = T_A(x_0^\sharp - x_1x_2) = T_A(x_0^\sharp) - T_A(x_1x_2) = S_A(x_0) - T_A(x_1x_2) = S(x).$$

(iii) Since $x \times y = \frac{1}{2}(x\sharp y) = \frac{1}{2}(x_0\sharp y_0 - x_1y_2 - y_1x_2, \mu^{-1}(x_2\sharp y_2) - x_0y_1 - y_0x_1, \mu(x_1\sharp y_1) - x_2y_0 - y_2x_0)$, we obtain $T(x \times y) = T_A(x_0 \times y_0) - \frac{1}{2}T_A(x_1y_2) - \frac{1}{2}T_A(y_1x_2) = \frac{1}{2}(T_A(x_0)T_A(y_0) - T_A(x_0y_0) - T_A(x_1y_2) - T_A(y_1x_2)) = \frac{1}{2}(T(x)T(y) - T(xy))$.

□

Define operators $U_x, U_{x,y} : J(A, \mu) \to J(A, \mu)$ via

$$U_x(y) = T(x,y)x - x^\sharp\sharp y, \quad U_{x,y}(z) = U_{x+y}(z) - U_x(z) - U_y(z)$$

for all $z \in J(A, \mu)$.

Proposition 1. *(cf.* [11] *(Proposition 5.2.4) without factor $\frac{1}{2}$ because of slightly different terminology) For all $x, y \in J(A, \mu)$, we have $xy = \frac{1}{2}U_{x,y}(1)$.*

This generalizes the classical setup. Our proof is different to the one of [11] (Proposition 5.2.4), which also proves this result without the factor $\frac{1}{2}$ because of the slightly different definition of the multiplication.

Proof. We find that $U_x(1) = T(x,1)x - x^\sharp \sharp 1 = T(x)x - T(x^\sharp)1 + x^\sharp$; in the second equality, we have used Theorem 1 and the fact that $T(x,1) = T(x)$ by Theorem 1. So

$$\begin{aligned} U_{x,y}(1) &= U_{x+y}(1) - U_x(1) - U_y(1) \\ &= T(x+y)(x+y) - T((x+y)^\sharp)1 + (x+y)^\sharp - T(x)x + T(x^\sharp)1 - x^\sharp \\ &\quad - T(y)y + T(y^\sharp)1 - y^\sharp \\ &= T(x)y + T(y)x + x\sharp y - T(x\sharp y)1. \end{aligned}$$

We look at the first component of xy and $U_{x,y}(1)$: let $x = (x_0, x_1, x_2)$ and $y = (y_0, y_1, y_2)$. Then, the first component of $U_{x,y}(1) = T(x)y + T(y)x + x\sharp y - T(x\sharp y)1$ is

$$T_A(x_0)y_0 + T_A(y_0)x_0 + x_0\sharp y_0 - x_1y_2 - y_1x_2 - T_A(x_0\sharp y_0 - x_1y_2 - y_1x_2)1. \tag{19}$$

Using (10), the linearity of T_A and (6), we obtain—after some simplification—that (19) is equal to

$$2(x_0 \cdot y_0) + T_A(x_1y_2) - x_1y_2 + T_A(y_1x_2) - y_1x_2 = 2(x_0 \cdot y_0) + 2\,\overline{x_1y_2} + 2\,\overline{y_1x_2}.$$

This is equal to 2 times the first component of xy. Now, we look at the second component of xy and $U_{x,y}(1)$: the second component of $U_{x,y}(1) = T(x)y + T(y)x + x\sharp y - T(x\sharp y)1$ is

$$T_A(x_0)y_1 + T_A(y_0)x_1 + \mu^{-1}(x_2\sharp y_2) - x_0y_1 - y_0x_1 = 2\overline{x_0}y_1 + 2\overline{y_0}x_1 + 2\mu^{-1}(x_2 \times y_2).$$

This is precisely equal to 2 times the second component of xy. Finally, the third component of $2xy$ and $U_{x,y}(1)$ are equal, too. The third component of $U_{x,y}(1) = T(x)y + T(y)x + x\sharp y - T(x\sharp y)1$ is

$$T_A(x_0)y_2 + T_A(y_0)x_2 + \mu(x_1\sharp y_1) - x_2y_0 - y_2x_0 = 2x_2\overline{y_0} + 2y_2\overline{x_0} + 2\mu(x_1 \times y_1).$$

This is precisely equal to 2 times the third component of xy. □

Theorem 3. *If $\mu \in A^\times$ and $A \neq F$, then* $\mathrm{Nuc}_l(J(A,\mu)) = \mathrm{Nuc}_r(J(A,\mu)) = F$.

Proof. Let $(x_0, x_1, x_2) \in \mathrm{Nuc}_l(J(A,\mu))$, then

$$(x_0, x_1, x_2)[(0,1,0)(0,0,1)] = [(x_0, x_1, x_2)(0,1,0)](0,0,1)$$

implies that

$$(x_0, x_1, x_2) = (\overline{\overline{x_0}}, \mu^{-1}(\overline{\mu\overline{x_1}}), \overline{\overline{x_2}}),$$

that means $x_0 = \overline{\overline{x_0}}$ and $x_2 = \overline{\overline{x_2}}$. Using the definition of $\overline{x_0}$, we obtain $\overline{\overline{x_0}} = \frac{1}{4}(\mathrm{T}_A(x_0) + x_0)$, so $x_0 = \frac{1}{4}(\mathrm{T}_A(x_0) + x_0)$. Thus, $x_0 = \frac{1}{3}\mathrm{T}_A(x_0) \in F$. Furthermore, since $x_2 = \overline{\overline{x_2}}$, we find in a similar way that $x_2 = \frac{1}{3}\mathrm{T}_A(x_2) \in F$. Next, since $x = (x_0, x_1, x_2) \in \mathrm{Nuc}_l(J(A,\mu))$, we have that

$$(x_0, x_1, x_2)[(0,0,1)(0,1,0)] = [(x_0, x_1, x_2)(0,0,1)](0,1,0).$$

This implies that

$$(x_0, x_1, x_2) = (\overline{\overline{x_0}}, \overline{\overline{x_1}}, \mu(\overline{\mu^{-1}\overline{x_2}})),$$

and so $x_1 = \overline{\overline{x_1}}$. We now find in a similar way that $x_1 = \frac{1}{3}\mathrm{T}_A(x_1) \in F$, thus $\mathrm{Nuc}_l(J(A,\mu)) \subseteq \{(x_0, x_1, x_2) \in J \mid x_0, x_1, x_2 \in F\}$. Let $x = (x_0, x_1, x_2) \in \mathrm{Nuc}_l(J(A,\mu))$, and let $a \in A \setminus F$. Then

$$(x_0, x_1, x_2)[(0,0,1)(0,a,0)] = [(x_0, x_1, x_2)(0,0,1)](0,a,0)$$

which implies that

$$(x_0 \cdot \overline{a}, \overline{\overline{a}}x_1, x_2\overline{\overline{a}}) = (\overline{a\overline{x_0}}, \overline{\overline{x_1}}a, \mu(\overline{\mu^{-1}\overline{x_2}} \times a)),$$

and so $\bar{\bar{a}}x_1 = \overline{\overline{x_1}}a$. Assume towards a contradiction that $x_1 \neq 0$. Since $x_1 \in F$, this implies that x_1 is invertible and $\overline{\overline{x_1}} = x_1$. Thus, the condition $\bar{\bar{a}}x_1 = \overline{\overline{x_1}}a$ yields $a = \bar{\bar{a}}$, and so $a = \frac{1}{3}\,\mathrm{T}_A(a) \in F$ which is a contradiction. Next, since $(x_0, x_1, x_2) \in \mathrm{Nuc}_l(J(A,\mu))$, we know that

$$(x_0, x_1, x_2)[(0,1,0)(0,0,a)] = [(x_0, x_1, x_2)(0,1,0)](0,0,a)$$

which implies that

$$(x_0 \cdot \bar{a}, \bar{\bar{a}}x_1, x_2\bar{\bar{a}}) = (\overline{\overline{x_0}a}, \mu^{-1}(\mu\overline{x_1} \times a), a\overline{\overline{x_2}}),$$

and so $x_2\bar{\bar{a}} = a\overline{\overline{x_2}}$. Assume towards a contradiction that $x_2 \neq 0$. Then, since $x_2 \in F$, x_2 is invertible and $\overline{\overline{x_2}} = x_2$. Thus, the condition $x_2\bar{\bar{a}} = a\overline{\overline{x_2}}$ yields $a = \bar{\bar{a}}$, and so $a = \frac{1}{3}\,\mathrm{T}_A(a) \in F$ which is a contradiction. Therefore, $x = (x_0, 0, 0)$, $x_0 1 \in F$ which shows that $\mathrm{Nuc}_l(J(A,\mu)) = F$.

Let $(x_0, x_1, x_2) \in \mathrm{Nuc}_r(J(A,\mu))$. Then,

$$(0,0,1)[(0,1,0)(x_0, x_1, x_2)] = [(0,0,1)(0,1,0)](x_0, x_1, x_2)$$

implies that

$$(\overline{\overline{x_0}}, \mu^{-1}(\overline{\mu\overline{x_1}}), \overline{\overline{x_2}}) = (x_0, x_1, x_2).$$

Hence, $x_0 = \overline{\overline{x_0}}$ and $x_2 = \overline{\overline{x_2}}$. Using the definition of $\overline{\overline{x_0}}$, we find that $\overline{\overline{x_0}} = \frac{1}{4}(\mathrm{T}_A(x_0) + x_0)$, so the condition $x_0 = \overline{\overline{x_0}}$ gives that $x_0 = \frac{1}{4}(\mathrm{T}_A(x_0) + x_0)$. Thus, $x_0 = \frac{1}{3}\,\mathrm{T}_A(x_0) \in F$. Furthermore, since $x_2 = \overline{\overline{x_2}}$, we find in a similar way that $x_2 = \frac{1}{3}\,\mathrm{T}_A(x_2) \in F$. Next, since $x = (x_0, x_1, x_2) \in \mathrm{Nuc}_r(J(A,\mu))$, we have that

$$(0,1,0)[(0,0,1)(x_0, x_1, x_2)] = [(0,1,0)(0,0,1)](x_0, x_1, x_2).$$

This implies that

$$(\overline{\overline{x_0}}, \overline{\overline{x_1}}, \mu(\overline{\mu^{-1}\overline{x_2}})) = (x_0, x_1, x_2),$$

and thus $x_1 = \overline{\overline{x_1}}$. We find in a similar way that $x_1 = \frac{1}{3}\,\mathrm{T}_A(x_1) \in F$, i.e. $\mathrm{Nuc}_r(J(A,\mu)) \subseteq \{(x_0, x_1, x_2) \in J \mid x_0, x_1, x_2 \in F\}$.

Let $x = (x_0, x_1, x_2) \in \mathrm{Nuc}_r(J(A,\mu))$, and let $a \in A \setminus F$. Then, $(0,a,0)[(0,0,1)(x_0, x_1, x_2)] = [(0,a,0)(0,0,1)](x_0, x_1, x_2)$ which implies that

$$(a\overline{\overline{x_0}}, \overline{\overline{x_1}}a, \mu(a \times \mu^{-1}\overline{x_2})) = (\bar{a} \cdot x_0, \bar{\bar{a}}x_1, x_2\bar{\bar{a}});$$

therefore, $\bar{\bar{a}}x_1 = \overline{\overline{x_1}}a$. Assume towards a contradiction that $x_1 \neq 0$. Then, since $x_1 \in F$, x_1 is invertible and $\overline{\overline{x_1}} = x_1$. Thus, the condition $\bar{\bar{a}}x_1 = \overline{\overline{x_1}}a$ yields $a = \bar{\bar{a}}$, and so $a = \frac{1}{3}\,\mathrm{T}_A(a) \in F$ which is a contradiction. Next, since $(x_0, x_1, x_2) \in \mathrm{Nuc}_r(J(A,\mu))$, we know that

$$(0,0,a)[(0,1,0)(x_0, x_1, x_2)] = [(0,0,a)(0,1,0)](x_0, x_1, x_2)$$

which implies that

$$(\overline{\overline{x_0}a}, \mu^{-1}(a \times \mu\overline{x_1}), a\overline{\overline{x_2}}) = (\bar{a} \cdot x_0, \bar{\bar{a}}x_1, x_2\bar{\bar{a}}),$$

and so $x_2\bar{\bar{a}} = a\overline{\overline{x_2}}$. Assume towards a contradiction that $x_2 \neq 0$. Then, since $x_2 \in F$, x_2 is invertible and $\overline{\overline{x_2}} = x_2$. Thus, the condition $x_2\bar{\bar{a}} = a\overline{\overline{x_2}}$ yields $a = \bar{\bar{a}}$, and so $a = \frac{1}{3}\,\mathrm{T}_A(a) \in F$ which is a contradiction. Therefore, $x = (x_0, 0, 0) = x_0 1 \in F$ which shows the assertion. □

Theorem 4. *Let $A \neq F$ be a central simple division algebra of degree three and $\mu \in A^\times$. Then, $\mathrm{Nuc}_m(J(A,\mu)) = F$.*

Proof. Let $x = (x_0, x_1, x_2) \in \mathrm{Nuc}_m(J(A,\mu))$, and let $y_0 \notin C(A)$. Then, there exists $z_0 \in A$ such that $y_0 z_0 \neq z_0 y_0$. Since $(x_0, x_1, x_2) \in \mathrm{Nuc}_m(J(A,\mu))$, we know that

$$(y_0, 0, 0)[(x_0, x_1, x_2)(z_0, 0, 0)] = [(y_0, 0, 0)(x_0, x_1, x_2)](z_0, 0, 0)$$

which implies that

$$(y_0 \cdot (x_0 \cdot z_0), \overline{y_0}(\overline{z_0}x_1), (x_2\overline{z_0})\overline{y_0}) = ((y_0 \cdot x_0) \cdot z_0, \overline{z_0}(\overline{y_0}x_1), (x_2\overline{y_0})\overline{z_0}).$$

Comparing the second and third components yields

$$\overline{y_0}(\overline{z_0}x_1) = \overline{z_0}(\overline{y_0}x_1), \tag{20}$$

$$(x_2\overline{z_0})\overline{y_0} = (x_2\overline{y_0})\overline{z_0}. \tag{21}$$

Now, assume towards a contradiction that $x_1 \neq 0$. Since A is a division algebra, x_1 is invertible. Since A is associative, (20) implies that $\overline{y_0}\ \overline{z_0} = \overline{z_0}\ \overline{y_0}$. By definition, this yields

$$(T_A(y_0)1 - y_0)(T_A(z_0)1 - z_0) = (T_A(z_0)1 - z_0)(T_A(y_0)1 - y_0).$$

Hence, $y_0z_0 = z_0y_0$ which is a contradiction. Now, in a similar way we assume towards a contradiction that $x_2 \neq 0$. Then, since A is a division algebra, x_2 is invertible. Since A is associative, (21) implies again that $\overline{y_0}\ \overline{z_0} = \overline{z_0}\ \overline{y_0}$. Hence, $y_0z_0 = z_0y_0$ which is a contradiction. Next, since $x = (x_0, 0, 0) \in \mathrm{Nuc}_m(J(A, \mu))$, we also have that

$$(0,1,0)[(x_0,0,0)(0,0,y_2)] = [(0,1,0)(x_0,0,0)](0,0,y_2)$$

for each $y_2 \in A$. This implies $(\overline{y_2\overline{x_0}}, 0, 0) = (\overline{\overline{x_0}y_2}, 0, 0)$, and so $\overline{y_2\overline{x_0}} = \overline{\overline{x_0}y_2}$. By definition, this means that

$$\frac{1}{2}T_A(\overline{y_2}x_0)1 - \frac{1}{2}\overline{y_2}x_0 = \frac{1}{2}T_A(x_0\overline{y_2})1 - \frac{1}{2}x_0\overline{y_2}. \tag{22}$$

We know that $T_A(\overline{y_2}x_0) = T_A(x_0\overline{y_2})$ (see (6)), and so (22) gives that $\overline{y_2}x_0 = x_0\overline{y_2}$. By using the definition of $\overline{y_2}$, this implies that $y_2x_0 = x_0y_2$. Hence, $x_0 \in C(A)$. Therefore, $x = (x_0, 0, 0) = x_01 \in C(A)$. Since $F \subseteq \mathrm{Nuc}_m(J(A, \mu))$ this implies the assertion if A is a central simple division algebra. □

Theorem 5. ([18] *(Chapter IX, Section 12)*, [15] *(Chapter C.5))* *For $\mu \in F^\times$, $J(A, \mu)$ is a division algebra if and only if $\mu \notin N_A(A^\times)$ and A is a division algebra, if and only if N is anisotropic.*

The general situation is much harder to figure out and we were only able to obtain some obvious necessary conditions:

Theorem 6. *Let $\mu \in A^\times$.*

(i) If $J(A, \mu)$ is a division algebra, then $\mu \notin N_A(A^\times)$ and A is a division algebra.
(ii) Let A be a division algebra over F. If 1, μ, μ^2 are linearly independent over F then N is anisotropic.
(iii) If N is anisotropic then A is a division algebra and $\mu \notin N_A(A^\times)$.
(iv) Let $0 \neq x = (x_0, x_1, x_2) \in J(A, \mu)$. Then, $x^\sharp = 0$ implies that A has zero divisors, or A is a division algebra and $\mu \in N_A(A^\times)$.

Proof.

(i) Suppose that $J(A, \mu)$ is a division algebra, then so is A^+ and thus A (Lemma 1). Assume towards a contradiction that $\mu = N_A(x_0)1$ for some $x_0 \in A^\times$. Then, $\mu \in F^\times$ and $J(A, \mu)$ is not a division algebra by Theorem 5. Hence, $\mu \notin N_A(A)1$.
(ii) Since A is a division algebra, N_A is anisotropic. So, let $N((x_0, x_1, x_2)) = 0$; then, the assumption means that $N(x_0) = 0$, which implies that $x_0 = 0$. This immediately means that $x_1 = x_2 = 0$, too.
(iii) If N is anisotropic, then so is N_A; so, A is clearly a division algebra. Moreover, $\mu \notin N_A(A^\times)$ by Theorem 5.

(iv) Let $0 \neq x = (x_0, x_1, x_2) \in J(A, \mu)$. Then, $x^\sharp = 0$ implies that

$$x_0^\sharp = x_1 x_2 \tag{23}$$
$$\mu^{-1} x_2^\sharp = x_0 x_1 \tag{24}$$
$$\mu x_1^\sharp = x_2 x_0. \tag{25}$$

We can now multiply (23) (resp. (24), (25)) by x_0 (resp. x_2, x_1) on the right and left to obtain two new equations. Additionally, using the fact that $N_A(x_i) = x_i x_i^\sharp = x_i^\sharp x_i$ for all $i = 0, 1, 2$, we obtain the following six equations:

$$\begin{aligned} N_A(x_0) &= x_1 x_2 x_0 & N_A(x_0) &= x_0 x_1 x_2 \\ \mu^{-1} N_A(x_2) &= x_0 x_1 x_2 & \mu^{-1} N_A(x_2) &= x_2 x_0 x_1 \\ \mu N_A(x_1) &= x_2 x_0 x_1 & \mu N_A(x_1) &= x_1 x_2 x_0. \end{aligned} \tag{26}$$

These imply that $N_A(x_0) = \mu^{-1} N_A(x_2) = \mu N_A(x_1)$. This means that either $N_A(x_0) = \mu^{-1} N_A(x_2) = \mu N_A(x_1) = 0$ and so N_A is isotropic, or $N_A(x_0) = \mu^{-1} N_A(x_2) = \mu N_A(x_1) \neq 0$ and N_A is anisotropic. In the later case, x_0, x_1, x_2 are all invertible in A, $N_A(x_i) \neq 0$ for all $i = 0, 1, 2$ and it follows that $\mu \in N_A(A^\times)$. This proves the assertion.

□

In other words: If A is a division algebra and $\mu \notin N_A(A^\times)$, $0 \neq x = (x_0, x_1, x_2) \in J(A, \mu)$, then $x^\sharp \neq 0$. Note that (iv) was a substantial part of the classical result that if $\mu \in F^\times$, $\mu \notin N_A(A^\times)$ and A is a division algebra, then N is anisotropic. What is missing in order to generalize this result to the generalized first Tits construction is the adjoint identity $(x^\sharp)^\sharp = N(x)x$. This identity only holds in very special cases—see Lemma 4 below. It would be of course desirable to have conditions on when (or if at all) $J(A, \mu)$ is a division algebra.

4. Some More Identities

Lemma 2. *Let $x = (x_0, x_1, x_2)$, $y = (y_0, y_1, y_2)$, $z = (z_0, z_1, z_2) \in J(A, \mu)$ be such that one of x_1, y_1, z_1 is equal to zero and one of x_2, y_2, z_2 is equal to zero. Then, $T(x \times y, z) = T(x, y \times z)$.*

Proof. We find that

$$\begin{aligned} T(x \times y, z) =& \frac{1}{2} T_A((x_0 \sharp y_0) z_0 - x_1 y_2 z_0 - y_1 x_2 z_0) \\ &+ \frac{1}{2} T_A(\mu^{-1}(x_2 \sharp y_2) z_2 - x_0 y_1 z_2 - y_0 x_1 z_2) \\ &+ \frac{1}{2} T_A(\mu(x_1 \sharp y_1) z_1 - x_2 y_0 z_1 - y_2 x_0 z_1) \end{aligned} \tag{27}$$

and

$$\begin{aligned} T(x, y \times z) =& \frac{1}{2} T_A(x_0(y_0 \sharp z_0) - x_0 y_1 z_2 - x_0 z_1 y_2) \\ &+ \frac{1}{2} T_A(x_1 \mu(y_1 \sharp z_1) - x_1 y_2 z_0 - x_1 z_2 y_0) \\ &+ \frac{1}{2} T_A(x_2 \mu^{-1}(y_2 \sharp z_2) - x_2 y_0 z_1 - x_2 z_0 y_1). \end{aligned} \tag{28}$$

Using the definitions, we can show that $T_A((x_0 \sharp y_0) z_0) = T_A(x_0(y_0 \sharp z_0))$. Furthermore, since one of x_1, y_1, z_1 is equal to zero, we have that $T_A(\mu(x_1 \sharp y_1) z_1) = 0 = T_A(x_1 \mu(y_1 \sharp z_1))$. Finally, since one of x_2, y_2, z_2 is equal to zero, $T_A(\mu^{-1}(x_2 \sharp y_2) z_2) = 0 = T_A(x_2 \mu^{-1}(y_2 \sharp z_2))$. Therefore, applying these equalities and using (6), we deduce that (27) and (28) are equal, so $T(x \times y, z) = T(x, y \times z)$. □

We know that $xx^\sharp = x^\sharp x = N(x)1$ holds for all $x \in J(A,\mu)$ if $\mu \in F^\times$. We now show for which $x \in J(A,\mu)$ we still obtain $xx^\sharp = x^\sharp x = N(x)1$:

Lemma 3. *Let $\mu \in A^\times$ and suppose that $x \in J(A,\mu)$, such that one of the following holds:*

(i) $x = (x_0, 0, x_2) \in J(A,\mu)$, $x_0\mu = \mu x_0$ *and* $N_A(x_2) = 0$.

(ii) $x = (x_0, x_1, 0) \in J(A,\mu)$, $x_1\mu = \mu x_1$ *and* $N_A(x_1) = 0$.

Then, we have

$$xx^\sharp = x^\sharp x = N(x)1. \tag{29}$$

Moreover, assume that one of the following holds:

(iii) $x = (x_0, 0, x_2) \in J(A,\mu)$, $x_0\mu = \mu x_0$ *and* $N_A(x_2) \neq 0$.

(iv) $x = (x_0, x_1, 0) \in J(A,\mu)$, $x_1\mu = \mu x_1$ *and* $N_A(x_1) \neq 0$.

Then, $xx^\sharp = x^\sharp x = N(x)1$ *if and only if* $\mu \in F^\times$.

Proof. Let $x = (x_0, x_1, x_2) \in J(A,\mu)$, and let $xx^\sharp = (a_0, a_1, a_2)$; then, $x^\sharp = (x_0^\sharp - x_1x_2, \mu^{-1}x_2^\sharp - x_0x_1, \mu x_1^\sharp - x_2x_0)$. Thus, we have

$$\begin{aligned} a_0 = &\frac{1}{2}(x_0x_0^\sharp - x_0x_1x_2 + x_0^\sharp x_0 - x_1x_2x_0) \\ &+ \frac{1}{2}(T_A(x_1\mu x_1^\sharp - x_1x_2x_0)1 - x_1\mu x_1^\sharp + x_1x_2x_0) \\ &+ \frac{1}{2}(T_A(\mu^{-1}x_2^\sharp x_2 - x_0x_1x_2)1 - \mu^{-1}x_2^\sharp x_2 + x_0x_1x_2), \end{aligned} \tag{30}$$

$$\begin{aligned} a_1 = &\frac{1}{2}(T_A(x_0) - x_0)(\mu^{-1}x_2^\sharp - x_0x_1) + \frac{1}{2}(T_A(x_0^\sharp - x_1x_2) - x_0^\sharp + x_1x_2)x_1 \\ &+ \mu^{-1}(x_2 \times (\mu x_1^\sharp - x_2x_0)), \end{aligned} \tag{31}$$

$$\begin{aligned} a_2 = &\frac{1}{2}x_2(T_A(x_0^\sharp - x_1x_2) - x_0^\sharp + x_1x_2) + \frac{1}{2}(\mu x_1^\sharp - x_2x_0)(T_A(x_0) - x_0) \\ &+ \mu(x_1 \times (\mu^{-1}x_2^\sharp - x_0x_1)) \end{aligned} \tag{32}$$

by the definition of the multiplication on $J(A,\mu)$.

(i) If $x_1 = 0$ and $N_A(x_2) = 0$, using the fact that $x_ix_i^\sharp = x_i^\sharp x_i = N_A(x_i)1$ for all $i = 0,1,2$ (see (5)), (30) simplifies to $a_0 = N_A(x_0)1 = N(x)$. Since we have $x_0\mu^{-1} = \mu^{-1}x_0$, (31) gives that $a_1 = \frac{1}{2}\mu^{-1}(\mathrm{T}_A(x_0) - x_0)x_2^\sharp - \mu^{-1}(x_2 \times (x_2x_0))$. By (10),

$$x_2^\sharp \sharp x_0 = x_2^\sharp x_0 + x_0x_2^\sharp - T_A(x_2^\sharp)x_0 - T_A(x_0)x_2^\sharp + (T_A(x_2^\sharp)T_A(x_0) - T_A(x_2^\sharp x_0))1. \tag{33}$$

Using the fact that $T_A(x_2^\sharp) = S_A(x_2)$ (by (8)) on the right-hand side of (33), we further obtain after some simplification that

$$x_2^\sharp \sharp x_0 = x_2^2x_0 - T_A(x_2)x_2x_0 + x_0x_2^\sharp - T_A(x_0)x_2^\sharp - T_A(x_2^2x_0)1 + T_A(x_2x_0)1. \tag{34}$$

Now, combining (13) with (34) yields $T_A(x_0)x_2^\sharp - x_0x_2^\sharp = x_2^2x_0 + x_2x_0x_2 - T_A(x_2)x_2x_0 - T_A(x_2x_0)x_2 + (T_A(x_2)T_A(x_2x_0) - T_A(x_2^2x_0))1 = 2(x_2 \times (x_2x_0))$, so $x_2 \times (x_2x_0) = \frac{1}{2}(T_A(x_0)x_2^\sharp - x_0x_2^\sharp)$. Hence, (4) implies $a_1 = 0$. For a_2, (32) yields $a_2 = \frac{1}{2}x_2(T_A(x_0^\sharp) - x_0^\sharp) - \frac{1}{2}x_2(T_A(x_0)x_0 - x_0^2)$. Then, using the definition of $x_0^\sharp$ and the fact that $2S_A(x_0) = \mathrm{T}_A(x_0)^2 - \mathrm{T}_A(x_0^2)$, we find that $\mathrm{T}_A(x_0^\sharp) - x_0^\sharp = \mathrm{T}_A(x_0)x_0 - x_0^2$. Therefore, $a_2 = 0$.

(ii) In this case, we have $x_2 = 0$, $x_1\mu = \mu x_1$ and $N_A(x_1) = 0$. So, (30) simplifies to $a_0 = N_A(x_0)1 = N(x)$. For a_1, (31) simplifies to $a_1 = -\frac{1}{2}(\mathrm{T}_A(x_0)x_0 - x_0^2)x_1 + \frac{1}{2}(\mathrm{T}_A(x_0^\sharp) - x_0^\sharp)x_1$. Then, in a similar way to how we found a_2 in (i), we find here that $a_1 = 0$.

For a_2, (32) simplifies to $a_2 = \frac{1}{2}\mu x_1^\sharp(T_A(x_0) - x_0) - \mu(x_1 \times (x_0 x_1))$. We now find in a similar way to how we found a_1 in (i) that $a_2 = 0$.

To prove that the claimed equivalence holds assuming (iii) or (iv), we only need to show the forward direction since we know from the classical first Tits construction that the reverse direction holds:

(iii) Here, (30) yields $a_0 = N_A(x_0)1 + \frac{1}{2}(\mathrm{T}_A(\mu^{-1})N_A(x_2) - \mu^{-1}N_A(x_2))$; thus, $xx^\sharp = N(x)1 = (N_A(x_0)1 + \mu^{-1}N_A(x_2))1$ gives that $N_A(x_0)1 + \frac{1}{2}(\mathrm{T}_A(\mu^{-1}) N_A(x_2) - \mu^{-1}N_A(x_2)) = a_0 = N_A(x_0)1 + \mu^{-1}N_A(x_2)$. Therefore, we have $\mu^{-1} = \frac{1}{3}\mathrm{T}_A(\mu^{-1}) \in F^\times$, so $\mu \in F^\times$.

(iv) In this case, (30) yields $a_0 = N_A(x_0)1 + \frac{1}{2}(\mathrm{T}_A(\mu)N_A(x_1) - \mu N_A(x_1))$; thus, $xx^\sharp = N(x)1 = (N_A(x_0)1 + \mu N_A(x_1))1$ yields $N_A(x_0)1 + \frac{1}{2}(\mathrm{T}_A(\mu)N_A(x_1) - \mu N_A(x_1)) = a_0 = N_A(x_0)1 + \mu N_A(x_1)$. Therefore, we obtain $\mu = \frac{1}{3}\mathrm{T}_A(\mu) \in F^\times$. The proof that $x^\sharp x = N(x)1$ is performed similarly.

□

Corollary 1. *Let $\mu \in A^\times$. Suppose that $x \in J(A,\mu)$ satisfies $N(x) \neq 0$, and assume that one of the following holds:*

(i) $x = (x_0, x_1, 0) \in J(A,\mu)$, $x_1\mu = \mu x_1$ *and* $N_A(x_1) = 0$.

(ii) $x = (x_0, 0, x_2) \in J(A,\mu)$, $x_0\mu = \mu x_0$ *and* $N_A(x_2) = 0$.

Then, x is invertible in $J(A,\mu)$ with $x^{-1} = N(x)^{-1}x^\sharp$.

Proof. Let $\mu \in A^\times$ and suppose that $x \in J(A,\mu)$ satisfies (i) or (ii); then, $xx^\sharp = x^\sharp x = N(x)1$. Since $F = C(J(A,\mu))$ this yields the assertion. □

In particular, if N is anisotropic, then every $0 \neq xx = (x_0, x_1, 0) \in J(A,\mu)$ in (i) or (ii) is of the type $x = (x_0, 0, 0) \in J(A,\mu)$, i.e., lies in A; so, this result then becomes trivial.

Corollary 2. *Let $\mu \in A^\times$ and suppose that $x \in J(A,\mu)$, such that one of the following holds:*

(i) $x = (x_0, 0, x_2) \in J(A,\mu)$, $x_0\mu = \mu x_0$ *and* $N_A(x_2) = 0$.

(ii) $x = (x_0, x_1, 0) \in J(A,\mu)$, $x_1\mu = \mu x_1$ *and* $N_A(x_1) = 0$.

Then, we have

$$x^3 - T(x)x^2 + S(x)x - N(x)1 = 0.$$

Proof. Using the fact that $x^\sharp = x^2 - T(x)x + S(x)1$ from Theorem 2 (i), we have that $x^3 - T(x)x^2 + S(x)x - N(x)1 = 0$ if and only if $xx^\sharp = x^\sharp x = N(x)1$. Thus, the result now follows as a consequence of Lemma 3. □

Theorem 7. *The identity $xx^\sharp = x^\sharp x = N(x)1$ holds for all $x \in J(A,\mu)$ if and only if $\mu \in F^\times$.*

Proof. If $\mu \in F^\times$, then $xx^\sharp = x^\sharp x = (N(x), 0, 0)$ for all $x \in J(A,\mu)$. Conversely, suppose that $xx^\sharp = x^\sharp x = (N(x), 0, 0)$ holds for all $x \in J(A,\mu)$. Take $x = (0, 1, 0)$. Then, $x^\sharp = (0, 0, \mu)$, and so

$$xx^\sharp = (\bar{\mu}, 0, 0) = (\frac{1}{2}(T_A(\mu)1 - \mu), 0, 0).$$

We also know that by definition, $N(x) = \mu N_A(1) = \mu$, so the condition $xx^\sharp = (N(x), 0, 0)$ gives that $\mu = \frac{1}{2}(T_A(\mu)1 - \mu)$. Hence $\mu = \frac{1}{3}T_A(\mu)1 \in F^\times$. □

We know that the adjoint identity $(x^\sharp)^\sharp = N(x)x$ holds for all $x \in J(A,\mu)$, if $\mu \in F^\times$ [15] (Chapter C.4). In the general construction, it holds only in very special cases:

Lemma 4. *Let $\mu \in A^\times$ and suppose that $x \in J(A,\mu)$, such that one of the following holds:*

(i) $x = (0, x_1, 0) \in J(A,\mu)$ *and* $N_A(x_1) = 0$.

(ii) $x = (x_0, x_1, 0) \in J(A,\mu)$ *and* $N_A(x_1) = 0$ *and* $x_1\mu = \mu x_1$.

(iii) $x = (x_0, 0, x_2) \in J(A, \mu)$ *and* $N_A(x_2) = 0$ *and* $x_0\mu = \mu x_0$.
Then, we have $(x^\sharp)^\sharp = N(x)x$.
Moreover, if one of the following holds:
(iv) $x = (x_0, x_1, 0) \in J(A, \mu)$, $N_A(x_1) \neq 0$, $x_0\mu = \mu x_0$ *and* $x_1\mu = \mu x_1$.
(v) $x = (x_0, 0, x_2) \in J(A, \mu)$, $N_A(x_2) \neq 0$, $x_0\mu = \mu x_0$ *and* $x_2\mu = \mu x_2$.
Then, $(x^\sharp)^\sharp = N(x)x$ *for all* $x \in J(A, \mu)$ *if and only if* $N_A(\mu) = \mu^3$.

Proof. Let $x = (x_0, x_1, x_2) \in J(A, \mu)$ and $(x^\sharp)^\sharp = (a_0, a_1, a_2)$. By definition, $x^\sharp = (x_0^\sharp - x_1x_2, \mu^{-1}x_2^\sharp - x_0x_1, \mu x_1^\sharp - x_2x_0)$, so $a_0 = (x_0^\sharp - x_1x_2)^\sharp - (\mu^{-1}x_2^\sharp - x_0x_1)(\mu x_1^\sharp - x_2x_0)$. Now, using (9) and (10), it is easy to show that

$$\begin{aligned}(x_0^\sharp - x_1x_2)^\sharp &= (x_0^\sharp - x_1x_2)^2 - T_A(x_0^\sharp - x_1x_2)(x_0^\sharp - x_1x_2) + S_A(x_0^\sharp - x_1x_2) \\ &= (x_0^\sharp)^\sharp - x_0^\sharp\sharp(x_1x_2) + (x_1x_2)^\sharp.\end{aligned}$$

Hence,

$$\begin{aligned}a_0 &= (x_0^\sharp - x_1x_2)^\sharp - (\mu^{-1}x_2^\sharp - x_0x_1)(\mu x_1^\sharp - x_2x_0) \\ &= (x_0^\sharp)^\sharp - x_0^\sharp\sharp(x_1x_2) + (x_1x_2)^\sharp - \mu^{-1}x_2^\sharp\mu x_1^\sharp + \mu^{-1}x_2^\sharp x_2x_0 + x_0x_1\mu x_1^\sharp - x_0x_1x_2x_0. \quad (35)\end{aligned}$$

Similarly, we find that

$$\begin{aligned}a_1 &= \mu^{-1}(\mu x_1^\sharp - x_2x_0)^\sharp - (x_0^\sharp - x_1x_2)(\mu^{-1}x_2^\sharp - x_0x_1) \\ &= \mu^{-1}((\mu x_1^\sharp)^\sharp - (\mu x_1^\sharp)\sharp(x_2x_0) + (x_2x_0)^\sharp) \\ &\quad - x_0^\sharp\mu^{-1}x_2^\sharp + x_0^\sharp x_0x_1 + x_1x_2\mu^{-1}x_2^\sharp - x_1x_2x_0x_1 \quad (36)\end{aligned}$$

and

$$\begin{aligned}a_2 &= \mu(\mu^{-1}x_2^\sharp - x_0x_1)^\sharp - (\mu x_1^\sharp - x_2x_0)(x_0^\sharp - x_1x_2) \\ &= \mu((\mu^{-1}x_2^\sharp)^\sharp - (\mu^{-1}x_2^\sharp)\sharp(x_0x_1) + (x_0x_1)^\sharp) \\ &\quad - \mu x_1^\sharp x_0^\sharp + \mu x_1^\sharp x_1x_2 + x_2x_0x_0^\sharp - x_2x_0x_1x_2. \quad (37)\end{aligned}$$

(i) Here, $x_0 = x_2 = 0$; therefore, (35) implies $a_0 = 0$ and (36) gives that $a_1 = \mu^{-1}(\mu x_1^\sharp)^\sharp = \mu^{-1}N_A(x_1)x_1\mu^\sharp = 0 = N(x)x_1$. Finally, (37) gives that $a_2 = 0$ as required.
(ii) Since $x_2 = 0$, $x_1\mu = \mu x_1$ and $N_A(x_1) = 0$, we find by (35) that $a_0 = (x_0^\sharp)^\sharp + x_0\mu x_1x_1^\sharp = N_A(x_0)x_0 + x_0\mu N_A(x_1) = N(x)x_0$. Now, (36) gives that $a_1 = \mu^{-1}(\mu x_1^\sharp)^\sharp + x_0^\sharp x_0x_1 = \mu^{-1}N_A(x_1)x_1\mu^\sharp + N_A(x_0)x_1 = N(x)x_1$, and by (37), we obtain $a_2 = \mu(x_0x_1)^\sharp - \mu x_1^\sharp x_0^\sharp = 0 = N(x)0$.
(iii) Since $x_1 = 0$ and $N_A(x_2) = 0$, (35) yields $a_0 = (x_0^\sharp)^\sharp + \mu^{-1}x_2^\sharp x_2x_0 = N_A(x_0)x_0 + \mu^{-1}N_A(x_2)x_0 = N(x)x_0$. Now, since $x_0\mu^{-1} = \mu^{-1}x_0$, we have that $x_0^\sharp\mu^{-1} = \mu^{-1}x_0^\sharp$, so (36) gives that $a_1 = \mu^{-1}(x_2x_0)^\sharp - \mu^{-1}x_0^\sharp x_2^\sharp = 0 = N(x)0$. Finally, (37) gives that $a_2 = \mu(\mu^{-1}x_2^\sharp)^\sharp + x_2x_0x_0^\sharp = \mu N_A(x_2)x_2(\mu^{-1})^\sharp + N_A(x_0)x_2 = N(x)x_2$.
(iv) Since $x_2 = 0$, $x_0\mu = \mu x_0$ and $x_1\mu = \mu x_1$, (35) yields $a_0 = (x_0^\sharp)^\sharp + \mu x_0x_1x_1^\sharp = N_A(x_0)x_0 + \mu N_A(x_1)x_0 = N(x)x_0$. Now, (37) gives that $a_2 = \mu(x_0x_1)^\sharp - \mu x_1^\sharp x_0^\sharp = 0$. Finally, (36) gives that $a_1 = \mu^{-1}(\mu x_1^\sharp)^\sharp + x_0^\sharp x_0x_1 = \mu^{-1}N_A(x_1)x_1\mu^\sharp + N_A(x_0)x_1$. Thus, $a_1 = N(x)x_1$ if and only if $\mu^{-1}N_A(x_1)x_1\mu^\sharp + N_A(x_0)x_1 = N(x)x_1$, which occurs if and only if $\mu^{-1}N_A(x_1)x_1\mu^\sharp = \mu N_A(x_1)x_1$. Since $N_A(x_1) \neq 0$ and $x_1\mu^\sharp = \mu^\sharp x_1$, this occurs if and only if $\mu^\sharp x_1 = \mu^2 x_1$. Finally, $N_A(x_1) \neq 0$ implies that x_1 is invertible, so $\mu^\sharp x_1 = \mu^2 x_1$ if and only if $N_A(\mu) = \mu\mu^\sharp = \mu^3$.

(v) Since $x_1 = 0$, (35) yields $a_0 = (x_0^\sharp)^\sharp + \mu^{-1}x_2^\sharp x_2 x_0 = N(x)x_0$. Furthermore, since x_0 commutes with μ, $x_0^\sharp$ commutes with μ. So, $x_0^\sharp \mu^{-1} = \mu^{-1}x_0^\sharp$. Hence, (36) gives that $a_1 = \mu^{-1}(x_2x_0)^\sharp - \mu^{-1}x_0^\sharp x_2^\sharp = 0 = N(x)0$. Finally, (37) yields $a_2 = \mu(\mu^{-1}x_2^\sharp)^\sharp + x_2x_0x_0^\sharp = \mu N_A(x_2)x_2(\mu^{-1})^\sharp + N_A(x_0)x_2$. Thus, $a_2 = N(x)x_2$ if and only if $\mu N_A(x_2)x_2(\mu^{-1})^\sharp + N_A(x_0)x_2 = N(x)x_2$, which occurs if and only if $\mu N_A(x_2)x_2(\mu^{-1})^\sharp = \mu^{-1}N_A(x_2)x_2$. Since $N_A(x_2) \neq 0$ and $x_2(\mu^{-1})^\sharp = (\mu^{-1})^\sharp x_2$, this occurs if and only if $(\mu^{-1})^\sharp x_2 = \mu^{-2}x_2$. Finally, $N_A(x_2) \neq 0$ implies that x_2 is invertible, so $(\mu^{-1})^\sharp x_2 = \mu^{-2}x_2$ if and only if $N_A(\mu^{-1}) = \mu^{-1}(\mu^{-1})^\sharp = \mu^{-3}$. This is equivalent to $N_A(\mu) = \mu^3$.

□

Proposition 2. *Let A be a central simple algebra over F. Then, $(x^\sharp)^\sharp = N(x)$ for all $x \in J(A,\mu)$ if and only if $\mu \in F^\times$.*

Proof. Let $\mu \in F^\times$ then by Lemma 4, the adjoint identity holds for all $x \in J(A,\mu)$. Suppose now that the adjoint identity holds for all $x \in J(A,\mu)$. Let $x = (x_0, 1, 0) \in J(A,\mu)$ for some $x_0 \in A$. Then, $x^\sharp = (x_0^\sharp, -x_0, \mu)$ and so

$$(x^\sharp)^\sharp = ((x_0^\sharp)^\sharp + x_0\mu, \mu^{-1}\mu^\sharp + (x_0^\sharp)^\sharp x_0, 0). \tag{38}$$

Furthermore, $N(x) = N_A(x_0)1 + \mu$. Since the adjoint identity holds by assumption, we see that by using (38),

$$((x_0^\sharp)^\sharp + x_0\mu, \mu^{-1}\mu^\sharp + (x_0^\sharp)^\sharp x_0, 0) = (N_A(x_0)x_0 + \mu x_0, N_A(x_0) + \mu, 0). \tag{39}$$

We know that $(x_0^\sharp)^\sharp = N_A(x_0)x_0$ for all $x_0 \in A$ by (12), and so by comparing the first components of (39), we find that $x_0\mu = \mu x_0$ for all $x_0 \in A$. Hence, $\mu \in C(A)$, and since A is a central simple algebra by assumption, $\mu \in F^\times$. □

If $\mu \in F^\times$, then the norm N *permits Jordan composition*, i.e. $N(U_x y) = N_A(x)^2 N(y)$ for all $x, y \in J(A,a)$. The following result is a corrected version of [11] (Theorem 5.2.5), and a weak generalization of the Jordan composition for $\mu \in A^\times \setminus F$:

Theorem 8. *Let $x = (x_0, 0, 0) \in A$, $y = (y_0, y_1, y_2) \in J(A,\mu)$ and suppose that one of the following holds:*

(i) $T_A(y_0y_1y_2) = T_A(N_A(y_0)x_0^\sharp y_1 y_2 x_0^\sharp)$.
(ii) $y_0y_1y_2 = N_A(y_0)x_0^\sharp y_1 y_2 x_0^\sharp$.
(iii) $y_i = 0$ *for some* $i = 0, 1, 2$.

Then, $N(U_x(y)) = N(x)^2 N(y)$.

Proof. Using the definitions, we see that $T(x,y) = T_A(x_0y_0)$ and $x^\sharp \sharp y = (x_0^\sharp \sharp y_0, -x_0^\sharp y_1, -y_2 x_0^\sharp)$. So $U_x(y) = T(x,y)x - x^\sharp \sharp y = (U_{x_0}(y_0), x_0^\sharp y_1, y_2 x_0^\sharp)$. This yields

$$\begin{aligned} N(U_x(y)) &= N_A(U_{x_0}(y_0))1 + \mu N_A(x_0^\sharp y_1) + \mu^{-1}N_A(y_2x_0^\sharp) - T_A(U_{x_0}(y_0)x_0^\sharp y_1 y_2 x_0^\sharp)1 \\ &= N_A(x_0)^2(N_A(y_0)1 + \mu N_A(y_1) + \mu^{-1}N_A(y_2) - T_A(N_A(y_0)x_0^\sharp y_1 y_2 x_0^\sharp)1) \\ &= N(x)^2(N(y) + T_A(y_0y_1y_2)1 - T_A(N_A(y_0)x_0^\sharp y_1 y_2 x_0^\sharp)1), \end{aligned}$$

where in the second equality we have used the fact that $N_A(x_0^\sharp) = N_A(x_0)^2$, and that $N_A(U_{x_0}(y_0)) = N_A(x_0)^2 N_A(y_0)$. Therefore, $N(U_x(y)) = N(x)^2N(y)$, if and only if $T_A(y_0y_1y_2)1 = T_A(N_A(y_0)x_0^\sharp y_1 y_2 x_0^\sharp)$.
(ii) and (iii) are examples where this is the case. □

Remark 2. *Let $f : J(A,\mu) \to J(A,\mu)$ be an automorphism. Then,*

$$f((x_0,x_1,x_2)) = f((x_0,0,0)) + f((0,x_1,0)) + f((0,0,x_2)). \tag{40}$$

Now, for each $x \in A$, we have $f((0,\overline{x},0)) = f((x,0,0))f((0,1,0))$, and $f((0,0,\overline{x})) = f((x,0,0))f((0,0,1))$. On the other hand, by using the definition of $\overline{x}$,

$$f((0,\overline{x},0)) = \frac{1}{2}\operatorname{Tr}_A(x)f((0,1,0)) - \frac{1}{2}f((0,x,0)),$$
$$f((0,0,\overline{x})) = \frac{1}{2}\operatorname{Tr}_A(x)f((0,0,1)) - \frac{1}{2}f((0,0,x)).$$

Hence,

$$f((0,x,0)) = f((0,1,0))(\operatorname{Tr}_A(x) - 2f((x,0,0))), \tag{41}$$
$$f((0,0,x)) = f((0,0,1))(\operatorname{Tr}_A(x) - 2f((x,0,0))). \tag{42}$$

So, by (40)–(42), we see that any automorphism of $J(A,\mu)$ is determined by its restriction on A^+, and its value on $(0,1,0)$ and $(0,0,1)$. Let $f : J(A,\mu) \to J(A,\mu)$ be an automorphism that fixes A^+; then, $f|_{A^+} = \tau$ is either an automorphism or an anti-automorphism of A. Moreover, clearly $f((1,0,0)) = (1,0,0)$, so

$$f((x_0,x_1,x_2)) = (\tau(x_0),0,0) + (\tau(x_1),0,0)f((0,1,0)) + (\tau(x_2),0,0)f((0,0,1)).$$

Calculation to try gain some deeper understanding on the automorphisms are tedious and did not lead us anywhere so far.

5. The Nine-Dimensional Non-Associative Algebras $J(K,\mu)$

Let K/F be a separable cubic field extension with $\operatorname{Gal}(K/F) = \langle\sigma\rangle$, norm N_K, and trace T_K. For all $x_0 \in K$, we have $x_0^\sharp = \sigma(x_0)\sigma^2(x_0)$ and $\overline{x_0} = \frac{1}{2}(\sigma(x_0) + \sigma^2(x_0))$. Assume $\mu \in K^\times$.

Let us compare the first Tits construction $J(K,\mu)$ with the algebra D^+ for a (perhaps non-associative) cyclic algebra $D = (K/F,\sigma,\mu)$ over F of degree three. Consider D as a left K-vector space with basis $\{1,z,z^2\}$. Write R_x for the matrix of right multiplication by $x = x_0 + x_1z + x_2z^2$, $x_i \in K$, with respect to the basis $\{1,z,z^2\}$, then the cubic map $N_D : D \to K$, $N_D(x) = \det(R_x)$ (which is the reduced norm of the central simple algebra D if $\mu \in F^\times$), is given by

$$N_D(x) = N_K(x_0) + \mu N_K(x_1) + \mu^2 N_K(x_2) - \mu T_K(x_0\sigma(x_1)\sigma^2(x_2)).$$

If N_D is anisotropic then D is a division algebra over F. If $\mu \in K \setminus F$, we obtain $N_D(lx) = N_K(l)N_D(x)$ for all $x \in D$, $l \in K$ [11] (Propositions 4.2.2 and 4.2.3).

On the other hand, $J(K,\mu)$ is a nine-dimensional non-associative unital algebra over F with multiplication

$$xy = (x_0 \cdot y_0 + \overline{x_1y_2} + \overline{x_2y_1}, \overline{x_0}y_1 + \overline{y_0}x_1 + \mu^{-1}(x_2 \times y_2), \overline{x_0}y_2 + \overline{y_0}x_2 + \mu(x_1 \times y_1))$$

for $x = (x_0,x_1,x_2), y = (y_0,y_1,y_2) \in J(K,\mu)$, cubic norm map

$$N((x_0,x_1,x_2)) = N_K(x_0) + \mu N_K(x_1) + \mu^{-1}N_K(x_2) - T_K(x_0x_1x_2),$$

and trace $T(x) = T_K(x_0)$. Moreover, we have

$$x^\sharp = (\sigma(x_0)\sigma^2(x_0) - x_1x_2, \mu^{-1}\sigma(x_2)\sigma^2(x_2) - x_0x_1, \mu\sigma(x_1)\sigma^2(x_1) - x_2x_0).$$

If $\mu \in F^\times$, then $D = (K/F, \sigma, \mu)$ is an associative cyclic algebra over F of degree three and $J(K, \mu) \cong D^+$ is a special cubic Jordan algebra. It is well known that the isomorphism $G : D^+ = (K/F, \sigma, \mu)^+ \to J(K, \mu)$ is given by

$$x_0 + x_1 z + x_2 z^2 \mapsto (x_0, \sigma(x_1), \mu\sigma^2(x_2)).$$

However, if $\mu \in K \setminus F$, then the map $G : D^+ \to J(K, \mu)$ is not an algebra isomorphism between $(K/F, \sigma, \mu)^+$ and $J(K, \mu)$, where now $(K/F, \sigma, \mu)$ is a non-associative cyclic algebra, since $\sigma(\mu) \neq \mu$. However, for $\mu \in K \setminus F$, the map $G : D^+ \to J(K, \mu)$ still yields an isometry of norms, since

$$\begin{aligned} N((x_0, \sigma(x_1), \mu\sigma^2(x_2)) &= N_K(x_0) + \mu N_K(x_1) + \mu^{-1} N_K(x_2) - \mu T_K(x_0 \sigma(x_1) \sigma(x_2)) \\ &= N_D((x_0, x_1, x_2)); \end{aligned}$$

hence, the norms of the two nonisomorphic non-associative algebras $D^+ = (K/F, \sigma, \mu)^+$ and $J(K, \mu)$ are isometric.

6. Conclusions

We looked at the following canonical question: "what happens if we choose the element μ that is used in the first Tits construction $J(A, \mu)$ in $A^\times$ instead of in $F^\times$?" We showed that the basic ingredients for an interesting theory are in place: our new algebras $J(A, \mu)$ carry maps that can be understood as generalizations of the classical norms and traces, and that behave surprisingly similar to the norms and traces of their classical counterparts; we have a function N on $J(A, \mu)$ that extends the cubic norm of A (however, it has values in A), a trace function $T : J(A, \mu) \to F$, and a quadratic map $\sharp : J(A, \mu) \to J(A, \mu)$. Operations like $x \sharp y$ can easily be defined. Some of the main identities from the classical setup hold (Theorems 1 and 2), some others hold only for some elements, e.g., Lemmas 2 and 3, Corollaries 1 and 2, but not in general, and some hold if—and only if—$\mu \in F^\times$ (Proposition 2, Theorem 7), i.e., they hold only in the classical case.

It seems a hard problem to check when the algebras $J(A, \mu)$ are division algebras. It would also be interesting to compute their automorphisms; however, we expect the automorphism group to be "small". Here is one indication as to why this is the case: For Albert algebras over fields F of characteristic not 2 or 3, we know that the similarities of their norms are given either by scalar multiplications or the U operators [4]. Using Theorem 8 (iii), we see that for $J(A, \mu)$ with $\mu \in A^\times \setminus F$, scalar multiplications still give similarities; the U-operators, however, do not.

Even partial results on automorphisms or similarities could give an insight on what is happening in this general context, and it would be interesting to address questions of whether there are inner automorphisms, whether there are cubic subfields fixed by automorphisms like in the classical case [2], etc.

The fact that two nonisomorphic algebras $D^+ = (K/F, \sigma, \mu)^+$ and $J(K, \mu)$ have isometric norms is an example of how rich the structure theory for non-associative algebras really is (Section 4).

This is an exploratory paper, but our results show that the algebras $J(A, \mu)$ obtained via a generalized first Tits construction merit a closer look. As one referee pointed out, they also show the weaknesses of the language that we have at our disposal, which describes highly non-associative structures.

7. Materials and Methods

We used classical methods from algebra.

Author Contributions: Conceptualization, S.P.; Methodology, S.P. and T.M.; Investigation, S.P. and T.M.; Writing—Original Draft Preparation, S.P. and T.M.; Writing—Review and Editing, S.P.; Supervision, S.P. All authors have read and agreed to the published version of the manuscript.

Funding: This paper was written while the second author was a visitor at the University of Ottawa. The second author acknowledges support for her stay from the Centre de Recherches Mathématiques for giving a colloquium talk, and from Monica Nevins' NSERC Discovery Grant RGPIN-2020-05020.

Data Availability Statement: The data presented in this study are available in article.

Acknowledgments: The second author would like to thank the Department of Mathematics and Statistics for its hospitality. The authors thank the anonymous referees for their valuable comments which greatly helped improve the paper and write the conclusions section.

Conflicts of Interest: The author has no relevant financial or non-financial interests to disclose.

References

1. Knus, M.A.; Merkurjev, A.; Rost, M.; Tignol, J.-P. *The Book of Involutions*; AMS Colloquium Publications: Providence, RI, USA, 1998; Volume 44.
2. Thakur, M. On R-triviality of F_4. *Isr. J. Math.* **2021**, *244*, 145–161. [CrossRef]
3. Thakur, M. On R-triviality of F_4, II. *Münster J. Math.* **2021**, *14*, 497–507.
4. Thakur, M. Automorphisms of Albert algebras and a conjecture of Tits and Weiss II. *Trans. Amer. Math. Soc.* **2019**, *372*, 4701–4728. [CrossRef]
5. Thakur, M. The cyclicity problem for Albert algebras. *Isr. J. Math.* **2021**, *241*, 139–145. [CrossRef]
6. Garibaldi, S.; Petersson, H. P.; Racine, M. L. Albert algebras over $\mathbb{Z}$ and other rings. *Forum. Math. Sigma* **2023**, *11*. [CrossRef]
7. Sandler, R. Autotopism groups of some finite nonassociative algebras. *AMS J. Math.* **1962**, *84*, 239–264. [CrossRef]
8. Brown, C.; Pumplün, S. Nonassociative cyclic extensions of fields and central simple algebras. *J. Pure Appl. Algebra* **2019**, *223*, 2401–2412. [CrossRef]
9. Pumplün, S. The automorphisms of generalized cyclic Azumaya algebras. *J. Pure Appl. Algebra* **2021**, *225*, 106540. [CrossRef]
10. Steele, A. Nonassociative cyclic algebras. *Isr. J. Math.* **2014**, *200*, 361–387. [CrossRef]
11. Steele, A. Some New Classes of Algebras. Ph.D. Thesis, University of Nottingham, Nottingham, UK, 2013. Available online: http://eprints.nottingham.ac.uk/13934/1/PhdthesisFinal.pdf (accessed on 25 March 2024).
12. Pumplün S.; Unger, T. Space-time block codes from nonassociative division algebras. *Adv. Math. Commun.* **2011**, *5*, 609–629. [CrossRef]
13. Steele, A.; Pumplün, S.; Oggier, F. MIDO space-time codes from associative and non-associative cyclic algebras. In Proceedings of the 2012 IEEE Information Theory Workshop, Lausanne, Switzerland, 3–7 September 2012; pp. 192–196.
14. Schafer, R.D. Forms permitting composition. *Adv. Math.* **1970**, *4*, 127–148. [CrossRef]
15. McCrimmon, K. *A Taste of Jordan Algebras*; Springer: New York, NY, USA, 2004.
16. Thakur, M. Automorphisms of Albert algebras and a conjecture of Tits and Weiss. *Trans. Amer. Math.* **2013**, *365*, 3041–3068. [CrossRef]
17. Petersson, H.-P.; Racine, M.-L. Jordan algebras of degree 3 and the Tits process. *J. Algebra* **1986**, *98*, 211–243. [CrossRef]
18. Jacobson, N. *Structure and Representations of Jordan Algebras*; AMS. Providence, AMS. Colloquium Publications: Providence, RI, USA, 1968; Volume XXXIX.

axioms

MDPI

Article

Ideals and Filters on Neutrosophic Topologies Generated by Neutrosophic Relations

Ravi P. Agarwal [1,2,*], Soheyb Milles [3], Brahim Ziane [4], Abdelaziz Mennouni [5] and Lemnaouar Zedam [6]

1 Department of Mathematics, Texas A & M University-Kingsville, Kingsville, TX 78363, USA
2 Department of Mathematics and Systems Engineering, Florida Institute of Technology, Melbourne, FL 32901, USA
3 Department of Mathematics, Institute of Science, University Center of Barika, Barika 05400, Algeria; soheyb.milles@cu-barika.dz
4 Laboratoire de Mathématique et Physique Appliques, École Normale Supérieure de Bousaada, Bousaada 28200, Algeria; ziane.brahim@ens-bousaada.dz
5 Department of Mathematics, University of Batna 2, Mostefa Ben Boulaïd, Fesdis, Batna 05078, Algeria; a.mennouni@univ-batna2.dz
6 Department of Mathematics, Laboratory of Pure and Applied Mathematics, University of M'sila, M'sila 28000, Algeria; lemnaouar.zedam@univ-msila.dz
* Correspondence: ravi.agarwal@tamuk.edu

Abstract: Recently, Milles and Hammami presented and studied the concept of a neutrosophic topology generated by a neutrosophic relation. As a continuation in the same direction, this paper studies the concepts of neutrosophic ideals and neutrosophic filters on that topology. More precisely, we offer the lattice structure of neutrosophic open sets of a neutrosophic topology generated via a neutrosophic relation and examine its different characteristics. Furthermore, we enlarge to this lattice structure the notions of ideals (respectively, filters) and characterize them with regard to the lattice operations. We end this work by studying the prime neutrosophic ideal and prime neutrosophic filter as interesting types of neutrosophic ideals and neutrosophic filters.

Keywords: binary relation; filter; ideal; lattice; neutrosophic set; topology

MSC: 06B10; 54A10; 54A40

check for updates

Citation: Agarwal, R.P.; Milles, S.; Ziane, B.; Mennouni, A.; Zedam, L. Ideals and Filters on Neutrosophic Topologies Generated by Neutrosophic Relations. *Axioms* **2024**, *13*, 292. https://doi.org/10.3390/axioms13050292

Academic Editor: Feliz Manuel Minhós

Received: 28 February 2024
Revised: 1 April 2024
Accepted: 22 April 2024
Published: 25 April 2024

1. Introduction

The concept of neutrosophic sets was introduced by Smarandache [1] as a generalization of the concepts of fuzzy sets and intuitionistic fuzzy sets. The notion of a neutrosophic set is described by three degrees, truth membership function (T), indeterminacy membership function (I) and falsity membership function (F), in the non-standard unit interval, and it accomplished tremendous success in various areas of applications [2–4]. In particular, Wang et al. [5] presented the concept of a single-valued neutrosophic set as a subclass of the neutrosophic set which can be used in the field of scientific and engineering applications.

In the literature, there are many approaches to the concept of neutrosophic topological space. In [6], Smarandache presented neutrosophic topology on the non-standard interval. Later, Lupiáñez [7,8] proposed some notes about the relationship between Smarandache's concept of neutrsophic topology and intuitionistic fuzzy topology. Others, such as Salama and Alblowi [9,10] studied neutrosophic topological spaces with various basic properties and characteristics. Recently, El-Gayyar [11] introduced the notion of smooth topological space in the setting of neutrosophic sets. For more details, see [12–17].

One of the essential tools in many branches of mathematics is the concepts of ideal and filter. For instance, ideals and filters appear in topology, boolean algebra, the extensive theory of representation of distributive lattices and in algebraic structures. In addition to their theoretical uses, ideals and filters are used in some branches of applied mathematics.

In a neutrosophic setting, many researchers have examined and studied the neutrosophic ideals and neutrosophic filters in various frameworks and structures [18–21].

In this work, we apply Smarandache's neutrosophic set to the notion of ideals and filters in a neutrosophic open-set lattice on neutrosophic topology generated by neutrosophic relation. We study its various properties and characterizations. We finally characterize them with regard to this lattice of meet and join operations.

The content of the present work is structured as follows. Section 2 provides an overview introduction to neutrosophic sets and relations. We recall the concept of a neutrosophic topology generated by a neutrosophic relation in Section 3, and then describe the lattice structure of neutrosophic open sets on a topology generated by a neutrosophic relation in Section 4. In Section 5, we establish the notions of neutrosophic ideals (respectively, neutrosophic filter) on the lattice of neutrosophic open sets, and some characterizations in terms of this lattice of meet and join operations and in terms of the corresponding level sets are given. In Section 6, we examine and characterize the notion of the prime neutrosophic ideal and prime neutrosophic filter as interesting types of neutrosophic ideals and neutrosophic filters. Section 7 concludes with some thoughts and suggestions for future works.

2. Preliminaries

This part contains some concepts and properties of neutrosophic sets and several related definitions that will be required throughout this work.

2.1. Neutrosophic Sets

The fuzzy set notion was defined by Zadeh [22].

Definition 1 ([22])**.** *Assume that $\mathcal{E}$ is a crisp set. A fuzzy set $\Omega = \{\langle \varsigma, \daleth_\Omega(\varsigma)\rangle \mid \varsigma \in \mathcal{E}\}$ is defined by a function of membership $\daleth_\Omega : \mathcal{E} \to [0,1]$, with $\daleth_\Omega(\varsigma)$ as the degree of membership of an element ς in the fuzzy subset Ω for all $\varsigma \in \mathcal{E}$.*

As a generalization of the idea of a fuzzy set, K, Atanassov proposed the intuitionistic fuzzy set in [23,24].

Definition 2 ([23])**.** *Assume that $\mathcal{E}$ is a classical set. An intuitionistic fuzzy set (IFS) Ω of $\mathcal{E}$ is an object of the model*

$$\Omega = \{\langle \varsigma, \daleth_\Omega(\varsigma), \digamma_\Omega(\varsigma)\rangle \mid \varsigma \in \mathcal{E}\}$$

defined by a membership mapping $\daleth_\Omega : \mathcal{E} \to [0,1]$ and a non-membership mapping $\digamma_\Omega : \mathcal{E} \to [0,1]$, such that

$$0 \leqslant \daleth_\Omega(\varsigma) + \digamma_\Omega(\varsigma) \leqslant 1, \textit{ for all } \varsigma \in \mathcal{E}.$$

In [1], the author suggested the approach of a neutrosophic set as an extension of the approach of the IF-set. For an applied use of neutrosophic sets, the authors of [5] proposed a subclass of neutrosophic sets, which is the single-valued neutrosophic set (SVNS).

Definition 3 ([1])**.** *Assume that $\mathcal{E}$ is a classical set. A neutrosophic set (NS) Ω of $\mathcal{E}$ is an object of the model*

$$\Omega = \{\langle \varsigma, \daleth_\Omega(\varsigma), \beth_\Omega(\varsigma), \digamma_\Omega(\varsigma)\rangle \mid \varsigma \in \mathcal{E}\}$$

defined by a membership mapping $\daleth_\Omega$ from $\mathcal{E}$ to $\mathcal{J} :=]^-0, 1^+[$ and an indeterminacy mapping $\beth_\Omega$ from $\mathcal{E}$ to $\mathcal{J}$. Also, it is a non-membership mapping $\digamma_\Omega$ from $\mathcal{E}$ to $\mathcal{J}$ such that

$$^-0 \leqslant \daleth_\Omega(\varsigma) + \beth_\Omega(\varsigma) + \digamma_\Omega(\varsigma) \leqslant 3^+, \textit{ for all } \varsigma \in \mathcal{E}.$$

Remark 1. *In the literature of neutrosophic logic, different notations are used to represent the functions introduced earlier. The most widely used symbols are μ (membership function), σ (indeterminacy function) and v (non-membership function). See Figure 1.*

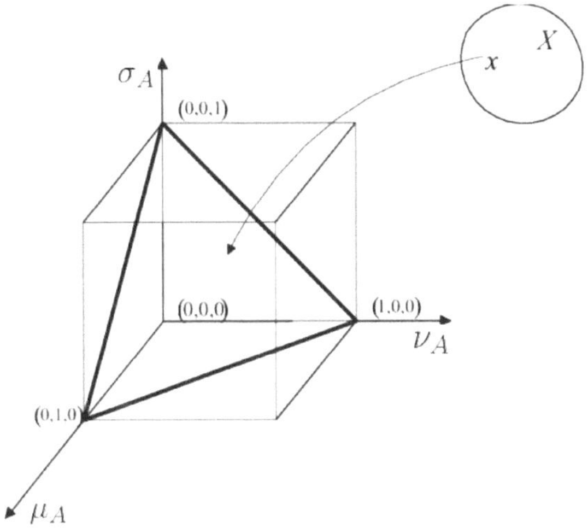

Figure 1. Representation of a neutrosophic set.

Definition 4 ([5]). *Assume that $\mathcal{E}$ is a classical set. Define a single-valued neutrosophic set (SVNS) Ω of $\mathcal{E}$ as an object of the model*

$$\Omega = \{\langle \varsigma, \daleth_\Omega(\varsigma), \gimel_\Omega(\varsigma), \digamma_\Omega(\varsigma)\rangle \mid \varsigma \in \mathcal{E}\}$$

defined by a truth membership mapping $\daleth_\Omega : \mathcal{E} \to [0,1]$, an indeterminacy membership mapping $\gimel_\Omega : \mathcal{E} \to [0,1]$ and a falsity membership mapping $\digamma_\Omega : \mathcal{E} \to [0,1]$.

Obviously, IF-set is a neutrosophic set by setting $\gimel_\Omega(\varsigma) = 1 - \daleth_\Omega(\varsigma) - \digamma_\Omega(\varsigma)$. The family of all neutrosophic sets of the set $\mathcal{E}$ is indicated by $NS(\mathcal{E})$.

For every two neutrosophic sets Ω and Δ of $\mathcal{E}$, many operations are defined (see, e.g., [5,25–29]). Only those relevant to the current work are presented below:

(i) $\Omega \subseteq \Delta$ if $\daleth_\Omega(\varsigma) \leqslant \daleth_\Delta(\varsigma)$ and $\gimel_\Omega(\varsigma) \leqslant \gimel_\Delta(\varsigma)$ and $\digamma_\Omega(\varsigma) \geqslant \digamma_\Delta(\varsigma)$, for all $\varsigma \in \mathcal{E}$;
(ii) $\Omega = \Delta$ if $\daleth_\Omega(\varsigma) = \daleth_\Delta(\varsigma)$ and $\gimel_\Omega(\varsigma) = \gimel_\Delta(\varsigma)$ and $\digamma_\Omega(\varsigma) = \digamma_\Delta(\varsigma)$, for all $\varsigma \in \mathcal{E}$;
(iii) $\Omega \cap \Delta = \{\langle \varsigma, \daleth_\Omega(\varsigma) \curlywedge \daleth_\Delta(\varsigma), \gimel_\Omega(\varsigma) \curlywedge \gimel_\Delta(\varsigma), \digamma_\Omega(\varsigma) \curlyvee \digamma_\Delta(\varsigma)\rangle \mid \varsigma \in \mathcal{E}\}$;
(iv) $\Omega \cup \Delta = \{\langle \varsigma, \daleth_\Omega(\varsigma) \curlyvee \daleth_\Delta(\varsigma), \gimel_\Omega(\varsigma) \curlyvee \gimel_\Delta(\varsigma), \digamma_\Omega(\varsigma) \curlywedge \digamma_\Delta(\varsigma)\rangle \mid \varsigma \in \mathcal{E}\}$;
(v) $\overline{\Omega} = \{\langle \varsigma, \digamma_\Omega(\varsigma), \gimel_\Omega(\varsigma), \daleth_\Omega(\varsigma)\rangle \mid \varsigma \in \mathcal{E}\}$;
(vi) $[\Omega] = \{\langle \varsigma, \daleth_\Omega(\varsigma), \gimel_\Omega(\varsigma), 1 - \daleth_\Omega(\varsigma)\rangle \mid \varsigma \in \mathcal{E}\}$;
(vii) $\langle \Omega \rangle = \{\langle \varsigma, 1 - \digamma_\Omega(\varsigma), \gimel_\Omega(\varsigma), \digamma_\Omega(\varsigma)\rangle \mid \varsigma \in \mathcal{E}\}$.

Additionally, we need the following concept of (α, β, γ)-cuts (which is also called "level sets") of a neutrosophic set.

Definition 5. *Assume that Ω is a neutrosophic set of $\mathcal{E}$. The (α, β, γ)-cut of Ω is a classical subset*

$$\Omega_{\alpha,\beta,\gamma} = \{\varsigma \in \mathcal{E} \mid \daleth_\Omega(\varsigma) \geqslant \alpha \text{ and } \gimel_\Omega(\varsigma) \geqslant \beta \text{ and } \digamma_\Omega(\varsigma) \leqslant \gamma\},$$

for some $0 < \alpha, \beta, \gamma \leq 1$.

Definition 6. *Assume that Ω is a neutrosophic set of $\mathcal{E}$. The support of Ω is the classical subset of $\mathcal{E}$, given by*

$$\mathcal{S}(\Omega) := \{\varsigma \in \mathcal{E} \mid \daleth_\Omega(\varsigma) \neq 0 \text{ and } \gimel_\Omega(\varsigma) \neq 0 \text{ and } \digamma_\Omega(\varsigma) \neq 0\}.$$

2.2. Neutrosophic Relations

In [30], the authors proposed the approach of neutrosophic relation as a generalization of fuzzy and IF-relation.

Definition 7 ([30])**.** *A neutrosophic binary relation (or, a neutrosophic relation, for short) from a set $\mathcal{E}$ to a set $\mathcal{Z}$ is a neutrosophic subset of $\mathcal{E} \times \mathcal{Z}$, i.e., it is an expression $\mathcal{N}$ expressed by*

$$\mathcal{N} = \{\langle(\varsigma,\sigma), \daleth_{\mathcal{N}}(\varsigma,\sigma), \beth_{\mathcal{N}}(\varsigma,\sigma), \digamma_{\mathcal{N}}(\varsigma,\sigma)\rangle \mid (\varsigma,\sigma) \in \mathcal{E} \times \mathcal{Z}\},$$

where $\daleth_{\mathcal{N}} : \mathcal{E} \times \mathcal{Z} \to [0,1]$, and $\beth_{\mathcal{N}} : \mathcal{E} \times \mathcal{Z} \to [0,1]$ and $\digamma_{\Omega} : \mathcal{E} \times \mathcal{Z} \to [0,1]$.

For any $(\varsigma,\sigma) \in \mathcal{E} \times \mathcal{Z}$, the value $\daleth_{\mathcal{N}}(\varsigma,\sigma)$ is named the degree of a membership of (ς,σ) in $\mathcal{N}$; $\beth_{\mathcal{N}}(\varsigma,\sigma)$ is named the degree of indeterminacy of (ς,σ) in $\mathcal{N}$; and $\digamma_{\mathcal{N}}(\varsigma,\sigma)$ is said to be the degree of non-membership of (ς,σ) in $\mathcal{N}$.

Example 1. *Suppose $\mathcal{E} = \{\rho_1, \rho_2, \rho_3, \rho_4, \rho_5\}$. Then, the neutrosophic relation $\mathcal{N}$ of $\mathcal{E}$ is given by*

$$\mathcal{N} = \{\langle(\varsigma,\sigma), \daleth_{\mathcal{N}}(\varsigma,\sigma), \beth_{\mathcal{N}}(\varsigma,\sigma), \digamma_{\mathcal{N}}(\varsigma,\sigma)\rangle \mid \varsigma,\sigma \in \mathcal{E}\},$$

such that $\daleth_{\mathcal{N}}$, $\beth_{\mathcal{N}}$ and $\digamma_{\mathcal{N}}$ are given by the following tables.

$\daleth_R(.,.)$	ρ_1	ρ_2	ρ_3	ρ_4	ρ_5
ρ_1	3.5×10^{-1}	0	0	3.5×10^{-1}	3×10^{-1}
ρ_2	0	4×10^{-1}	0	3.5×10^{-1}	4.5×10^{-1}
ρ_3	2×10^{-1}	0	6.5×10^{-1}	0	7×10^{-1}
ρ_4	0	0	0	1	0
ρ_5	2.5×10^{-1}	3.5×10^{-1}	0	0	6×10^{-1}

$\beth_R(.,.)$	ρ_1	ρ_2	ρ_3	ρ_4	ρ_5
ρ_1	5×10^{-1}	5×10^{-1}	4.2×10^{-1}	2×10^{-1}	0
ρ_2	6×10^{-1}	1.2×10^{-1}	4×10^{-1}	8×10^{-1}	1×10^{-1}
ρ_3	0	1	2×10^{-2}	7.5×10^{-1}	1.5×10^{-1}
ρ_4	3.3×10^{-1}	1	8.8×10^{-1}	0	1×10^{-1}
ρ_5	2×10^{-1}	5.5×10^{-1}	1	5.5×10^{-1}	3×10^{-1}

$\digamma_R(.,.)$	ρ_1	ρ_2	ρ_3	ρ_4	ρ_5
ρ_1	0	1	4×10^{-1}	2.5×10^{-1}	2.5×10^{-1}
ρ_2	3×10^{-1}	3.5×10^{-1}	2×10^{-1}	3.5×10^{-1}	1×10^{-1}
ρ_3	8×10^{-1}	1	0	8.5×10^{-1}	1.5×10^{-1}
ρ_4	1	1	1	0	1
ρ_5	7×10^{-1}	5.5×10^{-1}	1	9×10^{-1}	3×10^{-1}

Next, the following notions need to be recalled.

Definition 8 ([31])**.** *Let $\mathcal{N}$ and $\mathcal{M}$ be two neutrosophic relations from a set $\mathcal{E}$ to a set $\mathcal{Z}$.*

(i) The transpose (inverse) $\mathcal{N}^t$ of $\mathcal{N}$ is the neutrosophic relation from the universe $\mathcal{Z}$ to the universe $\mathcal{E}$ defined by

$$\mathcal{N}^t = \{\langle(\varsigma,\sigma), \daleth_{\mathcal{N}^t}(\varsigma,\sigma), \beth_{\mathcal{N}^t}(\varsigma,\sigma), \digamma_{\mathcal{N}^t}(\varsigma,\sigma)\rangle \mid (\varsigma,\sigma) \in \mathcal{E} \times \mathcal{Z}\},$$

where

$$\begin{cases} \daleth_{\mathcal{N}^t}(\varsigma,\sigma) = \daleth_{\mathcal{N}}(\sigma,\varsigma) \\ \text{and} \\ \beth_{\mathcal{N}^t}(\varsigma,\sigma) = \beth_{\mathcal{N}}(\sigma,\varsigma) \\ \text{and} \\ \digamma_{\mathcal{N}^t}(\varsigma,\sigma) = \digamma_{\mathcal{N}}(\sigma,\varsigma) \end{cases}$$

for every $(\varsigma,\sigma) \in \mathcal{E} \times \mathcal{Z}$.

(ii) $\mathcal{N}$ *is said to be contained in* $\mathcal{M}$ *(or we say that* $\mathcal{M}$ *contains* $\mathcal{N}$*) and is indicated by* $\mathcal{N} \subseteq \mathcal{M}$*; if for all* $(\varsigma,\sigma) \in \mathcal{E} \times \mathcal{Z}$*, it holds that*

$$\daleth_{\mathcal{N}}(\varsigma,\sigma) \leqslant \daleth_{\mathcal{M}}(\varsigma,\sigma),\ \beth_{\mathcal{N}}(\varsigma,\sigma) \leqslant \beth_{\mathcal{M}}(\varsigma,\sigma) \text{ and } \digamma_{\mathcal{N}}(\varsigma,\sigma) \geqslant \digamma_{\mathcal{M}}(\varsigma,\sigma).$$

(iii) *The intersection (respectively,* the union*) of two neutrosophic relations* $\mathcal{N}$ *and* $\mathcal{M}$ *from a universe* $\mathcal{E}$ *to a universe* $\mathcal{Z}$ *is a neutrosophic relation defined as*

$$\begin{aligned}\mathcal{N} \cap \mathcal{M} = \{\langle(\varsigma,\sigma), &\min(\daleth_{\mathcal{N}}(\varsigma,\sigma), \daleth_{\mathcal{M}}(\varsigma,\sigma)), \min(\beth_{\mathcal{N}}(\varsigma,\sigma), \beth_{\mathcal{M}}(\varsigma,\sigma)),\\ &\max(\digamma_{\mathcal{N}}(\varsigma,\sigma), \digamma_{\mathcal{M}}(\varsigma,\sigma))\rangle \mid (\varsigma,\sigma) \in \mathcal{E} \times \mathcal{Z}\}\end{aligned}$$

and

$$\begin{aligned}\mathcal{N} \cup \mathcal{M} = \{\langle(\varsigma,\sigma), &\max(\daleth_{\mathcal{N}}(\varsigma,\sigma), \daleth_{\mathcal{M}}(\varsigma,\sigma)) \max(\beth_{\mathcal{N}}(\varsigma,\sigma), \beth_{\mathcal{M}}(\varsigma,\sigma)),\\ &\min(\digamma_{\mathcal{N}}(\varsigma,\sigma), \digamma_{\mathcal{M}}(\varsigma,\sigma))\rangle \mid (\varsigma,\sigma) \in \mathcal{E} \times \mathcal{Z}\}.\end{aligned}$$

Definition 9 ([31])**.** *Let* $\mathcal{N}$ *be a neutrosophic relation from a set* $\mathcal{E}$ *into itself.*

(i) *Reflexivity:* $\daleth_{\mathcal{N}}(\varsigma,\varsigma) = \beth_{\mathcal{N}}(\varsigma,\varsigma) = 1$ *and* $\digamma_{\mathcal{N}}(\varsigma,\varsigma) = 0$*, for all* $\varsigma \in \mathcal{E}$.

(ii) *Symmetry: for all* $\varsigma,\sigma \in \mathcal{E}$*, then*

$$\begin{cases} \daleth_{\mathcal{N}}(\varsigma,\sigma) = \daleth_{\mathcal{N}}(\sigma,\varsigma) \\ \beth_{\mathcal{N}}(\varsigma,\sigma) = \beth_{\mathcal{N}}(\sigma,\varsigma) \\ \digamma_{\mathcal{N}}(\varsigma,\sigma) = \digamma_{\mathcal{N}}(\sigma,\varsigma) \end{cases}.$$

(iii) *Antisymmetry: for all* $\varsigma,\sigma \in \mathcal{E}$, $\varsigma \neq \sigma$*, then*

$$\begin{cases} \daleth_{\mathcal{N}}(\varsigma,\sigma) \neq \daleth_{\mathcal{N}}(\sigma,\varsigma) \\ \beth_{\mathcal{N}}(\varsigma,\sigma) \neq \beth_{\mathcal{N}}(\sigma,\varsigma) \\ \digamma_{\mathcal{N}}(\varsigma,\sigma) \neq \digamma_{\mathcal{N}}(\sigma,\varsigma) \end{cases}.$$

(iv) *Transitivity:* $\mathcal{N} \circ \mathcal{N} \subset \mathcal{N}$*, i.e.,* $\mathcal{N}^2 \subset \mathcal{N}$.

3. Neutrosophic Topology Generated by Neutrosophic Relation

In this part, we will recall the concept of topology generated by relation in a neutrosophic setting [32] as an extension of the fuzzy topology generated by the fuzzy relation given in [33]. Moreover, several properties of this structure are investigated.

Definition 10. *Let* $\mathcal{E}$ *be a universe and* $\mathcal{N} = \{\langle(\varsigma,\sigma), \daleth_{\mathcal{N}}(\varsigma,\sigma), \beth_{\mathcal{N}}(\varsigma,\sigma), \digamma_{\mathcal{N}}(\varsigma,\sigma)\rangle \mid \varsigma,\sigma \in \mathcal{E}\}$ *be a neutrosophic relation of* $\mathcal{E}$*. Then, for all* $\varsigma \in \mathcal{E}$*, the neutrosophic sets* $\mathcal{L}_\varsigma$ *and* $\mathcal{R}_\varsigma$ *are defined by*

$\daleth_{\mathcal{L}_\varsigma}(\sigma) = \daleth_{\mathcal{N}}(\sigma,\varsigma)$, $\beth_{\mathcal{L}_\varsigma}(\sigma) = \beth_{\mathcal{N}}(\sigma,\varsigma)$ *and* $\digamma_{\mathcal{L}_\varsigma}(\sigma) = \digamma_{\mathcal{N}}(\sigma,\varsigma)$*, for every* $\sigma \in \mathcal{E}$*;*

$\daleth_{\mathcal{R}_\varsigma}(\sigma) = \daleth_{\mathcal{N}}(\varsigma,\sigma)$, $\beth_{\mathcal{R}_\varsigma}(\sigma) = \beth_{\mathcal{N}}(\varsigma,\sigma)$ *and* $\digamma_{\mathcal{R}_\varsigma}(\sigma) = \digamma_{\mathcal{N}}(\varsigma,\sigma)$*, for every* $\sigma \in \mathcal{E}$*;*

they are named, respectively, the lower and the upper contours of ς.

We symbolize the neutrosophic topology generated by the family of all lower contours with τ_1, and the neutrosophic topology generated by the family of all upper contours with τ_2. Therefore, we symbolize the neutrosophic topology generated by S, the family of all lower and upper contours, with $\tau_{\mathcal{N}}$, and it is named the neutrosophic topology generated by $\mathcal{N}$.

Remark 2. *Since the neutrosophic set $\mathcal{L}_\varsigma$ (respectively, $\mathcal{R}_\varsigma$) is defined from the neutrosophic relation $\mathcal{N}$, then, in that case*

$$0 \leqslant \urcorner_{\mathcal{L}_\varsigma} + \beth_{\mathcal{L}_\varsigma} + \digamma_{\mathcal{L}_\varsigma} \leqslant 3,$$

respectively,

$$0 \leqslant \urcorner_{\mathcal{R}_\varsigma} + \beth_{\mathcal{R}_\varsigma} + \digamma_{\mathcal{R}_\varsigma} \leqslant 3,$$

for all $\varsigma \in \mathcal{E}$.

Example 2. *Suppose $\mathcal{E} = \{\varsigma, \sigma\}$ and $\mathcal{N}$ is a neutrosophic relation of $\mathcal{E}$, given by*

$\urcorner_{\mathcal{N}}(.,.)$	ς	σ
ς	0.6	0.8
σ	0.3	0.7

$\beth_{\mathcal{N}}(.,.)$	ς	σ
ς	0.3	0.1
σ	0.6	0.2

$\digamma_{\mathcal{N}}(.,.)$	ς	σ
ς	0.3	0.1
σ	0.6	0.2

So, $\mathcal{L}_\varsigma$, $\mathcal{L}_\sigma$, $\mathcal{R}_\varsigma$ and $\mathcal{R}_\sigma$ are the neutrosophic sets of $\mathcal{E}$ given by the following values:

$$\begin{aligned}
\mathcal{L}_\varsigma &= \{\langle \varsigma, 0.6, 0.3, 0.3\rangle; \langle \sigma, 0.3, 0.6, 0.6\rangle\}; \\
\mathcal{L}_\sigma &= \{\langle \varsigma, 0.8, 0.1, 0.1\rangle; \langle \sigma, 0.7, 0.2, 0.2\rangle\}; \\
\mathcal{R}_\varsigma &= \{\langle \varsigma, 0.6, 0.3, 0.3\rangle; \langle \sigma, 0.8, 0.1, 0.1\rangle\}; \\
\mathcal{R}_\sigma &= \{\langle \varsigma, 0.3, 0.6, 0.6\rangle; \langle \sigma, 0.7, 0.2, 0.2\rangle\}.
\end{aligned}$$

Note that

$$\mathcal{L}_\varsigma \subset \mathcal{L}_\sigma, \ \mathcal{L}_\varsigma \subset \mathcal{R}_\sigma, \ \mathcal{R}_\sigma \subset \mathcal{R}_\varsigma \ \text{ and } \ \mathcal{R}_\sigma \subset \mathcal{L}_\sigma.$$

Then, the neutrosophic topology $\tau_{\mathcal{R}}$ is generated by

$$S = \{\mathcal{L}_\varsigma, \mathcal{L}_\sigma\} \cup \{\mathcal{R}_\varsigma, \mathcal{R}_\sigma\}.$$

Hence,

$$\tau_{\mathcal{R}} = \{\emptyset, \mathcal{E}, \mathcal{L}_\varsigma, \mathcal{L}_\sigma, \mathcal{R}_\varsigma, \mathcal{R}_\sigma, \mathcal{L}_\varsigma \cap \mathcal{R}_\sigma, \mathcal{L}_\sigma \cap \mathcal{R}_\varsigma, \mathcal{L}_\varsigma \cup \mathcal{R}_\sigma, \mathcal{L}_\sigma \cup R_\varsigma\}.$$

Proposition 1. *Assume that $\mathcal{E}$ is a classical set and $\mathcal{N}$ is a neutrosophic symmetric relation of $\mathcal{E}$. Then, it holds that $\tau_1 = \tau_2$.*

Proof. Assume that $\mathcal{N}$ is a neutrosophic symmetric relation of $\mathcal{E}$; so for every $\varsigma, \sigma \in \mathcal{E}$, it holds that

$$\urcorner_{\mathcal{N}}(\varsigma, \sigma) = \urcorner_{\mathcal{N}}(\sigma, \varsigma), \ \beth_{\mathcal{N}}(\varsigma, \sigma) = \beth_{\mathcal{N}}(\sigma, \varsigma) \ \text{ and } \ \digamma_{\mathcal{N}}(\varsigma, \sigma) = \digamma_{\mathcal{N}}(\sigma, \varsigma).$$

Then, in such a case,

$$\urcorner_{\mathcal{L}_\varsigma}(\sigma) = \urcorner_{\mathcal{R}_\varsigma}(\sigma), \ \beth_{\mathcal{L}_\varsigma}(\sigma) = \beth_{\mathcal{R}_\varsigma}(\sigma) \ \text{ and } \ \digamma_{\mathcal{L}_\varsigma}(\sigma) = \digamma_{\mathcal{R}_\varsigma}(\sigma).$$

Therefore, $\mathcal{L}_\varsigma = \mathcal{R}_\varsigma$, for all $\varsigma \in \mathcal{E}$. We can determine that $\tau_1 = \tau_2$. □

Remark 3. *If $\mathcal{N}$ is a neutrosophic preorder relation, then the neutrosophic topology generated by $\mathcal{N}$ is a generalization of the Alexandrov topology introduced in [34].*

4. The Lattice of Neutrosophic Open Sets on a Topology Generated by a Neutrosophic Relation

The purpose of this part is to study the lattice structure of neutrosophic open sets on a topology generated by a neutrosophic relation. First, we introduce the notion of neutrosophic intersection and union between neutrosophic open sets.

Definition 11. *Let $\tau_{\mathcal{N}}$ be the neutrosophic topology of the set $\mathcal{E}$ generated by the relation $\mathcal{N}$ and let $\mathcal{W}_1$ and $\mathcal{W}_2$ be two neutrosophic open sets of $\tau_{\mathcal{N}}$. The intersection of $\mathcal{W}_1$ and $\mathcal{W}_2$ (in symbols, $\mathcal{W}_1 \Cap \mathcal{W}_2$) is a neutrosophic open set V such that*

$$\begin{aligned} \urcorner_V(\varsigma_i) &= \min(\urcorner_{\mathcal{W}_1}(\varsigma_i), \urcorner_{\mathcal{W}_2}(\varsigma_i)), \\ \beth_V(\varsigma_i) &= \min(\beth_{\mathcal{W}_1}(\varsigma_i), \beth_{\mathcal{W}_2}(\varsigma_i)), \\ F_V(\varsigma_i) &= \max(F_{\mathcal{W}_1}(\varsigma_i), F_{\mathcal{W}_2}(\varsigma_i)) \end{aligned}$$

for all $x_i \in \mathcal{E}$. Furthermore, $\Cap_{i \in I} \mathcal{W}_i$ is the neutrosophic open set of $\mathcal{E}$ containing all $\mathcal{W}_i$.

Definition 12. *Let $\tau_{\mathcal{N}}$ be the neutrosophic topology of the set $\mathcal{E}$ generated by the relation $\mathcal{N}$ and let $\mathcal{W}_1$ and $\mathcal{W}_2$ be two neutrosophic open sets of $\tau_{\mathcal{N}}$. The union of $\mathcal{W}_1$ and $\mathcal{W}_2$ (in symbols, $\mathcal{W}_1 \Cup \mathcal{W}_2$) is a neutrosophic open set V such that*

$$\begin{aligned} \urcorner_V(\varsigma_i) &= \max(\urcorner_{\mathcal{W}_1}(\varsigma_i), \urcorner_{\mathcal{W}_2}(\varsigma_i)), \\ \beth_V(\varsigma_i) &= \max(\beth_{\mathcal{W}_1}(\varsigma_i), \beth_{\mathcal{W}_2}(\varsigma_i)), \\ F_V(\varsigma_i) &= \min(F_{\mathcal{W}_1}(\varsigma_i), F_{\mathcal{W}_2}(\varsigma_i)) \end{aligned}$$

for all $\varsigma_i \in \mathcal{E}$. Furthermore, $\Cup_{i \in I} \mathcal{W}_i$ is a greater neutrosophic open set of $\mathcal{E}$ containing all $\mathcal{W}_i$.

In the following theorem, we provide the lattice of neutrosophic open sets of a neutrosophic topology generated by neutrosophic relation.

Theorem 1. *Let $\mathcal{E}$ be a universe, $\mathcal{N}$ be a neutrosophic relation of $\mathcal{E}$ and $\tau_{\mathcal{N}}$ be a neutrosophic topology generated by $\mathcal{N}$. Then, the family*

$$\mathfrak{L} = \{\mathcal{W}_i \mid \mathcal{W}_i \text{ is a neutrosophic open set on } \tau_{\mathcal{N}}\}$$

is a lattice.

Proof. Assume that $\{\mathcal{W}_i\}$ is a set of neutrosophic open sets of $\tau_{\mathcal{N}}$. Definition of neutrosophic topology guarantees that $\{\mathcal{W}_i\}$ is a non-empty set.
Now, let $\mathcal{W}_1$ and $\mathcal{W}_2$ be two neutrosophic open sets. It is easy to check that $\mathcal{W}_1 \Subset \mathcal{W}_1$, i.e., the neutrosophic reflexivity, and if we assume that $\mathcal{W}_1 \Subset \mathcal{W}_2$ and $\mathcal{W}_2 \Subset \mathcal{W}_1$, in which case, $\mathcal{W}_1 = \mathcal{W}_2$, i.e., the neutrosophic antisymmetry.
To verify the neutrosophic transitivity, we assume that $\mathcal{W}_1 \Subset \mathcal{W}_2$ and $\mathcal{W}_2 \Subset \mathcal{W}_3$, in which case $\mathcal{W}_1 \Subset \mathcal{W}_3$, i.e., the neutrosophic transitivity. Hence, $(\mathfrak{L}, \Subset)$ is a neutrosophic poset of $\mathcal{E}$. Also, the least upper bound (respectively, the greatest lower bound) of $\mathcal{W}_1$ and $\mathcal{W}_2$ coincides with the intersection of neutrosophic open sets (respectively, the union of neutrosophic open sets), i.e.,

$$\mathcal{W}_1 \curlywedge \mathcal{W}_2 = \mathcal{W}_1 \Cap \mathcal{W}_2, \quad (\text{resp.} \mathcal{W}_1 \curlyvee \mathcal{W}_2 = \mathcal{W}_1 \Cup \mathcal{W}_2).$$

Then, we can determine that $(\mathfrak{L}, \Subset)$ is a lattice of $\mathcal{E}$. □

Hence, $(\mathfrak{L}, \Subset)$ is a neutrosophic poset of $\mathcal{E}$. Also, the greatest lower bound (respectively, the least upper bound) of $\mathcal{W}_1$ and $\mathcal{W}_2$ coincides with the union of neutrosophic open sets (respectively, the intersection of neutrosophic open sets), i.e.,

$$(\text{resp. } \mathcal{W}_1 \curlyvee \mathcal{W}_2 = \mathcal{W}_1 \Cup \mathcal{W}_2), \quad \mathcal{W}_1 \curlywedge \mathcal{W}_2 = \mathcal{W}_1 \Cap \mathcal{W}_2.$$

Example 3. *Let $\mathcal{E} = \{\varsigma, \sigma\}$ and $\mathcal{N}$ be a neutrosophic relation of $\mathcal{E}$ given by the following:*

$\daleth_{\mathcal{N}}(.,.)$	ς	σ
ς	0.6	0.8
σ	0.3	0.7

$\beth_{\mathcal{N}}(.,.)$	ς	σ
ς	0.3	0.1
σ	0.6	0.2

$\digamma_{\mathcal{N}}(.,.)$	ς	σ
ς	0.3	0.1
σ	0.6	0.2

Consider the neutrosophic topology $\tau_{\mathcal{N}}$ of Example 2. Then, $\mathfrak{L} = \{\mathcal{W}_i \mid \mathcal{W}_i$ is a neutrosophic open set and $\tau_{\mathcal{N}}\}$ is a lattice.

Remark 4. *To avoid the confusion, we will use the symbols $(\Subset, \Cup, \Cap)$ to refer to the order,* max, *and* min *on the lattice structure $\mathfrak{L}$ and $(\leqslant, \curlyvee, \curlywedge)$ to refer to the usual order,* max, *and* min *on the unit interval* $[0,1]$.

Proposition 2. *Let $\mathcal{E}$ be a finite universe and $\mathfrak{L} = \{\mathcal{W}_i\}$ is the lattice structure of all neutrosophic open sets on topology $\tau_{\mathcal{N}}$ generated by neutrosophic relation $\mathcal{N}$. Then, $\mathfrak{L}$ is complete.*

Proof. Let $\mathfrak{L} = \{\mathcal{W}_i\}$ be the lattice of neutrosophic open sets on neutrosophic topology τ_R generated by the neutrosophic relation $\mathcal{N}$. Let $\Omega = \{\mathcal{W}_j\}$ be a subset of $\mathfrak{L}$ under the neutrosophic inclusion between the neutrosophic open sets defined above. Since $\mathfrak{L}$ is a finite lattice, then $\Cap U_j \in \mathfrak{L}$, which shows that Ω has an infimum. Thus, $\mathfrak{L}$ is complete. □

Corollary 1. *Let $\mathfrak{L}$ be the complete lattice of all neutrosophic open sets of neutrosophic topology generated by neutrosophic relation; then $\mathfrak{L}$ is bounded. Indeed, the least element of $\mathfrak{L}$ is $0_{\mathfrak{L}} = \emptyset = \Cap U_i$ and the greatest element of $\mathfrak{L}$ is $1_{\mathfrak{L}} = \mathcal{E} = \Cup U_i$.*

Corollary 2. *Let $\mathfrak{L}$ be the lattice of neutrosophic open sets of neutrosophic topology τ_R generated by neutrosophic relation $\mathcal{N}$, then $\mathfrak{L}$ is distributive and therefore modular.*

Hartmanis in 1958 proved that the lattice structure of all topologies on a finite universe is complemented. The following proposition shows that the lattice structure of neutrosophic open sets of a topology generated by neutrosophic relation is also complemented.

Proposition 3. *Let $\mathfrak{L}$ be the lattice of open neutrosophic sets of neutrosophic topology $\tau_{\mathcal{N}}$ generated by the neutrosophic relation $\mathcal{N}$, then $\mathfrak{L}$ is complemented.*

Proof. Indeed, every element $\mathcal{W}_{i_0}$ has a complement $\mathcal{W}_{j_0}$ such that $\mathcal{W}_{i_0} \Cap \mathcal{W}_{j_0} = 0_{\mathfrak{L}}$ and $\mathcal{W}_{i_0} \Cup \mathcal{W}_{j_0} = 1_{\mathfrak{L}}$. Hence, $\mathfrak{L}$ is complemented. □

Corollary 3. *The fact that $\mathfrak{L}$ is a distributive lattice and complemented with the least element $0_{\mathfrak{L}} = \emptyset$ and the greatest element $1_{\mathfrak{L}=\mathcal{E}}$, then $\mathfrak{L}$ is a boolean algebra indicated by $(\mathfrak{L}, \Cap, \Cup, 0_{\mathfrak{L}}, 1_{\mathfrak{L}})$.*

Proof. Directly from Corollary 2 and Proposition 3. □

5. Ideals and Filters on the Lattice of Neutrosophic Open Sets

The study of ideals and neutrosophic filters on the lattice structure of neutrosophic open sets is presented in this section. We describe them both in terms of the corresponding level sets and terms of lattice structure operations.

5.1. Definitions and Properties

Definition 13. *A neutrosophic set $\mathcal{D}$ of $\mathfrak{L}$ is named a neutrosophic ideal if for all $\Phi, \Psi \in \mathfrak{L}$, the following conditions hold:*

(i) $\daleth_{\mathcal{D}}(\Phi \cup \Psi) \geqslant \daleth_{\mathcal{D}}(\Phi) \curlywedge \daleth_{\mathcal{D}}(\Psi)$;
(ii) $\daleth_{\mathcal{D}}(\Phi \cap \Psi) \geqslant \daleth_{\mathcal{D}}(\Phi) \curlyvee \daleth_{\mathcal{D}}(\Psi)$;
(iii) $\beth_{\mathcal{D}}(\Phi \cup \Psi) \geqslant \beth_{\mathcal{D}}(\Phi) \curlywedge \beth_{\mathcal{D}}(\Psi)$;
(iv) $\beth_{\mathcal{D}}(\Phi \cap \Psi) \geqslant \beth_{\mathcal{D}}(\Phi) \curlyvee \beth_{\mathcal{D}}(\Psi)$;
(v) $\digamma_{\mathcal{D}}(\Phi \cup \Psi) \leqslant \digamma_{\mathcal{D}}(\Phi) \curlyvee \digamma_{\mathcal{D}}(\Psi)$;
(vi) $\digamma_{\mathcal{D}}(\Phi \cap \Psi) \leqslant \digamma_{\mathcal{D}}(\Phi) \curlywedge \digamma_{\mathcal{D}}(\Psi)$.

Definition 14. *A neutrosophic set F of $\mathfrak{L}$ is said to be a neutrosophic filter if for all $\Phi, \Psi \in \mathfrak{L}$, the following conditions hold:*

(i) $\daleth_{F}(\Phi \cup \Psi) \geqslant \daleth_{F}(\Phi) \curlyvee \daleth_{F}(\Psi)$;
(ii) $\daleth_{F}(\Phi \cap \Psi) \geqslant \daleth_{F}(\Phi) \curlywedge \daleth_{F}(\Psi)$;
(iii) $\beth_{F}(\Phi \cup \Psi) \geqslant \beth_{F}(\Phi) \curlyvee \beth_{F}(\Psi)$;
(iv) $\beth_{F}(\Phi \cap \Psi) \geqslant \beth_{F}(\Phi) \curlywedge \beth_{F}(\Psi)$;
(v) $\digamma_{F}(\Phi \cup \Psi) \leqslant \digamma_{F}(\Phi) \curlywedge \digamma_{F}(\Psi)$;
(vi) $\digamma_{F}(\Phi \cap \Psi) \leqslant \digamma_{F}(\Phi) \curlyvee \digamma_{F}(\Psi)$.

In the following proposition, we show the relationship between ideal and filter on a lattice structure of neutrosophic open sets.

Proposition 4. *Let $\mathfrak{L}$ be the lattice structure of neutrosophic open sets, $\mathfrak{L}^d$ be the dual-order lattice, and let $\Phi \in S(\mathfrak{L})$. So, it holds that Φ is a neutrosophic ideal of $\mathfrak{L}$ if and only if Φ is a neutrosophic filter of $\mathfrak{L}^d$ and vice versa.*

Proof. Let Φ be a neutrosophic ideal of $\mathfrak{L}$, then the six conditions of Definition 13 hold. From the principle of duality, which we obtained by replacing each meet operation (respectively, join operation) by its dual, we then obtained the six conditions of Definition 14. Therefore, Φ becomes a neutrosophic filter of $\mathfrak{L}^d$. □

This result will be useful in the following.

Proposition 5. *Let $\mathfrak{L}$ be the lattice structure of neutrosophic open sets, and Φ and Ψ be two neutrosophic sets of $\mathfrak{L}$. Then, we have the following:*

(i) *If Φ and Ψ are two neutrosophic ideals of $\mathfrak{L}$, then $\Phi \Cap \Psi$ is a neutrosophic ideal of $\mathfrak{L}$;*
(ii) *If Φ and Ψ are two neutrosophic filters of $\mathfrak{L}$, then $\Phi \Cap \Psi$ is a neutrosophic filter of $\mathfrak{L}$.*

5.2. Characterizations of Neutrosophic Ideals and Filters in Terms of Their Level Sets

The following result discusses the relationship between neutrosophic ideal and neutrosophic filter and their support on the lattice of open sets.

Proposition 6. *Let $\mathcal{D}$ and F be two neutrosophic sets of $\mathfrak{L}$. Then, the following hold:*

(i) *If $\mathcal{D}$ is a neutrosophic ideal, then the support of $\mathcal{D}$ is an ideal of $\mathfrak{L}$.*

(ii) *If F is a neutrosophic filter, then the support F is a filter of $\mathfrak{L}$.*

Proof. (i) Let $\mathcal{D}$ be a neutrosophic ideal of $\mathfrak{L}$. We prove that $\mathcal{S}(\mathcal{D})$ is an ideal of $\mathfrak{L}$.
(a) Assume that $\Phi \in \mathcal{S}(\mathcal{D})$ and $\Psi \Subset \Phi$. Therefore, it implies that

$$\daleth_{\mathcal{D}}(\Phi) \neq 0,\ \gimel_{\mathcal{D}}(\Phi) \neq 0,\ \digamma_{\mathcal{D}}(\Phi) \neq 0.$$

Because $\Psi \Subset \Phi$, we have $\Phi \Cap \Psi = \Psi$. Consequently,

$$\daleth_{\mathcal{D}}(\Psi) = \daleth_{\mathcal{D}}(\Phi \Cap \Psi) \geqslant \daleth_{\mathcal{D}}(\Phi) \curlyvee \daleth_{\mathcal{D}}(\Psi).$$

So,

$$\daleth_{\mathcal{D}}(\Psi) \geqslant \daleth_{\mathcal{D}}(\Phi) \neq 0.$$

Similarly, we can determine that

$$\gimel_{\mathcal{D}}(\Phi) \neq 0 \text{ and } \digamma_{\mathcal{D}}(\Phi) \neq 0.$$

Hence, $\Psi \in \mathcal{S}(\mathcal{D})$.
(b) Assume that $\Phi, \Psi \in \mathcal{S}(\mathcal{D})$. We prove that $\Phi \Cup \Psi \in \mathcal{S}(\mathcal{D})$. The fact that $\mathcal{D}$ is a neutrosophic ideal, it thus holds by Definition 13 that

$$\daleth_{\mathcal{D}}(\Phi \Cup \Psi) \geqslant \daleth_{\mathcal{D}}(\Phi) \curlywedge \daleth_{\mathcal{D}}(\Psi) \neq 0.$$

Similarly, we show that

$$\gimel_{\mathcal{D}}(\Phi \Cup \Psi) \neq 0 \quad \text{and} \quad \digamma_{\mathcal{D}}(\Phi \Cup \Psi) \neq 0.$$

Thus, $\Phi \Cup \Psi \in \mathcal{S}(\mathcal{D})$. Therefore, $\mathcal{S}(\mathcal{D})$ is an ideal of $\mathfrak{L}$.
(ii) Analogously from (i) and Proposition 4. □

We establish the concept of ideal and filter on the lattice structure of open sets in terms of its level sets in the following result.

Theorem 2. *Let $\mathcal{D}$ and F be two neutrosophic sets of $\mathfrak{L}$:*

(i) *$\mathcal{D}$ is a neutrosophic ideal equivalent to that when its level sets are ideals of $\mathfrak{L}$;*
(ii) *F is a neutrosophic filter equivalent to that when its level sets are filters of $\mathfrak{L}$.*

Proof. (i) Let Φ be a neutrosophic ideal of $\mathfrak{L}$ and $\mathcal{D}_{\alpha,\beta,\gamma}$ their level sets, with $0 < \alpha, \beta, \gamma \leq 1$.
(a) Assume that $\Phi \in \mathcal{D}_{\alpha,\beta,\gamma}$ and $\Psi \Subset \Phi$. By Definition 13 of a neutrosophic ideal, it states that

$$\daleth_{\mathcal{D}}(\Psi) \geqslant \daleth_{\mathcal{D}}(\Phi),\ \gimel_{\mathcal{D}}(\Psi) \geqslant \gimel_{\mathcal{D}}(\Phi) \text{ and } \digamma_{\mathcal{D}}(\Psi) \leqslant \digamma_{\mathcal{D}}(\Phi).$$

Since,

$$\daleth_{\mathcal{D}}(\Phi) \geqslant \alpha,\ \gimel_{\mathcal{D}}(\Phi) \geqslant \beta \text{ and } \digamma_{\mathcal{D}}(\Phi) \leqslant \gamma,$$

we obtain

$$\daleth_{\mathcal{D}}(\Psi) \geqslant \alpha,\ \gimel_{\mathcal{D}}(\Psi) \geqslant \beta \text{ and } \digamma_{\mathcal{D}}(\Psi) \leqslant \gamma.$$

Hence, $\Psi \in \mathcal{D}_{\alpha,\beta,\gamma}$.
(b) Let $\Phi, \Psi \in \mathcal{D}_{\alpha,\beta,\gamma}$, then it holds that

$$\daleth_{\mathcal{D}}(\Phi) \geqslant \alpha,\ \gimel_{\mathcal{D}}(\Phi) \geqslant \beta,\ \digamma_{\mathcal{D}}(\Phi) \leqslant \gamma$$

and

$$\daleth_{\mathcal{D}}(\Psi) \geqslant \alpha,\ \gimel_{\mathcal{D}}(\Psi) \geqslant \beta,\ \digamma_{\mathcal{D}}(\Psi) \leqslant \gamma.$$

By Definition 13 of a neutrosophic ideal, it holds that

$$\begin{aligned}\urcorner_{\mathcal{D}}(\Phi \Cup \Psi) &\geqslant \urcorner_{\mathcal{D}}(\Phi) \curlywedge \urcorner_{\mathcal{D}}(\Psi) \geqslant \alpha,\\ \rbrack_{\mathcal{D}}(\Phi \Cup \Psi) &\geqslant \rbrack_{\mathcal{D}}(\Phi) \curlywedge \rbrack_{\mathcal{D}}(\Psi) \geqslant \beta,\\ \digamma_{\mathcal{D}}(\Phi \Cup \Psi) &\leqslant \digamma_{\mathcal{D}}(\Phi) \curlyvee \digamma_{\mathcal{D}}(\Psi) \leqslant \gamma.\end{aligned}$$

Hence, $\Phi \Cup \Psi \in \mathcal{D}_{\alpha,\beta,\gamma}$.
Consequently, $\mathcal{D}_{\alpha,\beta,\gamma}$ is an ideal of $\mathfrak{L}$, for all $0 < \alpha, \beta, \gamma \leq 1$.

Inversely, we suppose that all level sets of $\mathcal{D}$ are ideals of $\mathfrak{L}$. We prove that $\mathcal{D}$ is a neutrosophic ideal of $\mathfrak{L}$. Let $\Phi, \Psi \in \mathfrak{L}$ with

$$\alpha = \urcorner_{\mathcal{D}}(\Phi) \curlywedge \urcorner_{\mathcal{D}}(\Psi), \quad \beta = \rbrack_{\mathcal{D}}(\Phi) \curlywedge \rbrack_{\mathcal{D}}(\Psi) \quad \text{and} \quad \gamma = \digamma_{\mathcal{D}}(\Phi) \curlyvee \digamma_{\mathcal{D}}(\Psi).$$

The fact that $\mathcal{D}_{\alpha,\beta,\gamma}$ is an ideal of $\mathfrak{L}$ assures that $\Phi \Cup \Psi \in \mathcal{D}_{\alpha,\beta,\gamma}$, for all $0 < \alpha, \beta, \gamma \leq 1$. Then, we can determine that

$$\urcorner_{\mathcal{D}}(\Phi \Cup \Psi) \geqslant \alpha, \quad \rbrack_{\mathcal{D}}(\Phi \Cup \Psi) \geqslant \beta \quad \text{and} \quad \digamma_{\mathcal{D}}(\Phi \Cup \Psi) \leqslant \gamma.$$

Thus,

$$\begin{aligned}\urcorner_{\mathcal{D}}(\Phi \Cup \Psi) &\geqslant \urcorner_{\mathcal{D}}(\Phi) \curlywedge \urcorner_{\mathcal{D}}(\Psi),\\ \rbrack_{\mathcal{D}}(\Phi \Cup \Psi) &\geqslant \rbrack_{\mathcal{D}}(\Phi) \curlywedge \rbrack_{\mathcal{D}}(\Psi),\\ \digamma_{\mathcal{D}}(\Phi \Cup \Psi) &\leqslant \digamma_{\mathcal{D}}(\Phi) \curlyvee \digamma_{\mathcal{D}}(\Psi).\end{aligned}$$

Similarly, we can prove conditions (ii), (iv) and (vi) on Definition 13. Therefore, $\mathcal{D}$ is a neutrosophic ideal of $\mathfrak{L}$.
(ii) It follows in the same way by using Proposition 4 and (i). □

5.3. Basic Characterizations of Neutrosophic Ideals (Respectively, Filters)

This part provides a significant characterization of neutrosophic ideals (respectively, filters).

Theorem 3. *Let $\mathfrak{L}$ be the lattice structure of neutrosophic open sets. Then, it holds that $\mathcal{D}$ is a neutrosophic ideal of $\mathfrak{L}$ if and only if the following conditions are satisfied:*
(i) $\urcorner_{\mathcal{D}}(\Phi \Cup \Psi) = \urcorner_{\mathcal{D}}(\Phi) \curlywedge \urcorner_{\mathcal{D}}(\Psi)$;
(ii) $\rbrack_{\mathcal{D}}(\Phi \Cup \Psi) = \urcorner_{\mathcal{D}}(\Phi) \curlywedge \urcorner_{\mathcal{D}}(\Psi)$;
(iii) $\digamma_{\mathcal{D}}(\Phi \Cup \Psi) = \digamma_{\mathcal{D}}(\Phi) \curlyvee \digamma_{\mathcal{D}}(\Psi)$, *for all* $\Phi, \Psi \in \mathfrak{L}$.

Proof. Let $\mathcal{D}$ be a neutrosophic ideal of $\mathfrak{L}$, then for all $\Phi, \Psi \in \mathfrak{L}$. Then

$$\begin{aligned}\urcorner_{\mathcal{D}}(\Phi \Cup \Psi) &\geqslant \urcorner_{\mathcal{D}}(\Phi) \curlywedge \urcorner_{\mathcal{D}}(\Psi),\\ \rbrack_{\mathcal{D}}(\Phi \Cup \Psi) &\geqslant \rbrack_{\mathcal{D}}(\Phi) \curlywedge \rbrack_{\mathcal{D}}(\Psi),\\ \digamma_{\mathcal{D}}(\Phi \Cup \Psi) &\leqslant \digamma_{\mathcal{D}}(\Phi) \curlyvee \digamma_{\mathcal{D}}(\Psi).\end{aligned}$$

Since $\Phi \Subset \Phi \Cup \Psi$ and $\Psi \Subset \Phi \Cup \Psi$, it follows by the monotonicity that

$$\urcorner_{\mathcal{D}}(\Phi) \geqslant \urcorner_{\mathcal{D}}(\Phi \Cup \Psi), \quad \rbrack_{\mathcal{D}}(\Phi) \geqslant \rbrack_{\mathcal{D}}(\Phi \Cup \Psi)$$

and

$$\urcorner_{\mathcal{D}}(\Psi) \geqslant \urcorner_{\mathcal{D}}(\Phi \Cup \Psi), \quad \rbrack_{\mathcal{D}}(\Psi) \geqslant \rbrack_{\mathcal{D}}(\Phi \Cup \Psi).$$

Hence,

$$\urcorner_{\mathcal{D}}(\Phi) \curlywedge \urcorner_{\mathcal{D}}(\Phi) \geqslant \urcorner_{\mathcal{D}}(\Phi \Cup \Psi) \ \textit{and} \ \rbrack_{\mathcal{D}}(\Phi) \curlywedge \rbrack_{\mathcal{D}}(\Psi) \geqslant \rbrack_{\mathcal{D}}(\Phi \Cup \Psi).$$

Thus,

$$\daleth_{\mathcal{D}}(\Phi \Cup \Psi) = \daleth_{\mathcal{D}}(\Phi) \curlywedge \daleth_{\mathcal{D}}(\Psi) \ \ and \ \ \gimel_{\mathcal{D}}(\Phi \Cup \Psi) = \gimel_{\mathcal{D}}(\Phi) \curlywedge \gimel_{\mathcal{D}}(\Psi).$$

Also, since

$$\Phi \Subset \Phi \Cup \Psi \ \text{ and } \ \Psi \Subset \Phi \Cup \Psi,$$

we obtain from the monotonicity that

$$\digamma_{\mathcal{D}}(\Phi) \leqslant \digamma_{\mathcal{D}}(\Phi \Cup \Psi) \ \ and \ \ \digamma_{\mathcal{D}}(\Psi) \leqslant \digamma_{\mathcal{D}}(\Phi \Cup \Psi).$$

Hence,

$$\digamma_{\mathcal{D}}(\Phi) \curlyvee \digamma_{\mathcal{D}}(\Delta) \leqslant \digamma_{\mathcal{D}}(\Phi \Cup \Delta).$$

Thus,

$$\digamma_{\mathcal{D}}(\Phi \Cup \Psi) = \digamma_{\mathcal{D}}(\Phi) \curlyvee \digamma_{\mathcal{D}}(\Psi).$$

Inversely, assume that

$$\begin{aligned} \daleth_{\mathcal{D}}(\Phi \Cup \Psi) &= \daleth_{\mathcal{D}}(\Phi) \curlywedge \daleth_{\mathcal{D}}(\Psi), \\ \gimel_{\mathcal{D}}(\Phi \Cup \Psi) &= \gimel_{\mathcal{D}}(\Phi) \curlywedge \gimel_{\mathcal{D}}(\Delta), \\ \digamma_{\mathcal{D}}(\Phi \Cup \Psi) &= \digamma_{\mathcal{D}}(\Phi) \curlyvee \digamma_{\mathcal{D}}(\Psi), \quad \text{for all } \Phi, \Psi \in \mathfrak{L}. \end{aligned}$$

Easily, we can see that

$$\begin{aligned} \daleth_{\mathcal{D}}(\Phi \Cup \Psi) &\geqslant \daleth_{\mathcal{D}}(\Phi) \curlywedge \daleth_{\mathcal{D}}(\Psi), \\ \gimel_{\mathcal{D}}(\Phi \Cup \Psi) &\geqslant \gimel_{\mathcal{D}}(\Phi) \curlywedge \gimel_{\mathcal{D}}(\Psi), \\ \digamma_{\mathcal{D}}(\Phi \Cup \Psi) &\leqslant \digamma_{\mathcal{D}}(\Phi) \curlyvee \digamma_{\mathcal{D}}(\Psi), \quad \text{for all } \Phi, \Psi \in \mathfrak{L}. \end{aligned}$$

Now, we show that

$$\begin{aligned} \daleth_{\mathcal{D}}(\Phi \Cap \Psi) &\geqslant \daleth_{\mathcal{D}}(\Phi) \curlyvee \daleth_{\mathcal{D}}(\Psi), \\ \gimel_{\mathcal{D}}(\Phi \Cap \Psi) &\geqslant \gimel_{\mathcal{D}}(\Phi) \curlyvee \gimel_{\mathcal{D}}(\Psi), \\ \digamma_{\mathcal{D}}(\Phi \Cap \Psi) &\leqslant \digamma_{\mathcal{D}}(\Phi) \curlywedge \digamma_{\mathcal{D}}(\Phi), \quad \text{for all } \Phi, \Psi \in \mathfrak{L}. \end{aligned}$$

Since

$$\Psi \Cup (\Phi \Cap \Psi) = \Phi \ \text{ and } \ \Psi \Cup (\Phi \Cap \Psi) = \Psi,$$

we can determine that

$$\begin{aligned} \daleth_{\mathcal{D}}(\Phi \Cup (\Phi \Cap \Psi)) &= \daleth_{\mathcal{D}}(\Phi), \\ \gimel_{\mathcal{D}}(\Phi \Cup (\Phi \Cap \Psi)) &= \gimel_{\mathcal{D}}(\Phi), \\ \daleth_{\mathcal{D}}(\Psi \Cup (\Phi \Cap \Psi)) &= \daleth_{\mathcal{D}}(\Psi), \\ \gimel_{\mathcal{D}}(\Psi \Cup (\Phi \Cap \Psi)) &= \gimel_{\mathcal{D}}(\Psi). \end{aligned}$$

From conditions (i) and (ii), we conclude that

$$\begin{aligned} \daleth_{\mathcal{D}}(\Phi) \curlywedge \daleth_{\mathcal{D}}(\Phi \Cap \Psi) &= \daleth_{\mathcal{D}}(\Phi), \\ \gimel_{\mathcal{D}}(\Phi) \curlywedge \gimel_{\mathcal{D}}(\Phi \Cap \Psi) &= \gimel_{\mathcal{D}}(\Phi), \\ \daleth_{\mathcal{D}}(\Psi) \curlywedge \daleth_{\mathcal{D}}(\Phi \Cap \Psi) &= \daleth_{\mathcal{D}}(\Psi), \\ \gimel_{\mathcal{D}}(\Psi) \curlywedge \gimel_{\mathcal{D}}(\Phi \Cap \Psi) &= \gimel_{\mathcal{D}}(\Psi). \end{aligned}$$

Hence,

$$\begin{aligned}\daleth_{\mathcal{D}}(\Phi \Cap \Psi) &\geqslant \daleth_{\mathcal{D}}(\Phi),\\ \gimel_{\mathcal{D}}(\Phi \Cap \Psi) &\geqslant \gimel_{\mathcal{D}}(\Phi),\\ \daleth_{\mathcal{D}}(\Phi \Cap \Psi) &\geqslant \daleth_{\mathcal{D}}(\Psi),\\ \gimel_{\mathcal{D}}(\Phi \Cap \Psi) &\geqslant \gimel_{\mathcal{D}}(\Psi).\end{aligned}$$

Thus,

$$\begin{aligned}\daleth_{\mathcal{D}}(\Phi \Cap \Psi) &\geqslant \daleth_{\mathcal{D}}(\Phi) \curlyvee \daleth_{\mathcal{D}}(\Psi),\\ \gimel_{\mathcal{D}}(\Phi \Cap \Psi) &\geqslant \gimel_{\mathcal{D}}(\Phi) \curlyvee \gimel_{\mathcal{D}}(\Psi), \quad \text{for all } \Phi, \Psi \in \mathfrak{L}.\end{aligned}$$

In the same way, we obtain that

$$\digamma_{\mathcal{D}}(\Phi \Cap \Psi) \leqslant \digamma_{\mathcal{D}}(\Phi) \curlywedge \digamma_{\mathcal{D}}(\Psi), \quad \text{for all } \Phi, \Psi \in \mathfrak{L}.$$

Therefore, $\mathcal{D}$ is a neutrosophic of $\mathfrak{L}$. □

Similarly, the following result provides a characterization of neutrosophic filters of neutrosophic open-set lattice in terms of its operation.

Theorem 4. *Let $\mathfrak{L}$ be the lattice of neutrosophic open sets. Then, it holds that F is a neutrosophic filter of $\mathfrak{L}$ if and only if the following conditions are satisfied:*
(i) $\daleth_F(\Phi \Cap \Psi) = \daleth_F(\Phi) \curlywedge \daleth_F(\Psi)$;
(ii) $\gimel_F(\Phi \Cap \Psi) = \gimel_F(\Phi) \curlywedge \gimel_F(\Psi)$;
(iii) $\digamma_F(\Phi \Cap \Psi) = \digamma_F(\Phi) \curlyvee \digamma_F(\Psi)$ *for all* $\Phi, \Psi \in \mathfrak{L}$.

Proof. Directly from Theorem 3 and Proposition 4. □

As results of the above theorems, we can obtain the following properties of ideals and filters on a neutrosophic open-set lattice.

Corollary 4. *Let $\mathcal{D}$ be a neutrosophic ideal of $\mathfrak{L}$ and $\Phi, \Psi \in \mathfrak{L}$. If $\Phi \subseteq \Psi$, then*

$$\daleth_{\mathcal{D}}(\Phi) \geqslant \daleth_{\mathcal{D}}(\Psi), \; \gimel_{\mathcal{D}}(\Phi) \geqslant \gimel_{\mathcal{D}}(\Psi) \; \text{ and } \; \digamma_{\mathcal{D}}(\Phi) \leqslant \digamma_{\mathcal{D}}(\Psi),$$

i.e., the mappings $\daleth_{\mathcal{D}}, \gimel_{\mathcal{D}}$ are antitone and $\digamma_{\mathcal{D}}$ is monotone.

Corollary 5. *Let F be a neutrosophic filter of $\mathfrak{L}$ and $\Phi, \Psi \in \mathfrak{L}$. If $\Phi \subseteq \Psi$, then*

$$\daleth_F(\Phi) \leqslant \daleth_F(\Psi), \; \gimel_F(\Phi) \leqslant \gimel_F(\Psi) \; \text{ and } \; \digamma_F(\Phi) \geqslant \digamma_F(\Psi),$$

i.e., the mappings $\daleth_F, \gimel_F$ are monotone and $\digamma_F$ is antitone.

The following result characterizes fuzzy ideals (respectively, fuzzy filters) of open-set lattice.

Corollary 6. *For every fuzzy set $\mathcal{D}$ and F of $\mathfrak{L}$, the following equivalences hold:*
(i) *$\mathcal{D}$ is a fuzzy ideal of $\mathfrak{L}$ equivalent to* $\daleth_{\mathcal{D}}(\Phi \Cup \Psi) = \daleth_{\mathcal{D}}(\Phi) \curlywedge \daleth_{\mathcal{D}}(\Psi)$;
(ii) *F is a fuzzy filter of $\mathfrak{L}$ equivalent to* $\daleth_F(\Phi \Cap \Psi) = \daleth_F(\Phi) \curlywedge \daleth_F(\Psi)$, *for all* $\Phi, \Psi \in \mathfrak{L}$.

Proof. (i) The fact that fuzzy ideal is a neutrosophic ideal of $\mathfrak{L}$ by setting $\gimel_{\mathcal{D}}(\Phi) = 0$ and $\digamma_{\mathcal{D}}(\Phi) = 1 - \daleth_{\mathcal{D}}(\Phi)$, Theorem 3 assures that $\mathcal{D}$ is a fuzzy ideal of $\mathfrak{L}$ if and only if $\daleth_{\mathcal{D}}(\Phi \Cup \Psi) = \daleth_{\mathcal{D}}(\Phi) \curlywedge \daleth_{\mathcal{D}}(\Psi)$, for all $\Phi, \Psi \in \mathfrak{L}$.

(ii) It follows from Proposition 4 and (i). □

Similarly, the following result shows a characterization of intuitionistic fuzzy ideals and filters of the open-set lattice.

Corollary 7. *For any intuitionistic fuzzy sets $\mathcal{D}$ and F of $\mathfrak{L}$, the following equivalences hold:*

(i) *$\mathcal{D}$ is an intuitionistic fuzzy ideal of $\mathfrak{L}$ if and only if for all $\Phi, \Psi \in \mathfrak{L}$, the following conditions are satisfied:*

(a) $\text{⅂}_{\mathcal{D}}(\Phi \Cup \Psi) = \text{⅂}_{\mathcal{D}}(\Phi) \curlywedge \text{⅂}_{\mathcal{D}}(\Psi)$;

(b) $\text{Ⅎ}_{\mathcal{D}}(\Phi \Cup \Psi) = \text{Ⅎ}_{\mathcal{D}}(\Phi) \curlyvee \text{Ⅎ}_{\mathcal{D}}(\Psi)$.

(ii) *F is an intuitionistic fuzzy filter of $\mathfrak{L}$ if and only if for all $\Phi, \Psi \in \mathfrak{L}$, the following conditions are satisfied:*

(a) $\text{⅂}_{F}(\Phi \Cap \Psi) = \text{⅂}_{F}(\Phi) \curlywedge \text{⅂}_{F}(\Psi)$;

(b) $\text{Ⅎ}_{F}(\Phi \Cap \Psi) = \text{Ⅎ}_{F}(\Phi) \curlyvee \text{Ⅎ}_{F}(\Psi)$.

Proof. (i) Since every intuitionistic fuzzy ideal is a neutrosophic ideal of $\mathfrak{L}$ by putting $\text{⅃}_{\mathcal{D}}(\Phi) = 1 - \text{⅂}_{\mathcal{D}}(\Phi) - \text{Ⅎ}_{\mathcal{D}}(\Phi)$, it holds by Theorem 3 that $\mathcal{D}$ is an intuitionistic fuzzy ideal of $\mathfrak{L}$ if and only if for all $\Phi, \Psi \in \mathfrak{L}$, the following conditions hold:
(a) $\text{⅂}_{\mathcal{D}}(\Phi \Cup \Psi) = \text{⅂}_{\mathcal{D}}(\Phi) \curlywedge \text{⅂}_{\mathcal{D}}(\Psi)$;
(b) $\text{Ⅎ}_{\mathcal{D}}(\Phi \Cup \Psi) = \text{Ⅎ}_{\mathcal{D}}(\Phi) \curlyvee \text{Ⅎ}_{\mathcal{D}}(\Psi)$.

(ii) Directly via (i) and Proposition 4. □

6. Prime Neutrosophic Ideals and Filters of $\mathfrak{L}$

In this part of the paper, we study the concept of prime neutrosophic ideals (respectively, prime neutrosophic filters) of $\mathfrak{L}$ as interesting types of neutrosophic ideals (respectively, neutrosophic filters).

6.1. Characterizations of Prime Neutrosophic Ideals and Filters

We apply the previous characterizations of neutrosophic ideals (respectively, neutrosophic filters) to the prime neutrosophic ideals (respectively, prime neutrosophic filters) of $\mathfrak{L}$.

Definition 15. *A neutrosophic ideal $\mathcal{D}$ of the lattice $\mathfrak{L}$ is said to be a prime neutrosophic ideal if, for all $\Phi, \Psi \in \mathfrak{L}$, the following conditions apply:*

(i) $\text{⅂}_{\mathcal{D}}(\Phi \Cap \Psi) \leqslant \text{⅂}_{\mathcal{D}}(\Phi) \curlyvee \text{⅂}_{\mathcal{D}}(\Psi)$;

(ii) $\text{⅃}_{\mathcal{D}}(\Phi \Cap \Psi) \leqslant \text{⅃}_{\mathcal{D}}(\Phi) \curlyvee \text{⅃}_{\mathcal{D}}(\Psi)$;

(iii) $\text{Ⅎ}_{\mathcal{D}}(\Phi \Cap \Psi) \geqslant \text{Ⅎ}_{\mathcal{D}}(\Phi) \curlywedge \text{Ⅎ}_{\mathcal{D}}(\Psi)$.

Definition 16. *A neutrosophic filter F of the lattice $\mathfrak{L}$ is said to be a prime neutrosophic filter if, for all $\Phi, \Psi \in \mathfrak{L}$, the following conditions apply:*

(i) $\text{⅂}_{F}(\Phi \Cup \Psi) \leqslant \text{⅂}_{F}(\Phi) \curlyvee \text{⅂}_{F}(\Psi)$;

(ii) $\text{⅃}_{F}(\Phi \Cup \Psi) \leqslant \text{⅃}_{F}(\Phi) \curlyvee \text{⅃}_{F}(\Psi)$;

(iii) $\text{Ⅎ}_{F}(\Phi \Cup \Psi) \geqslant \text{Ⅎ}_{F}(\Phi) \curlywedge \text{Ⅎ}_{F}(\Psi)$.

The next theorem shows a basic characterization of prime neutrosophic ideals.

Theorem 5. *Let $\mathcal{D}$ be a neutrosophic subset of $\mathfrak{L}$. Then,*
$\mathcal{D}$ is a prime neutrosophic ideal of $\mathfrak{L}$ if and only if the following conditions hold:

(i) $\text{⅂}_{\mathcal{D}}(\Phi \Cup \Psi) = \text{⅂}_{\mathcal{D}}(\Phi) \curlywedge \text{⅂}_{\mathcal{D}}(\Psi)$;

(ii) $\text{⅂}_{\mathcal{D}}(\Phi \Cap \Psi) = \text{⅂}_{\mathcal{D}}(\Phi) \curlyvee \text{⅂}_{\mathcal{D}}(\Psi)$;

(iii) $\text{⅃}_{\mathcal{D}}(\Phi \Cup \Psi) = \text{⅃}_{\mathcal{D}}(\Phi) \curlywedge \text{⅃}_{\mathcal{D}}(\Psi)$;

(iv) $\text{⅃}_{\mathcal{D}}(\Phi \Cap \Psi) = \text{⅃}_{\mathcal{D}}(\Phi) \curlyvee \text{⅃}_{\mathcal{D}}(\Psi)$;

(v) $\text{Ⅎ}_{\mathcal{D}}(\Phi \Cup \Psi) = \text{Ⅎ}_{\mathcal{D}}(\Phi) \curlyvee \text{Ⅎ}_{\mathcal{D}}(\Psi)$;

(vi) $\text{Ⅎ}_{\mathcal{D}}(\Phi \Cap \Psi) = \text{Ⅎ}_{\mathcal{D}}(\Phi) \curlywedge \text{Ⅎ}_{\mathcal{D}}(\Psi)$, *for all* $\Phi, \Psi \in \mathfrak{L}$.

Proof. Let $\mathcal{D}$ be a prime neutrosophic ideal of $\mathfrak{L}$. We prove (i), as the others can be proved similarly. By the aforementioned hypothesis, we have that

$$\urcorner_{\mathcal{D}}(\Phi \Cup \Psi) \geqslant \urcorner_{\mathcal{D}}(\Phi) \curlywedge \urcorner_{\mathcal{D}}(\Psi), \quad \text{for every } \Phi, \Psi \in \mathfrak{L}.$$

It follows by Definition 13 that

$$\urcorner_{\mathcal{D}}(\Phi) = \urcorner_{\mathcal{D}}(\Phi \Cap (\Omega \Cup \Psi)) \geqslant \urcorner_{\mathcal{D}}(\Phi \Cup \Psi) \text{ and } \urcorner_{\mathcal{D}}(\Psi) = \urcorner_{\mathcal{D}}(\Psi \Cap (\Phi \Cup \Psi)) \geqslant \urcorner_{\mathcal{D}}(\Phi \Cup \Psi).$$

Thus,

$$\urcorner_{\mathcal{D}}(\Phi) \curlywedge \urcorner_{\mathcal{D}}(\Psi) \geqslant \urcorner_{\mathcal{D}}(\Phi \Cup \Psi).$$

Therefore,

$$\urcorner_{\mathcal{D}}(\Phi \Cup \Psi) = \urcorner_{\mathcal{D}}(\Phi) \curlywedge \urcorner_{\mathcal{D}}(\Psi).$$

Inversely, if we assume that $\urcorner_{\mathcal{D}}$, $\beth_{\mathcal{D}}$ and $\digamma_{\mathcal{D}}$ satisfy the above conditions, then it is clear that $\mathcal{D}$ is a prime neutrosophic ideal of $\mathfrak{L}$. □

Similarly, the following theorem shows a characterization of prime neutrosophic filters.

Theorem 6. *Let $\mathcal{D}$ be a neutrosophic subset of $\mathfrak{L}$. Then, $\mathcal{D}$ is a prime neutrosophic filter of $\mathfrak{L}$ if and only if the following conditions hold:*

(i) $\urcorner_F(\Phi \Cup \Psi) = \urcorner_F(\Phi) \curlyvee \urcorner_F(\Psi)$;
(ii) $\urcorner_F(\Phi \Cap \Psi) = \urcorner_F(\Phi) \curlywedge \urcorner_F(\Psi)$;
(iii) $\beth_F(\Phi \Cup \Psi) = \beth_F(\Phi) \curlyvee \beth_F(\Psi)$;
(iv) $\beth_F(\Phi \Cap \Psi) = \beth_F(\Phi) \curlywedge \beth_F(\Psi)$;
(v) $\digamma_F(\Phi \Cup \Psi) = \digamma_F(\Phi) \curlywedge \digamma_F(\Psi)$;
(vi) $\digamma_F(\Phi \Cap \Psi) = \digamma_F(\Phi) \curlyvee \digamma_F(\Psi)$.

Proof. Direct application of Proposition 4 and Theorem 5. □

Example 4. *Let $\mathcal{E} = \{a, b\}$ and $\mathfrak{L} = \{\phi, \Phi, \Psi, \mathcal{E}\}$ be a lattice of $\mathcal{E}$ with $\Phi = \{\langle a, 0.4, 0.3, 0.1\rangle \mid a \in \mathcal{E}\}$ and $\Psi = \{\langle b, 0.1, 0.3, 0.4\rangle \mid b \in \mathcal{E}\}$. Then, according to Definitions 15 and 16, we have the following:*

(i) $\mathcal{D} = \{\langle a, 0.2, 0.3, 0.1\rangle, \langle b, 0.3, 0.4, 0.1\rangle \mid a, b \in \mathcal{E}\}$ *is a prime neutrosophic ideal of* $\mathfrak{L}$.
(ii) $F = \{\langle a, 0.5, 0.2, 0.3\rangle, \langle b, 0.4, 0.1, 0.2\rangle \mid a, b \in \mathcal{E}\}$ *is a prime neutrosophic filter of* $\mathfrak{L}$.

6.2. Operations of Prime Neutrosophic Ideals and Prime Neutrosophic Filters

We present some basic operations of prime neutrosophic ideals (respectively, prime neutrosophic filters).

Proposition 7. *Suppose $(\Phi_i)_{i\in I}$ is a set of neutrosophic sets of $\mathfrak{L}$:*

(i) *If Φ_i is a prime neutrosophic ideal of $\mathfrak{L}$, then $\bigcap_{i\in I} \Phi_i$ is a prime neutrosophic ideal of $\mathfrak{L}$;*
(ii) *If Φ_i is a prime neutrosophic filter of $\mathfrak{L}$, then $\bigcap_{i\in I} \Phi_i$ is a prime neutrosophic filter of $\mathfrak{L}$.*

Proof. (i) Let Φ_i be a prime neutrosophic ideal of $\mathfrak{L}$. From Proposition 5, it holds that $\bigcap_{i\in I} \Phi_i$ is a neutrosophic ideal of $\mathfrak{L}$. Now, we show that $\bigcap_{i\in I} \Phi_i$ is prime. Let $\Phi, \Psi \in \mathfrak{L}$ with $\Phi \Cap \Psi \in \bigcap_{i\in I} \Phi_i$. Then, in that case, $\Phi \Cap \Psi \in \Phi_i$. Since for all $i \in I$, Φ_i is a prime neutrosophic ideal, in that case

$$\begin{aligned}
&\urcorner_{\Phi_i}(\Phi \Cap \Psi) \leqslant \urcorner_{\Phi_i}(\Phi) \curlyvee \urcorner_{\Phi_i}(\Psi),\\
&\beth_{\Phi_i}(\Phi \Cap \Psi) \leqslant \beth_{\Phi_i}(\Phi) \curlyvee \beth_{\Phi_i}(\Psi),\\
&\digamma_{\Phi_i}(\Phi \Cap \Psi) \geqslant \digamma_{\Phi_i}(\Phi) \curlywedge \digamma_{\mathcal{D}}(\Psi), \quad \text{for every } i \in I.
\end{aligned}$$

We can determine that

$$\begin{aligned}
\rceil_{\bigcap_{i\in I}\Phi_i}(\Phi \Cap \Psi) &\leqslant \rceil_{\Phi_i}(\Phi \Cap \Psi) \leqslant \rceil_{\Phi_i}(\Phi) \curlyvee \rceil_{\Phi_i}(\Psi),\\
\gimel_{\bigcap_{i\in I}\Phi_i}(\Phi \Cap \Psi) &\leqslant \gimel_{\Phi_i}(\Phi \Cap \Psi) \leqslant \gimel_{\Phi_i}(\Phi) \curlyvee \gimel_{\Phi_i}(\Psi),\\
\digamma_{\bigcap_{i\in I}\Phi_i}(\Phi \Cap \Psi) &\geqslant \digamma_{\Phi_i}(\Phi \Cap \Delta) \geqslant \digamma_{\Phi_i}(\Phi) \curlywedge \digamma_{\mathcal{D}}(\Delta), \quad \text{for every } i \in I.
\end{aligned}$$

Hence,

$$\begin{aligned}
\rceil_{\bigcap_{i\in I}\Phi_i}(\Phi \Cap \Psi) &\leqslant \bigwedge_{i\in I}(\rceil_{\Phi_i}(\Phi) \curlyvee \rceil_{\Phi_i}(\Psi)),\\
\gimel_{\bigcap_{i\in I}\Phi_i}(\Phi \Cap \Psi) &\leqslant \bigwedge_{i\in I}(\gimel_{\Phi_i}(\Phi) \curlyvee \gimel_{\Phi_i}(\Psi)),\\
\digamma_{\bigcap_{i\in I}\Phi_i}(\Phi \Cap \Psi) &\geqslant \bigvee_{i\in I}(\digamma_{\Phi_i}(\Phi) \curlywedge \digamma_{\mathcal{D}}(\Psi)).
\end{aligned}$$

Therefore,

$$\begin{aligned}
\rceil_{\bigcap_{i\in I}\Phi_i}(\Phi \Cap \Psi) &\leqslant \rceil_{\bigcap_{i\in I}\Phi_i}(\Omega) \curlyvee \rceil_{\bigcap_{i\in I}\Phi_i}(\Psi),\\
\gimel_{\bigcap_{i\in I}\Phi_i}(\Phi \Cap \Psi) &\leqslant \gimel_{\bigcap_{i\in I}\Phi_i}(\Phi) \curlyvee \gimel_{\bigcap_{i\in I}\Phi_i}(\Psi),\\
\digamma_{\bigcap_{i\in I}\Phi_i}(\Omega \Cap \Psi) &\geqslant \digamma_{\bigcap_{i\in I}\Phi_i}(\Phi) \curlywedge \digamma_{\bigcap_{i\in I}\Phi_i}(\Psi).
\end{aligned}$$

We conclude that $\bigcap_{i\in I}\Phi_i$ is a prime neutrosophic ideal of $\mathfrak{L}$.
(ii) Directly by Proposition 4 and (i). □

Next, we study the complement property between the prime neutrosophic ideal and prime neutrosophic filter.

Proposition 8. *Let $\mathcal{D}$ be a neutrosophic set of $\mathfrak{L}$; the following equivalences hold:*

(i) $\mathcal{D}$ is a prime neutrosophic ideal if and only if $\overline{\mathcal{D}}$ is a prime neutrosophic filter of $\mathfrak{L}$;
(ii) $\mathcal{D}$ is a prime neutrosophic filter if and only if $\overline{\mathcal{D}}$ is a prime neutrosophic ideal of $\mathfrak{L}$.

Proof. (i) Let $\mathcal{D}$ be a prime neutrosophic ideal, for all $\Phi, \Psi \in \mathfrak{L}$, Proposition 5 provides that

$$\rceil_{\overline{\mathcal{D}}}(\Phi \Cup \Psi) = \digamma_{\mathcal{D}}(\Phi \Cup \Psi) = \digamma_{\mathcal{D}}(\Phi) \curlyvee \digamma_{\mathcal{D}}(\Psi) = \rceil_{\overline{\mathcal{D}}}(\Phi) \curlyvee \rceil_{\overline{\mathcal{D}}}(\Psi)$$

and

$$\rceil_{\overline{\mathcal{D}}}(\Phi \Cap \Psi) = \digamma_{\mathcal{D}}(\Phi \Cap \Psi) = \digamma_{\mathcal{D}}(\Phi) \curlywedge \digamma_{\mathcal{D}}(\Psi) = \rceil_{\overline{\mathcal{D}}}(\Phi) \curlywedge \rceil_{\overline{\mathcal{D}}}(\Psi).$$

Similarly, we show that

$$\begin{aligned}
\gimel_{\overline{\mathcal{D}}}(\Phi \Cup \Psi) &= \gimel_{\overline{\mathcal{D}}}(\Phi) \curlyvee \gimel_{\overline{\mathcal{D}}}(\Psi),\\
\gimel_{\overline{\mathcal{D}}}(\Phi \Cap \Psi) &= \gimel_{\overline{\mathcal{D}}}(\Phi) \curlywedge \gimel_{\overline{\mathcal{D}}}(\Psi),\\
\digamma_{\overline{\mathcal{D}}}(\Phi \Cup \Psi) &= \digamma_{\overline{\mathcal{D}}}(\Phi) \curlywedge \digamma_{\overline{\mathcal{D}}}(\Psi),\\
\digamma_{\overline{\mathcal{D}}}(\Phi \Cap \Psi) &= \digamma_{\overline{\mathcal{D}}}(\Phi) \curlyvee \digamma_{\overline{\mathcal{D}}}(\Psi).
\end{aligned}$$

By Proposition 6, $\overline{\mathcal{D}}$ is a prime neutrosophic filter of $\mathfrak{L}$. The inverse follows from Proposition 4 and the first implication.
(ii) Directly by the concerned that $\mathcal{D} = \overline{\overline{\mathcal{D}}}$ and (i). □

Example 5. *Consider the prime neutrosophic ideal $\mathcal{D}$ of $\mathfrak{L} = \{\phi, \Phi, \Psi, \mathcal{E}\}$ given in Example 4. Then, according to Definition 16, the complement*

$$\overline{\mathcal{D}} = \{\langle a, 0.1, 0.3, 0.2\rangle, \langle b, 0.3, 0.4, 0.1\rangle \mid a, b \in \mathcal{E}\}$$

is a prime neutrosophic filter of $\mathfrak{L}$.

Proposition 9. *Let $\mathcal{D}$ and F be two neutrosophic sets of $\mathfrak{L}$; the following equivalences hold:*

(i) $\mathcal{D}$ is a prime neutrosophic ideal if and only if $[\mathcal{D}]$ is a prime neutrosophic ideal;
(ii) F is a prime neutrosophic filter if and only if $[F]$ is a prime neutrosophic filter.

Proof. (i) Let $\mathcal{D}$ be a prime neutrosophic ideal of a lattice $\mathfrak{L}$. It is obvious that $[\mathcal{D}] = \{\langle \Phi, \daleth_{\mathcal{D}}(\Phi), \gimel_{\mathcal{D}}(\Phi), 1 - \daleth_{\mathcal{D}}(\Phi)\rangle \mid \Phi \in \mathfrak{L}\}$ is a neutrosophic ideal of $\mathfrak{L}$. Now, we show that $[\mathcal{D}]$ is prime. We have that

$$\daleth_{[\mathcal{D}]}(\Phi \Cap \Psi) = \daleth_{\mathcal{D}}(\Phi \Cap \Psi) = \daleth_{\mathcal{D}}(\Phi) \curlyvee \daleth_{\Phi}(\Psi) = \daleth_{[\mathcal{D}]}(\Phi) \curlyvee \daleth_{[\mathcal{D}]}(\Psi)$$

and

$$\gimel_{[\mathcal{D}]}(\Phi \Cap \Psi) = \gimel_{\mathcal{D}}(\Phi \Cap \Psi) = \gimel_{\mathcal{D}}(\Phi) \curlyvee \gimel_{\mathcal{D}}(\Psi) = \gimel_{[\mathcal{D}]}(\Phi) \curlyvee \gimel_{[\mathcal{D}]}(\Psi).$$

Also,

$$\begin{aligned} \digamma_{[\mathcal{D}]}(\Phi \Cap \Psi) &= 1 - \daleth_{\mathcal{D}}(\Phi \Cap \Psi) \\ &= 1 - (\daleth_{\mathcal{D}}(\Phi) \curlyvee \daleth_{\mathcal{D}}(\Psi)) \\ &= (1 - \daleth_{\mathcal{D}}(\Phi)) \curlywedge (1 - \daleth_{\mathcal{D}}(\Psi)) \\ &= \digamma_{[\mathcal{D}]}(\Phi) \curlywedge \digamma_{[\mathcal{D}]}(\Psi). \end{aligned}$$

We can determine that $[\mathcal{D}]$ is a prime neutrosophic ideal of $\mathfrak{L}$. Inversely, let $[\mathcal{D}]$ be a prime neutrosophic ideal. By using the same proof, we conclude that $\mathcal{D}$ is a prime neutrosophic ideal of $\mathfrak{L}$.
(ii) It follows from Proposition 4 and (i). □

Proposition 10. *Let $\mathcal{D}$ and F be two neutrosophic sets of $\mathfrak{L}$:*

(i) $\mathcal{D}$ is a prime neutrosophic ideal if and only if $\langle \mathcal{D}\rangle$ is a prime neutrosophic ideal;
(ii) F is a prime neutrosophic filter if and only if $\langle F\rangle$ is a prime neutrosophic filter.

Proof. The proof of this property is analogous to that of Proposition 9 by using the definition of $\langle \mathcal{D}\rangle$ instead of $[\mathcal{D}]$. □

The following result discusses the relationship between the prime neutrosophic ideal (respectively, prime neutrosophic filter) and its support of the lattice of open sets.

Proposition 11. *Let $\mathcal{D}$ and F be two neutrosophic sets of $\mathfrak{L}$:*

(i) If $\mathcal{D}$ is a prime neutrosophic ideal, then the support $\mathcal{S}(\mathcal{D})$ is a prime ideal of $\mathfrak{L}$.
(ii) If F is a prime neutrosophic filter, then the support $\mathcal{S}(F)$ is a prime filter of $\mathfrak{L}$.

Proof. (i) Let $\mathcal{D}$ be a prime neutrosophic ideal of the lattice $\mathfrak{L}$. Proposition 6 confirms that $\mathcal{S}(\mathcal{D})$ is an ideal of $\mathfrak{L}$.

Now, we show that $\mathcal{S}(\mathcal{D})$ is prime. Let $\Phi, \Psi \in \mathfrak{L}$ with $\Phi \Cap \Psi \in \mathcal{S}(\mathcal{D})$. We have

$$\daleth_{\mathcal{D}}(\Phi \Cap \Psi) \neq 0,$$
$$\gimel_{\mathcal{D}}(\Phi \Cap \Psi) \neq 0,$$
$$\digamma_{\mathcal{D}}(\Phi \Cap \Psi) \neq 0.$$

Since $\mathcal{D}$ is a prime neutrosophic ideal of $\mathfrak{L}$, then

$$\begin{aligned}\daleth_{\mathcal{D}}(\Phi) \curlyvee \daleth_{\mathcal{D}}(\Psi) &= \daleth_{\mathcal{D}}(\Phi \Cap \Psi) \neq 0,\\ \gimel_{\mathcal{D}}(\Phi) \curlyvee \gimel_{\mathcal{D}}(\Psi) &= \gimel_{\mathcal{D}}(\Phi \Cap \Psi) \neq 0,\\ \Finv_{\mathcal{D}}(\Phi) \curlywedge \Finv_{\mathcal{D}}(\Psi) &= \Finv_{\mathcal{D}}(\Phi \Cap \Psi) \neq 0.\end{aligned}$$

This implies that either ($\daleth_{\mathcal{D}}(\Phi) \neq 0$, $\gimel_{\mathcal{D}}(\Phi) \neq 0$ and $\Finv_{\mathcal{D}}(\Phi) \neq 0$) or ($\daleth_{\mathcal{D}}(\Psi) \neq 0$, $\gimel_{\mathcal{D}}(\Psi) \neq 0$ and $\Finv_{\mathcal{D}}(\Psi) \neq 0$). Thus, either $\Phi \in \mathcal{S}(\mathcal{D})$ or $\Psi \in \mathcal{S}(\mathcal{D})$. Therefore, $\mathcal{S}(\mathcal{D})$ is a prime ideal of $\mathfrak{L}$.

(ii) Directly by using Proposition 4 and (i). □

Similarly, we obtain the following agreement that describes the level sets of the prime neutrosophic ideals, (respectively, prime neutrosophic filters).

Theorem 7. *Let $\mathcal{D}$ and F be two neutrosophic sets of $\mathfrak{L}$. Then, the following hold:*

(i) $\mathcal{D}$ is a prime neutrosophic ideal if and only if its level sets are prime ideals.
(ii) F is a prime neutrosophic filter if and only if its level sets are prime filters.

Proof. (i) By Proposition 2, $\mathcal{D}$ is a neutrosophic ideal of $\mathfrak{L}$ if and only if $\mathcal{D}_{\alpha,\beta,\gamma}$ are ideals of $\mathfrak{L}$ for all $0 < \alpha, \beta, \gamma \leq 1$. We shall prove the primality property. Let $\mathcal{D}$ be a prime neutrosophic ideal of $\mathfrak{L}$, and let $\Phi, \Psi \in \mathfrak{L}$ with $\Phi \Cap \Psi \in \mathcal{D}_{\alpha,\beta,\gamma}$. Then, from Theorem 5, it holds that

$$\begin{aligned}(\daleth_{\mathcal{D}}(\Phi \Cap \Psi) &= \daleth_{\mathcal{D}}(\Phi) \curlyvee \daleth_{\mathcal{D}}(\Psi) \geqslant \alpha,\\ \gimel_{\mathcal{D}}(\Phi \Cap \Psi) &= \gimel_{\mathcal{D}}(\Phi) \curlyvee \gimel_{\mathcal{D}}(\Psi) \geqslant \beta,\\ \Finv_{\mathcal{D}}(\Phi \Cap \Psi) &= \Finv_{\mathcal{D}}(\Phi) \curlywedge \Finv_{\mathcal{D}}(\Psi) \leqslant \gamma).\end{aligned}$$

This implies that either ($\daleth_{\mathcal{D}}(\Phi) \geqslant \alpha$, $\gimel_{\mathcal{D}}(\Phi) \geqslant \beta$ and $\Finv_{\mathcal{D}}(\Phi) \leqslant \gamma$) or ($\daleth_{\mathcal{D}}(\Psi) \geqslant \alpha$, $\gimel_{\mathcal{D}}(\Psi) \geqslant \beta$ and $\Finv_{\mathcal{D}}(\Psi) \leqslant \gamma$). Thus, either $\Phi \in \mathcal{D}_{\alpha,\beta,\gamma}$ or $\Psi \in \mathcal{D}_{\alpha,\beta,\gamma}$. Therefore, $\mathcal{D}_{\alpha,\beta,\gamma}$ are prime ideals for all $0 < \alpha, \beta, \gamma \leq 1$. Inversely, let $\mathcal{D}_{\alpha,\beta,\gamma}$ be prime ideals for all $0 < \alpha, \beta, \gamma \leq 1$ where $\mathcal{D}$ is not a prime neutrosophic ideal of $\mathfrak{L}$. Then, it follows that there exist $\Phi, \Psi \in \mathfrak{L}$ such that

$$\begin{aligned}\daleth_{\mathcal{D}}(\Phi \Cap \Psi) &> \daleth_{\mathcal{D}}(\Phi) \curlyvee \daleth_{\mathcal{D}}(\Psi),\\ \gimel_{\mathcal{D}}(\Phi \Cap \Psi) &> \gimel_{\mathcal{D}}(\Phi) \curlyvee \gimel_{\mathcal{D}}(\Psi),\\ \Finv_{\mathcal{D}}(\Phi \Cap \Psi) &< \Finv_{\mathcal{D}}(\Phi) \curlywedge \Finv_{\mathcal{D}}(\Psi).\end{aligned}$$

This implies that

$$\begin{aligned}\daleth_{\mathcal{D}}(\Phi \Cap \Psi) &> \daleth_{\mathcal{D}}(\Phi) \quad \text{and } \daleth_{\mathcal{D}}(\Phi \Cap \Psi) > \daleth_{\mathcal{D}}(\Psi),\\ \gimel_{\mathcal{D}}(\Phi \Cap \Psi) &> \gimel_{\mathcal{D}}(\Phi) \quad \text{and } \gimel_{\mathcal{D}}(\Phi \Cap \Psi) > \gimel_{\mathcal{D}}(\Psi),\\ \Finv_{\mathcal{D}}(\Phi \Cap \Psi) &< \Finv_{\mathcal{D}}(\Phi) \quad \text{and } \Finv_{\mathcal{D}}(\Phi \Cap \Psi) < \Finv_{\mathcal{D}}(\Psi).\end{aligned}$$

If we put

$$\begin{aligned}\daleth_{\mathcal{D}}(\Phi \Cap \Psi) &= \alpha,\\ \gimel_{\mathcal{D}}(\Phi \Cap \Psi) &= \beta,\\ \Finv_{\mathcal{D}}(\Phi \Cap \Psi) &= \gamma\end{aligned}$$

we obtain

$$\begin{aligned} \daleth_{\mathcal{D}}(\Phi) &< \alpha, \\ \beth_{\mathcal{D}}(\Phi) &< \beta, \\ F_{\mathcal{D}}(\Phi) &> \gamma, \end{aligned}$$

and

$$\begin{aligned} \daleth_{\mathcal{D}}(\Psi) &< \alpha, \\ \beth_{\mathcal{D}}(\Psi) &< \beta, \\ F_{\mathcal{D}}(\Psi) &> \gamma. \end{aligned}$$

Hence,

$$\Phi \Cap \Psi \in \mathcal{D}_{\alpha,\beta,\gamma} \quad \text{and} \quad \Phi, \Psi \notin \mathcal{D}_{\alpha,\beta,\gamma},$$

which contradicts the concerned that $\mathcal{D}_{\alpha,\beta,\gamma}$ are prime ideals of $\mathfrak{L}$ for all $0 < \alpha, \beta, \gamma \leq 1$. Consequently, $\mathcal{D}$ is a prime neutrosophic ideal.
(ii) Derive through Proposition 4 and (i). □

Example 6. *Let us consider the lattice $\mathfrak{L} = \{\phi, \Phi, \Psi, \mathcal{E}\}$ given in Example 4 and let*

$$\mathcal{D} = \{\langle a, 0.2, 0.3, 0.1\rangle, \langle b, 0.3, 0.4, 0.1\rangle \mid a, b \in \mathcal{E}\}$$

be a prime neutrosophic ideal of $\mathfrak{L}$. Then, for any $0 < \alpha, \beta, \gamma \leq 1$, $\mathcal{D}_{\alpha,\beta,\gamma}$ are crisp ideals of $\mathfrak{L}$.

7. Conclusions

The structure of the neutrosophic open-set lattice on a topology generated by a neutrosophic relation is described in this study. We have defined the concepts of neutrosophic ideals and neutrosophic filters on that lattice in terms of their level sets and meet and join operations. In addition, we have examined and defined the concepts of prime neutrosophic filters and ideals as fascinating subsets of neutrosophic ideals and filters. This work mostly discussed neutrosophic ideals and neutrosophic filters on the lattice structure of neutrosophic open sets. However, we think that other types of neutrosophic ideals and neutrosophic filters will also be very interesting in more general structures in future works.

Author Contributions: Methodology, R.P.A., S.M., B.Z., A.M. and L.Z.; Software, R.P.A., S.M., B.Z., A.M. and L.Z.; Validation, R.P.A., S.M., B.Z., A.M. and L.Z.; Formal analysis, R.P.A., S.M., B.Z., A.M. and L.Z.; Investigation, R.P.A., S.M., B.Z., A.M. and L.Z.; Resources, R.P.A., S.M. and B.Z.; Data curation, R.P.A. and S.M.; Writing—original draft, R.P.A., S.M., B.Z., A.M. and L.Z.; Writing—review and editing, R.P.A., S.M., B.Z., A.M. and L.Z.; Visualization, R.P.A., S.M., B.Z., A.M. and L.Z.; Supervision, R.P.A., S.M., B.Z., A.M. and L.Z.; Project administration, R.P.A., S.M., B.Z., A.M. and L.Z.; Funding acquisition, R.P.A. All authors have read and agreed to the published version of the manuscript.

Funding: This research received no external funding.

Data Availability Statement: Data are contained within the article.

Conflicts of Interest: The authors declare no conflicts of interest.

References

1. Smarandache, F. *Neutrosophy. Neutrosophic Property, Sets, and Logic*; American Research Press: Rehoboth, DE, USA, 1998.
2. Guo, Y.; Cheng, H.D. New neutrosophic approach to image segmentation. *Pattern Recognit.* **2009**, *42*, 587–595. [CrossRef]
3. Liu, P.D.; Li, H.G. Multiple attribute decision making method based on some normal neutrosophic Bonferroni mean operators. *Neural Comput. Appl.* **2017**, *28*, 179–194. [CrossRef]
4. Mondal, K.; Pramanik, S. A study on problems of Hijras in West Bengal based on neutrosophic cognitive maps. *Neutrosophic Sets Syst.* **2014**, *5*, 21–26.
5. Wang, H.; Smarandache, F.; Zhang, Y.Q.; Sunderraman, R. Single valued neutrosophic sets. *Multispace Multistruct* **2010**, *4*, 410–413.

6. Smarandache, F. A unifying field in Logics: Neutrosophic Logic. *Mult.-Valued Log.* **2002**, *8*, 385–438.
7. Lupiáñez, F.G. On neutrosophic topology. *Kybernetes* **2008**, *37*, 797–800. [CrossRef]
8. Lupiáñez F.G. On neutrosophic sets and topology. *Procedia Comput. Sci.* **2017**, *120*, 975–982. [CrossRef]
9. Salama, A.A.; Alblowi, S.A. Neutrosophic set and neutrosophic topological spaces. *IOSR J. Math.* **2012**, *3*, 31–35. [CrossRef]
10. Salama, A.A.; Eisa, M.; Abdelmoghny, M. Neutrosophic Relations Database. *Int. J. Inf. Sci. Intell. Syst.* **2014**, *3*, 33–46.
11. El-Gayyar, M. Smooth Neutrosophic Topological Spaces. *Neutrosophic Sets Syst.* **2016**, *65*, 65–72.
12. Gündüz, C.; Bayramov, S. Neutrosophic Soft Continuity in Neutrosophic Soft Topological Spaces. *Filomat* **2020**, *34*, 3495–3506. [CrossRef]
13. Kandil, A.; Saleh, S.; Yakout, M.M. Fuzzy topology on fuzzy sets: Regularity and separation axioms. *Am. Acad. Sch. Res. J.* **2012**, *4*.
14. Latreche, A.; Barkat, O.; Milles, S.; Ismail, F. Single valued neutrosophic mappings defined by single valued neutrosophic relations with applications. *Neutrosophic Sets Syst.* **2020**, *32*, 203–220.
15. Milles, S.; Latreche, A.; Barkat, O. Completeness and Compactness in Standard Single Valued Neutrosophic Metric Spaces. *Int. J. Neutrosophic Sci.* **2020**, *12*, 96–104.
16. Milles, S. The Lattice of intuitionistic fuzzy topologies generated by intuitionistic fuzzy relations. *Appl. Appl. Math.* **2020**, *15*, 942–956.
17. Saadaoui, K.; Milles, S.; Zedam, L. Fuzzy ideals and fuzzy filters on topologies generated by fuzzy relations. *Int. J. Anal. Appl.* **2022**, *20*, 1–9. [CrossRef]
18. Bennoui, A.; Zedam, L.; Milles, S. Several types of single-valued neutrosophic ideals and filters on a lattice. *TWMS J. App. Eng. Math.* **2023**, *13*, 175–188.
19. Öztürk, M.A.; Jun, Y.B. Neutrosophic ideals in BCK/BCI-algebras based on neutrosophic points. *J. Int. Math. Virtual Inst.* **2018**, *8*, 117.
20. Salama, A.A.; Smarandache, F. Fliters via neutrosophic crisp sets. *Neutrosophic Sets Syst.* **2013**, *1*, 34–37.
21. Zedam, L.; Milles, S.; Bennoui, A. Ideals and filters on a lattice in neutrosophic setting. *Appl. Appl. Math.* **2021**, *16*, 1140–1154.
22. Zadeh, L.A. Fuzzy sets. *Inf. Control* **1965**, *8*, 331–352. [CrossRef]
23. Atanassov, K. *Intuitionistic Fuzzy Sets, Sofia, VII ITKRs Scientific Session*; Springer: Berlin/Heidelberg, Germany, 1983.
24. Atanassov, K. *Intuitionistic Fuzzy Sets*, Springer: New York, NY, USA; Berlin/Heidelberg, Germany, 1999.
25. Arockiarani, I.; Sumathi, I.R.; Martina Jency, J. Fuzzy neutrosophic soft topological spaces. *Int. J. Appl. Math. Arch.* **2013**, *4*, 225–238.
26. Smarandache, F.; Pramanik, S. (Eds.) *New Trends in Neutrosophic Theory and Applications*; Pons Editions: Brussels, Belgium, 2016.
27. Ye, J. Improved correlation coefficients of single-valued neutrosophic sets and interval neutrosophic sets for multiple attribute decision making. *J. Intell. Fuzzy Syst.* **2014**, *27*, 2453–2462. [CrossRef]
28. Ye, J. Multicriteria decision-making method using aggregation operators for simplified neutrosophic sets. *J. Intell. Fuzzy Syst.* **2014**, *26*, 2450–2466. [CrossRef]
29. Ziane, B.; Amroune, A. Representation and construction of intuitionistic fuzzy t-preorders and fuzzy weak t-orders. *Discuss. Math. Gen. Algebra Appl.* **2021**, *41*, 81–101.
30. Kim, J.; Lim, P.K.; Lee, J.G.; Hur, K. Single valued neutrosophic relations. *Ann. Fuzzy Math. Inform.* **2018**, *16*, 201–221. [CrossRef]
31. Salama, A.A.; Smarandache, F. *Neutrosophic Crisp Set Theory*; The Educational Publisher: Columbus, OH, USA, 2015.
32. Milles, S.; Hammami, N. Neutrosophic topologies generated by neutrosophic relations. *Alger. J. Eng. Archit. Urban.* **2021**, *5*, 417–426.
33. Mishra, S.; Srivastava, R. Fuzzy topologies generated by fuzzy relations. *Soft Comput.* **2018**, *22*, 373–385. [CrossRef]
34. Kim, Y.C. Alexandrov L topologies. *Int. J. Pure Appl. Math.* **2014**, *93*, 165–179. [CrossRef]

axioms

MDPI

Article

Monotonic Random Variables According to a Direction

José Juan Quesada-Molina [1,†] and Manuel Úbeda-Flores [2,*,†]

1 Department of Applied Mathematics, University of Granada, 18071 Granada, Spain; jquesada@ugr.es
2 Department of Mathematics, University of Almería, 04120 Almeria, Spain
* Correspondence: mubeda@ual.es
† These authors contributed equally to this work.

Abstract: In this paper, we introduce the concept of monotonicity according to a direction for a set of random variables. This concept extends well-known multivariate dependence notions, such as corner set monotonicity, and can be used to detect dependence in multivariate distributions not detected by other known concepts of dependence. Additionally, we establish relationships with other known multivariate dependence concepts, outline some of their salient properties, and provide several examples.

Keywords: monotonic dependence; random variable; total positivity

MSC: 60E15; 62H05

check for updates

Citation: Quesada-Molina, J.J.; Úbeda-Flores, M. Monotonic Random Variables According to a Direction. *Axioms* **2024**, *13*, 275. https://doi.org/10.3390/axioms13040275

Academic Editors: Cristina Flaut, Dana Piciu and Murat Tosun

Received: 26 February 2024
Revised: 6 April 2024
Accepted: 17 April 2024
Published: 20 April 2024

1. Introduction

There are numerous methodologies and approaches available for the exploration and analysis of the intricate relationships of dependence among random variables. As underscored by Jogdeo [1], this area stands as a cornerstone of extensive research within the expansive domains of probability theory and statistics. The investigation of dependence among variables is fundamental in understanding the underlying structure and behavior of complex systems, making it a focal point of study across various scientific disciplines.

When delving into the examination of a multivariate model, it becomes imperative to conduct a thorough analysis of the specific type of dependence structure it encapsulates. This meticulous scrutiny is essential for discerning the suitability of a particular model for a given dataset or practical application. By comprehensively understanding the nature of dependence presents, researchers can make informed decisions regarding model selection and parameter estimation, thereby enhancing the robustness and reliability of their analyses.

Within the vast landscape of studied dependence types, our attention is particularly drawn to the nuanced distinctions between positive and negative dependence. Positive dependence expresses a tendency for the variables to move in the same direction, exhibiting a mutual influence that often reflects synergistic relationships. Conversely, negative dependence denotes an inverse relationship, where the movement of one variable is accompanied by a corresponding opposite movement in another, indicative of regulatory or inhibitory interactions.

By elucidating the intricacies of positive and negative dependence, researchers gain valuable insights into the underlying dynamics of the systems under study. This deeper understanding not only enriches theoretical frameworks but also has practical implications in various fields, including finance, engineering, and epidemiology. Moreover, it underscores the importance of considering diverse dependence structures in statistical modeling, ensuring that analyses accurately capture the complexities of real-world phenomena.

Positive dependence is defined by any criterion capable of mathematically characterizing the inclination of components within an n-variate random vector to assume concordant values [2]. As emphasized by Barlow and Proschan [3], the concepts of (positive) dependence in the multivariate context are more extensive and intricate compared to the bivariate case.

The literature contains various extensions of the bivariate dependence concepts to the multivariate domain (we refer to [4–7] for more details). Our objective in this study is to extend certain established notions of multivariate positive and negative dependence. This includes the exploration of concepts such as orthant dependence and corner set monotonicity, investigating their connections with other dependence concepts and presenting several associated properties.

The paper is organized as follows. We begin with some preliminaries (Section 2) pertaining to the properties of multivariate dependence. This section serves to lay the foundation for our subsequent analyses by elucidating key concepts and frameworks, essential for understanding the complexities of dependence structures among random variables. Following the preliminaries, in Section 3, we delve into the concept of monotonic random variables with respect to a given direction. This extends the notion of corner set monotonicity and provides a more nuanced understanding of the directional dependence present in multivariate systems. We further explore several properties pertaining to these monotonic random variables and provide some examples. Finally, Section 4 is dedicated to presenting our conclusions drawn from the analyses and discussions shown in the preceding sections.

2. Preliminaries

In the sequel, by convention, we will indistinctly use "increasing" (respectively, "decreasing") and "nondecreasing" (respectively, "nonincreasing"). In addition, a subset $A \subseteq \mathbb{R}^d$, with $d \geq 1$, is an *increasing set* if its indicator function χ_A is increasing.

Let $n \geq 2$ be a natural number. Let $(\Omega, \mathcal{F}, \mathbb{P})$ be a probability space, where Ω is a nonempty set, $\mathcal{F}$ is a σ-algebra of subsets of Ω, and $\mathbb{P}$ is a probability measure on $\mathcal{F}$, and let $\mathbf{X} = (X_1, X_2, \ldots, X_n)$ be an n-dimensional random vector from Ω to $\overline{\mathbb{R}}^n = [-\infty, \infty]^n$.

The orthant dependence according to a direction is defined as follows [8]: Let $\alpha = (\alpha_1, \alpha_2, \ldots, \alpha_n)$ be a vector in $\mathbb{R}^n$ such that $|\alpha_i| = 1$ for all $i = 1, 2, \ldots, n$. An n-dimensional random vector $\mathbf{X}$—or its joint distribution function—is said to be *orthant positive* (respectively, *negative*) *dependent according to direction* α—written PD(α) (respectively, ND(α))—if

$$\mathbb{P}\left[\bigcap_{i=1}^{n}(\alpha_i X_i > x_i)\right] \geq \prod_{i=1}^{n} \mathbb{P}[\alpha_i X_i > x_i] \text{ for all } (x_1, x_2, \ldots, x_n) \in \overline{\mathbb{R}}^n \quad (1)$$

(respectively, with the reversed inequality in (1)).

Note that for some elections of direction α—e.g., for $\alpha = \mathbf{1} = (1, 1, \ldots, 1)$ or $\alpha = -\mathbf{1} = (-1, -1, \ldots, -1)$—we obtain different known (bivariate and multivariate) dependence concepts in the literature, as positive quadrant dependence, positive upper orthant dependence, etc. (we refer to [2,7,9–12] for more details).

Let $\mathbf{X}$ be an n-dimensional random vector. The following two multivariate positive dependence notions—on corner set monotonicity—were introduced in [13], where the expression "nonincreasing in $\mathbf{x}$"—and similarly for nondecreasing—means that it is nonincreasing in each of the components of $\mathbf{x}$, and $\mathbf{X} \leq \mathbf{x}$ means $X_i \leq x_i$ for all $i = 1, 2, \ldots, n$:

1. $\mathbf{X}$ is *left corner set decreasing*, denoted by LCSD($\mathbf{X}$), if

$$\mathbb{P}[\mathbf{X} \leq \mathbf{x} | \mathbf{X} \leq \mathbf{x}'] \text{ is nonincreasing in } \mathbf{x}' \text{ for all } \mathbf{x}. \quad (2)$$

2. $\mathbf{X}$ is *right corner set increasing*, denoted by RCSI($\mathbf{X}$), if

$$\mathbb{P}[\mathbf{X} > \mathbf{x} | \mathbf{X} > \mathbf{x}'] \text{ is nondecreasing in } \mathbf{x}' \text{ for all } \mathbf{x}. \quad (3)$$

The corresponding negative dependence concepts LCSI($\mathbf{X}$) (*left corner set increasing*) and RCSD($\mathbf{X}$) (*right corner set decreasing*) are defined in a similar manner by exchanging "nondecreasing" and "nonincreasing" in (2) and (3), respectively.

Let H be the joint distribution function of $\mathbf{X}$. We note that condition (2) can be written as

$$\frac{H(\mathbf{x} \wedge \mathbf{x}')}{H(\mathbf{x}')} \text{ is nonincreasing in } \mathbf{x}' \text{ for all } \mathbf{x},$$

where $\mathbf{x} \wedge \mathbf{x}' = (\min\{x_1, x_1'\}, \min\{x_2, x_2'\}, \ldots, \min\{x_n, x_n'\})$. Denoting by $\overline{H}$ the survival function of H, i.e., $\overline{H}(\mathbf{x}) = \mathbb{P}[\mathbf{X} > \mathbf{x}]$, condition (3) can be written as

$$\frac{\overline{H}(\mathbf{x} \vee \mathbf{x}')}{\overline{H}(\mathbf{x}')} \text{ is nondecreasing in } \mathbf{x}' \text{ for all } \mathbf{x},$$

where $\mathbf{x} \vee \mathbf{x}' = (\max\{x_1, x_1'\}, \max\{x_2, x_2'\}, \ldots, \max\{x_n, x_n'\})$.

For properties of these notions and relationships with other multivariate dependence concepts, see, e.g., refs. [7,14].

3. Monotonic Dependence According to a Direction

In this section, we undertake a comprehensive examination of the concepts of left-corner set and right-corner set dependence in sequence according to a direction, delineating their definitions within the framework of directional dependence for a set of random variables. Building upon the foundations laid out in Section 2, where the concepts of LCSD and RCSI were recalled, we extend these notions to incorporate directional considerations, thus offering a more nuanced understanding of dependence structures. It is worth noting that a similar analytical approach could be applied to explore negative dependence concepts, mirroring the methodology employed for positive dependence. Furthermore, we not only define these directional dependence concepts but also delve into some of their salient properties.

3.1. Definition

We begin with the key definition of this work, in which for a direction α and an n-dimensional random vector $\mathbf{X}$, $\alpha\mathbf{X}$ denotes the vector $(\alpha_1 X_1, \alpha_2 X_2, \ldots, \alpha_n X_n)$.

Definition 1. *Let* $\mathbf{X}$ *be an n-dimensional random vector and* $\alpha = (\alpha_1, \alpha_2, \ldots, \alpha_n) \in \mathbb{R}^n$ *such that* $|\alpha_i| = 1$ *for all* $i = 1, 2, \ldots, n$. *The random vector* $\mathbf{X}$*—or its joint distribution function—is said to be increasing (respectively, decreasing) according to the direction* α*—denoted by I(*α*) (respectively D(*α*))—if*

$$\mathbb{P}\left[\alpha\mathbf{X} > \mathbf{x} | \alpha\mathbf{X} > \mathbf{x}'\right]$$

is nondecreasing (respectively, nonincreasing) in $\mathbf{x}'$ *for all* $\mathbf{x}$.

In the sequel, we focus on the I(α) concept. Similar results can be obtained for the D(α) concept, so we omit them.

Observe that the I(α) concept generalizes the LCSD and RCSI concepts defined in Section 2; that is, I($-\mathbf{1}$) (respectively, I($\mathbf{1}$)) corresponds to LCSD (respectively, RCSI).

We wish to emphasize that, in general, the I(α) concept signifies positive dependence. This means that large values of the variables X_j, for $j \in J$, are associated with small values of the variables X_j, for $j \in I \backslash J$, where $I = \{1, 2, \ldots, n\}$ and $J = \{i \in I : \alpha_i = 1\}$. Therefore, if a random vector $\mathbf{X}$ is I(α), then

$$\mathbb{P}\left[\bigcap_{j \in J} (X_j > x_j), \bigcap_{j \in I \backslash J} (X_j \le x_j) | \bigcap_{j \in J} \left(X_j > x_j'\right), \bigcap_{j \in I \backslash J} \left(X_j \le x_j'\right)\right]$$

is nondecreasing in each x_j' for $j \in J$, and nonincreasing in each x_j' for $j \in I \backslash J$, for all $\mathbf{x}$.

3.2. Relationships with Other Multivariate Dependence Concepts

In this subsection, our focus lies on exploring the connections between the I(α) dependence notion and several established multivariate dependence concepts within the context of directional analysis. By examining these relationships, we aim to elucidate how the I(α) concept aligns with or diverges from other well-known measures of dependence, thus providing a more comprehensive understanding of their interplay. Through this investigation, we seek to uncover potential insights into the nature of multivariate dependence and its implications in various analytical scenarios.

We begin our study by recalling the increasingness in the sequence dependence concept.

Definition 2 ([15]). *Let $X_1, X_2, \ldots, X_n$ be n random variables and $\alpha = (\alpha_1, \alpha_2, \ldots, \alpha_n) \in \mathbb{R}^n$ such that $|\alpha_i| = 1$ for all $i = 1, 2, \ldots, n$. The random variables $X_1, X_2, \ldots, X_n$ are said to be increasing in sequence according to direction α—denoted by IS(α)—if, for any $x_i \in \mathbb{R}$,*

$$\mathbb{P}[\alpha_i X_i > x_i | \alpha_1 X_1 > x_1, \ldots, \alpha_{i-1} X_{i-1} > x_{i-1}]$$

is nondecreasing in $x_1, x_2, \ldots, x_{i-1} \in \mathbb{R}$ for all $i = 2, 3, \ldots, n$.

The relationship between I(α) and IS(α) dependence concepts is given in the following result.

Proposition 1. *If a random vector $\mathbf{X}$ is I(α), then it is IS(α).*

Proof. Let $x_1, x_2, \ldots, x_n, x_1', x_2', \ldots, x_n' \in \mathbb{R}$ such that $x_i \leq x_i'$ for $1 \leq i \leq n$. Since $\mathbf{X}$ is I(α), for any i, $2 \leq i \leq n$, we have

$$\begin{aligned}
\mathbb{P}\left[\alpha_i X_i > x_i | \bigcap_{j=1}^{i-1} (\alpha_j X_j > x_j)\right] &= \mathbb{P}\left[\bigcap_{j=1}^{n} (\alpha_j X_j > t_j) | \bigcap_{j=1}^{n} (\alpha_j X_j > s_j)\right] \\
&\leq \mathbb{P}\left[\bigcap_{j=1}^{n} (\alpha_j X_j > t_j) | \bigcap_{j=1}^{n} \left(\alpha_j X_j > s_j'\right)\right] \\
&= \mathbb{P}\left[\alpha_i X_i > x_i | \bigcap_{j=1}^{i-1} (\alpha_j X_j > x_j')\right]
\end{aligned}$$

where

$$t_j = \begin{cases} x_i, & j = i, \\ -\infty, & j \neq i, \end{cases}$$

$$s_j = \begin{cases} x_j, & \text{for } j = 1, 2, \ldots, i-1, \\ -\infty, & \text{for } j = i, \ldots, n, \end{cases}$$

and

$$s_j' = \begin{cases} x_j', & \text{for } j = 1, 2, \ldots, i-1, \\ -\infty, & \text{for } j = i, \ldots, n; \end{cases}$$

whence $\mathbf{X}$ is IS(α), which completes the proof. □

The converse of Proposition 1 does not hold in general: see, for instance, (Ref. [16], Exercise 5.33) for a counterexample in the bivariate case.

In [15], the authors establish a significant result demonstrating that the IS(α) condition implies PD(α). Building upon this crucial insight, we can readily derive the following result, thereby highlighting the logical consequence of this implication.

Corollary 1. *If a random vector $\mathbf{X}$ is I(α), then it is PD(α).*

The next definition involves the concept of multivariate totally positive of order two.

Definition 3 ([17]). *Let* $\mathbf{X}$ *be an n-dimensional random vector with joint density function f, and* $\alpha \in \mathbb{R}^n$, *with* $|\alpha_i| = 1$ *for all* $i = 1, 2, \ldots, n$. *Then,* $\mathbf{X}$ *is said to be multivariate totally positive of order two according to direction α—denoted by* $MTP_2(\alpha)$*—if*

$$f(\alpha(\mathbf{x} \vee \mathbf{y}))f(\alpha(\mathbf{x} \wedge \mathbf{y})) \geq f(\alpha\mathbf{x})f(\alpha\mathbf{y}) \quad (4)$$

for all $\mathbf{x}, \mathbf{y} \in \overline{\mathbb{R}}^n$.

The relationship between the notions I(α) and $\mathrm{MTP}_2(\alpha)$ is given in the following result.

Proposition 2. *If a random vector* $\mathbf{X}$ *is* $MTP_2(\alpha)$, *then it is I(α).*

Proof. Let $\mathbf{X} = (X_1, X_2, \ldots, X_n)$ be an n-dimensional random vector such that $\mathbf{X}$ is $\mathrm{MTP}_2(\alpha)$. Given $x_i, x_i' \in \overline{\mathbb{R}}$, for $i = 1, 2, \ldots, n$, we consider three cases:

1. If $x_i > x_i'$ for all $i = 1, 2, \ldots, n$, we have that

$$\mathbb{P}\left[\bigcap_{i=1}^{n}(\alpha_i X_i > x_i) | \bigcap_{i=1}^{n}(\alpha_i X_i > x_i')\right] = \frac{\mathbb{P}\left[\bigcap_{i=1}^{n}(\alpha_i X_i > x_i)\right]}{\mathbb{P}\left[\bigcap_{i=1}^{n}(\alpha_i X_i > x_i')\right]}$$

is nondecreasing in $x_1', x_2', \ldots, x_n'$.

2. If $x_i \leq x_i'$ for all $i = 1, 2, \ldots, n$, we have

$$\mathbb{P}\left[\bigcap_{i=1}^{n}(\alpha_i X_i > x_i) | \bigcap_{i=1}^{n}(\alpha_i X_i > x_i')\right] = 1,$$

and hence it is nondecreasing in $x_1', x_2', \ldots, x_n'$.

3. Given $j \in \{1, 2, \ldots, n\}$, consider, without loss of generality, $x_i \leq x_i'$ for $1 \leq i \leq j$ and $x_i > x_i'$ for $j + 1 \leq i \leq n$. Then, we have

$$\begin{aligned}\mathbb{P}[\alpha\mathbf{X} > \mathbf{x} | \alpha\mathbf{X} > \mathbf{x}'] &= \frac{\mathbb{P}\left[\bigcap_{i=1}^{n}(\alpha_i X_i > x_i), \bigcap_{i=1}^{n}(\alpha_i X_i > x_i')\right]}{\mathbb{P}\left[\bigcap_{i=1}^{n}(\alpha_i X_i > x_i')\right]} \\ &= \frac{\mathbb{P}\left[\bigcap_{i=1}^{j}(\alpha_i X_i > x_i'), \bigcap_{i=j+1}^{n}(\alpha_i X_i > x_i)\right]}{\mathbb{P}\left[\bigcap_{i=1}^{n}(\alpha_i X_i > x_i')\right]}. \end{aligned} \quad (5)$$

Since

$$\mathbb{P}\left[\bigcap_{i-1}^{n}(\alpha_i X_i > x_i')\right] \geq \mathbb{P}\left[\bigcap_{i=1}^{n}(\alpha_i X_i > x_i'')\right]$$

for all $x_i', x_i'' \in \overline{\mathbb{R}}$ such that $x_i' \leq x_i''$ for $1 \leq i \leq n$, we have that (5) is nondecreasing in $x_{j+1}', \ldots, x_n'$. In order to prove that (5) is also nondecreasing in $x_1', \ldots, x_j'$, considering $x_1'', \ldots, x_j'' \in \overline{\mathbb{R}}$ such that $x_i' \leq x_i''$ for $1 \leq i \leq j$, we need to verify

$$\mathbb{P}\left[\bigcap_{i=j+1}^{n}(\alpha_i X_i > x_i) | \bigcap_{i=1}^{n}(\alpha_i X_i > x_i')\right] \leq \mathbb{P}\left[\bigcap_{i=j+1}^{n}(\alpha_i X_i > x_i) | \bigcap_{i=1}^{j}(\alpha_i X_i > x_i''), \bigcap_{i=j+1}^{n}(\alpha_i X_i > x_i')\right]. \quad (6)$$

For that, it suffices to show that the determinant

$$D = \begin{vmatrix} \mathbb{P}\left[\bigcap_{i=1}^{j}(\alpha_i X_i > x_i'), \bigcap_{i=j+1}^{n}(\alpha_i X_i > x_i)\right] & \mathbb{P}\left[\bigcap_{i=1}^{j}(\alpha_i X_i > x_i''), \bigcap_{i=j+1}^{n}(\alpha_i X_i > x_i)\right] \\ \mathbb{P}\left[\bigcap_{i=1}^{n}(\alpha_i X_i > x_i')\right] & \mathbb{P}\left[\bigcap_{i=1}^{j}(\alpha_i X_i > x_i''), \bigcap_{i=j+1}^{n}(\alpha_i X_i > x_i')\right] \end{vmatrix}$$

is non-positive (note that, in this case, the quotient between the elements of the first column would be less than the quotient between the elements of the second column, obtaining (6)). First of all, if we add the second column changed of sign to the first column, we have

$$D = \begin{vmatrix} \mathbb{P}\left[\bigcap_{i=1}^{j}(x_i' < \alpha_i X_i \le x_i''), \bigcap_{i=j+1}^{n}(\alpha_i X_i > x_i)\right] & \mathbb{P}\left[\bigcap_{i=1}^{j}(\alpha_i X_i > x_i''), \bigcap_{i=j+1}^{n}(\alpha_i X_i > x_i)\right] \\ \mathbb{P}\left[\bigcap_{i=1}^{j}(x_i' < \alpha_i X_i \le x_i''), \bigcap_{i=j+1}^{n}(\alpha_i X_i > x_i')\right] & \mathbb{P}\left[\bigcap_{i=1}^{j}(\alpha_i X_i > x_i''), \bigcap_{i=j+1}^{n}(\alpha_i X_i > x_i')\right] \end{vmatrix},$$

and now adding to the second row, the first row with a changed sign, we obtain

$$D = \begin{vmatrix} \mathbb{P}\left[\bigcap_{i=1}^{j}(x_i' < \alpha_i X_i \le x_i''), \bigcap_{i=j+1}^{n}(\alpha_i X_i > x_i)\right] & \mathbb{P}\left[\bigcap_{i=1}^{j}(\alpha_i X_i > x_i''), \bigcap_{i=j+1}^{n}(\alpha_i X_i > x_i)\right] \\ \mathbb{P}\left[\bigcap_{i=1}^{j}(x_i' < \alpha_i X_i \le x_i''), \bigcap_{i=j+1}^{n}(x_i' < \alpha_i X_i \le x_i)\right] & \mathbb{P}\left[\bigcap_{i=1}^{j}(\alpha_i X_i > x_i''), \bigcap_{i=j+1}^{n}(x_i' < \alpha_i X_i \le x_i)\right] \end{vmatrix}. \tag{7}$$

Since $\mathbf{X}$ is $\mathrm{MTP}_2(\alpha)$, from Ref. [17] (Propositions 2 and 4), we have

$$h(\mathbf{y})h(\mathbf{y}') \ge h\left(\mathbf{y}'^j\right)h\left(\mathbf{y}^j\right), \tag{8}$$

for any pair of vectors $\mathbf{y}, \mathbf{y}' \in \overline{\mathbb{R}}^n$ such that $y_i \le y_i'$ for all $i = 1, 2, \ldots, n$, and for any $1 \le j \le n-1$, where $\mathbf{y}'^j = \left(y_1', \ldots, y_j', y_{j+1}, \ldots, y_n\right)$ and $\mathbf{y}^j = \left(y_1, \ldots, y_j, y_{j+1}', \ldots, y_n'\right)$, and h is the joint density function of the random vector $(\alpha_1 X_1, \alpha_2 X_2, \ldots, \alpha_n X_n)$. By integrating both sides of (8) in $\mathbf{y}, \mathbf{y}'$, with $x_i' < y_i \le x_i'' < y_i'$ for $i = 1, 2, \ldots, j$ and $x_i' < y_i \le x_i < y_i'$ for $i = j+1, \ldots, n$, we obtain

$$\begin{aligned} &\int_{x_1'}^{x_1''} \cdots \int_{x_j'}^{x_j''} \int_{x_{j+1}'}^{x_{j+1}} \cdots \int_{x_n'}^{x_n} \int_{x_1''}^{+\infty} \cdots \int_{x_j''}^{+\infty} \int_{x_{j+1}}^{+\infty} \cdots \int_{x_n}^{+\infty} h(\mathbf{y})h(\mathbf{y}')\mathbf{dy}\mathbf{dy}' \\ &\ge \int_{x_1'}^{x_1''} \cdots \int_{x_j'}^{x_j''} \int_{x_{j+1}'}^{x_{j+1}} \cdots \int_{x_n'}^{x_n} \int_{x_1''}^{+\infty} \cdots \int_{x_j''}^{+\infty} \int_{x_{j+1}}^{+\infty} \cdots \int_{x_n}^{+\infty} h\left(\mathbf{y}'^j\right)h\left(\mathbf{y}^j\right)\mathbf{dy}\mathbf{dy}'. \end{aligned}$$

It easily follows that the determinant D in (7) is non-positive.

In the three cases, we obtain that $\mathbf{X}$ is $\mathrm{I}(\alpha)$, which completes the proof. □

In order to conclude this subsection, we summarize the relationships among the different dependence concepts outlined above in the following scheme:

$$\mathrm{MTP}_2(\alpha) \Rightarrow \mathrm{I}(\alpha) \Rightarrow \mathrm{IS}(\alpha) \Rightarrow \mathrm{PD}(\alpha).$$

3.3. Properties

The subsequent results presented herein encapsulate essential properties inherent to the I(α) families. These properties span a diverse range of scenarios, encompassing not only the behavior of independent random variables but also extending to subsets of the newly introduced concept IS(α), as well as the concatenation of I(α) random vectors. Furthermore, these results touch upon topics, such as weak convergence, thereby providing a comprehensive framework for analyzing and understanding the dynamics of multivariate dependence within the realm of I(α) families.

Proposition 3. *Every set of independent random variables is I(α) for any $\alpha \in \mathbb{R}^n$.*

Proof. If the random variables $X_1, X_2, \ldots, X_n$ are independent, then for any $\alpha \in \mathbb{R}^n$ and for all $\mathbf{x}, \mathbf{x}' \in \overline{\mathbb{R}}^n$, we have

$$\mathbb{P}\left[\alpha\mathbf{X} > \mathbf{x} | \alpha\mathbf{X} > \mathbf{x}'\right] = \prod_{i=1}^{n} \mathbb{P}\left[\alpha_i X_i > x_i | \alpha_i X_i > x_i'\right].$$

Given $i \in \{1, 2, \ldots, n\}$, consider the probability $\mathbb{P}\left[\alpha_i X_i > x_i | \alpha_i X_i > x_i'\right]$. We study two cases:

1. If $x_i \leq x_i'$, we have
$$\mathbb{P}\left[\alpha_i X_i > x_i | \alpha_i X_i > x_i'\right] = 1.$$
2. If $x_i > x_i'$, we have
$$\mathbb{P}\left[\alpha_i X_i > x_i | \alpha_i X_i > x_i'\right] = \frac{\mathbb{P}[\alpha_i X_i > x_i]}{\mathbb{P}\left[\alpha_i X_i > x_i'\right]}.$$

   We consider two subcases:

   (a) If $x_i' \leq x_i'' \leq x_i$, then we have
   $$\mathbb{P}\left[\alpha_i X_i > x_i'\right] \geq \mathbb{P}\left[\alpha_i X_i > x_i''\right],$$
   and therefore
   $$\mathbb{P}\left[\alpha_i X_i > x_i | \alpha_i X_i > x_i'\right] \leq \mathbb{P}\left[\alpha_i X_i > x_i | \alpha_i X_i > x_i''\right].$$

   (b) If $x_i' \leq x_i \leq x_i''$, then we have
   $$\mathbb{P}\left[\alpha_i X_i > x_i | \alpha_i X_i > x_i'\right] \leq 1 = \mathbb{P}\left[\alpha_i X_i > x_i | \alpha_i X_i > x_i''\right].$$

In any case, we obtain that the probability $\mathbb{P}\left[\alpha_i X_i > x_i | \alpha_i X_i > x_i'\right]$ is nondecreasing in x_i' for any $x_i \in \overline{\mathbb{R}}$ and for all $i = 1, 2, \ldots, n$, whence the result follows. □

Exploring the interplay of stochastic processes, we delve into the transformation of subsets of I(α) random variables.

Proposition 4. *Every subset of I(α) random variables is I(α^*), where α^* is the vector attained by excluding from α the components associated with the random variables not included in the subset.*

Proof. Assume that $\mathbf{X} = (X_1, X_2, \ldots, X_n)$ is I(α), and let $\mathbf{X}_k = (X_{i_1}, X_{i_2}, \ldots, X_{i_k})$ be a subvector of $\mathbf{X}$. Let $I = \{1, 2, \ldots, n\}$. For any $x_{i_1}, x_{i_2}, \ldots, x_{i_k}, x_{i_1}', x_{i_2}', \ldots, x_{i_k}' \in \overline{\mathbb{R}}$, and by considering $x_i = x_i' = -\infty$ for every $i \in I \backslash \{i_1, i_2, \ldots, i_k\}$, we have

$$\mathbb{P}\left[\bigcap_{j=1}^{k}\left(\alpha_{i_j} X_{i_j} > x_{i_j}\right) | \bigcap_{j=1}^{k}\left(\alpha_{i_j} X_{i_j} > x_{i_j}'\right)\right] = \mathbb{P}\left[\bigcap_{i=1}^{n}(\alpha_i X_i > x_i) | \bigcap_{i=1}^{n}(\alpha_i X_i > x_i')\right].$$

Thus, given $x''_{i_j} \in \overline{\mathbb{R}}$, $1 \leq j \leq k$, such that $x'_{i_j} \leq x''_{i_j}$, and taking $x''_i = -\infty$ for every $i \in I \backslash \{i_1, i_2, \ldots, i_k\}$, we obtain

$$\mathbb{P}\left[\bigcap_{i=1}^{n}(\alpha_i X_i > x_i) | \bigcap_{i=1}^{n}(\alpha_i X_i > x''_i)\right] = \mathbb{P}\left[\bigcap_{j=1}^{k}\left(\alpha_{i_j} X_{i_j} > x_{i_j}\right) | \bigcap_{j=1}^{k}\left(\alpha_{i_j} X_{i_j} > x''_{i_j}\right)\right].$$

Since $\mathbf{X}$ is I(α), we conclude that $\mathbf{X}_k$ is $\mathrm{I}(\alpha_{i_1}, \alpha_{i_2}, \ldots, \alpha_{i_k})$, completing the proof. □

Within the domain of stochastic processes, we now show that when applying strictly increasing functions to the components of an I(α) random vector, the I(α) property is retained.

Proposition 5. *If the random vector* $\mathbf{X} = (X_1, X_2, \ldots, X_n)$ *is I(α), and* $g_1, g_2, \ldots, g_n$ *are n real-valued and strictly increasing functions, then the random vector* $(g_1(X_1), g_2(X_2), \ldots, g_n(X_n))$ *is I(α).*

Proof. Let $\mathbf{y}, \mathbf{y}', \mathbf{y}'' \in \overline{\mathbb{R}}^n$ such that $y'_i \leq y''_i$ for all $i = 1, 2, \ldots, n$. Since $X_1, X_2, \ldots, X_n$ are I(α) and $\alpha_i g_i^{-1}(\alpha_i y'_i) \leq \alpha_i g_i^{-1}(\alpha_i y''_i)$ for every $i = 1, 2, \ldots, n$, we have

$$\begin{aligned}
\mathbb{P}\left[\bigcap_{i=1}^{n}(\alpha_i g_i(X_i) > y_i) | \bigcap_{i=1}^{n}(\alpha_i g_i(X_i) > y'_i)\right] &= \mathbb{P}\left[\bigcap_{i=1}^{n}(\alpha_i X_i > \alpha_i g_i^{-1}(\alpha_i y_i)) | \bigcap_{i=1}^{n}(\alpha_i X_i > \alpha_i g_i^{-1}(\alpha_i y'_i))\right] \\
&\leq \mathbb{P}\left[\bigcap_{i=1}^{n}(\alpha_i X_i > \alpha_i g_i^{-1}(\alpha_i y_i)) | \bigcap_{i=1}^{n}(\alpha_i X_i > \alpha_i g_i^{-1}(\alpha_i y''_i))\right] \\
&= \mathbb{P}\left[\bigcap_{i=1}^{n}(\alpha_i g_i(X_i) > y_i) | \bigcap_{i=1}^{n}(\alpha_i g_i(X_i) > y''_i)\right],
\end{aligned}$$

i.e., $(g_1(X_1), g_2(X_2), \ldots, g_n(X_n))$ is I(α), which completes the proof. □

For the next result, we need some additional notations. Given $\alpha = (\alpha_1, \alpha_2, \ldots, \alpha_n) \in \mathbb{R}^n$ and $\beta = (\beta_1, \beta_2, \ldots, \beta_m) \in \mathbb{R}^m$, (α, β) will denote *concatenation*, that is, $(\alpha, \beta) = (\alpha_1, \ldots, \alpha_n, \beta_1, \ldots, \beta_m) \in \mathbb{R}^{n+m}$. Similar notation will be used in the case of random vectors.

Proposition 6. *If* $\mathbf{X} = (X_1, X_2, \ldots, X_n)$ *is I(α),* $\mathbf{Y} = (Y_1, Y_2, \ldots, Y_m)$ *is I(β), and* $\mathbf{X}$ *and* $\mathbf{Y}$ *are independent, then* $(\mathbf{X}, \mathbf{Y})$ *is I(α, β).*

Proof. Let $\mathbf{x}, \mathbf{x}', \mathbf{x}'' \in \overline{\mathbb{R}}^n$ and $\mathbf{y}, \mathbf{y}', \mathbf{y}'' \in \overline{\mathbb{R}}^m$ such that $\mathbf{x}' \leq \mathbf{x}''$ and $\mathbf{y}' \leq \mathbf{y}''$. Since $\mathbf{X}$ is I(α), $\mathbf{Y}$ is I(β), and $\mathbf{X}$ and $\mathbf{Y}$ are independent, then we have

$$\begin{aligned}
&\mathbb{P}\left[\bigcap_{i=1}^{n}(\alpha_i X_i > x_i), \bigcap_{j=1}^{m}(\beta_j Y_j > y_j) | \bigcap_{i=1}^{n}(\alpha_i X_i > x'_i), \bigcap_{j=1}^{m}(\beta_j Y_j > y'_j)\right] \\
&= \mathbb{P}\left[\bigcap_{i=1}^{n}(\alpha_i X_i > x_i) | \bigcap_{i=1}^{n}(\alpha_i X_i > x'_i)\right] \cdot \mathbb{P}\left[\bigcap_{j=1}^{m}(\beta_j Y_j > y_j) | \bigcap_{j=1}^{m}(\beta_j Y_j > y'_j)\right] \\
&\leq \mathbb{P}\left[\bigcap_{i=1}^{n}(\alpha_i X_i > x_i) | \bigcap_{i=1}^{n}(\alpha_i X_i > x''_i)\right] \cdot \mathbb{P}\left[\bigcap_{j=1}^{m}(\beta_j Y_j > y_j) | \bigcap_{j=1}^{m}(\beta_j Y_j > y''_j)\right] \\
&= \mathbb{P}\left[\bigcap_{i=1}^{n}(\alpha_i X_i > x_i), \bigcap_{j=1}^{m}(\beta_j Y_j > y_j) | \bigcap_{i=1}^{n}(\alpha_i X_i > x''_i), \bigcap_{j=1}^{m}(\beta_j Y_j > y''_j)\right],
\end{aligned}$$

whence $(\mathbf{X}, \mathbf{Y})$ is I(α, β). □

The following result pertains to a closure property of the I(α) family of multivariate distributions and, similarly, of the D(α) family.

Proposition 7. *The family of I(α) distribution functions is closed under weak convergence.*

Proof. Let $\{\mathbf{X}_n\}_{n\in\mathbb{N}}$ be a sequence of p-dimensional random vectors such that $\mathbf{X}_n = (X_{1n}, X_{2n}, \ldots, X_{pn})$ is I(α) for all $n \in \mathbb{N}$, and$\{\mathbf{X}_n\}_{n\in\mathbb{N}}$ converges weakly to $\mathbf{X}$. If $\mathbf{x}, \mathbf{x}', \mathbf{x}'' \in \overline{\mathbb{R}}^p$ are such that $x_i' \leq x_i''$ for all $i = 1, 2, \ldots, p$, then we have

$$\begin{aligned}
\mathbb{P}\left[\bigcap_{i=1}^{p}(\alpha_i X_i > x_i) | \bigcap_{i=1}^{p}(\alpha_i X_i > x_i')\right] &= \lim_{n\to+\infty} \mathbb{P}\left[\bigcap_{i=1}^{p}(\alpha_i X_{in} > x_i) | \bigcap_{i=1}^{p}(\alpha_i X_{in} > x_i')\right] \\
&\leq \lim_{n\to+\infty} \mathbb{P}\left[\bigcap_{i=1}^{p}(\alpha_i X_{in} > x_i) | \bigcap_{i=1}^{p}(\alpha_i X_{in} > x_i'')\right] \\
&= \mathbb{P}\left[\bigcap_{i=1}^{p}(\alpha_i X_i > x_i) | \bigcap_{i=1}^{p}(\alpha_i X_i > x_i'')\right];
\end{aligned}$$

therefore, $\mathbf{X}$ is I(α), whence the result follows. □

3.4. Examples

In this section, we delve into examples that illustrate the I(α) concept of dependence. Through the following three examples—involving both continuous and discrete cases—, we aim to elucidate the behavior and implications of this type of dependence in various contexts. These examples serve to elucidate the impact on statistical analysis, decision-making processes, and other pertinent areas of study.

Example 1. *Let $\mathbf{X} = (X_1, X_2, \ldots, X_n)$ be a random vector with multivariate Normal distribution $N(\mu, \Sigma)$, where $\mu = (\mu_1, \mu_2, \ldots, \mu_n)$ and Σ is the covariance matrix. Let $(r_{ij}) = \Sigma^{-1}$ such that $r_{ij} < 0$ for all (i, j) with $1 \leq i < j \leq n$—a similar study can be conducted by considering $r_{ij} > 0$. The probability density function of $\mathbf{X}$ is given by*

$$f(x_1, x_2, \ldots, x_n) = (2\pi)^{-n/2}|\Sigma|^{-1/2}\exp\left(-\frac{1}{2}\sum_{i=1}^{n}\sum_{j=1}^{n} r_{ij}(x_i - \mu_i)(x_j - \mu_j)\right).$$

Then, for every pair (i, j) with $1 \leq i < j \leq n$, we can express the probability density function as follows:

$$f(x_1, x_2, \ldots, x_n) = f_1\left(x^{(i)}\right) f_2\left(x^{(j)}\right)\exp(-r_{ij}x_i x_j),$$

where $x^{(k)} = (x_1, \ldots, x_{k-1}, x_{k+1}, \ldots, x_n)$ for $k = i, j$ and appropriate functions f_1, f_2. Now, given x_i, x_j, x_i', x_j' such that $x_i \leq x_i'$ and $x_j \leq x_j'$, and (α_i, α_j) such that $|\alpha_k| = 1$ for $k = i, j$, we have

$$\begin{aligned}
& f(x_1, \ldots, \alpha_i x_i, \ldots, \alpha_j x_j, \ldots, x_n) f\left(x_1, \ldots, \alpha_i x_i', \ldots, \alpha_j x_j', \ldots, x_n\right) \\
& - f(x_1, \ldots, \alpha_i x_i', \ldots, \alpha_j x_j, \ldots, x_n) f\left(x_1, \ldots, \alpha_i x_i, \ldots, \alpha_j x_j', \ldots, x_n\right) \\
& = f_1\left(x^{(i)}\right) f_1\left(x^{(i')}\right) f_2\left(x^{(j)}\right) f_2\left(x^{(j')}\right) \\
& \cdot \left[\exp(-r_{ij}\alpha_i\alpha_j(x_i x_j + x_i' x_j')) - \exp(-r_{ij}\alpha_i\alpha_j(x_i' x_j + x_i x_j'))\right].
\end{aligned} \tag{9}$$

Since

$$\alpha_i\alpha_j(x_i x_j + x_i' x_j' - x_i' x_j - x_i x_j') = \alpha_i\alpha_j[(x_i' - x_i)(x_j' - x_j)] \geq 0,$$

as long as $\alpha_i\alpha_j > 0$, then (9) is non-negative if, and only if, $\alpha_i\alpha_j > 0$. Then we have that, for any $\alpha = (\alpha_1, \alpha_2, \ldots, \alpha_n) \in \mathbb{R}^n$ such that $|\alpha_i| = 1$ for all $i = 1, 2, \ldots, n$, the random vector $\mathbf{X}$ is MTP$_2$(α) if, and only if, $\alpha_i\alpha_j > 0$ for any election of (i, j)—see Theorem 3 of [17]. From Proposition 2, we conclude that $\mathbf{X}$ is I(α) for $\alpha = \mathbf{1}$ and $\alpha = -\mathbf{1}$.

Example 2. *Let* $\mathbf{X} = (X_1, X_2, \ldots, X_n)$ *be a random vector with Dirichlet distribution* $\mathrm{Dir}(\gamma)$, *with* $\gamma = (\gamma_1, \gamma_2, \ldots, \gamma_n; \gamma_{n+1})$, *and such that* $\gamma_i > 0$ *for all* $i = 1, 2, \ldots, n$ *and* $\gamma_{n+1} \geq 1$. *The probability density function is given by*

$$f(x_1, x_2, \ldots, x_n) = \frac{\Gamma\left(\sum_{i=1}^{n+1} \gamma_i\right)}{\prod_{i=1}^{n+1} \Gamma(\gamma_i)} \prod_{i=1}^{n} x_i^{\gamma_i - 1} \left(1 - \sum_{i=1}^{n} x_i\right)^{\gamma_{n+1} - 1},$$

with $x_i \geq 0$ *and* $\sum_{i=1}^{n} x_i \leq 1$. *Given any selection of* (i, j), *with* $1 \leq i < j \leq n$, *and any real numbers* x_i, x_j, x_i', x_j' *such that* $x_i \leq x_i'$ *and* $x_j \leq x_j'$, *we have*

$$\begin{aligned}
& f(x_1, \ldots, x_i, \ldots, x_j, \ldots, x_d) f\left(x_1, \ldots, x_i', \ldots, x_j', \ldots, x_d\right) \\
& - f(x_1, \ldots, x_i', \ldots, x_j, \ldots, x_d) f(x_1, \ldots, x_i, \ldots, x_j', \ldots, x_d) \\
& = \left[\frac{\Gamma\left(\sum_{i=1}^{n+1} \gamma_i\right)}{\prod_{i=1}^{n+1} \Gamma(\gamma_i)}\right]^2 \prod_{\substack{k=1 \\ k \neq i,j}}^{n} x_k^{2(\gamma_k - 1)} x_i^{\gamma_i - 1} (x_i')^{\gamma_i - 1} x_j^{\gamma_j - 1} (x_j')^{\gamma_j - 1} \\
& \cdot \left\{ \left[\left(1 - \sum_{\substack{k=1 \\ k \neq i,j}}^{n} x_k - x_i - x_j\right)\left(1 - \sum_{\substack{k=1 \\ k \neq i,j}}^{n} x_k - x_i' - x_j'\right)\right]^{\gamma_{n+1} - 1} \right. \\
& \left. - \left[\left(1 - \sum_{\substack{k=1 \\ k \neq i,j}}^{n} x_k - x_i' - x_j\right)\left(1 - \sum_{\substack{k=1 \\ k \neq i,j}}^{n} x_k - x_i - x_j'\right)\right]^{\gamma_{n+1} - 1} \right\}.
\end{aligned} \tag{10}$$

Since

$$\begin{aligned}
& \left(1 - \sum_{\substack{k=1 \\ k \neq i,j}}^{n} x_k - x_i - x_j\right)\left(1 - \sum_{\substack{k=1 \\ k \neq i,j}}^{n} x_k - x_i' - x_j'\right) \\
& - \left(1 - \sum_{\substack{k=1 \\ k \neq i,j}}^{n} x_k - x_i' - x_j\right)\left(1 - \sum_{\substack{k=1 \\ k \neq i,j}}^{n} x_k - x_i - x_j'\right) \\
& = x_i x_j' + x_i' x_j - x_i' x_j' - x_i x_j = -(x_i' - x_i)(x_j' - x_j) \leq 0
\end{aligned}$$

and $\gamma_{n+1} \geq 1$, *then (10) is non-positive; therefore, we have that* $\mathbf{X}$ *is MRR*$_2$(**1**), *that is,* $\mathbf{X}$ *is a multivariate reverse rule of order two—the corresponding negative analog to* (4) *by reversing the inequality sign in (Ref. [17], Theorem 3)—according to the direction* $(1, 1, \ldots, 1)$. *Thus, by applying the corresponding negative dependence concept, in a manner similar to that provided in Proposition 2 for the corresponding positive dependence concept, we conclude that* $\mathbf{X}$ *is* $D(\mathbf{1})$.

Example 3. *Let* $\mathbf{X} = (X_1, X_2, \ldots, X_n)$ *be a random vector with a multinomial distribution with parameters N (number of trials) and* $p = (p_1, p_2, \ldots, p_n)$ *(event probabilities) such that* $p_i \geq 0$ *for all* $i = 1, 2, \ldots, n$ *and* $0 < \sum_{i=1}^{n} p_i < 1$. *The joint probability mass function is given by*

$$f(x_1, x_2, \ldots, x_n) = \frac{N!}{\prod_{i=1}^{n} x_i! (N - \sum_{i=1}^{n} x_i)!} \prod_{i=1}^{n} p_i^{x_i} \left(1 - \sum_{i=1}^{n} p_i\right)^{N - \sum_{i=1}^{n} x_i},$$

where $\sum_{i=1}^{n} x_i \leq N$. *The multinomial distribution function is the conditional distribution function of independent Poisson random variables given their sum. As a consequence of (Ref. [5], Theorem 4.3) and (Ref. [17], Theorem 3), we have that* $\mathbf{X}$ *is MRR*$_2$(**1**). *Thus, we conclude that* $\mathbf{X}$ *is* $D(\mathbf{1})$.

Remark 1. *We want to note that by considering a similar reasoning to that given in Example 3, we have that any random vector with multivariate hypergeometric distribution—the conditional distribution function of independent binomial random variables given their sum—is also* $D(\mathbf{1})$.

Now we provide an illustrative example demonstrating the application of Proposition 7 regarding weak convergence.

Example 4. *Let* $\mathbf{X} = (X_1, X_2, \ldots, X_n)$ *be a random vector with joint distribution function*

$$H_\theta(\mathbf{x}) = \exp\left[-\left(\sum_{i=1}^{n} e^{-\theta x_i}\right)^{1/\theta}\right]$$

for all $\mathbf{x} \in \overline{\mathbb{R}}^n$, *and* $\theta \geq 1$. *This parametric family of distribution functions is a multivariate generalization of the Type B bivariate extreme-value distributions (see [16,18]). By applying (Ref. [19], Theorem 2.11)—which involves log-convex functions [20]—we have that the random vector* $\mathbf{X}$ *is* $I(-\mathbf{1})$. *Consider the sequence of distribution functions* $\{H_\theta\}_{\theta\in\mathbb{N}}$. *When* θ *goes to* ∞, *we get* $H_\infty(\mathbf{x}) = \min(F_1(x_1), F_2(x_2), \ldots, F_n(x_n))$, *where* F_i, *with* $i = 1, 2, \ldots, n$, *are the one-dimensional marginals of* H_θ; *therefore, as a consequence of Proposition 7, we obtain that* H_θ *is* $I(-\mathbf{1})$ *as well.*

4. Conclusions

In this paper, we have undertaken a significant endeavor by introducing a novel concept of monotonicity, characterized by its directionality, for a set of random variables. This extension of existing multivariate dependence concepts represents a substantial contribution to the field, offering a more nuanced understanding of dependence structures. Moreover, we have not only defined this directional monotonicity concept but also delved into its implications by establishing relationships with other well-known multivariate dependence concepts. These comparative analyses shed light on the interconnectedness and compatibility between different analytical approaches, enriching our understanding of multivariate dependence. The exploration of I(α) stochastic orders—closely resembling those studied in [21]—is ongoing and represents a fertile ground for future research.

Author Contributions: Conceptualization, J.J.Q.-M.; methodology, J.J.Q.-M. and M.Ú.-F.; validation, J.J.Q.-M. and M.Ú.-F.; investigation, J.J.Q.-M. and M.Ú.-F.; writing—original draft preparation, M.Ú.-F.; writing—review and editing, M.Ú.-F.; visualization, J.J.Q.-M. and M.Ú.-F.; supervision, J.J.Q.-M. and M.Ú.-F. All authors have read and agreed to the published version of the manuscript.

Funding: This research was funded by the Ministry of Science and Innovation (Spain) grant number PID2021-122657OB-I00.

Data Availability Statement: Data are contained within the article.

Acknowledgments: The authors thank the comments provided by three anonymous reviewers.

Conflicts of Interest: The authors declare no conflicts of interest.

References

1. Jogdeo, K. Concepts of dependence. In *Encyclopedia of Statistical Sciences*; Kotz, S., Johnson, N.L., Eds.; Wiley: New York, NY, USA, 1982; Volume 1; pp. 324–334.
2. Colangelo, A.; Scarsini, M.; Shaked, M. Some notions of multivariate positive dependence. *Insur. Math. Econ.* **2005**, *37*, 13–26. [CrossRef]
3. Barlow, R.E.; Proschan, F. *Statistical Theory of Reability and Life Testing: Probability Models*; To Begin With: Silver Spring, MD, USA, 1981.
4. Block, H.W.; Ting, M.-L. Some concepts of multivariate dependence. *Comm. Statist. A Theory Methods* **1981**, *10*, 749–762. [CrossRef]
5. Block, H.W.; Savits, T.H.; Shaked, M. Some concepts of negative dependence. *Ann. Probab.* **1982**, *10*, 765–772. [CrossRef]
6. Colangelo, A.; Müller, A.; Scarsini, M. Positive dependence and weak convergence. *J. Appl. Prob.* **2006**, *43*, 48–59. [CrossRef]
7. Joe, H. *Multivariate Models and Dependence Concepts*; Chapman & Hall: London, UK, 1997.
8. Quesada-Molina, J.J.; Úbeda-Flores, M. Directional dependence of random vectors. *Inf. Sci.* **2012**, *215*, 67–74. [CrossRef]
9. Kimeldorf, G.; Sampson, A.R. A framework for positive dependence. *Ann. Inst. Statist. Math.* **1989**, *41*, 31–45. [CrossRef]
10. Lehmann, E.L. Some concepts of dependence. *Ann. Math. Statist.* **1966**, *37*, 1137–1153. [CrossRef]
11. Shaked, M. A general theory of some positive dependence notions. *J. Multivariate Anal.* **1982**, *12*, 199–218. [CrossRef]
12. Karlin, S.; Rinott, Y. Classes of orderings of measures and related correlation inequalities. I. Multivariate totally positive distributions. *J. Multivariate Anal.* **1980**, *10*, 467–498. [CrossRef]

13. Harris, R. A multivariate definition for increasing hazard rate distribution functions. *Ann. Math. Statist.* **1970**, *41*, 713–717. [CrossRef]
14. Popović, B.V.; Ristić, M.M.; Genç, A.İ. Dependence properties of multivariate distributions with proportional hazard rate marginals. *Appl. Math. Model.* **2020**, *77*, 182–198. [CrossRef]
15. Quesada-Molina, J.J.; Úbeda-Flores, M. Monotonic in sequence random variables according to a direction. University of Almería, Almería, Spain. 2024, to be submitted.
16. Nelsen, R.B. *An Introduction to Copulas*, 2nd ed.; Springer: New York, NY, USA, 2006.
17. de Amo, E.; Quesada-Molina, J.J.; Úbeda-Flores, M. Total positivity and dependence of order statistics. *AIMS Math.* **2023**, *8*, 30717–30730. [CrossRef]
18. Johnson, N.L.; Kotz, S. *Distributions in Statistics: Continuous Multivariate Distributions*; John Wiley & Sons: New York, NY, USA, 1972.
19. Müller, A.; Scarsini, M. Archimedean copulae and positive dependence. *J. Multivar. Anal.* **2005**, *93*, 434–445. [CrossRef]
20. Kingman, J.F.C. A convexity property of positive matrices. *Quart. J. Math. Oxford* **1961**, *12*, 283–284. [CrossRef]
21. de Amo, E.; Rodríguez-Griñolo, M.R.; Úbeda-Flores, M. Directional dependence orders of random vectors. *Mathematics* **2024**, *12*, 419. [CrossRef]

MDPI AG
Grosspeteranlage 5
4052 Basel
Switzerland
Tel.: +41 61 683 77 34

Axioms Editorial Office
E-mail: axioms@mdpi.com
www.mdpi.com/journal/axioms

www.ingramcontent.com/pod-product-compliance
Lightning Source LLC
LaVergne TN
LVHW072326090526
838202LV00019B/2360
* 9 7 8 3 7 2 5 8 3 5 8 0 5 *